13.50

Disability Rights Handbook

30th Edition
April 2005 - April 2006

by Ian Greaves

Address list compiled by
Michèle Holland

Acknowledgements

We would like to acknowledge the valuable contribution of all the contributors and checkers of this edition of the Handbook.

Thanks also to colleagues at Disability Alliance for their work on Handbook sales administration and distribution, and for their practical help and advice. Particular thanks to Vanessa Davis (for editing the address list), Michael Odedairo, Libia Killeen and Irene Musoke – their assistance has been invaluable.

Thanks also to Paula McDiarmid for her patience and efficiency in co-ordinating the writing and checking of the Handbook and for her copy-editing skill.

Design and print production management is by Debbie Kamofsky, Anderson Fraser Partnership. Typesetting is by Humphrey Weightman. I am most grateful to them for their professional support and high-quality work.

Special acknowledgements go to Judith Paterson who wrote the Disability Rights Handbook from the 19th through to the 26th edition and to her predecessor Sally Robertson.

We do our best to ensure the information in the Handbook is correct. However, changes in the law after April 2005 might affect the accuracy of some of the information. Where this could be important to you, you should check the details with a local advice centre or your local social security or Jobcentre Plus office.

If you think anything in the Handbook is incorrect, please write and tell us. Thanks to all those who wrote in to us this year with comments and suggestions on the Handbook. Your contributions are always very welcome.

To the memory of Paul Bradley and John Hargreaves.

Contributors
Miranda Bayliss
Tony Bowman
Mike Ellison
Daphne Hall
Pauline Hunter
Michael Mandelstam
Alan Markey
Clive Martin
Ben Moore
Paul Moorhouse
Amanda Palmer
Judith Paterson
Simon Robinson
Vicky Routledge
Fiona Seymour
David Simmons
Derek Sinclair
Carl Smith
Kate Smith
Rebecca Walker
Sally West
Chris White
Helen Winfield

Checkers
David Allsop
(Ferret Information Systems)
Gina Antczak (Tax Aid)
Ron Armour
Douglas Campbell
(Disabled Drivers' Association)
Louise Curtis
(Disability Rights Commission)
Teresa Davies
(National Assembly for Wales)
Pamela Fitzpatrick
Joan Greening (RNIB)
Helen Healy
Martin Inch
David Malcolm
(National Union of Students)
Paul Martin
(Independent Living Fund)
Jim Pearson
(Alzheimer Scotland)
Lorna Reith
Sylvia Saxton
Andrew Sim
(Age Concern Scotland)
Stephen Spencer
Pauline Thompson
(Age Concern England)
Pauline Wardman
and Jo Morrigan
(Department for Work and Pensions)
Mick Wilson and his team at the
Inland Revenue (Preston)

and staff at
Compensation Recovery Unit
Department for Education and Skills
Department for Transport Local
Government and the Regions
Department for Work and Pensions
Department of Health
Inland Revenue
Jobcentre Plus
Veterans Agency

Disability Rights Handbook
30th Edition
April 2005 - April 2006
ISBN 1-903335-22-1

Published by Disability Alliance

Contents

Benefits checklist

This is a quick guide to help you see which benefits you might be entitled to. It is not a guide to the benefits themselves – you still need to read the relevant chapters. More than one of the circumstances below may apply to you and you may well qualify for more than one benefit, especially if you have low savings and income. Box A.2 in Chapter 1 tells you which benefits depend on your national insurance (NI) record and which are affected by other income.

Circumstance	Benefit	Chapter
Incapable of work		
■ employed	**statutory sick pay (SSP)**	**13**
■ not employed or after 28 weeks SSP – if you've paid enough NI contributions	**incapacity benefit (IB)**	**14**
■ after 28 weeks incapacity if you are aged 16 to 20 (or 25 for students/trainees) – no NI contributions required	**incapacity benefit**	**14**
■ you can't get SSP or IB, or can, but still do not have enough to live on	**income support**	**3**
Unemployed or working less than 16 hours a week		
■ payable for 26 weeks if you've paid enough NI contributions	**contribution-based jobseeker's allowance (JSA)**	**17**
■ if you've not paid enough NI contributions, or your contribution-based JSA has run out or is not enough to live on	**income-based jobseeker's allowance**	**17**
■ if you don't have to sign on for work (eg you're incapable of work, disabled, a carer or a lone parent) and any income or savings are low	**income support**	**3**
Working at least 16 hours a week		
■ you have a child	**child tax credit**	**18**
■ you are 50 or over and returning to work, or you have a child, or you have a disability and get a qualifying disability benefit or recently got a qualifying incapacity benefit, or you are 25 or over and are working at least 30 hours a week	**working tax credit**	**18**
Injured or contracted disease in work		
■ you are disabled through an industrial accident or prescribed disease	**industrial injuries disablement benefit**	**44**
■ the industrial accident or disease occurred before 1.10.90 and your earnings capacity is reduced	**reduced earnings allowance**	**44**
■ replaces reduced earnings allowance when you give up regular employment after state pension age	**retirement allowance**	**44**
Disabled due to vaccine damage	**vaccine damage payment**	**47**
Injured due to violent crime	**criminal injuries compensation**	**46**
War disablement		
■ injured because of service in the Armed Forces (prior to 6.4.05), or a civilian disabled due to the 1939-45 war	**war disablement pension**	**45**
■ your spouse died because of the war, or because of service in the Armed Forces	**war widow(er)'s pension**	**45**
■ injured because of service in the Armed Forces on or after 6.4.05	**Armed Forces Compensation scheme**	**45**
Retirement		
■ from age 60 for women or 65 for men	**state pension**	**42**
■ from age 60 to top up your pension	**pension credit**	**41**
■ from age 80 and little or no state pension before	**non-contributory state pension**	**42**
Need help with NHS costs, glasses, hospital fares	**health benefits**	**52**
Caring		
■ you care for a disabled person for at least 35 hours a week	**carer's allowance**	**23**
■ you or your partner get carer's allowance or would do but for an overlapping benefit	**carer premium with means-tested benefits**	**4**
Practical help at home		
■ practical help if you are disabled	**care services, eg home care, meals on wheels**	**25**
■ equipment and adaptations	**help from social services or the NHS**	**27**

Circumstance	Benefit	Chapter
Problems with walking		
■ aged under 65 when you claim	**disability living allowance mobility component**	20
■ hire or buy a car using the mobility component	**Motability**	22
■ if you get higher rate mobility component	**road tax exemption**	22
■ parking concessions	**Blue Badge scheme**	22
Need help with personal care		
■ aged under 65 when you claim	**disability living allowance care component**	20
■ aged 65 or over when you claim	**attendance allowance**	21
■ severely disabled and need help with personal care or household assistance	**Independent Living Funds**	26
Housing problems		
■ repairs, adaptations, improvements	**housing grants**	28
■ help with the mortgage	**income support**	3
	income-based jobseeker's allowance	17
	pension credit, guarantee credit	41
■ help with the rent	**housing benefit**	7
■ help with the council tax	**council tax benefit**	7
	disability reduction or discount schemes	8
Pregnancy		
■ employed	**statutory maternity pay (SMP)**	34
■ recently employed or self-employed, but not entitled to SMP	**maternity allowance**	34
■ incapable of work	**incapacity benefit**	14
■ if income and savings are low	**income support**	3
■ help with maternity expenses	**Sure Start maternity grant**	9
■ for free milk and vitamins	**health benefits**	52
Responsibility for children		
■ employed	**statutory paternity pay (SPP)**	34
■ employed (responsible for adopted child)	**statutory adoption pay (SAP)**	34
■ responsible for a child under 16, or 16-19 in full-time, non-advanced education	**child benefit**	36
	child tax credit	18
■ responsible for an orphan	**guardian's allowance**	36
■ disabled child	**disability living allowance,**	35
	Family Fund	35
■ for free milk and vitamins	**health benefits**	52
Death		
■ widow under 60 or widower under 65, or whose husband or wife did not get state pension	**bereavement payment**	51
■ widow or widower with a dependent child	**widowed parent's allowance**	51
■ paid for 52 weeks to a widow or widower aged 45 or over but under state pension age when spouse dies	**bereavement allowance**	51
■ help with the cost of a funeral	**social fund funeral payment**	9
If you do not have enough to live on		
■ not working, or working less than 16 hours a week	**income support**	3
■ if you have to sign on for work	**income-based jobseeker's allowance**	17
■ from age 60	**pension credit**	41
■ working at least 16 hours a week (see above)	**working tax credit & child tax credit**	18
■ paying rent for your home	**housing benefit**	7
■ paying council tax	**council tax benefit**	7
If you have needs difficult to meet out of regular income		
■ if you get income support, income-based jobseeker's allowance or pension credit	**social fund community care grant**	10
■ if you've had income support, income-based jobseeker's allowance or pension credit for at least 26 weeks	**social fund budgeting loan**	10
■ following emergency or disaster	**social fund crisis loan**	10

Abbreviations

Most abbreviations used in the Handbook are explained here. If you come across one that isn't listed, you will usually find it explained towards the beginning of the chapter, towards the beginning of the section in a chapter, or in a box headed 'For more information'.

AA	attendance allowance
AIP	assessed income period
BEL	Benefit Enquiry Line
CA	carer's allowance
CAA	constant attendance allowance
CB	child benefit
CBEP	child benefit extension period
CCG	community care grant
CLS	Community Legal Service
CRAG	Charging for Residential Accommodation Guide
CTB	council tax benefit
CTC	child tax credit
DBC	Disability Benefits Centre
DBU	Disability Benefits Unit
DDA	Disability Discrimination Act
DEA	disability employment adviser
DfES	Department for Education and Skills
DHP	discretionary housing payment
DIAL	Disability Information and Advice Line
DLA	disability living allowance
DMG	Decision Makers' Guide
DP	disability premium
DSA	disabled students' allowance
DWP	Department for Work and Pensions
EC	European Community
EEA	European Economic Area
EMP	examining medical practitioner
GB	Great Britain (England, Scotland and Wales)
GP	general practitioner
HB	housing benefit
HBD	Health Benefits Division
HRP	home responsibilities protection
HRT	habitual residence test
IAP	intensive activity period
IB	incapacity benefit
IIDB	industrial injuries disablement benefit
ILF	Independent Living Fund
IR	Inland Revenue
IS	income support
JSA	jobseeker's allowance
LEA	local education authority
MA	maternity allowance
NASS	National Asylum Support Service
NDDP	New Deal for Disabled People
NHS	National Health Service
NI	national insurance
NIHE	Northern Ireland Housing Executive
p./para	paragraph in a schedule to an Act or set of Regulations, or in a Guidance Manual
PAYE	pay as you earn
PC	pension credit
PCA	personal capability assessment
PIW	period of incapacity for work
RA	retirement allowance
REA	reduced earnings allowance
Reg	regulation in a set of Regulations
S.	section of an Act of Parliament
SAAS	Student Awards Agency for Scotland
SAP	statutory adoption pay
Sch.	schedule, at the end of an Act or a set of Regulations
SDA	severe disablement allowance
SDP	severe disability premium
SERPS	state earnings-related pension scheme
SF	social fund
SMP	statutory maternity pay
SPP	statutory paternity pay
S2P	second state pension
SSP	statutory sick pay
TAS	The Appeals Service
UK	United Kingdom (England, Northern Ireland, Scotland, Wales)
VA	Veterans Agency
WBLA	Work-Based Learning for Adults
WPA	widowed parent's allowance
WTC	working tax credit

This section of the Handbook looks at:

Overview A

1 Introduction

1. What does the Handbook include?

This Handbook is intended as a comprehensive guide to social security and related benefits for disabled people, their families and carers and the many professionals who work with them. The Handbook is aimed at disabled people, whether their impairment is physical, mental or sensory. You may find it helpful to start by looking at the benefits checklist (pages 4-5). In addition to social security benefits and tax credits, the Handbook covers practical help and services and other essential matters such as community care, income tax, council tax and housing grants. A list of the abbreviations used in the Handbook is included opposite.

2. What's new in this edition?

Following the upheavals in 2003 when the introduction of the tax credits and pension credit transformed the landscape of social security, the last year has been one of quiet consolidation. That said, the process of change brought on by the introduction of tax credits is still not complete. While financial support for children is now provided through child tax credit for new claims, there are still substantial numbers of income support and income-based jobseeker's allowance claimants with children who have yet to be moved onto child tax credit. Changes have already been made, however, to housing benefit and council tax benefit so that any income and capital your children have is ignored when calculating your entitlement to these benefits. This brings housing benefit and council tax benefit into line with child tax credit. We have introduced these changes into Chapters 5 and 7.

The transformation of old-style social security offices into new, more work-focused Jobcentre Plus offices should be complete by April 2006. One aspect of this focus on work is the expansion of the 'Pathways to Work' scheme. This affects claimants on all incapacity benefits in pilot areas covering a large section of the country. We describe Pathways to Work in more detail in Box F.2 in Chapter 16.

Other changes in this Handbook:

- ❑ The 'personal capability assessment', which is used in deciding whether or not you can remain on incapacity benefits, has been considerably changed by a Court of Appeal decision (*Howker*). We describe the latest version of the personal capability assessment in Chapter 11.
- ❑ A significant change has been made to the appeals process. Appeals can no longer be struck out if they are 'misconceived'. The appeals process is described in Chapter 58.

3. Disability Rights Bulletin

Besides the Handbook, we publish the *Disability Rights Bulletin* three times a year. The *Bulletin* updates the Handbook and deals with changes in the law or administrative practices. It also carries articles on social policy issues affecting disabled people.

The 31st edition of the Handbook will be published in May 2006.

PLEASE REMEMBER TO ORDER THE 31ST EDITION OF THIS HANDBOOK BEFORE APRIL 2006.

4. Disability and benefits

What is disability?

Few of your rights depend on what your condition is called. In most cases, your right to a benefit or service depends on the effect of the disability on your life.

Within the benefits and tax credits systems there are 5 main tests of disability:

A.1 The costs of disability

Disability inevitably leads to extra costs. It is far more difficult for a disabled person to manage on the same income as someone of the same age who is not disabled. Yet the average disabled person has a much lower income than the average non-disabled person. And despite the range of benefits and other help available to people with disabilities, not all people manage to work their way through the maze and claim their full legal entitlements. The weekly loss can be substantial.

Even among people who have claimed all they are entitled to, there are still anomalies. People who are equally severely disabled can be entitled to different amounts of non-means-tested income. How old you were when you became disabled; how you became disabled; the effects of your disability; how long you have lived in the UK; and whether you worked and paid the right national insurance contributions at the right time: all can make a difference to the total amount you may be entitled to.

The disability gap

Without going through any means test, different people who are equally and extremely severely disabled, could be entitled to:

- ■ a maximum of £472.75 a week from the War Disablement scheme;
- ■ a maximum of £364.42 a week from the Industrial Injuries scheme and disability living allowance (DLA);
- ■ a maximum of £195.40 a week from incapacity benefit and DLA;
- ■ a maximum of £102.90 a week from DLA alone.

The gap between the maximum and minimum help available without going through a means test now stands at £369.85 a week.

- **incapacity for work** – used for statutory sick pay, incapacity benefit, severe disablement allowance, income support and the unemployability supplement under the Industrial Injuries and War Disablement schemes. There are different tests of incapacity depending on the benefit you claim;
- **needing care, supervision or watching over by another person** – used for disability living allowance care component and attendance allowance. A similar test is used for constant attendance allowance under the Industrial Injuries and War Disablement schemes;
- **unable or virtually unable to walk** – used for disability living allowance mobility component and war pensioners' mobility supplement;

A.2 Benefits affected by other income or NI contributions

Means-tested benefits

The following means-tested or income-related benefits are affected by most other types of income and by the amount of savings you have. However, child tax credit and working tax credit are only affected by the income from your savings, not by the actual level of savings. Your national insurance (NI) contribution record does not matter.

- Child tax credit
- Council tax benefit
- Housing benefit
- Income-based jobseeker's allowance
- Income support
- Pension credit
- Social fund
- Working tax credit

Non-means-tested benefits

The following non-means-tested benefits are not usually affected by other money that you have, although those marked (*) can be affected by your earnings or your occupational or private pension. See the relevant chapter for details. For some of these benefits, your NI record does not matter and they are listed here as non-contributory benefits. However, for the other benefits you must have sufficient NI contributions and they are listed here as contributory benefits.

Non-contributory benefits

- Attendance allowance
- Carer's allowance*
- Child benefit
- Disability living allowance
- Guardian's allowance
- Industrial injuries benefits
- State pension: Category D
- Statutory adoption pay
- Statutory maternity pay
- Statutory paternity pay
- Statutory sick pay
- War disablement pensions

Contributory benefits

- Bereavement allowance
- Bereavement payment
- Contribution-based jobseeker's allowance*
- Incapacity benefit*
- Maternity allowance*
- State pension: Category A or B
- Widowed parent's allowance

- **degree of disablement** – used for industrial injuries disablement benefit, war disablement pension and vaccine damage payments;
- **at a disadvantage in getting a job** – used for the disability element of working tax credit.

In addition, there are two other definitions in use:

- **substantially and permanently disabled** – used for registering as disabled with a local authority social services department and for getting a disability reduction in your council tax;
- **physical or mental impairment which has a substantial and long-term adverse effect on ability to carry out normal day-to-day activities** – used to define those covered by the Disability Discrimination Act 1995.

Besides these main tests of disability, there may be other criteria you must satisfy to get a particular benefit or service. The individual chapters give details of these.

The different types of benefits

Benefits can be divided into three broad categories:

- those which are intended to replace earnings;
- those which compensate for extra costs;
- those which help alleviate poverty.

The first category includes those benefits that compensate you if you are unable to work because of sickness, disability, unemployment, pregnancy, retirement or caring responsibilities. In general, these benefits are not subject to a means test, but some will depend on your national insurance contribution (NI) record (see Box A.2).

Benefits intended to contribute towards the extra costs of disability or the extra cost of children are not means tested, nor do they depend on NI contributions.

Benefits intended to alleviate poverty by providing a basic income or topping up a low income are subject to a means test.

5. The law

Every decision on any claim for benefit depends on something in the law. Primary legislation, in Acts of Parliament, sets out the framework for the law and gives the Secretary of State specific powers to make regulations giving detailed provisions. The Acts of Parliament most commonly referred to in the Handbook are the Social Security Contributions and Benefits Act 1992, the Social Security Administration Act 1992, the Social Security Act 1998, the State Pension Credit Act 2002 and the Tax Credits Act 2002. These largely cover entitlement conditions and administration for most benefits. Box R.9 in Chapter 58 tells you where you can find the legislation and suggests useful reference books.

Case law

Besides the Acts and Regulations, you may need to consider case law. Social Security Commissioners hear appeals against decisions of appeal tribunals. Decisions made by these Commissioners, as well as decisions of the courts, make up social security case law. Case law clarifies any doubt about the meaning of the law or its application to individual cases. Where case law sets up a general principal, it also sets a precedent that should be followed in similar cases.

The way decisions are referred to (eg R(IB)2/99 or CA/140/85) is explained in Box R.7 in Chapter 58. Box R.9 in that chapter tells you how to get copies of relevant decisions.

Practice – getting answers

If in doubt, check the actual law rather than guidebooks. Always check to see if a word or phrase is being used in a technical way. It may be defined in an Act or in Regulations, or it may have been considered in case law. If a word or phrase has not been defined in legislation or case law, it has its ordinary English meaning: check a good dictionary.

If you are not sure about something, contact the office dealing with the claim concerned (see Box A.3). Ask for an explanation and outline of the exact basis (with references) for what has been, or is, happening.

It is always worth contacting an advice agency, which may have copies of the law and relevant text books. Your local library may also be able to assist.

You can also find the Acts and Regulations (in *The Law Relating to Social Security*) and official guidance on our website: www.disabilityalliance.org/links.htm. Remember, if you feel a decision about your benefit is wrong you may be able to appeal (see Chapter 58).

2 The benefits system

1. Department for Work and Pensions

The Department for Work and Pensions (DWP) is responsible for most of the help available for disabled people. Responsibility for policy making lies with the DWP, while services are delivered to the public by six service delivery organisations.

2. The structure of the DWP

The day-to-day running of the benefits system is undertaken by six service delivery organisations: Jobcentre Plus, the Disability & Carers Directorate, The Pension Service, the Child Support Agency, Debt Management and The Appeals Service.

- **Jobcentre Plus** – provides services to people of working age, administering the majority of benefits they can claim. It was created by merging the Employment Service, which ran Jobcentres, with those parts of the Benefits Agency that provided services to people of working age through social security offices. Over time, existing social security offices and Jobcentres will be upgraded to provide a full Jobcentre Plus service. This service aims to provide 'a work focus' to the benefits system. The upgrading is scheduled to be complete for 2006. In the meantime, some offices will continue to display the old 'Social Security' or 'Jobcentre' signs outside.
- **Disability & Carers Directorate** – administers disability living allowance, attendance allowance, carer's allowance and vaccine damage payments through a network of 11 regional Disability Benefits Centres, as well as the central units at Blackpool and Preston. The initial contact for these benefits will usually be through the Jobcentre Plus network (ie your local social security or Jobcentre Plus office).
- **The Pension Service** – provides a centralised benefits service for pensioners and people planning for retirement, through largely telephone-based pension centres supported by a local service network. The local service network provides appointment-based meetings in such places as libraries and community centres. The Pension Service administers the state pension, pension credit and winter fuel payments.
- **Child Support Agency** – administers the system that pursues maintenance from non-resident parents.
- **Debt Management** – is responsible for the recovery of debts from claimants.
- **The Appeals Service** – administers the independent tribunals which hear appeals on social security benefits and, for the time being, tax credits.

Most benefits are administered by the DWP, although tax credits, child benefit and guardian's allowance are administered by the Inland Revenue.

The DWP contracts out some of its functions to private companies; for example, Atos Origin has a contract to provide medical advice and examinations.

In this Handbook we refer to the system as a DWP system – eg 'write to the DWP', 'DWP doctor', etc. This reflects the legal reality. However, when we talk about the local office that you need to deal with, we usually refer to 'your local Jobcentre Plus office'. Although social security benefits in your area might still be administered by one of the old social security offices (at least until April 2006), you will be able to find the address of this under Jobcentre Plus.

3. Northern Ireland

In Northern Ireland, the Department for Social Development is responsible for social security matters, and benefits are administered by the Social Security Agency.

Northern Ireland has its own legislation, and the structure and organisation of the system is different from Great Britain (GB). However, the rates of benefits and qualifying conditions are similar to those in GB, except that you have rate rebates instead of council tax benefit (see Chapter 7(28)).

A.3 Contacting the DWP

Contact details of your nearest Jobcentre Plus office, Jobcentre or social security office will be in the phone book. Alternatively, you can find details of local offices on the website: www.jobcentreplus.gov.uk. The Pension Service has its own website: www.thepensionservice.gov .uk. The addresses of the DWP central units are listed on the inside back cover of this Handbook.

Northern Ireland – To find your local social security office, look in the phone book under 'Social Security'.

Benefit Enquiry Line (BEL)

This is a confidential telephone advice and information line for people with disabilities, their carers and representatives. It covers England, Scotland and Wales. BEL can provide general benefits advice and information, but staff do not have access to any claimant records and are therefore unable to give information on the progress of a claim or benefits you are already receiving. It is a confidential service and nothing you ask or say will go on your file.

For certain disability-related benefit claims, staff can arrange to fill in your form over the phone and send it to you to check and sign. The form can be in Braille or large print. The service covers carer's allowance, IB50 forms (see Chapter 11(8)), disability living allowance, attendance allowance and industrial injuries disablement benefit.

Ring the enquiry line on 0800 882200 or Textphone 0800 243355. Lines are open 8.30am-6.30pm Monday to Friday and 9am-1pm Saturday. From a landline your call is free.

Northern Ireland Benefit Enquiry Line (BEL)

Ring 0800 220674 or Textphone 0800 243787. Staff give general advice on benefits for disabled people and offer a forms-completion service. Both lines are open 9am-5pm Monday to Friday.

4. Who's who in the benefits system

The services are organised in slightly different ways. What follows is a rough sketch – you'll find more details in the chapters on the individual benefits. The main rules about claims, payments, decision making and appeals are covered in Chapters 57 and 58.

In all cases you have a right to expect a good standard of service. Jobcentre Plus, the Disability & Carers Directorate, The Pension Service, the Child Support Agency and The Appeals Service each have customer charters, which explain the standards; you can get a copy from the local office of each organisation. If you want to complain about something or have suggestions about how services could be improved, see Chapter 60.

If you want to know how your local office is organised, ask to speak to a Customer Services Manager or Office Manager, who can explain things and send you relevant information.

Administrative staff

The people you talk to when you visit or phone a local office are not always legally responsible for making a decision on your claim. Although they will do the support and maintenance work for claims, and may handle many routine claims, particularly for means-tested benefits, decisions must, in law, be made by a decision maker authorised by the Secretary of State.

Secretary of State

The Secretary of State is responsible for decisions on your social security benefit entitlement. In practice this is delegated to decision makers who are officers acting under the Secretary of State's authority. In a few cases the Secretary of State delegates decision-making responsibility to officers of the Inland Revenue (eg for some national insurance credits decisions).

Decision makers

Decision makers are officers acting under the authority of the Secretary of State. They make decisions on your entitlement to benefits but won't always be based in your local office. So it may be best to write rather than phone. If you are not satisfied with a decision, you can ask for an explanation of the decision, ask for a revision of the decision, or appeal to an independent tribunal. The letter giving you the decision must always explain what you can do next.

Appeal tribunals

Appeal tribunals hear appeals against decisions of the Secretary of State. They also hear appeals against local authority decisions on housing benefit and council tax benefit and appeals against decisions made by the Inland Revenue on tax credits. The role and powers of appeal tribunals are explained in Chapter 58.

Social Security Commissioners

If an appeal tribunal refuses your appeal, you can apply for permission to appeal (on a point of law) to the Social Security Commissioners, who are lawyers of at least 10 years' standing, with the same status as High Court judges. Their decisions set precedents and form case law. We quote a few useful decisions in this Handbook: eg R(IB)2/99 and CDLA/265/97. Box R.7 in Chapter 58 explains what each reference means. Chapter 58(18) explains more about appealing to the Commissioners.

Social fund decision makers

Access to the social fund is through the Jobcentre Plus network (ie your local Jobcentre Plus office). For the discretionary social fund there is a different decision-making system. Initial decisions are taken by a decision maker authorised to do so by the Secretary of State. There is an ultimate right of review by a social fund inspector (see Chapter 10).

5. The Inland Revenue

The Inland Revenue is responsible for decisions on national insurance contributions and statutory sick, maternity, paternity and adoption pay. The right of appeal on such decisions is to the Income Tax General Commissioners. The Inland Revenue is also responsible for decisions on tax credits, child benefit and guardian's allowance, which are made by decision makers based in either the Tax Credit Office in Preston or the Child Benefit Office in Newcastle-upon-Tyne. Until the reform of the tax appeal system is complete, appeals for these will continue to be heard by appeal tribunals administered by The Appeals Service.

At some time in 2005 the Inland Revenue will be merging with HM Customs and Excise to form a single new department called HM Revenue and Customs. The Inland Revenue is likely to maintain an independent identity within this new department, under the name 'Revenue'.

Income support B

3 Who can get income support?

1. What is income support?

Income support (IS) is a means-tested or income-related benefit intended to provide for basic living expenses for you and, if you have one, your partner. It does not depend on your national insurance contributions. It can be paid on its own if you have no other income, or it can top up other benefits or earnings from part-time work up to the basic amount the law says you need to live on. If you don't have much money coming in, it is always worth checking to see if you might qualify for IS. IS has been replaced by pension credit for people aged 60 or over (see Chapter 41). If you have children, their basic living expenses can be met by child tax credit (see Chapter 18).

IS is for people who are not required to sign on for work – eg those incapable of work through ill-health or disability, carers or lone parents. Box B.1 lists the groups of eligible people. If you are not in one of these groups, you are not eligible for IS and should claim income-based jobseeker's allowance instead (see Chapter 17).

IS can help towards mortgage interest payments and certain other housing costs. If you get IS, you may also get housing benefit and council tax benefit to help with your rent and council tax. You won't have to go through a separate means test (see Chapter 7).

Getting IS may entitle you to other types of benefit such as:

- free prescriptions and dental treatment (Chapter 52);
- housing grants (Chapter 28);
- help from the social fund (Chapters 9 and 10);
- free school meals (Chapter 35);
- help with hospital fares (Chapter 32).

For details of how to work out your IS entitlement, see Chapter 4. Chapter 5 deals with the way your income and capital are assessed. Chapter 6 provides you with information on how to claim.

2. The starting conditions

To qualify for IS there are 8 key starting conditions. You are generally eligible for IS if you meet all these conditions, which are:

- you must be in Great Britain (see 3); *and*
- you must be aged 16 or over (see 4); *and*
- you must be aged under 60. If you are aged 60 or over, claim pension credit (PC) instead (see Chapter 41). If your partner receives PC you cannot claim IS; *and*
- you must not be in full-time education, though there are exceptions (see 4 and 5); *and*
- you must not be working 16 or more hours a week (see 6); *and*
- if you have a partner, they must not be working 24 or more hours a week (see 6); *and*
- your capital (and any belonging to a partner, but not to a dependent child) must be no more than £8,000, or £12,000 if you have a partner aged 60 or over, or £16,000 if you live permanently in a care home (see Chapter 5); *and*
- you must be in one of the categories of people who can claim IS (see Box B.1).

If you meet these 8 conditions, you'll be entitled to IS if your income, worked out under IS rules, is less than your 'applicable amount' (the amount the law says you need to live on – see Chapter 4(2)). Note the following points.

- ❑ If you have no income at all, you'll be paid the full amount of your IS applicable amount.
- ❑ If you have some income, but it is less than your IS applicable amount, IS is payable to bridge the gap between that income and your IS applicable amount.
- ❑ If your income is higher than your IS applicable amount, you won't be entitled to IS. But you may be entitled to housing benefit and/or council tax benefit (see Chapter 7).
- ❑ If you are classed as a person 'subject to immigration control', you are generally not entitled to IS, although there are limited exceptions (see 7).
- ❑ For some groups of people there are special rules. IS rules for those in care homes are explained in Chapter 30.

Claiming jobseeker's allowance (JSA)? – If you are claiming either income-based or contribution-based JSA or your partner is claiming income-based JSA, you cannot get IS at the same time. You can switch claims if you find you've made the wrong choice (see Chapter 6(3)).

3. Presence in Great Britain

IS can only be paid for the first 4 or 8 weeks of a temporary absence from Great Britain (GB) (see Chapter 50(4)).

As well as being present in GB, you must also be 'habitually resident' in the UK, Channel Islands, Isle of Man or Republic of Ireland (see Chapter 49(2)).

4. Aged 16 or over

If you are aged under 16 you cannot get IS in your own right in any circumstances.

If you are under 19 and still at school or doing a non-advanced course at college, you are usually excluded from IS – your parents can claim child benefit and child tax credit for you. But in some circumstances you can claim IS in your own right while you are at school (see 5 below).

If you are under 19 and on a full-time advanced course, see Chapter 38(3) for details of IS entitlement.

Once you've left school, from the first Monday after the end of the school holiday following your school leaving date, you are eligible to claim IS if you fit into one of the groups outlined in Box B.1. If you don't fit into one of these groups, you should claim jobseeker's allowance (JSA) instead. But there are additional conditions for 16- and 17-year-olds claiming JSA (see Chapter 17(19)).

Care leavers – If you are a care leaver your local authority has a duty to support you until your 18th birthday. In most cases, therefore, you would be excluded from IS (and JSA). This does not apply, however, if you are:

- a lone parent or a single foster parent; *or*
- incapable of work (or appealing against a decision that you are not incapable of work); *or*
- a disabled worker with reduced hours or pay because of your disability (see 6); *or*
- blind; *or*
- a full-time disabled student eligible to claim IS (see Chapter 38(3)); *or*
- at school or doing a non-advanced college course for 12 hours or more a week and you would be unlikely to find work within a year due to a severe disability.

Reg 2 Children (Leaving Care) Social Security Benefits Regs 2001

5. Full-time education

You are excluded from IS if you are aged 16, 17 or 18 and are at school or doing a non-advanced course at college for 12 or more hours a week (and are thus treated as a child for child benefit purposes – see Chapter 36). But even if you are at school, you won't be excluded from IS in this way if you:

- are severely mentally or physically disabled and your disability means that you would be unlikely to find work within a year if you were to leave school now and sign on for work; *or*
- get child benefit for a child living with you (provided no one gets child benefit for you); *or*
- are a refugee on an English course (see Box B.1); *or*
- have no parent, and no one is legally responsible for you or acting in place of your parents; *or*
- are living away from your parents (and anyone acting in their place) and they cannot support you as they are chronically sick or disabled, in custody, or prohibited from coming into Great Britain: seek advice; *or*
- have to live away from your parents (and anyone acting in their place) because:
  - you are estranged from them; *or*
  - you are in physical or moral danger; *or*
  - there is a serious risk to your physical or mental health; *or*
- have left local authority care and have to live away from your parents (and anyone acting in their place).

Reg 13, IS (General) Regulations

If you are aged 19 or over and on a full-time course, you will be treated as a student whether your course is advanced or non-advanced. Chapter 38 explains which students are entitled to IS.

B.1 Who can claim income support?

You can only claim IS if one of the categories below applies to you. You are eligible for the whole benefit week if the category applies for at least one day. To be entitled to IS you must also pass the means test (explained in Chapter 4) and other IS conditions described in this chapter (see 2). IS is only for people who are not expected to sign on as available for work. If none of the categories below apply to you, you cannot get IS and should claim jobseeker's allowance (JSA) instead. These categories are set out in Schedule 1B of the IS (General) Regulations 1987.

Sickness or disability

- ❑ You are entitled to statutory sick pay (SSP).
- ❑ You are incapable of work.
  This is assessed under the 'own occupation test' or 'personal capability assessment' (PCA) (see Chapter 11). You must send in medical certificates until you are assessed under (or exempted from) the PCA. You can be treated as incapable of work even if you are able to work in some circumstances (see Chapter 11(4)). You are eligible for IS even if you are treated as capable of work because of misconduct, failure without good cause to accept medical treatment, or failure to observe certain rules of behaviour (see Chapter 11(13)).
- ❑ You have appealed against a decision under a determination that you are capable of work. This category continues to apply until the final decision on your appeal (eg by the Commissioner if you further appeal the decision of the appeal tribunal). This category depends on which test of incapacity was applied:
  - if the decision is under the own occupation test you must continue to send in medical certificates. IS is paid at the normal rate;
  - if the decision is under the PCA, you don't need to send in medical certificates. IS will be reduced by 20% of the single person's personal allowance for your age group (unless you are eligible for IS under one of the other categories in this box, eg you are a carer). If you win your appeal, the reduction will be repaid. See Chapter 17(8), as you may be better off claiming JSA. If you were getting invalidity benefit or severe disablement allowance on 12.4.95, or were continuously incapable of work for 28 weeks before 13.4.95, and this is the first time the PCA has been applied (or previously the 'all work' test), this reduction won't be made;
  - you are not eligible for IS under this category while you are appealing against a decision treating you as capable of work because you failed without good cause to return the incapacity for work questionnaire (form IB50) or attend a medical examination, or you were doing work that was not permitted. You should claim JSA instead, unless any of the other categories in this box apply.

Para 24, Sch 1B and reg 22A, IS (General) Regs

- ❑ You are registered as blind (in Scotland, certified as blind). If you regain your sight, you don't have to sign on during the 28 weeks after you are taken off the register.
- ❑ You are mentally or physically disabled and are not treated as being in remunerative work because your hours or earnings are 75% or less than that of a person without your disability in the same job (see 6).
- ❑ You are in employment while living in (or temporarily absent from) a care home in which you receive care.

Caring

- ❑ You are *'regularly and substantially engaged in caring for another person'* and either you are getting carer's allowance (CA), or the person you are looking after gets attendance allowance (AA) or constant attendance allowance, or the middle or highest rate of disability living allowance (DLA) care component.
  If the person you are looking after has claimed DLA or AA you'll be eligible for up to 26 weeks while you are waiting for their claim to be processed. You are eligible if they have an advance award of DLA middle or highest rate care component or AA but are still in the qualifying period. If CA entitlement stops, or the person you are looking after stops getting AA or the middle or highest rate of DLA care component, you continue to be eligible for 8 weeks.
- ❑ If you would have been eligible for IS as a carer had you made a claim for IS, then you are eligible for IS for 8 weeks from the date your CA and/or the disabled person's qualifying benefit stops.

6. Full-time or part-time work

You are excluded from IS if you or your partner are in 'remunerative work'. This means that you are not entitled to IS if you, the claimant, work for 16 hours or more a week or if your partner works for 24 hours or more a week. But there are exceptions (see below).

To count as 'remunerative' it must be work *'for which payment is made or which is done in expectation of payment'*.

Lunch breaks, if you are paid for them, count towards the 16 or 24 hours.

Some people may be treated as being in full-time work: eg if they are off work because of a holiday or during a period covered by pay in lieu of notice. But if you are off work because you are ill or on maternity leave, you are not treated as being in remunerative work, even if you are getting sick pay or maternity pay from your employer. You are also not treated as being in remunerative work if you are off work because you are on paternity or adoption leave.

Once you have stopped working, you are not excluded from IS during a period covered by your last normal earnings.

Exceptions to the 16-hour/24-hour rule

If you come within one of the exceptions listed below, you can qualify for IS even if you are working for 16 hours or more a week. If your partner is working 24 hours or more a week, they must come within one of these exceptions.

Although you are not excluded from IS on account of the number of hours you work in these cases, any earnings are taken into account in the usual way (see Chapter 5(4)).

Unless you are a carer (see below), if you have an additional occupation which is not in one of these exceptions, the hours you work in that occupation do count towards the 16-hour or 24-hour remunerative work limit.

You are not treated as being in remunerative work in the following circumstances.

❑ **Less hours or pay because of disability** – Because of your disability, physical or mental, *either:*

- your earnings are reduced to 75% or less of what someone without your disability would reasonably be expected to earn if they worked the same number of hours in your type of job or in a comparable job in the area; *or*
- your hours of work are 75% or less of what someone without your disability would reasonably be expected to undertake in your type of job, or in a comparable job in the area.

DWP guidance advises that your own evidence of reduced earnings or hours should normally be accepted. But the decision maker may get more evidence from employment agencies, social services departments or disability charities

❑ You are looking after your partner or a child who you are responsible for who is *'temporarily ill'*.

Childcare responsibility

❑ You are a lone parent and responsible for a child under 16 who is a member of your household.

❑ You are taking unpaid statutory parental leave to look after a child who lives with you. You must have been entitled to housing benefit (HB), council tax benefit (CTB), working tax credit (WTC) or child tax credit (CTC – payable at a higher rate than the family element) on the day before your leave began.

❑ You are taking unpaid statutory paternity leave and you do not receive statutory paternity pay, and/or you were entitled to HB, CTB, WTC or CTC (payable at a higher rate than the family element) on the day before your leave began.

❑ You are single or a lone parent and are fostering a child under 16 through a local authority or voluntary organisation.

❑ You are looking after a child under 16 because the child's parent, or the person who usually looks after the child, is ill, or is temporarily away from their home.

❑ Your partner is temporarily outside the UK and you are responsible for a child under 16 who is a member of your household.

Education and training

❑ You are entitled to IS while at school or in full-time non-advanced education, eg if your severe disability means you would be unlikely to get a job within the next 12 months (see 5).

❑ You are a student and your applicable amount includes the disability premium or severe disability premium; or you have been incapable of work (or entitled to SSP) for at least 28 weeks (2 or more periods of incapacity can be added together provided they are no more than 8 weeks apart).

❑ You are a student who gets a disabled students' allowance because of your deafness (see Chapter 38).

❑ You are on Work-Based Learning for Young People (see Chapter 16(3)).

❑ You are a refugee and start attending an English course for over 15 hours a week during your first year in Great Britain (to help you obtain employment); you are eligible under this category for up to 9 months only.

Pregnancy

❑ You are pregnant and incapable of work because of your pregnancy.

❑ You are pregnant and due to have your baby within the next 11 weeks.

❑ You have had a baby within the last 15 weeks.

Bereavement

❑ You are aged under 60; you were aged at least 55 on 9.4.01, your husband or wife died on or after that date and you claim IS for yourself as a single person.

Age

❑ You are aged under 60; you were aged at least 50 on 6.10.96 or at any time in the 8 weeks before 6.10.96, and receiving IS. In the previous 10 years you had not worked for 16 hours or more in any week, had no prospect of getting work, and would not have been made to sign on if you had claimed IS or supplementary benefit. You cannot re-claim under this category if you stop claiming IS for more than 8 weeks. If you re-claim within 8 weeks you are still covered unless you worked for 16 hours or more in any week.

Other

❑ You are getting IS urgent cases payments as a *'person subject to immigration control'* (see Chapter 49(3)).

❑ You have been granted refugee status. This is limited up to the time of the asylum decision, allowing backdated IS to be paid from the date of your asylum application (see Chapter 49(3)).

❑ You have started work and are eligible for the first 4 weeks of mortgage interest run-on (see Chapter 15(4)).

❑ You are required to attend court as a JP, juror, witness, defendant or plaintiff.

❑ You are remanded or committed in custody for trial or sentencing (however, you can only get IS to cover housing costs; see Chapter 4(11)).

❑ You are held to be involved in a trade dispute.

if they need this to make a comparison.

- ❑ **Living in a care home** – You are in employment and live in, or are temporarily away from, a care home, in which you receive care.
- ❑ **Volunteering** – You are a volunteer or working for a charity or voluntary organisation, but only if the only payment you receive or expect to receive is a payment to cover your actual expenses. If you are paid anything else, even if it is below your earnings disregard, all your hours of work go into the melting pot. If your average hours are 16 or more a week, you'll be excluded from IS. If the decision maker is not *'satisfied that it is reasonable for [you] to provide [your] services free of charge'*, they may treat you as having 'notional' earnings (see Chapter 5(14)).
- ❑ **Caring** – You are eligible for IS because you are caring for a person who gets attendance allowance (AA), or the middle or highest rate of disability living allowance care component, or you get carer's allowance (see Box B.1).
  If this exception applies, then you are not excluded from IS even if you have another job. For example, if you care for your mother during the day and she gets AA, and you also work 20 hours a week in a supermarket in the evenings, because you are a carer none of your hours count, not even the 20 hours evening work. (For jobseeker's allowance (JSA) only the hours you spend caring are disregarded and you must not be employed as a paid carer.)
- ❑ **Foster or respite care** – You are a foster carer or you are paid by a health body, local authority or voluntary organisation to provide respite care in your own home for someone who does not normally live with you.
- ❑ **Childminding** – You are working as a childminder in your home. (Note that for JSA childminding does count as remunerative work.)
- ❑ **Other** – You are not treated as being in remunerative work if you:
- ■ are getting a state training allowance;
- ■ are receiving assistance through the New Deal self-employment route;
- ■ are starting work and are eligible for the first 4 weeks mortgage interest run-on (see Chapter 15(4));
- ■ are working as a local authority councillor, a part-time firefighter, a member of the Territorial Army or reserve forces, a lifeboat crew member, or running or launching a lifeboat, or as an auxiliary coastguard involved in coast rescue duties;
- ■ are held to be involved in a trade dispute (but not during the first 7 days after the day you stopped work);
- ■ get or are due to get a Sports Council National Lottery award (and no other payment for that sporting activity).

Reg 6, IS (General) Regulations

7. Subject to immigration control

With very few exceptions, if you are 'subject to immigration control' you are not entitled to ordinary IS, although some people may be able to get an urgent cases payment. People who have been granted refugee status, or indefinite or exceptional leave to remain or enter, are not subject to immigration control and are eligible for ordinary IS.

If you're a British citizen or have right of abode or are a European Economic Area national, you are also eligible for IS. See Chapter 49(3) for more details. You must also be accepted as 'habitually resident' (see Chapter 49(2)).

4 Income support amounts

In this chapter we look at:

1. How do you work out your entitlement?

The amount of IS you get depends on your income and capital, whether you have a partner, your age, whether you (or your partner) have a disability or are a carer, and whether you have certain housing costs. If you are a single person, only your needs and resources will be relevant. If you are one of a couple (married or living together as husband and wife), then the needs and resources of both of you will be relevant. It is planned that from December 2005 registered same-sex couples will be treated in the same way. If you have dependent children living with you, their needs and resources will be ignored. That is because support for children is now provided through child tax credit (see Chapter 18). To check whether you are eligible for IS, see Chapter 3.

Set amounts for different needs are added together to reach the total amount the law says you need to live on. This is called your 'applicable amount'. Any income worked out under IS rules is deducted from your applicable amount. This leaves the amount of IS you are entitled to.

Step 1: Add up your total capital resources – see Chapter 5(2)

You won't be entitled to IS if your capital, and any capital belonging to your partner, is more than £8,000, or £12,000 if your partner is aged 60 or over, or £16,000 if you live in a care home.

Step 2: Work out your applicable amount – see 2

- ❑ Add up all your personal allowances (see 3).
- ❑ Add up your entitlement to the premiums (see 4-10).
- ❑ Add up any IS housing costs (see 11-14).

The sum total of all these is your IS applicable amount.

Step 3: Add up your total income resources – see Chapter 5(2)

Don't forget the tariff income if you have capital over £3,000, or £6,000 if your partner is aged 60 or over, or £10,000 (if you are in a care home) (see Box B.2, Chapter 5).

Step 4: Deduct your income from your applicable amount

If your income is less than your applicable amount, IS makes up the difference in full, provided you meet the other qualifying conditions (see Chapter 3(2)).

Example: Mr Davies, aged 53, is disabled. He gets the higher rate mobility component and middle rate care component of disability living allowance (DLA). He lives alone.

His applicable amount is:

Personal allowance	£56.20
Disability premium	£23.95
Severe disability premium	£45.50
Applicable amount	*£125.65*

His income is:	
Incapacity benefit	£92.50
(DLA is disregarded)	
Applicable amount	£125.65
Less income	£92.50
IS entitlement	*£33.15*

He will be paid IS of £33.15 as well as incapacity benefit of £92.50 and his DLA.

2. What is your applicable amount?

The applicable amount, set by Parliament, is the amount the law says you need to live on. It consists of:

- personal allowances – for a single claimant or for a couple (see 3);
- premiums – flat-rate extra amounts if you satisfy certain conditions (see 4);
- certain housing costs (see 11).

Your entitlement to all of these is taken into account when your IS claim is assessed. The DWP will add up your total applicable amount. They will also assess your income under the IS rules. If your income is lower than your applicable amount, the difference is payable as IS, as long as all other qualifying conditions are met (see Chapter 3(2)).

If you want to check that your IS has been correctly worked out, ask for a detailed notice of assessment (on form A124 – see Chapter 6(6)).

Special groups

In some circumstances your IS may be worked out differently or paid at a reduced rate.

Children: pre-April 2004 claims – If your claim for IS began before April 2004 and you have dependent children living with you, your IS may still include amounts payable for the children. These will include personal allowances for each child, as well as a family premium, and disabled child premiums and enhanced disability premiums for any disabled children.

The child allowances and premiums are similar to those that still exist for housing benefit and council tax benefit (see Chapter 7(25)). It is intended that some time after April 2005, any amounts payable in your IS for your children will be removed and child tax credit will become payable instead.

Care homes – If you live permanently in a care home, the capital limits are higher (see Box B.2, Chapter 5).

Hospital – If you or a member of your family are in hospital, your applicable amount may be reduced (see Chapter 33).

Urgent cases – If you are in one of the groups of people who can claim IS on an 'urgent need' basis, it is worked out under different rules (see Chapter 49(3)).

Incapacity appeals – Generally, IS is reduced while you are appealing against a decision under the 'personal capability assessment' that you are capable of work (see Box B.1).

Jobcentre Plus interviews – You (or your partner) may be asked to attend a work-focused meeting with a personal adviser. If you fail to attend without good cause, your IS will be paid at a reduced rate. See Box R.1 in Chapter 57.

Mortgage interest run-on – For the first 4 weeks after starting work, you may continue to get housing costs met by IS (see Chapter 15(4)).

Child support – IS can be paid at a reduced rate if you refuse to apply for child support maintenance or fail to provide the Child Support Agency with any information or authorisation they require.

Sanctions – IS can be paid at a reduced rate for 13 weeks through sanctions, which can be applied if either you or your partner are convicted of more than one benefit offence within a 3-year period (see Chapter 57(6)).

3. The personal allowances

The personal allowances are part of your applicable amount (see 2). For IS, the decision maker takes into account your age and whether you are one of a married or unmarried couple.

Personal allowances		per week
Couple	both aged 18 or over [1]	£88.15
	both under 18 [2]	£67.15
	one aged 25 or over [3]	£56.20
	one aged 18-24 [3]	£44.50
Lone parent	aged 18 or over	£56.20
	aged under 18 (higher rate)	£44.50
	aged under 18 (lower rate)	£33.85
Single person	aged 25 or over	£56.20
	aged 18-24	£44.50
	aged under 18 (higher rate)	£44.50
	aged under 18 (lower rate)	£33.85

If you are aged under 18

The rate you get depends on meeting other conditions.

Couples – In the table of rates above, the reference numbers mean:

1: includes couples where one is under 18 but is: eligible for IS or would be if they were single; or eligible for income-based jobseeker's allowance (JSA) or discretionary JSA (see Chapter 17(19));

2: only if one is responsible for a child; or each would be eligible for IS if they were single; or the claimant's partner is eligible for income-based JSA or discretionary JSA. If only one of the couple is eligible for IS, etc, the single person's allowance of £33.85 (or £44.50 if you fall into one of the groups of people listed below) would apply;

3: only if the other is under 18 and would not be eligible for IS (even if they were single), income-based JSA or discretionary JSA.

Single person or lone parent – You get the higher rate of £44.50 if you qualify for a disability premium or you fall into one of these groups of people:

- you have no parent nor anyone acting in place of your parents;
- you are not living with your parents, or anyone acting in their place, *and*
  - before you reached 16 you were placed in the care of someone other than a 'close relative' (see 7 below) by a local authority; or were in custody; *or*
  - you moved into your accommodation under the supervision of the probation service or a local authority as part of a rehabilitation or resettlement programme; or to avoid physical or sexual abuse; or because of a mental or physical handicap or illness and you need that accommodation because of your disability;
- you are living away from your parents (and anyone acting in their place), they are unable financially to support you – and they are chronically sick or mentally or physically disabled, or detained in custody, or prohibited from coming into Great Britain;
- you *'of necessity'* have to live away from your parents (and anyone acting in their place), because you are estranged from them; or you are in physical or moral danger; or there is a serious risk to your physical or mental health.

Part 1, Schedule 2, IS (General) Regulations

4. The premiums

There are 6 different premiums, each one having specific qualifying conditions, as detailed in 5 to 10 below. The premiums are part of your applicable amount (see 2). Some premiums overlap with each other and you can only get one of these at a time; you get the one that is worth the most (overlapping premiums). Others you can get in addition to any other premium (add-on premiums).

Overlapping premiums – You may get just one of the following premiums. If you qualify for more than one, you will only get the highest.

Premiums – per week	single	couple
Disability premium	£23.95	£34.20
Pensioner premium	–	£78.90
Bereavement premium	£25.85	–

Add-on premiums – In addition, you may get any or all of the following premiums (except that if you qualify for a pensioner premium you cannot get an enhanced disability premium for yourself or your partner).

Add-on premiums		per week
Carer premium		£25.80
Severe disability premium	single	£45.50
	couple (one qualifies)	£45.50
	couple (both qualify)	£91.00
Enhanced disability premium	single	£11.70
	couple	£16.90

5. The disability premium

The disability premium for a single claimant aged 16 or over is £23.95. For a couple the disability premium is £34.20, whether one or both of the couple count as disabled.

The disability premium can be awarded on top of an enhanced disability premium, carer premium and severe disability premium.

The disability premium is payable only while the person who qualifies is aged under 60. So if you are the IS claimant but it is your partner who qualifies for the disability premium and they reach the age of 60 before you do, if they choose not to claim pension credit, then a claim for IS could technically continue (until you also reach the age of 60) but with a pensioner premium payable instead of the disability premium.

There are two ways of qualifying for the disability premium:

- you (or your partner) must meet at least one of the disability conditions; *or*
- the person who is, or becomes, the IS claimant meets the incapacity condition.

The disability conditions (claimant or partner)

You (or your partner) must be:

- registered as blind, or taken off that register in the past 28 weeks; *or*
- getting one of the following qualifying benefits:
  - attendance allowance
  - disability living allowance (DLA)
  - long-term incapacity benefit (IB)
  - severe disablement allowance (SDA)
  - the disability element or severe disability element of working tax credit
  - war pensioner's mobility supplement
  - constant attendance allowance

(but you or your partner must satisfy the conditions for getting that benefit yourselves. It doesn't count if you are paid someone else's benefit as an appointee.)

Points to note – If your DLA stops when you are in hospital, you won't lose the disability premium as well (unless your personal allowance is reduced – see Box L.1, Chapter 33).

If you have been getting long-term IB or SDA, and have already qualified for the disability premium, the premium won't be withdrawn if you go on a government training course such as Work-based Learning for Adults or for any period in which you receive a training allowance. Nor will the premium be withdrawn if the overlapping benefit rules mean that you cannot be paid your long-term IB or SDA (eg because you start to receive a bereavement allowance).

Applying for the premium – If you get one of these qualifying benefits backdated, write to the IS section at your local Jobcentre Plus office and ask them to include the disability premium from either the start of your IS claim or the start of your award of the qualifying benefit, whichever is the later.

If your IS claim is turned down while you are still waiting for a decision on a claim for one of these qualifying benefits, you must make sure that you make another IS claim within 3 months of the decision awarding the qualifying benefit so that you don't lose out on backdated IS. See Chapter 6(2) for more details.

The incapacity condition (claimant only)

You must be the IS claimant. If you are one of a couple, you must become the IS claimant (see Chapter 6(3)). But you don't have to have been the IS claimant during the qualifying period for a disability premium under this incapacity condition. To qualify under the incapacity condition, you must:

- have been incapable of work or entitled to statutory sick pay during the qualifying period of 52 weeks (or 28 weeks if you are terminally ill); *and*
- still be incapable of work. See Chapter 11 for details of the assessment of incapacity for work.

During the qualifying period – You don't have to be in receipt of IS during the 52-week qualifying period, so if you have already been incapable of work for 52 weeks before you claim, the disability premium will be included immediately.

There are linking rules that allow gaps in your incapacity during the qualifying period to be ignored (see below).

The qualifying period is 28 weeks if you are terminally ill. You count as terminally ill if you *'suffer from a progressive disease and [your] death can reasonably be expected within 6 months'*.

After you have qualified – If you stop being incapable of work, you will lose the disability premium unless you can pass the 'disability condition' (eg you get one of the qualifying benefits) – see above. But you will be able to go straight back onto the disability premium if you become incapable of work again and the two spells of incapacity are linked (see below).

If you go on a government training course such as Work-Based Learning for Adults or you receive a training allowance, you will not lose the disability premium.

8-week linking rule – Gaps of up to 8 weeks in your incapacity (for any reason) are ignored. When you become incapable of work again, the two spells of incapacity are linked together. If you had already served the qualifying period, the disability premium is included again immediately. If you are still in the qualifying period, you pick up where you left off.

52-week linking rule – If your incapacity stops because you begin work or training, you may be a 'welfare to work beneficiary' if you meet other rules (see Chapter 15(12)). Starting from the day after your last day of incapacity, there is a 52-week linking period during which your entitlement to the disability premium is protected if you become incapable of work again. If you are part-way through the qualifying period when you start work or training, you only need to serve the remainder of the qualifying period before the disability premium is included.

Applying for the premium – Send in the claim pack, SC1, which you can get from your local Jobcentre Plus office, together with a medical certificate from your doctor on form Med 3. If you have been incapable of work for some time but not sending in medical certificates, ask your doctor for a backdated medical certificate on form Med 5. If you are already getting IS, send a covering letter with the SC1 claim-pack and medical certificate stating that you wish to claim the IS disability premium on the grounds of incapacity.

If you are refused backdated IB because you claimed late, this does not prevent days of incapacity in that past period counting towards the disability premium.

If you are claiming on release from prison, note that days of incapacity while in prison count towards the disability premium. Get a backdated medical certificate.

Incapacity before 13.4.95 – Before 13.4.95, rules on the qualifying period and on assessing incapacity for work were different. See *Disability Rights Handbook* 19th edition.

6. The enhanced disability premium

This is £11.70 for a single person and £16.90 for a couple where one or both qualify. You or your partner qualify for the enhanced disability premium if you or they are paid disability living allowance (DLA) highest rate care component. It can be awarded on top of a disability premium. The enhanced disability premium is payable only while the person who qualifies is aged under 60.

If your DLA stops when you are in hospital, you won't lose the enhanced disability premium (unless your personal allowance is reduced – see Box L.1, Chapter 33).

7. The severe disability premium

The severe disability premium (SDP) can be awarded on top of the disability premium and any enhanced disability premium, or the pensioner premium. It is £45.50 for each person who qualifies. To qualify:

- you must get disability living allowance (DLA) care component at the middle or highest rate, or attendance allowance (AA) (or constant attendance allowance); *and*
- no one gets carer's allowance (CA) for looking after you; *and*
- you technically count as living alone (see below).

Couples – If you are one of a couple, you can qualify for the SDP if:

- both you and your partner get DLA care component at the middle or highest rate, or AA (or constant attendance allowance); *and*
- you technically count as living alone; *and either*
- someone gets CA for looking after just one of you; *or*
- no one gets CA for looking after either of you.

If your partner is registered blind you can still qualify for the SDP even if they do not get DLA or AA. You are treated as if you were a single person.

If you both get middle or highest rate care component or AA, and no one gets CA for looking after either you or your partner, your SDP will be £91.

If you both get middle or highest rate DLA care component or AA, and one person gets CA for looking after you (or your partner), your SDP will be £45.50. If two people are getting CA for looking after you and your partner, you won't get any SDP. Note that it is quite possible for you and your partner to each get CA for looking after each other. Normally this would disqualify you both from getting the SDP. However, when CA cannot actually be paid because of the overlapping benefit rules (see 8 below) then the SDP would not be affected. If you both have overlapping benefits such that neither of you are actually paid CA, then not only could you get the higher SDP of £91, but you could also get two carer premiums.

Is someone caring for you?

If someone gets CA for looking after you, that excludes you from the SDP. If CA is not actually payable to your carer, for whatever reason, you can get the SDP. For example, if CA cannot be paid to your carer because they get another non-means-tested benefit (such as incapacity benefit) which cancels out CA under the overlapping benefit rules, you will be entitled to the SDP. In this example, your carer may also qualify for a carer premium (see 8 below).

Neither you nor your carer can be forced to claim CA. Although the DWP will ask you if anyone is caring for you, and will send you the CA claim-form to give to your carer, nothing should happen if a non-resident carer decides not to claim CA. By the same token, you cannot stop your carer claiming CA, as long as they meet, or are able to meet, the qualifying conditions for getting CA. If, however, they spend less than 35 hours from Sunday through to Saturday looking after you, they won't normally be eligible for CA.

Note that the deprivation of income and notional income rules apply also to CA (see Chapter 5(14)). Seek expert advice if you or your carer fall foul of these rules (see also para 28608, Vol 5, *Decision Makers Guide* – see Box R.9, Chapter 58).

Your premium is only affected once CA is actually awarded. Arrears of CA for any period before the date of the award will not affect your SDP.

Living alone?

You cannot qualify for the SDP if you have a partner who is not also getting the middle or highest rate of DLA care component or AA (unless your partner is registered blind), or if you have people living with you who are classed as 'non-dependants'. A non-dependant is someone who lives in your home – usually an adult son or daughter, friend or relative.

The following people are not classed as non-dependants, however, and therefore their presence in your home is ignored:

- anyone aged under 18;
- a dependent child aged 18 who is part of your family and still in full-time non-advanced education (see Chapter 36(1));
- someone who gets the middle or highest rate DLA care component or AA (or constant attendance allowance);
- anyone who is registered blind;
- someone who does not *'normally'* reside with you – because they normally live elsewhere, they cannot count as a non-dependant (there is no definition of 'normally resides' in terms of time, frequency or anything else – see CSIS/100/93 and CIS/14850/96);
- someone who is not a *'close relative'* and *'jointly occupies'* your dwelling as a co-owner or who is sharing legal liability to make 'rent' payments – a joint occupier, such as a joint tenant, cannot count as a non-dependant. If a co-owner or joint tenant is a close relative of you (or your partner), they will count as a non-dependant (and so exclude you from the SDP) unless:
  – the co-ownership or joint liability began before 11.4.88; *or*
  – the co-ownership or joint liability began after 11.4.88 but began *'on or before the date upon which [you or your] partner first occupied the dwelling in question'*;

Reg 3(2C) IS (General) Regulations

- someone who is not a close relative and who is your resident landlord sharing living accommodation with you – to whom you or your partner are *'liable to make payments on a commercial basis in respect of [your] occupation of [his or her] dwelling'*;
- someone who is not a close relative and who shares living accommodation with you and is *'liable to make payments on a commercial basis to [you or your partner] in respect of [his or her] occupation of [your] dwelling'* – a licensee, tenant or sub-tenant cannot count as a non-dependant;
- a live-in helper who has been placed with you by a charitable or voluntary body (not by a public or local authority), where the organisation (not the helper) charges you for that help – the charge need only be nominal.

If you are already getting the SDP and someone else joins your household *'for the first time in order to care for [you or your partner]'*, the SDP continues for up to 12 weeks after the date they join your household. This is to give them time to claim CA. Once CA is awarded, the SDP stops.

Close relatives and living arrangements

A 'close relative' means a parent, parent-in-law, son, daughter, son/daughter-in-law, step-parent, stepson/daughter, brother, sister, or the (married or unmarried) partner of any of those. If you have a licence or tenancy agreement with a relative who is not a close relative, you (or they) would only be excluded from the SDP while you were residing with them if your occupancy agreement was not on a commercial basis.

Living independently? – If you have entirely separate living accommodation, you cannot be said to 'normally reside' with other people living under the same roof. For example, if you live in a separate granny flat, your right to the SDP is not affected, even if a close relative lives under the same roof.

If you are living under the same roof as other people, with a separate bedroom, kitchen and living room, you won't count as residing with those other people – so you can qualify for the SDP. It makes no difference if you share a bathroom, lavatory or any communal area (which does not include any communal rooms, unless you are living in sheltered accommodation).

Separate liability – If you share a living room or kitchen with other people but are *'separately liable to make payments in respect of [your] occupation of the dwelling to the landlord'*, you won't count as residing with those other people even if they are close relatives. The DWP sees this as typically covering someone in supported lodgings.

Protecting pre-21.10.91 SDP – If you are a co-owner or joint tenant with a close relative and had an award of IS, including an SDP, in the week before 21.10.91, your position is protected. Protection will survive changes in the type of agreement, in the parties to the agreement, and even a move of home (see reg 4(9) IS (General) Amendment (No. 6) Regs 1991). It cannot survive a carer getting CA or a non-dependant joining your home. If you have a break off IS, you can regain your protected SDP if:

- the break is no more than 8 weeks or less (for any reason); *or*
- the break is no more than 12 weeks (covered by the work 'trial period' provisions); *or*
- you have just finished employment training or an employment rehabilitation course and you re-claim IS immediately.

Hospital

If you enter hospital, the SDP will be withdrawn once your DLA care component or AA is withdrawn – usually once you've been in hospital for 4 weeks.

For couples, if both of you get DLA care component or AA, and one or both of you enters hospital, you will still get the SDP even after the care component or AA is withdrawn, but the SDP will only be paid at the rate of £44.50.

If your carer enters hospital and loses CA, you may qualify for the SDP while they are in hospital.

8. The carer premium

The carer premium can be awarded in addition to any of the other premiums covered in this chapter. It is £25.80 a week for each person who qualifies.

You'll qualify for a carer premium if you or your partner:

- are actually paid an amount of carer's allowance (CA); *or*
- have an underlying entitlement to CA: you are entitled to CA but it cannot be paid because of the overlapping benefit rules.

Overlapping benefits – You must be entitled to CA, so that some CA would be paid but for the overlapping benefit rules. These rules mean you cannot be paid the full amount of CA at the same time as receiving the full amount of your entitlement to incapacity benefit, state pension, severe disablement allowance, maternity allowance, widows' or bereavement benefits, unemployability supplement or contribution-based jobseeker's allowance (JSA). In general, CA is reduced by the amount of the other listed benefits payable for the same period. Unless you receive less than £45.70 a week from a listed benefit, your CA will be cancelled out.

Although you can get the carer premium whether or not your CA is overlapped, the person you are caring for will lose their SDP if you are paid CA. The person you are caring for can only qualify for the SDP if you can't be paid CA (either because CA is completely overlapped, or you haven't claimed it).

8-week extension

The carer premium can continue for 8 weeks after you stop getting CA or lose an underlying entitlement to it. Your caring role can have ended temporarily or permanently and for any reason at all, with one exception: where the person you are caring for dies (see below). During this 8-week extension of the carer premium you continue to be eligible for IS as a carer. After this you will be expected to sign on and claim JSA instead, unless you are eligible for IS in another way (see Box B.1, Chapter 3).

If the person you care for dies – In this case, since CA can also be extended for 8 weeks, the carer premium can continue during the same period and is limited to that period. Thus, it must finish 8 weeks after the death of the person being cared for.

9. The pensioner premium

Now that pension credit (PC) has replaced IS for claimants aged 60 or over, there are only limited circumstances in which the pensioner premium will be relevant to an IS claim. It will be payable only when the IS claimant is under 60 and their partner reaches the age of 60 first and chooses not to claim PC instead (see Chapter 41). Since PC has a number of features that make it more attractive than IS (particularly with respect to the way in which capital and savings are treated), this is not likely to occur very often. The pensioner premium is still, however, significant with respect to housing benefit (HB) and council tax benefit (CTB). The pensioner premium is £78.90 for a couple (and, in the case of income-based jobseeker's allowance, HB and CTB, £53.25 for a single person).

Enhanced and higher pensioner premiums – The pensioner premium was originally paid at three different levels: the pensioner, enhanced, and higher pensioner premiums. Although these separate premiums still technically exist, they are now all paid at the same rate – ie the amount you get is the same whichever one you qualify for. The difference occasionally becomes important (we point out when it does).

❑ **Pensioner premium** – You qualify for this if you or your partner are aged 60-74 (inclusive).

❑ **Enhanced pensioner premium** – You qualify for this if you or your partner are aged 75-79 (inclusive).

❑ **Higher pensioner premium** – You qualify for this if:

- you or your partner are aged 80 or over; *or*
- you or your partner are aged 60 or over and also satisfy the 'disability condition' for a disability premium (see 5).

  There are other ways to qualify for the higher pensioner premium. For details see *Disability Rights Handbook* 25th edition, page 20.

10. The bereavement premium

Bereavement benefits were introduced on 9.4.01 to replace the old system of widows' benefits. For the next 5 years, special arrangements allow men and women who were aged

55 to 59 on 9.4.01 and widowed since that date, to claim IS, which includes an extra bereavement premium once any bereavement allowance has ended.

The bereavement premium is £25.85 a week. It can be awarded in addition to a carer premium, severe disability premium or enhanced disability premium. It overlaps with a disability premium, so if you are eligible for both you will get the bereavement premium, as it is worth more.

You can get a bereavement premium with your IS if you:

- were aged 55-59 (inclusive) on 9.4.01; *and*
- were getting a bereavement allowance that has now ended (see Chapter 51); *and*
- are claiming IS for yourself as a single person.

If you do not already get IS, you must claim no more than 8 weeks after the last day of entitlement to bereavement allowance. If you leave it any later, although you may still qualify for IS, you will not qualify for a bereavement premium.

If at any time in the future you claim for a new partner you will lose entitlement to the bereavement premium.

11. Housing costs

If you pay rent, you may get housing benefit (HB) (see Chapter 7). For help with the cost of a care home, see Chapter 30. Mortgage interest payments and certain other housing costs are covered by IS. Housing costs for income-based jobseeker's allowance (JSA) and for pension credit are treated in a similar way as for IS. Where there are differences, these are noted.

The basic rules

Housing costs may be included in your IS applicable amount if:

- you or your partner are liable for the housing costs at the home you normally live in – see below; *and*
- the type of housing costs is covered by IS – see below; *and*
- your mortgage was not taken out while you or your partner were on IS or income-based JSA or between claims (there are some exceptions) – see 12.

The amount of housing costs met by IS is worked out taking into account the following factors:

- the ceiling on loans of £100,000 (there are some exceptions) – see 13;
- the standard rate of interest applied to loans – see 13;
- the waiting period (ie the number of weeks you must be entitled to IS before housing costs are included in your applicable amount) – see 14;
- whether your housing costs are 'excessive' – see 13;
- deductions for any 'non-dependants' living with you (eg adult son or daughter, friend or relative). The law assumes they are contributing towards your housing costs, whether they are paying anything or not. Unless your circumstances, or your non-dependant's, exempt you from the deduction, an amount is deducted from your assessed housing costs. IS rules are almost the same as for HB (see Chapter 7(22)). No deduction is made from your IS housing costs if a deduction for that non-dependant is already being made from your HB.

Liability for housing costs

You (or your partner) must be liable for housing costs for the home you live in. You are still treated as liable if the person normally liable for the costs is not meeting them and you have to meet them in order to carry on living in your home, as long as it is considered reasonable to do so.

Absence from home

Generally, you can only get help on one home at a time and this must be the home you occupy. In some situations you are treated as occupying your home when you are not actually present there – eg during a temporary absence of up to 13 weeks (or 52 weeks in some cases), or for up to 4 weeks when moving home. Chapter 7(6) and (7) cover the extra conditions – the HB rules are almost the same as the IS rules.

Housing costs covered by IS

The following housing costs can be included as part of your IS applicable amount:

- mortgage interest payments (see 12);
- interest on loans for certain repairs and improvements (see 12);
- service charges – these are charges payable as a condition of your occupancy (eg under a lease) that relate to the provision of adequate accommodation. House insurance can be included if payments are made under the terms of the lease (rather than as a condition of the mortgage). Service charges for repairs and improvements listed in 12 below are not met by IS, although you can get help to pay interest on a loan taken out to pay these charges. Service charges are not met where these would be ineligible under the HB rules (see Chapter 7(8));
- ground rent or other rent payable under a long lease of over 21 years;
- payments under a co-ownership scheme;
- rent if you are a Crown tenant;
- payments on a tent;
- rentcharges – this is a nominal rent that may be charged to a freeholder.

Paragraphs 15–17, Schedule 3, IS (General) Regulations

Housing costs not covered by IS

IS personal allowances are intended to cover day-to-day living expenses, including the cost of water and fuel. For this reason water and fuel charges cannot be additionally included as housing costs. Other housing costs not covered by IS include:

- housing costs covered by HB;
- ineligible service charges – see Chapter 7(8);
- endowment premiums or capital repayments payable on a mortgage;
- mortgage interest on a new or additional loan taken out while you were on IS or income-based JSA or between claims (but there are exceptions) – see 12.

Following changes to the rules on 2.10.95, some previously eligible housings costs are no longer covered by IS: arrears of mortgage interest payments; loans for certain repairs and improvements; and extra help to separated couples with loans secured on the home. If, in the benefit week including 1.10.95, your applicable amount included interest for such a loan, it will continue to be covered as long as you or your partner remain on IS, disregarding any breaks in IS entitlement of 12 weeks or less. If you separate from your partner, you keep this protection. If you are a 'welfare to work beneficiary' (see Chapter 15(12)) this protection should be maintained on a new claim where you become incapable of work again within your 52-week linking period.

12. Which mortgages and loans are covered?

IS only covers interest on mortgages (or higher purchase agreements or other loans) used:

- to buy your home – this includes buying your home jointly with others, buying the freehold if you are a leaseholder, or buying out a joint owner;
- to pay off an earlier loan, but only to the extent that the earlier loan would have been covered by IS. For example, if your outstanding mortgage was £10,000 and you borrow £12,000 to repay that first mortgage, IS can only cover the interest on £10,000 of the second loan;
- for certain repairs and improvements (see below).

Where a loan is taken out partly for a different purpose (eg a business loan), IS will not cover that part of the loan.

If your loan is covered by IS, an amount is added to your applicable amount, worked out according to the rules in 13 below. (See 14 below for when entitlement to housing costs can begin.) If your lender is part of the Mortgage Direct scheme this amount is not paid to you but is deducted from your benefit and paid 4-weekly in arrears directly to your lender.

Mortgages taken out while on IS or income-based JSA or between claims

The general rule is that IS does not meet mortgage interest on a loan taken out to buy a home while you or your partner were on IS or income-based jobseeker's allowance (JSA) (or on certain New Deal options) or within a break in entitlement of 26 weeks or less. The intention is to restrict your entitlement to the level of help (if any) you were already entitled to, either from IS, JSA or housing benefit (HB). Once a restriction is made, it continues to apply until you have a break in entitlement to IS or income-based JSA of over 26 weeks. Some loans are exempt from the restrictions (see below). These restrictions do not apply to loans for repairs and improvements.

Replacement or additional loans – If you already have a mortgage and you increase it or take out an additional loan while on IS or between claims (eg if you take on a bigger mortgage to move home or buy out a joint owner), IS does not meet the additional amount. You can replace one mortgage with another provided the new mortgage is for the same amount or less. Where your new mortgage has been used to buy a home, and you pay off all or part of an earlier eligible loan in respect of another property from the sale of that property, then IS on the new mortgage is restricted to the amount of the earlier loan. This allows separated couples who sell their home to each have IS paid for mortgage interest on a new home at the full amount of the previous mortgage.

If you were previously getting HB – If you take on a mortgage while on IS, income-based JSA, or between claims, the amount of IS for mortgage interest and for other housing costs (such as service charges and ground rent) is restricted to the level of HB payable to you or your partner in the week before the week you buy the home. If you were getting both HB and IS/JSA housing costs in that week, perhaps because you were on a shared ownership scheme, the restriction is to the total of the HB payable plus the IS/JSA housing costs included in your applicable amount. The restricted amount can only subsequently go up to take account of increases in the standard rate of mortgage interest (see 13 below) or increases in other housing costs (service charges, etc).

If in the week before you buy the home you were not getting any HB, for example you lived in your parents' home, then none of the mortgage interest is met by IS.

If your applicable amount previously included only housing costs other than for loan interest (eg service charges or ground rent) – If you take on a mortgage while on IS or income-based JSA or when you are between claims, IS is restricted to the level of housing costs included in your applicable amount in the week before the week you buy a home. The restricted amount can only then increase if the standard rate of mortgage interest goes up or there is an increase in service charges or ground rent, etc.

Loans exempt from restrictions – In the following cases, loans are exempt from the restrictions described above, and IS for housing costs is worked out under the usual rules:

- any loan taken out before 3.5.94;
- a loan taken out, or an existing loan increased, to buy *'alternative accommodation more suited to the special needs of a disabled person'* than your previous home (see below for who counts as a disabled person). This could include moving home to be nearer a carer (CIS/14551/96) or moving to sheltered housing;
- an additional or increased loan taken out because you've sold your home to buy another solely in order to provide separate bedrooms for children of different sexes aged 10 or over who are part of your family.

Paragraph 4, Schedule 3, IS (General) Regulations

Who counts as a 'disabled person'? – Someone is considered to be 'a disabled person' if they satisfy the conditions for a disability premium, disabled child premium, enhanced or higher pensioner premium at the date the loan is taken out, but they don't actually have to be getting any of these premiums or be entitled to IS. The disabled person could be you (the IS claimant) or a member of your family or someone else who lives with you or who will be living with you. When considering which loans are exempt from restriction for pension credit purposes, the definition of a 'disabled person' is slightly different. They must be someone who:

– is aged 75 or over; *or*
– had they qualified for IS, would have qualified for the higher pensioner or disability premium; *or*
– is under 19 who you or your partner are responsible for who gets disability living allowance (or would get it were they not in hospital) or is registered as blind.

Loans for repairs and improvements

IS covers the interest on loans taken out and used within 6 months to pay for repairs and improvements to your home. These must be *'undertaken with a view to maintaining the fitness of the dwelling for human habitation'* and fall within the following categories:

- adapting your home for *'the special needs of a disabled person'* – see above for who counts as 'a disabled person' for this rule;
- provision of a bath, shower, sink, lavatory, ventilation, natural lighting, electric lighting and sockets, or insulation of the home;
- provision of facilities for preparing and cooking food, storing fuel or refuse, or for drainage;
- provision of separate bedrooms for children of different sexes aged 10 or over who are part of your family;
- repairs to existing heating systems or of unsafe structural defects;
- damp proof measures.

Loans to pay service charges for any of these works are covered, as are loans used to pay off an existing loan for repairs but only to the extent that the existing loan would have qualified.

Paragraph 16, Schedule 3, IS (General) Regulations

If your loan is covered by IS, an amount is added to your applicable amount, worked out according to the rules in 13 below.

13. The assessment of mortgage and loan interest

There is a limit of £100,000 on the amount of eligible loans on which interest payments are met by IS. Provided the total amount of outstanding capital on your mortgage(s) and/or loan(s) is no more than £100,000 and your housing costs are not 'excessive', the interest to be met by IS is worked out on the whole of the eligible capital, using the standard rate of interest. In most cases, there is a waiting period before the loan interest is included in your applicable amount (see 14 below).

Once interest is included, reductions to the amount of eligible capital owing (eg if you reduce it with capital repayments) are only taken into account after a year and then annually. This also applies if you move between IS and income-based jobseeker's allowance (JSA) or onto pension credit; reductions in capital are taken into account annually from the date housing costs were first included in whichever benefit was first claimed, providing there is no more than 12 weeks between claims (longer in certain circumstances).

The ceiling

If your loan (or the total of your loans) is above the ceiling of £100,000, the interest to be met by IS is worked out only on the first £100,000. Loans taken out to adapt the home *'for the special needs of a disabled person'* are exempt and do not count towards this limit (see 'Loans for repairs and improvements' in 12 above). If you are eligible for IS for housing costs on two homes, the ceiling is applied separately to each home. Any payments from a mortgage protection insurance policy to cover the interest on the part of a loan above the ceiling are disregarded as income for IS (see Chapter 5(9)).

The £100,000 ceiling applies to IS claims made from 9.4.95. If you have been on IS or income-based JSA continuously since before this, existing loans will be met up to the level of the ceiling that applied at the time you made your claim: £125,000 between 11.4.94 and 8.4.95; £150,000 between 2.8.93 and 10.4.94; no limit prior to 2.8.93. Loans that you take out or increase while on IS are subject to whichever ceiling applies at the time you do so. Generally, a break off IS or income-based JSA of just one day is enough to end this protection. However, if you are covered by the 52-week benefit protection as a 'welfare to work beneficiary' (see Chapter 15(12)) this protection is maintained on a new claim where you become incapable of work again within your 52-week linking period.

Excessive housing costs

The amount of housing costs met by IS may be restricted if they are regarded as 'excessive', ie your home is larger than you need for your household, or the area is more expensive than other areas in which there is suitable alternative accommodation, or your housing costs are higher than those for suitable alternative accommodation in the area.

But no restriction is made if it is not reasonable to expect you to move, taking into account the availability of suitable alternative accommodation and the level of housing costs in the area, and the circumstances of you and your family. In particular, the age and health of yourself and your family must be considered, as well as your employment prospects, and the effect of a move on the children's education. But other factors could also be relevant – eg whether you provide care, or rely on the care or support of someone nearby.

No restriction is made for the first 26 weeks of your claim or after a decision is made to introduce a restriction, if you could afford the costs when you took them on; nor for a further 26 weeks if you're doing your best to find cheaper accommodation. The 26 weeks continues to run during a break in IS of 12 weeks or less.

Where a restriction is applied, the amount of loan to be met is restricted to the amount you need to obtain suitable alternative accommodation.

Calculating the interest

Once the amount of capital outstanding on your eligible loan/s has been established, the interest to be included in your IS applicable amount is calculated on that capital using, in most cases, a standard interest rate. The rate is set with reference to the Bank of England base rate plus 1.58% (prior to 28.11.04 it was linked to an average of the interest rates charged by the top building societies).

The standard interest rate is applied in all cases, with one exception. Where your actual interest rate was less than 5% on the day your housing costs were first included in your IS applicable amount (and this was prior to 28.11.04), it is your actual interest rate on that day that is applied. Changes in actual interest rate are ignored for 12 months from that day, unless it increases to at least 5% or if your housing costs are re-assessed. The standard interest rate will then be applied.

Arrears of interest cannot be met.

Prior to 2.10.95, IS housing costs were worked out using actual interest rates. There is transitional protection (called 'add back') for those who would otherwise have lost out when the rules changed. See *Disability Rights Handbook* 24th edition, page 23.

14. When does entitlement to housing costs begin?

In most cases there is a waiting period from the start of your IS entitlement before housing costs are included in your applicable amount. Generally, the length of the waiting period depends on whether you took out your mortgage or other housing costs before or after 2.10.95.

Note that the waiting period begins from the start of your IS entitlement even if you have no housing costs at the time. So if you take out a loan while on IS having already served the waiting period, and you are eligible for help with the costs (see 12 above), housing costs can be included immediately.

If you are not entitled to IS because your income or capital is over the limit, or there is a break in your claim, see below. In some cases the waiting period can run even though you are not getting IS.

No waiting period

If your partner is aged 60 or over – Eligible housing costs are included in your applicable amount from the beginning of your IS entitlement, or from the day your partner reaches 60 if you are part-way through the waiting period. Similarly, there is no waiting period for housing costs to be included in pension credit (PC).

Certain housing costs – There is no waiting period for payments under a co-ownership scheme, rent for a Crown tenant or payments on a tent. These are included from the start of your IS entitlement.

8 to 26-week waiting period

Housing costs agreements made before 2.10.95 – If your loan or other housing costs arose under an agreement made before 2.10.95, your housing costs are included in your IS applicable amount as follows. If you've been continuously entitled to IS (or treated as entitled to IS – see below if you're not entitled to IS during the waiting period) for:

- less than 8 weeks – no housing costs are met;
- at least 8 weeks but less than 26 weeks – 50% of assessed housing costs are met;
- 26 weeks or more – 100% of assessed housing costs are met.

Replacement loans – If, on or after 2.10.95, you replace one mortgage or loan with another, the 8–26-week waiting period applies only where the new loan is between the same parties, for the same property and for the same amount or less, and replaces a loan that was taken out before 2.10.95. Otherwise the 39-week waiting period applies.

Special circumstances – If your loan or housing costs agreement was made on or after 2.10.95, the 8–26-week waiting period still applies if, when you claim IS you:

- are eligible for IS as a carer (see Box B.1, Chapter 3); *or*
- have been refused payments under a mortgage protection insurance policy because you have a pre-existing medical condition or because you are HIV-positive; *or*
- are a prisoner on remand; *or*
- have a child and are claiming IS because your partner has died or has 'abandoned' you. Some women forced to move out because of their partner's violence have argued successfully that they have effectively been 'abandoned'. But it does not apply if your partner has been imprisoned. If you become one of a couple and you have not yet been

on IS for 39 weeks, you lose this protection and the 39-week waiting period applies instead.

39-week waiting period
If your loan or other housing costs arose under an agreement made on or after 2.10.95, 100% of assessed housing costs are included in your applicable amount after you have been continuously entitled to IS (or treated as entitled – see below) for 39 weeks. You get no help with housing costs for the first 39 weeks of your claim, unless you come under one of the special circumstances above, when the 8–26-week waiting period applies instead.

If you are not entitled to IS during the waiting period
Throughout the waiting period, you must be entitled to IS – although breaks in entitlement of 12 weeks or less are ignored. A break in IS entitlement of more than 12 weeks puts you back to the start. But there are linking rules that, in some situations, allow the period in between the end of one IS claim and the beginning of another to count towards the waiting period as though you had been entitled to IS throughout. Others allow a period when your partner was the claimant to count.

If you have other income or your capital is over £8,000, you might not be entitled to IS until your applicable amount goes up after the waiting period when the housing costs are included. In this case, the waiting period can run while you are entitled to certain benefits or national insurance (NI) credits, or if you are a carer or single parent (see below).

During a break in IS claims, or a change of claimant – You are treated as entitled to IS:

- for any time you are entitled to income-based jobseeker's allowance (JSA);
- during a gap between claims for IS or income-based JSA of 12 weeks or less;
- during a gap between IS claims of up to 52 weeks if you are protected under the back-to-work linking rule (see below);
- during a gap between IS claims of up to 52 weeks if you are a 'welfare to work beneficiary' (see Chapter 15(12)) and become incapable of work again;
- for any period in which it is decided you were entitled to IS or income-based JSA;
- during the time your partner was getting IS or income-based JSA for both of you if you swap to become the claimant yourself;
- during a gap between claims of 26 weeks or less where your last claim included full housing costs, your IS or income-based JSA stopped because of child support payments and you re-claim later because the child support payments are either reduced or terminated;
- during a gap between claims while you or your partner are on a government training scheme or employment rehabilitation scheme or certain New Deal options;
- for the same period your ex-partner was getting IS, income-based JSA or PC for both of you, if you claim within 12 weeks of separating;
- during the time someone was claiming IS or income-based JSA for you as their dependent child, if you claim within 12 weeks of the end of the claim and your claim includes a child who was also their dependant;
- for the same period that your new partner was getting IS or income-based JSA as a single person or lone parent, if you claim within 12 weeks of becoming a couple.

In the last three cases the 12-week linking period is extended to 52 weeks if the back-to-work linking rule applies, or you (or in the last case, your partner) are a 'welfare to work beneficiary' and you become incapable of work again (see below).

If your income or capital is over the IS limit – If you cannot get IS only because your income is higher than your applicable amount and/or your capital is over £8,000 you are treated as entitled to IS for up to 39 weeks if you satisfy one of the following conditions on each day (but gaps of up to 12 weeks are allowed):

- you are entitled to contribution-based JSA, statutory sick pay or incapacity benefit; *or*
- you are entitled to NI credits for incapacity for work or unemployment (see Chapter 12(2)); *or*
- you are treated as entitled to IS during a break in IS claims, or because of a change in claimant (see rules above); *or*
- you are eligible for IS as a carer (see Box B.1, Chapter 3) or you are a lone parent – provided you are not working 16 hours or more a week, your partner is not working 24 hours or more a week, you are not a student who is excluded from IS (see 38(3)), and you're not absent from the UK other than in circumstances described in Chapter 50(4).

The 39 weeks runs from when your IS claim is refused, so don't delay putting in your claim.

If you also have a mortgage protection policy, the 39 weeks is extended to cover the period that payments are made under the policy, provided your capital is within the limit of £8,000 throughout.

Once you have qualified for housing costs
You will not have to serve the waiting period again if you have a break in your claim of 12 weeks or less, or your claims can be linked under one of the other linking rules described above.

Back-to-work linking rule – If your IS stops because you or your partner start work (employed or self-employed) or your working hours or earnings increase, you do not have to serve the waiting period again on a new claim if the break in claims is no longer than 52 weeks. Housing costs can be included from the start of your new claim. Similar protection will be afforded if your participation in certain New Deal options takes you off IS. If you had already qualified for the 50% help with housing costs before starting work or the New Deal option, you are also covered by the linking rule.

If this linking rule does not help you, the 52-week linking rule for 'welfare to work beneficiaries' might apply (see Chapter 15(12)). This gives you extra protections, eg against the £100,000 ceiling on loans if a higher ceiling applied in your earlier claim.

When you start work, you may continue to get IS for housing costs for the first 4 weeks ('mortgage interest run-on' – see Chapter 15(4)).

Insurance payments – If you have a break in claim of 26 weeks or less and payments from an insurance policy for unemployment have run out, your two claims are linked and the period in between during which you were receiving the insurance payments is ignored. Consequently housing costs will resume from the start of your linked claim.

5 Income and capital

1. Introduction

In this chapter we look at the rules for working out income and capital for income support (IS). You can also use this chapter to work out income and capital for these other means-tested or income-related benefits:

- income-based jobseeker's allowance (JSA);
- housing benefit and council tax benefit, as long as you (and your partner) are under 60 or still claiming IS or income-based JSA (otherwise the rules are similar to pension credit – see Chapter 41(5 & 6)).

Where the income and capital rules for these benefits differ significantly from those of IS, we will point this out.

2. What are your resources?

The IS assessment takes into account your income and capital. All income is considered, including earnings, benefits and pensions. But your income or capital may then be disregarded, partially disregarded or taken fully into account.

If you have earnings, the amount disregarded generally depends on the premiums you are entitled to. In 4 and 5 below we outline the assessment of earnings and how much is disregarded.

If you have income other than earnings (eg other benefits or pensions), see 6 to 9 below to check whether any (or all) of your income may be disregarded.

Capital includes savings, investments, some lump-sum payments and the value of property and land (but if you own the home you live in, the value of your home, garden, garage and outbuildings is not taken into account).

If you borrow money, that will almost always count as money you possess (generally as capital if it is a one-off loan or, in some cases, as income if it is part of a series of payments). If you intend to borrow a sum to use for a specific purpose, wait until you actually need to spend that money – don't borrow in advance of your need.

Seek expert advice if credit, loans or capital you possess outside the UK is taken into account.

If you have capital of over a set lower limit (usually £3,000 – see Box B.2 for details), look at 12 below to see if any can be disregarded, and Box B.2 for the way in which it affects the amount of benefit you get.

Generally, it will be clear if a particular resource is income or capital. But in some cases, capital is treated as income and vice versa (see 13 below).

In some cases you can be treated as possessing income or capital that you don't actually have (see 14 and 15 below).

There are specific rules for students (see Chapter 38) and urgent cases payments. We do not cover the latter, so seek advice if these apply.

3. Whose income and capital is included?

If you are one of a couple (married or living together as husband and wife, or after December 2005 in a registered same-sex partnership), your partner's income and capital are added to your own. Otherwise only your own income and capital are taken into account; any income or capital belonging to dependent children is disregarded.

4. Earnings from employment

How earnings from employment are assessed

The IS assessment is normally based on your actual earnings in respect of a particular week. If you are paid monthly, that month's pay is multiplied by 12 and then divided by 52 to provide a weekly amount. However, if the amount of your income varies from week to week, there is discretion to take a more representative period and work out your average earnings over that period. If you have a regular pattern, or cycle, of working some weeks on, some weeks off, your average weekly earnings may be worked out over your working cycle: that average is then also taken into account in your off weeks.

Reg 32(1) and 32(6), IS (General) Regulations

If you have just retired, or your job has ended, or your job has been interrupted for some other reason (but not if you have been suspended from work), your last normal earnings as an employee will usually be disregarded. You cannot be excluded from IS during the period covered by normal last earnings. However, you will be excluded during a period covered by pay in lieu of notice, holiday pay within a set period, or pay in lieu of remuneration (but not a periodic redundancy payment). The period covered by a last payment of sick pay affects the amount of IS you get, but does not exclude you from IS. In the IS assessment, sick pay is taken into account in full less any tax, national insurance (NI) contributions and half of any pension contributions you make, for the same length of time for which it was paid but measured forwards from the date of payment.

If you are not being paid, or are underpaid for a service, 'notional' earnings may be taken into account (see 14).

Reg 42(5) and 42(6), IS (General) Regulations

Housing benefit (HB)/council tax benefit (CTB) – Your average weekly earnings are estimated over the 5 weeks before your HB/CTB claim if you are paid weekly, or the 2 months before your HB/CTB claim if you are paid monthly. But in either case, your local authority should average them over another period if that would give a more accurate estimate.

Working out net earnings

Do not count any payment in kind (see 9) or *'any payment in respect of expenses wholly, exclusively and necessarily incurred in the performance of the duties of the employment'*. Occupational pensions are not treated as earnings, but are normally taken into account in full (as income) less tax payable (see 6).

For IS and income-based jobseeker's allowance (JSA), don't count as earnings any sick pay, maternity pay, paternity pay or adoption pay from your employer, nor any statutory sick pay (SSP), statutory maternity pay (SMP), statutory paternity pay (SPP) or statutory adoption pay (SAP). Instead, these are counted in full (as income) less any tax, NI contributions and half of any contributions you make towards an occupational or personal pension. For HB/CTB, unlike for IS, sick pay, maternity pay, paternity pay or adoption pay from your employer, and SSP, SMP, SPP and SAP are all counted as earnings.

An advance of earnings, or a loan, counts as capital. Count any other payment from your employer as earnings: for example, bonuses, commission, payments towards travel expenses between your home and workplace or towards

childminding fees, retainers (from your employer or from a boarder), pay in lieu of notice, and holiday pay (unless you get it more than 4 weeks after you last worked). Most non-cash vouchers count as earnings, but not childcare vouchers.
Reg 35, IS (General) Regulations

Deduct from your earnings income tax, NI contributions and half of any contribution you make towards an occupational or personal pension scheme.

Earnings disregards
Once you have worked out your total earnings as above, you now deduct the appropriate 'earnings disregard'.

For IS and income-based JSA, this is limited to an overall maximum of £20 a week of a single person's earnings or joint earnings of a couple. But you have to qualify for the £20 overall maximum earnings disregard (see below). If you do not qualify for the £20 earnings disregard, you are limited to an earnings disregard of £5 if you are single or £10 for a couple.

For HB/CTB, the rules are the same as for IS, except lone parents can have £25 disregarded from earnings, and there are two extra disregards – childcare costs and the 16- or 30-hours earnings disregard (see below).

For contribution-based JSA, the earnings disregard is normally limited to £5 a week (see Chapter 17(13)).

The £20 earnings disregard – Deduct £20 a week from your earnings or joint earnings with your partner if any of the following apply.

- ❑ You qualify for a disability premium.
- ❑ You qualify for a carer premium. The disregard applies to the earnings of the carer; if you are the carer and your earnings are less than £20, up to £5 can be disregarded from your partner's earnings, subject to the overall £20 maximum.
- ❑ You are a lone parent. Note that for HB/CTB only, the disregard for lone parents is £25.
- ❑ You qualify for the higher pensioner premium – but only where you or your partner were working part time immediately before reaching 60 and were then entitled to the £20 disability premium earnings disregard. Since then, you or your partner must have continued in part-time employment, although breaks of up to 8 weeks when you were not getting IS are ignored.
- ❑ You are one of a couple and your IS would include a disability premium but for the fact that the higher pensioner premium is applicable. Either you or your partner must be under 60 with either one of you in part-time employment.
- ❑ If you are working in one of the jobs listed below, up to £20 of those earnings are disregarded:
  - ■ a part-time firefighter;
  - ■ an auxiliary coastguard on coast rescue activities;
  - ■ part-time crewing or launching of a lifeboat;
  - ■ a member of any territorial or reserve force.

  If you are part of a couple and you are both doing one of those jobs, you are still restricted to the joint earnings disregard of £20. If you are doing one of those jobs, your earnings are less than £20, and your partner is doing an ordinary part-time job, up to £5 can be disregarded from your partner's earnings, subject to the overall £20 maximum.

If you do not qualify for the £20 earnings disregard – Deduct £5 from earnings if you are single. Deduct £10 from joint earnings if you are in a couple, whether one or both of you are working.

Childcare costs earnings disregard – only in HB/CTB
For HB/CTB, and only for these benefits, you may get an extra earnings disregard for childcare costs.

- ❑ You must be:
  - ■ a lone parent working at least 16 hours a week; *or*
  - ■ in a couple and you both work at least 16 hours a week; *or*
  - ■ in a couple and one of you works at least 16 hours a week and the other counts as 'incapacitated', is a hospital in-patient or is in prison. You count as 'incapacitated' if:
    - – you get short-term higher rate or long-term incapacity benefit (IB) or severe disablement allowance (SDA); *or*
    - – you get attendance allowance (AA), disability living allowance (DLA), constant attendance allowance or mobility supplement (or payment has stopped because you are a patient); *or*
    - – your HB/CTB includes a disability premium on account of your incapacity; *or*
    - – you are the claimant and have been incapable of work for at least 28 weeks (ignoring gaps of 8 weeks or less); *or*
    - – you are aged 80 or over, or you satisfy the qualifying conditions for the higher pensioner premium.

  In each of these three categories you are still treated as working for up to 28 weeks when you are off sick and claiming statutory sick pay, short-term lower rate IB, and IS or NI credits on the grounds of incapacity.
- ❑ Your child must be aged 15 or younger, or aged 16 or younger if they are eligible for a disabled child premium (see Chapter 7(25)). The disregard is available until the day before the first Monday in September after their 15th or 16th birthday.
- ❑ The childcare must meet certain requirements. You must be paying an approved or registered childcare provider, including out-of-school-hours schemes run on school premises or provided by local authorities. If a relative of the child is providing the care, it needs to be done away from your home.

Deduct from your earnings childcare payments up to a maximum of £175 weekly for one child, or £300 weekly for two or more children. If you get working tax credit (WTC) or child tax credit (CTC) and your earnings, once other earnings disregards have been taken off, are less than the deduction for childcare costs, then the deduction is made from the total of your earnings and your tax credits added together.

Extra earnings disregard – only in HB/CTB
There is an extra earnings disregard, only in HB/CTB, for certain groups of people who work on average either 16 or 30 hours or more a week. Deduct an extra £14.50 from earnings if:

- ■ you (or your partner) receive the 30-hour element within your WTC (see Chapter 18(7)); *or*
- ■ you (or your partner) are aged at least 25 and work at least 30 hours a week; *or*
- ■ you (or your partner) work at least 16 hours a week; *and*
  - – are responsible for a child or young person; *or*
  - – are a lone parent; *or*
  - – your HB/CTB includes a disability premium or higher pensioner premium. If you are the one eligible for the premium, then you must be the one who is working for at least 16 hours a week; *or*
  - – are at least 50, have recently started work and would satisfy the conditions for the 50-plus element of WTC (see Chapter 18(7)).

Only one such £14.50 deduction can be made from earnings or from a couple's joint earnings.

If your earnings are less than the sum of all the relevant earnings disregards and deductible childcare charges, then the £14.50 can be disregarded from WTC taken into account instead.

5. Self-employed earnings

There are specific rules to work out income from self-employment. It is based on the net cash flow of your business or of your share of the business. If you get royalties or copyright payments, seek advice.

Step 1: Take full gross receipts of the business
This is all the money you receive in respect of and generated by the business over a specific trading period. This is normally one year; but if you've recently started self-employment or there has been a change that is likely to affect the normal pattern of business, the DWP can pick a different period which is more representative of your average weekly earnings.

For housing benefit (HB)/council tax benefit (CTB), earnings are usually assessed over the period covered by your last year's trading accounts. A different period can be used if appropriate, as long as it's no longer than a year.

Step 2: Work out net profit – deduct:

- *'any expenses wholly and exclusively defrayed [ie actually paid] in that period for the purposes of that employment'*: this is subject to some exceptions and extra rules, eg the expenses must be 'reasonably incurred', and business entertainment is specifically excluded. Note that expenses can be apportioned between business and personal use (see R(FC)1/91 and R(IS)13/91);
- a repayment of capital on any loan used for replacing equipment or machinery, or for repairing existing business assets (less any insurance payments);
- the excess of any VAT paid, over VAT received;
- expenditure out of income to repair an existing business asset (less any insurance payment);
- interest (but not capital) payments on a loan taken out for the purposes of the employment.

The sum left after these deductions is your net profit. If you work as a childminder, however, simply deduct two-thirds of those earnings.

Reg 38 IS (General) Regulations

Step 3: From your net profit, deduct:

- income tax – this is based on your appropriate personal tax allowances, on a pro rata basis if necessary (see Chapter 54);
- Class 2 and Class 4 contributions (see Chapter 12(1));
- half of any contribution to a personal pension scheme.

Step 4: See which earnings disregards apply
Check to see which earnings disregards apply (see 4 above). The disregards are the same as those for employed earners.

6. Income from benefits and pensions

Most benefits are taken into account in full in the IS assessment (less any income tax payable). However, some benefits are either completely or partly disregarded.

Benefits that are completely disregarded

The following benefits are completely disregarded:

- housing benefit (HB);
- council tax benefit (CTB);
- child benefit;
- guardian's allowance;
- attendance allowance (AA);
- disability living allowance (DLA);
- constant attendance allowance, severe disablement occupational allowance, exceptionally severe disablement allowance (payable under the War Pensions or Industrial Disablement schemes only);
- war pensioners' mobility supplement;
- any ex-gratia payment made to compensate for the non-payment of DLA, mobility allowance or supplement, AA, IS or jobseeker's allowance (JSA);
- any social fund payment;
- any payment(s) of the £10 Christmas bonus;
- certain special war widow's or widower's payments or supplementary pensions;
- any payment or repayment of health benefits and any payment made instead of milk tokens or vitamins (see Chapter 52);
- dependants' additions to non-means-tested benefits if the dependant is not a member of your family.

HB/CTB – For HB/CTB, the list is the same excluding, however, child benefit. If you are in receipt of IS, income-based JSA or the guarantee credit of pension credit (PC), all your income and capital are disregarded anyway.

If you save your benefit – Although these benefits are disregarded as income in the IS assessment, if there is any money left over after the end of the period for which the benefit is paid, it will be regarded as capital and, in most cases, will then count in with any other savings. (Benefit can be disregarded as capital in limited cases – see 12 below.) For example, if you save up your mobility component towards a wheelchair, the savings will count as capital. This will only affect your benefit if it takes your capital above the lower limit for tariff income (see Box B.2).

Benefits that are partly disregarded

For IS/JSA, deduct up to £10 of:

- widowed parent's allowance;
- widowed mother's allowance;
- a war disablement pension (including a 'service attributable pension' or tax-free service invaliding pension);
- a guaranteed income payment made under the new Armed Forces and Reserve Forces Compensation scheme;
- war widow/widower's pension;
- comparable pensions paid under non-UK social security legislation, or to victims of Nazi persecution.

For HB/CTB, the rule is the same except that £15 is disregarded from the widowed parent's or widowed mother's allowance. Local authorities can choose to run a local scheme under which they disregard more than £10 of a war pension in HB/CTB. Your local authority can tell you if it runs a scheme and how much it disregards.

If £10 of a war pension or (for IS/JSA) a widowed mother's or widowed parent's allowance is disregarded, you can also have £10 of a regular charitable payment disregarded. This is because, taken together, there is an overall maximum disregard of £20 for such payments (see 7).

Tax credits

Working tax credit (WTC) is taken into account in full for IS/JSA. Child tax credit (CTC) is completely disregarded. For HB/CTB both WTC and CTC are taken into account in full. They will be reduced, however, by any deduction which is being made in order to recover an overpayment of tax credit which arose in a previous year.

Additionally, for HB/CTB, if your earnings are less than the sum of all the relevant earnings disregards and deductible childcare charges, then the WTC taken into account can be reduced by the £14.50 extra earnings disregard (see 4 above).

Statutory sick pay and statutory maternity/paternity/adoption pay

IS/JSA – Statutory sick pay (SSP), statutory maternity pay (SMP), statutory paternity pay (SPP) and statutory adoption pay (SAP) are taken into account in full for IS and income-based JSA, less any Class 1 national insurance contributions, tax, and half of any contributions you make towards an occupational or personal pension scheme.

HB/CTB – SSP, SMP, SPP and SAP are counted as earnings for HB/CTB. So when you go on sick leave, maternity leave, paternity leave or adoption leave your SSP, SMP, SPP or SAP are added in with any actual earnings you continue to receive. All the rules on assessing earnings then apply. In particular, you get an 'earnings disregard' (see 4) even if you receive only SSP, SMP, SPP or SAP.

Occupational and personal pensions

Occupational, personal and state pensions are normally taken into account in full, less any tax payable. For HB/CTB, if you are aged 60 or over, income from an occupational or personal pension that would be available to you on application, or from a pension fund that could be turned into an annuity, may be taken into account as 'notional income' (see 14). The same applies to your partner.

7. Charitable and voluntary payments

Some types of charitable and voluntary payments are completely disregarded as income. Others are partly disregarded. The disregards do not apply, however, to payments made to strikers. For maintenance payments, see 8 below. For payments made towards the cost of a care home, see 9 below. It is planned that from October 2005 all charitable, voluntary and personal injury payments will be disregarded for housing benefit and council tax benefit.

Disregarded regular payments

Any charitable or voluntary payments made (or due to be made) regularly to you or your partner should be completely disregarded as income if they are intended and used for items other than everyday living expenses.

Everyday living expenses – These are defined as:

- food;
- ordinary clothing or footwear;
- household fuel;
- council tax;
- water charges;
- rent (for which HB could be payable) or any housing costs (which could be met by IS).

Ordinary clothing or footwear includes items for normal daily use, but does not include school uniforms, or clothing or footwear used solely for sporting activities.

Examples of disregarded payments – These could include those intended and used for: annual veterinary check-ups and inoculations for a pet; annual service charges for electrical and gas equipment and appliances; and hire purchase or other regular payments for a car, wheelchair, electrical and gas equipment and appliances, furniture and furnishings. However, paying for adaptations to your car is almost certainly a one-off payment. It would normally be treated as capital and taken into account, but would only affect benefit if it took existing capital above the lower capital limit (see Box B.2). On the other hand, if it was paid to a third party (eg a garage), it would be disregarded (see 9 below).

Note that you must use the whole of the payment for the allowable item or need: any cash left over after you have paid for the item would be taken into account as income, subject to the £20 disregard (see below).

Payments in kind (eg a regular box of groceries) are wholly disregarded.

Partly disregarded regular payments

If it cannot be completely disregarded under the rules above, then up to £20 a week of any regular charitable or voluntary payment is disregarded as income. The maximum that can be disregarded in any week is £20, no matter how many such payments are made.

There are also individual disregards for the following:

- £5 from student's covenant income;
- £10 from a student loan;
- £20 from a student's Access to Learning Fund payment (or equivalent in Scotland, Wales, etc – see Chapter 38(1)).

There is an overriding limit of £20 for the combined disregards of any partly disregarded benefits (see 6), of these student payments and of any charitable or voluntary payments.

Payments made to a third party (rather than to yourself) are dealt with under the 'third party' rules (see 9 below).

Irregular payments

If charitable or voluntary payments are not made or not due to be made to you (rather than to a third party – see 9) at regular intervals, they will be treated as capital. Irregular gifts in kind from a charity are disregarded.

Payments from specific trusts

Any payments in kind or cash made by the Macfarlane Trusts, the Fund, the Eileen Trust, the Skipton Fund or the Independent Living Funds are disregarded.

Any payment made by or on behalf of a person with haemophilia (or their partner) who received money from any of these trusts or funds, or from the Skipton Fund, is disregarded in full if it originates from that trust or fund. To qualify for the disregard, the payment must be made to (or for the benefit of) the partner or former partner of the person who is making the payment (unless you are estranged or divorced), or to dependent children (if they are a member of the donor's family, or were, but are now a member of the claimant's family). If the person making the payment has no partner or dependent children, a payment (including a payment from their estate if they are now dead) to their parent, step-parent, or guardian is disregarded for a period of 2 years after their death, as long as the payment originates from any of these trusts.

Personal injury payments

Personal injury payments include vaccine damage payments (Chapter 47) and criminal injuries compensation payments (Chapter 46), as well as payments from insurance companies and damages awards by the courts. Any personal injury payments, as long as they are put into a trust fund or they receive a structured settlement (eg through a court judgment), are completely disregarded when used for items other than everyday living expenses (see above). When such a payment is used for everyday living expenses then up to £20 of it can be disregarded.

8. Maintenance payments

Under recent reforms to the child support system a maximum of £10 a week will be disregarded from maintenance payments (including those made voluntarily) for IS and income-based jobseeker's allowance. This disregard, known as the child maintenance premium, only applies initially to new child support cases from 3.3.03 and new voluntary arrangements from 16.2.04. Old cases will have the disregard included at a later date. Payments for more than one child will be added together and treated as a single payment, so only one disregard can apply.

For housing benefit/council tax benefit, any maintenance you receive is counted in full as income unless there is at least one child in your family, in which case £15 is disregarded.

If you pay maintenance, there is no disregard for your payments.

9. Other kinds of income

For IS purposes, other kinds of income are generally taken into account in full less any tax payable. But some kinds of income can be disregarded in full or in part.

Payments to third parties

A payment of income made to a third party in respect of you or your partner can be taken into account but only to the extent that it is used for everyday living expenses (see 7). If it is not used for everyday living expenses, its value will be disregarded (eg paying a garage for your car to be repaired or adapted, or paying a grocer to supply you with cat food, or paying the shop for your TV rental).

Any payment made to a third party towards the cost of your care home is treated as your income. But some of this income may be disregarded under other rules (see below).

A payment to a third party from an occupational or personal pension is taken into account even when it is not used for everyday living expenses.

Payments in kind

Any income in kind is disregarded (eg a free bus pass, food, cigarettes, petrol, etc) unless you are involved in a trade dispute (for IS and jobseeker's allowance (JSA)).

Although non-cash vouchers which are liable for Class 1 national insurance contributions are not treated as payments in kind, vouchers which are not liable for contributions (eg certain childcare and charitable vouchers) are, and are thus disregarded.

Training and employment schemes

If you are on a government training programme or employment scheme (under either s.2 of the Employment and Training Act 1973 or s.2 of the Enterprise and New Towns (Scotland) Act 1990) any payment is disregarded unless:

- it is made as a substitute for IS, JSA, incapacity benefit or severe disablement allowance (eg the basic rate of New Deal allowance);
- it is a young person's bridging allowance;
- it is intended to meet the cost of everyday living expenses (see 7) while you are participating in the programme or scheme; *or*
- it is intended to meet the cost of living away from home, where the payment is to cover rent charged for the accommodation where you are staying, for which housing benefit is payable.

The following are also disregarded:

- payments to help a disabled person get or keep work, made under the Disabled Persons (Employment) Act 1944 (or the equivalent for training) – eg Access to Work payments – but not if it is a state training allowance;
- Employment Zone discretionary payments;
- special account payments made under the New Deal self-employment route to meet necessary expenses or maintain loan repayments;
- lone parent work-search premium;
- return to work credit and in-work credit (HB/CTB only).

Payments towards education

The following are disregarded:

- educational maintenance allowance paid to you or your dependent child;
- maintenance payments to the school or college for a dependent child from someone outside your family (IS/JSA only);
- for housing benefit (HB)/council tax benefit (CTB), if you make assessed parental contributions to a student son or daughter, the amount you pay is disregarded from your income – unless the student gets a discretionary grant or gets no grant or loan, in which case the disregard from your income is limited to £44.50 a week (less the amount of any discretionary grant);
- certain amounts of a student grant or loan, Access Fund payment or Career Development Loan can be disregarded (see Chapter 38(3));
- repayments of student loans under the Education Act 2002 to certain newly qualified teachers.

Payments for your home

The following payments related to your home are disregarded:

- payments under a mortgage protection policy used to meet repayments on a mortgage or on a loan for eligible repairs and improvements (see Chapter 4(12)) up to the amount of loan interest not met in your applicable amount, plus the amount due in capital repayments or endowment premiums, premiums on the mortgage protection policy and premiums on a buildings insurance policy (IS/JSA only);
- payments under an insurance policy taken out against the risk of being unable to maintain repayments on a loan secured on your home, and used to maintain repayments and premiums on that policy and any premiums for buildings insurance if this is a requirement of the loan (HB/CTB only);
- payments (from any source) made to you that are intended and used as a contribution towards:
  - payments due on a loan secured on your home which are not covered by IS (see Chapter 4(12));
  - housing costs covered by IS but not met in your applicable amount;
  - capital repayments or endowment premiums on loans covered by IS;
  - premiums on a policy taken out to meet any of the above costs or for buildings insurance;
  - any rent not met by HB (IS/JSA only);
- the part of a home income plan annuity which covers the net interest payable on the loan used to buy the annuity – the full qualifying conditions are listed in para 17, Schedule 9, IS (General) Regs. Income from any other type of annuity counts in full;
- discretionary housing payments made under the Discretionary Financial Assistance Regulations 2001.

Income from tenants and lodgers

Disregard the following income from tenants and lodgers:

- contributions towards living and accommodation costs made to you by someone living as a member of your household (but not if they are a commercial boarder or a sub-tenant);
- if you have a sub-tenant or tenant (but not if that person lives as a member of your household, nor if you provide them with meals):
  - £4 from the rent they pay you; *plus*
  - £10.55 if that rent includes an amount for heating;
- if you provide board and lodging in your own home, £20 and half of the remainder of the weekly charge paid by each person provided with such accommodation (even if that person lodges with you for just one night).

Payments for care homes

Some payments towards the cost of your care can be disregarded as income for IS. See also Chapter 30.

If the local authority arranged your care – Payments made by the local authority towards the cost of care home charges are fully disregarded.

Para 66, Schedule 9, IS (General) Regulations

If the local authority has arranged your preferred choice of care home and it is more expensive than the local authority would usually pay, any charitable or voluntary payment made or due to be made at regular intervals to meet the difference is disregarded as income. See Chapter 29(4).

Para 15A, Schedule 9, IS (General) Regulations

If the local authority did not arrange your care – Any payment intended for and used to meet the care home charge is partly disregarded. The amount disregarded is the weekly accommodation charge less your IS applicable amount. The payment need not be from a charity nor be a voluntary payment.

Para 30A, Schedule 9, IS (General) Regulations

Payments for children

The following payments for children or young people in your care are disregarded:

B.2 Capital limits

For IS, as well as for housing benefit (HB)/council tax benefit (CTB) and income-based jobseeker's allowance (JSA), you are excluded from benefit if your capital is above the upper limit (eg if it is £8,000.01 or more). Capital at or below the lower limit does not affect your benefit. If your capital is between the limits, an amount of 'tariff income' from capital is assumed, worked out using a fixed formula (see below). If you move permanently into a care home, the capital limits go up to £10,000 (lower) and £16,000 (upper) – see Chapter 30. If your stay is only temporary, the higher limits do not apply.

Capital limits	lower limit	upper limit
Under age 60		
IS/income-based JSA	£3,000	£8,000
HB/CTB	£3,000	£16,000
Aged 60 or over (see below)		
IS/income-based JSA	£6,000	£12,000
HB/CTB	£6,000	£16,000
Permanently in a care home		
IS/income-based JSA	£10,000	£16,000
HB	£10,000	£16,000

Aged 60 or over

The capital limits are higher (in IS/JSA and HB/CTB) if either you or your partner are aged 60 or over, so you can have more savings and still qualify for benefit. If you are in receipt of IS and reach the age of 60 you can no longer claim IS and will need to claim pension credit (PC) instead, which has more generous rules on capital (see Chapter 41). However, if you are aged under 60 and your partner reaches the age of 60, should they choose not to claim PC, then you could continue to claim IS (until you also reach the age of 60), in which case the IS capital limits will continue to apply, but at the higher level. The higher level capital limits will also apply if you or your partner are aged 60 or over and claiming HB or CTB (unless you or your partner are in receipt of the guarantee credit of PC, in which case all your capital will be disregarded anyway; see Chapter 7(26)).

Tariff income

If your capital is between the lower and upper limits, a 'tariff income' is assumed. One pound a week for every £250 (or part of £250) above the lower limit is included as your income. For example, for IS, if you have capital of between £3,250.01 and £3,500, £2 a week is included as your income. Each time capital gets into the next block of £250 (even by as little as one penny) an additional £1 is included as income. For HB/CTB, if you or your partner are aged 60 or over (and not claiming IS or income-based JSA), the assumed tariff income is one pound a week for every £500 (or part of £500) above the lower limit.

If tariff income is included in your assessment, notify the DWP if the amount of your capital changes. If your savings drop to the next lower tariff income band and you haven't told the DWP, you will be getting too little IS. If your savings have increased to the next higher tariff income band and you haven't told the DWP, you will have been overpaid benefit. Watch out for the 'notional capital rule' (see 15). It is sensible to keep records and all receipts to show how and why you spent your savings.

- fostering allowances (for official arrangements only);
- adoption and residence order allowances. However, for HB/CTB, only the amount of allowance that exceeds the child's personal allowance and disabled child premium is disregarded;
- special guardianship payments;
- discretionary payments from social services or social work departments to help children in need or to provide help to young care leavers.

Miscellaneous income

The following types of income are also disregarded:

- expenses paid to a volunteer, including advance payments to cover expenses – but only if you are paid nothing else by the charity or organisation, and aren't treated as having 'notional' earnings (see 14);
- payments in respect of a person who is not normally a member of your household but is temporarily in your care, made by a health body, voluntary organisation or local authority (or by a person placed with you by the local authority). This covers respite care payments for overnight (or longer) stays or for just a few hours in the day. It does not cover any direct payments of housing benefit made to you;
- any community care direct payments;
- payments to a juror or witness in respect of attendance at court (but not if they are to compensate for loss of earnings or loss of benefit);
- payments under the Assisted Prison Visits scheme;
- payments from a local authority under the Supporting People scheme;
- payments under an insurance policy taken out against the risk of being unable to maintain repayments under a credit agreement, hire purchase or conditional sale agreement, up to the amount used to maintain the repayments and pay premiums on that policy;
- income abroad while transfer to the UK is prohibited;
- charges for currency conversion if income is not paid in sterling;
- Sports Council National Lottery award, except for amounts awarded for everyday living expenses (see 7, although 'food' in this case does not include vitamins, minerals or other special dietary supplements intended to enhance performance);
- Victoria Cross/George Cross annuities and analogous payments.

Schedule 9, IS (General) Regulations

10. Capital limits

There is a lower capital limit and an upper capital limit. While the value of all your capital resources (or notional capital resources) is above the upper limit you are excluded from benefit. If your capital is at or below the lower limit, your benefit is not affected. If your capital is between these limits, a tariff income is assumed. See Box B.2 for details of the capital limits and the effect of capital on benefit. Some types of capital are disregarded for these capital limits (see 12 below).

11. How is capital valued?

Capital is calculated at its current market or surrender value, less 10% if there would be costs involved in selling and less any mortgage or debt secured on the property.

Jointly owned capital – If you own property or other capital jointly with one or more others, you are treated as though you own an equal share. Thus, if 4 people jointly possess an item of capital in an actual split of 80%, 10%, 5% and 5%, each of you will be treated as possessing 25% of that capital. Your deemed equal share is valued under normal IS rules. However, if you share the property as tenants-in-common rather than as joint tenants, following a recent court of appeal ruling, the share that you are treated as owning should reflect the actual split.

R v Hourigan 2002 EWCA Civ 1890

The decision maker must establish the market value or price that a willing buyer would pay to a willing seller for the share that you possess. The market value could be low or even nil if other joint owners would not be prepared to sell the property as a whole or to buy the share themselves.

12. What capital is disregarded?

Benefits

Arrears (or an ex-gratia payment) of the following benefits are disregarded for 52 weeks after you get them: disability living allowance (DLA), attendance allowance (AA) (or equivalent under the Industrial Injuries or War Pensions schemes), housing benefit (HB), council tax benefit (CTB), IS, income-based jobseeker's allowance (JSA), disabled person's tax credit, working families' tax credit, child tax credit, working tax credit, special war widow's payment, mobility allowance, mobility supplement, community charge benefit, supplementary benefit or family income supplement. Arrears of HB are not disregarded for CTB, however, and vice versa.

Where the arrears have been made to rectify or compensate for an official error, amount to £5,000 or more, and have been awarded in full since 14.10.01, they can be disregarded for 52 weeks from the date of receipt or for the remaining period of the IS award, whichever is the longer period.

Any payment or repayment of a health benefit in respect of NHS prescription charges, dental charges or hospital travelling expenses is disregarded for 52 weeks after you receive the money. Any payment made instead of milk tokens or free vitamins is disregarded for 52 weeks after receipt.

Any social fund payment is completely disregarded.

For HB/CTB, a back-to-work bonus and a child maintenance bonus are disregarded for 52 weeks.

Personal possessions

The value of any personal possessions is disregarded except those bought to reduce your capital in order to get more benefit. A compensation payment for loss of or damage to personal possessions, which is to be used for repair or replacements, is disregarded for 26 weeks, or longer if that is reasonable.

Trust funds

A trust fund created from payments for a personal or criminal injury is completely disregarded. 'Personal injury' includes a disease and injury suffered as a result of a disease (R(SB)2/89). Trusts created from compensation and vaccine damage payments are covered, so too may a trust of funds collected for a person because of their personal injuries. Where capital is administered by the courts, damages awarded for personal injury and, for under 18s, compensation for the loss of a parent ('infant funds in court') are disregarded. Actual payments from a trust fund can count in full as capital, though may be partly or wholly disregarded as income.

The value of the right to receive any income under a life interest or from a life rent (this is a type of trust in Scotland) is disregarded. Actual income received counts in full as income.

Any payment made under the Macfarlane Trusts, the Fund, the Eileen Trust, the Skipton Fund or the Independent Living Funds is disregarded. Any payment made by or on behalf of a person with haemophilia may be disregarded under the same rules as income (see 7 above).

A payment from the government-funded trust for people with variant Creutzfeldt-Jakob disease (vCJD) paid to a person with vCJD or their partner is disregarded for life. If the trust payment is made to a parent or child of a person with vCJD (including payment from the estate if they are now dead) it is disregarded for 2 years from the date it is paid or until the child reaches age 19 or leaves full-time education, whichever is the latest.

Training and employment

Disregard the following:

- payments (but not a state training allowance) made under the Disabled Persons (Employment) Act 1944 (or the equivalent for training) to help a disabled person get or keep work;
- start-up capital under the Blind Homeworkers' scheme;
- business assets while you are 'engaged as a self-employed earner'. If you've ceased that self-employment, the assets will be disregarded for as long as is reasonable in the circumstances to allow you to dispose of them. However, if sickness or disability means you cannot work as a self-employed earner, your business assets will be disregarded for 26 weeks from your date of claim, or longer if that is reasonable in the circumstances. You must intend to start or resume work in that business as soon as you are able to or as soon as you recover;
- business assets while you are on the self-employment route of the New Deal, and for as long as is reasonable after the self-employment ends.

Disregard for 52 weeks from the date of receipt the following:

- any payment from a government training programme or employment scheme (under either s.2 of the Employment and Training Act 1973 or s.2 of the Enterprise and New Towns (Scotland) Act 1990);
- any business capital under the New Deal self-employment route;
- any discretionary payment or arrears of subsistence allowance from an Employment Zone contractor.

Your home

The following items are disregarded:

- the value of your own home;
- the value of any premises occupied wholly or partly by your partner or by a relative, if they are aged 60 or over, or incapacitated; or former partner if you are not estranged or divorced;
- the value of your former home for 26 weeks after you left it because of divorce or estrangement from your former partner. If the former partner is a lone parent, the value is disregarded for as long as they occupy your former home;
- the value of premises you've acquired, if you intend to move in within 26 weeks of the date of purchase. More time is allowed if that is reasonable in the circumstances to enable you to get possession and move in;
- any sum directly attributable to the proceeds of the sale of your former home that you intend to use to buy another home within 26 weeks of that sale, or *'such longer period as is reasonable in the circumstances to enable [you] to complete the purchase'*;
- any sum paid to you because of damage to, or loss of, the home or any personal possession and intended for its repair or replacement, or any sum given or loaned to you expressly for essential repairs or improvements to the home, will be disregarded for 26 weeks if you are going to use that sum for its intended purpose, or for longer if that is reasonable in the circumstances;
- any sum deposited with a housing association as a condition of occupying the home. If you've removed that deposit and intend to use it to buy another home it can be disregarded on the same basis as the proceeds of the sale of a former home;
- the value of premises which you are taking reasonable

steps to dispose of, for 26 weeks from *'the date on which [you] first took such steps, or such longer period as is reasonable in the circumstances to enable [you] to dispose of those premises'*;

- the value of premises which you intend to occupy as your home if you are taking steps to obtain possession and have either sought legal advice or commenced legal proceedings in order to obtain possession. The value is disregarded for 26 weeks from the date on which you first sought such advice, or started proceedings (whichever is earlier), but it may be disregarded for a longer period if that is reasonable in the circumstances;
- the value of premises you intend to occupy as your home once *'essential repairs or alterations'* make the premises *'fit for such occupation'*, for 26 weeks from the date on which you first took steps to get the premises repaired or altered, or such longer period as is reasonable in the circumstances to enable the works to be carried out and for you to move in. This can help if you need to make adaptations because of a disability (eg install a ground floor bathroom);
- any grant made by a local authority (if you are one of its tenants) to be used to buy premises you intend to live in as your home, or to do repairs or alterations needed to make the premises fit for you to live in. The grant is disregarded for 26 weeks, or such longer period as is reasonable in the circumstances, to enable you to complete buying, repairing or altering the premises;
- arrears of discretionary housing payments made under the Discretionary Financial Assistance Regulations 2001 for 52 weeks from the date received.

Right to receive income or payment in future

Certain forms of capital can be released at some stage in order to provide you with income or payment in the future. The following types are disregarded for IS:

- any future interest in property other than land or premises on which you have been granted a lease or tenancy;
- the capital value of the right to receive any income under an annuity, and the surrender value of an annuity;
- the capital value of the right to receive any income that is disregarded because it is frozen abroad;
- the value of the right to receive an occupational or personal pension, and the value of any funds held under a personal pension scheme or retirement annuity contract;
- the value of the right to receive any rent except where you have a future interest in the property;
- the full surrender value of any life insurance policy.

Other capital

The following types of capital are disregarded for IS:

- discretionary payments from social services or social work departments to help children in need or to provide help to young care leavers;
- any payment made under the para.3, S4, Adoption and Children Act 2002;
- any special guardianship payment;
- payments from local authorities under the Supporting People scheme;
- any community care direct payments;
- a refund of tax that was deducted on loan interest if that loan was taken out in order to buy the home or to carry out repairs or improvements to the home;
- payments in kind made by a charity (see 9);
- payments made to a juror or witness in respect of attendance at a court (but not if it was to compensate for loss of earnings or loss of benefit);
- where any payment of capital *'falls to be made by instalments, the value of the right to receive any outstanding instalments'* (see also 13 below, 'Capital treated as income');
- payment to you as holder of the Victoria Cross or George Cross;
- any Sports Council National Lottery award, less everyday living expenses (see 7, although 'food' in this case does not include vitamins, minerals or other special dietary supplements intended to enhance performance), for 26 weeks after you receive payment of the award;
- £10,000 special payment made to you or your partner (or for a deceased spouse or partner's deceased spouse) because of internment by the Japanese during the Second World War;
- payments made to you or your partner (or for a deceased spouse or partner's deceased spouse) to compensate for being a slave labourer or a forced labourer, suffering property loss or personal injury or being the parent of a child who had died, during the Second World War;
- any charge for currency conversion if your capital is not held in sterling.

Disregard the following for 52 weeks after you receive payment of them:

- an educational maintenance allowance bonus;
- payments made under the Assisted Prison Visits scheme.

Schedule 10, IS (General) Regulations

13. Income or capital?

There is usually no problem deciding whether a particular resource is income or capital. But the distinction is not defined in the regulations. Where it is unclear, the general principle (developed in case law) is that payments of income recur periodically and do not include ad hoc payments, whereas capital payments are one-off and not linked to a particular period (although capital may be paid in instalments). In some cases the rules treat capital as income and vice versa (see below).

Income generated from capital

Income derived from capital is generally not treated as income but added to your capital from the date it is normally due to be credited to you. However, income derived from the following items of disregarded capital (see 12) is treated as income:

- your home;
- premises you've acquired to live in, but have not yet been able to move in to;
- premises occupied by a partner or relative who is aged 60 or over, or is incapacitated, or an ex-partner (but not if estranged or divorced);
- your former home if you are estranged or divorced;
- premises you are taking reasonable steps to sell;
- premises you intend to occupy and are taking legal steps to obtain possession of;
- premises you intend to occupy but which need essential repairs or alterations;
- business assets;
- a trust fund from compensation for personal injury.

Reg 48(4) IS (General) Regulations

During the period in which you receive income from those premises, any mortgage payments made, or council tax or water charges paid, in respect of the disregarded premises (other than the home you live in) can be offset against that income. The amount above this is taken into account as income.

Para 22(2), Schedule 9, IS (General) Regulations

If you let out your property and it is not covered under one of the disregards above, rent is treated as capital, not as income. The full amount is taken into account as capital without any deductions for mortgage payments, etc.

Income treated as capital

The following payments of income are treated as capital:

- income derived from capital (but see above);
- income tax refunds;*
- irregular charitable or voluntary payments (other than payments made under the Macfarlane Trusts, the Fund, the Eileen Trusts or the Independent Living Funds);*
- holiday pay which is payable more than 4 weeks after the employment ends or is interrupted;*
- advance of earnings or a loan from an employer;*
- compensation for loss of full-time employment if it is less than a week's legal maximum (IS only);
- payment for a discharged prisoner (for IS/jobseeker's allowance (JSA));
- arrears of child tax credit and working tax credit (for housing benefit (HB)/council tax benefit (CTB));
- lump-sum payment of arrears of Employment Zone subsistence allowance;
- gross business receipts payable into New Deal self-employment route special accounts (HB/CTB only);
- a bounty paid no more than once a year to a part-time fire fighter, for coast rescue duties or running a lifeboat, or to a member of the Territorial Army or reserves.

* except for those involved in a trade dispute (for IS/JSA)

Reg 48, IS (General) Regulations

Capital treated as income

If any capital is payable by instalments, each instalment outstanding when your claim is decided (or on the first day for which IS is paid if this is earlier) or at a later supersession, is treated as income if the total of all your capital, including the outstanding instalments, adds up to more than the upper capital limit. If your total capital adds up to less than or equal to the upper capital limit, each instalment is treated as a payment of capital (see Box B.2 for details of the upper capital limits).

A similar rule applies to other means-tested benefits, where outstanding instalments of capital would bring you above the relevant capital limit for that benefit (see Box B.2) and these are outstanding on the following days: for HB/CTB on the date of claim or the date of a later review; for JSA, the first day for which income-based JSA is paid or the date of a supersession.

Any periodical personal injury payments are treated as income.

Any payment under an annuity is treated as income.

If you or your partner have been involved in a trade dispute, any tax refund is treated as income (IS only).

Any capital treated as income is disregarded as capital.

Reg 41 IS (General) Regulations

14. Notional income

Income that you do not actually possess may be taken into account in some circumstances.

❑ **Deprivation of income** – You are treated as possessing any income of which you have deprived yourself in order to get IS or increase your IS.

❑ **Income available if applied for** – You are treated as possessing any income from the date that you could expect to receive it. This also applies to most social security benefits (but only up until the time you put in a claim). The rule does not apply to:

- jobseeker's allowance (JSA) – for IS only;
- working tax credit and child tax credit;
- payments from a discretionary trust or a personal injury compensation trust;
- compensation administered by the courts for personal injury or the death of a parent of a child under 18;
- employment rehabilitation allowances;
- income from a personal pension scheme, or retirement annuity contract as long as you are aged under 60. If you are 60 or over and fail to purchase an annuity or draw an income from the pension, you are assumed to have notional income;
- any Category A or B state pension, additional state pension or graduated retirement benefit which has been deferred – see Chapter 42(4) (for HB/CTB only).

❑ **Notional earnings** – If you are a volunteer, or engaged by a charitable or voluntary organisation, notional earnings cannot be assumed if it is reasonable for you to provide your services free of charge. (A carer may count as a 'volunteer' – see CIS/93/91 – but see CIS/701/94 for exemptions.)

If it is reasonable to expect you to charge for your services, or you are performing a service for someone else in some other capacity, you are treated as having *'such earnings (if any) as is reasonable for that employment unless [you] satisfy [the decision maker] that the means of that person are insufficient for him to pay or to pay more for the service'*. Decision makers are advised to assume earnings of at least the relevant national minimum wage.

If notional earnings are assumed, seek expert help with your appeal.

❑ **Income owed** – For IS and JSA only, you are treated as possessing any income owing to you, but there are exceptions (eg income from a discretionary or personal injury trust, or delays in social security benefits).

❑ **Care homes** – Any payment made towards the cost of your care home is treated as your income, but some of this may be disregarded (see 9).

Reg 42, IS (General) Regulations

15. Notional capital

If you are held to have deprived yourself of some capital in order to get IS or extra benefit, the law says that capital must be treated as if you still had it. This is called 'notional' capital. In some cases, the amount of notional capital along with your actual capital will exclude you from benefit. Or you may still be entitled to benefit, but because of your notional capital, the assessment is based on a higher tariff income than your actual capital warrants (see Box B.2).

A similar deprivation of capital rule applies to other means-tested benefits.

If there were good and sensible reasons for spending your capital, and getting IS (or more IS) wasn't a significant motive for spending part of your savings, you should be alright. It is worth appealing if capital you no longer have is taken into account, but do seek expert advice and check Commissioners' decisions R(IS)1/91, R(SB)11/82, R(SB)38/85, R(SB)40/85, R(SB)9/91 and CIS/242/93.

If you are held to have notional capital on this basis, you won't be excluded from IS permanently, nor will a tariff income be based permanently on the higher amount of notional capital. The DWP will apply the 'diminishing capital rule', which reduces the amount of notional capital over time (see below). It is not possible to deprive yourself of notional capital – only actual capital is subject to this rule.

Chapter 57(6) covers the separate diminishing capital rule for overpayments.

Reducing 'notional' capital

Your notional capital is treated as having been reduced by the amount of benefit 'lost' over a set period.

If you are held to have deprived yourself of an amount of capital, the DWP will work out:

- how much benefit you would have been entitled to in the normal way if you had no notional capital – (A)
- how much benefit, if any, you are entitled to on the basis of your notional capital (as well as actual capital) – (B)
- (A) minus (B) = the benefit you have lost – (LB 1).

If you have also lost any of the other means-tested benefits, the DWP (or local authority) will add on those amounts of lost benefit, eg LB 1 (income support) + LB 2 (housing benefit) + LB 3 (council tax benefit) = total lost benefit (TLB).

Your notional capital is treated as being reduced each week by your total lost benefit.

When you claim a means-tested benefit, the decision on your claim will include the amount of that particular benefit which you have lost because of notional capital. Keep that decision letter – you may need to produce it when you claim any of the other means-tested benefits in case you are held to have deprived yourself of some capital in order to get any of these benefits as well.

For example, if you are excluded from IS because of notional capital and you are also held to have deprived yourself of some capital to get housing benefit (HB) and/or council tax benefit (CTB), you will need to show the IS decision letter to the local authority sections dealing with your HB/CTB claims. Note that it is quite possible to have completely different decisions on deprivation of capital, and different amounts of notional capital, for each benefit.

If you still get benefit – Each time your notional capital goes below another tariff income step, you will be entitled to more benefit. A change of circumstances may also increase or reduce your benefit. Both (A) and (B) will be re-calculated, giving you a new amount of lost benefit (LB 1.2). For any other means-tested benefits, the amount of 'lost' benefit may also change – so you will add these on (LB 1.2 + LB 2.2 etc). Your notional capital will now be treated as being reduced by your current total lost benefit (TLB 2).

If you don't get benefit – Once your total lost benefit is worked out, it cannot be reduced. It can only be increased so as to enable your notional capital to diminish faster. Unless you have a change of circumstances, your total lost benefit can only be re-calculated after 26 weeks. The onus is on you to make a fresh claim for each benefit affected by the deprivation of capital rule and to produce the decision letters showing the amount(s) of the other lost benefit(s). If there is only a small amount of notional capital, you might become entitled to some benefit within a matter of weeks.

You do not have to wait 26 weeks before making a fresh claim. That time limit is only relevant for re-calculating total lost benefit if there have been no changes of circumstances affecting your entitlement beforehand.

Reg 51A, IS (General) Regulations

More deprivation? – If you have actual capital as well as notional capital, you should still be careful about how you spend your actual capital. Obviously you will have to draw on actual capital to help supplement your income and to cover expenses that cannot be met by benefit. But the deprivation of capital rule can be re-applied to the actual capital spent.

6 Claiming income support

In this chapter we look at: page

1. How do you claim income support?

You can start off your claim for income support (IS) by phoning your local Jobcentre Plus office. They will send you a claim-form, the A1. You can also download the claim-form from the DWP website: www.dwp.gov.uk. If you do this, you should also ring your local Jobcentre Plus office to tell them you intend to claim IS, so that your benefit can be backdated to the date of your phone call. You can fill in the form yourself, but don't hesitate to ask the Jobcentre Plus office for help as soon as you need it.

You must give all the information and send in all the supporting documents specified in the claim-form for your claim to be accepted as properly made. As long as you do this within one month of the date you first notified the DWP of your intention to claim, your date of claim will be the date of that first contact. If you have problems getting the necessary information or evidence within one month, tell the DWP straightaway and send in your claim-form anyway. If your difficulty is for certain specified reasons then your claim will still be treated as made on the date of your first contact – for more details see Chapter 57(2).

Your IS claim may also depend on you attending a Jobcentre Plus interview with a personal adviser about work prospects (see Box R.1, Chapter 57). Your IS claim will lapse if you don't take part, unless you have good cause. If you are claiming IS for a partner as well, they may also have to attend a similar interview after you have been on IS for at least 6 months.

If you re-claim IS after a break in benefit of no more than 12 weeks, you can re-claim the benefit under a rapid reclaim process using a much shorter claim-form.

2. Backdating

If you think you were entitled to IS before you put in your claim, ask, in writing, for your claim to be backdated. IS can be backdated for up to 3 months if there are 'special reasons' why you couldn't reasonably have been expected to claim earlier (see Chapter 57(3)).

Waiting for a decision on another benefit? – Sometimes entitlement to another benefit can mean you become entitled to IS, or to more IS, because your applicable amount (see Chapter 4(2)) goes up. For example, if you or your partner get carer's allowance, that qualifies you for a carer premium with IS. If you or your partner get disability living allowance (DLA), that qualifies you for a disability premium.

If you already get IS – Ask for your award to be revised or superseded once you get the decision on the DLA or other qualifying benefit. Arrears of any extra IS you are entitled to are paid for the same period as the award of the qualifying benefit.

If you do not already get IS – To make sure you do not miss out on benefit, you may need to make two IS claims. (We use the example of DLA here, but the process is the same for any other benefit that allows you to qualify for IS.)

Do not delay making an IS claim while you are waiting for a decision on the DLA claim, as DLA claims can sometimes take a long time to be decided. This IS claim will be turned down if entitlement depends on DLA being awarded (eg without a disability premium your income is higher than your applicable amount). You are later awarded DLA, possibly after a revision or appeal if your DLA is refused initially. If you claim IS again within 3 months of the date of the decision to award DLA, IS can be backdated to the date from which DLA was first payable (or the date of the first IS claim if that is later).

Note that if the DLA claim is made more than 10 days after your first IS claim, the second IS claim cannot be backdated in this way (the DWP says this means 10 working days). If you did not make an IS claim at the right time, claim as soon as you can and ask for it to be backdated for up to 3 months if there are 'special reasons' (see Chapter 57(3)).

If your IS is stopped – Where IS entitlement depends on getting another qualifying benefit like DLA, and the qualifying benefit is stopped, your IS will also stop. But if you challenge the decision on the qualifying benefit and it is reinstated, claim IS again within 3 months and it will be fully backdated.

3. Who should make the claim?

You can make the claim yourself, or if necessary someone can make the claim on your behalf. If you are unable to act for yourself, the Secretary of State can appoint someone else (a parent or carer) to take over the management of your claim.

Couples

Only married couples, or a man and woman living together as husband and wife, count as a couple for IS. From December 2005, registered same-sex partners will be treated in the same way.

If one is eligible for IS – If you are eligible for IS but your partner would be required to sign on for benefit, you can choose which of you should make a claim. Either you claim IS or your partner claims jobseeker's allowance (JSA). However, where you are within the joint-claim age group for JSA (see Chapter 17(2)), either you claim IS or you both claim JSA jointly. You can't get IS and JSA at the same time unless your partner is only claiming contribution-based JSA. In this case you can claim IS to top up the JSA.

Whether you claim IS or JSA, the amount of benefit is usually the same, but note that:

- IS is tax free whereas JSA is taxable;
- JSA is not payable for the first 3 'waiting days' at the start of the claim;
- you avoid the risk of JSA sanctions if you claim IS instead (see Chapter 17(9));
- if the only way you can qualify for the disability premium is through being incapable of work (because you don't get a qualifying benefit – see Chapter 4(5)), you should claim IS.

If you claim IS, your partner can sign on voluntarily at the Jobcentre Plus office to secure national insurance credits.

If you find you've made the wrong choice, simply put in a claim for IS. The DWP will stop the JSA award if your IS claim is successful.

If both are eligible for IS – You can choose which of you should make the claim. There are some points to consider in deciding which of you should be the IS claimant.

- ❑ If the only way you can qualify for a disability premium is because you are incapable of work (but not receiving a qualifying benefit), you have to be the claimant (see Chapter 4(5)).
- ❑ If you are appealing against a personal capability assessment incapacity decision and are subject to a reduction in IS, generally your partner should be the claimant so that full-rate IS can be paid (see Box B.1, Chapter 3). But if the only way you qualified for the disability premium was because you were incapable of work but not receiving a qualifying benefit, you should be the claimant to protect your entitlement to arrears of the premium if your appeal is successful. In this case, you should consider claiming JSA instead to avoid the benefit reduction.

You can switch roles at any time. Your partner just has to put in a claim for IS with your agreement that they should make the claim, or vice versa.

4. How is IS paid?

Payment of IS is usually made directly into a bank, building society or post office account (see Chapter 57(5)). If you need money urgently at the start of your claim, the DWP should make the first payment by giro.

Payment is usually made in arrears, but if you're getting certain other benefits, it may be paid in advance (see 5).

Small payments – If you are entitled to less than £1 a week in IS, it will be paid to you weekly only if it can be paid along with another benefit. Otherwise, it will usually be paid in one sum every 13 weeks (but never less frequently).

The minimum payment of IS is 10p a week. If you are entitled to IS of 9p or less a week, that can only be paid to you if it can be paid along with another benefit. If you cannot be paid IS because of this minimum payment rule, you don't count as being 'on IS' for housing benefit or council tax benefit purposes; you have to go through the separate benefit assessments (see Chapter 7).

Third party deductions from benefit – IS for mortgage interest is paid direct to the lender when they are a member of the Mortgage Interest Direct scheme. For other costs, part of your benefit (up to a ceiling) may be deducted and paid direct to a third party if you have enough benefit, and usually where you have built up a debt.

The order of priority for direct payment deductions is: housing costs, rent arrears, fuel costs, water charges, community charge and council tax, court fines and compensation orders, and maintenance payments.

5. Benefit weeks and pay days

Your IS is normally paid on the same day and at the same intervals as any other benefit you get. In most cases, IS is paid in arrears. It is only paid in advance where you are getting widows' or bereavement benefits (but not if you are providing medical evidence of incapacity) or returning to work after a trade dispute.

When you are paid in arrears your 'benefit week' is the period of 7 days ending with your IS pay day, and you can be paid from the date your claim was received (or treated as received) in the Jobcentre Plus office. If there is a change of circumstances, your IS will alter from the first day of the week in which the change occurs.

6. Revisions and appeals

When you first claim, or when there is a major change in your applicable amount or resources, and thus a change in the amount of benefit you get, you will be sent a short notice of assessment (form A14). You can ask for a more detailed notice of assessment (on form A124) at any time.

If your IS claim is turned down, or you don't think you've been awarded the right amount, you can appeal to an appeal tribunal. The time limit for appealing is one month from the date the decision was sent to you. You should apply on form GL24 (see Chapter 58(8)).

You can ask for an A124 to show you how the DWP worked things out. If the decision did not include reasons, you can also ask for a written statement of reasons for the decision within one month. If the statement is provided within one month the appeal time limit will be extended by 14 days; if it is provided outside one month the appeal time limit will be extended until 14 days after the statement is provided. It is not always clear, however, whether the original decision did or did not include reasons, so if there is any doubt, the best advice is to make sure you appeal within the one-month time limit – even if you are still waiting for a written statement of reasons.

If you are running out of time and can't get a written appeal in within the deadline, you can ring your local Jobcentre Plus office, still within the month, and ask them to revise the decision. Where the decision maker revises the decision you will be given a new decision with new appeal rights; where they don't revise the decision, you will be informed and told that you have one month in which to appeal against the original decision.

If you are out of time, you can still ask for the past decision to be reconsidered (see Box R.5, Chapter 58). However, unless there are special circumstances for admitting your late application (see Chapter 58(5)), the decision maker will only change the decision from the date of your request (thus limiting any arrears payable to this date; see Box R.4, Chapter 58 for exceptions). You will have the right of appeal against the new decision.

There is more detail in Chapter 58 about how to challenge a decision.

C Housing and council tax benefits

This section of the Handbook looks at:

7 Housing benefit and council tax benefit

1. What is housing benefit?

Housing benefit (HB) helps people pay their rent. It can also be known as rent rebate or rent allowance. In Northern Ireland, where the rates scheme still applies, it helps people pay their rates. Council tax was not introduced in Northern Ireland (see 28 for details of the rate rebate scheme).

In nearly all cases, local authorities run the HB scheme. But in a few cases, other organisations run the scheme for their tenants, and in some areas local authorities have contracted out part of the administration to private firms. In Northern Ireland, the Northern Ireland Housing Executive and the Rate Collection Agency (an executive agency within the Department of Finance and Personnel) administer the scheme for tenants and owner occupiers respectively.

Rules and regulations

In England, Wales and Scotland, the framework for the scheme is in the Social Security Contributions and Benefits Act 1992, the Social Security Administration Act 1992 and the Child Support, Pensions and Social Security Act 2000. The details are in the Housing Benefit (General) Regulations 1987 (as amended), the Housing Benefit and Council Tax Benefit (State Pension Credit) Regulations 2003 and the Housing Benefit and Council Tax Benefit (Decisions and Appeals) Regulations 2001. Local authorities have a duty to allow members of the public to inspect the Acts and Regulations. There is corresponding legislation in Northern Ireland for the Scheme.

2. Who can get HB?

You can get HB if you satisfy all the following conditions:

- you are not excluded from getting HB (see below and Box C.1);
- you are liable to pay rent on your normal home (see 5);
- with the exception of some pensioners, your capital is no more than £16,000 (see 23);
- you are on income support, income-based jobseeker's allowance, the guarantee credit of pension credit, or have a fairly low income (see 21);
- you claim and provide the information requested (see 14).

People who cannot get housing benefit

If you are in any of the following groups, you are excluded altogether from getting HB.

- **Care leavers under 18** – if social services are responsible for accommodating you. There are rare exceptions: seek further advice if you are in this situation.
- **People in care homes** – There are rare exceptions (see Chapter 30(3)).
- **'Persons from abroad' or 'subject to immigration control'** – This does not cover every non-UK national, and it does cover some UK nationals who do not habitually reside in the UK. See Chapter 49 for details.
- **Many full-time students** – Full-time students cannot get HB unless they fall within certain groups – eg disabled students (see Chapter 38(4) for details). If you are in a couple and only one of you is a full-time student, the other one can get HB for you both.
- **Members of religious orders** – if you are maintained by the order.
- **Other groups** – See Box C.1 for details of other people who cannot get HB.

3. What is rent?

You can get HB towards almost any kind of rent, whether you pay it to a local authority (including a health authority), the Northern Ireland Housing Executive, Scottish Homes, a housing association, a co-op, a hostel, a bed and breakfast hotel, a private company, or a private individual (including a resident landlord – but see Box C.1). This is true whether your letting is a 'tenancy' or 'licence'; whether your payments are for 'rent' or for 'use and occupation' or for 'mesne profits' or 'violent profits'; and whether you have a written letting agreement or an agreement entered into by word of mouth. If you are buying a share of your local authority or housing association home, but still pay rent, you can get HB towards the rent (and you may be able to get income support, income-based jobseeker's allowance or pension credit towards your mortgage interest). You can also get HB towards the following, which all count as 'rent' for HB purposes:

- mooring charges and/or berthing fees for a houseboat (as well as your rent, if you do not own it);
- site fees for a caravan or mobile home (as well as your rent, if you do not own it);
- payments to a charitable almshouse;
- payments under a 'rental purchase' agreement;
- payments (in Scotland) on a croft or croft land.

4. Housing costs that HB cannot meet

You cannot get HB towards any of the following – although some of them may be met by income support, income-based jobseeker's allowance or pension credit (see Chapter 4(11), Chapter 17(20) and Chapter 41(3)):

- any payments you make on your home if you own it or have a long lease (over 21 years);
- any payments you make in a co-ownership scheme where, if you left, you would be entitled to a sum based on the value of your home;
- rent if you are a Crown tenant (there is a separate scheme for Crown tenants). But tenants of the Crown Estate Commissioners and the Duchies of Cornwall and Lancaster can get HB;
- hire purchase or credit sale agreements;
- conditional sale agreements (unless for land);
- payments on a tent.

5. Liability for rent on your normal home

The general rule is that, to get HB, you must be personally liable to pay the rent on your home. You can usually only get HB on one home at a time, which is the dwelling *'normally occupied'* by yourself and any members of your family. (Seek advice if you live in more than one dwelling due to the size of your family.) However, there are exceptions to these points as described in the next few paragraphs.

Couples – If you are in a couple, either one of you can get HB towards the rent on your normal home, even if the letting agreement is in one name only.

Joint occupiers – We use 'joint occupiers' to mean two or more people (other than a couple) who are jointly liable to pay the rent on their home. If you are a joint occupier, you can get HB towards a share of the rent on your normal home. This 'share' is assessed by taking into account the number of joint occupiers, how much each of you pays and how many rooms you each occupy in order to fairly apportion the rent between you.

If you take over paying someone else's rent – If the person who is liable for the rent on your home stops paying it, and you take over the payments in order to continue living there, you can get HB towards the rent – even though you are not legally liable for it. This applies if your partner has left you, and in any other reasonable case.

Repairs to your home – If your landlord agrees not to collect rent while you do repairs to your home, you can carry on getting HB for the first 8 weeks. After that, you cannot get HB until you start paying rent again.

C.1 Who cannot get HB?

The rules in this box apply in addition to those in the main text (see 2). If you have difficulties getting HB because of these rules, seek advice.

Your letting is not on a commercial basis – You cannot get HB if your letting is not on a commercial basis. This rule applies whether you live with your landlord or somewhere else. Factors to be considered when deciding this include: the relationship and agreement between the parties; the living arrangements; the amount of rent; and whether the agreement contains terms enforceable by law.

You live with your landlord who is a close relative – You cannot get HB if you live with your landlord and they are a 'close relative'. Sharing just a bathroom, toilet, hallway, stairs or passageways does not count as living with your landlord. A 'close relative' means only a parent, parent-in-law, step-parent, son, daughter, son/daughter-in-law, stepson/daughter, sister, brother or the (married or unmarried) partner of any of those. The term 'partner' does not currently apply to same-sex couples (although this may change when the Civil Partnership Act comes into effect in December 2005).

Your landlord is an ex-partner – You cannot get HB if you rent your home from:

- your ex-partner, and you used to live there with that ex-partner; *or*
- your (current) partner's ex-partner, and your (current) partner used to live there with that ex-partner.

Your landlord is the parent of your child – You cannot get HB if you or your partner are responsible for a child whose father or mother is your landlord. You (or your partner) count as 'responsible' for any child who normally lives with you.

Your landlord is a company or a trust connected with you – You cannot get HB if your landlord is a company or a trust of which any of the directors or employees (of the company), or trustees or beneficiaries (of the trust) is:

- you or your partner, or an ex-partner of either of you; *or*
- a person who lives with you and who is a 'close relative' of you or your partner (see above).

But this rule does not apply if your letting agreement was created for a genuine reason (rather than to take advantage of the HB scheme). What counts as 'taking advantage of the HB scheme' can be open to argument.

Your landlord is a trust connected with your child – You cannot get HB if your landlord is a trust of which your, or your (current) partner's, child is a beneficiary. For this rule, you cannot get HB even if your letting agreement was created for a genuine reason.

You used to be a non-dependant – You cannot get HB if:

- you lived in your home before you began renting it; *and*
- at that time you were a non-dependant (see 22) of a person who then lived in your home; *and*
- that person still lives in your home.

But this rule does not apply if your letting agreement was created for a genuine reason (rather than to take advantage of the HB scheme). What counts as 'taking advantage of the HB scheme' can be open to argument.

You used to own the home you rent – You cannot get HB if you or your partner used to own the home you are now renting. But this rule only applies if you owned it within the past 5 years and have lived there continuously since you owned it. It does not apply if you or your partner would have to have left your home if it was not sold. For example, this rule should not apply if you are renting your home under a 'mortgage rescue scheme'.

Tied accommodation – You cannot get HB if you or your partner are employed by your landlord and have to live in your home as a condition of that employment.

Contrived lettings – In addition to all the above rules, you cannot get HB if your or your landlord's principal or dominant purpose in creating your letting agreement was to take advantage of the HB scheme. The motives and intentions of landlord and tenant may be considered in order to determine this.

If you have to move into temporary accommodation while your normal home is being repaired, you can get HB on the property for which you are liable to make payments – but only if you are not liable for payments on the other home.

Bail or probation hostels – If you are required to reside in a bail or probation hostel, you will not be treated as occupying that dwelling as your home, and so will be unable to claim HB for any rent charged.

6. Temporary absence

You can continue to get HB while you are temporarily absent from your normal home in the circumstances described below.

The 13-week rule

You can get HB for up to 13 weeks during a temporary absence from your normal home if:

- you intend to return to occupy it as your home; *and*
- the part you normally occupy has not been let or sub-let; *and*
- your absence is unlikely to exceed 13 continuous weeks.

This rule applies to all absences (including absences outside the UK). In calculating the length of a prison sentence, the length of the sentence includes periods of temporary release, but should be reduced by any remission allowable for good behaviour.

The 52-week rule

You can get HB for up to 52 weeks during a temporary absence from your normal home if:

- you intend to return to occupy it as your home; *and*
- the part you normally occupy has not been let or sub-let; *and*
- your absence is unlikely to exceed 52 weeks or, in exceptional circumstances, is unlikely to substantially exceed 52 weeks; *and*
- your absence is for any of the reasons listed below.

Who the rule applies to – You can get HB under this rule if you are:

- a patient in a hospital or similar institution;
- receiving medical treatment or medically-approved care or convalescence (other than in a care home) in the UK or abroad;
- accompanying your child or partner who is receiving the above (but not care);
- providing care to a child whose parent or guardian is absent from home due to receiving medically approved care or medical treatment;
- providing medically approved care to anyone in the UK or abroad;
- receiving care in a care home (but not for a trial period – see below);
- on an approved training course in the UK or abroad;
- on remand awaiting trial or sentencing or required to reside in a hostel or property other than your home as a condition of bail;
- a student who is eligible for HB/council tax benefit (see Chapter 38(4));
- in fear of violence (the conditions are the same as in the rule for getting HB on two homes in such cases – see 7).

Your period of absence

If your absence is likely to exceed the 13 or 52 continuous weeks, you cannot get HB for any time you are away. If you cannot make an estimate of the length of your absence, you are unlikely to get HB during any of it. So, if possible, always give your local authority an estimate.

Any re-occupation of the home (other than a prisoner's temporary release) will break the period of absence – a stay of 24 hours is usually enough, although your local authority has to be satisfied that your stay at home was genuine.

As soon as it becomes likely that the absence will exceed the 13 or 52 week limit, your HB will stop.

Trial periods in care homes

You can get HB for up to 13 weeks during an absence from your normal home if:

- you are trying out a care home to see whether it suits your needs; *and*
- you intend to return to your normal home if it does not; *and*
- the part you normally occupy has not been let or sub-let.

7. Moving home and getting HB on two homes

The general rule

When you move from one rented home to another, you can get HB on both homes for up to 4 weeks if you have actually moved into the new home but your local authority agrees that you could not reasonably have avoided liability for rent on both your new home and your old home (eg because you have had to move unexpectedly and have to give notice on your old home). This general rule applies only if you have actually moved into the new home. Exactly what it means to *'move in'* can be interpreted in different ways, so it is often worth getting advice. This 4-week rule also applies if you move to a new home where you are not liable for rent but continue to have a rental liability on your old property.

Different rules apply if you move for one of the following reasons.

Fear of violence – This rule applies if you move because of fear that violence may occur:

- in your old home – in this case the rule applies regardless of who might cause the violence; *or*
- in the locality – in this case only if the violence would be caused by a (former) partner or member of your family.

In either case, you can get HB on both homes for up to 52 weeks – as long as you intend to return to your old home at some point and your local authority agrees it is reasonable to pay HB on both. You do not have to say exactly when you intend to return: it should be sufficient if you intend to return when it becomes safe to do so. If you do not intend to return, you continue to get HB on your former property for up to 4 weeks – if the continuing liability was unavoidable.

Waiting for your new home to be adapted – If you do not move into a new rented home straight away because you have to wait for it to be adapted to meet your disablement needs or those of any member of your family, and your local authority agrees the delay is reasonable, you can get HB for up to 4 weeks before you actually move in. If you are liable for rent on your old home, you can get HB on both during those 4 weeks.

Waiting for a social fund payment before moving home – If you do not move into a new rented home straight away because you have asked for a social fund payment to help with the move or with setting up home, and your local authority agrees the delay is reasonable, you can get HB for up to 4 weeks before you actually move in. But this rule only applies if there is a child under the age of 6 in your family, or if you or your partner are aged 60 or over, or if you qualify for one of the HB disability, disabled child or pensioner premiums – see 25 and Chapter 4(4) to (9). Under this rule you cannot get HB on your old home at the same time.

When you leave hospital or a care home – If you do not move into a new rented home straight away because you are waiting to leave hospital or a care home, and your local authority agrees the delay is reasonable, you can get HB for up to 4 weeks before you actually move in.

Claiming on time – In the above 3 cases, you must make your claim straight away: it is not enough to wait until you have actually moved in (unless your local authority backdates your claim – see 17). If your local authority rejects that claim, but you re-apply within 4 weeks of actually moving in, the rejected claim must be reconsidered.

Large families – If your family is so large that your local authority has arranged for you to be housed in two homes, you can get HB on both.

Students – Some students with partners who have to maintain two homes can get HB on both (if they are eligible for HB in the first place) – see Chapter 38(4).

8. How much of your rent is taken into account?

Your rent may include things like water charges, fuel, meals or other services; or you may rent a garage with your home. As detailed below, HB cannot be awarded towards all of these things. The HB calculation is based on your weekly 'eligible rent'. This means:

- the actual rent on your home,
- plus in some cases the rent on a garage,
- minus amounts for water, fuel, meals and certain other services.

Exceptions – In certain cases, the HB calculation is based instead on a lower figure (see 9).

To convert rent due monthly to a weekly figure, multiply by 12 (giving an annual figure), then divide by 365 (giving a daily figure), then multiply by 7.

Garages

If you rent a garage, this is included as part of the rent on your home only if you were obliged to rent the garage from the beginning of your letting agreement, or you are making (or have made) all reasonable efforts to stop renting it.

Water charges and council tax included in your rent

If your rent includes water or sewerage charges, the actual amount of the charge for your home (or if your water is metered, an estimate) is deducted. If your rent includes a contribution towards the council tax because your landlord pays it, not you, this is included as part of your eligible rent.

Service charges: general conditions

The rules for several types of service charge are given below, saying whether they can be taken into account as part of your eligible rent. But even when they can, there are two further conditions.

- The amount of the charge must be reasonable for the service provided. If it is not reasonable, the unreasonable part is deducted.
- Payment of the charge must be a condition of occupying your home – whether from the beginning of your letting agreement or from later on. If it is not a condition of occupying the home, the whole charge is deducted.

Exception – If the rent officer fixes a maximum rent for your home, they also fix a value for some of the services (see 9).

Fuel and related charges

If your rent includes fuel of any kind, the actual amount of the fuel charge is deducted if there is evidence of how much it is (eg in your rent book or letting agreement). If there is no evidence of the amount, a flat-rate amount is deducted for the various things the fuel is for; the amounts are given below.

Whenever your local authority makes flat-rate deductions, it must write inviting you to provide evidence of the actual amount. If you can provide reasonable evidence (which need not be from your landlord), your local authority must estimate the actual amount and deduct that instead of the flat rate.

Exceptions – A fuel charge for a communal area (including communal rooms in sheltered accommodation) is included as part of your eligible rent as long as it is separately specified in your rent book or letting agreement. The same is true for a separately specified charge for providing a heating system.

Flat-rate deductions – If you rent more than one room (not counting any shared accommodation), these are:

Deductions	per week
Heating	£10.55
Hot water	£1.25
Lighting	£0.85
Cooking	£1.25

If you rent only one room (not counting a shared kitchen, bathroom or toilet), the flat-rate deduction for heating is £6.33. If you get a flat-rate deduction for heating, there is no further deduction for hot water or lighting, but the figure for cooking is as above.

Meal charges

If your rent includes meals (the preparation of food or the provision of food) a flat-rate amount is deducted for these. The flat rate is always used, regardless of how much you are actually charged for meals. One flat-rate deduction is made for each person (even if not a member of your family) whose meals are included in your rent. The amount for each person depends on their age and what meals they get.

Weekly deductions per person	aged 16	under 16
For at least 3 meals every day	£20.05	£10.15
For breakfast only	£2.45	£2.45
For any other arrangement	£13.35	£6.70

Note that for these purposes, a person does not count as aged 16+ until the first Monday in the September following their 16th birthday.

Other services

Cleaning and window cleaning – A charge for cleaning and window cleaning of communal areas is included in your eligible rent; so is a charge for exterior window cleaning if neither you nor anyone in your household can do it. A charge for any other cleaning and window cleaning (estimated if necessary) is deducted.

Furniture and household equipment – A charge for these is included in your eligible rent as long as your landlord has not agreed that they will become part of your personal property.

General support charges – Before April 2003, 'support charges' could be included in your eligible rent if you lived in supported accommodation. This has now ceased but you may be able to get help from the Supporting People scheme (see Chapter 25(5)).

Medical, nursing and personal care – A charge for any of these (estimated if necessary) is deducted. (Even before April

C.2 Why housing benefit may not cover all your rent

Your HB may not cover all of your rent. This could be because:

- your rent includes service charges or other things which have to be deducted in the calculation of HB (see 8);
- you have one or more non-dependant(s) in your home and a deduction has to be made because of this (see 22);
- your HB is restricted (eg because a 'maximum rent' applies) (see 9);
- the level of your income means you do not qualify for the whole of your rent to be met (see 21).

2003, these could not be met by HB.)

Communal or accommodation-related services – Most charges for these are included in your eligible rent. Examples are: TV/radio aerial and relay (with exceptions for satellite or cable), refuse removal, lifts, communal telephones, entry phones, children's play areas, garden maintenance necessary for the provision of adequate accommodation and communal laundry facilities.

Day-to-day living expenses, etc – Charges for these (estimated if necessary) are deducted. Examples are: TV/radio rental and licence, laundering (ie if washing is done for you), transport, sports facilities, leisure items, and any other service not related to the provision of adequate accommodation.

9. HB restrictions

There are several rules about how your local authority can restrict (in other words, reduce) your eligible rent. They depend on whether you rent from your local authority, from a housing association, or from any other landlord (including a private landlord). If you live in a pilot area where local housing allowances are being introduced see Box C.3, as the following paragraphs will not apply to you.

Note: When you look at the following, don't forget the rules about joint occupiers (see 5); and don't forget to convert your rent (and the other figures mentioned below) to a weekly amount.

If you rent from your local authority

If you rent from the local authority, it will administer your HB claim, and it is very unlikely that your eligible rent will be restricted. If you rent from any other authority (such as a non-metropolitan county council), look instead at 'If you rent from any other landlord, including a private landlord'.

If you rent from a housing association

If you rent from a registered housing association (or any other registered social landlord), it is possible (though fairly unlikely) that your eligible rent will be restricted. If your local authority considers that your rent is unreasonably expensive or your accommodation is unreasonably large, they may refer your details to the rent officer.

- If they do this, all the rules relating to people who rent from a private landlord will apply to you (see below).
- If they do not do this, they should not restrict your eligible rent at all.

If you rent from an unregistered housing association (which is not a registered social landlord), all the rules relating to people who rent from a private landlord will apply to you (see below).

Note: Don't forget to look at the exceptions given later: they can mean you qualify for more HB.

If you rent from any other landlord, including a private landlord

In this case, your eligible rent is restricted to a figure called your 'maximum rent' – unless you fall within certain protected groups or qualify for a discretionary housing payment (see 17 below).

To find out your maximum rent, your local authority must pass details of your rent and other circumstances to the rent officer before deciding your claim for HB. Rent officers are independent of the local authority. They look at your rent and various other matters and then give the local authority various figures to use in the calculation of your maximum rent. In Northern Ireland there are no rent officers so the Northern Ireland Housing Executive (NIHE) decides the amount of rent to be used in the calculation of maximum rent.

Note: Don't forget to look at the exceptions given later: they can mean you qualify for more HB.

The rent officer's figures – The rent officer may give your local authority one or more of the following figures:

- a 'claim-related rent' – this is based either on the rent officer's valuation of a reasonable market rent for your home or (if they regard your home as being too large) for a smaller home. It might be your actual rent or, if the rent officer thinks this is too high, a lower figure;
- a 'local reference rent' – this is based on the rent officer's valuation of the midpoint of all rents in your area (ignoring extreme cases) for homes that are in a reasonable state of repair and which are the same size as yours or (if they regard your home as being too large) for smaller homes;
- a 'single room rent' – this is based on the rent officer's valuation of the midpoint of all rents in your area (ignoring extreme cases) for homes that are in a reasonable state of repair and which are just one room (eg a bedsit) with shared use of a toilet and shared use (or no use) of a kitchen. This is the case even if you live somewhere bigger. But it only applies if you count as a 'young individual' (see below).

How to calculate your maximum rent

Step 1: If you are a joint occupier, adjust the 'claim-related rent' and (if one is given) the 'local reference rent', as described earlier (see 5). Never adjust the 'single room rent' in this way.

Step 2: If your actual rent includes meals, subtract the correct amount for meals from the 'claim-related rent' and (if one is given) from the 'local reference rent'. (Never deduct a figure for meals from a 'single room rent'.) Note that no deduction is made for fuel, water or any other ineligible services (because the rent officer has already done this).

Step 3: Your maximum rent is the lowest of the 'claim-related rent', 'local reference rent' and 'single room rent' (adjusted as just described) – or if only one is given, it is that one (adjusted as described).

'Young individuals' – You count as a 'young individual' if you are single (not a lone parent or in a couple) and are under the age of 25. However, there are 5 exceptions; you do not count as a young individual if you:

- satisfy the conditions for a severe disability premium in the calculation of your HB, income support or income-based jobseeker's allowance (see Chapter 4(7)); *or*
- have one or more non-dependant(s) living in your home (see 22); *or*
- are under the age of 22 and were previously in the care of your social services department under a court order (as long as the court order applied, or continued to apply, to you after your 16th birthday); *or*
- are under the age of 22 and used to be accommodated by your social services department at any time before your 18th birthday; *or*
- rent from a registered housing association (or other registered social landlord).

More information – You can get full information about all the above figures, categories, etc (but only those which have been used in calculating your HB entitlement) from your local authority by asking for a written statement (see 20, under 'Notice of decisions'). If you ask for reasons (and this is recommended), the rent officer should give these and your local authority should send these on to you; in Northern Ireland, these functions are carried out by NIHE. If you write asking the authority to reconsider any of the figures supplied by the rent officer and used in the calculation of your claim (see 20), your letter will be referred to the rent officer for a re-determination. This could result in your maximum rent being increased or decreased.

Example: A claimant and his family have just moved into a flat which they rent for £180 a week. This includes fuel and water charges. The rent officer thinks the property is too big

for their needs and so gives a claim-related rent of £160 a week. The local reference rent is £150 a week.
Calculation: No adjustments need to be made for meals, so the maximum rent is the lower of the rent officer's figures, which is the local reference rent of £150 a week.

Example: A 'young individual' has just moved into a flat which she rents for £50 a week. This does not include any service charges. The rent officer gives a single room rent of £45 a week.
Calculation: No adjustments need to be made for meals, so the maximum rent is simply the single room rent of £45 a week.

When is a case referred to the rent officer?
New claims for HB will be referred to the rent officer, unless less than 52 weeks have passed since the last referral and there has been no relevant change of circumstances. If a relevant change of circumstances has occurred, a claim can be referred back to the rent officer even if less than 52 weeks have passed since the last referral. A claim can always be referred whenever 52 weeks have passed since the last referral.

Will your rent be restricted?
Your local authority must restrict your eligible rent to the maximum rent as calculated above (but see 'Protections for certain people' below, and 17). The local authority can restrict

C.3 Local housing allowance

Pathfinder areas

The local housing allowance (LHA) Pathfinder project is part of a programme of reforms to housing benefit (HB). The initial 9 Pathfinder projects commenced in 2003/04 and will run for 2 years; 9 more projects start in April 2005.

People living in private sector rented accommodation in the Pathfinder areas have their entitlement to HB assessed in a different way. The initial Pathfinder areas are: Blackpool, Lewisham, Coventry, Teignbridge, Brighton and Hove, Edinburgh, North-East Lincolnshire, Conwy and Leeds. From April 2005 the following areas will also operate the scheme: Argyll & Bute, East Riding of Yorkshire, Guildford, Norwich, Pembrokeshire, Salford, South Norfolk, St Helens and Wandsworth.

HB for LHA claimants is based on a flat rate that is determined by the area their property is in and the number of people living in the property. The actual allowance paid is subject to a means test (as with 'normal' HB) but the standard allowance is the same for everyone in the area, regardless of property size or the actual rent charged. Joint tenants will receive a proportion of the rate payable for a property of the size applicable to all the tenants together. There is some protection for certain existing tenants in these areas who may otherwise be worse off because of the change.

Benefit payment

The Government intends for all payments to be made direct to the tenant, although payment can be made to the landlord at the local authority's discretion. This could be considered, for example, where the claimant has a learning disability or significant rent arrears.

Government aims

The Government's intention is to increase tenant choice and to make the system fairer. It believes tenants will be able to choose between staying in a property that is larger than they need, but more desirable, or moving to a cheaper, less attractive property. The fact that the allowance is standard across all properties also means it will be easier for a claimant to decide whether to take on a particular tenancy. The process of actually paying the allowance should also be speeded up, as 'eligible rents' will all be the same. The projects starting in 2005 will have a particular focus on operational issues, such as testing enhanced computer software packages.

It is clear from government announcements that it intends to 'roll-out' the scheme nationally in the private rented sector. No firm date has been set but it seems unlikely this will be earlier than 2008. It also intends to extend the scheme to the registered social landlord sector at a later date.

Rate of the LHA

Rent officers determine the rate of the LHA. A claimant can then decide to rent a property where the rent is lower than the LHA and keep the difference. Alternatively, they can take a more expensive property but will have to make up the shortfall. Initial government estimates suggested that around 60% of tenants would gain from the scheme.

Exempt tenancies

Tenancies that are currently exempt are:

- registered social landlord tenancies;
- protected cases, such as supported housing provided by certain local authorities, social landlords, charities and voluntary organisations;
- tenancies which are excluded from current rent restrictions (eg pre-1989 tenancies);
- exceptional cases, such as caravans, houseboats and hostels;
- cases where the rent officer judges that a substantial part of the rent is attributable to board and attendance (eg hotel accommodation).

Property size criteria

The size criteria used when determining the property size rates are the same as those used by rent officers in other cases. That is:

- ❑ One bedroom for:
- every adult couple;
- any other adult (aged 16 or over);
- any two children under 10;
- any two children of the same sex aged 10 to 15;
- for any other child.
- ❑ Living rooms:
- 1-3 occupiers are entitled to 1 living room;
- 4-6 occupiers are entitled to 2 living rooms;
- 7 or more occupiers are entitled to 3 living rooms.

Based on the size criteria, a couple with a 12-year-old daughter, for example, would be eligible for the 3-room property rate (2 bedrooms and 1 living room).

Young people and couples without children

Single claimants under the age of 25 defined as 'young individuals' (see 9) will only be entitled to the rate for one room in shared accommodation (as under the current 'single room rent' rules). Single claimants over the age of 25, disabled young people and couples without children will be entitled to the 2-room property rate (eg a 1-bedroom flat).

Appeals

There is no right of appeal against the level of the LHA in any area. There is the right to appeal against the actual HB assessment but not against the LHA set by the rent officer.

A
B
C
D
E
F
G
H
I
J
K
L
M
N
O
P
Q
R
S

your eligible rent further if it considers the maximum rent is unreasonable in all the circumstances of your case. If this happens, seek advice.

Protections for certain people

Your local authority must not use the maximum rent figure described above in the following two cases. (For how your eligible rent is calculated in these cases, see 8.)

- If you and/or any member of your household could afford the financial commitments of your home when you first entered into them, and you have not received HB during the 52 weeks before your current claim, your authority must not use the maximum rent figure for the first 13 weeks of your claim.
- If any member of your household has died, and you have not moved since then, your authority must not use the maximum rent figure until a year after the date of that death (unless there was already a maximum rent figure that applied before that death, in which case that continues).

Although your local authority cannot use the maximum rent figure in the above circumstances, it can restrict your eligible rent if it considers it is unreasonable in all the circumstances of your case. If this happens, seek advice.

For the purposes of the above protections, all the following count as a member of your household:

- each member of your family: yourself, your partner if you are in a couple, children under 16, and children aged 16, 17 or 18 for whom child benefit is payable (see 25, under 'Your family');
- any other relative of yours (or your partner) who lives with you but does not have an independent right to do so. A 'relative' means only a parent, parent-in-law, step-parent, son, daughter, son/daughter-in-law, stepson/daughter, sister, brother or the (married or unmarried) partner of any of those; or a grandparent, grandchild, uncle, aunt, niece or nephew.

Exceptions to the above rules

The following exceptions to the rent restriction rules may apply to you if you rent from a housing association or from any other private landlord. If you fall within more than one of the following exceptions, just look at the first one that applies to you.

The exceptions can be complicated in some cases (and in rare cases there are yet further rules). It is often worth seeking advice. Don't forget to also check the points in 'Protections for certain people' (above).

Pre-January 1989 tenancies – This applies to you if your letting began before 15.1.89 in England and Wales or 2.1.89 in Scotland. In these cases, your local authority must not refer your details to the rent officer, and it is very unlikely they will restrict your eligible rent.

People in accommodation where care, support or supervision is provided – This applies to you if:

- your home is provided by a non-metropolitan county council, housing association, registered social landlord, registered charity, non-profit-making voluntary organisation or certain similar bodies; *and*
- your landlord provides you with 'care, support or supervision' or has arranged for you to be provided with this.

This exception also applies to you if your home is a resettlement hostel.

In these cases, your local authority can only restrict your eligible rent if they themselves have evidence that your rent is unreasonably expensive, or that your home is unreasonably large.

There are several further rules which give protection to certain vulnerable people – if you have difficulties seek further advice.

If you have been on HB since 1.1.96 – This applies to you if you:

- were getting HB on 1.1.96 (in Northern Ireland on 1.4.96); *and*
- have been on HB continuously since that date (ignoring either gaps of no more than 52 weeks if you or your partner are a 'welfare to work beneficiary' – see Chapter 15(12) – or gaps of no more than 4 weeks for anyone else); *and*
- have not moved since that date (unless as a result of a fire, flood, explosion or natural catastrophe).

If your partner or another member of your household previously satisfied these conditions, you may be able to take advantage of these rules – seek further advice.

In the above cases, your local authority can only restrict your eligible rent if it has evidence that your rent is unreasonably expensive or that your home is unreasonably large.

There are several further rules which give protection to certain vulnerable people – if you have difficulties seek further advice.

If you have been on HB since 5.10.97 – This applies to you if:

- you were getting HB on 5.10.97; *and*
- you have been on HB continuously since that date, ignoring gaps of no more than 52 weeks if you or your partner are a 'welfare to work beneficiary' (see Chapter 15(12)). No gaps are allowed for anyone else; *and*
- you have not moved since that date (regardless of the reason for the move); *and*
- the rent officer has provided a local reference rent for your claim.

In these cases, your local authority may have to use a higher maximum rent when it assesses your eligible rent. If this applies to you, seek further advice.

Getting information before you sign up for a letting

Are you thinking of taking up a letting at a new address? Or are you considering whether to sign a new letting agreement with your landlord (and at least 12 months have passed since you last signed an agreement with them)? And would you like to know whether your eligible rent is likely to be restricted if you claim HB? If 'yes', you have the right to a 'Pre-tenancy determination'.

Get a form from your local authority or NIHE (in some areas the forms may also be available from your landlord or a local advice agency). Fill in the form, sign it, get the landlord of the accommodation to sign it, and give it or send it to your local authority.

The rent officer, your local authority or NIHE will then write to you (and the landlord of the accommodation) to say whether there will be a maximum rent in your case. You should hear within 9 days in most cases (or sooner in some areas).

This maximum rent will apply for at least one year (as long as your circumstances –eg family size – do not change). Although this is not a guarantee of the amount of your HB, it can be a good guide. Your local authority will usually be able to give you further advice about this.

Note: The form you fill in asking for a 'Pre-tenancy determination' is not a claim for HB. You must make a claim for HB separately. As always: do not delay; make an HB claim as soon as you can to avoid losing any HB.

You cannot get a 'Pre-tenancy determination' for a local authority or NIHE letting. In practice, it is unlikely that the landlord will agree to you getting one if the landlord is a registered housing association.

10. What is council tax benefit?

Council tax benefit (CTB) helps people pay their council tax. There are two types of CTB, but you can only get one type at a time: see 27 under 'The better buy'. 'Main council tax benefit'

(Main CTB) is the more common type and is described below. 'Second adult rebate' is much less common (see 27).

In all cases, local authorities run the CTB scheme, although some have contracted out part of the administration to private firms. (There is no council tax, and so no CTB, in Northern Ireland.)

Rules and regulations – The framework for the scheme is in the Social Security Contributions and Benefits Act 1992, the Social Security Administration Act 1992 and the Child Support, Pensions and Social Security Act 2000. The details are in the Council Tax Benefit (General) Regulations 1992 (as amended), the Housing Benefit and Council Tax Benefit (State Pension Credit) Regulations 2003 and the Housing Benefit and Council Tax Benefit (Decisions and Appeals) Regulations 2001. Local authorities have a duty to allow members of the public to inspect the Acts and Regulations. There is corresponding legislation in Northern Ireland for the scheme.

11. Who can get Main CTB?

You can get Main CTB if you satisfy all the following conditions:

- you are not excluded from getting Main CTB (see below);
- you are liable to pay council tax on your normal home (see 12);
- you claim and provide the information requested (see 14);
- you are on income support, income-based jobseeker's allowance, the guarantee credit of pension credit, or you have a fairly low income (see 21);
- with the exception of some pensioners, your capital is no more than £16,000 (see 23).

People who cannot get Main CTB

The following groups are excluded altogether from getting Main CTB.

- ❑ **'Persons from abroad' or 'subject to immigration control'** – This does not include every non-UK national, but it does cover some UK nationals who do not habitually reside in the UK. See Chapter 49 for details.
- ❑ **Many full-time students** – Full-time students cannot get Main CTB unless they fall within certain groups (although they can get second adult rebate). Many students with disabilities do, however, fall within one of those groups. See Chapter 38(4) for details. If you are in a couple and only one of you is a full-time student, the other can get Main CTB for you both.

12. Liability for council tax on your normal home

To claim CTB, you must be personally liable to pay the council tax on your normal home. For most purposes, your 'normal home' means wherever you are treated as being *'resident'* under council tax rules (see Chapter 8(6)). Most home owners and rent payers are liable for council tax and so can claim CTB. But note the following points.

- ❑ **Exempt dwellings** – If your dwelling is exempt from council tax (see Chapter 8(4)), you cannot get CTB on it.
- ❑ **If you rent non-self-contained accommodation** – You are not liable for council tax (your landlord is), so you are not eligible for CTB.
- ❑ **Water charges** – You cannot get CTB towards water charges or (in Scotland) towards the council water charge.
- ❑ **Couples** – If you are in a couple and you are jointly liable for council tax on your home, either one of you can get CTB towards this. If only one of you is liable, that one can get CTB on behalf of you both (see Chapter 8(5)).
- ❑ **Joint occupiers** – We use 'joint occupiers' to mean two or more people (other than a couple) who are jointly liable to pay the council tax on their home (see Chapter 8(5)). If you are a joint occupier, you can get Main CTB towards a share of the council tax on your home. This share is always found by dividing the total council tax bill by the number of people who are liable.
- ❑ **Absences from home** – The rules for whether you can get CTB during a temporary absence from home have, from 4.4.05, been realigned with those of HB (see 6).
- ❑ **Moving home and occupying two homes** – You can only ever get CTB on one home at a time. This is wherever you are treated as being resident under the council tax rules (see Chapter 8(6)).

13. How much of your council tax is taken into account?

The CTB calculation is based on your weekly *'eligible council tax'*. For Main CTB purposes, this means whatever you are liable to pay after you have been awarded any reduction for disabilities, discount or transitional reduction (see Chapter 8(7), (8) and (9)).

CTB is worked out on a weekly basis, so your council tax liability has to be converted. Divide the annual figure by 365 (giving a daily figure), then multiply by 7. If your bill is not for a full year, divide it by the number of days it covers, then multiply by 7.

14. How to claim HB and CTB

The following applies to HB for rent and CTB (both Main CTB and second adult rebate). For HB help with rates in Northern Ireland, see 28. Whether or not you get income support (IS), incapacity benefit (IB), jobseeker's allowance (JSA) or pension credit (PC) you must make a written claim for HB and/or CTB.

Getting someone to claim for you

If you are incapable of managing your own affairs, an appointee can take over the responsibilities of claiming for you and dealing with any further matters relating to your claim. That person (who must be aged 18 or over) should write to your local authority to request approval to act as your appointee. Permission should not be withheld unreasonably.

Keeping a record

If possible keep a copy, or at least a record including the date, when you send in any of the claim-forms described below or any information you have been asked for. If you take in forms instead of posting them, get a receipt or an acknowledgement from whoever you give them to. Forms do sometimes go astray, and without a record it can be hard to convince your local authority that you submitted a form that has been lost. A form which your local authority accepts it has lost is treated as though it was received (although you may have to fill in a replacement for their records).

Where to claim

Usually you need to complete a claim-form and return it to the office responsible for administering the HB scheme. However, if you are claiming IS, income-based JSA or PC, you can send your claim for HB/CTB to the relevant DWP office, as well as the HB office. (If your HB/CTB claim is on a separate form from the claim for the other benefits, the DWP must forward it on within 2 days.) When you claim IS or income-based JSA, you should be given a claim-form for HB and CTB. This is usually called an HCTB1 (but see 'Other names of claim-forms' below). If you are claiming PC, since first contact is usually by phone, you should be asked if you want to claim HB or CTB. If you do, an HCTB1(PC) form should be sent to you.

Other names of claim-forms – Forms have changed a lot recently. Here are the forms you may be given instead of the HCTB1 form to claim HB and CTB. However, the time limits and other rules mentioned above and below apply in just the same way.

- The HCTB1(PC) is a shorter form for people aged 60 and over.
- In certain areas you can claim HB and CTB on the same claim-form as IS/JSA/IB. In these areas, Jobcentre Plus will take your details over the phone and will provide you with a statement of your circumstances to sign. This statement should be returned to Jobcentre Plus, which will send details to your local authority.
- If you reclaim IS or income-based JSA within 12 weeks of last receiving them, you should be given a form HBRR1 (instead of the HCTB1 form) to claim HB and CTB. This is sometimes also called a 'rapid reclaim' form.
- In some areas you will receive your local authority's own version of the HCTB1.

Making a claim

If you are not claiming one of the benefits above, you should ask your local authority for a claim-form, complete it and send it back to them as soon as possible. Most (if not all) local authorities have one combined form for claiming both HB and CTB. You can phone and ask for the form. It is planned that from April 2005, as long as a written claim is made within 4 weeks of this call, the claim can be treated as having been made at the time of this first contact, and benefit backdated accordingly (at time of writing, regulations have not been put into effect on this matter).

If you cannot easily get the claim-form, write to your local authority: give your name and address, say you wish to claim HB and/or CTB, and date it. Your local authority should then send you the claim-form. Make sure you get it back to your local authority within 4 weeks of the date it was sent out.

The claim-form asks you to provide various documents (eg your rent book in the case of a claim for HB). If you do not have all the information or documents requested, send the form back as soon as possible, and write on it that you will send the further information or documents as soon as you can. It is also a good idea to explain any reasons for the delay. Sometimes your local authority may write with further questions. Always ensure your reply reaches them within 4 weeks of when they sent the letter out.

If you do not keep to the 4-week time limit for sending information back to your local authority (or for sending in the form if you originally sent a letter), they can agree a delay of whatever period is *'reasonable'*. This will mean you are treated as having claimed within the time limits (see below).

Date of claim

If your claim for IS, income-based JSA or the guarantee credit of PC is successful, and your HB/CTB claim is received within the 4-week time limit, your HB will start from the same date as the IS, JSA or PC.

If your claim for IS, income-based JSA or the guarantee credit of PC is unsuccessful, your HB starts from the date your local authority or DWP office received your HB/CTB form. The 4-week time limit for returning your HCTB1 form is strict. If you do not keep within it, your date of claim will be the day the HCTB1 form actually reached the HB office.

If you claimed HB/CTB on the same form as IB or contribution-based JSA, your HB/CTB starts on the day the DWP office received your form.

In all other cases, your claim begins on the day your claim-form is received by the HB office. However, in all cases you may qualify for your claim for HB/CTB to be backdated under the 'good cause' rule (see 17).

The Government has stated that from April 2005 the rules on backdating HB/CTB claims will be put into line with those of other benefits. Consequently, a claim for HB/CTB will be treated as having been made at the time of first contact as long as a written claim is made within 4 weeks of this contact. Benefit will be backdated accordingly. At time of writing, however, regulations have not been put into effect on this matter.

15. When your HB/CTB starts, changes and ends

Your first day of entitlement

The usual rule is that HB and/or CTB start on the Monday after your date of claim for HB/CTB (this date was described above). Even if that date was itself a Monday, HB and/or CTB start the following Monday.

The exception is if your date of claim for HB/CTB is in the same benefit week (Monday to Sunday) as you moved into your home (or first became liable for rent or council tax for any other reason). In that case, your CTB starts on the exact day you became liable for council tax; your HB starts on the Monday of that week (if your rent is due weekly, fortnightly or 4-weekly) or on the exact day your rent liability began (if your rent is due daily or monthly).

The length of your claim

Prior to April 2004, most claims for HB/CTB were awarded for a fixed period only (typically 6 months or one year) after which time a renewal claim had to be made to continue the award.

From April 2004, fixed period awards no longer apply, so your claim for HB/CTB will continue to run for as long as you remain entitled to the benefit.

When your benefit ends

You will cease to be entitled to HB/CTB if a change in your circumstances means you no longer qualify. Your HB/CTB will also end if you have been receiving IS, income-based JSA, IB or severe disablement allowance for at least 26 weeks, and that benefit ends due to you or your partner starting work or increasing your hours/earnings. You will need to re-claim HB/CTB in these circumstances. (However, you should qualify for an extended payment of HB/CTB in such circumstances, to continue your award at the same rate for a period of 4 weeks – see Chapter 15(6) for more details.)

If your IS, income-based JSA, IB or SDA ends for any other reason, this will not bring your HB/CTB claim to an end. However, your claim will need to be re-assessed due to the change in your circumstances.

Change of circumstances

Although HB/CTB is awarded for an indefinite period, you still have a duty to notify your local authority about any change in your circumstances that may affect your HB/CTB entitlement. Your local authority will advise you of the changes that you should notify.

If a change in your circumstances means that you qualify for more HB/CTB, write to your local authority promptly. If you take more than one calendar month and you have no good reason for the delay, you will lose money because the increase will only be given to you from the Monday following the day your letter reached them. If you do have a good reason for delaying more than a month, explain this when you write in with your change, as otherwise this may not be taken into account. In all cases, if you take more than 13 months you will definitely lose money, because 13 months is the absolute limit for notifying changes.

If a change in your circumstances means that you qualify for less HB/CTB, write to your local authority promptly, otherwise you will probably be asked to repay any overpayment (see 19).

16. How your HB/CTB is paid

HB if you pay rent to the local authority

Your HB is awarded as a rebate towards your rent account

– which is why it is also called a 'rent rebate'. In other words, the rent you have to pay will be reduced. This will also apply if you pay your rent to the Northern Ireland Housing Executive.

HB for everyone else
Your HB is paid in a cheque, giro, etc – which is why it is also called a 'rent allowance'. Your local authority must take into account your *'reasonable needs and convenience'* in choosing the method of payment, so it should not insist on paying you by crossed cheques if you do not have a bank account.

Your first payment of HB – The law says that your local authority should make your first payment within 14 days of when they receive your properly completed claim or, *'if that is not reasonably practicable, as soon as possible thereafter'*. This must be either the correct amount of your entitlement or, if that is not yet known, an estimated amount, known as a 'payment on account' – which will be adjusted when the correct amount is known. The law is also clear that you should not have to ask the authority for a prompt first payment; though of course if you do not get one, it is sensible to get in touch with them and remind them of their duties. They do not, however, have to make a prompt first payment if you have not supplied the information and documents they have requested, unless you can show that your failure to do so is 'reasonable' (eg if the delay in providing these is outside your control).

Paying your HB to your landlord – Your HB is paid to your landlord, instead of to you, in the following main circumstances:

- if you request or consent to this; *or*
- if it is in your or your family's best interests; *or*
- if your landlord requests it and can show your local authority that you have at least 8 weeks of rent arrears (6 weeks in Northern Ireland).

In the first 2 cases, your local authority does not have to agree. In the third case, they have to agree (until the rent arrears reduce to below 8 weeks) unless there are overriding reasons for refusing, or if the landlord is deemed not to be a 'fit and proper' person to receive payment. Your local authority can also choose to pay your first payment of HB to your landlord (regardless of whether you agree) if they consider this appropriate.

Council tax benefit
Your CTB is awarded as a rebate towards your council tax liability. In other words, your bill for council tax will be reduced. If, however, by the end of the financial year (31 March) your authority owes you any outstanding CTB, you can ask for it to be paid to you in a cheque, giro, etc. If you do not do this, it is usually carried over and rebated against the new financial year's council tax bill.

17. Getting more benefit

Discretionary housing payments
Discretionary housing payments (DHPs) are technically not a kind of HB or CTB, but they are administered by the same authorities and can only be given to people who qualify for at least some HB or Main CTB.

The local authority can give you a DHP if you *'appear to [the] authority to require some further financial assistance... in order to meet housing costs'*. DHPs are discretionary (no one has a right to one) – as is the amount of DHP (if any) and the period it is granted for. However, the combined amount of your HB, CTB and DHP in any one week cannot exceed your 'eligible rent' (see 8) and 'eligible council tax' (see 13). DHPs cannot be used for any of the following:

- service charges (including support charges) which HB cannot meet (see 8);
- water and sewage charges;
- your rent liability if you qualify only for CTB;
- your council tax liability if you qualify only for HB, or only for second adult rebate.

In Northern Ireland a DHP is paid only to claimants whose rent has been restricted and who seem in need of further financial assistance. It is not intended to meet anything other than the shortfall between the rent being requested by a landlord and the restricted rent. It does not apply to the rate rebate scheme.

Most local authorities have a form on which to request a DHP. If your local authority does not, write a letter instead. Your local authority may ask for detailed information about your circumstances and those of your household. You should explain these fully. For example, the local authority could take into account disability needs, and it could also take into account the fact that you receive state benefits such as disability living allowance for these (even if the HB rules would normally ignore these). The availability of DHPs varies widely from authority to authority. The HB and CTB appeals system does not apply to DHPs, but you have the right to ask the local authority to look again at their decision if you are dissatisfied. It is your duty to report changes in your circumstances which could affect the payment of a DHP.

Getting your benefit backdated
If you can show that you (not anyone else – eg your landlord) had continuous 'good cause' for having delayed making your claim, your local authority must backdate your HB and/or CTB. You have to ask in writing for your claim to be backdated. Benefit can only be backdated for a maximum of one year before the date this written request is received by your local authority.

'Good cause' means some fact or facts, which *'having regard to all the circumstances (including the claimant's state of health and the information which he had received and that which he might have obtained) would probably have caused a reasonable person of his age and experience to act (or fail to act) as the claimant did'*. For example, you may have good cause if you are ill and have no one to help you make the claim, or if you are unable to manage your own affairs and you don't have an appointee. Ignorance of the law on its own is not normally good cause unless there are exceptional circumstances (eg mental health or learning disabilities, educational limitations, youthfulness, language difficulties, or a combination of these and other factors). Generally, you are expected to make reasonable enquiries about your right to benefit. You will normally be able to show good cause if you ask the DWP or local authority for advice and then act on the basis of their wrong or misleading advice, or if you reasonably misunderstood the advice you were given.

If your claim was delayed for over a year and the delay was your local authority's fault, you can ask for an ex-gratia compensation payment to cover the period remaining after the maximum 52 week backdate.

In line with the rules for pension credit (see Chapter 41) if you or your partner are aged 60 or over, your claim for HB/CTB can be backdated automatically for 12 months as long as you met the rules of entitlement throughout the period.

18. Underpayments

If your local authority has awarded you less HB or CTB than they should have, due to official error, they must make up the difference. An *'official error'* means a mistake by your local authority or by your Jobcentre Plus office or by the Inland Revenue. There is no limit to the period for which arrears may be paid in these cases.

However, if you were awarded less HB or CTB because you failed to tell the authority something, see 15.

19. Overpayments

Overpayments are amounts of HB/CTB you were awarded

but which you weren't entitled to – perhaps because you did not tell your local authority something you should have, or because your local authority or Jobcentre Plus office made a mistake, or for some unavoidable reason. Different rules apply to different types of overpayment, as follows.

How much is the overpayment?
If you qualified for at least some HB or CTB during the period for which you were overpaid, your authority should allow you to keep that (even if you didn't claim it or tell them everything you should have at the time). They should normally only recover the difference between what you were paid and what you should have been paid.

Although this rule has applied since October 2000, there are still problems with its application in some areas; if you have difficulties, seek advice. (There are also circumstances in which the authority cannot recover anything – see below.)

Overpayments of CTB due to a change in your council tax liability
If you get a backdated reduction for disabilities or discount (see Chapter 8), and you were getting CTB, you will have been overpaid CTB. When your local authority adjusts your council tax bill, they will adjust your entitlement to CTB at the same time to recover the overpayment. Overpayments caused by such adjustments are always recoverable.

Overpayments of HB payments on account
If you were granted a payment on account (see 16) and it turned out to be greater than your actual entitlement to HB, the overpayment will be recovered from your future HB entitlement.

If it turns out you were not entitled to any HB, the following rules apply.

Overpayments of HB or CTB due to official error
An 'official error' means a mistake by your local authority or by your Jobcentre Plus office, or by the Inland Revenue.

The main example of a mistake made by a Jobcentre Plus office which counts as official error is when they tell your local authority that you qualify for income support (IS) or income-based jobseeker's allowance (JSA) when in fact you do not.

If your Jobcentre Plus office does not tell your local authority that you have come off IS or income-based JSA (or started receiving any other benefit), this may count as an official error, but because the law says it is your duty to tell your local authority about the change – it should not be deemed as having caused the overpayment. If the error does not cause the overpayment it will be recoverable from you.

Your local authority must not recover an overpayment due to official error unless you (or someone acting for you, or the person who received the payment – such as your landlord if your HB is paid to them) could *'reasonably have been expected to realise that it was an overpayment'* at the time the payment or any notification about it was received. Your local authority should take into account what you (or the other person) personally could have been expected to realise.

Overpayments due to a mistake about capital
An overpayment of more than 13 weeks of HB or CTB due to a mistake about capital may not be recoverable in full. There are 'diminishing capital' rules which treat the capital as gradually reducing (described in Chapter 57(6)).

All other overpayments
Any overpayment of HB or CTB not mentioned above may be recovered by your local authority. This includes overpayments due to a failure or mistake by you, and even overpayments which were unavoidable (such as overpayments due to a backdated pay rise or a backdated social security benefit).

Discretion and hardship
Even if an overpayment is recoverable, your local authority can exercise their discretion not to recover it (eg if you can show that you would otherwise suffer hardship).

Notifications and appeals
In all cases, if your local authority decides to recover an overpayment, they must write notifying you of all the details and of your appeal rights. You can use the appeal procedure (see below) if you are dissatisfied with their decision.

How are overpayments recovered?
If an overpayment is recoverable, it can be recovered from you or your partner (as long as you were a couple at the time of both the overpayment and the recovery) or (in most cases) the person who received the payment (eg your landlord) or the person who caused the overpayment. It can be recovered as follows:

- by reducing your future HB entitlement (but not, if you are a local authority or Northern Ireland Housing Executive (NIHE) tenant, by simply turning the amount into arrears of rent). The most your authority can recover in this way is currently £8.55 a week (although this can be increased in certain cases if you are now working or receive a war widow's or war disablement pension or charitable or voluntary income, or have committed fraud);
- by adding the amount back to your council tax account. Therefore you will have more council tax to pay;
- if the above methods are not possible, by making deductions from almost any other social security benefit.

In all cases, you can agree to repay the overpayment in cash or by cheques, giros, etc. As a last resort, your local authority can take action in the courts to recover an overpayment.

Note that if an HB overpayment is recovered from your landlord, then (unless you rent your home from the local authority or NIHE), your landlord is legally allowed to treat the amount repaid as rent arrears due from you.

20. Decisions, reconsiderations and appeals

The following rules have applied to HB and CTB since July 2001. For more detail, see Chapter 58.

Notice of decisions
Your local authority has a duty to send you a written notice about the decision it makes on your HB and/or CTB claim. If you do not qualify, the notice will say why not. If your local authority makes further decisions during the course of your claim (eg about a change of circumstances or an overpayment), it must send you a written notice about that. In each case, it will also explain your right to get more information and to appeal.

If you want more information about how your entitlement to HB or CTB (or lack of it) was worked out, write to your local authority and ask for a written statement. You can do this at any time (though if you are also thinking about asking the authority to reconsider their decision, or about making an appeal, bear in mind the time limits mentioned below). You can ask about specific things or ask for full details of how your claim was assessed. Your local authority should reply in writing within 14 days, or as soon as possible after that.

Exceptions – In certain circumstances, your local authority does not have to make a decision, and the tribunal does not have to deal with an appeal. This is called 'staying' a decision or appeal. It arises when a test case is pending, the result of which could affect your case (see Chapter 58(6) for details).

Asking the authority to reconsider their decision
You have the right to ask your local authority to reconsider

their decision on almost all matters relating to your HB and/or CTB claim (for example, how much you qualify for, whether you should have to repay an overpayment, and so on). If your letter arrives within the 'dispute period' (see below), your local authority must reconsider their decision, taking account of what you say. They should give you a written notice saying whether they are changing or sticking to their original decision, and giving their reasons. But if you were requesting a reconsideration of a maximum rent fixed by the rent officer (see 9), it will take longer because it will be sent to the rent officer to consider.

Appeals to a tribunal
Either instead of, or after, asking your local authority to reconsider their decision (see above), you can appeal to an independent appeal tribunal. See Chapter 58 for the details of appeals to a tribunal and for how to make a further challenge to the Commissioners or courts.

Exceptions – There is no right of appeal to a tribunal about:

- most administrative decisions about claims and payments of HB/CTB, although you can appeal to a tribunal about when your HB/CTB should begin and whether your claim should be backdated;
- whether your local authority should run a local scheme for war widow/widower's pensions and war disablement pensions (see Chapter 5(6) under 'Benefits that are partly disregarded');
- your maximum rent if the rent officer or Northern Ireland Housing Executive (NIHE) fixed one for your home (see 9);
- discretionary housing payments (see 17).

In each case, however, you can ask the local authority to reconsider their decision.

The dispute period
Whether you are asking the local authority to reconsider a decision or asking for an appeal, your letter should reach your local authority within one calendar month of the day they sent out the notice about the decision. If you have asked for a written statement, the time they took to deal with that is ignored in adding up the month. For example, if you asked for a written statement in late July, 10 days after your local authority's notice was sent out, you have 21 days left from the date they reply to write requesting them to reconsider.

Also, your local authority (or the tribunal, in the case of an appeal) can agree to extend the one-month time limit if the delay was caused by special circumstances (see Chapter 58(3)). If this is the case, explain what the special circumstances are when you write, as otherwise they may not be taken into account. In all cases, 13 months is the absolute limit for asking for the decision to be changed.

The Ombudsman
You can make a complaint to the Ombudsman if you feel the local authority or NIHE administered your claim unfairly or caused unreasonable delays. This is separate from the appeal procedures. See Chapter 60.

21. How much benefit?

We explain below how to work out your entitlement to HB and Main CTB. We give the rules for people on income support (IS), income-based jobseeker's allowance (JSA) or the guarantee credit of pension credit (PC) first, then the rules for other people. (For how to work out the other kind of CTB, second adult rebate, see 27. For how to calculate HB for rates in Northern Ireland, see 28.)

People on IS, income-based JSA or PC (guarantee credit)
If you (or your partner if you are in a couple) are on IS, income-based JSA or PC (guarantee credit), there are a few simple steps to follow.

Step 1: Work out your eligible rent and council tax
HB is worked out on your weekly eligible rent. This can be less than your actual rent (see 8 and 9). Main CTB is worked out on your weekly eligible council tax (see 13).

Step 2: Deduct amounts for non-dependants
If you have one or more non-dependants in your home, your HB and Main CTB are reduced by flat-rate amounts (though there are exceptions to this). For who counts as a non-dependant and the other details, see 22.

Step 3: Amount of benefit per week
HB equals your weekly eligible rent minus any amounts for non-dependants. Main CTB equals your weekly eligible council tax minus any amounts for non-dependants.

Examples
HB: If your weekly eligible rent is £90 and you have no non-dependants, the weekly amount of your HB is £90. But if you have one non-dependant, and a flat-rate deduction of £47.75 applies, the weekly amount of your HB is £42.25.

Main CTB: If your weekly eligible council tax is £15 and you have no non-dependants, the weekly amount of your Main CTB is £15. But if you have one non-dependant and a flat-rate deduction of £6.95 applies, the weekly amount of your Main CTB is £8.05.

People not on IS, income-based JSA or PC (guarantee credit)
If you (or your partner if you are in a couple) are not on IS, income-based JSA or PC (guarantee credit) there are several steps to follow.

Step 1: Your capital
If your capital (including your partner's) is more than £16,000 you cannot get HB or Main CTB. Not all capital counts. For how to work out your capital, see 23 and 26. Even if your capital is over £16,000, you may be able to get second adult rebate (see 27).

Step 2: Your eligible rent and council tax
HB is worked out on your weekly eligible rent. This can be less than your actual rent (see 8 and 9). Main CTB is worked out on your weekly eligible council tax (see 13).

Step 3: Deduct amounts for non-dependants
If you have one or more non-dependants in your home, your HB and Main CTB are reduced by flat-rate amounts (though there are exceptions to this). For who counts as a non-dependant and the other details, see 22.

Step 4: Work out your weekly income
This includes your (and your partner's) income from some, but not all, sources. For how to work out your weekly income, see 24 and 26.

Step 5: Work out your applicable amount
This figure represents your weekly living needs. For how to work out your applicable amount, see 25 and Chapter 4.

Step 6: Have you got 'excess income'?
If your income is *less* than, or equal to, your applicable amount, you do not have 'excess income'. See Step 7.

If your income is *greater* than your applicable amount, you have 'excess income'. The amount of your excess income is the difference between your income and your applicable amount. See Step 8.

Step 7: Amount of benefit per week if you do not have excess income
HB equals your weekly eligible rent less any amounts for non-dependants.

Main CTB equals your weekly eligible council tax less any amounts for non-dependants.

This is exactly the same as for people who are on IS, income-based JSA or PC (guarantee credit). For examples, see above.

Step 8: Amount of benefit per week if you have 'excess income'
HB equals your weekly eligible rent less any amounts for non-dependants and less 65% of your excess income. If the result is less than 50p you will not be awarded HB. See below, 'Points to note'.

Main CTB equals your weekly eligible council tax less any amounts for non-dependants and less 20% of your excess income. You might get more using the second adult rebate calculation (see 27).

For other points to note see below.

Examples if you have excess income
HB: If your weekly eligible rent is £90, you have no non-dependants, and you have excess income of £20, the weekly amount of your HB is:

Eligible rent	£90.00
Less 65% of £20 excess income	£13.00
Weekly HB	*£77.00*

But if you have one non-dependant and a flat-rate deduction of £7.40 applies, the weekly amount of your HB is:

Eligible rent	£90.00
Less non-dependant deduction	£7.40
Less 65% of £20 excess income	£13.00
Weekly HB	*£69.60*

Main CTB: If your weekly eligible council tax is £15, you have no non-dependants, and you have excess income of £20, the weekly amount of your Main CTB is:

Eligible council tax	£15.00
Less 20% of £20 excess income	£4.00
Weekly Main CTB	*£11.00*

But if you have one non-dependant and a flat-rate deduction of £2.30 applies, your weekly Main CTB is:

Eligible council tax	£15.00
Less non-dependant deduction	£2.30
Less 20% of £20 excess income	£4.00
Weekly Main CTB	*£8.70*

Points to note
The percentages (65% in HB and 20% in Main CTB) are also called 'tapers' because of how they work: as your excess income goes up, your benefit goes down. You can have so much excess income that you do not qualify for any benefit. The amount(s) of your non-dependant deduction(s) can also mean you do not qualify for any benefit.

The minimum award of HB is 50p a week. So if the calculation comes out at less than 50p, you will not get any HB. There is no minimum award of Main CTB: you can get as little as 1p a year.

22. Non-dependants

Whether or not you are on income support (IS), income-based jobseeker's allowance (JSA) or the guarantee credit of pension credit (PC), deductions are made from your HB and/or Main CTB if you have one or more non-dependants. The law assumes they will contribute towards your rent and/or council tax, whether or not they actually do so. A deduction cannot be cancelled on the grounds that your non-dependant pays you nothing. But there are cases when the law says that no deduction must be made.

Who is a non-dependant?
A non-dependant is someone who normally lives in your home on a non-commercial basis – usually an adult son, daughter, friend or relative. None of the following are your non-dependants (and so there is no deduction for any of them):

- your *'family'* (see 25). For example, an 18-year-old who is still included in your family is not your non-dependant;
- foster children;
- someone with whom you share just a bathroom, toilet, communal area (or in sheltered accommodation, a communal room);
- your joint occupier(s), tenant(s) or sub-tenant(s), resident landlord/landlady, and members of their households;
- your or your partner's carer if they are provided by a charity or voluntary organisation who charge you for this (even if someone else pays the charge for you).

Almost anyone else who lives with you is your non-dependant.

No non-dependant deduction
Your (or your partner's) circumstances – There is no deduction for any non-dependants you have (no matter how many) if you or your partner:

- are registered as blind or ceased to be registered within the last 28 weeks; *or*
- get the care component of disability living allowance (DLA; any rate) or attendance allowance (AA) or constant attendance allowance.

Your non-dependant's circumstances – There is no deduction for any individual non-dependant you have if they:

- are under 18; *or*
- in calculating HB, are under 25 and on IS or income-based JSA; *or*
- from 4.4.05 are on PC (whether guarantee or savings credit); *or*
- in calculating Main CTB, are any age and on IS or income-based JSA; *or*
- get a Work-Based Learning for Young People training allowance; *or*
- have been in an NHS hospital for over 52 weeks; *or*
- are detained in prison or a similar institution; *or*
- have their normal home elsewhere; *or*
- are a full-time student (see Chapter 38(4)) – but in calculating HB only, there is a deduction in the summer vacation if they take up remunerative work (see below), unless they (or their partner) are 65 or over; *or*
- in calculating Main CTB only, are in any of the groups who are 'disregarded' for the purposes of the council tax discount rules (see Box C.6).

The amounts of the deductions

- ❑ **Non-dependants aged 25 or over on IS or income-based JSA** – The weekly amount in calculating HB is £7.40, but there is no deduction in calculating Main CTB.
- ❑ **Non-dependants on PC** – From 4.4.05, no deduction.
- ❑ **Other non-dependants not in remunerative work** – Regardless of the level of your non-dependant's income, the weekly amount is £7.40 in HB and £2.30 in Main CTB.
- ❑ **Non-dependants in remunerative work (excluding those on PC)** – The weekly amount depends on the level of your non-dependant's weekly gross income.

Weekly gross income	HB	Main CTB
£322 or more	£47.75	£6.95
£258 to £321.99	£43.50	£5.80
£194 to £257.99	£38.20	£4.60
£150 to £193.99	£23.35	£4.60
£101 to £149.99	£17.00	£2.30
Under £101	£7.40	£2.30

If you cannot provide evidence of your non-dependant's gross income (and they are in remunerative work and not in receipt of PC), your local authority will make the highest of the above deductions. If you later provide evidence showing that the deduction should have been lower, your local authority should award you arrears of HB/Main CTB because you have been underpaid (but act quickly – see 15).

Which non-dependants are in remunerative work?
'Remunerative work' means work that averages 16 or more hours a week. If your non-dependant is on maternity leave, paternity leave, adoption leave or sick leave, they are not counted as being in remunerative work (even if paid full pay or statutory maternity/paternity/adoption/sick pay). If your non-dependant gets IS or income-based JSA for more than 3 days in any benefit week (Monday to Sunday) they are not counted as being in remunerative work.

Your non-dependant's gross income
Your non-dependant's income is relevant if they are in remunerative work. It is assessed gross, which, in the case of earnings, means before tax, national insurance and any other deductions are made. All other income is counted, except DLA, AA, constant attendance allowance and payments from the Macfarlane Trusts, the Eileen Trust, the Independent Living Fund and the Fund. If your non-dependant has capital, only the interest is counted as gross income. If your non-dependant is in a couple, add in their partner's gross income (but see below).

Other points about non-dependants
You get a deduction for each non-dependant you have (apart from those for whom no deduction applies).

But if you have non-dependants who are a couple, you get only one deduction for the two of them. This is the higher figure of the two amounts that would have applied to them if each was single and each had the income of both.

If you are a joint occupier (see 5 and 12), and your non-dependant is also a non-dependant of the other joint occupier(s), the deduction is shared between you and the other joint occupier(s).

Concession if you are aged 65 or over
If you or your partner are aged 65 or over, special non-dependant deduction rules apply. If a non-dependant comes to live with you, their income will be ignored for HB/CTB purposes for a period of 26 weeks. If you already have a non-dependant living with you and their circumstances or income change (meaning a higher deduction applies), the local authority will not increase the amount of the deduction for a 26-week period. Where changes occur more than once, the 26-week period runs from the date of the first change. If your non-dependant's income decreases, the authority should reduce the deduction immediately if appropriate.

23. Capital

Your local authority needs to assess your capital if you are not on income support (IS), income-based jobseeker's allowance or the guarantee credit of pension credit (PC). If you are in a couple, your partner's capital is counted in with yours. The rules about how capital is assessed for HB and Main CTB purposes are almost the same as for IS (see Chapter 5). Where they differ and this could make a difference to you, we say so in Chapter 5.

There are different capital rules for claimants aged 60 and over, which are intended to reflect the more generous provisions of PC (see 26 below).

If your capital is over £16,000, you cannot get HB or Main CTB (but you may still get second adult rebate – see 27). If your capital is £3,000 or less (or £6,000 or less if you or your partner are aged 60 or over), it is totally ignored in assessing your HB/CTB. If it is a higher figure (but not over £16,000), you are treated as having income – known as 'tariff income' (see Box B.2, Chapter 5). In rare cases, some people in care homes are entitled to HB (see Chapter 30(3)). For them, the first £10,000 (instead of £3,000 or £6,000) of capital is ignored.

If a child in your family has capital of their own, it is disregarded.

24. Income

Your local authority needs to assess your income if you are not on income support (IS), income-based jobseeker's allowance or the guarantee credit of pension credit (PC). If you are in a couple, your partner's income is counted in with yours. The rules about how income is assessed for HB and Main CTB purposes are almost the same as for IS (see Chapter 5). Where they differ and this could make a difference to you, we say so in Chapter 5. Income rules for claimants aged 60 and over are intended to reflect the more generous provisions of PC and differ in some respects (see 26 below).

If your income is greater than your applicable amount, this affects the amount of HB and Main CTB you get (see 21). It does not affect second adult rebate (see 27).

25. Applicable amounts

Your local authority needs to assess your applicable amount if you are not on income support (IS), income-based jobseeker's allowance (JSA) or the guarantee credit of pension credit. An 'applicable amount' is a figure set by Parliament which is intended to reflect your weekly living needs and those of your family. Your applicable amount is made up of:

- **personal allowances** – you get one or more of these for the various members of your family, including children; *plus*
- **premiums** – many, but not all, people get one or more premiums to take account of family responsibilities, age, disabilities and responsibilities as a carer.

These include the same premiums as for IS (see Chapter 4(4) to (10)), with additional premiums payable for a family and disabled child(ren).

You have to satisfy conditions for each part of the applicable amount. The premiums for disabilities are the most complex. It's a good idea to ask for a written statement from your local authority about what premiums you have been awarded and why. You can check these and, if you think any have been missed, you should ask for a reconsideration or lodge an appeal (see 20).

Your family
Applicable amounts are based on the circumstances of your 'family'. 'Family' is used in a technical sense in HB/CTB. It means:

- you (the claimant); *and*
- your partner of the opposite sex if you are married and are members of the same household or if you are unmarried and living together as husband and wife (after December 2005 registered same-sex partners should be treated in the same way); *and*
- any dependent child(ren) who are members of your household, and are either under the age of 16 or are aged 16, 17 or 18 if child benefit is still payable. The definition of a dependent child includes your natural and adopted children and other children for whom you are responsible (eg a grandchild). Foster children are not usually included. If a child who is normally in local authority care spends time with you at home, your local authority can either include that child or not as a member of your family for the benefit week(s) (Monday to Sunday) when the child stays with you. This is an 'all or nothing' rule: your local authority cannot give you just part of a personal allowance or family premium.

Personal allowances

Personal allowances for people aged 18 or over are the same as for IS (see Chapter 4(3)). For people aged under 18, the rules are somewhat simpler (see table below).

Allowances for children, although removed from IS and JSA following the introduction of child tax credit, have been retained in the applicable amounts for HB and CTB. They are paid for each dependent child under the age of 19 for whom you are responsible (see above).

Personal allowances		per week
Couple	one or both aged 18 or over	£88.15
	both under 18	£67.15
Lone parent	aged 18 or over	£56.20
	aged under 18	£44.50
Single person	aged 25 or over	£56.20
	aged 16-24	£44.50
Dependent child		£43.88

The premiums

The following table shows the weekly rates for the additional premiums payable for children and families within HB/CTB. Rates for the other premiums are shown at Chapter 4(4).

Premium	per week
Family premium	£16.10
Family premium (lone parent rate)	£22.20
Disabled child premium	£43.89
Enhanced disability premium (child)	£17.71

The family premium

This is awarded if you have a dependent child aged under 19. The ordinary rate of £16.10 is awarded if you are one of a couple or a lone parent, unless you have transitional protection for the higher lone parent rate of £22.20 (see below). The ordinary rate can be awarded in addition to any other premium.

To qualify for the family premium – Your HB/CTB family must include a child aged under 19. The family premium is fixed at £16.10 (or £22.20) regardless of the number of children you have. If your family includes a child under the age of one year, you will receive an additional £10.50.

If you have just one child, and get the full personal allowance for that child, you will also be entitled to the family premium.

If you have just one child and they do not count as a member of your family, you won't get the child's personal allowance, nor will you get the family premium, disabled child premium or enhanced disability premium for that child. This would happen, for example, where your former partner gets child benefit in respect of that child.

Protected lone parent rate – The lone parent rate was abolished on 6.4.98 but existing claimants can continue to get it. You must have been a lone parent entitled (or treated as entitled) to HB or CTB on 5.4.98 and have continued to be entitled to it. You must not cease to be or become entitled to either IS or income-based JSA. If you are or become entitled to a disability premium or any pensioner premium, your family premium switches to the ordinary rate. But you regain the lone parent rate if the disability premium or pensioner premium stops.

Disabled child premium

The disabled child premium can be awarded in addition to any of the other premiums. The disabled child premium is £43.89 for each child who lives with you and counts as disabled. Your child counts as disabled if they:

- are registered blind, or were taken off that register within the past 28 weeks; *or*
- get disability living allowance (DLA); *or*
- no longer get DLA because they are in hospital – as long as they are still treated as a member of your HB family.

There is no lower age limit in law for registering a child as blind. Apply (in writing) to your social services (or social work) department for registration as soon as you are given a diagnosis, or you think one likely. Contact the RNIB (see Address List) if you experience difficulty. If a delay in registration is unreasonable, consider complaining to the Local Government Ombudsman (see Chapter 60).

If a child is not registered as blind and is not terminally ill, the earliest age at which you can get the disabled child premium for them is 3 months (when DLA care component normally first becomes payable). If they qualify only for DLA mobility component, the disabled child premium would be paid from their 3rd birthday at the earliest.

The enhanced disability premium (child)

This premium is paid at the rate of £17.71 for each child who qualifies.

A child qualifies for the enhanced disability premium if they are paid DLA highest rate care component. It can be awarded on top of a disabled child premium.

If a child is in hospital, you keep the enhanced disability premium for as long as the child is treated as a member of your family (see Box L.1 in Chapter 32).

26. Rules for people in receipt of pension credit or aged 60 or over

New rules were introduced on 6.10.03 for claimants who are aged 60 and over. These are intended to reflect the more generous provisions of pension credit (PC – see Chapter 41), which was introduced on that date. The main changes are listed below.

Your applicable amount

Your personal allowance will be based on the 'standard minimum guarantee' and, in addition (if you or your partner are aged 65 or over), the 'maximum savings credit' (see Chapter 41(3 & 4)). For a single claimant the personal allowance is £109.45, or £125.90 if you are aged 65 or over. For a couple it is £167.05, or £188.60 if either of you is aged 65 or over.

The following extra sums can be included in your applicable amount following the usual HB/CTB rules:

- personal allowances for dependent children and young people (see 25 above);
- family premium (see 25 above);
- severe disability premium (see Chapter 4(7));
- enhanced disability premium (for any qualifying dependent child or young person, not for yourself or your partner) (see 25 above);
- disabled child premium (see 25 above);
- carer premium (see Chapter 4(8)).

Income and capital

There are different rules about how income and capital affect the amount of HB/CTB you get, depending on whether or not you receive PC and which elements of it are in payment (see Chapter 41).

Guarantee credit – If you or your partner receive the guarantee credit of PC, the whole of your capital and income will be disregarded and you will receive full HB/CTB. This applies even if your capital exceeds the usual HB/CTB limit of £16,000. Since there is no capital limit for PC, it is possible to receive the guarantee credit even though your savings would exceed the HB/CTB limit.

Savings credit only – If you or your partner are aged 65 or over and receive the savings credit but not the guarantee credit of PC and do not have more than £16,000 capital, then the local authority will use the assessment of your income and capital which the DWP used to calculate your savings credit (see Chapter 41(4)). The local authority will then adjust this figure to reflect the following special rules.

- Any of your partner's income or capital which was not taken into account in the PC calculation will be taken into account.
- Any income of a non-dependant which can be treated as yours under HB/CTB regulations will be included.
- Any PC savings credit will be taken into account.
- The higher HB/CTB disregards of lone parent's earnings, maintenance payments and the 30-hour element of working tax credit will apply.
- The normal HB/CTB disregard of childcare costs will apply (see Chapter 5(4)).
- Any discretionary disregard of war pensions allowed by your local authority will be applied to your income.

No PC payable – If you or your partner are aged 60 or over but do not receive PC (savings credit or guarantee credit) your income and capital will be assessed by the local authority in much the same way as it is for PC (See Chapter 41(5 & 6)).

27. Second adult rebate

This type of CTB is known in the law as *'alternative maximum council tax benefit'*, but we use the more common term 'second adult rebate'. It is completely different from Main CTB described earlier. One of the unique features of second adult rebate is that you can get it regardless of how much income and capital you have. You cannot get second adult rebate and Main CTB at the same time, but if you satisfy the rules for both, your local authority will grant whichever is the higher amount.

Note: If you qualify for Main CTB equal to at least 35% of your council tax liability, you need not consider second adult rebate because you could never get that much second adult rebate.

Claims

You should not have to make a separate claim for second adult rebate: your claim for CTB should be treated as a claim for both Main CTB and second adult rebate. However, some local authorities have a special claim-form to use if you want to be considered for second adult rebate only (eg if your capital is way over £16,000).

Who is eligible?

You can get second adult rebate if you satisfy all these conditions:

- you are not excluded from getting CTB by the rule about 'persons from abroad' (see 11);
- you are liable to pay council tax on your normal home (see Chapter 8(5));
- there are one or more 'second adult(s)' in your home (see below);
- the second adult(s) are on income support (IS), pension credit (PC) or income-based jobseeker's allowance (JSA) or have a fairly low income (see below);
- you meet conditions to do with certain types of households (see below);
- your entitlement to second adult rebate is greater than any entitlement to Main CTB (see below, 'The better buy');
- you claim and provide the information requested (see 14).

Note: If you are a student, you can get second adult rebate even if you are excluded from getting Main CTB (see Chapter 38(4)).

Who is a 'second adult'?

You must have at least one 'second adult' in your home to get second adult rebate. A person is a 'second adult' if they are:

- aged 18 or more; *and*
- your non-dependant (see 22); *and*
- not in any of the groups who are 'disregarded' for the purposes of the council tax discount rules. Those groups are listed in Box C.6.

If your non-dependant is in one of the 'disregarded' groups, this should have been taken into account in considering whether you qualify for a council tax discount (see Chapter 8(9)); this is why you can only get second adult rebate if you have a non-dependant who is not 'disregarded'. (The note on carers under 'Extra rules' below gives the one exception to the above definition of a 'second adult'.)

Extra rules for certain types of households

Single claimants and lone parents – If you alone are liable for the council tax on your home, there are no extra rules. But if you are jointly liable for the council tax, see below.

Couples – If you are in a couple there is an extra rule. Either you or your partner (or both of you) must be 'disregarded' for the purposes of the council tax discount rules (see Box C.6). If you are jointly liable for the council tax with someone other than just your partner, see below.

Jointly liable for council tax – If you and others are jointly liable for the council tax on your home there is an extra rule. Either all, or all but one, of the jointly liable people must be 'disregarded' for the purposes of the council tax discount rules (see Box C.6). The amount of second adult rebate is worked out for the whole dwelling and you will get a share, which is calculated by dividing the total amount by the number of jointly liable people.

All claimants who have tenants, sub-tenants or boarders in their home – In addition to the rules mentioned above, there is an overriding rule that you cannot get second adult rebate if you personally receive rent from a tenant, sub-tenant or boarder aged 18 or over in your home.

Carers – Many carers are 'disregarded' for the purposes of the council tax discount rules (see Box C.6) so they cannot be second adults. But if you or your partner have a carer who is not 'disregarded' and who is provided by a charity or voluntary organisation that charges you for this, the carer is a 'second adult'. This is the only case in which someone who is not a non-dependant can be a 'second adult'.

Amount of second adult rebate

The amount of your second adult rebate depends only on the income of your second adult(s).

- If you have just one second adult, you get the highest amount of second adult rebate if they are on IS, PC or income-based JSA. In all other cases the amount depends on their gross income.
- If you have two or more second adults, you get the highest amount of second adult rebate if they are all on IS, PC or income-based JSA. In all other cases, the amount depends on the combined gross income of all of them apart from those on IS, PC or income-based JSA.

Income of second adult(s)	rebate
Second adult(s) is on IS, PC or income-based JSA	25%
Weekly gross income of second adult(s) is:	
Under £150	15%
£150 to £193.99	$7\frac{1}{2}$%
£194 or more	nil

Your second adult rebate is shown in the above table as a percentage of your eligible council tax. For example, if the 15% figure applies to you, your second adult rebate is 15% of your eligible council tax – ie your bill is cut by 15%.

Your eligible council tax – For second adult rebate purposes, your eligible council tax is the same as for Main CTB purposes (see 13).

Exceptions if you also qualify for a discount – There is one special rule that applies only for second adult rebate (not Main CTB) and only if you qualify for a council tax discount (see Chapter 8(9)). If this applies to you, your eligible council tax is worked out as though you did not get that discount. (You do not lose the discount: it is ignored only for the purposes of calculating your second adult rebate.) The following example may explain this.

Example: Mr Young owns his home. He is 'severely mentally impaired'. He has savings over £16,000 and so cannot get Main CTB. His adult son lives with him (but does not provide personal care). His son works and has a gross income of £110 a week. The home falls in council tax band D: this year the full council tax for band D in his area is £800.

Mr Young asks for a council tax discount. The local authority agrees he is a 'disregarded person' (see Box C.6, Chapter 8), but his son is not. So Mr Young qualifies for a 25% council tax discount (see Chapter 8(9)). This is £200 a year.

Mr Young also claims second adult rebate. The local authority agrees that he qualifies for second adult rebate: his son is the 'second adult'. Based on his son's gross income, the amount of the second adult rebate is 15% of his eligible council tax. This means 15% of his council tax before the discount is awarded, in other words 15% of £800. This is £120 a year.

Mr Young's council tax reduction:	per year	per week
Total council tax bill	£800	£15.34
Less 25% discount	£200	£3.84
Less 15% second adult rebate	£120	£2.30
Amount of council tax due	*£480*	*£9.20*

Your second adult's gross income

The second adult's income is relevant whether or not they are in remunerative work (but not if they are on IS, PC or income-based JSA). It is assessed gross, which, in the case of earnings, means before tax, national insurance and any other deductions are made. All other income is counted, except disability living allowance, attendance allowance, constant attendance allowance and payments from the Macfarlane Trusts, the Eileen Trust, the Independent Living Fund and the Fund. If the second adult has capital, only the actual interest is counted as gross income. If they are in a couple, add in their partner's gross income (even if the partner is not classified as a second adult).

The 'better buy'

If you qualify under the above rules for second adult rebate, and you also qualify under the earlier rules for Main CTB, there is one final step – often known as a 'better buy' calculation.

This is because you cannot get both Main CTB and second adult rebate at the same time: you will only get the one that is worth most. You should get a full notification explaining this if it applies to you, and can ask for a written statement if you want more information (see 20).

C.4 For more information

Your local Citizens Advice Bureau has detailed information on housing benefit, council tax benefit and the council tax rules. They should be able to advise you. If you want to look at the law, see CPAG's *Housing Benefit and Council Tax Benefit Legislation 2004/2005* or visit www.hbinfo.org. For further information see the *Guide to Housing Benefit and Council Tax Benefit 2005/2006* and other publications listed in Chapter 61.

28. Rate rebates in Northern Ireland

Rates are payable on domestic properties in Northern Ireland: there is no council tax. You can get help through HB towards the rates you are liable to pay on your normal home – whether you pay rent for your home (in which case you can get a rate rebate as well as HB for your rent) or whether you own your home (in which case you can get only a rate rebate).

The conditions for getting a rate rebate are similar to those for getting HB for rent, described at the start of this chapter. The method of claiming a rate rebate is also similar to that for HB for rent (see 14). Your rate rebate is awarded towards your rates liability.

However, if you rent from a private landlord or housing association, and your landlord (not you) pays the rates, the amount of your rate rebate is usually paid to you, along with your HB for rent, in a cheque, giro, etc. Recoverable overpayments may be recovered by adding the amount back to your rates bill. Other rules (eg about appeals) are the same as the rules about HB for rent (see 20).

Amount of rebate

If you (or your partner) are on income support (IS), income-based jobseeker's allowance (JSA) or the guarantee credit of pension credit (PC) your rate rebate equals:

- the weekly amount of your rates liability;
- less any amount for non-dependants.

The amounts for non-dependants are the same as the figures used in England and Wales for council tax benefit (see 22).

If you (or your partner) are not on IS, income-based JSA or PC (guarantee credit) your rate rebate equals:

- the weekly amount of your rates liability;
- less any amount for non-dependants;
- less 20% of your excess income.

The amounts for non-dependants are the same as for CTB (see 22). For whether you have excess income, see 21.

8 Council tax

1. What is council tax?

Council tax is a domestic property-based tax paid to the local authority to help pay for the services it provides. It applies only in England, Wales and Scotland. In Northern Ireland, domestic rates are payable (see Chapter 7(28)).

Rules and regulations – The council tax framework is contained in the Local Government Finance Act 1992. Regulations have been subject to numerous amendments. You can get details of the current provisions from your local authority or an advice agency.

2. Your dwelling

Council tax is only charged on domestic properties or 'dwellings'. A 'dwelling' is a self-contained unit of living accommodation, such as a house, flat, bungalow, houseboat or mobile home. It does not matter whether the dwelling is owned or rented. One council tax bill is due on each dwelling, unless it is exempt (see 4).

Points to note – If a property is divided into self-contained units (eg flats), each unit is a separate dwelling and gets a separate bill (unless it is exempt). If a property contains non-self-contained units (eg a house with a number of rooms with different people in each, but they all share some accommodation) the property is one dwelling and gets one bill (unless it is exempt). A self-contained unit is defined as *'a building or part of a building which has been constructed or adapted for use as separate living accommodation'*. If a property contains both living and business accommodation, one amount of council tax is due for the domestic part (unless it is exempt) and the business part is subject to non-domestic rates.

3. How much council tax?

Council tax bands

Every property in each local authority area is placed into one of 8 valuation bands labelled from A (the lowest) to H (the highest), depending on its value. The higher the band, the more council tax you are liable to pay.

Values – The value of a dwelling does not relate to its current market value. It is based on April 1991 property values, and on several other assumptions such as that it is in a reasonable state of repair. In England and Wales dwellings are valued by the Valuation Office, and in Scotland by the local assessor. (The Valuation Office or local assessor also decides what counts as a dwelling and how many dwellings there are in a property.)

Note: The Government intends to start reviewing English property values in 2005, with council tax bills based on updated values being issued in 2007. It also intends that local authorities will have regulatory powers to create additional valuation bands. In Wales, revaluation has already taken place and new bandings will apply from 1.4.05.

Challenges and appeals

You have the right to propose a change to the valuation of your dwelling if within 6 months you have become newly liable for council tax there (eg through moving) or if there has been a material reduction in its value (eg through partial demolition or its adaptation for use by a disabled person). You can also ask for a change if part of the property begins to be used for business purposes. If the proposal is not agreed by the Valuation Office or local assessor it is referred to the Valuation Tribunal (England and Wales) or Valuation Appeal Committee (Scotland).

You can also appeal within 6 months of a successful challenge on a comparable dwelling (eg another property on the same street or on a new estate) if this suggests that the value of your own property should be changed.

In other circumstances, you can ask the Valuation Office or local assessor to reconsider the band for your dwelling and, if it is clearly wrong, they may alter it. But if they do not agree, you do not have the right of appeal.

C.5 Summary of council tax exemptions for dwellings

Note: Since April 2004 authorities have been required to take reasonable steps to check whether any discounts apply before deciding on the chargeable amount.

❑ **A substantially unfurnished, unoccupied dwelling is exempt if:**

- structural or major repair works are needed, are in hand, or have been recently completed (for up to 12 months in total); *or*
- it is unoccupied for any other reason (which could be that it has just been built), and has been for less than 6 months.

❑ **An unoccupied dwelling (whether furnished or not) can be exempt if it is:**

- left empty by persons in prison or a similar institution;
- left empty by persons now resident in a hospital, a care home or a hostel where personal care is provided;
- left empty by persons now resident elsewhere for the purpose of receiving or providing personal care due to old age, disablement, illness, past or present alcohol or drug dependence, or past or present mental disorder;
- left empty by deceased persons where probate or letters of administration have not been granted, or less than 6 months have passed since the granting of probate or letters of administration;
- the responsibility of a bankrupt's trustees;
- to be occupied by ministers of religion; *or*
- a pitch or mooring that is not occupied by a caravan or boat.

❑ **A dwelling is also exempt if it is:**

- wholly occupied by a person (or persons) who is *'severely mentally impaired'* (see Box C.6) and no one else could be liable. (Note: You do not lose the exemption if a student or students also occupy or own the dwelling);
- wholly occupied by people under the age of 18;
- unoccupied, and is part of a property containing another dwelling where someone resides, and letting it separately would be difficult;
- in Scotland and is a housing association trial flat for pensioners or for people with disabilities;
- unoccupied and occupation is prohibited by law (eg it is unfit for habitation or subject to a compulsory purchase order);
- under charitable ownership and has been unoccupied for less than 6 months;
- an armed forces barracks or married quarters or used as visiting forces accommodation;
- a repossessed property;
- a student hall of residence; *or*
- currently wholly occupied by students (including students temporarily absent from their course) or is now unoccupied and was last occupied by students.

❑ **In England and Wales only**

There is a further exemption where there are at least two dwellings (ie two self-contained units) within a single property and one occupant is a *'dependent relative'* of someone who is resident in another part of the property. The exemption applies only to the part of the property where the dependent relative is resident. The definition of 'relative' is quite straightforward and includes quite distant relatives (eg great-great-grandchild) and common-law relations. If there is a dispute about your status as a relative you should seek advice.

The dependent relative must be:

- aged 65 or over; *or*
- *'severely mentally impaired'* (see Box C.6); *or*
- *'substantially and permanently disabled'*, the definition of which is open to wide interpretation.

4. Exempt dwellings

If your home is an exempt dwelling, no council tax is due on it. Most exemptions are for unoccupied dwellings. The main conditions for exemptions are given in Box C.5.

Getting an exemption, and backdating – If the local authority has not awarded an exemption you can ask for one. Your local authority may have a standard form you can fill in. An exemption can be backdated to the date it should have first applied. There is no time limit and no need to show 'good cause' for applying late.

Appeals – Appeals about whether a dwelling is exempt go first to your local authority. There is no time limit for lodging the appeal. If this is refused you can make a further appeal, to the Valuation Tribunal (England and Wales) or Valuation Appeal Committee (Scotland). Time limits apply to the second appeal.

5. Who is liable to pay?

Unless a dwelling is exempt, someone will be liable to pay council tax on it. This usually depends on who is *'resident'* there (see 6). The rules for the dwelling in which you are resident are given below. If you own or rent a dwelling that has no residents, you are usually liable for council tax there (whether or not you are also liable on the dwelling in which you are resident).

Backdating

If you were liable for council tax in the past, but were not billed, a bill can be backdated. There is no time limit, although the local authority will be unable to obtain a liability order through the courts after 6 years have expired.

Appeals

Appeals about who is liable for council tax go first to your local authority. There is no time limit for lodging the appeal. If this is refused you can make a further appeal to the Valuation Tribunal (England and Wales) or Valuation Appeal Committee (Scotland). Time limits apply to the second appeal.

General rules for the dwelling in which you reside

The following rules apply to the dwelling in which you are 'resident' (see 6).

If you own it – You are liable for council tax. Your partner, if resident with you, is jointly liable with you (even if not a joint owner). Any other joint owners resident with you are also jointly liable.

If you rent it and do not have a resident landlord – You are liable for council tax. Your partner, if resident with you, is jointly liable with you (even if not included on the letting agreement). Any other residents who rent it on the same letting agreement are also jointly liable.

If you rent from a resident landlord – Your landlord is liable.

If you rent non-self-contained accommodation and/or any others who rent it have separate letting agreements – Your landlord is liable, even if they are not resident there.

If it is a care home or (in most cases) a hostel – The landlord is liable.

If you are an asylum seeker receiving asylum support (other than temporary support) from either the National Asylum Support Service or your local authority – The landlord is liable.

Special cases

If you are 'severely mentally impaired' (see Box C.6) – If you and any other occupiers are *'severely mentally impaired'* or are students, then the dwelling in which you are resident is exempt (see Box C.5). If anyone else lives with you, including carers, the property will no longer be exempt. However, you may still be eligible for a discount (see 9).

If you are under 18 – You are not liable for council tax on any dwelling in which you are resident. The other resident(s) aged 18 or over are liable instead. If there are none, the dwelling is exempt (see Box C.5).

6. Who is a resident of a dwelling?

You are a *'resident'* of a dwelling if it is your *'sole or main residence'*. You can only be a resident of one dwelling at a time. Deciding where you are resident is usually straightforward. In difficult cases, your local authority should take into account how much time you spend at different addresses, where you work, where your children go to school, how much security of tenure you have at different addresses, and other relevant information.

Appeals

Appeals about where you are resident go first to your local authority. There is no time limit for lodging the appeal. If it is refused you can make a further appeal to the Valuation Tribunal (England and Wales) or Valuation Appeal Committee (Scotland). Time limits apply to the second appeal.

7. How to pay less council tax

There are three different schemes for reducing council tax bills. You can get help through all three schemes at the same time if you satisfy the relevant conditions for all of them. The three schemes are:

- the disability reduction scheme (see 8);
- the discount scheme (see 9);
- the council tax benefit scheme (see Chapter 7).

Some dwellings are exempt from council tax (see 4).

8. The disability reduction scheme

You can get a disability reduction if you or any other *'resident'* (see 6) in your dwelling is *'substantially and permanently disabled'*. This can be an adult or a child of any age, whether or not they are related to you. At least one of the next three conditions must also be met:

- you have an additional bathroom or kitchen needed by the disabled person; *or*
- you have a room (other than a bathroom, kitchen or toilet) needed by and predominantly used by that person; *or*
- you have enough space in your dwelling for that person to use a wheelchair indoors.

Disability reductions are available in all types of dwellings, including care homes and hostels.

In Scotland, the council water charge can also be reduced under this scheme.

Comments – There is no general test of who counts as *'substantially and permanently disabled'*, although it is clear that it includes people who have been disabled for life and also those who have become disabled later in life. There is also no general test of what it means for the disabled person to 'need' the room or the wheelchair, except that they must be *'essential or of major importance to [his or her] well-being by reason of the nature and extent of [his or her] disability'*.

However, it is clear that disability reductions are not limited to dwellings specially constructed or adapted to provide a room or wheelchair space.

Guidance given to local authorities suggests they should consider how difficult life would be for the disabled person without the facilities being available.

How much is it worth?

If you qualify for a disability reduction, your council tax bill is reduced to the amount payable for a dwelling in the valuation band below yours. So if your home is in band F, the bill will be reduced to the amount for band E. Since 1.4.00, if your dwelling is in band A, you get a reduction of one-sixth of your bill.

Getting a reduction, and backdating

The person liable for council tax (not necessarily the disabled person), has to make an application. Your local authority may have a standard form for this (and in some areas you may have to make a separate application for each financial year). If you should have been given a disability reduction in the past, but were not, it should be backdated. There is no time limit at present.

Appeals

Appeals about disability reductions go first to your local authority. There is no time limit for lodging the appeal. If it is refused you can make a further appeal, to the Valuation Tribunal (England and Wales) or Valuation Appeal Committee (Scotland). Time limits apply to the second appeal.

9. The discount scheme

The council tax discount scheme is for dwellings where less than two adults are 'resident' (see 6). You can get a discount if:

- there is only one resident in your dwelling: in this case your discount equals 25% of your council tax liability; *or*
- there are no residents in your dwelling: in this case your discount equals 50% of your council tax liability (except in certain cases in Wales, where local authorities can set the discount at 50%, 25% or nil). If your home is empty, you may be able to qualify for exemption instead of a discount (see 4) – but see point 10 below.

C.6 People who are disregarded for council tax discount purposes

People who are 'severely mentally impaired'

This means anyone who:

- *'has a severe impairment of intelligence and social functioning (however caused) which appears to be permanent'; and*
- has a certificate from a registered medical practitioner confirming this (which may cover a past, present or future period); *and*
- is entitled to one of the following benefits:
  - disability living allowance (DLA) middle or highest rate care component;
  - attendance allowance (AA), constant attendance allowance (or an equivalent benefit);
  - incapacity benefit (any rate);
  - severe disablement allowance (SDA);
  - income support including a disability premium due to incapacity, or whose partner has a disability premium for them included in their income-based jobseeker's allowance; *or*
  - is over state pension age and would have been entitled to one of the above benefits if under state pension age.

Carers

There are three different types of carer who are disregarded.

First type of carer – All the following conditions must be met.

- ❑ The carer provides care for at least 35 hours a week on average. (The law refers to *'care'*, not *'support'*.)
- ❑ The carer is 'resident' (see 6) in the same dwelling as the person cared for.
- ❑ The carer is not the partner of the person cared for (ie neither married nor living together as husband and wife).
- ❑ The carer is not the parent of the person cared for, if the person cared for is aged under 18.
- ❑ The person cared for is entitled to one of the following: the highest rate of the care component of DLA, the higher rate of AA, or constant attendance allowance.

Second type of carer – All the following conditions must be met.

- ❑ The carer provides *'care or support'* or a combination of both for at least 24 hours a week.
- ❑ The carer is employed by the person cared for.
- ❑ The carer is paid no more than £36 a week for the work.
- ❑ The carer is 'resident' (see 6), for the better performance of the work, in accommodation (not necessarily the same dwelling) provided by the person cared for.
- ❑ The carer was introduced to the person cared for by a local authority, government department or charity.

Third type of carer – All the following conditions must be met.

- ❑ The carer provides *'care or support'* or a combination of both for at least 24 hours a week.
- ❑ The carer is paid no more than £36 a week for the work.
- ❑ The carer provides the care or support on behalf of a local authority, government department or charity.
- ❑ The carer is 'resident' (see 6), for the better performance of the work, in accommodation (not necessarily the same dwelling) provided by or on behalf of the body just mentioned.

People in a hospital, a care home, or certain kinds of hostel

In the case of hospital, the person must be 'resident' there (see 6), so short stays are rarely sufficient. In the case of a care home, it is sufficient that the person is receiving care or treatment there. In the case of a hostel, the person must be receiving care or treatment, and it must be a hostel where the owner (not the residents) is liable for council tax or a bail or probation hostel.

Anyone whose 'sole or main residence' is elsewhere

For where someone is 'resident', see 6.

Young people, students, student nurses, youth trainees, apprentices, and others

The following individuals or groups are ignored:

- everyone under the age of 18;
- 18-year-olds for whom child benefit is payable (see Chapter 36);
- education-leavers under 20 (but only if they left on or after 1st May, and then only until 31 October inclusive that year);
- school or college-level students aged under 20, if their term-time study normally amounts to 12 or more hours a week;
- students at university or an equivalent level of study, if their study amounts to 21 hours or more a week for 24 or more weeks a year;
- student nurses whose academic course means they count as a 'student', or who are studying for their first nursing registration;
- foreign language assistants;
- trainees under the age of 25 on Work-Based Learning for Young People;
- apprentices undertaking training that leads to an accredited qualification (eg an NVQ), subject to limitations on pay;
- people in prison or similar institutions;
- members of a religious community where the community provides for all the individuals needs;
- members of some international organisations or visiting forces;
- foreign spouses and dependants of students;
- diplomats and their spouses.

A B C D E F G H I J K L M N O P Q R S

Counting the residents
Several groups of people are disregarded when counting up the number of residents in your dwelling; they are sometimes called 'invisible'. The groups are outlined in Box C.6. This is important because it can mean that you qualify for a discount even if there are several people in your dwelling – as long as enough of them are 'disregarded'.

Example: If you are in a couple and have two children aged 17 and 20 at home, you might not expect to get a discount. But if your partner was severely mentally impaired or a carer (as defined in Box C.6), and the 20-year-old was a student, they would both be 'disregarded'. So would the 17-year-old (because of being under 18). That would leave you as the only resident who would be counted. Your council tax bill would be reduced by 25%.

Getting a discount, and backdating
Your local authority may automatically grant a discount but you can also apply for one. Your local authority may have a standard form for this. A discount can be backdated to the date it should have first applied. There is no time limit within which you can apply for the discount.

Appeals
Appeals about discounts go first to your local authority. There is no time limit for lodging the appeal. If this is refused you can make a further appeal, to the Valuation Tribunal (England and Wales) or Valuation Appeal Committee (Scotland). Time limits apply to the second appeal.

10. Second homes and long-term empty properties

From April 2004, local authorities have the power to reduce the discount offered on second homes from 50% to just 10%. They will also have the power to reduce or remove completely the discount offered on long-term empty properties. Local authorities will be able to keep any additional money raised in this way to directly fund local services.

11. Additional help for those aged 65 or over

Two different payments will be available to older people over the winter period of 2005/06 to help towards council tax bills. The first payment is £50, payable if you are aged 70 or over and in receipt of the guarantee credit of pension credit. It is designed to help with additional living expenses, including council tax. The second, announced in the March 2005 Budget, is a payment of £200, payable if you are aged 65 or over and *not* in receipt of the guarantee credit of pension credit. This payment is designed specifically to help with council tax. It will be administered by the DWP and will be made at the same time as the winter fuel payment (see Chapter 9(5)).

Social fund D

9 Regulated social fund

1. What is the regulated social fund?

The regulated social fund is a government fund which makes payments to people in need to cover specific costs. It provides Sure Start maternity grants and funeral, cold weather and winter fuel payments. You are legally entitled to a payment if you satisfy the regulations.

2. Sure Start maternity grants

You are entitled to a Sure Start maternity grant of £500 for each child if:

- you (or a member of your family) are pregnant, or have given birth in the last 3 months (including stillbirth after 24 weeks of pregnancy), or have an adopted child under the age of one, or have been granted a parental order for a child born to a surrogate mother; *and*
- you have been awarded one of the following qualifying benefits in respect of the day you claim a maternity grant: income support, pension credit, income-based jobseeker's allowance, child tax credit paid at a rate which exceeds the family element (see Chapter 19(2)) or working tax credit which includes the disability or severe disability element (see Chapter 18(7 and 8)); *and*
- you have received health and welfare advice about maternal and child health matters (see below); *and*
- you claim within the time limits (see below).

How and when to claim

Claim on form SF100, available from your local Jobcentre Plus office or antenatal clinic.

You must claim in the 11 weeks before your expected week of confinement, or in the 3 months following the date of the birth, adoption or parental order. If you are waiting for a decision about a qualifying benefit, claim within the time limits and if your claim is refused because you are not getting a qualifying benefit, re-claim within 3 months of being awarded the qualifying benefit.

The form must be signed by a health professional to confirm you have received health and welfare advice about maternal and child health matters.

3. Funeral payments

You are entitled to a funeral payment if:

- you or your partner accept responsibility for the costs of a funeral (ie you have paid or are liable to pay them) that takes place in the UK (or another European Economic Area country (see Chapter 49(1)) or Switzerland, if you or a member of your family are classified as a 'worker' or have the right to reside in the UK under European Community law – see Chapter 49(2)); *and*
- you or your partner have been awarded one of the following qualifying benefits in respect of the day you claim a funeral payment: income support, pension credit, income-based jobseeker's allowance, child tax credit paid at a rate that exceeds the family element (see Chapter 19(2)), working tax credit that includes the disability or severe disability element (see Chapter 18(7 and 8)), housing benefit or council tax benefit; *and*
- the deceased was ordinarily resident in the UK when they died; *and*
- you claim within the time limits (see below); *and*
- you fall into one of the groups of people who are eligible to claim (see below).

Who can claim?

You can only get a funeral payment if you fall into one of the following groups:

- ❑ You were the partner (married or unmarried, of the opposite sex) of the deceased when they died, or before either of you entered a care home.
- ❑ The deceased was a child for whom you were responsible and there is no 'absent parent' (unless they were getting one of the above qualifying benefits when the child died), or the deceased was a stillborn child.
- ❑ You were a 'close relative' or close friend of the deceased and it is reasonable for you to accept responsibility for the funeral costs, given the nature and extent of your contact with the deceased. Close relative means parent (or parent-in-law), son (-in-law), daughter (-in-law), brother (-in-law), sister (-in-law), stepson/daughter (-in-law) or step-parent.

You cannot get a payment as a close relative or friend of the deceased if:

- the deceased had a partner when they died; *or*
- there is a parent, son or daughter of the deceased who is not:
  - getting a qualifying benefit (see above); *or*
  - in prison or hospital immediately following a period on a qualifying benefit; *or*
  - under 18; *or*
  - aged 18 or over and in full-time education; *or*
  - a fully maintained member of a religious order; *or*
  - someone who was estranged from the deceased; *or*
  - receiving asylum support from the National Asylum Support Services (see Chapter 49(4)); *or*
  - ordinarily resident outside the UK; *or*
- there is a close relative (see above) of the deceased, other than a person under 18 or ordinarily resident outside the UK, who was in closer contact with the deceased than you were, or had equally close contact and is not getting a qualifying benefit.

How much do you get?

The following costs can be met:

- the necessary costs of purchasing a new burial plot with exclusive rights plus necessary burial fees, or the necessary costs of cremation including medical fees;
- the cost of documentation required to release the deceased's assets;
- the reasonable costs of transport for the portion of journeys in excess of 50 miles, undertaken to transport the body within the UK to a funeral director's premises or a place of rest and to transport the coffin, bearers and mourners in two vehicles to the funeral;
- the necessary costs of one return journey from your home for you or your partner to arrange or attend the funeral if

you are responsible for the funeral costs;
- up to £700 for other funeral expenses (or £120 if you have a pre-paid funeral plan which does not cover these expenses).

The following amounts are deducted from an award of a funeral payment (note that a funeral payment is recoverable from the deceased's estate):
- any of the deceased's assets that are available to you without probate or letters of administration;
- any lump sum due to you on the death of the deceased from an insurance policy, occupational pension, war pension, burial club or similar scheme;
- any contribution towards the funeral costs from a charity or relative of yours or the deceased's;
- any amount from a pre-paid funeral plan or similar scheme.

Note that any payments from the Macfarlane, variant CJD, or Eileen Trusts, or the Fund or Skipton Fund are ignored.

How and when to claim

You must claim within 3 months of the date of the funeral (on form SF200, available from the DWP). If you are waiting for a decision on a qualifying benefit, claim within the time limit and if your claim is refused because you are not getting a qualifying benefit, re-claim within 3 months of being awarded the qualifying benefit.

4. Cold weather payments

These are automatic payments (you do not need to make a claim) made by the DWP of £8.50 for each qualifying week if:
- the average temperature recorded or forecast over 7 consecutive days by the designated weather station for your area is zero degrees Celsius (freezing) or less; *and*
- you have been awarded income support (IS) or income-based jobseeker's allowance (JSA) for at least one of those days and you are responsible for a child under the age of 5, or you are getting child tax credit which includes a disability or severe disability element, or your IS or JSA includes one of the disability or pensioner premiums; *or*
- you have been awarded pension credit for at least one of those days; *and*
- you are not resident in a care home.

5. Winter fuel payments

This is a lump-sum payment (for the winter of 2005/06) if you are aged 60 or over in the week beginning 19.9.05 (the 'qualifying week').

You are not entitled to a payment if during that week you:
- are subject to immigration control or not ordinarily resident in Great Britain (see Chapter 49(3)); *or*
- have been receiving free inpatient treatment in hospital (or similar institution) for more than 52 weeks; *or*
- are in custody serving a sentence imposed by a court; *or*
- are getting income-based jobseeker's allowance (JSA) or pension credit (PC) and you live in a care home and have been in the home for the 12 preceding weeks (disregarding temporary absences).

How much do you get?

Subject to the rules below, the winter fuel payment is £200 if you are aged 60-69 in the qualifying week, £250 if you are aged 70-79 or £300 if you are aged 80 or over.

If you share accommodation as a mutual home with another person who is also entitled to a payment, only one payment is made per household (£200 if you are both aged 60-69, £250 if one of you is aged 70-79 or £300 if one of you is aged 80 or over). If you have been living in a care home for at least 12 weeks preceding the qualifying week and are not getting income-based JSA or PC, you are entitled to £100 if you are aged 60-69, £125 if you are aged 70-79 or £150 if you are aged 80 or over.

Note: Additional payments for those aged 65 and over to help towards the council tax may be payable with the winter fuel payment for 2005/06. See Chapter 8(11) for details.

How do you claim?

You should automatically receive a payment without making a claim if you received a payment last year, or are getting a state pension or other social security benefit (apart from child benefit, housing benefit, or council tax benefit) in the qualifying week. Otherwise you must make a claim before 31.3.06. You can get a claim-form and other information by ringing the winter fuel payment helpline: 08459 15 1515.

6. Appeals

If you disagree with a decision relating to the regulated social fund, you can appeal to a tribunal (see Chapter 58).

10 Discretionary social fund

1. What is the discretionary social fund?

The discretionary social fund provides grants and interest-free loans for a variety of needs that are difficult to meet from weekly benefits. There are three types of payments.
- **Community care grants** are intended to promote community care by assisting people on income support (IS), income-based jobseeker's allowance (JSA) or pension credit (PC) to live independently in the community.
- **Budgeting loans** are interest-free loans to help people who have been on IS, income-based JSA or PC for at least 26 weeks to meet intermittent expenses for specified items for which it may be difficult to budget, enabling the cost to be spread over time.
- **Crisis loans** are interest-free loans for people (whether on benefit or not) who are unable to meet their immediate short-term needs in a crisis.

There are eligibility rules for each type of payment (see 4, 5 and 6 below). Unlike the regulated social fund, however, (see Chapter 9) there is no legal entitlement to a payment if the rules are satisfied. Payments are discretionary; each DWP district has an annual budget for grants and another for loans which must not be overspent and must be managed on a monthly basis so that funds are available throughout the financial year. Decisions are subject to review rather than appeal (see 7 below).

2. Applying for a payment

You should apply for a community care grant on form SF300, a budgeting loan on form SF500 and a crisis loan on form SF401, all available from your local Jobcentre Plus office and the DWP website: www.dwp.gov.uk. You can also apply for a crisis loan by ringing or calling at any local Jobcentre Plus office (you will only have to complete a form if you are offered a loan). An appointee, or someone with your written authority, can apply for a payment on your behalf. For further details of how to apply for a payment, see 4, 5 and 6 below.

You should always apply for a community care grant rather than a budgeting or crisis loan if you think you may be eligible. There is nothing to stop you from applying for a grant and a loan for the same item, and an application for a crisis loan can be treated as an application for a community care grant (and vice versa). You cannot, however, get a community care grant or crisis loan for an item if you have already received or been refused a grant or crisis loan for that item on an application made within the previous 26 weeks, unless there has been a relevant change of circumstances. Certain items are also excluded from grants or crisis loans (see Box D.1). There are no restrictions on re-applying for budgeting loans, but you can only apply for specified items (see 5 below).

3. How decisions are made

Decisions are made by decision makers based in Jobcentre Plus offices. Although payments are discretionary, decision makers are required to take the following matters into account:

- for community care grants and crisis loans, all the circumstances of each case and, in particular, the nature, extent and urgency of the need;
- for budgeting loans, specified personal circumstances only;
- whether the need can be met by other resources (excluding the disability living allowance mobility component) or by another person or body;
- the likelihood and timescale of repayment of a budgeting loan or crisis loan;
- the amount in the district budget (see 1 above);
- legally binding social fund 'directions', which set out the eligibility conditions for each type of payment, the criteria for managing the district budget (see below) and the procedure for reviews;
- national guidance on how to prioritise applications, exercise discretion and interpret the social fund directions, set out in the *Social Fund Guide* (see Box R.9 in Chapter 58) (the guidance is *not* legally binding, however, and although it gives examples of when payments may be appropriate, it stresses that the absence of guidance relating to a particular situation or item does not mean that a payment cannot be considered);
- local guidance issued to decision makers in each DWP district, which gives information on a monthly basis about the district budget and the priority of applications it can afford to meet. You can request a copy from your local Jobcentre Plus office.

Decisions should be made without delay and notified to you in writing with confirmation of your right to request a review. If there are unreasonable delays, you should complain to the social fund district manager and if necessary ask your MP to intervene.

Payments should normally be made to you, but the DWP can decide to pay a supplier directly.

4. Community care grants

To be eligible for a community care grant you must satisfy all the following conditions.

- You must be in receipt of (ie be the claimant of) income support (IS), pension credit (PC), or income-based jobseeker's allowance (JSA) when you apply for a grant (or be leaving institutional or residential care within 6 weeks and likely to get IS, PC, or income-based JSA when you leave). You satisfy this condition if you receive a backdated award of IS, PC or income-based JSA which covers the date of your grant application. For joint-claim couples (see Chapter 17(2)), only the partner who is paid JSA is eligible for a grant.
- The item you apply for is not excluded (see Box D.1).
- You or your partner must not be involved in a trade dispute, unless the claim is for travel expenses to visit a sick person.
- You must not have too much capital. Any award you get is reduced by any capital or savings that you or your partner have above £500 (or £1,000 if you or your partner are aged 60 or over). Capital is worked out in the same way as for IS, PC or income-based JSA, depending on which benefit you are getting, except that Family Fund payments are disregarded.
- You must need the grant for one or more of the purposes listed below, which are set out in social fund direction 4.

Leaving institutional or residential care

A grant can be given to help you, a member of your family or another person (for whom you or a member of your family will be providing care) to *'establish yourself or themselves in the community following a stay in institutional or residential accommodation in which you or they received care'* (social fund direction 4(a)(i)).

The *Social Fund Guide* advises that 'institutional or residential' care means places like hospitals, care homes, hostels, supported lodgings, prisons, youth centres and foster care, where there is significant and substantial care, protection or supervision provided to residents because they cannot live independently or might be a danger to others. If your accommodation would not usually be classed as institutional or residential care you may qualify on the grounds that a grant will help you to stay in the community (see below).

The *Social Fund Guide* says that a 'stay' in care normally means at least 3 months or a pattern of frequent or regular admission, but the High Court has ruled that *'Undue importance should not be attached to the reference to a 3-month period in... the guidance' (R v Secretary of State, ex parte Stitt, Sherwin and Roberts, 21.2.90).*

To qualify, you must be moving into the community, so you cannot get a grant under this provision if you are transferring from one care institution to another.

You should apply for what you need to set up home and live independently – eg furniture, household equipment, connection charges, bedding, clothing, removal expenses, storage charges or items needed because of a disability (as long as it is not an excluded item – see Box D.1).

Staying out of institutional or residential care

A grant can be given to help you, a member of your family, or someone you or a member of your family are caring for *'to remain in the community rather than enter institutional or residential accommodation in which you or they will receive care'* (direction 4(a)(ii)).

The grant does not have to prevent you going into care, and the risk of care does not have to be immediate, but you should show how a grant would improve your independence in the community and therefore reduce or delay the risk of admission into care. See above for what counts as institutional or residential care. The *Social Fund Guide* suggests that a higher priority should be given to applications where the threat of care is immediate or imminent or there is a direct link between the threat of care and the need in question.

If you have a history of admission into care, it should be easier to argue that the risk is significant. If you are elderly or have a disability and your medical condition or home circumstances are deteriorating, a grant should be considered.

The *Social Fund Guide* says a grant may be appropriate to help you improve your living conditions, or move to more suitable accommodation or nearer to people who will be supporting you (or whom you will be supporting). These are only examples, however, and you can ask for whatever you need to help you to remain independent (as long as it is not an excluded item – see Box D.1).

For example, to improve living conditions you may get a grant for redecoration, refurbishment, bedding (particularly for those who are housebound and need extra warmth or who are incontinent), reconnection charges, heaters, a washing machine (particularly for those who are bedridden or incontinent or can't do laundry by hand because of a disability), minor repairs and improvements. You could also get a grant for disability-related items such as a stairlift, a wheelchair, an orthopaedic mattress or an upright armchair. If you are moving home, you may get a grant for removal expenses, fares, furniture and household equipment, connection charges and installation charges.

Families under exceptional pressure
A grant can be given *'to ease exceptional pressures'* on you and your family (direction 4(a)(iii)). There is no legal definition of 'exceptional pressures'. You should always fully explain in your application all the pressures your family is experiencing and their cumulative effect. These could include problems relating to your physical or mental health, any disabilities you have, your accommodation, your finances or your children (eg behavioural problems or difficulties at school).

The *Social Fund Guide* advises that the term 'family' generally means couples with or without children, people caring for children, or women over 24 weeks pregnant. There is no legal definition, however, and you could argue you are a family if, for example, you live with a parent, adult child, a sister or brother, or a lesbian or gay partner. Decision makers are advised to be flexible in their interpretation, and to give higher priority to cases involving domestic violence.

The *Social Fund Guide* gives examples of circumstances in which a grant may be appropriate, including where there are high washing costs or excessive wear and tear on clothing because of a disabled child, or where minor structural repairs are needed to keep a home habitable, or for the safety of a child. These are only examples, however, and you can ask for any item that will ease the pressures on your family (as long as it is not an excluded item – see Box D.1).

Other purposes for which a grant can be awarded
A grant can be given to:

- allow you or your partner to care for a prisoner or young offender on temporary release (direction 4(a)(iv));
- help you set up home in the community as part of a planned programme of resettlement following a period of an unsettled way of life (direction 4(a)(v));
- help you or your family with travel expenses within the UK (including overnight accommodation) to visit a sick person, attend a relative's funeral, ease a domestic crisis, move to suitable accommodation, or visit a child who is with the other parent pending a court decision (direction 4(b)).

Decision making and priorities
A decision maker should firstly decide whether you are eligible for a grant under direction 4 and if so, the priority of your application. The local guidance (see 3) must specify whether the district budget can afford to meet high-, medium- or low-priority applications (usually only high).

The *Social Fund Guide* states that an application should normally be given high priority if a grant will have a substantial effect in the immediately foreseeable future in resolving or improving the circumstances of the applicant and meeting one of the purposes for which a grant can be awarded. Medium priority should normally be given if a grant will have a noticeable (but not substantial or immediate) effect in achieving the above aims, and low priority should normally be given if a grant will only have a minor effect in meeting the above aims.

The *Social Fund Guide* also gives examples of situations which would affect priority, including where a person has:

- restricted mobility or a physical disability;
- mental health problems or learning difficulties;
- chronic physical or mental illness;
- behavioural problems often associated with drug or alcohol abuse;
- unstable family circumstances or experience of abuse.

How much do you get?
The *Social Fund Guide* says the amount you ask for should normally be allowed if it is within the range of prices charged for the item in question by high street chain retailers and national catalogue outlets. There is no maximum amount that can be awarded but the minimum is £30, apart from travelling and daily living expenses, where there is no minimum.

Applying for a community care grant
Apply on form SF300, giving full details of your needs and circumstances. You must establish that you need a grant for one of the purposes set out in direction 4 (see above) and why your application should be given high priority, bearing in mind the guidance on priorities referred to above.

When listing the items you need, be as specific as possible. If, for example, you need bedding, specify what you need (eg two single sheets, one single duvet cover, two pillows, etc), giving the cost of each item. If you need carpets, state which

D.1 Which items are excluded?

You cannot get a community care grant or crisis loan for the following items (the exclusions do not apply to budgeting loans):

- maternity or funeral expenses;
- needs occurring outside the UK;
- educational or training needs, including clothing and tools;
- distinctive school uniform or equipment, or sports clothes for school use;
- travelling expenses to or from school;
- school meals taken during school holidays by children who are entitled to free school meals;
- expenses in connection with court (legal) proceedings (including a community service order) such as legal fees, court fees, fines, costs, damages, subsistence or travelling expenses (other than a crisis loan for emergency travelling expenses where an applicant is stranded away from home);
- removal or storage charges where an applicant is rehoused following the imposition of a compulsory purchase order or a redevelopment or closing order or a compulsory exchange of tenancies, or pursuant to a housing authority's statutory duty to the homeless under Part VII of the Housing Act 1996 or Part II of the Housing (Scotland) Act 1987;
- domestic assistance and respite care;
- any repair to property of any body mentioned in section 80(1) of the Housing Act 1985 or section 61(2)(a) of the Housing (Scotland) Act 1987 and, in the case of Scotland, any repair to property of any housing trust in existence on 13.11.53;
- work-related expenses;
- debts to government departments;
- investments;
- council tax, council water charges, arrears of community charge, collective community charge contributions or community water charges;
- costs of purchasing, renting or installing a telephone or call charges;
- medical, surgical, optical, aural or dental items or services (see below).

Medical items – Medical items are not defined, but an item of ordinary everyday use cannot be regarded as a medical item (*R v SFI ex parte Connick*, 8.6.93). This includes items such as cotton sheets, non-allergic bedding or curtains, built-up shoes, incontinence pads, beds with adaptations or lactose-free foods. If an item is not one of ordinary everyday use, it should only be treated as a medical item if its sole purpose is to cure, alleviate, treat, diagnose or prevent a medical condition, eg a nebuliser or insulin gun (*Social Fund Commissioner's Advice on Excluded* rooms they are for, the size of the rooms and the condition of any existing carpet. If you need curtains, specify the size, the rooms they are needed for, and whether the rooms are overlooked. For less common items, such as an orthopaedic bed and other disability-related items, it is best to back up your application with an estimate from a specialist supplier.

5. Budgeting loans

To be eligible for a budgeting loan you must satisfy all the following conditions.

- You must be in receipt of (ie be the claimant of) income support (IS), pension credit (PC) or income-based jobseeker's allowance (JSA) when your application for a budgeting loan is decided, and you and/or your partner must have been receiving IS, PC or income-based JSA throughout the 26 weeks before the decision (ignoring breaks of 28 days or less). The 3 waiting days at the start of a JSA claim do not count. For joint-claim couples (see Chapter 17(2)), only the partner who is paid JSA is eligible for a budgeting loan.
- You or your partner must not be involved in a trade dispute.
- You must not have too much capital. The rules are the same as for community care grants (see 4 above).
- Your application must be for one of the categories of expenses listed below.

What can you get a budgeting loan for?

You do not have to specify what item(s) you need the loan for, but it must fall into one of the following categories:

- furniture and household equipment;
- clothing and footwear;
- rent in advance and/or removal expenses to secure new accommodation;
- improvement, maintenance and security of the home;
- travelling expenses;
- expenses associated with seeking or re-entering work;
- HP and other debts for expenses associated with the above categories.

How is the amount of the loan calculated?

The maximum amount is determined by two factors:

- the 'weighting' of your application, which is dependent on specified 'personal circumstances' (see below); *and*
- the district budget, which determines the maximum amount of loan for each level of weighting.

The amount of loan you are offered may be less than the maximum (see below, 'How much do you get?').

Your personal circumstances – Your application is given a weighting, based on the following two 'initial criteria':

- the length of time you or your partner have been getting IS, PC or income-based JSA, subject to a minimum of 6 months and a maximum of 3 years (ignoring breaks of 28 days or less):
  - for 6 months, the minimum weighting of 1 applies;
  - for 3 years or more, the weighting is 1.5;
  - for any period between 6 months and 3 years, a pro rata weighting is given (eg if you have been on benefit for 21 months, halfway between the two, the weighting is 1.25);
- the size of your family for benefit purposes:
  - for you, the weighting is 1;
  - for a partner, add 1/3;
  - for a first child aged 18 or under, add 2/3;
  - for other children, add 1/3 for each child.

The total weighting for your application is made up of the weighting for the length of time on benefit multiplied by the weighting for the size of your family.

If, for example, you have been on IS for 3 years and have a partner and one child in your household, the weighting for your time on benefit is 1.5 and the weighting for your family size is 2 (1 for you, plus 1/3 for your partner, plus 2/3 for your child). The total weighting of your application is 1.5 multiplied by 2, which is 3.

The district budget – Local guidance (see 3) must specify the maximum amount payable for an application of the lowest weighting of 1 (single person on benefit for 6 months). To calculate the maximum amount you can get, you should multiply this figure by your total weighting. For example, if the amount specified in local guidance is £300 and your weighting is 3, then the maximum amount you can get is £900. The benchmark figure in local guidance may change from time to time, as the district budget is reassessed.

How much do you get? – The lowest award that can be made is £30 and the highest is £1,000. The actual amount you are offered may be less than the maximum for the following

Items, 18/6/01). Under this test, wheelchairs or stairlifts should not be treated as medical items. You will not get help, however, if they are available from the NHS or elsewhere.

Community care grants only

In addition, you cannot get a community care grant for:

- expenses which the local authority has a statutory duty to meet;
- costs of fuel consumption and any associated standing charges;
- housing costs – including repairs and improvements to the dwelling occupied as the home (including any garage, garden and outbuildings), deposits to secure accommodation, mortgage payments, water rates, sewerage rates, service charges, rent and all other charges for accommodation (whether or not such charges include payment for meals and/ or services) – other than:
  - minor repairs and improvements; *or*
  - charges for accommodation applied for under direction 4(b) (ie overnight accommodation included in a grant for travel expenses (see 4));
- daily living expenses such as food and groceries, except where:
  - such expenses are incurred in caring for a prisoner or young offender on release on temporary licence; *or*
  - a crisis loan cannot be awarded for such expenses because the maximum loan limit has been reached.

Crisis loans only

In addition, you cannot get a crisis loan for:

- mobility needs;
- holidays;
- a television or radio, or licence, aerial or rental charges for a television or radio;
- garaging, parking, purchase and running costs of any motor vehicle except where payment is being considered for emergency travelling expenses;
- housing costs (as for community care grants), other than:
  - payments for intermittent housing costs not met by housing benefit, income support, income-based jobseeker's allowance or pension credit, or for which direct payments cannot be implemented, such as the cost of emptying cesspits or septic tanks; *or*
  - rent in advance which is payable to secure fresh accommodation where the landlord is not a local authority; *or*
  - charges for board and lodging accommodation and residential charges for hostels (but not deposits, whether included in the total charge or not); *or*
  - minor repairs and improvements.

reasons.

- ❑ The repayment rules may prevent full payment (see below).
- ❑ The amount of the award is reduced if you have capital or savings over the limit (see above).
- ❑ If you or your partner have another budgeting loan outstanding, the maximum amount you can get is reduced by double the amount of your outstanding loan. If, for example, the maximum amount for your weighting is £900, but you have an existing budgeting loan outstanding of £250, the maximum you can borrow is reduced by £500 (2 x £250) to £400. This 'double debt' rule is due to be abolished in April 2006.

Wider criteria – If the above rules prevent you from being offered a loan of at least £30, the decision maker must apply the following wider criteria relating to your personal circumstances in addition to the initial criteria (see above) and reassess your weighting accordingly.

- ❑ The length of time you or your partner were in receipt of either housing benefit, council tax benefit, working families' tax credit, working tax credit (including a disability or severe disability element) or child tax credit (paid at a rate greater than the family element) immediately prior to being awarded IS, PC or income-based JSA (ignoring gaps of 28 days or less) is taken into account.
- ❑ If you or your partner are pregnant, the expected child (or children) counts as a member of your family.
- ❑ Anyone else who shares your home, such as an adult son or daughter, parent, friend or relative, who gets IS, PC or income-based JSA, and their partner and dependent children also count as members of your family.

Loans taken out while you were with an ex-partner can be disregarded if your application is a direct result of the separation. Note that if any loan of £30 or more can be made using the initial criteria alone, the decision maker will not apply the wider criteria even if that would result in a higher loan.

Repayment of budgeting loans

A decision maker can only award an amount you are likely to be able to repay. The loan will be scheduled for repayment within 78 weeks. If you have asked for a loan (within your maximum amount) that cannot be repaid within 78 weeks at standard repayment rates, the decision maker will give you up to three options, worked out using combinations of different repayment rates, amounts or number of weeks, and could include varying repayment rates on outstanding loans. Standard repayment rates are 5%, 10% or 15% of your IS or income-based JSA applicable amount or PC appropriate minimum guarantee (excluding, in each case, housing costs) depending on whether you have other financial commitments. The maximum repayment rate is 25%.

Decisions about repayment are not subject to review. If you have difficulty repaying the loan you can, however, ask for it to be rescheduled by writing to your local Jobcentre Plus office.

Loans are normally repaid by deductions from your or your partner's IS, PC or income-based JSA. If you don't get enough benefit, or your benefit stops, deductions can be made from most other social security benefits. Deductions cannot be made from disability living allowance, attendance allowance or child benefit.

Applying for a budgeting loan

You should apply on form SF500, making sure that you include all the information requested about your personal circumstances, including people living with you who are getting IS, PC or income-based JSA.

6. Crisis loans

To be eligible for a crisis loan you must satisfy all the following conditions.

- ❑ You must be aged 16 or over.
- ❑ The item you apply for must not be excluded (see Box D.1).
- ❑ The amount to be awarded must not be more than you can afford to repay.
- ❑ You must need the loan because of an emergency or disaster (where the loan would be the only means of preventing serious damage, or serious risk to the health or safety of yourself or a member of your family), or to pay rent in advance (see below 'When can you get a crisis loan?').
- ❑ You must be without sufficient resources to meet the immediate short-term needs of yourself and/or your family.

You do not have to be in receipt of a qualifying benefit to get a crisis loan but all your available resources are taken into account, including most types of savings, if it is reasonable to do so in the circumstances.

The *Social Fund Guide* gives examples of resources which normally should be ignored, including housing benefit, other social fund payments, business assets, personal possessions and payments from the Independent Living Fund, the Macfarlane and Variant CJD Trusts and the Skipton Fund. Disability living allowance mobility component must be ignored. Help from any other source can be taken into account if there is a realistic expectation that it would be available in time. Decision makers should not routinely refer applicants to charities, employers, relatives, close friends or social services, unless there is reason to believe that an offer of help will be forthcoming. Credit facilities should only be taken into account if you are not getting income support (IS), income-based JSA or pension credit (PC) and are likely to be able to afford the repayments.

Who cannot get a crisis loan?

You cannot get a crisis loan if you are:

- in a care home or hospital, unless you are going to be discharged within the following 2 weeks;
- a prisoner or in custody or released on temporary licence;
- a member of, and fully maintained by, a religious order;
- under 19 and in full-time non-advanced education and as a result not entitled to IS or income-based JSA.

When can you get a crisis loan?

A crisis loan may be paid to meet expenses *'in an emergency, or as a consequence of a disaster, provided that the provision of such assistance is the only means by which serious damage or serious risk to the health or safety of that person, or to a member of his family, may be prevented'* (social fund direction 3). If you are awarded a community care grant to enable you to return to the community after a stay in institutional or residential care, you may get a crisis loan to cover rent in advance (without having to show there is an emergency or disaster, or a risk to your health or safety).

The need for help will generally be for a specific item or service or for immediate living expenses for a short period not normally exceeding 14 days.

The *Social Fund Guide* does not define the terms 'emergency', 'disaster' or 'serious risk to health or safety'. The cause of the crisis is irrelevant and 'health' includes both physical and mental health. It is important to argue that your individual circumstances should be considered fully, as people may be affected differently by the same situation. Supporting evidence from a social worker, doctor or other professional may be helpful but you should not delay your application to get it. The guidance gives a number of examples where a crisis loan may be considered, including:

- loss of money;
- hardship due to payment of regular income in arrears;
- disaster (eg fire or flood) that has caused significant damage;
- emergency travel expenses (eg if you are stranded away from home);
- hardship due to compulsory unpaid holiday;
- fares to hospital for patients;
- fuel reconnection charges;
- homelessness.

Restrictions for certain groups

- If you are not entitled to IS, PC or income-based JSA because you are a full-time student or a 'person subject to immigration control', you can only get a crisis loan to alleviate the consequences of a disaster.
- If you or your partner are involved in a trade dispute, you can get a crisis loan only for items needed for cooking or heating, or to meet expenses arising from a disaster.
- If your JSA is sanctioned or disallowed and you are not getting hardship payments, you can only get a crisis loan for items needed for cooking or heating or to meet expenses arising from a disaster for the first 2 weeks of the sanction period, or for the whole sanction period in the case of a New Deal or work-focused interview sanction. Your partner can claim a crisis loan in the normal way but cannot get living expenses for you.

How much do you get?

The amount of any crisis loan awarded is the smallest amount needed to tide you over or remove the crisis. There is no minimum amount. The maximum amount that can be paid is £1,000 less any other social fund loan outstanding. You cannot be awarded more than you can afford to repay.

If you are applying for immediate living expenses (eg because of lost or stolen money) the maximum loan is:

- 75% of the IS personal allowance (single or couple rate); *plus*
- £43.88 for each dependent child.

Repayment of crisis loans

The rules are similar to budgeting loans (see 5 above), with most loans being recovered by weekly deductions from benefit over 78 weeks at the rate of 5%, 10% or 15% of your IS applicable amount or PC appropriate minimum guarantee (excluding, in each case, housing costs).

Applying for a crisis loan

You should apply for a crisis loan on form SF401, or by ringing or calling at the local Jobcentre Plus office where the need arises. You should always insist on making a formal application and being given a written decision (it is common for counter staff to put off potential applicants by telling them they will not be given a loan).

7. Reviews

Internal reviews

You can ask for a review of any decision made by a decision maker, including the refusal of a payment, or the amount awarded (you can accept the payment pending review of the amount). You must do this in writing within 28 days of the date the decision was issued to you. The time limit can be extended if there are 'special reasons'. There is no definition of, or guidance on, what counts as special reasons, so each case should be considered on its merits. A decision can also be reviewed at any time at the discretion of a decision maker.

Your application must explain why you disagree with the decision. The review is carried out by a reviewing officer in the Jobcentre Plus office that made the decision. If the decision is not revised in your favour, you will be asked if you want to attend an interview at the local office. You can take a representative with you to help present your case. Alternatively, the reviewing officer may conduct the review over the telephone, but this can only be done with your agreement, or where it is not practicable to interview you in person. You can ask to rearrange the date and time of a telephone interview so that you have time to prepare or get advice. The interview can be held at your home if you cannot attend the office.

For reviews concerning budgeting loans, the reviewing officer will only look at your circumstances at the time of the original decision (you can submit new evidence relating to the time of the decision). For other reviews, changes of circumstances since the decision can be taken into account, including changes in the level of the district budget.

There are no legal time limits for carrying out reviews but if there are unreasonable delays, you should complain to the social fund manager or ask your MP to intervene. You are entitled to a written decision, which must include confirmation of your right to request a further review.

Social fund inspector reviews

If you are not happy with a review decision made by a reviewing officer, you can ask for a further review by a social fund inspector based at the Independent Review Service in Birmingham. The inspectors are independent from the DWP but must take into account the same matters as decision makers when deciding whether to change a decision (see 3 above).

You must write to the office that made the review decision within 28 days of the day the decision was issued to you. That office will send your review letter and all the relevant papers to the Independent Review Service. The social fund inspector can accept a late application if there are special reasons (see above under 'Internal reviews).

Your application must explain why you are unhappy with the review decision. You can accept any grant or loan already offered while you are asking for a further review.

The Independent Review Service should write to you within a few days of receiving your application, setting out the main issues and asking you for further information or comments before a decision is made by an inspector. The decision will be notified to you in writing and may confirm or revise the original decision or (exceptionally) refer the case back to the DWP for re-determination.

If you are dissatisfied with an inspector's decision, you can ask the inspector to reconsider it, or you can apply for a judicial review in the High Court (you will need legal advice to do this and must act quickly).

E Unable to work?

This section of the Handbook looks at:

11 Incapacity for work

1. What help can you get?

If you are unable to work because of ill-health or disability, there are a number of benefits you could claim, depending on your situation.

Are you an employee? – If you have an employer and earn at least £82 a week, you are likely to get statutory sick pay (SSP), which can last for up to 28 weeks off sick (see Chapter 13 for details). If for any reason you don't get SSP, you may get incapacity benefit (IB) instead.

Are you self-employed or unemployed? – If yes, you cannot get SSP. Instead, you may get IB (see Chapter 14).

Do you have the right amount of national insurance (NI) contributions? – These do not matter for SSP, but they do for IB unless you claim under the rules for people incapable of work since before age 20 or 25 or widowed before 9.4.01. You must have paid or been credited with enough NI contributions in the right tax years (see Chapter 12).

Are you aged 16-19 (or 24 for students and trainees)? – If your incapacity for work begins before age 20, you can claim IB without needing any NI contributions once you have had 196 days continuous incapacity. While you are under age 19 you cannot usually qualify if you are in full-time education (see Chapter 37(3)). The age limit for claiming is extended to under 25 for certain students and trainees. See Chapter 14(3).

Are you off sick because of an industrial accident or disease? – Claim SSP or IB under the normal rules. You might also get industrial injuries disablement benefit (see Chapter 44).

Are you a widow or widower? – If you are a widow whose husband died before 9.4.01 and you were incapable of work before your husband's death or before the end of your widowed mother's allowance, and continue to be incapable of work, you may get IB even without the right NI contributions. A widower may also qualify. See Chapter 51(5).

Is your household income low and savings no more than £8,000? – You might qualify for income support (IS) to top up IB or other benefits or to provide a basic household income (see Chapter 3). If you have a partner, they must not be working for 24 hours or more a week. A disability premium may be included in your assessment if you receive a qualifying benefit, or you pass the 'incapacity condition' (see Chapter 4(5)). IS can provide help with mortgage interest. IS has been replaced by pension credit (see Chapter 41) for those aged 60 or over. This has no savings limit. For help with rent or council tax, see Chapter 7. For help with NHS costs, see Chapter 52.

Do you need help with personal care or mobility? – You might get disability living allowance (DLA – see Chapter 20). DLA is paid on its own or on top of other benefits to disabled people who need help with personal care or supervision. DLA is also paid to people with mobility difficulties. You can get DLA in work or out of work; it does not depend on your income, savings or NI contributions.

2. What is 'incapacity'?

Not all sickness and disability benefits depend on being incapable of work – eg disability living allowance and industrial injuries disablement benefit each have quite different qualifying tests. The rules and assessment of incapacity for work described in this chapter apply to:

- incapacity benefit (see Chapter 14);
- disability premium under the 'incapacity condition' with income support (IS), housing benefit and council tax benefit (see Chapter 4(5));
- eligibility for IS on grounds of incapacity for work (see Box B.1, Chapter 3);
- national insurance credits for incapacity for work (see Chapter 12(2)).

It is no longer possible to make a first claim for severe disablement allowance, but this chapter applies to existing claims.

Other chapters describe the rules and conditions for each benefit. Note that entitlement to statutory sick pay does depend on being unfit for work but the way this is assessed is different (see Chapter 13).

To show you are incapable of work you must *either*:

- satisfy the 'own occupation' test; *or*
- unless you are exempt, pass the incapacity test in the 'personal capability assessment'.

We look at how incapacity is assessed under these tests in 3 to 10 below.

Some *'specific'* disease or disablement

Your 'incapacity for work' must be because of *'some specific disease or bodily or mental disablement'*. This phrase is used in both the 'own occupation test' and the 'personal capability assessment'. 'Specific' is not the same as 'specified', so it may not be essential that the cause of the disease or disablement is identified (CS/7/82). For example, you may suffer pain, the cause of which has not yet been diagnosed. A normal pregnancy does not count as a disease or disablement, but conditions such as high blood pressure arising because of the pregnancy do count. Symptoms such as the pain experienced by those with 'chronic pain syndrome' or by those who are showing 'illness behaviour' are likely to be taken into account, as there is now sufficient medical consensus that these are 'specific' conditions (CIB/5435/2002).

3. How is your incapacity assessed?

There are two tests of incapacity.

- The 'own occupation test' looks at your ability to do your usual work.
- The 'personal capability assessment' (PCA) assesses your ability to do any work by focusing on a range of activities such as walking, standing and sitting, and includes an assessment of mental health where appropriate. See 6 to 10 below for details.

The decision on whether or not you are incapable of work on any day depends on passing these tests, unless either you can be 'treated' as incapable of work (see 4 below) or, if the PCA applies, you are in an exempt group (see 7 below).

When you make a claim for benefit, the DWP decides which test to apply by looking at whether you have done enough recent work.

If you have worked recently, then the own occupation test applies for the first 28 weeks of incapacity. It is based on medical certificates provided by your doctor. See 5 below for more details. After 28 weeks of incapacity, the PCA applies.

If you have not worked recently, the PCA applies from the start of your claim.

The DWP starts gathering information for the PCA up to 10 weeks before the time the assessment itself becomes applicable. This means that claimants who are still in receipt of statutory sick pay or assessed under the own occupation test may be sent a questionnaire (form IB50) to complete.

Prior to sending out the questionnaire the DWP first checks to see if they have enough information in their records and from your medical certificates to decide if you are exempt from the PCA (see 7 below); they may write to your doctor for more details of your condition. If you are not exempt, you are sent the questionnaire to fill in to assess your physical and mental abilities; you may also be called in for a medical examination. Until you have passed the incapacity test in the personal capability assessment, or the DWP has decided you are exempt, you must continue to send in medical certificates.

4. When are you treated as incapable of work?

You may be treated as incapable of work even if you are able to work. While you come into one of the groups below, you do not have to pass any further tests of incapacity. But you do have to satisfy all the other conditions for benefit. You must not actually work on the days for which you are claiming benefit unless it is exempt work (see 14 below).

You are treated as incapable of work on any day:

- you are an inpatient in hospital;
- you are pregnant and, to avoid serious risk of damage to your health or the baby's health, you must not work in your own occupation if the own occupation test applies, or in any work if the personal capability assessment (PCA) applies;
- you are pregnant or have recently given birth but are not entitled to maternity allowance or statutory maternity pay, from 6 weeks before the baby is due to 2 weeks after the birth (see Chapter 34(8));
- for up to 91 days if you are a 'welfare to work beneficiary' (see Chapter 15(12)) and you are re-claiming benefit within your 52-week linking period. If you had previously passed or been exempt from the PCA (or the 'all-work test'), it doesn't apply to you again for 91 days of a new claim; just send in medical certificates. If your claim doesn't last that long, you can carry over any remaining days to the next claim within the 52 weeks;
- you receive regular weekly peritoneal or haemodialysis for chronic renal failure; or weekly parenteral nutrition for gross impairment of enteric function; or treatment by plasmapheresis, parenteral chemotherapy with cytotoxic drugs, anti-tumour agents or immunosuppressive drugs or radiotherapy.

  Days of treatment can include any necessary recuperation specified in the treatment. If you are not able to work on the other days in the week, your incapacity on those days is assessed under either the own occupation test or PCA. If you are receiving dialysis or other treatment only on a limited number of days in a week, and could not pass the appropriate test on the other days, you might still be treated as incapable of work for the whole of the week. This is because you can benefit from the approach in R(IB) 2/99, which allows a *'broad view'* to be taken that considers the overall severity of the disablement and the frequency of occurrence of good and bad days (CIB/2397/2002).

  If you work on other days of the week, you are only treated as capable of work on the days you work, not for the whole week (see Box E.8, Chapter 14);
- you are under medical observation because you are a carrier of, or have been in contact with, an infectious disease, and a Medical Officer for Environmental Health has issued a certificate excluding you from work.

Regs 11 to 14, Social Security (Incapacity for Work) (General) Regs 1995

5. The own occupation test

When does the own occupation test apply?

If you have worked for more than 8 weeks out of the last 21 weeks before the first day for which a decision on incapacity needs to be made, then the own occupation test is applied. The work must have been for at least 16 hours a week. The 8 weeks do not need to be consecutive. You can be employed or self-employed provided you are paid or the work is done in expectation of payment. But it still counts if you are on paid or unpaid leave (eg sick leave).

Reg 4, Social Security (Incapacity for Work) (General) Regs 1995

More than one job? – The 16 hours a week can be made up of work in more than one job if it is the same kind of work. Or they can be made up of different contracts with one employer even if, in this case, it is different types of work.

But if you have more than one type of job that qualifies as 16 or more hours a week for more than 8 weeks during the 21 weeks and you're not working for the same employer, the own occupation test applies to the most recent, unless they both ended in the same week, in which case, the test must be satisfied in each. For example, if you worked for 10 years full time as a builder, followed by 9 weeks full time as a taxi driver, the own occupation test will be applied to the work you did as a taxi driver.

What is the own occupation test?

The own occupation test assesses whether you are incapable *'by reason of some specific disease or bodily or mental disablement of doing work which [you] could reasonably be expected to do in the course of the occupation in which [you were] engaged'.*

S.171B(2) Social Security Contributions and Benefits Act 1992

Normally, the DWP accepts your statement and your doctor's statement as proof that you are incapable of work. However, they might want a second opinion and may ask you to attend a medical examination by a DWP doctor. Box E.6 in Chapter 13 gives some idea of the stage at which a second opinion may be required.

After your 18th week of incapacity, the DWP will write to you about the personal capability assessment (PCA) and send you a questionnaire. But check 7 below to see if you may be exempt. The PCA will be applied after 28 weeks (196 days) of incapacity. You must continue to send in medical certificates until you have been assessed or accepted as exempt.

If there is a break in your claim of less than 8 weeks before the 196 days are up, when you reclaim the benefit the own occupation test will continue to apply for the remainder of the linked spell of 196 days.

6. When does the personal capability assessment apply?

The personal capability assessment (PCA) applies from the first day of incapacity for which you claim, unless you have worked recently enough for the own occupation test to apply (ie worked for 8 weeks in the last 21 weeks – see above).

If you have exhausted your entitlement to statutory sick pay (SSP) and are now claiming incapacity-related benefit, the PCA normally applies straight away. But if your incapacity is first tested under the own occupation test, the PCA applies after 28 weeks (196 days) of incapacity including time on SSP or maternity allowance.

The 196 days of incapacity need not be continuous. Four or more consecutive days (or 2 days, which need not be consecutive, out of 7, if you receive certain specified treatment, such as dialysis – see 4 above) separated by 8 weeks or less are linked together.

Until you are assessed under the PCA, you must carry on sending in medical certificates.

7. Are you exempt?

When the personal capability assessment (PCA) applies, the DWP checks to see if you are in an exempt group.

❑ **You are exempt from the PCA if you satisfy any one of these conditions:**

- you get highest rate care component of disability living allowance (DLA), or constant attendance allowance (intermediate or exceptional rate);
- you are assessed (or passported) as 80% disabled for severe disablement allowance, or are entitled to industrial injuries disablement benefit or war pension on the basis of at least 80% disablement;
- you are terminally ill and your death can *'reasonably be expected within 6 months'* (see Box H.4, Chapter 20 for details of the legal definition);
- you are registered blind;
- you have any of these conditions: tetraplegia; persistent vegetative state; dementia; paraplegia or *'uncontrollable involuntary movements or ataxia which effectively renders [you] functionally paraplegic'*.

❑ **You are exempt if there is medical evidence that you are suffering from any of the following conditions:**

- severe learning disability – this is defined as a *'condition which results from the arrested or incomplete physical development of the brain, or severe damage to the brain, and which involves severe impairment of intelligence and social functioning'* (this is less restrictive than the 'severe mental impairment' test for DLA mobility component in that it includes conditions such as head injury which arise later in life – see Chapter 20(21));
- severe and progressive neurological or muscle wasting disease (eg advanced conditions of: multiple sclerosis; Huntington's chorea; Parkinson's disease; motor neurone disease; muscular dystrophy);
- active and progressive form of inflammatory polyarthritis;
- progressive impairment of cardio-respiratory function which severely and persistently limits effort tolerance (eg from heart disease, emphysema);
- dense paralysis of the upper limb, trunk and lower limb on one side of the body (eg from a severe stroke);
- multiple effects of impairment of function of the brain or nervous system causing severe and irreversible motor, sensory and intellectual deficits (eg from a severe stroke, brain tumour, head injury);
- manifestations of severe and progressive immune deficiency states characterised by the occurrence of severe constitutional disease (eg loss of weight, CD4 count below 400, fever, night sweats) or opportunistic infections or tumour formation;
- severe mental illness involving the presence of mental disease which severely and adversely affects mood or behaviour, and severely restricts social functioning or awareness of immediate environment (but see below).

Reg 10, Social Security (Incapacity for Work) (General) Regs 1995

❑ **Exemption for those receiving severe disablement allowance (SDA) before 13.4.95**

You are exempt if you were in receipt of SDA on 12.4.95. The exemption continues if you have a break in your claim, as long as the 2 periods of incapacity are no more than 8 weeks apart, or 52 weeks if you are a 'welfare to work beneficiary' (see Chapter 15(12)).

Reg 31, Social Security (Incapacity Benefit) (Transitional) Regs 1995

Severe mental illness

If your medical certificates show you have mental health problems, the DWP writes to your doctor for more information about the severity of the disability arising from your mental health condition.

Guidance advises that severe mental health problems are suggested by a need for ongoing psychiatric care, which may include: sheltered residential facilities where the person receives regular medical or nursing care; day care at least one day a week in a centre where qualified nursing care is available; care at home with intervention at least one day a week by a qualified mental health care worker; or long-term medication with anti-psychotic drugs including depot neuroleptics or mood-modifying drugs, or equivalent oral medication. The guidance also suggests that exemption should be considered where your condition severely restricts your social functioning or means you are likely to pose a threat or danger to others.

Incapacity Benefit Handbook for Approved Doctors, p16

If your condition is assessed as not 'severe' enough to declare you exempt, you will be sent a questionnaire to assess any physical and mental disabilities you may have and then, if necessary, you will be offered a medical examination to test your incapacity for work. Prior to changes to the regulations introduced in 1996 the requirement for exemption was to have a 'severe mental illness' – the extra wording as above has been added. A recent Court of Appeal case (*Howker*) held that certain of these 1996 changes are *ultra vires* (ie outside the law) and it may be possible to argue that this change is too, and provided you can show you have a 'severe mental illness' you should be exempt.

Decisions on exemption

If there is enough information to decide you are exempt, then a decision is issued that you are incapable of work. You do not have to fill in a questionnaire and, in most cases (apart from the exemption for those receiving severe disablement allowance before 13.4.95), you do not need to send in any further medical certificates. If there is not enough information on your medical certificates, the DWP may write to your GP for more details.

The decision maker may make the decision on whether you have an exempt condition based solely on medical evidence from a DWP doctor. But where there is also evidence from your own doctor, the decision maker must decide on the basis of the most 'reliable' medical evidence available.

If you do not fall into an exempt group, or there is still doubt whether you could be exempt, you will be sent a questionnaire to fill in.

If you are not exempt but think you should be, you

can write to the DWP explaining why you fit into one of the exempt categories. It would help to have a letter from your doctor backing you up. Show your doctor the list of exemptions so they can focus specifically on how you fit into the relevant category. In the meantime, make sure you send back the questionnaire within the deadline. If you are ultimately found capable of work, you can also argue in your appeal that you should be exempt.

Reviews of exemption

The DWP doctor gives advice on prognosis to help the decision maker decide when (if at all) there might be a significant improvement in your condition. The exemption may not last indefinitely, but could be reconsidered after a period depending on the medical advice.

8. What is the personal capability assessment?

The personal capability assessment (previously called the 'all work' test) assesses the extent to which your condition affects your ability to perform a range of activities.

If you are not exempt, you will be sent a questionnaire (form IB50) which you must fill in. The questionnaire is mainly intended to ask you about the effects of any physical disabilities or health problems you may have, but also asks about mental health problems.

If you have a mental health problem or learning disability, you should still fill in the questionnaire. Unless you are found incapable of work on physical disability or ill-health grounds, you will be asked to attend a medical examination so that an additional mental health assessment can be carried out (see 10).

In the questionnaire, you are asked to tick the boxes that most closely match how difficult you find it to perform certain activities. Under each of these activities is a list of related tasks of varying degrees of difficulty. These tasks are called 'descriptors'. For a list of the activities and descriptors used in the questionnaire see Box E.1.

The descriptors are ranked so that within each activity there is a threshold at which you are found to be incapable of work and thus pass the test, and a lower threshold at which it is judged that the effects of your condition begin to impair your ability to work. For example, under the activity of walking are 7 descriptors, ranging from 'cannot walk at all' to 'no walking problem'. If you cannot walk more than 50 metres, you are above the threshold and pass the test. If you cannot walk more than 800 metres, this is below the lower threshold and is judged to have no effect on your ability to work. If your walking ability lies somewhere in the middle, this will not be enough on its own to pass the test, but can be combined with your ability under other activities to bring you above the qualifying threshold.

Changes to the regulations were introduced in 1996. Subsequently, the Court of Appeal (*Howker*) has held that some of these changes were *ultra vires*, ie outside the law. The wording for a number of the descriptors was also changed; some have already been accepted as *ultra vires* by Commissioners, but there are others where there may be scope to appeal if you have lost out as a result of the changes. The main descriptors where you may be able to challenge are 'lifting and carrying', and 'continence' under the physical descriptors, and descriptor (g) under 'completion of tasks' in the mental descriptors (see Box E.2). If you think you may benefit from this you should seek specialist advice.

How many points do you need? – The questionnaire does not tell you where the threshold lies. A points system is used by the DWP to determine whether you pass the test. Each descriptor is allocated a fixed number of points, ranging from 0 to 15. These points are not shown on the questionnaire. To pass the test you need a score of at least 15 points. Points are added together from the descriptor with the highest score that applies to you under each activity. Only the higher score from the two activities 'walking' and 'walking up and down stairs' may be counted, together with one descriptor for each other activity.

You don't have to score points in every activity. You will pass the test if you score 15 points in just one activity; or if the points under two or more different activities add up to 15 or more. There is a different way of adding the points and different thresholds where you are tested under the mental health assessment (see 10 below).

For a complete list of the activities and points allocated to each descriptor, see Box E.1.

9. Filling in the incapacity for work questionnaire

For each different activity (walking, sitting, etc), you are asked to tick whichever box applies to you. The boxes correspond to the descriptors for that activity. When deciding which descriptor most closely matches your situation, there are a number of factors that should be taken into account.

Mental or physical disability? – The mental health descriptors are of a general nature and many people might at times fit within some of them. But to score points in the mental health assessment, the problem must arise from *'some specific mental illness or disablement'*. This will usually require some corroborative evidence, preferably medical evidence. To score points in the physical disability assessment, the problem must arise from *'a specific bodily disease or disablement'*.

Normally it will be clear whether a problem should be assessed under the physical or mental assessment. For example, if your mental health problem means you are too frightened to go up a flight of stairs, you cannot score points in the physical disability assessment for that. However, ill-health is often the result of the complex interaction of physical and mental factors and the same condition will sometimes give rise to both physical and mental disablement. A physical symptom (such as dizziness) arising from a mental illness (such as depression or anxiety) may be counted as a bodily disablement, or a bodily disease, such as high blood pressure, may itself give rise to the depression. Symptoms such as the pain felt by those with chronic pain syndrome or similar conditions clearly, in practice, impose genuine physical limitations. In cases such as these it would be wrong to assess someone using the mental health descriptors where these would clearly be inappropriate. *'Bodily'* refers to the affected function, rather than the source of the condition, so whether a physical problem is caused by a mental illness or a condition which has both physical and mental causes, the symptoms will need to be assessed under the physical disabilities section of the test.

See R(IB) 2/98, CIB/4828/1999 and CIB/5435/2002

Artificial aids – The test takes into account your abilities when using any aid or appliance that you would normally use, such as glasses, a walking stick or a prosthesis.

Work – Your abilities are considered in the context of everyday life, rather than in a work setting. However, if you cannot do an activity reliably, with reasonable regularity, safely and at a reasonable speed, you should say so. If the difficulty is sufficiently serious or frequent, you should be considered unable to do the activity at all.

See CSIB/17/96 and CIB/14587/96

Reasonableness – The test is one of whether you reasonably can or cannot do the particular activities (CSIB/17/96). Things like safety, tiredness, pain and discomfort may mean that although you can actually perform the activity it is not reasonable to expect you to do so or although you could perform it occasionally you could not repeat it with reasonable regularity.

Risk – When a certain activity would be a real risk to your health, enough to put off any reasonable person from doing it, you may score points in the same way as if you couldn't do it at all (CSIB/12/96). If you've been advised by a doctor, physiotherapist, etc to avoid an activity, make sure you say this on the questionnaire.

Pain and fatigue – Pain, tiredness, stiffness, breathlessness, nausea, dizziness or balance problems might affect how difficult you find it to do things. If doing a particular task causes you too much pain or discomfort, you should be regarded as not able to do it at all (CIB/14587/96). Similarly, if you find it so tiring or painful to do a particular task that you could not repeat it within a reasonable time, or could only do it so slowly that you could not effectively complete the task, you should be regarded as if you cannot do it at all.

There is space on the questionnaire to give extra information, so use it to give details of how it affects you if you attempt to do a task. Say how often you would need to rest, whether you take pain killers, and explain the cumulative effects of exhaustion or pain on your ability to perform the tasks. If you do take pain-killing medication, say whether it affects your ability to complete tasks.

Variable conditions – The test is not a snapshot of your abilities on a particular day, but an assessment of your abilities over time. DWP doctors are under very clear guidance to take into account variations in symptoms.

Incapacity Benefit Handbook for Approved Doctors, pp52-3

The test of whether you cannot perform an activity is not

E.1 The personal capability assessment – physical disabilities

To pass the test you need 15 points. Add together the highest score from each activity that applies to you. The first two activities (walking on level ground and walking up and down stairs) count as one activity so if you score on both, just count the highest. See 8 and 9 for more details.

Descriptors	Points
Walking on level ground with a walking stick or other aid if such aid is normally used	
■ Cannot walk at all	15
■ Cannot walk more than a few steps without stopping or severe discomfort	15
■ Cannot walk more than 50 metres without stopping or severe discomfort	15
■ Cannot walk more than 200 metres without stopping or severe discomfort	7
■ Cannot walk more than 400 metres without stopping or severe discomfort	3
■ Cannot walk more than 800 metres without stopping or severe discomfort	0
■ No walking problem	0
Walking up and down stairs	
■ Cannot walk up and down one stair	15
■ Cannot walk up and down a flight of 12 stairs	15
■ Cannot walk up and down a flight of 12 stairs without holding on and taking a rest	7
■ Cannot walk up and down a flight of 12 stairs without holding on	3
■ Can only walk up and down a flight of 12 stairs if he goes sideways or one step at a time	3
■ No problem in walking up and down stairs	0
Sitting in an upright chair with a back, but no arms	
■ Cannot sit comfortably	15
■ Cannot sit comfortably for more than 10 minutes without having to move from the chair*	15
■ Cannot sit comfortably for more than 30 minutes without having to move from the chair*	7
■ Cannot sit comfortably for more than one hour without having to move from the chair*	3
■ Cannot sit comfortably for more than 2 hours without having to move from the chair*	0
■ No problem with sitting	0
Standing without the support of another person or the use of an aid except a walking stick	
■ Cannot stand unassisted	15
■ Cannot stand for more than a minute before needing to sit down	15
■ Cannot stand for more than 10 minutes before needing to sit down	15
■ Cannot stand for more than 30 minutes before needing to sit down	7
■ Cannot stand for more than 10 minutes before needing to move around	7
■ Cannot stand for more than 30 minutes before needing to move around	3
■ No problem standing	0
Rising from sitting in an upright chair with a back but no arms without the help of another person	
■ Cannot rise from sitting to standing	15
■ Cannot rise from sitting to standing without holding on to something	7
■ Sometimes cannot rise from sitting to standing without holding on to something	3
■ No problem with rising from sitting to standing	0
Bending and kneeling	
■ Cannot bend to touch his knees and straighten up again	15
■ Cannot either, bend or kneel, or bend and kneel as if to pick up a piece of paper from the floor and straighten up again	15
■ Sometimes cannot either, bend or kneel, or bend and kneel as if to pick up a piece of paper from the floor and straighten up again	3
■ No problem with bending or kneeling	0
Manual dexterity	
■ Cannot turn the pages of a book with either hand	15
■ Cannot turn a sink tap or the control knobs on a cooker with either hand	15
■ Cannot pick up a coin which is 2.5 cm or less in diameter with either hand	15
■ Cannot use a pen or pencil	15
■ Cannot tie a bow in laces or string	10
■ Cannot turn a sink tap or the control knobs on a cooker with one hand, but can with the other	6
■ Cannot pick up a coin which is 2.5 cm or less in diameter with one hand, but can with the other	6
■ No problem with manual dexterity	0
Lifting and carrying by the use of upper body and arms (excluding all other activities specified in Part I of this Schedule [ie this box])	
■ Cannot pick up a paperback book with either hand	15
■ Cannot pick up and carry a 0.5 litre carton of milk with either hand	15
■ Cannot pick up and pour from a full saucepan or kettle of 1.7 litre capacity with either hand	15
■ Cannot pick up and carry a 2.5 kg bag of potatoes with either hand	8

whether you can never do it. Rather, you should score points if you cannot carry out the activity most of the time, even if you have days when you are free of symptoms.

However, it may still be true to say that overall you 'cannot' do something even if you are able to do it on, say, 4 days out of 7. This is because a range of factors must be taken into account: that even on your better days you still have a lot of trouble; how many bad days you have; the length of time between bad spells; whether bad days are unpredictable, etc. It involves looking at the whole period and saying whether, in a more general sense, you can fairly be described as someone who meets the descriptor. It is an exercise in judgement rather than an arithmetical calculation of frequency.

If there are some occasions when you cannot perform tasks, then you should give full details in the questionnaire. It is best to tick the boxes in the questionnaire based on what you can or can't do. Then use the space below the boxes to explain more fully how your condition affects you.

If you have an intermittent condition with longer periods of no, or few, symptoms, you may have difficulty passing the test overall even though you may be incapable of work on your bad days.

R(IB)2/99, Moyna v Secretary of State for Work and Pensions HofL 31.7.2003.

Mental health problems – The DWP may know from your medical certificates if you have a mental health problem. If

- Cannot pick up and carry a 0.5 litre carton of milk with one hand, but can with the other 6
- Cannot pick up and carry a 2.5 kg bag of potatoes with one hand, but can with the other 0
- No problem with lifting and carrying 0

Reaching

- Cannot raise either arm as if to put something in the top pocket of a coat or jacket 15
- Cannot raise either arm to his head as if to put on a hat 15
- Cannot put either arm behind his back as if to put on a coat or jacket 15
- Cannot raise either arm above his head as if to reach for something 15
- Cannot raise one arm to his head as if to put on a hat, but can with the other 6
- Cannot raise one arm above his head as if to reach for something, but can with the other 0
- No problem with reaching 0

Speech

- Cannot speak 15
- Speech cannot be understood by family or friends 15
- Speech cannot be understood by strangers 15
- Strangers have great difficulty understanding speech 10
- Strangers have some difficulty understanding speech 8
- No problems with speech 0

Hearing with a hearing aid or other aid if normally worn

- Cannot hear sounds at all 15
- Cannot hear well enough to follow a television programme with the volume turned up 15
- Cannot hear well enough to understand someone talking in a loud voice in a quiet room 15
- Cannot hear well enough to understand someone talking in a normal voice in a quiet room 10
- Cannot hear well enough to understand someone talking in a normal voice on a busy street 8
- No problem with hearing 0

Vision in normal daylight or bright electric light with glasses or other aid to vision if such aid is normally worn

- Cannot tell light from dark 15
- Cannot see the shape of furniture in the room 15
- Cannot see well enough to read 16 point print at a distance greater than 20 cm 15
- Cannot see well enough to recognise a friend across the room at a distance of at least 5 metres 12
- Cannot see well enough to recognise a friend across the road at a distance of at least 15 metres 8
- No problem with vision 0

Continence (other than enuresis (bed wetting))

- No voluntary control over bowels 15
- No voluntary control over bladder 15
- Loses control of bowels at least once a week 15
- Loses control of bowels at least once a month 15
- Loses control of bowels occasionally 9
- Loses control of bladder at least once a month 3
- Loses control of bladder occasionally 0
- No problem with continence 0

Remaining conscious other than for normal periods of sleep**

- Has an involuntary episode of lost or altered consciousness at least once a day 15
- Has an involuntary episode of lost or altered consciousness at least once a week 15
- Has an involuntary episode of lost or altered consciousness at least once a month 15
- Has had an involuntary episode of lost or altered consciousness at least twice in the 6 months before the day in respect to which it falls to be determined whether he is incapable of work for the purposes of entitlement to any benefit, allowance or advantage 12
- Has had an involuntary episode of lost or altered consciousness once in the 6 months before the day in respect to which it falls to be determined whether he is incapable of work for the purposes of entitlement to any benefit, allowance or advantage 8
- Has had an involuntary episode of lost or altered consciousness once in the 3 years before the day in respect to which it falls to be determined whether he is incapable of work for the purposes of entitlement to any benefit, allowance or advantage 0
- Has no problems with consciousness 0

Part I, Schedule, Social Security (Incapacity for Work) (General) Regs 1995

** For periods of incapacity prior to 15.7.04, the wording: '...because the degree of discomfort makes it impossible to continue sitting' is added.*

*** For periods of incapacity prior to 23.1.04 the activity title is: 'Remaining conscious without having epileptic or similar seizures during waking moments'.*

your condition is not severe enough to exempt you from the test, you are sent the incapacity for work questionnaire. As well as determining the effects of any physical disability you may have, the questionnaire also asks you to describe any mental health problems you may have. See Box E.2 for areas that will score you points – there is space at the back of the form if you need more room to describe your problems.

If the information you put in the questionnaire is not enough on its own for you to pass the test, you are offered a medical examination so that a DWP doctor can go through the mental health assessment with you.

Sending back the questionnaire

With your questionnaire you are required to send in a medical statement, which you get from your doctor. This is a specific form, Med 4, in which your doctor is asked to give a diagnosis of your condition, its disabling effects and an opinion on your ability to carry out your usual occupation. The doctor is not asked to look at your questionnaire or make any comment on it. You should make a copy of the completed questionnaire before sending it off for future reference.

Your completed questionnaire should reach the DWP within 6 weeks from the day after it was sent out. After 4 weeks, you must be sent a reminder. If you have not returned it within the time limit, you will be treated as capable of work unless you can show you had 'good cause' for failing to return it.

When deciding whether you had good cause the DWP must take into account your health, disability and whether you were outside Britain. But other reasons could be valid. You have a right of appeal. If you return your form late and the DWP does not accept you had good cause, it may be treated as a new claim for benefit.

Normally, your completed questionnaire is sent to a DWP approved doctor (from Medical Services) to assess, but if it is clear that you are in an exempt group that does not require supporting medical evidence, the decision maker will make a decision without a further medical opinion. The DWP approved doctor considers all the evidence on your claim and may request further information from your own doctor and/or ask that you should be medically examined. You will not be found capable of work without either having a medical examination or having been offered one. If the decision maker cannot make a decision in your favour, you will be offered a medical examination.

10. Medical examinations

The DWP must give you at least 7 days' notice of the time and place for the examination. This may be arranged over the phone. If you cannot attend, you should inform the office that arranged the examination as soon as possible.

You can ask to be examined in your own home if you are too ill to get to the Medical Examination Centre. You can ask your doctor to note on form Med 4 (which accompanies the incapacity for work questionnaire) that you are not able to travel to the examination centre. However, don't assume they will agree to a home visit.

If you live in an area covered by a Pathways to Work pilot (see Box F.2, Chapter 16), you will also be told that a 'capability report' will be produced at the medical examination and will be sent to your personal adviser, who may then contact you (see Box E.3).

You can claim travel expenses for yourself and a companion. You will be given an expenses form to fill in. You must phone the Medical Examination Centre beforehand to check that they will meet expenses if you need to take a

E.2 The personal capability assessment – mental disabilities

Add all the points together for each descriptor that applies to you. To pass the test you need 10 points. If your score is between 6 and 9 points, you'll still pass if you also score at least 6 points for physical disabilities (see 10).

In the table below we give the codes that will be used by the DWP in any report about you. For example, if you are awarded 2 points because you need alcohol before midday, this will be referred to as descriptor DL(b).

Descriptors	Points
Completion of tasks (CT)	
(a) Cannot answer the telephone and reliably take a message	2
(b) Often sits for hours doing nothing	2
(c) Cannot concentrate to read a magazine article or follow a radio or television programme	1
(d) Cannot use a telephone book or other directory to find a number	1
(e) Mental condition prevents him from undertaking leisure activities previously enjoyed	1
(f) Overlooks or forgets the risk posed by domestic appliances or other common hazards due to poor concentration	1
(g) Agitation, confusion or forgetfulness has resulted in potentially dangerous accidents in the 3 months before the day in respect to which it falls to be determined whether he is incapable of work for the purposes of entitlement to any benefit, allowance or advantage	1
(h) Concentration can only be sustained by prompting	1
Daily living (DL)	
(a) Needs encouragement to get up and dress	2
(b) Needs alcohol before midday	2
(c) Is frequently distressed at some time of the day due to fluctuation of mood	1
(d) Does not care about his appearance and living conditions	1
(e) Sleep problems interfere with his daytime activities	1
Coping with pressure (CP)	
(a) Mental stress was a factor in making him stop work	2
(b) Frequently feels scared or panicky for no obvious reason	2
(c) Avoids carrying out routine activities because he is convinced they will prove too tiring or stressful	1
(d) Is unable to cope with changes in daily routine	1
(e) Frequently finds there are so many things to do that he gives up because of fatigue, apathy or disinterest	1
(f) Is scared or anxious that work would bring back or worsen his illness	1
Interaction with other people (OP)	
(a) Cannot look after himself without help from others	2
(b) Gets upset by ordinary events and it results in disruptive behavioural problems	2
(c) Mental problems impair ability to communicate with other people	2
(d) Gets irritated by things that would not have bothered him before he became ill	1
(e) Prefers to be left alone for 6 hours or more each day	1
(f) Is too frightened to go out alone	1

Part II, Schedule, Social Security (Incapacity for Work)(General) Regs 1995

taxi or if you want to claim for other expenses, such as loss of earnings for a carer who will accompany you. The phone number should be at the top of the letter confirming your appointment.

If you fail to attend – If you do not attend, you will be treated as capable of work unless you can show you had 'good cause' for not attending (see 9 above). Write to the local Jobcentre Plus office explaining your reasons. If the decision maker refuses to accept that you had good cause, you can appeal. You should also make a new claim for benefit in case your appeal is unsuccessful, although the decision maker has the discretion to treat your appeal as a new claim.

The examination

When the doctor is ready to see you, they will probably come to get you from the waiting area to take you into the examination room. Note that this gives them a chance to watch how you manage to rise from a chair and walk.

During the examination the doctor will identify the 'descriptors' that they consider apply to you and should provide a full explanation of their choice in their report (on form IB85) to the decision maker, particularly where their opinion differs from yours. To do this, they will ask you questions about daily activities including any hobbies or leisure activities you have, they will observe how you manage during the examination itself and will give you a clinical examination. The assessment will not simply involve asking you to perform the activities in the questionnaire.

Guidance to DWP-approved doctors suggests the kind of questions about daily living they might ask and what information they might get from observing you at the examination, eg:

- **sitting** – watching TV, sitting at meal times or in a car or bus (observing you at the examination);
- **rising from sitting** – getting on and off the toilet, in and out of a car, out of a chair or off the bed (observing you getting out of the chair when they call you in from the waiting area);
- **standing** – doing the washing up or cooking, queuing at the shops or bus stop, waiting to collect a child from school, standing at a football match;
- **walking** – how you got to the examination centre, walking around a supermarket, walking the dog (observing you walking from the waiting area to the examination room);
- **walking up and down stairs** – going upstairs to the toilet or bedroom, coping with stairs in shops or friends' homes, getting on and off public transport;
- **bending or kneeling** – putting on shoes, getting out of the bath, using a washing machine or low cupboards (observing you bend to pick up a handbag or put on shoes);
- **reaching** – dressing, washing hair, shaving, reaching up to shelves (observing you taking off your coat);
- **lifting and carrying** – lifting saucepans, taking shopping out of a trolley (observing you lifting a handbag);
- **manual dexterity** – filling in forms like the incapacity questionnaire, coping with buttons and zips, opening jars, doing crosswords, using a petrol cap (observing you using a pen, lacing up shoes, handling tablet bottles);
- **vision** – filling in forms, reading newspapers, driving;
- **hearing** – communicating in shops or at family occasions (observing your response to an ordinary or quiet voice);
- **speech** – socialising with friends or family, communicating in shops or public transport, using a phone (observing your quality of speech);
- **remaining conscious** – driving, potentially hazardous domestic activities like cooking;
- **continence** – frequency and length of shopping trips and social outings.

The doctor's opinion should not be based on a snapshot of your condition on the day of the examination. They should

E.3 Capability report

The information in this box affects you only if you live in a Pathways to Work area (see Box F.2, Chapter 16).

If you live in one of these areas you will be allocated a personal adviser when you make a claim for benefit. You may be obliged to attend a series of work-focused interviews with your personal adviser to discuss your work prospects – ie the first 8 weeks after your claim and then monthly after that for a further 5 months.

In Pathways to Work areas, when you are called in for a medical examination under the personal capability assessment, the doctor who examines you will produce two separate reports:

- an incapacity report (IB85); *and*
- a capability report (CR1).

For the incapacity report, the doctor gives an opinion on which of the descriptors apply to you in the assessment of physical disabilities (see Box E.1) and mental disabilities (see Box E.2). This part of the medical is the same as described in this chapter (see 10). The incapacity report is sent to the DWP decision maker to decide whether you are incapable of work for benefit purposes.

For the capability report, the doctor will ask you extra questions about any recent work you have done and about your capabilities and limitations over a range of work-related activities. This report is sent to your Jobcentre Plus personal adviser, not the DWP decision maker, and is used by the adviser to look at your work prospects. The CR1 covers:

- the main tasks and any health problems involved in recent work;
- your medical condition and prognosis;
- what tasks you are able to do despite your disability or ill-health, and where your limitations lie; this is much the same list of activities as those for the incapacity report;
- work-related capabilities (eg travel to work);
- health and safety risks at work;
- advice on workplace adjustments.

As well as the CR1, the personal adviser is sent a notice of the decision on your incapacity. You may then be called in for a work-focused interview. Even if the DWP has decided you are incapable of work for benefit purposes, you are still expected to attend this meeting. If you don't, and you cannot show that you have 'good cause' for not attending, your benefit will be reduced for a specified time or stopped altogether if this interview has been deferred (see Box R.1, Chapter 57).

Not everyone will be called in for a meeting. For example, the adviser may decide it is not appropriate given the severity of your condition, or that a meeting should be deferred for a time (see Box R.1, Chapter 57).

Points to note

- ❑ The CR1 is not sent to the DWP decision maker. It cannot in law be used in the decision on your incapacity for work for benefit purposes (reg 6(4) Social Security (Incapacity for Work) (General) Regs 1995)).
- ❑ You can ask the personal adviser for a copy of the CR1.
- ❑ The adviser may suggest you try a training course or work trial, but they cannot insist you take up their suggestion. Your benefit is not affected if you refuse.
- ❑ You won't be called in for a medical just to complete a CR1, only if an incapacity report is also required.

consider the effects of your condition over time.

Explain your abilities as fully as you can; do not assume the doctor will know that you can only perform the activity with discomfort, that your ability varies, etc. You should tell the doctor about any pain or tiredness you feel, or would feel, while carrying out these activities, both on the day of the examination and over time. How would you feel if you had to do the same activity repeatedly? Try not to overestimate your ability to do these tasks. Focus on the problems and difficulties you have, rather than on the ways you manage to deal with those difficulties.

The examination should last about 20 to 30 minutes. The doctor must also consider the exceptional circumstances outlined below. The decision on entitlement is taken by the decision maker.

Mental health assessment

In some cases it will be appropriate for the doctor to carry out a mental health assessment, not only if you have a mental health problem, but also, for example, if:

- your ability to complete tasks is affected by medication you take;
- you have a physical condition that affects your alertness or cognition;
- you have mild or moderate learning difficulties; *or*
- you have an alcohol or drug dependency problem that impairs your mental abilities.

At the medical examination, the doctor will ask how your condition affects your abilities in 4 main areas of activity: completion of tasks; daily living; coping with pressure; interaction with other people.

Like the questionnaire for physical abilities (see 8 above), there are a series of tasks ('descriptors') related to each activity, and a points system for determining whether you pass the test or not. For a list of the activities and points allocated to each descriptor, see Box E.2. For each of the descriptors that applies to you, you score either 1 or 2 points.

The doctor will interview you to assess how your medical condition affects your day-to-day life. From the interview, the doctor will decide which descriptors are appropriate. The interview will not consist of the doctor simply asking you whether or not each of the descriptors applies to you. Instead, they will ask about everyday activities and experiences, as well as experience of work and training. For example, they might ask you how you spend your time, about your social activities and what stops you from doing things.

Try and explain to the doctor if you can only manage things under certain conditions. For example, the doctor might ask if you read books. If you just say yes, the doctor might decide you have no problems concentrating to read. But it might be that it takes you a long time to read a book because you can't concentrate on it for any length of time. Or perhaps you watch TV but can't usually concentrate on the programmes.

You can take someone with you to the examination for support.

How many points do you need? – All the points are added together to see if you pass the threshold of 10 points for this assessment. If you score 10 points or more, you pass the test. If you score at least 6 points but not enough to pass the test, the mental health assessment and the physical/sensory assessment can be combined: 9 points are added from the mental health assessment (whatever your actual score was) to the total score on your physical/sensory assessment to see if you can meet the combined threshold of 15 points.

The doctor should also consider again whether you ought to be exempt on the grounds of severe mental illness (see 7), and also whether any of the exceptional circumstances below apply. The doctor then provides a report (on form IB85) for the decision maker who makes a decision on your entitlement.

Exceptional circumstances

Even if you do not score enough points to satisfy the personal capability assessment, you will be treated as incapable of work if any of the following circumstances apply to you:

- you suffer from a severe uncontrolled or uncontrollable disease;
- you have some specific disease or bodily or mental disablement and because of this there would be a substantial risk to the mental or physical health of anyone if you were found capable of work. (This condition has been reinstated following a Court of Appeal case (*Howker*) and may be particularly useful if you have health problems you feel would be exacerbated if you started working or searching for work, eg you have stress-related mental or physical problems.);
- you have a previously undiagnosed and potentially life-threatening condition which was discovered during your examination by the DWP doctor;
- you are due to have a major surgical operation, or other major therapeutic procedure, within 3 months of the DWP doctor's examination.

Reg 27, Social Security (Incapacity for Work) (General) Regs 1995 (original wording as reinstated following 'Howker')

There is no definition of 'major surgery' or 'therapeutic procedure', but DWP guidance suggests as examples a hip replacement, hysterectomy, a major cartilage operation on the knee, and an open cholecystectomy.

Incapacity Benefit Handbook for Approved Doctors, pp117-8

Decisions on exceptional circumstances – The decision maker decides if any of the exceptional circumstances apply, based on the report from the DWP doctor who examined you. But if there is also medical evidence from your own doctor they must consider this too and decide on the basis of *'the most reliable evidence available'*. You can appeal against the decision.

11. Appeals

You can appeal against a decision to stop benefit (or national insurance (NI) credit entitlement) when you are found to be capable of work under either the 'own occupation test' or the personal capability assessment (PCA). If you are receiving income support (IS) (as incapacity benefit or severe disablement allowance cannot be paid), you should receive two decisions when you are found capable of work; one on your IS and one on your NI credits. You should appeal against the decision that you are no longer entitled to NI credits; if you win this, the tribunal decision will be binding on your IS as well.

You must appeal within one month of the date the decision is sent to you, so check the decision letter and make sure you keep to the deadline. Don't worry if you can't get all the evidence straight away – you can send it in later.

Outside of one month it is difficult to get a late appeal admitted, but it is possible if there are special circumstances for the delay (see Chapter 58(7)). Otherwise, you must ask the decision maker to revise or supersede the decision and you must be able to show that certain grounds are satisfied – eg that the decision maker made a mistake about the facts of your case or about the law (see Chapter 58, Box R.5). You'll have another month in which to appeal against the new decision, even if it is unchanged, unless the decision maker believes that you have made a 'hopeless application' (see Chapter 58(4) under 'Appeal rights').

If you don't agree that you are fit for work it is well worth appealing. In 2002 at oral hearings 51% of appeals over PCAs were successful. See Box E.4 for ideas of points to consider in your appeal.

Chapter 58 gives more information on appeals.

While you are appealing

You can sign on as available for work for jobseeker's allowance (see Chapter 17). This does not prejudice your chance of winning an appeal on incapacity for work. By signing on, you will protect your right to NI credits, whether or not your appeal is successful.

You can, however, choose to claim IS without signing on while you are waiting for your appeal (only send in medical certificates if it is an own occupation test appeal), but there are disadvantages. Your IS personal allowance is reduced by 20% while you are awaiting an appeal against a decision under the PCA (if you win the appeal the reduction will be repaid to

E.4 Appeal tactics

If you are found capable of work under the 'own occupation test', carry on sending in medical certificates while you are appealing. Your doctor is not bound by the decision of the DWP, but is free to form their own opinion. If you are found capable of work under the personal capability assessment (PCA), however, it is not necessary to send in medical certificates while you are appealing.

For information on appeal procedures, see Chapter 58. For information on claiming benefit while appealing, see 11 and Chapter 17(8).

Your appeal is heard by an appeal tribunal (see Chapter 58(16)). To maximise your chances of success, the following points should be noted:

Appeal in time – Get form GL24 to make your appeal and make sure it is received at your local Jobcentre Plus office within the one-month time limit (but see Chapter 58(7) if you need to make a late appeal).

Get the medical report – If you are found capable of work under the PCA, attached to the decision will be a summary of the assessment telling you the activities in which it was decided you had some limitation, and the total number of points allocated (for list of descriptors and points, see Boxes E.1 and E.2). Unfortunately, this does not necessarily identify where there are areas of dispute. You should ask the DWP to send you a copy of the DWP doctor's medical report, form IB85. This will allow you to see where you might need to dispute it, or point out misunderstandings. If you have previously been assessed as incapable of work following a DWP doctor's examination and there has not been a significant change in your condition(s) since then, you should also request a copy of the earlier DWP doctor's medical report. A tribunal should take account of any previous assessments and reports (CIB/2338/2000, CIB/1972/2000, CIB/378/2001 and CIB/3985/2001).

Request an oral hearing – Your chances of success are very much higher if you go in person to the appeal hearing. When you receive the 'pre-hearing enquiry form', make sure to ask for an oral hearing of your appeal (see Chapter 58(12)). It may be possible for the appeal to be heard in your home in very limited circumstances (see Chapter 58(15)).

Prepare your case – Seek advice from a Citizens Advice Bureau, DIAL or other advice centre, if you haven't already done so. They can help you prepare your case and may be able to represent you at the tribunal. Here are some general guidelines to start with:

- ❑ Think about how your condition affects your capacity for work. If you have been assessed under the own occupation test, think about the tasks involved in the job – a job description may help, if you have one.
- ❑ If you have been assessed under the PCA, use Box E.1 and/or Box E.2 to see which descriptors apply to you, and add up the points. Remember to think about your ability to perform the task reliably, safely, repeatedly and at reasonable speed, and the effects of pain, fatigue, etc (see 9). You can use this information to gather good medical evidence (see below) and to help you clarify to the tribunal exactly where in the test you should score points.
- ❑ If you think one of the exempt categories or exceptional circumstances should apply, seek medical evidence (see below) to back up what you say about this. Argue that your doctor's evidence is the most reliable medical evidence. For example, your doctor probably knows you and how your condition affects you much better than the DWP doctor, or may be a specialist in the field.
- ❑ If your medication affects your ability to complete tasks, or your physical condition affects your alertness, check whether this has been properly assessed under the mental health assessment. Perhaps you have a mental health problem that has not been taken into account. For example, you may suffer from depression or anxiety but not seen your GP about it. If so, you will stand more chance of having this taken into account if you have evidence, preferably medical evidence, to back you up.
- ❑ If you have walking problems, remember that any distance you can walk after you begin to suffer 'severe discomfort' should be ignored (CIB/3013/97). See if the descriptor points you have been given reflects this.
- ❑ Regarding the effects of pain, fatigue, variable symptoms, etc you may want to refer the tribunal to case law and the *Incapacity Benefit Handbook for Approved Doctors* (see Box R.9, Chapter 58). The guidance in the latter is not binding, but you can argue that it should be taken into account.

Get medical evidence – Seek medical evidence in advance. An advice centre may be able to help you with this. Your doctor may want to charge a fee for providing evidence for you, so check on this first – you may be able to get Legal Aid to pay for it (see Chapter 58(13) and Chapter 59).

Ask your doctor, consultant, physiotherapist, etc to comment on the practical and functional problems you have regarding each descriptor that is at issue in your appeal.

- ❑ Where there is a dispute, what descriptors do they think should apply?
- ❑ Is your assessment of your limitations consistent with their understanding of your condition?
- ❑ Do you come under the exemption or exceptional circumstances rules?

It is very important that your evidence focuses on these things, not simply on what condition you have and the treatment you receive.

If your condition has changed since the decision that you are appealing against was made, remember that the tribunal cannot take that into account. So make sure that your evidence is about your condition as it was at the time of the decision (CIB/3126/02).

Remember, however, that you know your abilities better than anyone. The DWP doctor will only have seen you briefly so cannot know everything about you. What you say will count as evidence as long as it is not self-contradictory or implausible (R(I)2/51, R(SB)33/85). Your statements will, however, carry even more weight when supported by medical evidence.

At the tribunal hearing – The tribunal should be conducted in an informal manner and should consider all the medical and other evidence in making its decision, and reach its own conclusions on each descriptor that is at issue in the appeal, not simply adopt the report of the DWP doctor (CIB/14722/96). If you think you need more evidence from your own doctor, ask for an adjournment (although you have no automatic right to an adjournment for this reason and it is best to get all of your medical evidence ready before the hearing).

you). Furthermore, your right to NI credits is not protected unless your appeal is successful. See Box B.1 in Chapter 3. The reduction does not apply to own occupation test appeals.

What if you get worse? – Bear in mind that the appeal tribunal can only look at your situation as it was at the time of the decision you are appealing against. If your condition gets worse later, they can't take that into account.

To make sure that you don't lose out while you have an appeal pending, you should consider making a new claim if a change in circumstances means that you should become entitled to benefit. If this new claim is unsuccessful, it is very important to appeal against the new decision. If you don't, you will find that the appeal tribunal hearing your first appeal cannot consider the period covered by your second unsuccessful claim – even if you win the first appeal, you will still be treated as capable of work from the date of the later unsuccessful claim. Although a decision maker can revise the decision on the new claim following the successful first appeal, there is no guarantee that this will happen every time or that they will revise the decision in your favour. To be on the safe side, lodge the second appeal.

Note that if you are still within 6 months of the date of the decision, a new claim will normally be refused unless your condition is significantly worse than before or you have a different condition (see below).

12. What if you fall ill again?

If you re-claim benefit on the grounds of incapacity for work within 6 months of being found capable of work, medical certificates from your doctor will be sufficient evidence of your incapacity until you are assessed under the personal capability assessment (PCA), provided:

- you have a different condition; *or*
- your condition has significantly worsened since the decision.

It would be helpful if your medical certificates clearly showed that this was the case. This allows benefit to be paid pending a new decision under the PCA.

If you re-claim within 6 months for the same condition you will not get paid while you are waiting to be assessed. The decision maker may decide not to reassess you immediately. This cannot be appealed, but after the 6 months is up you should be paid on the basis of your medical certificates. Alternatively, the decision maker may decide that you fail the PCA without a new questionnaire or examination. If there is a new decision that you cannot have benefit or national insurance credits because you are capable of work then you have the right to appeal against this. If you missed the deadline for appealing against the earlier incapacity cut-off, this gives you another chance, although you may not get full arrears if successful.

Reg 28, Social Security (Incapacity for Work) (General) Regs 1995

13. Disqualification

You can be disqualified from incapacity benefit or severe disablement allowance, or treated as capable of work for other purposes (eg for disability premium), for up to 6 weeks in the situations outlined below. The maximum is 6 weeks, but the DWP can decide on a shorter period. You have the right to appeal against the disqualification itself, or to argue that a shorter period is appropriate.

You may be disqualified if:

- you become incapable of work through your own misconduct (but not if your incapacity is due to pregnancy or a sexually transmitted disease). Misconduct is a wilful act, eg recklessly and knowingly breaking accepted safety rules;
- you do not accept medical or other treatment (not including vaccination, inoculation or major surgery) recommended by a doctor or hospital that is treating you – but only if the treatment would be likely to make you capable of work and you do not have 'good cause' for your refusal;
- you behave in a way calculated to slow down your recovery, without having good cause;
- you are absent from home without leaving word where you can be found, without having good cause.

Reg 18, Social Security (Incapacity for Work) (General) Regs 1995

14. What work can you do while claiming?

The general rule is that you must not work at all while claiming an incapacity-related benefit. If you do, you are treated as capable of work and thus are not entitled to benefit. But some kinds of work are allowed. Chapter 15(3) explains the rules for voluntary work, permitted work and other kinds of work you can do while remaining on your incapacity-related benefit.

If you want to try out a job, there are linking rules allowing you to return to your incapacity-related benefit without losing out if you stop work again within a year (see Chapter 15(12)).

Councillors

Any work you do as a councillor is disregarded when deciding whether or not you are capable of work. This applies to members of county, district, parish or community councils, to London borough and City of London councils, and to regional or island councils.

Your allowances as a councillor are normally taken into account in full as income, even if you do not claim them, provided these allowances are paid under certain specified local government legislation. Most councillors now receive a basic allowance and some may receive a special responsibilities allowance. The DWP should ignore any further specific allowances, such as travel, subsistence, childcare or dependent carer's allowances, which are paid to you for expenses incurred in the performance of your duties. You can also deduct from the calculation of your income any other expenses *'reasonably incurred'* in connection with your work as a councillor. These expenses may need to be turned into an estimated weekly amount if they cover costs such as clothing or heating which arise irregularly. If your net allowance following these calculations is £78 a week or less, your incapacity benefit or severe disablement allowance will not be affected. If your net allowance is over £78 a week, the excess will be deducted from your benefit. For income support, pension credit, housing benefit and council tax benefit you will be allowed the appropriate earnings disregard (see Chapter 5(4)).

It is possible for your allowance to be high enough to completely cancel out your benefit. But you keep your underlying entitlement to benefit, so you would not break your period of incapacity for work even if your benefit was cancelled out for over 8 weeks.

Ss.171F and 30E Social Security Contributions and Benefits Act 1992, CIB/6331/1999, CIS/771/1993, CIB/4621/2002

12 Contributions and credits

1. National insurance contributions

There are 6 different classes of national insurance (NI) contributions. Only Classes 1, 2 and 3 count towards contributory benefits. Classes 1A and 1B are paid by employers only and do not count towards benefit entitlement. Class 4 contributions are normally paid by self-employed people on profits or gains above a certain level. The table below shows which class of contribution counts towards which benefit.

Benefit	Class 1	Class 2	Class 3
Contribution-based JSA	Yes	No	No
Incapacity benefit	Yes	Yes	No
Bereavement benefits	Yes	Yes	Yes
Basic state pension	Yes	Yes	Yes

Class 1 contributions

Class 1 contributions are paid by employees and employers. You are only liable to pay Class 1 contributions once your gross earnings exceed £94 a week. This is called the 'primary threshold'. If you are not contracted-out of the state pension scheme (see Box N.2, Chapter 42), your contribution will be 11% on earnings between £94.01 and £630 a week. The level of contributions is now 1% on earnings above that last figure, known as the 'upper earnings limit'.

Earnings per week	Level of NI contribution
Below £82	Nil
From £82 – £94	Nil (but treated as paid)
From £94.01 – £630	11%
£630.01 and above	1%

Treated as paid – The 'lower earnings limit' is the point at which you start to build up entitlement to contributory benefits. In the tax year 2005/06, the lower earnings limit is £82 a week, but you only start to pay contributions on earnings above £94 a week. Although you will not be paying contributions on earnings between £82 and £94, you will still be treated as having done so. These notional Class 1 contributions are not credits. The contribution conditions for any benefit are the same as Class 1 contributions actually paid. When we refer in this Handbook to people who have 'paid contributions', we are including those who are treated as having paid them.

Reduced rate for married women – If you are a married woman or widow and have kept your right to pay reduced-rate contributions and you earn over £94 a week (in 2005/06), you will pay Class 1 contributions of 4.85% on your earnings between £94.01 and £630 and 1% on earnings above £630.

However, reduced-rate contributions do not count towards contributory benefits. So it is worth considering giving up your right to pay reduced-rate contributions, particularly if you are not contracted-out of the state second pension – ask for advice from a Citizens Advice Bureau or the NI contributions office (see inside back cover).

Class 2 contributions

Class 2 contributions are flat-rate contributions paid by self-employed people. In the tax year 2005/06 they are £2.10 a week.

If your net profits or gains are below (or you expect them to be below) £4,345 in the 2005/06 tax year, you can apply for a certificate of exception on form CF10 which comes with leaflet CA02 (*Self-employed People With Small Earnings*) available from your local Jobcentre Plus office or Inland Revenue Enquiry Centre. If (and only if) you get this certificate, you do not have to pay Class 2 contributions. However, even if your net profits are below £4,345 and you have the certificate, you still have the right to pay Class 2 contributions. If you have low earnings from self-employment and want to pay contributions voluntarily, it is sensible to pay Class 2, rather than Class 3, contributions.

A married woman or widow who has kept her reduced-rate election, does not have to pay Class 2 contributions. However, if her taxable profits from self-employment are £4,895 a year or more, she will nevertheless be liable to pay Class 4 contributions.

Class 3 contributions

Class 3 contributions are completely voluntary, flat-rate contributions. In the 2005/06 tax year they are £7.35 a week. You may want to pay them if the other contributions you have paid (or been credited with) in a tax year are not enough to make that year count as a 'qualifying year' for state pension or bereavement benefits (see Box N.1, Chapter 42 and Chapter 51). If you are covered by home responsibilities protection for that complete tax year, you may not need to pay Class 3 contributions (see Chapter 43).

If you or your spouse have not paid enough contributions for the tax years 1996/7 to 2001/02 you can make up the deficit after reaching pensionable age, which may allow for late claims of both Category A and Category B state pensions (see Chapter 42(4)).

2. Contribution credits

Credits can count only towards the second contribution condition for any contributory benefit. They usually help towards the second contribution condition for state pension and bereavement benefits. Most types of credits also count for incapacity benefit (IB) and contribution-based jobseeker's allowance (JSA). If you are a married woman and have kept your right to pay the reduced-rate national insurance (NI) contributions, you cannot get Class 1 contribution credits. Widows in this position, however, can get credits. Class 1 credits are equal to the lower earnings limit. In any tax year (April to April) you can only get credits up to the minimum required to make the year count for benefit purposes.

Credits for incapacity for work

You will be credited with a Class 1 contribution for each complete week of incapacity for work – ie on each day of the week you are entitled to:

- IB; *or*
- statutory sick pay (SSP); *or*
- severe disablement allowance; *or*
- income support on the ground of incapacity for work; *or*
- maternity allowance.

If you are not entitled to any of these benefits or you claim late, you can still get credits if you are accepted as incapable of work. The rules for assessing incapacity for work are described in Chapter 11. You should apply for your credits before the end of the benefit year after the tax year in which you were incapable of work (see 3).

If you were getting SSP you will have paid or been treated as having paid Class 1 contributions if your employer also has an occupational sick pay scheme, which brings your

SSP to the lower earnings limit. But if you only got SSP and therefore did not earn enough to pay or be treated as paying contributions and your NI contribution record is deficient, the NI contributions office will tell you. You can then apply for credits.

You can also get a credit for each week for any part of which you received an unemployability supplement. A week for NI contribution purposes begins on a Sunday and ends on a Saturday.

Incapacity credits can help meet the second contribution condition for any benefit.

Credits for unemployment

You will be credited with a Class 1 contribution for each complete week you are paid JSA.

If you are not entitled to JSA, you can protect your NI contribution record by signing on at the Jobcentre Plus office for credits only. You will get a credit for each week in which you meet the basic JSA rules (other than the specific contribution-based or income-based conditions for receipt of benefit) – eg you are available for and actively seeking work (see Chapter 17(2)). You do not have to sign a jobseeker's agreement when you are signing on for credits only. If you are incapable of work for part of the week, you are still entitled to a credit.

However, you may not get a credit for any week in which your JSA is not paid because of a sanction, or a joint-claim JSA is reduced because you are subject to a sanction, or you get JSA hardship payments or you are on strike. If there is a gap in your contribution record, you can protect your state pension entitlement by paying voluntary Class 3 contributions.

Unemployment credits help meet the second contribution condition for any benefit.

Carer's allowance credits

You get a Class 1 credit for each week in which you are paid carer's allowance (CA), or in which you would be paid CA if you were not receiving bereavement benefit instead. CA credits count for any benefit.

Credits for tax credits

You get a Class 1 credit for each week in which you receive the disability element or severe disability element of working tax credit (WTC). These credits count for any benefit. You may also get a Class 1 credit, which counts for state pensions and bereavement benefits, for any week you receive WTC and are either:

- employed and earning less than the lower earnings limit for that year; *or*
- self-employed and are exempt from paying Class 2 contributions (see 1 above).

If you are a couple, the credit is awarded to the one who is earning; if you are both earning, it is awarded to the one being paid WTC.

Maternity and adoption pay period credits

If you were getting statutory maternity pay (SMP) or statutory adoption pay (SAP) and did not earn enough to pay or be treated as paying contributions on your SMP or SAP, you can apply for Class 1 credits if you need them. These credits count for any benefit.

Jury service credits

If you were on jury service for all or part of any week, you can apply for Class 1 credits if you need them. These credits count for any benefit.

Starting credits

To help meet the second contribution condition for basic state pension and bereavement benefits, you can get Class 3 credits for the tax year in which you reached 16 and for the two following years.

Termination of full-time education/training credits

To help meet the second contribution condition for contribution-based JSA or IB only, you can get Class 1 credits for one of the two tax years before your benefit year if in that tax year you were aged 18 or over and in full-time education, or on a training course, or in an apprenticeship, and the course (or apprenticeship), which must have begun before you became 21, has now ended. In the other year, you must have passed the second contribution condition in a different way.

Approved training credits

To help you meet the second contribution condition for any benefit, you can get Class 1 credits for each week you are on an approved training course. You must meet the following conditions.

The course must be full time, or 15 or more hours a week if you are disabled, or be an introductory course to one of those courses. It must not be part of your job. It must be intended to run for no longer than one year (unless it is a course provided by, or on behalf of, Jobcentre Plus and a longer period is reasonable because of your disability). Jobcentre Plus training courses automatically count, but for other courses you must apply for credits. Obtain form CA 4147 from your local Jobcentre Plus office or the NI contributions office (see inside back cover).

You must have reached 18 before the start of the tax year in which you require the credits.

60 or older credits

Men can get credits automatically for the tax year in which they reach 60 and the following 4 years, provided they are not out of the UK for 6 months or longer in the year. These credits cover gaps in your NI record for these years and count for all benefits. If you are unemployed, you don't have to sign on to get these credits. You must continue to pay Class 1 or Class 2 contributions for weeks where you are liable. When the state pension age is equalised, women will also become eligible for these credits.

Credits for widows and widowers

To help meet the second contribution condition for JSA or IB when your bereavement benefit or widowed mother's allowance ceases, you can get Class 1 credits for each year up to the year in which your bereavement benefit or widowed mother's allowance ended, except where your benefit stopped because of remarriage or cohabitation. Women who were getting widowed mother's allowance are also deemed to satisfy the first contribution condition for IB.

Credits for periods in prison

You can apply for credits for any weeks in which you were imprisoned or detained in legal custody for convictions or offences which were subsequently quashed by the courts, provided there were no other reasons for you being in prison or custody at that time. These credits count for all benefits.

3. Benefit year and contribution years

Your entitlement to incapacity benefit (IB) or contribution-based jobseeker's allowance (JSA) depends on:

- the 'benefit year' you are in; *and*
- the relevant tax years (or contribution years) for your benefit year.

Benefit years start on the first Sunday in January and end on the Saturday before the first Sunday in January the following year. The 2005 benefit year started on Sunday 2.1.05 and will end on Saturday 31.12.05. Once you know the correct benefit year for your claim, you will know the right contribution years for your claim.

Contribution years for IB

For IB, the contribution years for the second contribution condition are the two complete tax years (6 April to 5 April) before the beginning of the benefit year that includes the start of the 'period of incapacity for work' (PIW) that contains your claim.

For the first contribution condition (unless one of the exceptions apply – see 5 below), you must have paid enough contributions in any one of the last three contribution years. These are the three complete tax years before the beginning of the benefit year in which your PIW begins.

Usually the PIW begins on the first day you are incapable of work for which you claim IB. In this case, you count 3 years back from the start of your claim to work out the right contribution years. For example, if your claim starts in June 2005, your contribution years for the second condition are 6.4.02 to 5.4.03 and 6.4.03 to 5.4.04. These are the tax years in which you must have paid or been credited with enough contributions to pass the second contribution condition. Count one more year back to 6.4.01 to 5.4.02 to add the final year for the first contribution condition.

There are linking rules, however, which mean, in some circumstances, that your PIW begins before you actually claim. These rules are important, since it is the beginning of this period that determines which are the right contribution years for your claim.

Period of incapacity for work – A PIW is made up of at least 4 consecutive days of incapacity for work (or 2 days out of 7 if you receive certain regular treatments) and includes days of entitlement to maternity allowance (see Box E.8, Chapter 14). It lasts for as long as you remain incapable of work.

8-week linking rule – Any two PIWs separated by no more than 8 weeks are joined together into one single period. It is the beginning of the first linked period that determines which are the contribution years. This linking rule allows you, for example, to re-claim IB within 8 weeks of the end of a previous claim and get the same rate as before without serving any waiting period or re-satisfying any contribution conditions.

Example: You claim IB starting from 7.11.05. Your PIW begins on 7.11.05 so your contribution years are 2001-04. You return to work on 4.12.05 for 6 weeks and re-claim IB on 15.1.06. The two periods of incapacity are linked so your contribution years are still 2001-04.

Note: An exception to the 8-week linking rule helps you if you've failed the first or second contribution conditions for IB but you would have passed had you waited and claimed the following benefit year. You can re-claim in the next benefit year without waiting 8 weeks to break the link. The first claim is simply ignored.

52-week linking rule – If you were incapable of work for at least 28 weeks before starting work or training and you meet other conditions (see Chapter 15(12)), the linking rule is extended to 52 weeks. During the 52 weeks from starting work or training, if you become incapable of work again, the new period of incapacity links back to your pre-work or training period of incapacity; and any other periods of incapacity that begin during the 52 weeks are linked together. So if you are off work temporarily or between jobs or have had to give up completely, you can re-claim IB at the same rate as before without re-satisfying contribution conditions.

2-year linking rule – If you were incapable of work before going on a training course, or getting the working tax credit disability element, a 2-year linking rule provides a bridge between your earlier period of incapacity and a new claim for IB (see Chapter 16(5) and Chapter 18(8)).

Linking rules before 13.4.95 – PIWs were introduced on 13.4.95. See the *Disability Rights Handbook* 25th edition for a note on the linking rules that applied before then.

Contribution years for jobseeker's allowance

For contribution-based JSA, the contribution years are the two complete tax years before the beginning of the benefit year which includes either the start of the 'jobseeking period' that contains your claim, or the start of a 'linked period' if that is earlier (see below).

The start of the jobseeking period is usually just the day you claim JSA, and you count three years back from there to work out your contribution years. So if you claim in July 2005, your contribution years are 2002/03 and 2003/04. But there are linking rules that mean the jobseeking period may start earlier.

Jobseeking period and linking rules – The jobseeking period is any period for which you claim and satisfy the basic conditions of entitlement to JSA (see Chapter 17(2)), or you get a hardship payment, or you're not paid JSA but are signing on to protect your national insurance contribution record. A period where you lose entitlement because of failing to sign on or attend an appointment, or you are not entitled because you are involved in a trade dispute, is not included in the jobseeking period.

Any two jobseeking periods link together and are treated as one single jobseeking period if they are separated by:

- 12 weeks or less; *or*
- one or more linked periods; *or*
- a period on jury service.

Gaps of 12 weeks or less between jobseeking periods and linked periods, or in between linked periods are ignored.

Linked periods are periods when you are incapable of work, or entitled to maternity allowance, or training and getting a training allowance, or on certain New Deal options.

It is the beginning of the jobseeking period or any linked period that is used to decide which years you must satisfy the contribution conditions for JSA. For example, if your IB ends and you sign on for JSA instead, as long as you claim JSA within 12 weeks of the end of your IB claim, your contribution years for your JSA claim will be the same as they were for the second contribution condition in your earlier IB claim.

Another linking rule helps people who gave up work to care for someone to qualify for JSA on the basis of the contributions they paid when they were working. If you were getting carer's allowance (CA) and this ended within 12 weeks of the beginning of your jobseeking period (or linked period), the period of CA entitlement also links to the jobseeking period, if this would help you satisfy the contribution conditions for JSA. So your benefit year would be the year in which your CA entitlement began.

Linking rules before 7.10.96 – Jobseeking periods were introduced on 7.10.96. For a note on linking rules before this, see *Disability Rights Handbook* 25th edition.

4. Contribution conditions for benefit

There are two contribution conditions for most contributory benefits. The first condition depends on contributions that you have actually paid in the relevant tax year. For the second condition, credited contributions as well as paid contributions count.

Below we explain the conditions for contribution-based jobseeker's allowance and incapacity benefit (IB). Chapter 14(3) explains the special rules for people under 20 (under 25 if they were in education or training) to qualify for IB without the need to satisfy the contribution conditions. For state pension contribution conditions, see Box N.1, Chapter 42. For bereavement benefits, see Chapter 51.

A B C D E F G H I J K L M N O P Q R S

5. The first condition – paid contributions

Contribution-based jobseeker's allowance

You must actually have paid Class 1 national insurance (NI) contributions on earnings 25 times the lower earnings limit, in either one of the two complete tax years before the start of the benefit year in which you make your claim or in which your jobseeking period (or linked period) began (see 3 above).

So if you claim in the 2005 benefit year, you pass the first condition if you paid Class 1 contributions on earnings of £1,875 between April 2002 and April 2003, or on earnings of £1,925 between April 2003 and April 2004.

Incapacity benefit

For incapacity benefit (IB) you must actually have paid in the relevant tax year (see below):

- Class 1 contributions on earnings of 25 times the lower earnings limit for that tax year; *or*
- 25 Class 2 contributions; *or*
- a mixture of Class 1 and Class 2 contributions, totalling 25 times the lower earnings limit for that year; *or*
- before 6.4.75, 26 flat-rate Class 1 or Class 2 contributions.

Each Class 2 contribution counts as a contribution on earnings of the weekly amount of the lower earnings limit for that tax year – ie £82 for 2005/06.

Unless one of the exceptions below applies to you, you must satisfy the first condition in one of the last 3 complete tax years before the start of the benefit year in which you make your claim or in which your period of incapacity for work began (see 3 above).

Example: If you make your claim in the 2005 benefit year, you will pass if you have paid:

- Class 1 contributions on earnings of:
  - £1,800 between April 2001 and April 2002; *or*
  - £1,875 between April 2002 and April 2003; *or*
  - £1,925 between April 2003 and April 2004; *or*
- 25 Class 2 contributions in any one of these tax years.

The more restrictive 'last 3 years' condition was introduced on 6 April 2001. Before then, the first contribution condition for IB was satisfied by contributions paid *in any tax year.* There are exceptions for some people whose circumstances may have prevented them from working or paying enough contributions in the last 3 years.

Exceptions – You can satisfy the first condition with contributions paid in any complete tax year if you are in any of the following groups.

❑ **Carers** – You were entitled to carer's allowance (CA), or would have been getting it were it not overlapped by another benefit, for at least a week in the last complete tax year before the benefit year in which your period of incapacity for work begins. For example, for an IB claim made in the 2005 benefit year, if you were getting CA at any time between 6.4.03 and 5.4.04 you can pass the first condition based on contributions paid in any tax year.

❑ **Low-paid disabled workers** – You were working, qualified for the disability or severe disability elements within the working tax credit (WTC) calculation, and were getting some tax credits (over and above the basic family element within child tax credit), or were getting the previous disabled person's tax credit. You have to have been getting these for more than 2 years immediately before the first day of incapacity for which you are claiming. This helps you claim IB when your earnings were below the limit for NI contributions. Note that if you were working for less than 2 years, the WTC disability element 2-year linking rule may allow you to go straight back onto your pre-work IB at the same rate without needing to pass any contribution conditions (see Chapter 18(8)).

❑ **Previous IB claimants:**

- you were getting IB for at least one day in the last complete tax year before the benefit year in which you again become entitled to IB. For example, if you claim IB in the benefit year 2005, the first condition is satisfied by contributions paid in any year if you were getting IB at any time between 6.4.03 and 5.4.04; *or*
- your current period of incapacity for work began before 6.4.01. The previous 'any year' rule continues to apply to new claims if your periods of incapacity are linked (see 3). For example, if you re-claim no more than 8 weeks after the end of your previous claim the two periods are linked.

❑ **In prison or detention but conviction or offence quashed** – You are entitled to a credit for a period in prison or detention (see 2), or would be if you applied, for at least one week in any tax year before the benefit year in which you claim.

Lower earnings limits

1994/95	**£57**	1998/99	**£64**	2002/03	**£75**
1995/96	**£58**	1999/00	**£66**	2003/04	**£77**
1996/97	**£61**	2000/01	**£67**	2004/05	**£79**
1997/98	**£62**	2001/02	**£72**	2005/06	**£82**

6. The second condition – paid or credited contributions

In each of the two tax years before the start of your benefit year you must have paid or been credited with contributions. For incapacity benefit (IB) and contribution-based jobseeker's allowance (JSA) you must have paid, or been credited with, Class 1 contributions (Class 1 or Class 2 for IB) on earnings of 50 times the lower earnings limit for that tax year in each of the 2 tax years.

If your benefit year is 2005, you meet this condition if you paid contributions on earnings of £3,750 in the 2002/03 tax year, and of £3,850 in the 2003/04 tax year.

If your benefit year is 2006, you meet this condition if you paid contributions on earnings of £3,850 in the 2003/04 tax year, and of £3,950 in the 2004/05 tax year.

A credited contribution counts as a having earnings at the amount of the lower earnings limit for that tax year (see above). You can combine credits and paid contributions.

For decisions before 6.4.01, your incapacity or unemployment credits only counted for IB in certain circumstances (see Chapter 12(2), *Disability Rights Handbook* 25th edition).

13 Statutory sick pay

1. What is statutory sick pay?

Statutory sick pay (SSP) is paid to employees by their employers for up to 28 weeks in any period of sickness lasting for 4 or more days.

SSP does not depend on national insurance (NI) contributions. You can work full or part time, but you must earn at least the lower earnings limit (£82 from April 2005). SSP is taxable. There are no additions for dependants.

SSP is primarily the responsibility of employers. The scheme is operated by the Inland Revenue from their NI Contributions Offices, usually based in the local Jobcentre Plus office. Detailed guidance is in CA86 *Employees Guide to Statutory Sick Pay* and E14 *What to Do if Your Employee is Sick* (available from the Inland Revenue, including their website: www.inlandrevenue.gov.uk).

Unemployed and self-employed people are not covered by SSP. If you cannot get SSP, you may be able to claim incapacity benefit instead (see Chapter 14).

If your SSP and any other income you get is below your income support (IS) 'applicable amount', you can claim IS to top it up (see Chapter 3). If you don't get IS, you may nevertheless get housing benefit because SSP is treated more generously under that scheme (see Chapter 5(6) and Chapter 7).

2. Do you qualify?

There are three key terms that describe the qualifying conditions for SSP:

- SSP period of incapacity for work (PIW);
- period of entitlement;
- qualifying days.

You can only be paid SSP if you are sick on a qualifying day and your days of sickness form part of an SSP PIW that comes within a period of entitlement. These three different qualifying conditions are explained in 3 to 5 below.

3. SSP period of incapacity for work

The first qualifying condition for SSP is that there must be an SSP 'period of incapacity for work' (PIW). This means that you must be incapable of doing the job you're employed to do because of sickness or disability for at least 4 days in a row. Sundays and public holidays count – therefore, every day of the week can count towards an SSP PIW, including days when you wouldn't have worked even if you had been fit. SSP PIWs separated by 8 weeks or less are 'linked' and count as one PIW.

Your employer is entitled to ask for reasonable evidence of your incapacity for work. For the first 7 days of a spell of sickness, you may need to provide some type of self-certification – eg Inland Revenue form SC2 (*Employee's statement of sickness*) or a special form provided by your employer. During the first 7 days of a spell of sickness you cannot be asked to produce a doctor's certificate, but after that you will usually be expected to get one.

Note that there are some situations when you will qualify even if you are not actually sick on a particular day. You can be treated as incapable of work for days when you are under medical care in respect of some specific disease or bodily or mental disablement and a doctor has advised you not to work for precautionary or convalescent reasons, provided you do not work on those days. You are also treated as incapable of work if you are under medical observation because you are a carrier of, or have been in contact with, an infectious disease, and a Medical Officer for Environmental Health has issued a certificate excluding you from work.

The term 'period of incapacity for work' is also used for other benefits, in particular, incapacity benefit (IB). But the rules are different for SSP. If you are receiving certain types of treatment (eg radiotherapy) you may find that days of treatment do not form an SSP PIW, even though they do form a PIW for IB purposes. So you might qualify for IB instead. Days on SSP do count for some IB purposes (eg deciding when you move onto the higher rate) but do not count towards a PIW for any benefit other than SSP.

4. Period of entitlement

The second qualifying condition for SSP is that there has to be a 'period of entitlement'. This just means the actual period of time when you are entitled to SSP. It begins with the start of the SSP period of incapacity for work (PIW) and ends when your employer's liability to pay you SSP ends.

Your employer's liability to pay SSP ends if:

- you are no longer sick; *or*
- you have had 28 weeks of SSP, either in one go or linked; *or*
- your contract of employment comes to an end (unless your employer has dismissed you solely or mainly to avoid paying you SSP); *or*
- for pregnant women, you are at the start of the 'disqualifying period', which is the 26 weeks during which you are entitled to statutory maternity pay or maternity allowance. If you are entitled to neither, the start of the 26-week disqualifying period depends on whether you already get SSP:
  - if you are already getting SSP, it cannot be paid after the day your baby is born or, if earlier, after the first day you are off work sick with a pregnancy-related illness on or after the start of the 4th week before the expected week of confinement;
  - if you are not already getting SSP, it cannot be paid from the earlier of either the start of the week your baby is born or the start of the week you are first off sick with a pregnancy-related illness if this is after the beginning of the 4th week before your expected week of confinement; *or*
- you are taken into legal custody; *or*
- your linked SSP PIW has spanned 3 years.

SSP will also end if your employer no longer considers you to be incapable of work. In this case, you can appeal against the decision (see 10 below).

People who cannot get SSP

In some circumstances, you won't be entitled to SSP at all (so no period of entitlement can start). These circumstances are listed in Box E.5 – but remember that they have to apply on the first day of an SSP PIW for you to be excluded from SSP altogether.

5. Qualifying days

SSP is only paid for days that are 'qualifying days'. These are normally the days you would have been required to work under the terms of your contract if you hadn't been sick – but they don't have to be.

If your working pattern varies from one week to another, you and your employer can come to some other arrangement as to which days will be qualifying days. As long as you and your employer reach agreement, you have a free choice of qualifying days – as long as they are not fixed by reference to the actual days you are off sick and there is at least one qualifying day in each week.

If you can't reach agreement with your employer, the qualifying days are the days your contract would have required you to work if you hadn't fallen sick. If it isn't clear which days would be working days in a particular week, the law says every day of that week except days you and your employer agree are rest days should be SSP qualifying days.

If you wouldn't normally have worked in a particular week and don't have an agreement on qualifying days with your employer, the law says that the Wednesday of that week will be a qualifying day regardless.

If there are any doubts about qualifying days, it is important to sort this out with your employer.

SSP is not paid for the first 3 qualifying days of an SSP period of incapacity for work (PIW); these are known as 'waiting days'. However, you do not need to wait another 3 days if you re-claim SSP and your second spell of sickness (which must last for at least 4 days) starts no more than 8 weeks after the end of the first PIW. The different PIWs are linked together and count as one continuous PIW. If different PIWs are linked in this way, your right to SSP in the later linked PIWs depends on your circumstances at the start of the first one.

E.5 Who cannot get SSP?

You are not entitled to SSP if, on the first day of your SSP period of incapacity for work (PIW), any of the following apply.

- You are aged 65 or over. But if you become 65 during a period of entitlement and don't plan to retire immediately, SSP should continue to the end of that period of entitlement.
- You are not treated as an employee. This is highly unlikely as all employees aged 16 or over are covered. You are only likely to be excluded if you are regarded as being self-employed rather than an employee.
- Your average earnings are below £82 a week. But remember the PIW linking rule – the first day of the first linked PIW should be used when working out your average earnings. If a new tax year starts while you're receiving SSP, this makes no difference (but you will get any increase in payment).
- You've received incapacity benefit (IB) or severe disablement allowance (SDA) within the previous 57 days.
- You were previously entitled to IB or SDA and you are within the 52-week linking period during which your entitlement is protected as a 'welfare to work beneficiary' (see Chapter 15(12)).
- There is a stoppage of work at your workplace due to a trade dispute and you have a direct interest in the outcome.
- You have already received SSP from your employer for 28 weeks in the same PIW. If you moved jobs, see 14.
- You are pregnant and already into the 'disqualifying period' (see 4).
- You are employed in another country; however, you may be entitled if your employer is liable for Class 1 contributions in the UK for you, or would be if your earnings were high enough (see Chapter 50(3)).
- You are in legal custody.
- You have not yet done any work for your employer.

Remember that PIWs with the same employer which are separated by 8 weeks or less count as one continuous PIW (ie they are linked together).

You won't be entitled to SSP if you come into one of the above groups.

Once you have been off sick for 4 days in a row and your employer decides you cannot get SSP, they must give you form SSP1 so you can claim IB (see 13).

6. How much do you get?

SSP is £68.20 a week. There are no additions for dependants. To qualify, your average weekly earnings must be at least the level of the lower earnings limit (£82 from 6.4.05) – see Chapter 12(1). To get an average weekly figure, gross earnings are averaged over the 8 weeks ending with the last pay day before the start of the SSP period of incapacity for work.

SSP is subject to deductions for income tax and national insurance (NI) contributions. However, no NI deductions are due if SSP is the only payment you receive when you are sick because SSP is below the primary threshold for NI contributions (but you can still get credits – see Chapter 12(2)). Other normal deductions, such as union subs, can also be made from SSP. It is important to make sure your payslip shows details of any SSP payments you have received, together with any deductions made by your employer, so you can check that it's all correct.

Payment of SSP

You should normally be paid SSP at the same time and in the same way as you would have been paid wages for the same period. Note that SSP cannot be paid in kind or as board and lodging or through a service.

If there has been some disagreement with your employer about your entitlement to SSP and the Inland Revenue states you are entitled to it (provided you pass all the other tests), your employer must pay SSP within a certain time limit. These time limits are laid down in the law (see also 11). In certain circumstances, if your employer defaults on payment of SSP or becomes insolvent, liability for any outstanding SSP transfers to the Inland Revenue.

Occupational sick pay

If your employer has an occupational sick pay scheme, any sick pay you get under that scheme will count towards your SSP entitlement for a particular day. Similarly, SSP paid to you by your employer will count towards any pay due to you for a particular day. But if the occupational scheme pays less than your full SSP, your employer must make up the balance so that you get all the SSP you are due. Employers are not obliged to operate the rules of the SSP scheme provided they pay remuneration or occupational sick pay at or above the SSP rate. Employees retain an underlying right to SSP.

7. Does anything affect what you get?

Other benefits – You cannot get SSP while you are receiving incapacity benefit, severe disablement allowance, contribution-based jobseeker's allowance, statutory maternity pay or maternity allowance. You cannot get statutory paternity pay or statutory adoption pay while you are receiving SSP. Other benefits do not affect your entitlement to SSP. See Box E.5 for other circumstances when you cannot get SSP.

Earnings from another job – If your employer accepts you are incapable of doing the work they employ you to do, you can earn money from a different type of work while receiving SSP. For example, if a milkman injures his leg and can't deliver milk, he may be fit enough to, say, call bingo. If so, he can do that and get SSP from his first employer. There is no limit on what you can earn from a different type of job while receiving SSP. However, doing other work may lead an employer to doubt you are genuinely incapable of doing your usual job.

Hospital – Going into hospital won't affect entitlement to SSP.

8. How do you get SSP?

To obtain SSP, you must notify your employer that you're off sick; you may be asked to provide evidence that you're incapable of work. Your employer can decide what kind of evidence is needed, but cannot ask for a doctor's certificate for the first 7 days. The self-certificate form SC2 is available from a GP surgery or Inland Revenue office if your employer doesn't have a special form.

Notification of sickness absence

This means letting your employer know you are sick and incapable of work. To get SSP you must provide evidence that you are incapable of work if your employer requires you to do so (see 9).

These are the rules on notification of sickness laid down in the law and your employer's SSP procedures must conform to them. If you also get occupational sick pay, you'll have to keep to the rules of that scheme to safeguard those payments.

- ❑ Your employer has to make the rules clear to all the workforce in advance.
- ❑ Your employer cannot demand notification before the end of the first qualifying day of a period of incapacity for work.
- ❑ Your employer cannot demand notification in the form of medical evidence. But if you use medical evidence to notify your employer, it should be accepted.
- ❑ Your employer can't insist you use a special form.
- ❑ If you post your notification, your employer should treat it as having been given on the day it was posted.
- ❑ Your employer can't demand notification more than once a week during a spell of sickness.
- ❑ Your employer must accept notification from someone else on your behalf.
- ❑ If your employer doesn't make any rules about notification of sickness absence, or the rules don't conform with SSP law, your employer must nevertheless accept notification of sickness on a qualifying day, if it's given in writing no later than 7 days after that day.

Late notification – If your notification of sickness is late according to your employer's rules (and these rules comply with SSP law) you could be disqualified from SSP for any

E.6 Lengthy absences

If you are off work for a long time, your employer may ask the Inland Revenue (IR) for an opinion on your continuing incapacity for work, although employers are expected to try and resolve any problem themselves and make their own arrangements to get more medical advice. The IR will only assist if you give your consent and if they agree that the absence does seem unduly long. If a serious illness or injury has been diagnosed, the IR would not expect to help the employer.

The table below gives the IR's guide on the more common and less serious ailments (from booklet E14 supplement). This suggests the time by which your employer should have started some form of control action – although there is nothing in law to stop them taking action sooner.

If the IR agrees to help, they will refer the case to their Medical Services, who will ask your doctor for a report on your incapacity to work. They may further arrange for you to attend an examination by one of their doctors, who will produce a similar report. The Medical Services will reach an opinion on whether or not you are incapable of work on the basis of these reports. The reports will not be sent to your employer, who will only be told whether or not you are considered to be capable of work. This is not a decision, it is only to help your employer decide whether payment of SSP should continue. If your employer stops SSP and you disagree, see 10.

Illness or diagnosis	Control (by weeks)
Addiction (drugs or alcohol)	10
Anaemia (other than in pregnancy)	4
Anorexia	10
Arthritis (unspecified)	10
Back and spinal disorders – PID (prolapsed intervertebral disc), sciatica, spondylitis	10
Concussion	4
Debility	
– cardiac, nervous, post-op, post-partum	10
– other	4
Fainting	4
Fractures of upper limbs	10
Fractures of lower limbs	10
Gastro-enteritis, gastritis, diarrhoea and vomiting	4
Giddiness	4
Haemorrhage	4
Headache, migraine	4
Hernia (strangulated)	10
Inflammation and swelling	4
Insomnia	10
Investigation	10
Joint disorders, other than arthritis and rheumatism	10
Kidney and bladder disorders, cystitis, UTI (urinary tract infection)	4
Menstrual disorders, menorrhagia, D&C (dilation and curettage)	10
Mouth and throat disorders	4
No abnormality discovered	Immediate
Nervous illnesses	10
Not yet diagnosed	4
Obesity	Immediate
Observation	4
Post-natal conditions	10
Respiratory illness	
– asthma	10
– cold, coryza, URTI (upper respiratory tract infection), influenza	4
– bronchitis	4
Skin conditions, dermatitis, eczema	10
Sprains, strains, bruises	4
Tachycardia	10
Ulcers	
– perforated	10
– peptic, gastric, duodenal	4
– varicose	10
– corneal	4
Wounds, cuts, lacerations, abrasions, burns, blisters, splinters, FB (foreign bodies)	4

A B C D E F G H I J K L M N O P Q R S

day of incapacity notified late. But SSP can be paid if your employer accepts you have 'good cause' for late notification provided this is given within one month of the normal time limit. This can be extended to 91 days from the day of incapacity if the employer accepts that it was not reasonably practicable for you to contact them within the month. After that time, your employer need not pay SSP for that day even if you have good cause for late notification. If your employer withholds SSP because they do not accept there is good cause for late notification, you can ask the Inland Revenue for a decision (see 10).

9. Supporting evidence

Inland Revenue (IR) leaflet E14 supplement says a doctor's certificate is *'strong evidence of incapacity and should usually be accepted as conclusive unless there is evidence to the contrary'*. A medical certificate may be accepted from someone who is not a registered medical practitioner – eg an osteopath, acupuncturist, herbalist.

It is up to your employer to decide whether to accept the evidence that you are incapable of work. If they do not accept it SSP can be withheld. But you can write and ask the IR for a formal decision (see 10).

Employers can decide to either use their own self-certificates as evidence of incapacity or accept a written note from you as evidence for the first 7 days of sickness. It is important to come to some arrangement as to what type of evidence will be acceptable.

For SSP purposes, your employer cannot require initial notice of your sickness in the form of medical evidence, private or otherwise. But after the first 7 days of a spell off sick they can ask for supporting medical evidence.

If your employer wants more medical evidence they must arrange and pay for it – unless the IR agrees to help (see Box E.6). They can only do this with your consent.

Frequent short spells of sickness

If you are frequently off sick for periods of 4 to 7 days, you may not have seen your doctor, and all your absences will probably be self-certificated.

If you've had at least 4 sickness absences over 12 months, and your employer isn't satisfied you've really been incapable of work, they should discuss the matter with you, and try and resolve any problem internally.

This could involve sending you (with your consent) to a company doctor. If your employer still has any doubts, they can refer your case to the IR for help, but only with your consent. The IR will then forward your case to their Medical Services, who will either ask for a report from your doctor or arrange for you attend an examination by one of their doctors. In either case an opinion will be sought as to whether there are reasonable grounds for your frequent absences. Your employer would take this opinion into account on the next occasion you were off sick.

See Box E.6 if, given the cause of your sickness, you have been off sick for a long time.

10. Fit for work?

If your employer doesn't accept you are incapable of work, you have the right to ask them for a written statement setting out the reasons for this, and details of the dates when you won't receive SSP. You also have the right to apply to the Inland Revenue (IR) for a decision – write to the Inland Revenue Statutory Payments Team, Howard House, Castle Meadow Road, Nottingham NG2 1AB (or telephone 0115 974 0000). They will expect you to have discussed the matter with your employer where it is reasonable to do so, and to have gone through the agreed grievance procedure if one exists where you work.

Both you and your employer will be asked to send comments in writing to the IR. You can provide other evidence – eg further medical statements. A copy of the decision will be sent to both you and your employer. If the decision says you are incapable of work, your employer must pay you the correct amount of SSP within fixed time limits, providing that you pass the other tests for SSP.

Both you and your employer have the right to appeal against the decision to the Tax Commissioners. If your employer appeals, they do not have to pay SSP until a final decision has been given.

11. Enforcing a decision

If the Inland Revenue (IR) has issued a formal written decision that you are entitled to SSP, and your employer doesn't pay it within the time laid down by law and has not appealed, inform the IR Statutory Payments Team (see 10). In this situation, responsibility for paying SSP transfers to the IR, who will pay any SSP to which you are entitled.

12. What information will the DWP give?

In order to decide if you are entitled to SSP, your employer can ask the Jobcentre Plus office for limited information about you. Before disclosing it, the DWP should be satisfied that the enquiry comes from your employer and no one else. Employers are told that detailed personal information about employees will not be disclosed.

13. What happens when SSP ends?

If you are still sick at the start of the 23rd week of your period of entitlement to SSP, your employer has to complete and send you form SSP1 to help you transfer to incapacity benefit (IB).

In some cases, your employer will have to issue the SSP1 earlier – eg if your employer's liability to pay SSP is due to end before the 23rd week of sickness, or SSP ends unexpectedly, or if you are off sick for 4 or more days in a row but you are not entitled to SSP. The employer must issue the SSP1 within 7 days of your request for it, or if payroll arrangements make this impracticable, by the first pay day in the following tax month.

On the form, your employer must tick the reasons they consider you are no longer entitled to SSP. You must also complete form SC1 (the claim-form for IB), available from your local Jobcentre Plus office. You should send forms SSP1 and SC1 to your Jobcentre Plus office in order to claim IB. Your employer can issue their own version of the SSP1. If they do, you should send your employer's form to the Jobcentre Plus office with your SC1.

Box E.7 explains the rules for transferring to IB. If you are not sure if you will be off sick after 28 weeks, complete form SC1 anyway and send it with the SSP1. If you wait until the end of the SSP period before claiming IB, you are likely to have a gap in payments.

If your employer is holding any of your doctor's certificates covering days beyond the last day of your SSP entitlement, these should be returned to you with form SSP1. Send them to the DWP with the completed form and your SC1.

14. What if your job ends?

If you have had an SSP period of incapacity for work (PIW) which ended no more than 8 weeks before your current contract of service ends, and were paid SSP for at least one week, your employer must give you a leaver's statement if you ask for one, on form SSP1(L) or their own version of this form. It's up to you to ask your employer to give you the SSP1(L); they don't need to give it to you automatically. They must then supply the form within 7 days of your request, or if payroll arrangements make this impracticable, by the first pay day of the following tax month.

The leaver's statement will give the date of your first day

of sickness in that PIW. If you have a linked PIW, it will state the first day of incapacity in that linked PIW. It will also state the last day for which SSP was payable and the number of weeks of SSP payable during that PIW. Where you have odd days of SSP, 3 days will round down and 4 will round up, both to the nearest whole week.

Starting a new job
If you go to a new employer and fall sick again no later than 8 weeks after the end of your previous PIW, your position is partly protected. This happens where you have given your new employer a leaver's statement from your last job within 7 days of your first qualifying day for SSP in the new job. Your employer may have set a longer time limit. If you hand over your leaver's statement late (but within 91 days of the first qualifying day of sickness in the new job) your employer can take it into account if you have 'good cause' for your delay.

Your new employer can take into account the number of weeks of SSP you have already received in the previous PIW. If you have had, say, 15 weeks of SSP from your old employer, and the new spell off sick starts within 8 weeks of the previous spell, your new employer will only be liable to pay you 13 weeks of SSP during the remainder of the PIW with them. However, this is the only way in which a PIW can straddle a change of jobs. For all other purposes your right to SSP and the rate of payment depend on your situation on the first day of incapacity in the PIW with your new employer – eg you will have to serve 3 'waiting days' again and will be paid SSP from the 4th qualifying day.

No job to go to
If you had less than 28 weeks worth of SSP from your last employer, and are still incapable of work, you can claim lower rate short-term incapacity benefit (IB) on form SC1, which you should send with the SSP1. But note that if your employer is found to have dismissed you solely or mainly to avoid paying SSP, they remain liable to pay SSP until liability ends for some other reason. Whatever the reason for your dismissal, you should claim IB on form SC1. Seek advice if you have difficulties or would not qualify for IB.

Lower rate short-term IB is £10.55 a week less than SSP, but you might be able to claim an addition for an adult dependant (see Chapter 14(4)). If you are not getting income support, check to see if you are eligible (see Chapter 3).

After a total of 28 linked weeks on SSP and lower rate short-term IB, you can go onto higher rate short-term incapacity benefit. Box E.7 gives details.

E.7 Transfers to incapacity benefit

After 28 weeks on SSP

Short-term incapacity benefit (IB) – After 28 weeks on statutory sick pay (SSP) you may be able to claim IB – see 13 in this chapter for how to claim, and Chapter 14 for more information. To qualify you must pass the national insurance (NI) contribution conditions from the start of your IB 'period of incapacity for work', usually the first day for which you claim (see Chapter 12(3) and (4)).

Providing you also passed the contribution conditions from the start of your SSP claim, you go straight to the higher rate of short-term IB (paid at the same rate as SSP). If you are terminally ill or get disability living allowance (DLA) highest rate care component you are paid the long-term rate of IB at this stage.

If you didn't pass the contribution conditions from the start of your SSP claim, but you do from the start of your IB claim, you are still entitled but you'll be paid the lower rate of short-term IB. You move to the higher rate (or long-term rate if you are terminally ill or get DLA highest rate care component) once you've had 28 weeks SSP/IB from the day you first satisfied the contribution conditions.

If you do not pass the contribution conditions at all, you may qualify for IB if you are aged under 20, or under 25 if you are a student or trainee (see below). Otherwise, check to see if you are eligible for income support (IS) – see Chapter 3.

Long-term IB – The higher rate of short-term IB lasts for a further 24 weeks. If you are still unable to work after 52 weeks altogether, you can go onto long-term IB.

An age addition may be paid with long-term IB (see Chapter 14(4)). If you transfer from SSP, it is your age at the beginning of your SSP entitlement that counts. Once you are on the long-term rate, a disability premium is payable with IS, housing benefit and council tax benefit. So check to see if you are eligible.

Incapacity test – For any rate of IB, after 28 weeks on SSP, you must also pass the 'personal capability assessment' (PCA) to show you are incapable of work, unless you are exempt. The PCA involves completing an incapacity for work questionnaire, and you may have to attend a medical examination (see Chapter 11).

Over pension age – You can't usually transfer from SSP to IB if you are over pension age (see Chapter 40(3)).

SSP ends before 28 weeks

Your SSP may end before your employer has paid the maximum 28 weeks of SSP. This would typically be where your contract with your employer ended – eg because of your continuing ill-health. In this situation you will go on to lower rate short-term IB if you pass the contribution conditions.

When you send in your SSP1 and SC1 form, the DWP will check to see if incapacity will be assessed under the 'own occupation test' (see Chapter 11(5)) or the PCA.

You move to higher rate short-term IB after 28 weeks in total on SSP and lower rate short-term IB. Only the days on SSP after you have passed the contribution conditions count when working out when to move to the higher rate. If you have not already had the PCA, it will apply after you have had a total of 28 weeks on SSP and the lower rate. However, in this case, even SSP days before you passed the contribution conditions count.

Aged under 20 (or 25 for students/trainees)

If your incapacity for work began before you are aged 20 (or 25 for certain students and trainees), you can claim IB even if you do not pass the NI contribution test. However, you must have been incapable of work for a continuous period of 196 days. So it is only possible to transfer directly from SSP if you have received SSP for 28 weeks with no breaks at all.

Once you have served the initial 196-day qualifying period, IB is paid at the lower rate for 28 weeks, the higher rate for the next 24 weeks and then the long-term rate. (You get the long-term rate after 28 weeks if you are terminally ill or get DLA highest rate care component.)

See Chapter 14(3) for more details.

Working tax credit (WTC) disability element

If you qualified for the WTC disability element and were getting tax credits (over and above the basic child tax credit family element) when in work, you might be covered by the 2-year linking rule that allows you to get IB at the same rate you left it. See Chapter 18(8).

14 Incapacity benefit

1. What is incapacity benefit?

Incapacity benefit (IB) is for people unable to work because of illness or disability. Usually you must have paid enough national insurance contributions to qualify, but not if you are incapable of work before age 20, or 25 in some cases, and you claim in time. In this case you claim no-contribution IB. IB is not affected by savings or most kinds of income other than occupational and personal pensions. You should claim if you can't get statutory sick pay (SSP), eg you are not employed or you are self-employed, or if your SSP has run out (see Chapter 13).

Your incapacity for work is assessed for the first 28 weeks of incapacity under the 'own occupation test' (see Chapter 11(5)), which looks at your ability to do your usual job if you've worked recently. If you have not worked recently the 'personal capability assessment' (PCA) applies (see Chapter 11(8)). This involves completing an incapacity for work questionnaire, and you may be asked to attend a medical examination. Some people are exempt from the assessment.

2. Do you qualify?

You qualify for short-term IB if you satisfy the following conditions.

❑ You must meet *all* the following:

- you are 'incapable of work' (see Box E.8 and Chapter 11(2)); *and*
- you are in a 'period of incapacity for work' (see Box E.8); *and*
- you cannot get statutory sick pay (see Box E.5 in Chapter 13); *and*
- you are under state pension age (60 for women, 65 for men) – but see 6 below for an exception.

❑ You must also meet *at least one* of the following:

- you satisfy the national insurance contribution conditions (see Chapter 12(4)); *or*
- your incapacity for work began before age 20 (or 25 in some cases), you claim in time and satisfy other conditions, or you were under 20 (or 25) in a previous linked claim (see 3 and 10); *or*
- you claim under the special rules for men and women widowed before 9.4.01 (see Chapter 51(5)).

3. Claiming under age 20 (or 25)

People who have been incapable of work since before the age of 20, or 25 if they have been in education or training, can get IB without needing to satisfy the national insurance (NI) contribution conditions. This **'no-contribution IB'**, known officially as 'incapacity benefit in youth', replaced severe disablement allowance (SDA) for young people from 6.4.01. Those under the age of 20 on 5.4.01 who were getting SDA at that time were moved onto long-term IB from 6.4.02. Those over that age stayed on SDA. Box E.9 describes SDA for those who remain entitled to it.

The DWP will first check to see if you satisfy the usual NI contribution conditions for IB (see Chapter 12(4)). If you don't, you qualify for no-contribution IB if you meet all the following conditions:

- you are aged 16 or over (or 19, generally, if you are in full-time education) – see below; *and*
- you are aged under 20 (under 25 if you were in education or training) at the start of your period of incapacity for work (PIW) – see below; *and*
- you have been incapable of work for a continuous period of 196 days (28 weeks) immediately before the first day your award starts and are still incapable of work – see below; *and*
- you satisfy the residence and presence conditions – see Chapter 49; *and*
- you are not a *'person subject to immigration control'*, unless you fall within one of the exempt groups – (see Chapter 49(3)).

Once you are entitled to no-contribution IB, the normal IB rules described in this chapter apply.

Age limits

There is a lower age limit of 16 and an upper age limit of 20 (or 25 in some cases). You are eligible for no-contribution IB if you claim within these limits (see below for the latest you can start your claim). Once you have served the qualifying period, the lower rate of short-term IB starts from the first day of entitlement (there are no waiting days) and you can stay on IB right up until state pension age if you remain in the same PIW (see Box E.8). There are linking rules that allow you to re-claim if your benefit stops while you try out employment or training or because you go abroad (see 10).

Aged 16 or over – You must be aged at least 16 when you claim. If you are aged 16, 17 or 18, you will usually be excluded if you are at school or in full-time education of 21 hours or more a week. See Chapter 37(3) for details.

If you are 19 or over, the general rule is you cannot be excluded from IB solely because you are in full-time education, unless you claim under the age exception for under-25-year-olds. To avoid missing out on no-contribution IB, if you are excluded while you are aged under 19, claim as soon as you leave school or college, or on your 19th birthday if you are still in education. (Note that the kinds of activities involved in attending the course may be taken into account in the personal capability assessment if you are not exempt from the test.) If you don't claim before the age of 20 and later want to claim under the age exception for under-25-year-olds who started a course before the age of 20, you can only do so after you leave that course.

Aged under 20 – Your incapacity for work must begin before your 20th birthday and you must have been incapable of work for 196 days in a row (28 weeks) before you can be paid. The latest you can start your claim is immediately after the end of 196 days continuous incapacity that began no later than the day before your 20th birthday. You can submit your claim-form to the Jobcentre Plus office up to 3 months after that (see 7).

You can make a claim for no-contribution IB up to the age of 25 if you have been in education or training under the rules explained below. Otherwise, if you do not claim in time to qualify for no-contribution IB, you can only get IB in future if you have paid enough NI contributions.

Age exception for under- 25-year-olds – The age limit can be extended to under 25 if:

- you were on a course of education or training for at least 3 months before you reached your 20th birthday (you must have started your course within the first academic term after registration unless the delay was because of illness or a domestic emergency); *and*

- the course was:
  - full-time education of any level from secondary school to postgraduate, or part-time if you couldn't attend full time because of your disability; *or*
  - a government training course, or a non-government occupational skills or vocational course of at least 16 hours a week (this includes courses such as life skills for disabled trainees); *and*
- you finished attending the course within the last 2 complete tax years (6 April to 5 April) before the 'benefit year' (January to January, see Chapter 12(3)) in which you claim; *and*

E.8 Period of incapacity for work

To qualify for incapacity benefit (IB), each day of your claim must be a 'day of incapacity for work'. These days must be part of a 'period of incapacity for work' (PIW). This means that you must have at least 4 days of incapacity in a row before you can begin to qualify. The first 3 days of your claim are usually waiting days and you are not paid for these days (see 4 for exceptions).

Once you've qualified, if you have a gap in your incapacity of up to 8 weeks (or 52 weeks or 2 years if you meet one of the special rules described below) you can re-claim when you have another 4 or more days of incapacity and go straight back onto IB at the same rate without serving the 3 waiting days again.

You can't be paid for odd days of incapacity. But if you receive certain kinds of regular treatment such as dialysis, you can be paid if you are treated for 2 or more days a week, including days of recuperation if that is part of the treatment. In this case, you don't need to be incapable of work for 4 days in a row. But you'll only be paid for the actual days of treatment unless the other days of the week are also days of incapacity.

What is a 'day of incapacity'?

A day of incapacity is a day on which you are 'incapable of work'. This depends on passing either:

- the 'own occupation test', which looks at whether you are fit for your usual work if you have worked recently. This is based on information from your doctor, and may occasionally include a medical examination; *or*
- the 'personal capability assessment' (PCA) which assesses your ability to do any work. This is based on an 'incapacity for work' questionnaire which you fill in and, sometimes, information from your doctor and may include a medical examination. Some people are exempt.

These tests are explained in Chapter 11.

A day of incapacity also includes a day on which you are treated as incapable of work (eg you're in hospital, or receiving dialysis – Chapter 11(4)), or on which you are exempt from the PCA (Chapter 11(7)) or are entitled to maternity allowance.

For IB, days can only count as days of incapacity for work if you have actually claimed IB for those days. Days that you are not entitled to IB because of claiming late do not count as days of incapacity.

What is a 'period of incapacity for work' (PIW)?

Your days of incapacity must link together in a PIW which is made up of:

- 4 or more consecutive days of incapacity; *and/or*
- 2 or more days of incapacity, whether consecutive or not, out of 7 consecutive days (including Sunday), when your incapacity results from:
  - regular weekly peritoneal or haemodialysis for chronic renal failure; *or*
  - treatment by way of plasmapheresis, chemotherapy with cytotoxic drugs, anti-tumour agents or immunosuppressive drugs or radiotherapy; *or*
  - regular weekly treatment by way of total parenteral nutrition for gross impairment of enteric function.

Any two or more of these periods that are no more than 8 weeks apart are linked together and count as just one continuous PIW. Sundays count towards a PIW. For more on the linking rules, see Chapter 12(3). See below for the special linking rules for work and training.

The rules for statutory sick pay (SSP) are different. SSP PIWs are explained in Chapter 13. Days on SSP don't count towards an IB PIW. See Box E.7 in Chapter 13 for details of transferring from SSP to IB.

Why are periods of incapacity for work important?

PIWs are important for a number of reasons. We outline some key points below. If your PIW is linked with a period on SSP, see Box E.7 in Chapter 13.

- ❑ IB is not usually paid for the first 3 days of a PIW (waiting days), but if you fall sick again within 8 weeks the two spells are linked together and you don't have to wait another 3 days.
- ❑ The first day of your PIW determines which tax years are the ones in which you must have met the contribution conditions for IB (see Chapter 12(3)).
- ❑ If you had no-contribution IB (see 3) in your earlier claim, you can re-claim within the same PIW on the same basis without needing any national insurance contributions.
- ❑ If you are still in the same PIW as when you last got IB, you can go straight back on at the same rate if you fall sick again.
- ❑ If the first day of your PIW is before you reach state pension age, you can claim short-term IB beyond state pension age (see Chapter 40(3)).
- ❑ Your age on the first day of your current PIW determines entitlement to an age allowance with long-term IB.
- ❑ If you are still in the same PIW as when you last got IB, any protections from changes in the rules that applied to that claim continue to apply – eg protection against deduction of occupational pensions.

Special linking rules for work and training

The general linking rule is that PIWs which are no more than 8 weeks apart are linked and count as one single PIW, whatever the reason for the gap in incapacity.

But if you start work or training, there is a special 52-week linking rule that helps you to return to your IB if you become incapable of work again.

If you qualify as a 'welfare to work beneficiary', you have a 52-week linking period starting from the day after the end of your last PIW, during which any two or more PIWs are linked together. So if you become incapable of work again within your 52-week linking period, you can go back onto IB at the same rate as before without re-satisfying the contribution conditions. This applies whether or not you are still employed and no matter how many repeat claims you make during the 52-week linking period. Chapter 15(12) explains this linking rule.

In addition, there are 2-year linking rules for people re-claiming IB after either a period on tax credits where they have had the disability element included in the calculation (see Chapter 18(8)) or a period on a training scheme (see Chapter 16(5)).

E.9 Severe disablement allowance

What happened to SDA?

Severe disablement allowance (SDA) was abolished on 6.4.01. Young people incapable of work before the age of 20, or 25 in some cases, who claim in time are eligible for incapacity benefit (IB) without needing national insurance contributions (see 3 in this Chapter).

Anyone else who would otherwise have qualified for SDA (eg because they were 80% disabled) can now only claim IB, and they will qualify for that only if they have paid enough contributions.

If you were already getting, or were treated as getting, SDA by 5.4.01, you can continue to receive it, although people under 20 on 5.4.01 were moved onto long-term IB on 6.4.02.

Staying on SDA

If you are on SDA your entitlement will continue indefinitely as long as you continue to be incapable of work and satisfy the SDA conditions. All the old SDA rules continue to apply, although the amount of benefit, earnings limits, etc will be uprated each year.

Linking claims

A period of incapacity for work in a later claim links to an earlier one where the gap is no more than 8 weeks, or longer if the special rules for work and training apply (see Box E.8). So you can have up to 8 weeks off SDA for any reason (or up to 52 weeks/2 years off under special work and training rules) and still re-claim your SDA.

SDA rates		**per week**
For yourself		£46.20
Age addition	higher rate	£16.05
	middle rate	£10.30
	lower rate	£5.15
Adult dependant		£27.50
Child dependant	first child	£9.40
	each other child	£11.35

Earnings

Your partner's earnings do not affect your basic benefit but can affect entitlement to dependants' additions. The rules are the same as for IB (see 5).

You can only continue to receive an increase for a child dependant if you have not yet been transferred onto child tax credit for them.

SDA is not affected by any wages, sick pay or occupational or personal pension you may get. However, it is only possible to do very limited work and still be counted as incapable of work for SDA (see Chapter 15(3)).

Other benefits

If you get SDA, you may get a disability premium included in income support, council tax benefit and housing benefit. SDA overlaps with other benefits such as carer's allowance, maternity allowance, state pension, bereavement benefits and unemployability supplement. If you are entitled to more than one, you are paid the one that is worth the most.

Other SDA rules

More information about SDA can be found in Chapter 15, *Disability Rights Handbook*, 25th edition. If you do not have a copy, send us an A4-sized, stamped addressed envelope and we will send you a photocopy.

- you claim before your 25th birthday, or immediately after the end of 196 days of continuous incapacity that began before your 25th birthday.

You must have been incapable of work for 196 consecutive days before your claim. Generally, these days can fall while you are still attending the course. However, if it is a government training course and a training allowance is being paid, the 196-day qualifying period can only begin when you leave the course.

You can claim as soon as the course has ended or you have left it (although not if your studies are interrupted temporarily by illness or domestic emergency). However, according to the DWP, you cannot claim after one course has ended and stay on your benefit while you go straight on to attend a further course. The law does not spell this out, except for those paid a training allowance on a government training course who are clearly excluded. If you are turned down in these circumstances, seek advice.

196-day qualifying period

You must have been incapable of work for a continuous period of 196 days (28 weeks) before the first day you can be paid no-contribution IB. These can be days before your 16th birthday. When you are serving the qualifying period remember that just a one-day break (perhaps a day trying to see if you can manage a job) is enough to put you back to the beginning and start the 196 days all over again. Once you have served the initial qualifying period, you won't have to serve it again while your IB is in the same PIW.

4. How much do you get?

For the first 28 weeks you get the short-term lower rate of IB. If you are transferring from statutory sick pay (SSP), see Box E.7 in Chapter 13.

After 28 weeks on the lower rate, you move onto the short-term higher rate. This is paid from week 29 to week 52. If you are entitled to disability living allowance (DLA) highest rate care component or you are terminally ill, you are paid at the long-term rate after 28 weeks.

After 52 weeks the long-term rate becomes payable unless you are over state pension age.

Incapacity benefit		**per week**
Short term	lower rate	£57.65
weeks 1–28	adult dependant	£35.65
Short term	higher rate	£68.20
weeks 29–52	adult dependant	£35.65
	child dependant	
	– first child	£9.40
	– each other child	£11.35
Long term	basic rate	£76.45
after 52 weeks	adult dependant	£45.70
(or 28 weeks*)	child dependant	
	– first child	£9.40
	– each other child	£11.35
	age addition (under 35)	£16.05
	age addition (35-44)	£8.05

*Long-term rate is payable after 28 weeks, if you are entitled to DLA highest rate care component or are terminally ill.

If you were getting invalidity benefit before 13.4.95, your level of benefit is protected (see Box E.10).

If you are over state pension age, the rates are different (see Chapter 40(3)).

Waiting days

You cannot normally be paid benefit for the first 3 days of

your claim; these are called waiting days. However, you can be paid from the first day of your claim if:

- your claim is linked to an earlier period of incapacity for work (PIW – see Box E.8); *or*
- your claim is linked to a period on SSP; *or*
- you claim no-contribution IB (see 3).

Additions for dependants

Prior to the introduction of child tax credit (CTC) you could get extra benefit for any children living with you if you were on the higher rate of short-term IB or the long-term rate. If you were over state pension age, you could get an increase for children when you were on the lower rate as well. These increases were abolished for claims made on or after 6.4.03. However, if you were already getting such an increase on 5.4.03 you may continue to receive it for the time being. See Box G.1, Chapter 18 for more details.

If you have children living with you, you may be able to get extra benefit for your partner or someone who looks after your children. If you don't have children, you may be able to claim extra for your spouse if they are aged 60 or over.

Your partner's (or other dependant's) earnings may affect the additions (see 5).

The IB claim-pack has a section to fill in if you want to claim extra benefit for an adult.

Adult dependants – You qualify for an adult dependant's addition if:

- your spouse is aged 60 or over and either lives with you, or you contribute to their maintenance at least to the level of the adult dependant's addition; *or*
- you live with your spouse (of any age) and you are also entitled to child benefit for a dependent child; *or*
- you live with an adult (who may be your unmarried, or lesbian or gay partner, or a relative or friend) who looks after a child for whom you are entitled to child benefit; *or*
- you contribute to the maintenance of, or employ, an adult who does not live with you, to look after a child for whom you are entitled to child benefit, and you pay at least the amount of the adult dependant's addition to the person's maintenance or for caring for the child.

It is possible that following the introduction of the Civil Partnership Act in December 2005, registered same-sex partners will be treated in the same way as spouses.

Child dependants – You can only qualify for an addition for a dependent child if you were already receiving the increase on 5.4.03. Otherwise, you claim CTC instead (see Chapter 18). To continue receiving the addition you also need to continue meeting the qualifying conditions:

- you are entitled to child benefit for that child and either the child lives with you or you contribute to their maintenance at least to the amount of the addition plus the amount of child benefit; *or*
- you live with the child and the child's parent who gets child benefit; *and*
  - you are also the child's parent; *or*
  - you maintain the child at least to the level of the addition and before you were incapable of work you contributed more than half the actual cost of maintenance for the child if they were a dependant (eg you are a step-parent).

See Chapter 36 for details of child benefit entitlement.

Age addition

Age additions are payable only with the long-term rate. It is your age on the first day of your PIW that counts for determining whether an age addition is payable (see Box E.8). If you are under 35 on the first day of your PIW, you get the higher amount of £16.05. If you are at least 35 but have not reached your 45th birthday on the first day of your PIW, you get the lower amount of £8.05.

The addition is paid at the same rate while you are in the same period of incapacity. So if you are 45 or over and have a break in your claim of over 8 weeks you cannot regain the age addition, unless your claims are linked under special linking rules for work and training (see Box E.8).

If you are transferring from SSP, see Box E.7, Chapter 13.

Terminal illness

If you are terminally ill, you are paid at the long-term rate after 28 weeks instead of 52. You count as terminally ill if you *'suffer from a progressive disease and [your] death can reasonably be expected within 6 months'*. See Box H.4,

E.10 Transferred from invalidity benefit

Incapacity benefit (IB) was introduced on 13.4.95 to replace sickness benefit and invalidity benefit. If you were entitled to invalidity benefit on 12.4.95, the amount of your benefit is protected (your award is a 'transitional award'). This protection continues to apply until you have a break in your claim of over 8 weeks. Your award is also protected if you are covered by the special linking rules for work or training (see Box E.8).

Amounts for 2005/06		per week
Long-term IB		£76.45
Invalidity allowance	higher rate	£16.05
	middle rate	£10.30
	lower rate	£5.15
Dependants' addition		£45.70
Additional pension (SERPS)		*

* The amount of additional SERPS pension is based on your contribution record and frozen at your 1994/95 level.

Dependant's addition

You can no longer claim an addition for a wife or husband under the age of 60 unless you have children. But if an addition for an adult dependant was payable with your invalidity benefit at any time in the 8 weeks immediately before 13.4.95, you could keep the addition. Generally, this protection is lost if the addition is not payable for more than 8 weeks (eg if payment of the addition is extinguished by earnings). But you don't lose this protection if the dependant's addition is not paid simply because your dependant receives a personal benefit of their own (CIB/14383/96). Should their personal benefit stop, payment of the dependant's addition should resume. If you are covered by the special linking rules for work and training (see Box E.8), you also keep protection for the dependant's addition on a new claim.

Industrial injuries

If you received invalidity benefit on the grounds of industrial injury or disease, ie without having to pass any national insurance (NI) contribution conditions, your protected award ends if your incapacity for work is no longer a result of that injury or disease. But you can pick up the protected award again if you become incapable of work within 8 weeks through the same injury or disease. The provision to receive sickness benefit without passing the NI contribution conditions has not been carried forward to IB. So if your benefit is cut off, you can only re-qualify if you can pass the NI contribution conditions (see Chapter 12).

A B C D E F G H I J K L M N O P Q R S

Chapter 20 for the legal definition of terminal illness.

Disability living allowance
If you are entitled to DLA highest rate care component you are paid at the long-term rate, including any appropriate age additions, after 28 weeks instead of 52.

No-contribution IB
You are not paid IB during the 196-day qualifying period that applies to those claiming no-contribution IB under the age of 20 (or 25). You may be eligible for income support (see 5 below).

Once you have served the 196-day qualifying period, IB starts at the short-term lower rate as normal.

5. Does anything affect what you get?

Other benefits
You cannot get IB as well as state pension or jobseeker's allowance. Other benefits such as maternity allowance, carer's allowance (CA), bereavement benefits and unemployability supplement are known as overlapping benefits. You can receive an amount equal to the highest of any of these benefits to which you are entitled.

Other benefits can be paid on top, including disability living allowance (DLA), attendance allowance (AA) and industrial injuries disablement benefit. Working tax credit (WTC) can be paid on top, but IB is taken into account in the WTC assessment.

If your income is low, you might get income support (IS) to top it up. Ask the Jobcentre Plus office for a claim-form. If you get long-term IB, you could get the disability premium with IS, housing benefit (HB) or council tax benefit (CTB) – see Chapter 4(5). If your income is low and you are aged 60 or over, you need to claim pension credit instead of IS (see Chapter 41).

You can claim IS from the age of 16. Even if you can't get IB because of the type of schooling you attend, you may still be eligible for IS. For IS, you just need to show that because of your mental or physical disability you would be unlikely to get a job within the next year if you left school now. See Chapter 37 for more on benefits from age 16.

Occupational and personal pension
Your pension – Half of your occupational or personal pension above £85 a week is deducted from IB. For example, if your weekly occupational pension is £95 before tax, your IB is reduced by £5 a week. This reduction is not applied if one of the 4 exceptions below applies in your case.

If you have more than one pension, they are added together before the reduction is applied. In other words, two pensions that are separately below the £85 limit but when added together are above the limit will reduce your benefit.

Pension payments that are subject to the reduction are periodical payments (eg weekly or monthly payments but not one-off lump sums) under:

- a personal pension scheme (including a stakeholder pension and self-employed pension scheme);
- an occupational or public service pension scheme;
- a permanent health insurance scheme arranged by a former employer, but not if you paid more than 50% of the premiums and only once you have left that employment.

Your IB is not reduced in the following 4 cases:

- you are entitled to DLA highest rate care component; *or*
- the pension payments are in connection with the death of the pension scheme member; *or*
- you were entitled to IB before 6.4.01 and are still in the same period of incapacity for work. In this case there is no reduction for existing or future pensions unless you lose entitlement to IB for more than 8 weeks, or longer if the special linking rules for work and training apply (see Box E.8); *or*
- you were under the age of 20 on 5.4.01 and continued to be entitled to severe disablement allowance (SDA) until being transferred onto no-contribution IB after 5.4.02.

If you stop work some time before pension age, you may be better off opting for a larger lump sum and lower regular payments. Note, however, that means-tested benefits such as IS, HB and CTB are affected by both income and savings. Seek expert advice. You may need a mix of financial and benefits advice.

Your partner's pension – This counts as earnings and may affect a dependant's addition (see below), but does not affect your personal rate of IB or the age addition.

Other income
IB is not affected if you receive wages or contractual sick pay while you are off sick. You might have more income tax deducted from your pay or pension if you get the taxable short-term higher rate or long-term IB (see below).

Work
Generally, if you do any work you are treated as capable of work and cannot get IB. But some work is exempt from this rule (see Chapter 15(3)).

You may be eligible to be a 'welfare to work beneficiary' to protect your benefits while you try out a job. It means you can return to IB and certain other benefits at the same rate as before if you become incapable of work again within 52 weeks of starting work. Chapter 15(12) explains these rules.

If you live in certain pilot areas you may also be able to qualify for a 'return to work credit', a reward based on your receipt of IB prior to returning to work that is ignored as income for means-tested benefits and tax credits (see Box F.2, Chapter 16).

Disqualification
You can be disqualified from benefit for up to 6 weeks in certain situations (see Chapter 11(13)).

Income tax
Lower rate short-term IB is tax free. Higher rate short-term and long-term IB are taxable, as are any adult dependants' additions paid with these rates, unless you transferred in April 1995 from invalidity benefit to IB, in which case IB remains tax free. The child dependant's addition is tax free.

If you get an occupational pension or are still being paid by an employer, your tax code is adjusted to take into account the amount of your taxable benefit. Your IB is paid in full, but the tax is taken off your pay or pension. If IB is your main income, any tax due is taken off your benefit by the DWP before it is paid to you.

For tax queries, contact HM Inspector of Taxes, Leicester 4 District, Attenborough House, 109-119 Charles Street, Leicester LE1 1FZ (0116 242 7200, Minicom 0116 251 3764).

Hospital
You can carry on getting IB while in hospital. It will only be reduced when you have been in hospital for 52 weeks if you first entered hospital prior to April 2005 (see Chapter 33).

Partner's earnings
Your partner's earnings do not affect your basic benefit, but can affect the additions for children and dependent adults. Occupational and personal pensions count as earnings.

Earnings are taken into account after deductions for tax and national insurance (NI) contributions, and certain other disregards (see 'Calculating earnings' below).

Child dependant's addition – If, despite the introduction of child tax credit (CTC), you continue to be entitled to an increase for a child dependant because you were receiving this on 5.4.03, and you are living with your spouse, or partner of the opposite sex, your partner's earnings may affect the amount you get for dependent children.

If your partner earns £170 or more a week, you lose one addition for a dependent child. For each extra £22 that your partner earns above £170, you lose an addition for one other child.

If you lose the addition because of this rule but qualify for it again within 8 weeks (because your partner stops working or their earnings reduce) then you can re-qualify for it. Otherwise, you should claim for help with your children through CTC.

Adult dependant's addition – For short-term IB, you lose the addition if your partner earns more than £35.65 a week (or £43.95 if you are over state pension age). For long-term IB (including those paid the long-term rate due to terminal illness or receipt of DLA highest rate care component), you lose the addition once your partner earns over £56.20 a week, if your partner lives with you. If you maintain someone who does not live with you, you lose the addition paid with the long-term rate if they earn over £45.70.

You can get an addition for an adult who you employ to care for your child. If the person lives with you, any wages you pay them for caring for the child are disregarded. If the person does not live with you, all their earnings from any source are disregarded.

If your partner's earnings are over the limit, you lose the addition in the following week. If earnings are not over the limit, the addition is not affected and you will get it in full.

If your adult dependant gets a benefit in their own right, your addition for them may be reduced or not paid because of the overlapping benefit rules. For example, if your partner gets CA this cancels out the addition paid with long-term IB.

If you've been getting an addition for a wife, or a woman looking after a child, continuously since before 16.9.85 there is a more generous tapered earnings rule. See *Disability Rights Handbook*, 26th edition, page 92, for more details.

Calculating earnings

In working out how much of a partner's earnings are taken into account, certain deductions and disregards can be taken from gross earnings. The same applies when working out earnings from permitted work if you get IB or SDA.

Count any payment from your employer as earnings (eg bonus, commission, payments for childminding, retainer, pay in lieu of notice). Occupational and personal pensions count as earnings for dependants' additions. If you're self-employed, the rules on working out net profit follow the IS rules (see Chapter 5(5)).

From your gross weekly earnings (or net profit) deduct:

- income tax and NI contributions (Class 1, 2 or 4);
- half of any contribution you make to an occupational or personal pension;
- expenses *'wholly, exclusively and necessarily incurred in the performance of the duties of the employment'*, eg equipment, special clothing, travel between workplaces (but not travel between home and work);
- advance of earnings or a loan from your employer;
- childcare charges of up to £60 a week for children under 11 (see below);
- fostering allowance;
- payments from a local authority, health authority or voluntary organisation for someone temporarily in your care;
- £4 from rent paid to you by a subtenant plus £9.25 if heating is included;
- the first £20 a week plus half the rest of the income from a boarder;
- the whole of any contribution towards living and accommodation costs from someone living in your home (other than boarders and subtenants);
- earnings from employment payable abroad where transfer to the UK is prohibited;
- charges for currency conversion;
- annual bounty paid to part-time members of the fire brigade or lifeboat service, or to auxiliary coastguards or members of a territorial or reserve force.

The Social Security (Computation of Earnings) Regs 1996

If earnings paid in one week are over the limit, the dependant's addition is lost the following week. Monthly earnings are worked out on a weekly basis and affect benefit for the month ahead. If earnings fluctuate, they may be averaged over a recognisable cycle of work or over 5 weeks, but this is discretionary. One-off payments that are not for any specific period are divided by the relevant weekly earnings limit to work out the number of weeks your benefit will be affected.

Childcare charges – You can get this disregard if you are a lone parent, or one of a couple and either you are both working or one of you is working and the other is 'incapacitated'. For this purpose, you count as incapacitated if you get DLA or AA (or the equivalent for War Pensions or Industrial Injuries schemes), long-term IB or SDA, or if there is included in your HB or CTB a disability premium or higher pensioner premium based on your (not your partner's) disability.

You must be paying a registered childminder (or a childminder provided on Crown premises, or by schools, hospitals, etc where childminders don't have to be registered) for childcare for at least one child under the age of 11, or paying an out-of-school-hours scheme (run on school premises or provided by a local authority) to look after at least one child aged 8 or over but under 11. A maximum of £60 a week of these childcare payments is deducted from your earnings.

6. What happens on retirement?

Long-term IB

If you are over state pension age (60 for women, 65 for men), you cannot receive long-term IB. Your benefit stops the day you reach state pension age. You should claim state pension instead.

If you were getting an age addition with your IB within 8 weeks of reaching state pension age, this will be paid with your state pension (but the SERPS/S2P additional pension and the age addition overlap) – see Chapter 42(4) 'Extra state pension'.

Short-term IB

When you reach state pension age you can choose to stay on short-term IB rather than draw your state pension. Bear in mind that IB is worth less than a full-rate state pension, and any personal or occupational pension above £85 will reduce your IB but will not reduce a state pension. When short-term IB runs out, you cannot move onto long-term IB. See Chapter 40(3) for more information.

7. How do you claim?

Your first contact with the Jobcentre Plus office will usually be by telephone, with a follow-up interview to complete the claim-pack. For the first 7 days, you do not need a medical certificate. If you are incapable of work for more than 7 days, you must send a medical certificate (form Med 3) from your doctor. If you are under 20 (or 25) and claiming no-contribution IB, you will also need a backdated medical certificate covering the 28 weeks before the date from which you are claiming.

If you work for an employer and do not get statutory sick pay, you will also need to send in form SSP1, which you get from your employer; you may require a medical certificate from the first day of your claim.

It is important to keep your medical certificates up to date. Ask your doctor for a new certificate well before the old one runs out. If you are not covered by medical evidence for each day of your claim, benefit could be withheld. Until you have passed the incapacity test in the personal capability assessment or the DWP has decided you are exempt from the test, you must carry on sending in certificates. The DWP will let you know if this is no longer required.

The procedure for assessing your incapacity is explained in Chapter 11(3).

You are likely to be asked to attend a meeting with a personal adviser to discuss work prospects as a condition of receiving benefit (see Box R.1, Chapter 57). From October 2005 all new IB claimants will have a work-focused interview after 8 weeks of their claim and will have to complete an action plan. If you live in a Pathways to Work area (see Box F.2, Chapter 16) you must attend a series of work-focused interviews.

Backdating claims

Your claim can be backdated from a date up to 3 months prior to your claim-form being received at the local Jobcentre Plus office if you met all the entitlement conditions during that period. Ask your doctor for a backdated medical certificate (form Med 5). If you are claiming no-contribution IB (see 3) and would like it to be backdated, you should put on your form that you are claiming from 3 months earlier and include a medical certificate backdated for another 28 weeks beyond that to cover the qualifying period. Bear in mind however, that the 3-month backdated no-contribution IB would reduce (or end) any child tax credit payable to your parents over the same period, resulting in an overpayment of the tax credit.

Your claim can be backdated further if you had previously been getting IB and were found capable of work but by the time your IB entitlement ended you had claimed disability living allowance (DLA). In this case, if you are awarded DLA highest rate care component, you should re-claim IB within 3 months of the DLA decision. IB can be backdated to the end of your earlier entitlement. The same rule applies where constant attendance allowance is awarded at the intermediate or exceptional rate.

8. How are you paid?

IB is usually paid fortnightly in arrears. The DWP can consider weekly payments if fortnightly payments are causing hardship. If you've been getting IB since before April 1995 (see Box E.10), benefit is paid weekly in arrears as before. Where the amount of your IB is less than £5 a week because of pension reductions, it may be paid annually. You may be paid by direct credit transfer into a bank, building society or post office account, or by cheque (see Chapter 57(5)).

9. Decisions and appeals

The decision on your claim is made by a decision maker at the local Jobcentre Plus office. When they decide your claim, the decision maker may also fix a date to reassess your incapacity for work, depending on the advice given by the DWP doctor about your illness or disability. You are not told this date. You may then be asked to complete a further incapacity for work questionnaire and/or attend a medical examination.

If you disagree with a decision, you can appeal to an independent tribunal. You must appeal within one month of the decision being sent to you, so check the date on your decision letter and make sure you keep to the deadline. If you are appealing against a decision on your capacity for work, see Chapter 11(11) and Box E.4. For more details on challenging decisions, see Chapter 58.

10. Claiming after a break in benefit

It is possible to have a gap in your IB entitlement and re-claim on the same basis as before. Generally the rules are designed to allow you to try out some work or training. But there are extra rules to allow those getting no-contribution IB to re-claim after a spell abroad (see below).

You may be able to re-claim at the same rate and on the same basis as before if the gap is no more than:

- 8 weeks for any reason (see Box E.8);
- 52 weeks to try out a job if you are a 'welfare to work beneficiary' (see Chapter 15(12));
- 2 years if you have been getting the disability element within working tax credit (WTC) and meet the relevant conditions (see Chapter 18(8));
- 2 years if you have been on certain training schemes (see Chapter 16(5)).

The period of incapacity for work (PIW) on the new claim must link to the PIW on the earlier claim (see Box E.8). Note that for no-contribution IB, you won't have to re-serve the qualifying period.

Re-claiming no-contribution IB

As well as the rules above which allow you to re-claim your benefit on the same no-contribution basis as before (see 3) and at the same rate, there are two extra ways, explained below, to re-claim IB without needing to satisfy contribution conditions. If you cannot re-claim under any of these linking rules, you will only be able to get IB again in the future if you can pass the national insurance (NI) contribution conditions. However, in each of the two cases below you do not go back to your previous rates of benefit. Instead, your entitlement starts again from the short-term lower rate and there is no protection for the age addition.

❑ **Employment and training**

- your previous entitlement to no-contribution IB must have ended solely with a view to you taking up employment or training; *and*
- your earnings must have been less than 25 times the lower earnings limit in any one of the last 3 complete tax years (April to April) before the benefit year (January to January) in which you re-claim IB (see Chapter 12(3) and (4)). For example, if you re-claim in 2005, your earnings must have been below £1,800 in 2001/02, or £1,875 in 2002/03, or £1,925 in 2003/04; *and either*
  - you re-claim no later than 8 weeks after your last job ended; *or*
  - you have at least one NI credit for the disability element of WTC in the last complete tax year before the benefit year in which you claim (eg if you claim in 2005, you must have a WTC credit in 2003/04) and have paid or been credited with enough NI contributions to meet the second contribution condition for IB (see Chapter 12(4)).

❑ **Returning to Britain**

- your previous no-contribution IB must have ended because you were outside Great Britain (GB); *and*
- you have been incapable of work for 196 consecutive days from the day you returned to GB; *and*
- you re-claim within 3 months of the end of this 196-day period.

Going back to work

F

15 Benefits and work

1. Going back to work

This chapter looks at the effect on benefit entitlement of doing paid work or voluntary work and the linking rules that can help you return to benefit without losing out.

2. What happens to your DLA?

Disability living allowance and attendance allowance are payable whether or not you are working. They are not means tested, so earnings do not affect the amount of benefit you are entitled to (see Chapters 20 and 21).

Note: Starting a job may suggest that your care or mobility needs have changed, so your benefit entitlement could be reconsidered.

3. Can you work while claiming benefits for incapacity?

Generally, if you do any work, whether or not you expect to be paid, you are treated as capable of work for the week in which you do any work (Sunday to Saturday) and thus are not entitled to the following benefits:

- incapacity benefit (IB) or severe disablement allowance (SDA);
- income support (IS) based on incapacity for work (see Box B.1, Chapter 3);
- disability premium under the 'incapacity condition' (see Chapter 4(5));
- national insurance incapacity credits.

If you come off one of these benefits to start paid work, for the first year you can protect your right to return to benefit (see 12 below).

Exempt work – You are allowed to do the kinds of work described below while remaining on your incapacity-related benefit.

Regs 10A, 16 and 17, Social Security (Incapacity for Work) (General) Regs 1995

Although work that falls into the categories below is allowed, it may not be ignored completely. The sort of activities or tasks you are able to do, whether they are connected with the work or not, could be taken into account when deciding whether you pass the incapacity test under the personal capability assessment or the own occupation test. When you start work the decision maker may, in some cases, decide to refer your case to a DWP doctor for an opinion, and you may find yourself subject to another medical examination. But this should not happen routinely. You do not have to undergo a medical examination just because you are doing permitted work. However, any medical examination that may be due during a period of permitted work will go ahead.

Caring for a relative (in your own home or elsewhere) and domestic tasks in your own home are not regarded as work. A relative is a parent (or in-law or step-parent), son/daughter (in-law/step), brother, sister, or the partner of any of them; or a spouse or unmarried partner, grandparent, grandchild, uncle, aunt, nephew or niece.

Negligible amounts of work can be ignored. The example given in the *Decision Makers Guide* is of someone who occasionally does small jobs for a business (eg signing cheques).

Permitted work

You are allowed to do the following types of 'permitted' work.

Permitted work lower limit – You can earn no more than £20 a week. You do not need prior permission from your doctor; there is no need for the work to be therapeutic in any way. You can do such work even between periods when you are on the other forms of permitted work described below. The £20 limit means that such work should not interfere with your entitlement to means-tested benefits such as IS, housing benefit (HB) or council tax benefit (CTB) if you qualify for the disability premium. You must notify the DWP before you cease doing the work, but it is a good idea to do this when you start work.

Supported permitted work – You may undertake work which is supervised by a person employed by a public or local authority or voluntary organisation which provides or arranges work opportunities for people with disabilities. The support must be ongoing and regular but the frequency of contact can vary depending on the needs. The means of contact can vary, and be either face to face or by phone. The work can be in the community or a sheltered workshop. Supported permitted work can also be work as part of a treatment programme, done under medical supervision while you are an inpatient or outpatient at a hospital or similar institution. The following rules apply.

- ❑ Theoretically there is no limit on your weekly hours of work, though with the national minimum wage, you effectively will not be able to work more than 16 hours a week.
- ❑ You can earn no more than £78 a week after any allowable deductions (see Chapter 14(5)).
- ❑ Technically, you must only notify the DWP before you cease doing the work. In practice, however, it is advisable to let the DWP know as soon as possible. The DWP can check to see if the work can actually be classified as supported permitted work. If you are receiving means-tested benefits such as IS, HB or CTB your earnings may affect how much of these benefits you are paid. Generally, any earnings above the disregard appropriate to you will be deducted from those benefits (see Chapter 5(4)). If you are only receiving HB and/or CTB you should contact the local authority instead.

Permitted work higher limit – You can only do this for a set period of time – it is designed for you to test your ability to work before you consider moving permanently into employment. The rules are as follows:

- you can only work for less than 16 hours a week; *and*
- you can earn no more than £78 a week after any allowable deductions (see Chapter 14(5)); *and*
- you can normally only work for 26 weeks; *and*
- you must notify the DWP that you have started work within 6 weeks of doing so.

16-hour limit – You must work for less than 16 hours a week. If you work for 16 or more hours in one week, in calculating your hours for that week, your hours are averaged over the current week and the 4 preceding weeks, or over the period of a 'recognisable cycle' of work.

Extension to the 26-week period – You may be allowed to work for more than 26 weeks, up to an overriding limit of 52 weeks, if there is evidence that prolonging your work would increase your chances of getting a full-time job. The Government proposes to change the permitted work rules to allow claimants to work for 52 weeks with a review at 26 weeks; people with the most limiting health conditions will be allowed to work for longer than 52 weeks. It is likely these changes will take place in April 2006; if you start work after October 2005 you may benefit from them.

Further periods – If you have had a break in your benefit of more than 8 weeks you can repeat the 26-week period of permitted work. Otherwise you can do further permitted work only after a gap of more than 52 weeks since you last did it and if there is evidence that such work will improve your chances of getting a full-time job. This new period of permitted work will have an overriding limit of 52 weeks.

If your earnings from these forms of permitted work are below the £78 limit, your IB or SDA will not be affected. But if you get IS, HB or CTB, earnings are taken into account as income and may reduce that benefit (see above).

Other kinds of work

The following kinds of work are also allowed:

- voluntary work (not for a close relative) – see 11 below;
- work done as a councillor – see Chapter 11(14) for the effect on benefits of councillors' allowances;
- any activity undertaken during an emergency, to protect another person, or to prevent serious damage to property or livestock;
- duties undertaken as a 'disability member' of an appeal tribunal or the DLA Advisory Board – but only one day a week is allowed;
- an approved work trial arranged in writing with the employer by an officer of the DWP (or an organisation providing services to the DWP) for which you will receive no wages.

Dialysis, radiotherapy and other weekly treatments

If you receive certain specified types of regular weekly treatment for 2 or more days a week, you can work on the other days and continue to receive IB or SDA for the days of treatment (including days of preparation and recuperation specified as part of the treatment). See Chapter 11(4) and Box E.8, Chapter 14.

Reg 13, Social Security (Incapacity for Work) (General) Regs 1995

If your partner works

Your partner's earnings do not affect the basic amount of IB or SDA you get but can affect an adult dependant's addition (see Chapter 14(5)). Your partner's earnings affect IS and income-based jobseeker's allowance (see 4 and 7 below).

4. What happens to income support?

If you get income support (IS) on the grounds of incapacity for work, you may do permitted work of less than 16 hours or other exempt work (see 3 above). If you get IS on any other grounds (eg because you are registered blind or a lone parent) you can work for less than 16 hours in any job.

In some cases there is no limit on the hours you can work – eg if your earnings or hours are 75% or less of what someone

F.1 Going back to work – a checklist

This is a guide to the main help available if you are in work or looking for work. Where there is more information in this or other chapters, we refer you to the right place in the Handbook. To find out more about other kinds of help, ask at your local Jobcentre or Jobcentre Plus office. A disability employment adviser can provide specialist advice on employment and training.

It is worthwhile asking for a 'better-off' calculation before taking a job. You can ask a local advice agency or an adviser at the Jobcentre Plus office. For a given level of earnings and other income they can work out how much benefit you might get. You can then compare your income in work and out of work.

Working 16 hours a week or more

Tax credits – Top up earnings if you are in low-paid work, with extra support for disabled people, those with children, and those over 50 starting work (see Chapter 18).

Income support (IS) – You can stay on IS in some circumstances – eg, your hours or earnings are reduced to 75% or less than those of a person without your disability in the same job; you live in a care home; or you are a carer. Keep up to £20 a week of earnings. IS helps with mortgage interest (tax credits do not). See Chapter 3(6).

Housing benefit and council tax benefit – Help with rent and council tax. See Chapter 7.

Working under 16 hours a week

Permitted work – Incapacity benefit (IB) and severe disablement allowance (SDA) can be paid on top of agreed permitted work earnings of up to a maximum of £78 a week (see 3).

Income support – You can stay on IS if work is permitted or you are eligible for a reason other than incapacity for work. Keep up to £20 a week of earnings. See 4.

Jobseeker's allowance (JSA) – Keep up to £20 a week of earnings. You must still look for full-time work. See Chapter 17.

Housing benefit and council tax benefit – Help with rent and council tax (see Chapter 7).

When you start work

Child maintenance bonus – One-off payment of up to £1,000 if you get child support and come off IS or income-based JSA. Applies to claims of IS or income-based JSA made prior to 3.3.03. Claim within 28 days. See 4.

Housing benefit and council tax benefit extended payments – Existing rate paid for first 4 weeks of coming off IS or income-based JSA. See 6.

Mortgage interest run-on – Existing housing costs paid for the first 4 weeks of coming off IS or income-based JSA. See 4.

Welfare to work benefit protection – If you re-claim benefit for incapacity in the first 52 weeks of work, this lets you pick up your pre-work benefits at the same rate. See 12.

Other benefit protection – Various linking rules help you re-claim benefit on the same terms as before if you have to stop work again. See 12.

Job grant – One-off payment if you start full-time work after at least 26 weeks on IS, JSA, IB, or SDA. See 4.

Equipment and support at work

Access to Work – Can help pay for equipment and adaptations at work and cover extra disability-related costs such as travel to work and support workers. See Chapter 16(2).

Workstep – Provides job support for disabled people who face more complex barriers to finding and keeping work. See Chapter 16(2).

without your disability would expect to earn or to work in a comparable job (see Chapter 3(6)).

If you are the claimant and your partner works, their hours must be less than 24 hours a week, although there are some exceptions (see Chapter 3(6)).

In each case you can only keep a maximum of £20 of your earnings or joint earnings for a couple (see Chapter 5(4)).

Mortgage interest run-on

If your IS or income-based jobseeker's allowance (JSA) stops because you or your partner get a job or more hours or more pay, any housing costs you were getting can be paid for an extra 4 weeks at the existing rate whatever your earnings, provided your job is expected to last at least 5 weeks. You may be able to get this help if you or your partner were getting IS or income-based JSA for at least 26 weeks. You do not have to make a separate claim. Simply inform your local Jobcentre Plus office that you are starting work.

Back to work bonus

This scheme for people working part time while on IS or JSA allowed you to build up entitlement to a lump-sum bonus of up to £1,000, payable when your work took you off benefit. It was abolished on 25.10.04, but if you were claiming on that date you can claim back any bonus you accrued up until 28.1.05, provided you claim your bonus by 28.1.06 (see Chapter 15(4) *Disability Rights Handbook,* 29th edition).

Child maintenance bonus

Prior to the introduction of the child support scheme 'new rules' on 3.3.03, if you were on IS or income-based JSA you could build up an entitlement to a bonus of up to £1,000, using up to £5 a week of any child maintenance payable. You can continue to build up entitlement to the bonus if, prior to 3.3.03, you were already on IS or income-based JSA and receiving child maintenance payments (whether through the Child Support Agency or under a voluntary agreement or court order). You can claim the bonus within 28 days of either benefit stopping, or up to 6 months if you have good cause for the delay.

Job grant

This provides help to bridge the gap between leaving benefit and receiving a wage. It is a one-off tax-free payment for people who have been claiming IS, JSA, incapacity benefit or severe disablement allowance for at least 26 weeks and who are moving into remunerative work of at least 16 hours a week, provided your job is expected to last 5 weeks or more. The grant is worth £100, or £250 if you have children. If you have been claiming JSA then you must be aged 25 or over to qualify.

5. What about carer's allowance?

You can work and claim carer's allowance (CA) at the same time, as long as your earnings (less any allowable deductions) are no more than £82 a week. There is no limit on the number of hours you can work, although you must continue to provide care for at least 35 hours a week.

CA is not means tested. Provided your earnings are below the limit, the full amount of CA is payable. Caring costs of up to half your net earnings can be disregarded if you pay someone other than a close relative to look after the disabled person you care for or a child under 16 (for whom you get child benefit). Your partner's earnings do not affect the basic

Adviser Discretion Fund – Discretionary grants for items that could facilitate your return to work such as clothing or work equipment. See Chapter 16(2).

Trying out a job

Benefit linking rules – Various linking rules help you re-claim benefit without losing out after a trial period at work. See 12.
Work trials – If you have been unemployed for 6 months you can do a work trial, which allows you to remain in receipt of benefit and receive travel and meal allowances for up to 15 working days while you and the employer see whether you will be suitable for a job.
Work Preparation – For people out of the job market for some time due to ill-health or disability, this is a programme to build confidence and work skills. You may be able to stay on your existing benefits or claim an allowance. See Chapter 16(2).
Employment on Trial – Your JSA will not be sanctioned for leaving a job voluntarily during the trial period. See Chapter 17(9).
Job Introduction Scheme – Your new employer applies to the Jobcentre for payments towards your wages for the first few weeks to give you a trial period in the job. See Chapter 16(2)
Return to work credit and in-work credit – Return to work credit is £40 a week, payable for a year in Pathways to Work areas to assist people on incapacity benefits into work. A similar in-work credit for lone parents is being tested in different pilot areas (and in London is being extended to couples with children). See Box F.2 and Chapter 16(2).

Starting a business

Self-Employment Provision (SEP) – There is a range of advice and support available (usually only to those aged 25 or over) to help you set up your own business.

Looking for work

Jobseeker's allowance – Weekly benefit providing a basic income if you have to sign on as available for work. If you are not required to sign on – eg because of incapacity or caring responsibilities – claim IS instead. See Chapter 17.
Access to Work – Travel costs, support workers and communicator support at interviews paid through the Access to Work scheme. See Chapter 16(2).
Social fund budgeting loan – You may be able to get a loan towards expenses of looking for work or starting work if you have been getting IS or income-based JSA for at least 26 weeks. See Chapter 10(5).
Work search premium – £20 premium available for up to 6 months to lone parents in pilot areas who have been on IS or income-based JSA for over a year. See Chapter 16(2).
Job preparation premium – £20 premium available to IB, IS and SDA claimants in Pathways to Work areas (see Box F.2, Chapter 16).

Childcare costs

Working tax credit – Includes a childcare tax credit of 70% of certain childcare costs. See Chapter 18.
Housing benefit and council tax benefit – Certain childcare costs can be ignored from your earnings in the benefit assessment. See Chapter 5(4).

Employment rights

Disability Discrimination Act – See Chapter 55.
Minimum wage – £4.85 an hour for workers aged 22 and over (£5.05 from October 2005), £4.10 if aged 18 to 21 (£4.25 from October 2005), and £3 if aged 16 or 17.
Other rights at work – Contact your trade union or ACAS (Advisory, Conciliation and Arbitration Service)

amount of CA you get but can affect an adult dependant or child dependant's addition. See Chapter 23(5) for more details.

Income support to top up your CA is affected in a different way. For carers, there is no limit on the number of hours you work, but only £20 of your net earnings can be disregarded (see Chapter 5(4)).

6. Getting housing and council tax benefit

You can claim housing benefit (HB) and council tax benefit (CTB) whether or not you are in work (see Chapter 7). These are means-tested benefits, so the amount you get depends on the level of your (and your partner's) income and savings. See Chapter 5(4) for the way earnings are assessed, and what earnings are disregarded.

If your income support (IS) or income-based jobseeker's allowance (JSA) ends because you have started work, your existing HB and CTB entitlement will also end. You should tell the local authority that your benefit has stopped and complete and return a new HB/CTB claim-form as soon as possible. You might also qualify for 'extended payments'.

Extended payments

If your IS or income-based JSA stops because you (or your partner) get a job or more hours or pay, your HB and CTB may carry on for an extra 4 weeks at the existing rate whatever your earnings, provided your job is expected to last 5 weeks or more. To be eligible, you or your partner must have been getting IS, or contribution- or income-based JSA, or a combination of these, for at least 26 weeks. You do not have to make a separate claim. Simply inform your local Jobcentre Plus office or local authority within 4 weeks that you or your partner have started or are about to start work or your earnings/hours have increased.

If you do not get IS, a similar extended payment can be made if you have received incapacity benefit or severe disablement allowance for at least 26 weeks, get a job, or your pay or hours increase. You must inform your local authority of the change within 4 weeks. The qualifying rules are the same as for IS/JSA, but there is no provision to combine periods on the different groups of benefits.

7. Jobseeker's allowance

If your income-based jobseeker's allowance (JSA) stops because you or your partner get a job or more hours or earnings, you may continue to get housing costs paid for up to 4 weeks under the mortgage interest run-on (see 4).

If you are working less than 16 hours a week, you are eligible for JSA. If your partner works and you get income-based JSA, they must work less than 24 hours a week. You must still sign on for work and actively look for, and be available to take up, a full-time job. Earnings above the earnings disregard affect the amount that you get. For income-based JSA only, your partner's earnings also affect the amount of your benefit (see Chapter 17(18)).

8. Tax credits

You may qualify for tax credits if you are in work or have dependent children and your income is low enough (see Chapter 18).

If you qualify for tax credits you are unlikely to be worse off in work, but it is worth getting advice so you know just how your income would be affected before taking a job. It is important to note that, unlike income support and income-based jobseeker's allowance, tax credits do not help with mortgage interest.

Child tax credit includes a basic family element paid to most families with children; it also includes other elements for children and disabled children.

Working tax credit (WTC) includes extra elements if you are a lone parent or have a partner, or work (or are treated as working) 30 hours a week or more, or are disabled, or aged 50 or over and starting work. Up to 70% of certain childcare costs can also be included in the calculation of your WTC.

If you stop work again and were getting the disability element within WTC included in the calculation of your tax credits, a special linking rule may allow you to return to your incapacity benefit on the same terms as before (see Chapter 18(8)).

9. Health benefits

You may qualify for help with prescription charges, hospital travel costs, dental treatment and glasses.

If your income and savings are low, claim on form HC1, which you get from the doctor, dentist or optician. If you get income support or income-based jobseeker's allowance, you qualify automatically. If you get tax credits you may qualify, depending on the level of earnings. See Chapter 52.

10. Industrial injuries benefit

Industrial injuries disablement benefit is not affected by any work or earnings you might have.

11. Voluntary work

If you get incapacity benefit, severe disablement allowance or other incapacity-related benefit

You are allowed to do voluntary work for anyone other than a parent (or in-law or step-parent), son/daughter (in-law/step), brother, sister, or partner of any of them. You must not be paid for your work, other than expenses *'reasonably incurred by [you] in connection with that work'*. Permitted expenses could include travel, childminding or the costs of caring for another dependant, equipment needed for work and use of a telephone. You may be treated as a volunteer if you're doing community service. There is no limit on the number of hours you can volunteer.

If you get income support (IS)

You can do voluntary work without your IS being affected. For this purpose, a volunteer is someone who, without legal obligation, performs a service for another person without expectation of payment, or someone working for a charity or voluntary organisation. The only payment you get or expect to get must be to cover your actual expenses.

If the DWP thinks it is not reasonable for you to provide your services free of charge, they may treat you as having notional earnings (Chapter 5(14)). If you are paid anything other than actual expenses, you are treated as being in paid work, and excluded from IS if you work 16 hours or more a week (24 hours or more if it is your partner who is the volunteer). See also Chapter 3(6).

If you get IS on the basis of being incapable of work then, as for incapacity benefit, the work must be for someone other than a close relative, otherwise you will be regarded as capable of work. Care you provide for a close relative will not count as work.

12. Stopping work again

If you stop claiming one or more benefits to begin work, but then stop working and re-claim benefit, there are linking rules that may allow you to go back to your previous benefit on the same terms as before. We outline some of the main rules below. There may be other linking rules that apply to your benefit entitlement. Often these arise when there is a change in the law for which transitional protection is given for existing claimants. Seek advice if you think these may apply. More than one linking rule may apply to you at the same time, so you should use whichever is best for you.

Rapid reclaim

There is a 'rapid reclaim' process for income support (IS), income-based jobseeker's allowance (JSA), housing benefit (HB) and council tax benefit (CTB). You should be able to take advantage of it if you have to reclaim these benefits within 12 weeks of a previous claim (eg if you started work but then couldn't cope with it). You are allowed to complete simpler, shorter benefit claim-forms. Your circumstances must be broadly the same as when you made your previous claim (eg any payment of working tax credit (WTC) made to you because you started work would not be treated as a change of circumstances).

8-week linking rule

Two periods of incapacity separated by a gap of 8 weeks or less can be linked together and treated as one period of incapacity. This means that if you are off work because of illness or disability within 8 weeks of the end of your last severe disablement allowance (SDA) or incapacity benefit (IB) award, you'll go back onto your SDA or IB at the same rate and on the same terms as before.

For IB, if the gap in your period of incapacity for work is 8 weeks or less, you are not required to satisfy or re-satisfy the contribution conditions.

This rule also applies to the disability premium paid within IS, HB or CTB. If you become incapable of work again within 8 weeks, you'll go straight back onto the disability premium without having to serve the 52-week qualifying period again. If you hadn't served the full 52 weeks on your earlier claim, you don't have to start at the beginning again but will pick up where you left off. See Chapter 4(5).

There is a similar 8-week linking rule for statutory sick pay (SSP) – see Chapter 13(3).

52-week linking rule

If you start work or training, a 52-week linking rule allows you to return to your incapacity-related benefit at the same rate as before if you become incapable of work again.

You are eligible for this protection if:

- you have been incapable of work for more than 196 days (gaps of up to 8 weeks are ignored); *and*
- your entitlement to any 'benefit, allowance or advantage' awarded on the basis of incapacity for work (other than SSP) stops at the end of your period of incapacity; *and*
- you start work or training (see below) within one week of entitlement to this benefit ending; *and*
- you notify the DWP within one month of entitlement to benefit ending that you have started work or training. You must notify them once you have actually started even if you already told them you intended to start. This notification is not required if you have successfully appealed against a decision that you are capable of work under the personal capability assessment or own occupation test.

The linking rule applies to full-time or part-time work for which you are paid or you do in expectation of payment and to government training programmes for which a training allowance is paid. There is also a 2-year linking rule covering these training programmes as well as some non-government programmes (see Chapter 16(5)).

Welfare to work beneficiary – If you meet the above conditions, you are classed as a 'welfare to work beneficiary' for a period of 52 weeks starting from the day after your last day of incapacity. You should receive a letter confirming this and giving you the date the 52-week protection ends. The protection applies to any number of repeat claims made during the 52-week linking period, so you could try a number of different jobs, or move from training into work, and your benefit is protected each time you claim. For income-based JSA claimants to benefit from this linking rule, it must be the claimant's partner who is the welfare to work beneficiary.

You are not a welfare to work beneficiary if your last period of incapacity ended because you were found (or treated as) capable of work (and do not successfully appeal the decision).

If you are off work or stop work within your 52-week linking period, get a medical certificate from your doctor and put in a claim for the benefit or benefits that you were getting before. The linking rule means that:

- Any two or more periods of incapacity for work which are no more than 52 weeks apart are linked and count as one period of incapacity.
- IB is paid at the same rate as before, including any age addition and dependants' additions. You won't need to re-satisfy the national insurance (NI) contribution conditions. If you had been getting no-contribution IB for those incapable of work since before age 20 (or 25), you go back on without re-serving the qualifying period (see Chapter 14(3)).
- You can re-claim SDA and it is paid at the same rate as before, including the age addition and any dependants' additions (see Box E.9, Chapter 14).
- The disability premium is included in your IS, HB or CTB immediately without serving the qualifying period again – if you were part-way through the qualifying period you pick up where you left off (Chapter 4(5)).
- You will normally be accepted as incapable of work for the first 13 weeks of your claim provided you send in medical certificates from your doctor (Chapter 11(4)).
- Mortgage interest or other housing costs can be included in your IS immediately without serving the waiting period again – if you were part-way through the waiting period, you pick up where you left off (Chapter 4(14)). You also keep transitional protection for the amount of housing costs included – ie against the £100,000 ceiling on loans and for the 'add back' (Chapter 4(13)).
- If you were getting an age addition with your IB within 52 weeks of reaching state pension age, this is paid with your state pension (Chapter 42(4)).

In general, your benefits are only protected if you become incapable of work again. However, for HB, you also regain transitional protection from rent restrictions (Chapter 7(9)) if you claim within the 52-week linking period for another reason – eg your wages decrease.

If neither linking rule applies

If you are not a welfare-to-work beneficiary and it has been 8 weeks and one day, or longer, since the end of your last incapacity-based award, and you fall sick again, you may get SSP from your employer if you are still employed. If you can't get SSP or are self-employed, you may get lower rate short-term IB but you must usually have enough NI contributions. The 2-year WTC disability element linking rule might help you go back to your IB or SDA (see below).

You may be eligible for IS to top up a low income. You are not excluded from IS while you are off work sick even if you normally work 16 hours or more a week.

Other linking rules

Check first to see if the 52-week linking rule might apply. Often this will give you a better deal.

2-year training linking rule – You may re-qualify for the higher rate short-term or long-term IB or SDA if you had a break in your claim of less than 2 years while you were participating in certain types of training courses (see Chapter 16(5)).

2-year WTC disability element linking rule – If you are receiving tax credits (apart from just the family element of child tax credit) and the WTC disability element has been included in your tax credit calculation when you stop work, you may be able to go back onto your IB or SDA under the

WTC disability element 2-year linking rule (see Chapter 18(8)).

No-contribution IB – You may be able to re-claim IB on the same no-contribution basis as before (ie where the original claim was before age 20 or 25 in some cases) if your earnings were below a certain limit. See Chapter 14(10).

IS/JSA housing costs – You will not have to serve a further waiting period before housing costs are included in your benefit, provided you re-claim within 52 weeks (12 weeks for some people) of the end of your earlier claim. See Chapter 4(14).

Housing benefit – If you have been claiming HB continuously since before 1996, you are exempt from the rent restrictions described in Chapter 7(9). To keep the exemption, any break in claim must be no longer than 4 weeks.

16 Employment and training

1. Introduction

In this chapter we look at some of the services and programmes designed to help you get and remain in work.

2. Jobcentre Plus

Jobcentre Plus was created by merging the Employment Service, which ran Jobcentres, with most of what was the Benefits Agency, which ran social security offices. All existing Jobcentres will be upgraded to provide a full Jobcentre Plus service by April 2006.

One of the major changes under Jobcentre Plus is that everyone of working age who is claiming benefits will have a personal adviser who will deal with benefits claims and provide information on work and training opportunities. Consequently, if you are between 16 and 60 and claiming income support (IS), incapacity benefit (IB), carer's allowance, severe disablement allowance (SDA) or any bereavement benefit you will be required to have a work-focused interview. Your partner can also be required to have a work-focused interview if your benefit is paid at a higher rate because they are included in the claim. These requirements, however, can be waived or deferred if it would not be of assistance to you (or your partner) or it would not be appropriate in the circumstances of your case.

Disability employment advisers (DEAs) can be contacted through your local Jobcentre or Jobcentre Plus office and can provide employment assessment, job-seeking advice and referral to training courses, as well as advice and information on Jobcentre Plus programmes for people with disabilities. The personal adviser and DEA roles are complementary. If you wish to be referred to a DEA, who may have more specialist experience, you should make this clear and your request should not be refused. The DEA should be able to provide you with information about all the schemes listed below.

Jobcentre Plus administers the welfare-to-work strategy, a package of schemes and rules designed to encourage claimants to find jobs. Some schemes pay allowances or provide services to make finding work easier, others seek to compel you to find work by cutting or removing your benefit if you do not take particular actions recommended by your personal adviser.

The welfare-to-work strategy is evolving and has pilot schemes in different parts of the country. Depending on where you live, you may be compelled to take actions or be offered services which do not apply in other areas. We cover the most important pilots in some detail, others we simply make reference to. We will cover any new pilots introduced after publication of this Handbook in the *Disability Rights Bulletin* (see Chapter 61).

Job Introduction Scheme

The Job Introduction Scheme (JIS) is for disabled people who, in the opinion of the DEA, are suited to a job but need to demonstrate their capabilities to a new employer. The scheme pays £75 a week to your employer during your initial period of employment – usually 6 weeks, but in some cases 13. The employment must be expected to last at least 26 weeks including the JIS period.

Access to Work

Access to Work provides practical advice to help overcome work-related obstacles resulting from disability and also grants towards extra employment costs, including:

- special aids or equipment for employment;
- adaptations to premises and existing equipment;
- help with travel to work if public transport can't be used;
- a support worker (eg a reader) to provide help in the workplace;
- a communicator for support at job interviews.

The programme is flexible to meet your needs in your job. Contact your local Jobcentre or Jobcentre Plus office and ask to talk to an Access to Work adviser or a DEA for advice and an application form.

Who can get help? – You may be eligible if you are unemployed, employed or self-employed, and you are disabled. Access to Work defines 'disability' as in the Disability Discrimination Act (see Chapter 55) but extends it to include disabilities that are only apparent in the workplace. The amount of support depends on what is needed because of your disability, and is granted for a maximum 3-year period, after which you can re-apply. If you have been in a job for less than 6 weeks or are about to start work, Access to Work will cover up to 100% of approved costs. If you have been in your job for 6 weeks or more when you first apply for help, Access to Work will cover up to 80% of approved costs above a threshold of £300 and below a ceiling of £10,000, and all costs above £10,000 over the 3-year period. All the extra costs of travel to work, support workers and communicator support for job interviews, and all the extra costs if you are self-employed, are met under Access to Work.

Work Preparation

Jobcentre Plus can provide individually tailored programmes of Work Preparation to help you get work by addressing employment-related needs arising from your disability and which prevent you taking up employment or training that would otherwise be suitable. Work Preparation can also help if you are at risk of losing your job because of your disability.

You may stay on your existing benefits or claim an allowance and travel expenses. The DEA can advise you on your best option. If you choose to claim the allowance, at the end of the programme you can re-claim your IB or SDA and regain your former rate of benefit without having to serve any qualifying periods, provided you are still incapable of work (see 'The 2-year linking rule', under 5 below).

Workstep

Workstep provides tailored support for disabled people who face more complex barriers to finding and keeping a job but who can work effectively with the right support. It enables eligible disabled people to realise their full potential to work in a commercial environment, giving them, wherever possible, an opportunity to progress into unsupported employment.

Workstep offers a variety of different job opportunities with a range of organisations from small high street shops to national companies. Some supported employees are also employed in supported factories and businesses. You will get the same wage as colleagues doing the same or similar work. You can agree a development plan with your employer to ensure you have the necessary training and support to learn to do your job and to develop to the best of your ability.

A DEA can explain about the entry conditions and discuss whether Workstep would be the right choice for you.

Adviser Discretion Fund

This fund allows Jobcentre Plus personal advisers to remove some small barriers that prevent people getting employment – eg help with clothing, work equipment, travel and transport issues. There is no automatic entitlement and decisions on use of the fund are made by the personal adviser. Personal advisers in Pathways to Work areas (see Box F.2) can access the fund at any time; elsewhere, you cannot have money from the fund until you have been on benefit for at least 13 weeks.

Pathways to Work for lone parents

Two schemes are being tested in certain pilot areas for lone parents looking to move into work: work search premium and in-work credit. In the pilot areas, lone parents should be able to access improved childcare and will be encouraged to participate in the New Deal for Lone Parents (see 4 below). In some of these areas they will also be required to attend 4 work-focused interviews a year if their youngest child is aged at least 12 (see Box R.1, Chapter 57).

Work search premium – The work search premium provides £20 a week on top of existing benefits to lone parents who have been on IS for more than a year, are on the New Deal for Lone Parents and who are actively searching for a job. It is ignored for means-tested benefits and tax credits.

In-work credit – This is paid to lone parents who have been on IS or jobseeker's allowance for over a year and have started working at least 16 hours a week. It is £40 a week for the first year of the new job and is ignored for means-tested benefits and tax credits. In-work credit is being extended to couples in London with dependent children.

3. Training

There are a variety of government training programmes; we outline two here. You can find out about other options from your local Jobcentre or Jobcentre Plus office or, if you are under age 20, from the Careers Service or the Connexions Service.

Support for disabled people – A range of help is available to enable you to take part in a government training programme, including individually tailored programmes, aids, equipment, adaptations to premises and equipment, a readership service for blind people, and an interpreter service for deaf people. Contact your local Careers Service or Connexions Service (for young people) or a disability employment adviser.

Minimum wage – Trainees aged 18 and over who receive wages from the employer must be paid at least the national minimum wage. The trade union in your workplace can advise you on which rate applies, or you can call the national minimum wage enquiry line: 0845 600 0678.

Work-Based Learning for Young People

Recruitment to Work-Based Learning (WBL), or Skillseekers in Scotland, is usually through the Connexions Service/ Careers Service. The training provided by it should lead to a recognised vocational qualification.

Most 16- and 17-year-olds are excluded from jobseeker's allowance (JSA) in the expectation that they will take up a 'guaranteed' place in WBL. You may also be offered a place in WBL if you are aged 18-24 and disability or a

F.2 Pathways to Work pilots

Pathways to Work was introduced in 7 Jobcentre Plus districts between October 2003 and April 2004. The districts involved are: Bridgend/Rhonda, Cynon Taff; Renfrewshire, Inverclyde, Argyll and Bute; Derbyshire; East Lancashire; Gateshead and South Teesside; Somerset; and Essex.

Pilots will also operate in the following areas from October 2005: Durham; Tees Valley; Lancashire West; Lanarkshire and East Dumbarton; Staffordshire; Barnsley and Rotherham (to be merged with Doncaster); Manchester (to be merged with Salford and Trafford); Cumbria; Greater Mersey; Liverpool (to be merged with Wirral); Eastern Valleys; Swansea Bay (to be merged with West Wales); Glasgow; and City of Sunderland.

If you live in one of these areas, are aged between 18 and 60, and claim a specified benefit – ie incapacity benefit, severe disablement allowance or income support as a person incapable of work (or while appealing a decision that you are not incapable of work) – then the following rules apply:

Work-focused Interviews – You normally must attend a compulsory work-focused interview (WFI) (see Box R1, Chapter 57) 8 weeks after your claim, then up to 5 further WFIs over the next 6 months. If you are already receiving one of the specified benefits you may need to attend a series of three WFIs. If you do not attend a WFI without good cause, the DWP can sanction you by deducting £11.24 a week from your benefit. If you are exempt from the personal capability assessment (PCA) because you have a serious illness or receive the highest rate care component of disability living allowance you will not have to attend an initial WFI. If your personal adviser decides at the initial WFI that you are only likely to be on benefit for a short time they can exempt you from subsequent WFIs.

Capability report – When you are called in for a medical examination under the PCA (see Chapter 11(8)), the doctor who examines you will also produce a separate 'capability report' (see Box E.3, Chapter 11).

Personal advisers – You will be allocated a personal adviser who will encourage you to draw up a return-to-work action plan and to take up various forms of help which form part of the 'choices' package. These include access to other New Deal programmes (see 4), job grants, Access to Work, Work-Based Learning for Adults, work trials and Workstep (see Box F.1, Chapter 15 for further information on these schemes).

Condition management programmes – Your adviser may refer you to one of these NHS programmes, which are meant to help claimants who have moderate mental health conditions, cardio-respiratory conditions or musculoskeletal conditions to control and cope with those symptoms that most affect their ability to work.

Adviser Discretionary Funds – Your adviser will have immediate access to up to £300 for items that facilitate a return to work (see Chapter 16(2)).

Job preparation premium – If you have agreed to and follow a return to work action plan, you can be paid a job preparation premium of up £20 a week for up to 26 weeks.

Return to work credit – If you take a job of at least 16 hours a week after claiming a Pathways to Work specified benefit for 13 weeks, you can be paid a 'return to work credit' for up to 52 weeks. Your earnings (but not any other income) must be less than £15,000 and your job should be expected to last at least 5 weeks. The £40 a week credit will be disregarded for tax credits and means-tested benefits.

health condition meant that you could not take part earlier or were unable to complete a course. In Scotland the rules are different: contact your local Careers Service for further information.

In WBL, you may be a trainee or you may have employed status. Being an employee could give you far more legal rights than a trainee, and you will receive wages instead of the basic training allowance.

Training allowance – For those who are not employed while training, the minimum training allowance is £40 a week. In many cases the levels are higher because of employer contributions.

Benefits – A trainee can claim income support (IS) to top up their training allowance. The whole £40 is taken into account as income. In practice, a 16- or 17-year-old is only likely to qualify for an IS top-up if they are entitled to a premium or if they are entitled to the higher rate of IS personal allowance (see Chapter 4(3)).

Once you leave the programme you are no longer eligible for IS, unless you are covered by one of the other situations listed in Box B.1, Chapter 3. You should claim JSA instead. If you don't complete the programme and you don't have 'good cause' for leaving, your JSA may be paid at a reduced rate.

Young person's bridging allowance – If you cannot get IS or JSA and are registered with the Connexions Service/ Careers Service for a place on a WBL programme, and you are disabled, you can get a bridging allowance of £15 a week paid for Monday to Friday from the end of the child benefit extension period up to your 18th birthday. Claim on form BA1, available from the Connexions Service/Careers Service office. In all other cases, the bridging allowance is for a maximum of 40 days (8 weeks) within a 52-week period and you can apply only if you are between jobs or training programmes.

Work-Based Learning for Adults

Work-Based Learning for Adults (WBLA) in England and Wales (Training for Work in Scotland) is a voluntary programme available through Jobcentre Plus and delivered by nationally approved training organisations. WBLA provides work experience and, where relevant, allows you to obtain work-related qualifications. As well as local opportunities, there is a range of residential courses leading to nationally recognised qualifications. If you want to become self-employed, you can get advice and support and the chance to test trade while still receiving benefit.

Generally, to qualify for a training programme you need to be aged 25 or over and unemployed continuously for 26 weeks (including time in receipt of incapacity-related benefits). People with disabilities and certain others may qualify before 26 weeks. If you are aged 18-24 and have a disability and are receiving benefits other than JSA you may be eligible to join WBLA. However, access to the programme is at the discretion of the Jobcentre Plus adviser.

Benefits – You receive a training allowance equivalent to your weekly benefit plus a £10 training premium. The premium does not affect the calculation of entitlement to working tax credit, child tax credit, housing benefit or council tax benefit.

As WBLA is a voluntary programme, JSA is not affected automatically if you refuse a place or leave a programme early. If, however, a jobseeker's direction has been used, JSA payments can be sanctioned for failure to comply (see Chapter 17(9)).

4. New Deal

There are 6 main New Deal programmes. The detailed rules of these are beyond the scope of this Handbook, but basic information is available at www.newdeal.gov.uk.

New Deal for Young People and New Deal 25 Plus are compulsory if you are claiming jobseeker's allowance (JSA), and your benefit will be suspended under a sanction if you do not comply (see Chapter 17(9)). All other New Deals are voluntary.

Early entry – Certain people claiming JSA, including anyone with a disability, can choose early entry to the New Deal for Young People or New Deal 25 Plus. But once you enter you cannot opt out without risk of being sanctioned.

New Deal for Young People

If you are aged between 18 and 24 and have been claiming JSA continuously for 6 months you will be required to enter the New Deal Gateway, a period of up to 4 months of help from a personal adviser to find a job. If you don't find a job in this period, you then have 4 options, lasting between 13 and 52 weeks, designed to help you get into work. Depending which option you are on, you could be paid a wage by an employer (when you will be an employed earner for benefit purposes) or a New Deal allowance (plus a token 10p a week income-based JSA to give you access to passported benefits):

- **employment option** – up to 26 weeks of either subsidised employment or self-employment;
- **voluntary sector option** – up to 13 weeks' work with a voluntary organisation;
- **environment task force option** – up to 13 weeks' work on an environmental project;
- **full-time education and training option** – up to one year, leading to N/SVQ Level 2 or equivalent qualification and including work experience.

If you can't attend your chosen option because of your disability, this will be accepted as good cause for leaving. You will be expected to take up an alternative.

If you have not found a job after your option period, you will need to re-claim JSA and enter the follow-through stage of the New Deal programme with further job search help.

New Deal 25 Plus

If you are aged 25 or over and have been claiming JSA for 18 months continuously or claiming JSA for 18 out of the previous 21 months, you automatically enter the New Deal Gateway. For up to 4 months, you meet regularly with a personal adviser who provides help to get a job.

If you do not find a job during this period, you are referred to the 'intensive activity period' lasting between 13 and 26 weeks, which may include work placements, basic skills training or support for self-employment, combined with an intensive job search. You can choose whether to participate if you are aged 50 or over, but for others this is compulsory and your JSA is sanctioned if you do not participate (see Chapter 17(9)).

If you have still not found a job you enter the follow-through period, which is 6 weeks of intensive job matching and weekly interviews.

Benefits – You stay on JSA except during the intensive activity period, when you move onto a training allowance equivalent to your benefit entitlement plus a top-up payment.

New Deal for Partners

If your partner has been claiming JSA for you for 6 months, you will receive a letter inviting you to an interview with an adviser at the Jobcentre or Jobcentre Plus office for advice on work and training opportunities.

This New Deal is not compulsory. However, if you are a member of a 'joint-claim couple' (see Chapter 17(2)) both of you are expected to sign on for JSA and meet the other conditions of benefit including attending the appropriate New Deal.

New Deal for Disabled People

New Deal for Disabled People (NDDP) is voluntary and offers support to people on disability and incapacity benefits who want to work. It is delivered through a network of job brokers who agree with you the most appropriate route into employment. Job brokers will work closely with providers of training and other services to meet your specific needs, and with employers to support you during your first 6 months of employment.

To find out more, and who your local job brokers are, ring the NDDP Helpline (0800 137177, Textphone 0800 435550), go to www.newdeal.gov.uk/nddp or visit your local Jobcentre or Jobcentre Plus office.

New Deal for Lone Parents (NDLP)
NDLP is a voluntary programme. However, if you are a lone parent on income support (IS) you will be required to attend compulsory work-focused interviews at regular intervals to discuss work and training opportunities. All lone parents participating in NDLP may be eligible to apply for help with training and exam fees, costs for books and equipment, and help with travel and registered childcare costs to attend NDLP/employer interviews or approved activities. NDLP participants are also eligible for a payment to cover childcare costs in the week immediately before starting work (of at least 8 hours a week) under the Childcare Assist scheme. Participants in receipt of IS and other qualifying allowances or benefits may be eligible for a £15 a week premium while on approved training.

New Deal for over-50s
You are eligible if you are aged 50 or over and you (or your partner) have been claiming IS, JSA, IB or SDA for at least 6 months, or you move onto one of these benefits after 6 months or more on carer's allowance or bereavement allowances. It is entirely voluntary. A personal adviser at the Jobcentre or Jobcentre Plus office will help you look for work. For those taking up work (including self-employment), there is a training grant of up to £1,500.

5. Benefits and training allowances

Disability living allowance (DLA) – DLA mobility component is not affected if you get a training allowance. DLA care component is not affected if you are living at home and attending the training programme daily. However, you will not be able to get the care component for the days you stay in a care home in order to attend the programme, nor if your training allowance includes a 'living away from home' allowance. The care component stops after 28 days in such accommodation (see Chapter 20(8)). You can get the care component for any days spent at home.

Although DLA can be paid at the same time as a training allowance, your ability to start a programme may suggest a lessening in your care or mobility needs: so your benefit may be reconsidered (see Chapter 20).

Disability premium – If you were getting a disability premium before beginning the programme, it won't be withdrawn even though you may now no longer be receiving the qualifying benefit. At the end of the programme, you will only continue to receive the disability premium if you satisfy the entitlement criteria (see Chapter 4(5)).

Incapacity benefit (IB) and severe disablement allowance SDA – A day in receipt of a state training allowance (other than just travel and meals expenses) cannot, in law, count as a day of incapacity for work. This means that you will cease to be entitled to IB or SDA on starting your programme (but see 2 above if you are going on a Work Preparation course). At the end of your programme, you may be able to get IB or SDA at the rate you were getting before your course started (see below).

If you do not find a job at the end of your programme, and are capable of work, you can sign on and claim jobseeker's allowance (JSA) – see Chapter 17.

The 2-year linking rule – If you are unable to work because of illness or disability at the end of your programme, there is a 2-year linking rule which enables you to go back on the same level of IB or SDA (with annual increases).

To qualify you must have been entitled to higher rate short-term or long-term IB or SDA for at least one day during the 8 weeks before your programme started, and be accepted as incapable of work (see Chapter 11) on the day your programme stops, and this day must be within 2 years of the last day you were entitled to benefit.

The 2-year rule applies to certain Jobcentre Plus programmes including Work Preparation, New Deal, and Work-Based Learning. But it also applies to non-government courses where the primary purpose is the teaching of occupational or vocational skills and you attend for 16 or more hours a week.

Non-government training courses
Note that a non-government training course is different from a 'state training scheme'. If your course is funded by the European Social Fund, seek advice.

You may be paid an allowance, but it is treated in a different way from a state training allowance. It will be taken into account in full as income for income support (IS) and other means-tested benefits unless some or all of it can be disregarded under the normal rules.

You may be regarded as a student for benefit purposes. Most full-time students are excluded from IS and JSA (see Chapter 38). The rules can be quite complicated, so seek advice on how your benefit rights might be affected.

There are no specific rules preventing someone studying or training on non-government courses and receiving IB or SDA. However, the assessment of your ability to undertake the activities in the personal capability assessment will take into account how you manage on your course. Starting a course may lead to your incapacity for work being reassessed if the DWP thinks there is some doubt about your incapacity for work.

17 Jobseeker's allowance

In this chapter we look at:

A. GENERAL CONDITIONS

1. What is jobseeker's allowance?

Jobseeker's allowance (JSA) is for people who are unemployed or working less than 16 hours a week, and who are available, and actively looking, for work.

People who don't have to sign on for work (eg those who are incapable of work or lone parents) should claim income support instead (see Box B.1, Chapter 3).

There are two forms of JSA.

- ❑ **Contribution-based JSA:** this is a personal flat-rate allowance with entitlement based on your national insurance contribution record; it is payable for up to 6 months (182 days) and is taxable.
- ❑ **Income-based JSA:** this is means tested and taxable, payable if you have no income or a low income, no more than £8,000 savings (£12,000 if you or your partner are aged 60 or over) and your partner (if you have one) is not working or is working less than 24 hours a week. It can top up contribution-based JSA.

One set of general labour market conditions of entitlement applies to JSA as a whole, so you must sign on as available for work, take active steps to look for work, and have a current jobseeker's agreement.

2. The basic rules

You are entitled to jobseeker's allowance if you:

- are available for work (see 4); *and*
- are actively seeking work (see 5); *and*
- have entered into a jobseeker's agreement which remains in force – see 6; *and*
- are not working 16 hours or more a week (see 7); *and*
- are capable of work (see 8); *and*
- are under state pension age (60 for women, 65 for men); *and*
- are not in full-time education – see Chapter 38(4) for exceptions; *and*
- are in Great Britain (GB) – see Chapter 50(6) for exceptions; *and*
- for contribution-based JSA, pass the contribution-based conditions (see 11); *or*
- for income-based JSA, pass the income-based conditions (see 15).

If you satisfy the conditions for both, you may be entitled to contribution-based JSA topped up with income-based JSA (see 20).

Couples

For contribution-based JSA, each member of a couple can claim separately and you each qualify for JSA based on your own contribution record. For income-based JSA, unless you are in a joint-claim couple (see below), one of you must claim for the both of you and that person is the one who must sign on as available for work and meet all the other conditions for benefit.

Joint-claim couples – Some couples must make a joint claim for income-based JSA. At present, these rules only apply to couples without dependent children, where one or both of the couple is aged at least 18 and was born after 28.10.57. If you are one of a joint-claim couple, you and your partner must both sign on as available for work and meet all the other basic rules above, unless one of you is 'excused'. You and your partner decide which one of you gets paid JSA.

In general, if one of you does not meet all the JSA conditions, JSA is paid at the rate for a single person. But if one of you would be eligible for income support (IS) instead (see Box B.1, Chapter 3), that person is excused from meeting the JSA conditions. In this case, you have a choice whether to claim IS or JSA. The person eligible can either claim IS for both of you (and the other can sign on voluntarily for national insurance credits), or you claim JSA jointly but with only one of you needing to meet the JSA conditions to get paid the full couple rate. Note that if the only way you can qualify for a disability premium is through being incapable of work (rather than having a qualifying benefit or being registered blind) you are better off claiming IS.

There are a few further exceptions in which only one member of the couple is expected to meet JSA conditions, including, in brief, where one of you is a full-time student, is or has been pregnant (for the same period that maternity allowance is payable), is not habitually resident in GB, or is working at least 16 hours but less than 24 hours a week.

3. How do you claim?

On the first day you become unemployed, you should make a claim for JSA. Don't delay, otherwise you will lose benefit unless you can show you have 'special reasons' for the delay (see Chapter 57(3)).

JSA is administered by Jobcentre Plus. By April 2006, all existing Jobcentres will be upgraded to provide a full Jobcentre Plus service, with the same offices administering all benefits for people of working age. Until then some offices will still be operated as old-style Jobcentres. Whichever type of Jobcentre you claim at, you should first register your claim by phone (although if you are unable to use a phone for any reason you can still visit the Jobcentre).

At Jobcentres – If your claim is made to an old-style Jobcentre, an appointment for a New Jobseeker Interview will then be made. You'll be issued with a JSA claim-pack to complete at home. The interview should take place within 5 days (although under the rapid reclaim process, if you are re-claiming JSA after a break of no more than 12 weeks, you should be interviewed the same or the next day).

The first part of the pack (form JSA1) asks for details to check whether you satisfy the contribution-based and income-based conditions. This form has to be completed by the time of your interview for the claim to be backdated to the time you first contacted the Jobcentre about the claim. If you do not complete it properly, your benefit may only date from when you do so (see Chapter 57(2)). If you need help to complete the form, tell the Jobcentre.

The second part of the pack (form ES2 *Helping You Back To Work*) contains detailed questions about the type of work you are looking for, the hours you are available for work, the pay you will accept, the distance you are prepared to travel to work and the types of steps you will take to find work or improve your prospects. You should take care when filling in this form, because if you put 'unreasonable' restrictions on what you are prepared to accept your answers could lead to doubts about whether you are 'available for work' (see 4 and 5 below).

At the New Jobseeker Interview, the adviser will check that you meet the 'labour market conditions' for benefit, ie whether you are capable of and available for work and what you intend to do to look for work. You will also be asked to discuss, agree and sign the jobseeker's agreement (see 6). This is compulsory and details the type of work you are looking for and what you are expected to do to find work or improve your prospects, as well as any restrictions on your availability for work that are agreed. It will be based on the answers you've given in the ES2 form. Once it has been established that you meet the basic labour market conditions for benefit, your claim will be assessed for the specific contribution-based or income-based conditions of entitlement to benefit. If your health or disability means that you need specialist advice and help, you can be referred to a disability employment adviser.

At Jobcentre Plus offices – If you are in an area with new Jobcentre Plus offices, you will need to ring your local claim number – an 0845 number, usually charged at local rate. You can get the number from your local office, the website (www.jobcentreplus.gov.uk) or the phone book, under Jobcentre Plus.

During your initial telephone call some basic details will be taken from you, you will be told if you appear to have an entitlement to JSA (or any other benefit), and a time arranged when you will be phoned back. During this second call Jobcentre Plus will complete your claim-form while collecting information from you and then book an appointment for you to see a financial assessor and a personal adviser. The financial assessor will be discussing your benefit entitlement and the personal adviser will be discussing your employment options and whether you meet the labour market conditions. These appointments will take place consecutively at your local Jobcentre Plus office.

Problems? – If there is a delay in your claim being decided, or benefit is suspended or disallowed, or a sanction is applied, or you are told you can't claim, seek advice. You should continue to sign on if possible while you are challenging any decision. You might be able to get hardship payments in the meantime (see 10). If you are not happy with the decision about your entitlement to benefit you can ask for a revision, or appeal to an appeal tribunal, within one month. Outside of this time limit, in limited circumstances, you may be able to request a late revision or a supersession. See Chapter 58.

During your claim – JSA is paid every 2 weeks in arrears, usually directly into a bank or building society account (see Chapter 57(5)).

You are normally expected to sign on at the Jobcentre every fortnight. You can be asked to sign on more frequently, even daily, if, for example, you are suspected of working without declaring it, or as a way of keeping in contact with you if you are homeless. You have to sign weekly for 6 weeks once you have been claiming JSA for 13 weeks. The Government is testing new patterns of signing on and telephone contact with new claimants in pilot areas between January and July 2005.

If you miss your signing-on day, your benefit entitlement will stop, unless you show within 5 working days that you have had 'good cause' for failing to sign on (eg you had a doctor's appointment or job interview). If you are in one of the circumstances in which you are 'treated' as though you are available for work, you will have 'good cause' for not signing on (see 5, under 'Absences, emergencies and other circumstances').

Each time you sign on you will be asked to explain what you have done to look for work or improve your prospects of finding work. You should keep a record of your jobseeking steps so you can demonstrate that you meet the 'actively seeking work' conditions (see 5).

Periodically there will be more in-depth interviews where, in particular, the jobseeker's agreement will be reviewed and updated if necessary. This is likely to happen after 13 weeks and then every 6 months, but you can be called in for an in-depth interview at any time. If you do not attend, your benefit entitlement will stop, unless you can show within 5 working days that you had 'good cause'.

Jobseeker's direction – At an in-depth interview, the employment officer may issue a 'jobseeker's direction' requiring you to undertake a specific activity related to improving your job prospects. For example, you could be directed to attend a course or to take steps to improve the way you present yourself to employers. If you don't comply with a jobseeker's direction, unless you have good cause, a sanction is applied stopping your benefit for 2 weeks, or 4 weeks if this is the second time a sanction has been applied (see 9).

New Deal – If you are aged 18-24 and have been claiming JSA for 6 months, or you are aged 25 or over and have been claiming JSA for 18 months, you will be referred to the New Deal (see Chapter 16(4)). Once on the New Deal, failure to comply with the requirements can result in your benefit being sanctioned.

4. Available for work

In general, you must be willing and able to take up immediately any paid employment of at least 40 hours a week (see below for restrictions you are allowed to make).

You are not regarded as available for work and therefore not entitled to JSA if you:

- get maternity allowance or statutory maternity pay; *or*
- are on paternity or adoption leave; *or*
- are a full-time student – there are limited exceptions (see Chapter 38(4)); *or*
- are a prisoner on temporary release.

At the start of your claim – For a 'permitted period' of up to 13 weeks from the beginning of your claim, you may be allowed to restrict your availability and jobseeking to your usual occupation and/or to your usual pay. After this you must be prepared to widen your availability for work and job searching activity. You are still allowed to restrict your availability under the rules described below, as long as (in most cases) you have reasonable prospects of securing employment.

Can you restrict the hours you are available for work?

The 40 hours rule – Generally, you must be prepared to take up employment of at least 40 hours a week and less than 40 hours if required to do so. In most cases, you don't have to accept a job of less than 24 hours a week (see 'What is good cause' in 9 below).

JSA is a 7-day benefit, so you must fulfil the conditions of entitlement on each day of the week. This does not mean you must be prepared to work 7 days a week. You can restrict the times in the week you are available to take up work (eg Monday to Saturday, 9am to 6pm) provided your 'pattern of availability' would give you 'reasonable prospects of employment' (see below), your job prospects are not considerably less than they would be if you were available at all times, and your available hours are at least 40 a week. Under the rules described below, you can specify fewer than 40 hours a week if that is reasonable given your disability, or you are a carer or on short-time working.

Carers – If you care for a child or an elderly person or someone *'whose physical or mental condition requires [him or her] to be cared for'* who is a 'close relative' or a member of your household, you may restrict the hours you are available for work to less than 40 hours, but not less than 16 hours a week. You must be available for as many hours, and at the times that your caring responsibilities allow, taking into account the times you spend caring, whether the caring is shared, and the age and physical and mental condition of the person you care for. You must also show you have 'reasonable prospects of securing employment' (see below). A 'close relative' means a partner, parent, parent-in-law, step-parent, son, daughter, son/daughter-in-law, stepson/daughter, grandparent, grandchild, brother or sister, or the partner of any of those.

If you care for a disabled person, or you are a lone parent you may be eligible for income support (IS) instead of JSA (see Box B.1, Chapter 3). For IS, there is no requirement to look for or take up work, although if you live in an area covered by Jobcentre Plus or are a lone parent you may have to attend a 'work-focused' interview (see Box R.1, Chapter 57). However, if you have income or capital you may be better off on contribution-based JSA until it runs out. Also, for carers who don't get carer's allowance, you may need to sign on in order to protect your national insurance contribution record.

Laid off or short-time working – For the first 13 weeks you are treated as available for work provided you are available to take on casual employment to top up any hours you actually work to at least 40 hours a week, and you are prepared to resume immediately the work you were laid off from, or return full time to the job in which you are being kept on short time. After 13 weeks, this concession no longer applies, so if you want to continue to restrict the hours you are available for work you will have to show you have reasonable prospects of employment.

Can you put any other restrictions on the type of work you'll accept?
Provided you can show you have 'reasonable prospects of securing employment' (see below), you can restrict:
- the nature of the employment (eg due to sincerely held religious or conscientious objections);
- the terms and conditions of employment;
- the rate of pay – but only for the first 6 months of your claim (after 6 months you can't insist on a rate of pay higher than the relevant national minimum wage);
- the localities you will work in – generally you are expected to be prepared to travel for up to one-and-a-half hours both to and from work, but you may restrict this to one hour for the first 13 weeks of your claim.

Disability-related restrictions – You can restrict your availability in any way (eg pay, hours, travel time, type of work), providing the restrictions are reasonable given your physical or mental condition. In this case, it is not relevant whether the restrictions affect your employment prospects, providing you do not put other non-disability-related restrictions on your availability as well. If you do, you will have to show you have reasonable employment prospects given all the restrictions. If you restrict the rate of pay you are prepared to accept, this is not subject to the general 6-month limit, but applies for as long as the restriction is reasonable given your physical or mental condition. If you refuse a job offer where the hours of work or other conditions of the job are beyond your agreed restrictions, you won't generally be sanctioned for doing so (see 9).

Reasonable prospects of employment
If you put any restrictions on your availability, unless these are solely disability-related, you must show you have reasonable prospects of securing employment. The decision maker must consider all the evidence and in particular:
- your skills, qualifications and experience;
- the type and number of vacancies within daily travelling distance;
- how long you have been unemployed;
- your job applications and their outcome; *and*
- if the restrictions are on the nature of the work, whether you are prepared to move home to take up work.

It is important to consider carefully before you put restrictions on your availability. If you can't show you have reasonable employment prospects, your benefit is disallowed.

Can you delay taking up an offer of employment?
Generally you must be able to take up employment immediately within your pattern of availability. There are exceptions for carers and volunteers. If you are a carer (see above) then you must be able to take up employment given 48 hours' notice. If you are a volunteer you must be able to take up employment given one week's notice and attend any employment opportunity interview given 48 hours' notice.

If you are providing a service (paid or unpaid) you must be able to take up work given 24 hours' notice. If you are employed for less than 16 hours a week, you must be able to take up work immediately after the statutory minimum notice period (rather than any contractual notice) that your employer is entitled to – usually one week.

Absences, emergencies and other circumstances
You may be treated as available for work while any of the following circumstances apply. In each case, you are also treated as actively seeking work for the week if the situation applies to you for at least 3 days in the week.

❑ **Absences from home**
- you are at a work camp – for up to 2 weeks, once in 12 months;
- you are on a Venture Trust programme – for up to 4 weeks, once in 12 months;
- you are on an Open University residential course – for up to one week per course;
- you are absent from Great Britain (GB) to attend a job interview (up to one week); or for a child's medical treatment (up to 8 weeks); or your partner is over 60 or disabled and you are both abroad (up to 4 weeks) – see Chapter 50(6).

❑ **Emergencies**
- you need time to deal with a death or serious illness or funeral of a close relative or close friend; or a domestic emergency affecting you, a close relative or close friend; or the person you have been caring for has died – for up to one week, no more than 4 times in 12 months;
- you are working as a part-time firefighter, or helping to run or launch a lifeboat;
- you are part of a group of people organised to respond to an emergency – eg part of an organised search for a missing person, or after a railway or other accident.

❑ **Other circumstances**
- you are sick for a short while, and treated as capable of work – see 8 below;
- you are a full-time student on an employment-related course and have prior approval from the employment officer – for up to 2 weeks, once in 12 months;
- you are looking after your child while your partner is temporarily absent from the UK – for up to 8 weeks;
- you are temporarily looking after a child because the usual carer is ill, temporarily away from home, or is looking after a member of your family who is ill – for up to 8 weeks;
- you've been discharged from prison – for one week from the date of release.

If you are on holiday in GB, you must still be available for work during your time away (although you might not have to be actively seeking work – see below). You must show that you can be contacted regularly while you are away, and how, and be willing to return at once to start work. Before you go away, send the *Going on holiday within Great Britain* form (ES674) to the Jobcentre or Jobcentre Plus office. If you go abroad on holiday, you are not usually entitled to JSA (see Chapter 50(6)).

5. Actively seeking work

As well as being available for work, you are expected to take such steps, usually at least 3 a week, as you can *'reasonably be expected to have to take'* in order to have the best prospects of getting employment, eg:
- applying for jobs;
- looking for vacancies;
- registering with an employment agency;
- on referral from an employment officer, seeking specialist advice on improving your prospects with regard to your particular needs or disability;
- drawing up a CV or getting a reference;
- drawing up a list of relevant employers and seeking information from them;
- seeking information on an occupation.

Even where you've taken reasonable steps to look for work, they can be disregarded where, by your *'behaviour or appearance [you] otherwise undermined [your] prospects of securing the employment in question'*, or you acted in a violent or abusive way or you spoiled a job application. But it can't be held against you if these were due to circumstances beyond your control (eg because of mental health problems).

Absences, emergencies and other circumstances
In some circumstances for a limited time, you can be treated as actively seeking work. The circumstances in which you are treated as both actively seeking work and available for work are listed in 4 above, under 'Absences, emergencies and other circumstances'. There are other times when you are not expected to take any steps to look for work, although you must still be available to take up work.

If you are absent from home – In any 12-month period, you may be treated as actively seeking work for a maximum of:

- 2 weeks for any reason (eg a holiday) as long as you are away from home for at least one day each week; *or*
- 6 weeks if you are blind: the 6 weeks consists of a maximum of 4 weeks during which you are attending a training course in using a guide dog for at least 3 days a week, and a further 2 weeks for any reason as long as you are away from home for at least one day each week; *or*
- 3 weeks if you are attending an Outward Bound course for at least 3 days a week.

In each case you must give written notice that you intend to stay away from home for at least one day in each week and that you do not intend to actively seek work in that week.

The weeks don't have to be consecutive. You can't use more than one provision in any one 12-month period. For example, if you have had one week away on holiday and then within 12 months you go on an Outward Bound course, you can only have one more week in which you are treated as actively seeking work (ie your second week for any reason).

For the 2-week 'any reason' provision, once you've notified your intention, you'll be treated as actively seeking work. If you change your mind and don't go anywhere you must give written notice withdrawing your intention before the start of the week you were due to be away to make sure you don't use up a week unnecessarily.

Becoming self-employed – You are treated as actively seeking work for up to 8 weeks during which you're taking active steps to establish yourself in self-employment, starting with the week you are accepted on a specified government scheme for assisting people into self-employment.

6. Jobseeker's agreement

A jobseeker's agreement contains a description of the type of work you're looking for, the hours you are available and any 'pattern of availability', the action you're expected to take to look for work and to improve your job prospects, details of any restrictions on your availability for work (see 4) and the dates of any 'permitted period' (see 4). It is a condition of entitlement to JSA that you and the employment officer sign the jobseeker's agreement (joint-claim couples must each sign a jobseeker's agreement).

If you don't accept the proposed agreement, you have the right to ask the employment officer to refer it to a decision maker who should make a decision *'so far as practicable'* within 14 days. In the meantime, you are not entitled to benefit. You may qualify for hardship payments of reduced rate income-based JSA (see 10). The decision maker may decide to backdate the jobseeker's agreement but not necessarily back to your date of claim.

Varying an existing jobseeker's agreement – Either you or the employment officer can propose to vary the agreement. If there is a disagreement, the proposed agreement may be referred to a decision maker as above. Your benefit will continue to be paid while the decision maker is considering a variation. If the agreement is varied, you must sign within 21 days, otherwise the jobseeker's agreement may be terminated and your entitlement to benefit will stop.

7. Working full time or part time

You are excluded from JSA if you are in 'remunerative work'. This means work of (on average) 16 hours a week or more. Work counts if you are paid, or you work 'in expectation of payment'. The rules closely follow the income support (IS) rules and provide for specific circumstances in which work can be ignored or, conversely, in which you can be treated as working even when you're not (see Chapter 3(6)). If you stop work because of a trade dispute at your workplace, you are not eligible to claim JSA; your partner can claim income-based JSA or you can claim IS, but payment will be at a reduced rate.

Partners – For contribution-based JSA it makes no difference to your entitlement whether or not your partner works or how much they earn. For income-based JSA, see 18 below.

8. Capable of work

Generally you only need to state that you are capable of work and that is accepted as sufficient to satisfy the condition of entitlement.

If you are disabled or ill – If you are incapable of work through ill-health (unless it is a short illness – see below) or disability, you are not eligible for JSA, but you may be able to claim incapacity benefit (IB) or income support (IS) instead.

Under the rules for assessing incapacity (see Chapter 11) you may find you are regarded as incapable of work even though you want to sign on, and are willing and able to work. This may apply if, for example, you get disability living allowance highest rate care component, are registered blind, are terminally ill, or you are tetraplegic or paraplegic, or if you were assessed as incapable of work under the personal capability assessment and your condition has not improved. In this case, to be regarded as capable of work and thus eligible for JSA, you must pass an extra condition. You must have worked or been in education or training to prepare for work while you had the same illness or disability and it has not worsened since then, or you must show you have 'a reasonable prospect of getting employment'. Once you have shown that you are eligible for JSA, any restrictions you wish to place on your availability for work because of your health or disability are treated as a separate issue.

Reg 17A, SS (Incapacity for Work)(General) Regs 1995

What if you are ill for a short while? – If you fall ill, you may choose to stay on JSA for up to 2 weeks instead of claiming IB. You need to fill in a form to declare that you are unfit for work and for how long. You may only do this twice in each 'jobseeking period' (ie period of entitlement to JSA – see 14 below). Or if you are entitled to JSA for over a year (ignoring breaks in entitlement of 12 weeks or less) you can only choose this option twice in each year. If you fall ill a third time or you are ill for longer than 2 weeks, you should claim IB or IS instead (see Chapter 11).

If you fall ill within 8 weeks of the end of an entitlement to IB, statutory sick pay, severe disablement allowance (SDA), or IS with a disability premium on incapacity grounds, you cannot stay on JSA. You should re-claim your previous benefit and, in most cases, you'll be entitled to your previous rate of benefit without re-serving any qualifying period (see Chapter 15(12)).

Incapacity cut-offs – If your IB, SDA or IS has been cut off because of a determination that you are capable of work, you may claim JSA instead. If you disagree with the decision to stop your benefit and have appealed then, unless your appeal is successful, for the purposes of JSA the determination that you are capable of work will be conclusive. This does not prevent you making a new claim for IB or IS if your condition gets significantly worse, or if you begin to suffer from a different illness or disability (see Chapter 11(11) and (12)).

Reg 10, D&A Regs; reg 28, SS (Incapacity for Work)(General) Regs 1995

Claiming JSA while you are appealing the decision on incapacity does not prejudice your chances of winning the appeal. However, you may claim IS instead (without signing on) while you are appealing (see Box B.1, Chapter 3). The disadvantages of doing so are that it may be paid at a reduced rate and, if you lose your appeal, you won't be covered by national insurance contribution credits for this period.

If you claim JSA, while there will be no question about your capacity for work, you will be asked about your availability for work and the sort of work you are looking for. The rules allow you to impose any restrictions that are reasonable given your disability (see 4 above). You are not expected to take work that would cause significant harm to your health or that would be excessively stressful. It might be useful to discuss things with a disability employment adviser. Unusually, you may find you fall between IB and JSA if what you say about the restrictions imposed by your health and disabilities is not regarded as reasonable. Seek advice if this happens to you.

9. Sanctions

If you don't fulfil the basic labour market conditions to be available for work and actively seeking work, benefit is disallowed altogether (or paid at a single person's rate if one member of a joint-claim couple fails to meet the conditions and is not excused from doing so – see 2 above).

Even if you do satisfy the basic conditions, in some circumstances your benefit may be sanctioned and payment stopped (although you remain entitled) for a limited period. The period of the sanction normally runs from the beginning of the benefit week following the decision to apply the sanction. If a sanction is applied (or your benefit is disallowed), you may be eligible for hardship payments of reduced rate income-based JSA (see 10). For a joint-claim couple, if one of you is subject to a sanction, JSA is reduced to the rate for a single person, or a lower reduction if you are eligible for hardship payments.

2- or 4-weeks sanction

JSA is not payable for 2 weeks, or 4 weeks if this is the second sanction within 12 months (except that a first New Deal sanction and any sanction under Gateway to Work is always for 2 weeks), in the following circumstances.

- You refuse or fail to carry out a reasonable jobseeker's direction (see 3 above).
- You neglect to avail yourself of a reasonable place on a training scheme or employment programme.
- You refuse or fail to apply for, or take up a place on, a training scheme or employment programme notified to you by an employment officer.
- You give up a place on, or fail to attend, a training scheme or employment programme.
- You lose your place on a training scheme or employment programme through misconduct.

In any case other than misconduct, a sanction will not be applied if you can show you had 'good cause' for your action (see below).

Training schemes and employment programmes – Although these sanctions only apply to certain schemes, such as Gateway to Work or any of the options in the New Deal for Young People, you could also be sanctioned for not attending other schemes if you've been referred under a jobseeker's direction and you don't comply with the direction. If you are aged 25 or over and in full-time education or training under the New Deal provisions, you can be sanctioned if, once you have accepted the course, you do not fulfil the requirements of this option or you leave without good cause or due to misconduct.

'Good cause' – The following circumstances count as good cause (unless you refused or failed to carry out a reasonable 'jobseeker's direction' when the test is the same as for the 26-weeks sanction – see below).

- You could not attend because of your disability or ill-health, or attendance (or continued attendance) would put your health at risk.
- You have caring responsibilities, you could not make alternative arrangements and the person has no 'close relative' (see 4 above) or member of their household available to care for them.
- Travel time would be more than an hour and a half (one hour during the first 13 weeks of your claim) either way or if there is no scheme within this travel time, the travel time would be longer than to the nearest appropriate scheme.
- You had to deal with a domestic emergency.
- You were arranging or attending the funeral of a close friend or relative.
- You did not participate due to a sincerely held religious or conscientious objection.
- You were attending court as a party to the proceedings, a witness or juror.
- You were running or launching a lifeboat, or on duty as a part-time firefighter, or part of a group organised to provide assistance in an emergency.
- For New Deal for Young People options, you were not given prior written notice about the relevant option warning of the actions that could lead to a sanction.
- For full-time education and training under the New Deal 25 Plus, you were within the first 4 weeks, or you left because of a lack of ability or the course was not 'suitable'.

If none of these apply, other reasons can also be considered.

Sanctions for benefits fraud

Sanctions lasting 13 weeks are applied if either you or your partner are convicted of more than one benefit offence within a 3-year period (see Chapter 57(6)). The reduction is 40% of the single person's personal allowance rate for your age group, or 20% if you or any member of your family is pregnant or seriously ill.

26-weeks sanction

JSA is not payable for up to 26 weeks in the following circumstances.

- You lose your job through misconduct.
- You voluntarily leave your job without 'just cause'.
- You refuse or fail to apply for a vacancy or accept a job offer, notified to you by an employment officer, without 'good cause' (see below).
- You do not take up a job opportunity with an employer for whom you worked within the last 12 months, where the terms and conditions of employment are at least as good as before (eg you do not exercise your right to return to work after maternity leave), without 'good cause' (see below).
- You have already been sanctioned twice under the New Deal, and this is the third or subsequent sanction without good cause, each sanction being within 12 months of the previous one.

You will not be sanctioned if you are in a trial period (see below).

Entitlement to contribution-based JSA lasts for a maximum of 26 weeks. Since you continue to be entitled during the period of a sanction you could be left with no entitlement at all if the maximum 26-week sanction is applied. The 26-week maximum period is discretionary and the decision maker must consider all your circumstances, including:

- any physical or mental stress connected with a job you left voluntarily or with a job for a previous employer;
- the rate of pay and hours of work in a job you left voluntarily, if you worked 16 hours or less a week;
- the length of time a job was likely to have lasted, if this would be less than 26 weeks.

You can appeal against the decision (see Chapter 58); a tribunal could reduce the period of sanction. The minimum sanction is one week.

If you lose your job through misconduct – Being dismissed does not necessarily lead to a benefit sanction. When you claim benefit, your ex-employer will be sent a standard form asking whether you were sacked and why. If it looks as though a sanction may be applied, you will be sent a copy of your employer's reply. It is important to comment on this reply in detail. Your ex-employer will also see what you have said and can add further comments. You may also be making a claim of unfair dismissal to an Employment Tribunal. If someone is helping with this (eg your union representative) you should ask them for advice. If a sanction is applied, you can appeal (see Chapter 58).

If you leave your job voluntarily – The decision maker has to show that you left your job voluntarily, but once this is shown you must show you had 'just cause' for leaving if you want to avoid a sanction. 'Just cause' for leaving work is not the same as having a good reason for leaving. Your state of health (or the health of a close relative) may help you show just cause. Generally there must be something in the nature of your job or your domestic circumstances that meant it was no longer reasonable for you to continue working.

It helps if you can show that handing in your notice was the only thing you could do, given all the circumstances, including your attempts to resolve the problems. This may enable you to escape the sanction altogether. You should therefore try and resolve work-related problems (using the firm's grievance procedures if they have them) before handing in your notice. You should also try and look for other work before leaving, or find out if you can be transferred to lighter work. If possible, discuss your personal or domestic difficulties with your employer to see if you can resolve the difficulty without handing in your notice.

You should not normally be sanctioned for agreeing to take voluntary redundancy, as you are not regarded as having left your job voluntarily – but see Chapter 39 if you are considering taking early retirement. Nor should you be sanctioned if you left because your employer paid you less than the national minimum wage, and you had tried unsuccessfully to get them to pay it.

Trial period – There is a trial period of 12 weeks to allow you to try out a new job without risking benefit sanctions if it does not work out. You may not have a benefit sanction applied if you leave work voluntarily at any time from the start of the 5th week to the end of the 12th week in that job. The trial period will only apply if you have been unemployed for the 13 weeks before the employment starts.

What is 'good cause'? – In deciding if you have 'good cause' for failing to carry out a jobseeker's direction, or not applying for or accepting a job notified to you by an employment officer, or not taking up a job opportunity with a previous employer (see above), the decision maker must take all your relevant personal circumstances into account.

You are not expected to accept a job of less than 24 hours a week unless it has been agreed that you may restrict the hours you are available for work to less than 24 hours a week (eg because of a disability or caring responsibilities – see 4 above). In this case, you won't be sanctioned for refusing a job of less than 16 hours a week.

The level of pay (if it's at least the national minimum wage) cannot usually be taken into account in deciding whether you have good cause for refusing a job, even if the pay would not cover your financial commitments or would be less than your benefits. The only exception is where, under the availability for work rules, it has been agreed that you may restrict the level of pay you are prepared to accept (eg if this is reasonable given your disability, or during the 'permitted period' at the start of your claim – see 4). See below if there are high work-related expenses.

You will have good cause if your reason for refusing a job or not carrying out a jobseeker's direction is that you are only looking for work in your usual occupation during your 'permitted period' or that you are not required to be able to take up a job at once – eg you are a carer or a volunteer (see 4). The decision maker must take certain other factors into account when deciding whether you have good cause:

- any personal circumstances which suggest that a particular job or jobseeker's direction might cause significant harm to your health, or subject you to excessive physical or mental stress;
- any responsibility for caring for a 'close relative' (see 4) or someone in your household which might make it unreasonable for you to do a particular job, or carry out a jobseeker's direction;
- travel time to and from work, or to a place mentioned in the jobseeker's direction; but it won't count as good cause if the travel time is normally less than an hour and a half (one hour during the first 13 weeks of your claim) each way unless the time is unreasonable because of your health or caring responsibilities;
- any agreed restrictions on your availability for work (see 4), and differences between the work you are available for given those restrictions and the job requirements;
- any sincerely held religious or conscientious objections to taking the job or carrying out the jobseeker's direction;
- travel expenses and other necessary, exclusively work-related expenses if these are an unreasonably high proportion of the income from the job, or your income while carrying out a jobseeker's direction. However, nothing else to do with your income and outgoings, or your family's, can be taken into account, unless you have been allowed to restrict the level of pay you are prepared to accept because of your disability, or you are still in the 'permitted period' at the start of your claim (see 4), or if the job is paid only by commission or pays below the national minimum wage.

10. Hardship payments

If your benefit is sanctioned, suspended or disallowed, or there is a delay in making a decision on your claim, you may be entitled to reduced-rate hardship payments of income-based JSA. However, payment is not automatic. In most cases you must show that you or your family will suffer hardship unless benefit is paid. Unless you fall into a particular vulnerable group, no benefit will be paid for the first 2 weeks.

The applicable amount is reduced by 40% of the single person's personal allowance. But if you, your partner or your child are seriously ill or pregnant, the reduction is 20%. If your partner is entitled to income support, they can claim it for both of you. It is not subject to any reduction.

You may be entitled to hardship payments if you have no JSA in payment for one of the following reasons.

- ❑ There is a delay in the decision on your claim for JSA, because of a question whether you satisfy the availability, actively seeking work and jobseeker's agreement conditions for benefit.
- ❑ Your benefit has been sanctioned (eg you have left work voluntarily without just cause). During a New Deal sanction of 2, 4 or 26 weeks, you can only get hardship payments if you are in a vulnerable group.
- ❑ Your benefit has been suspended because of a doubt about whether you satisfy the availability, actively seeking work or jobseeker's agreement conditions.
- ❑ If you are not available for work or actively seeking work or don't have a current jobseeker's agreement, you may still get hardship payments, but you must also be in one of the vulnerable groups listed below even after the first 2 weeks. However, qualifying for a disability premium does not count here – you must fall into one of the other groups.

For the first 2 weeks – Hardship payments are not payable for the first 2 weeks unless you or your partner are:

- responsible for a child or young person; *or*

- pregnant; *or*
- a carer looking after someone who gets attendance allowance or disability living allowance middle or highest rate care component (or has claimed but is waiting for a decision), and you cannot continue to care for them unless you receive hardship payments. In this case you need not show hardship would result; *or*
- qualifying for a disability premium; *or*
- suffering from a *'chronic medical condition which results in functional capacity being limited or restricted by physical impairment'* which has lasted, or is likely to last, for at least 26 weeks, and the disabled person's health would probably decline during the first 2 weeks more than that of a healthy person; *or*
- under 18 and fall within one of the groups eligible for JSA while age 16 or 17 (see 19 below); *or*
- under 21 and have recently left local authority care.

In each case, other than the exception for carers, you must satisfy the decision maker that the vulnerable person will suffer hardship unless payments are made.

After 2 weeks – If you don't fit into one of the 'vulnerable' groups above, you are eligible for hardship payments only after the first 2 weeks after the sanction has been applied, or suspension made, etc. You must show that you or your partner will suffer hardship unless payment is made.

What is 'hardship'? – You must fill in an application form and set out your grounds for applying for a hardship payment. In deciding whether or not you will suffer hardship if no payment is made, the decision maker must take into account any resources likely to be available to you and the shortfall between these and the reduced rate of hardship payments. They must also look at whether there is a substantial risk that you will have much less, or lose altogether, essential items such as food, clothing, heating and accommodation. It is also relevant whether a disability premium, or disabled or severely disabled child elements of child tax credit, are payable. But they may also take other factors into account.

B. CONTRIBUTION-BASED JSA

11. Do you qualify?

In order to qualify for contribution-based JSA you must have paid enough national insurance (NI) contributions in the right tax years. This contribution condition is explained in Chapter 12. You must also satisfy the basic rules for JSA set out in 2 above.

Contribution-based JSA is a flat-rate personal benefit and is payable for a maximum of 6 months (182 days). If you don't have enough NI contributions, you may be entitled to income-based JSA instead. You may also be entitled to income-based JSA to top up your benefit (eg if you have a dependent partner or certain housing costs such as a mortgage) – see 15.

12. How much do you get?

Contribution-based JSA	per week
Aged under 18	£33.85
Aged 18-24	£44.50
Aged 25 or over	£56.20

13. Does anything affect what you get?

The amount you get may be affected by earnings, payments at the end of a job, or by an occupational or personal pension. Only your own earnings (and not those of any partner or other family member) are taken into account. Payment is not affected by any other income or savings you may have. If one or more of these sources of money mean you are not paid benefit you will still remain entitled (unless your earnings exceed your 'prescribed amount' – see below). Any day for which you are entitled but not paid will count towards your 182 days of entitlement (see below).

Earnings – Your weekly earnings from employment or self-employment are deducted in full from the amount of benefit due, apart from an earnings disregard of £5 (or £20 if you are working as a part-time firefighter, auxiliary coastguard, lifeboat operator, or a member of any territorial or reserve force). Except for this earnings disregard, the assessment of earnings is essentially the same as for income support (IS) – see Chapter 5(4). On days in any week when your earnings exceed your 'prescribed amount' (which is the amount payable for your age plus your earnings disregard minus one pence) you are not entitled to contribution-based JSA and these days do not count towards your 182 days of entitlement (see 14 below).

Occupational or personal pensions – Income from an occupational or personal pension of over £50 a week is deducted from the amount of benefit due – eg, if your pension is £55 a week, £5 is deducted from your benefit. On days when no contribution-based JSA is payable because the level of your pension reduces it to nil, you still remain entitled. These days count towards your 182 days of entitlement. A one-off lump-sum payment does not affect your benefit.

Other benefits – You cannot get more than one contributory benefit at the same time. Nor can you get IS while claiming contribution-based JSA, although you may be entitled to income-based JSA paid as a top-up. However, if you have a partner they may be entitled to claim IS for you both provided you only get contribution-based JSA. If this applies, you should check whether you will be better off if you claim income-based JSA or if your partner claims IS. For example, if your partner is incapable of work but does not get a qualifying benefit, they must claim IS to qualify for the disability premium (see Chapter 4(5)).

14. How long does contribution-based JSA last?

You cannot usually be paid JSA for the first 3 days of unemployment in any 'jobseeking period' – these are called 'waiting days'. These waiting days do not apply when a decision maker elects to move you to JSA from income support.

Entitlement to benefit lasts for a total of 6 months (182 days). This can be in one spell of unemployment lasting for 6 months, or it could be in more than one spell of unemployment where you make shorter claims for JSA but your entitlement in each of those claims is based on the same two tax years. Once your 182 days are exhausted, you can only re-qualify when you begin a new jobseeking period and your new JSA claim is based on different tax years (at least one of which is a later year). See Chapter 12(3) for details of the tax years on which your claim is based.

Jobseeking period

This is the period when you meet the conditions for JSA or a hardship payment, including time when you are sanctioned. Two jobseeking periods will be linked if your new claim is within 12 weeks of the end of an earlier entitlement to contribution- or income-based JSA, or a benefit paid on the basis of incapacity, or maternity allowance, or (in certain circumstances) carer's allowance, or a training allowance because you were engaged in training, or you were on certain New Deal options. If your new claim is linked to your previous jobseeking period you will not have to wait another 3 waiting days, but you will only be entitled to what remains of your 182 days of contribution-based JSA. See Chapter 12(3).

C. INCOME-BASED JSA

15. Do you qualify?

To qualify for income-based JSA, you must satisfy the basic rules for JSA set out in 2 above. In addition you must satisfy the following income-based rules, which are broadly the same as for income support (IS).

- You must have no income, or your income is below your 'applicable amount' (a set amount that depends on your circumstances) – see 16.
- Your capital must be no more than £8,000 (or £12,000 if you or your partner are aged 60 or over) – see 17.
- If you have a partner they must not be working for 24 hours or more a week (see 18).
- You must be aged 18 or over; or aged 16 or 17 and pass other tests (see 19).
- You must be 'habitually resident' and not subject to immigration control (see Chapter 49(2 and 3)).

Income-based JSA is means tested and taxable. You claim for yourself and your partner. If you are one of a couple, you can choose who should make the claim. But the one who claims must sign on and satisfy all the basic rules. (If you are part of a joint-claim couple, see 2 above.)

Entitlement to income-based JSA gives you access to other benefits and entitlements without going through another means test. So you may also be entitled to housing benefit, council tax benefit, free prescriptions, free dental treatment, and any other benefit to which IS would provide access.

16. If you have any income

If you are one of a couple (married or living together as husband and wife), your partner's income is added to your own. (It is planned that from December 2005 registered same-sex couples will be treated in the same way.) Otherwise only your own income is taken into account. Some types of income and part of any earnings may be ignored or disregarded. The rules for income-based JSA are very much the same as for income support. See Chapter 5 for details of how your resources are assessed.

17. If you have savings or other capital

If you or your partner have capital of over £8,000, or £12,000 if you or your partner are aged 60 or over, you won't be entitled to income-based JSA. If you live in a care home, the capital limit is £16,000 (see Chapter 30(5)).

If your capital is from £3,000.01 to £8,000, it is treated as producing a 'tariff income' – ie, £1 for every £250 or part of £250 that you have in capital above £3,000 is deducted from benefit. If you or your partner are aged 60 or over, tariff income starts at capital above £6,000. If you live in a care home, tariff income starts at capital above £10,000.

Your capital is worked out in the same way as for income support (see Chapter 5). Some types of capital are ignored partly or completely, and other kinds count towards the capital limit.

18. If your partner is working

You are not entitled to income-based JSA if your partner is in 'remunerative work'. This means work of (on average) 24 hours or more a week. Work counts if it is paid or done *'in expectation of payment'*. The rules closely follow the income support rules and provide for specific circumstances in which work can be ignored or conversely in which your partner can be treated as working even when they're not (see Chapter 3(6)). If your partner's work does not exclude you from entitlement, their earnings are taken into account in the assessment of your benefit.

19. If you are aged 16 or 17

If you are aged 16 or 17 you are only entitled to JSA if you are in certain specified groups, such as people estranged from their parents. You must register for work and training with the Careers Service or Connexions Service. You must also satisfy all the basic rules of entitlement (set out in 2 above) including being available to take up work and taking active steps to look for work and training. Provided you haven't been subject to a JSA sanction in the past, you can restrict your availability to work where the employer is providing suitable training – ie you can turn down a job if no such training is offered.

Severe hardship payments – If you don't fit into any of the circumstances outlined below in which JSA can be paid to you while aged 16 or 17, you can be paid JSA on a discretionary basis if you would otherwise suffer severe hardship. The direction to pay JSA will be for a temporary period (usually 8 weeks) and you must satisfy the basic rules of entitlement. Things such as your health, vulnerability, threat of homelessness, training or job prospects should be taken into account. In some situations (eg if you fail to complete a course of training without good cause) the amount you get is reduced for the first 2 weeks by 40% of the personal allowance (or 20% if you are seriously ill or pregnant).

Until age 18 (without time limit) – You are eligible for income-based JSA while aged 16 or 17 if you fall into one of the specified groups of people who are eligible for income support (but you choose to claim JSA instead) – see Box B.1, Chapter 3. You are also eligible if you are one of a couple and are treated as responsible for a child who lives with you, or if you are laid off or on short-time working (up to a maximum of 13 weeks).

If you are not covered by these rules, you may be eligible for a limited period which either ends with the date that child benefit finishes for school leavers, called the 'child benefit extension period', or begins with that date. For details see *Disability Rights Handbook* 26th edition, page 111.

20. How much do you get?

The amount you get is based on your 'applicable amount' and on how much income and capital you have. The rules for calculating your entitlement are broadly the same as for income support (IS). These are explained in detail in Chapters 4 and 5. Your applicable amount is made up of:

- **a personal allowance:** for yourself, or for a couple – see Chapter 4(3); *plus*
- **premiums:** intended to help with extra costs of disability, age and caring responsibilities (not everyone qualifies for a premium) – see Chapter 4(4). If you are aged 60 or over and single, you may claim JSA but not IS; in this situation you will be entitled to a £53.25 pensioner premium; *plus*
- **certain housing costs** (eg mortgage interest) – see Chapter 4(11).

Your income or capital will be assessed and may affect how much of your applicable amount you are entitled to (see Chapter 5).

The first 3 days of your claim are 'waiting days' and you cannot usually be paid for these days, unless your claim is linked to a previous 'jobseeking period' (see 14 above), a decision maker elects to move you to JSA from IS, or you claim within 12 weeks of the end of entitlement to incapacity benefit, IS or carer's allowance.

If you also satisfy the contribution-based conditions – You are paid contribution-based JSA if you satisfy the conditions. Your entitlement to income-based JSA is also calculated and if this amount exceeds the contribution-based JSA the extra amount is paid as a top-up.

G Tax credits

This section of the Handbook looks at:

18 Tax credits

1. What are tax credits?

Child tax credit (CTC) – is a means-tested or income-related payment for people, whether working or not, who are responsible for children. CTC replaced the children's tax credit and the increases for children within working families' tax credit (WFTC) and disabled person's tax credit (DPTC) from April 2003.

CTC also replaces the child allowances within income support (IS) and income-based jobseeker's allowance (JSA), and the increases for child dependants paid with non-means-tested benefits (such as incapacity benefit (IB) or state pension). The intention is that people with children who move between low-paid work and periods when they are unemployed or in receipt of IS will continue to receive a consistent payment for their children.

Working tax credit (WTC) – is a means-tested or income-related payment for those in low-paid work. It replaced WFTC and DPTC from April 2003, but also provides help to people who did not receive WFTC and DPTC, and payments can be made towards certain childcare costs.

See Box G.1 for details of the transitional rules around the introduction of CTC and WTC.

CTC and WTC are tax free and administered by the Inland Revenue.

The amount you get will depend on your income and family circumstances.

Will you be better off going back to work?

Going back to work usually means that some benefits stop (eg IB), some may carry on as normal (eg disability living allowance) and others may continue but at a reduced rate, depending on income – eg housing benefit (HB) and council tax benefit (CTB). Box F.1 in Chapter 15 outlines benefits and other help available when you start work.

To work out whether you might be better off on tax credits, these points may be important.

- ❑ You can earn up to £78 a week from permitted earnings on top of IB or severe disablement allowance (SDA). However, if you get IS, HB or CTB as well, only a maximum of £20 of such earnings can be ignored in those assessments. You might be better off staying on your IB or SDA and doing permitted work. See Chapter 15(3) for details.
- ❑ If you are a homeowner, your IS or income-based JSA may include mortgage interest payments. Tax credits do not pay towards mortgage interest.
- ❑ You keep the full amount of any maintenance payments on top of your tax credits, whereas on IS or income-based JSA you can only keep up to £10 a week of any maintenance paid for children (see Chapter 5(8)).
- ❑ Depending on your level of tax credits, you may be entitled to some of the help available to those on IS, including: free prescriptions and other health benefits (see Chapter 52); free legal help (see Chapter 59(2)); and home repair assistance (see Chapter 28).
- ❑ Tax credits (above the basic CTC family element) may give you access to Sure Start maternity grants and social fund funeral payments (see Chapter 9).
- ❑ IS entitles your children to free school meals, and free milk and vitamins if they are under 5, whereas with tax credits you are only entitled to these if your income is below a certain level.

2. Do you qualify for CTC?

You can get CTC if you meet all the following conditions when you make your claim:

- you are at least 16 years old;
- you, or your partner, are responsible for a child or young person who normally lives with you (see below);
- you satisfy the residence and presence conditions (see Chapter 49);
- your income must be within a set limit, which varies according to your family circumstances (see 9 below).

If you are part of a couple you claim jointly and your claim is called a 'joint claim'. Otherwise you claim as a single person. Your claim will end immediately if you are a couple who separate or if you are a single claimant who becomes part of a couple. Your entitlement will also usually end if you cease to be responsible for any children or young people (see below).

Tax Credits Act 2002, s.3

3. Responsible for a child or young person

A child is someone aged under 16. Once the child reaches 16 they will continue to be treated as a child for tax credit purposes until 1 September following their 16th birthday.

A young person is someone over 16 but under 19 who is in full-time, non-advanced education. Young people continue to count for tax credit purposes for the first 20 weeks after they leave full-time education if they are under the age of 18 and registered for work or training with the Careers Service, Connexions Service, the Department for Education and Skills, or Skillseekers in Scotland. Young people no longer count for tax credit purposes once they start work or training or claim income support, income-based jobseeker's allowance or incapacity benefit in their own right.

Where two or more households make a claim in respect of the same child (eg where the child of separated parents spends time with both) then the two households may agree and jointly elect who will receive CTC for that child. If they cannot agree, the Inland Revenue will decide which parent has the main responsibility for that child.

CTC will not normally be payable in respect of a child who:

- has been placed by a local authority in certain types of accommodation paid for by that local authority;
- has been placed for adoption with you by a local authority which is still paying towards their costs;
- is serving a custodial sentence of more than 4 months;
- is 16 or older and is claiming CTC themselves for their own child.

Young people no longer count for tax credit purposes once they start remunerative work (unless they are in full-time education).

If a qualifying child or young person dies during the period of an award, then CTC will continue in respect of them for 8 weeks following their death (or until an 18-year-old would have become 19, if that is earlier).

The Child Tax Credit Regulations 2002, regs 2 to 6

4. CTC elements

CTC is made up of a number of elements.

Family element – this is included in the calculation for all who qualify for CTC.

Family element (baby) – this extra amount is included where the family has a child under the age of one.

Child element – this is included for each child or young person in your family (see 3). It is set at a single fixed rate regardless of the age of the dependent child or young person.

Disabled child element – this is included where any child or young person:

- is in receipt of either element of disability living allowance (DLA) at any rate (or would be but for the fact that they are a hospital inpatient); *or*
- is registered as blind, or has ceased to be registered within 28 weeks of the claim to CTC being made.

Severely disabled child element – this is included where any child or young person is in receipt of DLA highest rate care component (or would be but for the fact that they are a hospital inpatient).

The Child Tax Credit Regulations 2002, regs 7 and 8

5. Do you qualify for WTC?

You can get WTC if you meet the following conditions at the time you make your claim:

❑ You must be at least 16 years old; *and*
either you, or your partner, are working for 16 or more hours a week, *and*
- you have a dependent child or young person; *or*
- you have a physical or mental disability that puts you at a disadvantage in getting a job and you were previously in receipt of some form of disability benefit; *or*
- you (or your partner) are aged 50 or over and qualify for the 50-plus element (see 7 below); *or*

you, or your partner, are aged 25 or over, and work at least 30 hours a week.

❑ You satisfy the residence and presence conditions (see Chapter 49).

❑ Your income is within a set limit, which varies according to your family circumstances (see 9 below).

If you are part of a couple you claim WTC jointly and your claim is called a joint claim. Otherwise you claim as a single person. Your claim will end immediately if you are a couple who separate or if you are a single claimant who becomes part of a couple. Your entitlement will also usually end immediately if you cease working the right number of hours to qualify (see below).

Tax Credits Act 2002, s.10 and The Working Tax Credit (Entitlement and Maximum Rate) Regulations 2002, reg 4

6. What does and does not count as work?

In order to be treated as being in *'qualifying remunerative work'* you must *either:*

- be working at the date of your claim, and the work must be expected to continue for at least 4 weeks after you have made the claim; *or*

G.1 Tax credits transitional rules

CTC replacing child allowances and premiums during 2005/06

CTC will eventually replace all the existing child elements paid to families with children within income support (IS) and jobseeker's allowance (JSA) – ie, the personal allowances for dependent children, the family premium, disabled child premiums and enhanced disability premiums for children. Families should not be disadvantaged by the transition and should receive the same amount for their children through either CTC or IS/JSA.

New claims for IS or income-based JSA

There is no provision for children within these benefits now. You will need to claim CTC to provide this income if you have not already done so.

Already getting IS or income-based JSA

It is planned that those families still getting the child elements within these means-tested benefits will be moved onto CTC from early 2005 onwards. Those who were eligible for pension credit (PC) were moved automatically onto CTC from October 2003 (as there is no provision for children within PC) by being treated as if they had made a claim for CTC. It is likely that the transfer from IS and income-based JSA will be made by the same method, and will probably take place on a staged basis. Initially the money may go to the IS/JSA claimant (usually the man in a couple) but at a later stage, when things are more settled, couples should be asked to make their own choice. This will often mean the woman in a couple receives the CTC. For more detail of this transition, see the *Disability Rights Bulletin*.

'Floating off' IS

It is possible that when you claim CTC you will 'float off' IS. This may happen where your income from other sources and your CTC come to more than your IS applicable amount. For example, maintenance is not treated as income for CTC purposes but is for IS purposes, so if you claim CTC your income from maintenance and CTC may be higher than your IS applicable amount.

Child dependency increases

Increases for child dependants within non-means-tested benefits such as incapacity benefit (IB), severe disablement allowance (SDA), bereavement benefits and state pension were abolished for new claimants from 6.4.03. You now claim CTC for your dependent children instead. However, if you were getting such an increase on 5.4.03 you can continue to receive it if you wish, although you may claim CTC instead. If you get such an increase with IB or SDA and you lose it because of the way the increase is means tested against the earnings of your partner, then you can have it restored to you if, within 8 weeks of you last having got it, your partner stops working or starts earning below the figure at which the increase would be removed (see also Chapter 14(5)).

- have an offer of work which you are expected to start within 7 days of making your claim, and the work must be expected to last for a total of at least 4 weeks.

'Work' means work that is done for payment or in expectation of payment. If you are an employee the number of hours that count will be the number of hours you normally work each week, including any overtime you regularly do. If you are self-employed the number of hours that will count will be those that you actually work in your self-employed capacity, although you can count time spent on activities not directly related to your actual self-employed activity, such as essential bookkeeping, distributing advertising flyers, etc. In calculating the number of hours you work towards the 16 or 30 hours a week limit you cannot include time spent in unpaid meal breaks or periods of customary or paid holiday.

Exceptionally, if you work in a school or otherwise do work on a seasonal basis, and you have a recognisable pattern of employment over the year, you may ignore the school holidays or other holiday periods. This rule benefits people like school assistants or dinner ladies who might otherwise be found not to be working enough hours to qualify.

When you are not treated as being in work – Some kinds of work do not count:

- work for a charitable or voluntary organisation or otherwise as a volunteer if you are only paid expenses;
- work on a training scheme where you are paid a training allowance (unless taxable as trade profit);
- work as part of intensive activity period activities or Employment Zone Programmes as a jobseeker;
- activities when you are in receipt of a sports award and no other form of payment is made to you;
- work where you are caring for someone who is temporarily living with you if the only payment you get is from a local authority, health authority, primary care trust or voluntary organisation and your income is below the taxable limit for this sort of work.

When you are treated as being in work – Provided that you have been accepted as being in *'qualifying remunerative work'* then usually you will continue to be treated as being in work for WTC purposes, with your number of hours being your usual working hours prior to the interruption. This applies in the following circumstances.

- ❑ You are not working because you are off sick. You will continue to be treated as being in work for a period of up to 28 weeks while you are receiving statutory sick pay (SSP), short-term lower rate incapacity benefit, or income support (or national insurance contribution credits only) on the basis of being incapable of work. If you are self-employed and off sick you will continue to be treated as being in work if you would have got SSP but for the fact that as a self-employed person you are not entitled to it.
- ❑ You are off work and getting maternity allowance, or statutory maternity, paternity or adoption pay, or you are on ordinary maternity leave, paternity leave or adoption leave.
- ❑ You are temporarily suspended from work while complaints or allegations against you are being investigated.
- ❑ You are on strike, but only for a period of up to 10 consecutive days on which you would normally have been working.

The Working Tax Credit (Entitlement and Maximum Rate) Regulations 2002, regs 4-7

7. WTC elements

WTC is also made up of a number of elements. If you are a couple and qualify for more than one disability, severe disability or 50-plus element, then more than one will be included in the calculation.

Basic element – This will be included in the calculation for all who qualify for WTC.

Couple element – This will be included where you are one of a couple (married or living together as husband and wife). From December 2005 registered same-sex partners can also be treated as a couple.

Lone parent element – This will be included where you are single and have a dependent child or young person.

30-hour element – This will be included where you are treated as working enough hours. This will be the case when:

- one person works enough hours because you and/or your partner (if you have one) work for at least 30 hours a week; *or*
- you are part of a couple and together you work enough hours because:
  - you have a dependent child or young person; *and*
  - between you, you work for at least 30 hours a week in total; *and*
  - at least one of you works for at least 16 hours a week.

Severe disability element – This will be included if you get either higher rate attendance allowance (AA) or disability living allowance (DLA) highest rate care component (or would but for the fact that you are in hospital). If you are part of a couple and one of you meets this test you get one severe disability element. If both of you meet this test you get two severe disability elements. The person who meets this test does not have to be the person who is working.

50-plus element – You will qualify for this if you, or your partner if you have one, are aged at least 50 and work at least 16 hours a week. If you are part of a couple and one of you meets this test you get one 50-plus element. If both of you meet this test you get two 50-plus elements. For at least 6 months before starting this work, you or your partner must have been getting:

- income support; *or*
- jobseeker's allowance (whether contribution- or income-based); *or*
- incapacity benefit (IB); *or*
- severe disablement allowance (SDA); *or*
- state pension topped up by pension credit; *or*
- a training allowance paid under Work-Based Learning for Adults or Training for Work; *or*
- another person was getting one of those benefits and claiming for you as their dependant; *or*
- you were getting national insurance contributions credits (eg if you were signing on as unemployed).

If you or your partner were getting carer's allowance or bereavement allowance or widowed parent's allowance before claiming one of the benefits in the list above then you can combine the time spent on the two sets of benefits to count towards the 6-month qualifying rule.

The 50-plus element is included in the calculation at two rates:

- a lower rate if you work at least 16 hours but less than 30 hours a week;
- a higher rate if you work for at least 30 hours a week.

The 50-plus element is payable for no more than 12 months where your employment is continuous, or, where your employment is not continuous, for a total of no more than 12 months provided that the gaps between any periods of entitlement are of less than 26 weeks.

Childcare element – You get a tax credit equal to 70% of eligible childcare costs up to a maximum of £175 childcare costs for one child, or £300 for two or more children. (So the highest childcare tax credit you could get is £122.50 for one child, or £210 for two or more.)

You include a childcare tax credit if:

- you are a lone parent working at least 16 hours a week; *or*
- you are one of a couple and both of you work at least 16 hours a week; *or*
- you are one of a couple and one of you works at least 16 hours a week and the other is 'incapacitated', a hospital

inpatient, or in prison.

If you are on maternity or adoption leave, the statutory period you are away from work will count as though you were still working. So you will be able to claim help with childcare costs for the new child provided you were working the hours as set out above before your break from work.

You count as 'incapacitated' if you receive any of the following:

- housing benefit (HB) or council tax benefit (CTB) which includes a disability premium or a higher pensioner premium, or where you have already been held to be incapacitated for the purposes of HB/CTB childcare costs; *or*
- short-term higher rate or long-term IB, AA, SDA, DLA, constant attendance allowance (payable with the Industrial Injuries or War Pensions schemes), or war pensions mobility supplement (or would get one of these benefits but for the fact that you are a hospital inpatient).

In order to qualify, your child or children must be aged 15 or younger, or aged 16 or younger if they meet the same rules as for the disabled child element within CTC. You can claim a childcare element up to the last day of the week containing the 1st September following their 15th birthday, or for a disabled child, their 16th birthday.

Your childcare must be provided by a registered childminder (or equivalent), or by a childminder approved by an accredited organisation, or by an out-of-school-hours scheme run by a school or local authority. Care provided by foster carers can count if the child being cared for is other than the one(s) being fostered. If you've arranged the childcare but it hasn't started by the time you make your claim, the amount is based on an estimate provided by the childcare provider.

If your childcare costs vary (eg you pay more during the school holidays) then it is your average weekly costs over the period covered by your award that will be taken into account in the calculation. If there is a change in the childcare provided while you are getting WTC and your childcare charges go down by £10 a week or more, or stop altogether, you must report this promptly. Your WTC will be recalculated as a result.

The Working Tax Credit (Entitlement and Maximum Rate) Regulations 2002, regs 3, 10, 16-18

8. WTC disability element

This element is a significant one for disabled people. In addition to working at least 16 hours a week you also have to satisfy two other tests, one relating to your disability, and one to your recent receipt of a qualifying benefit. It is the person who meets the work conditions who also has to meet the disability and qualifying benefit tests (so, if you are working and not disabled, but have a disabled partner who is not working, you will not receive the disability element). Conversely, if both you and your partner meet the rules about working and the rules about disability and qualifying benefits you can receive two disability elements.

The 'disability' test

To get the disability element of WTC included in your assessment, you must have a *'physical or mental disability which puts [you] at a disadvantage in getting a job'*. How this is assessed depends on whether you are making an initial claim or a renewal claim.

Initial claims – If you are claiming WTC for the first time you need to meet the rules set out in *either* Part 1 *or* Part 2 of Box G.2.

Renewal claims – If you are making a renewal claim for WTC you need to meet the rules set out in Part 1 of Box G.2.

The 'qualifying benefit' test

To get the disability element of WTC included in your

G.2 The 'disability' test

Disability which puts you at a disadvantage in getting a job

These are the ways you can pass the disability test for working tax credit (WTC).

On an initial claim, you will pass the disability test if any one (or more) of the conditions in Parts 1 or 2 apply to you.

On a renewal claim, you will pass the test if any one (or more) of the conditions in Part 1 apply to you.

Part 1

- ❑ When standing you cannot keep your balance unless you continually hold on to something.
- ❑ Using any crutches, walking frame, walking stick, prosthesis or similar walking aid which you habitually use, you cannot walk a continuous distance of 100 metres along level ground without stopping or without suffering severe pain.
- ❑ You can use neither of your hands behind your back as in the process of putting on a jacket or of tucking a shirt into trousers.
- ❑ You can extend neither of your arms in front of you so as to shake hands with another person without difficulty.
- ❑ You can put neither of your hands up to your head without difficulty so as to put on a hat.
- ❑ Due to lack of manual dexterity you cannot with one hand pick up a coin which is not more than 2.5 cm in diameter.
- ❑ You are not able to use your hands or arms to pick up a full jug of one litre capacity and pour from it into a cup, without difficulty.
- ❑ You can turn neither of your hands sideways through 180 degrees.
- ❑ You are registered as blind or partially sighted.
- ❑ You cannot see to read 16 point print at a distance greater than 20 centimetres, if appropriate, wearing the glasses you normally use.
- ❑ You cannot hear a telephone ring when you are in the same room as the telephone, if appropriate, using a hearing aid you normally use.
- ❑ In a quiet room you have difficulty hearing what someone talking in a loud voice at a distance of 2 metres says, if appropriate, using a hearing aid you normally use.
- ❑ People who know you well have difficulty in understanding what you say.
- ❑ When a person you know well speaks to you, you have difficulty in understanding what that person says.
- ❑ At least once a year during waking hours you have a coma or fit in which you lose consciousness.
- ❑ You have a mental illness for which you receive regular treatment under the supervision of a medically qualified person.
- ❑ Due to mental disability you are often confused or forgetful.
- ❑ You cannot do the simplest addition and subtraction.
- ❑ Due to mental disability you strike people or damage property or are unable to form normal social relationships.
- ❑ You cannot normally sustain an 8-hour working day or a 5-day working week due to a medical condition or intermittent or continuous severe pain.

Part 2

- ❑ As a result of an illness or accident you are undergoing a period of habilitation or rehabilitation.

Sch 1, Working Tax Credit (Entitlement and Maximum Rate) Regulations, 2002 assessment, you must also meet *one* of the following conditions.

- ❑ **Condition A** – At any time in the last 26 weeks before your claim for WTC you were getting: higher rate short-term or long-term incapacity benefit (IB), or severe disablement allowance (SDA).
- ❑ **Condition B** – At any time in the last 26 weeks before your claim for WTC you were getting the disability or higher pensioner premium in income support (IS), income-based jobseeker's allowance, housing benefit (HB) or council tax benefit (CTB).
- ❑ **Condition C** – On the date of your claim, you are getting disability living allowance (DLA – either component, any rate) or attendance allowance (or an Industrial Injuries or War Pensions scheme equivalent).
- ❑ **Condition D** – On the date of your claim, you have a Motability car.
- ❑ **Condition E: the 'Fast Track'** – This route to the disability element is referred to as the 'Fast Track' because it allows some of those who have been off work for a while to return to work without having either to have been off sick for a prolonged period, or to fit the qualifying rules for DLA, etc (as in Conditions A to D).

  At any time *in the last 8 weeks* before your WTC claim you had been getting, for at least 20 weeks, *either:*
  - statutory sick pay, occupational sick pay, lower rate short-term IB or IS on the basis that you were incapable of work; *or*
  - Class 1 or Class 2 national insurance (NI) contribution credits on the basis that you were incapable of work; *and*
  - you have a disability, at the date of claim, which is likely to last for at least 6 months (or for the rest of your life if your death is expected within 6 months); *and*
  - your gross earnings are less than they were before your disability began by at least 20% (or £15 a week; whichever is greater).
- ❑ **Condition F** – At any time in the last 8 weeks before your WTC claim you:
  - had been undertaking training for work (which means certain government training courses or a course of 16 hours or more a week learning occupational or vocational skills); *and*
  - within the 8 weeks prior to the start of the training course, had been getting higher rate short-term or long-term IB, or SDA.
- ❑ **Condition G** – This condition in effect relates to making a renewal claim. It provides that you will be treated as qualifying for the disability element if, within the 8 weeks before you make your claim, you had previously met Condition A, B, E or F. This should allow those who were getting a qualifying benefit such as IB, etc, to continue to get the WTC disability element for long after they stopped receiving that benefit. Note also that if you got the disability element because you met Condition C or D, as you were in receipt of, for example, DLA, you need to be still getting that benefit when you make your renewal claim.

The Working Tax Credit (Entitlement and Maximum Rate) Regulations 2002, reg 9

WTC disability element 2-year linking rule

There is a special WTC disability element 2-year linking rule which may help you to return to your former IB or SDA on the same basis as before, or help you move to a higher rate of benefit more quickly on a new claim. It does not help you return to the disability premium with IS, HB or CTB; you have to re-qualify for premiums.

For this linking rule to apply, you must:

- give up or lose your job (for any reason at all) or be off work sick; *and*
- be entitled to have the WTC disability element included in your tax credits assessment; *and*
- actually receive some tax credits (apart from just the family element of CTC) for the week that includes your last working day (eg the day before you went off sick); *and*
- be incapable of work on the first day after your last working day; *and*
- have a gap of no more than 2 years between your last day of entitlement to your pre-tax credits IB or SDA and the first day after giving up your job or self-employment.

If you meet these conditions, your days in receipt of tax credits count as days of incapacity for work. If your period of incapacity for work (PIW), including these days, links back to your previous award of IB or SDA, you go back on to the same level of IB or SDA as you had before. PIWs link if the gap between them is no more than 8 weeks (or 52 weeks if you are a 'welfare to work beneficiary' – see Chapter 15(12)).

If the new PIW does not link back (eg because your previous IB award ended more than 8 weeks before your tax credits began), you will have to re-satisfy the NI contribution conditions for a new IB claim, but the time on tax credits will count towards working out when you move onto the higher and long-term rates of benefit.

Social Security Contributions and Benefits Act 1992 s 30C (5) & (5A)

9. Income and savings

Unlike other means-tested benefits, CTC and WTC have no system of capital limits. There is thus no upper limit on savings above which CTC and/or WTC will not be payable. However, actual income from savings will be taken into account in the calculation (see below).

Income for tax credit purposes is similar to that counted for other means-tested benefits but not identical. The rules are largely based on income tax legislation. The broad principle is that all taxable income will be taken into account and any other income will be ignored.

Income which has the first £300 ignored

The following types of income will be included in the calculation, but the first £300 a year of the total of such income will be ignored:

- pension income, including taxable income from annuities and pensions paid by the Crown or a former employer, but excluding war disablement pensions, war pensioners mobility supplement and certain other war service pensions which are exempt from income tax;
- investment income, including taxable income from stocks and shares;
- property income, including taxable income from rents;
- foreign income, including any income arising from possessions or from securities abroad, whether or not this was remitted to the UK, converted into British pounds. This excludes any pensions or annuities paid under German or Austrian law to victims of National Socialist persecution and certain other non-taxable receipts. If you receive a foreign pension, whether or not it was remitted to the UK, 90% of the full amount received will be taken into account (in British pounds not the foreign currency);
- notional income, including:
  - various forms of income treated as notional income under tax legislation, eg stock dividends;
  - income which you have deprived yourself of in order to gain entitlement to, or increase the amount of, tax credit;
  - income which would be available to you if you applied for it;
  - income you have done without because you have provided a service to another person but not been paid for it or been paid less than the 'going rate' for it;
  - trust income that, under the income tax rules, is treated

as the income of another person, eg investment income of a child where the trust funds have been provided by the parent and the amount exceeds £100.

Employment income

All taxable income from employment is usually taken into account. In contrast to all other means-tested benefits, income from employment is taken into account gross, that is, before income tax and national insurance (NI) contributions have been deducted. Such income includes:

- PAYE income from an office or employment, including pay, holiday pay, bonus and commission;
- payment made in respect of expenses that are not *'wholly, exclusively and necessarily incurred'* in the performance of the job;
- any cash voucher, non-cash voucher or credit token (but not if for eligible childcare – see below);
- the value of a car made available for private use, and of car fuel;
- any goods or assets your employer gave you which you could sell for cash (eg gifts of food, drink, clothes, cigarettes) or any payments made by your employer that you should have paid yourself (eg if your employer paid your rent to your landlord or paid your personal phone, gas or electricity bills);
- redundancy payments to the extent they are subject to income tax;
- statutory sick pay (SSP);
- statutory maternity pay (SMP), statutory adoption pay (SAP) or statutory paternity pay (SPP) in excess of £100 a week;
- certain retainer fees or similar compensation for a restrictive undertaking;
- strike pay received as a member of a trade union;
- taxable gains from security options (eg company shares, bonds, government gilts) acquired as a result of your employment.

Some payments made from your earnings which are tax exempt are ignored in reckoning your gross income. These include:

- the gross amount of any contributions you make to a pension scheme or retirement annuity contract;
- fees and subscriptions to professional bodies and learned societies, employee liabilities and indemnity insurance;
- contributions made under the Gift Aid and Give-As-You-Earn payroll deduction schemes for payments to charity.

Disregarded employment income – The following specific types of income are disregarded as employment income. As such they are not treated as any form of income:

- payments in respect of expenses which are wholly, exclusively and necessarily incurred in the performance of the duties of the employment or which are qualifying travelling expenses for tax purposes;
- payment or reimbursement of expenses in connection with the use of a car parking space at your place of work, or for certain overnight expenses or for removal expenses;
- the first £500 worth of the benefit to you of any computer equipment provided by your employer;
- cash vouchers or equivalents that you are to use to pay for childcare costs of the sort which would be included for WTC purposes;
- the value of meal vouchers received as an employee;
- other extra statutory concessions which are regarded as not subject to tax by the Inland Revenue;
- certain taxable benefits provided by an employer which do not have to be reported for tax credit purposes, eg the provision of living accommodation and cheap loans.

Self-employment income

Your taxable profit for income tax purposes – whether as a sole trader or as a partner in a business – is taken into account for tax credit purposes. You can deduct the following items from your taxable profit for tax credit purposes:

- the gross amount of any contributions you made to a pension scheme or retirement annuity contract;
- any trading losses brought forward from a previous year under the tax credit rules;
- the gross amount of any Gift Aid payments you made.

If your business made a loss you should contact the Tax Credit Helpline, as there are special rules dealing with losses for tax credit purposes.

Benefit income

All benefit income is taken into account in full as income, except:

- attendance allowance and disability living allowance;
- back-to-work bonus and return to work credit;
- bereavement payment;
- child benefit;
- Christmas bonus;
- guardian's allowance;
- housing benefit (HB), council tax benefit (CTB) and discretionary housing payments (see Chapter 7(17));
- income support (IS), except to strikers;
- incapacity benefit (IB) which is either the short-term lower rate or that paid to those who were previously in receipt of invalidity benefit and are still in the same period of incapacity for work;
- industrial injuries benefits (except industrial death benefit);
- income-based jobseeker's allowance (JSA);
- maternity allowance;
- pension credit;
- severe disablement allowance;
- social fund payments;
- SMP, SAP and SPP where the first £100 a week will be ignored as income; anything above that will be taken into account (SSP is treated in full as income);
- certain compensation payments, including compensation payments for the non-payment of IS, JSA, or HB; *and*
- payments in lieu of milk tokens or vitamins.

Student grants

All student grants and loans (except supplementary dependants' grant) are ignored for tax credit purposes.

Other income

Most other forms of taxable income are to be included in the calculation. The following are ignored as income:

- mandatory top-up payments (and discretionary payments to help meet special needs) to those taking part in certain training or employment programmes;
- payments made to disabled people to help them obtain or retain employment;
- adoption allowances;
- fostering allowances to the extent that they do not exceed the exempt amount allowed for income tax purposes;
- maintenance payments;
- apart from notional income from trusts (described above), the income of any children or young people for whom you claim CTC.

This is not an exhaustive list.

The Tax Credits (Definition and Calculation of Income) Regulations 2002

10. Claiming tax credits

Claims for CTC or WTC are made on the same claim-form, TC600. This can be obtained by ringing the Tax Credit Helpline on 0845 300 3900 or Minicom 0845 300 3909 or by calling in at an Inland Revenue (IR) enquiry centre or Jobcentre Plus office. Alternatively, a claim can be made at the IR website: www.inlandrevenue.gov.uk.

Claimants must produce a valid national insurance number or provide information or evidence to enable one to be traced. If you are unable to make a claim on your own behalf, this can be done for you by your appointee or someone else legally empowered to act on your behalf.

Backdating claims – If you meet the qualifying conditions, tax credits can be backdated for a maximum of 3 months. If you were not awarded any tax credits, or did not get the disability, severe disability, disabled child or severely disabled child element within your tax credit award because you were waiting to hear the result of a claim for a qualifying benefit (eg disability living allowance) then there are special backdating rules. If your claim had been refused, it can be backdated to either the date of claim or the date from which you are paid the qualifying benefit, whichever is later. If your tax credit award had been paid at a lower rate than it should have been, it can be increased from the date the qualifying benefit was awarded. In either case, you must tell the IR within 3 months of the award of the qualifying benefit in order to be able to take advantage of these rules.

Renewal claims

If you got tax credits in 2004/05 you will be contacted by the IR from April 2005 onwards. This will be to ask for your details for 2005/06 and also to check what your circumstances actually were in 2004/05 so that any necessary adjustments can be made to your 2004/05 award. If you have difficulty giving details for 2004/05 (for example, because you were self-employed and do not yet have your accounts available) you will have until 30.9.05 to provide an estimate and until 31.1.06 to provide your actual details.

The Tax Credits (Claims and Notifications) Regulations 2002

11. Payment of tax credits

CTC, and any WTC payment towards childcare costs, will normally be paid direct to the main carer by the Inland Revenue (IR). WTC, apart from any help with childcare costs, will normally be paid to you by your employer in your wage packet if you are an employee and directly into your bank or similar account if you are self-employed. Where you and your partner are both working, WTC (less any help with childcare costs) will be paid to you via whichever of your employers you nominate. If you cannot agree on this, the IR will decide which employer should make the payments to you. The Government intends to phase out the payment of WTC through employers between November 2005 and April 2006.

Payments made to you by the IR will normally be made by credit transfer to a bank account or similar account. If you do not have such an account then you are expected to get one. If you do not get such an account, unless you can show that there were *'exceptional circumstances'* which prevented you from doing so, the IR can stop making payments to you. If you get a bank account after tax credits have stopped for this reason they can be backdated for up to 3 months. Payments into your account will be made either weekly or 4-weekly at your choice, unless the amount due to you is less than £2 a week, when payment may be made by lump sum.

The Tax Credits (Payments by the Board) Regulations 2002

12. Penalties

Tax credits contain a system of financial penalties, another idea borrowed from tax legislation.

A penalty of up to £3,000 can be imposed where you *'fraudulently or negligently'* make an incorrect statement or declaration or give incorrect information or evidence either in connection with your claim or when you are informing the Inland Revenue (IR) of a change of circumstances. Where you make a claim as a couple, the penalty can be imposed on either of you, unless one of you can show that you were not aware and could not *'reasonably have been expected'* to be aware that your partner was making a false statement or providing incorrect information or evidence about your claim. You can also be subject to this penalty if you make a false statement when you are acting for someone else.

A penalty of up to £300 can be imposed if you fail to provide information or evidence that you have been specifically asked to provide by the IR in connection with your claim. This penalty can be increased by up to £60 a day for each day that you continue to fail to provide the required information, but will not be imposed where you have a reasonable excuse for not providing it.

The Tax Credits Act 2002, s 31 & 32

13. Revisions and appeals

The Inland Revenue (IR) has broad powers to end or amend your award of tax credits at any time. They can do so because you have told them of a change in your circumstances. They can also do so where they have *'reasonable grounds'* for believing that you should be getting a different amount or even no tax credits at all (see Chapter 19(5)). In the case of an official error by the IR or DWP, the former can revise a decision in your favour up to 5 years after the end of the tax year to which the decision relates.

The rules on appeals are similar to, but not identical to, those for other social security benefits. Chapter 58 gives details of how to go about challenging a decision. Some specific differences are:

- You have 30 days to appeal to an appeal tribunal against a decision on your tax credits.
- Your notice of appeal must give the grounds of appeal. The tribunal may allow you to put forward grounds that were not specified in that notice, and take them into consideration, if they think that the omission was *'not wilful or unreasonable'*.
- There is no right of appeal against a decision to recover an overpayment as such, so arguments about *'misrepresentation'* or *'failure to disclose'* are irrelevant. However, you may be able to appeal against the underlying decision(s) which has led the IR to believe that they have overpaid you.

It is standard practice for the IR to contact you by phone to settle with you if you submit a valid appeal. You may persist with your appeal if you do not wish to negotiate in this way.

The Tax Credits Act 2002, s 38 & 39, The Tax Credits (Appeals) Regulations 2002, The Tax Credits (Notice of Appeal) Regulations 2002

19 Calculating tax credits

1. Introduction

Child tax credit (CTC) and working tax credit (WTC) will, as far as possible, be calculated and awarded on an annual basis. However, you can be entitled to tax credits at different rates for different periods during the course of the year.

Where that is the case, the figures used will be recalculated on a proportional, daily, basis. For example, if you qualify for 10 weeks only, ie 70 days, then the elements below would be divided by 365 days (or 366 in a leap year) to produce a daily rate. That daily rate would be rounded in your favour, then multiplied by the number of days in the entitlement period, in this case 70. This will give the correct figure for your maximum credit entitlement during that entitlement period.

Usually, the income which is taken into account will be your income in the April-to-April tax year preceding the April-to-April tax year for which you are awarded WTC/CTC. So if you are awarded WTC/CTC in 2005/06, it will be provisionally assessed on your income in 2004/05. (Exceptionally, for the first year of tax credits, 2003/04, it was your income in 2001/02 that was taken into account. This was because a significant number of awards were made prior to April 2003 and the only income details available in those cases were for 2001/02.)

Your award can be altered if your income has decreased, or increased, by more than a certain amount, since the year used in the assessment.

2. Rates of CTC and WTC

The various elements described in Chapter 18(4) and (7) for 2005/06 are detailed below.

CTC elements 2005/06	**yearly amount**
Family element (normal)	£545
Family element (baby)	£1,090
Child element	£1,690
Disabled child element	£2,285
Severely disabled child element	£920

WTC elements 2005/06	**yearly amount**
Basic element	£1,620
Couple element	£1,595
Lone parent element	£1,595
30-hour element	£660
Severe disability element	£920
50-plus element (16- to 30-hours rate)	£1,110
50-plus element (30-hours rate)	£1,660
Disability element	£2,165
Childcare element	
– maximum eligible cost (1 child)	£175
– maximum eligible cost (2 or more children)	£300
– percentage of eligible costs covered	70%

The Child Tax Credit Regulations 2002, reg 7; The Working Tax Credit (Entitlement and Maximum Rate) Regulations 2002, reg 20 and Sch 2

3. The steps in tax credit calculations

You work out your entitlement to tax credits as follows:
Step 1: Work out your annual income (see Chapter 18(9)). It is the previous year's income which will normally be used (2004/05 for 2005/06).
Step 2: Find the appropriate income threshold figure (see below)
Step 3: Compare the income to the threshold figure
If your normal income is below or the same as your income threshold, you'll get the maximum tax credit for your family. If your normal income is above your income threshold, deduct the threshold figure from the income: the result will be your 'excess income'. Then apply the correct taper to the resulting excess income.
Step 4: Work out the maximum tax credits for yourself and for your family
This will be the combination of all of the above CTC and WTC elements that apply to you.
Step 5: Deduct the result at Step 3 from your maximum tax credits (Step 4). The amount you are left with is your tax credit entitlement.

Note: This calculation effectively only gives an estimate of your entitlement, as it is your actual income in the year of the award which determines your true entitlement and this cannot usually be known accurately until after the year has ended. See Box G.4.

The Tax Credits (Income Thresholds and Determination of Rates) Regulations 2002, reg 7

G.3 Calculating tax credits

Example 1

Shirley is a lone parent working 20 hours a week. Her gross annual income is £9,000. She has two children aged 4 and 10. She gets disability living allowance (DLA) highest rate care component in respect of one of the children. She pays childcare costs of £30 a week (£1,560 a year).

Step 1: annual income	
Annual income	£9,000.00
Step 2: appropriate income threshold	
WTC income threshold	£5,220.00
Step 3: income compared to threshold	
Income exceeds threshold by	*£3,780.00*
Taper excess income (£3,780 x 37%)	£1,398.60
Step 4: maximum tax credit	
CTC family element	£545.00
CTC child element (£1,690 x 2)	£3,380.00
CTC disabled child element	£2,285.00
CTC severely disabled child element	£920.00
WTC basic element	£1,620.00
WTC lone parent element	£1,595.00
WTC childcare element (£1,560 x 70%)	£1,092.00
Maximum award	*£11,437.00*
Step 5: total tax credit payable	
Maximum award	£11,437.00
Less reduction in award	£1,398.60
Total tax credit payable	*£10,038.40*

Example 2

The effect of a change of circumstances

Farouk is single, 35, works full time and has a disability. His salary is £10,220 a year. At the start of the year he does not meet the conditions for the disability element, but after 5 months he is awarded the mobility component of DLA. He is not entitled to the disability element for the first 150 days of the year, but is for the remaining 215.

Step 1: annual income	
Annual income	£10,220.00
Step 2: income threshold	
WTC income threshold	£5,220.00
Step 3: income compared to threshold	
Income exceeds threshold by	*£5,000.00*
Taper excess income (£5,000 x 37%)	£1,850.00
Step 4a: maximum credit without disability element	
WTC basic element	£1,620.00
WTC 30-hour element	£660.00
Maximum award	*£2,280.00*
Step 4b: tax credit eligibility for first period	
Maximum award	£2,280.00
Less reduction in award	£1,850.00
Annual tax credit payable	*£430.00*
Step 5a: maximum credit with disability element	
WTC basic element	£1,620.00
WTC disability element	£2,165.00
WTC 30-hour element	£660.00
Maximum award	*£4,445.00*
Step 5b: tax credit eligibility for second period	
Maximum award	£4,445.00
Less reduction in award	£1,850.00
Annual tax credit payable	*£2,595.00*
Step 6: actual tax credits payable for each period	
Period 1 £430 x 150/365	£176.72
Period 2 £2,595 x 215/365	£1,528.57
Total	*£1,705.29*

Note: This example assumes Farouk's past circumstances were such that he cannot benefit from any £2,500 tolerance rule.

The income thresholds and tapers

The threshold figures used in the process described above are:

2005/06	income threshold figure
WTC	£5,220
CTC (only)	£13,910
CTC (family element only)	£50,000

If you qualify for both CTC and WTC, the WTC figure is used in the calculation.

You apply a taper to work out how much of any excess income above the threshold should be taken from your maximum tax credit entitlement. This taper is usually 37%. However, the family element of CTC is retained until income exceeds a further threshold of £50,000 a year (£961.53 a week). At that point the family element starts to be tapered away at a rate of 6.67% (roughly £1 for every £15 of gross income above £50,000). This normally runs out altogether when income reaches £58,000; or £66,000 if your family has a baby under one, as that entitles you to the higher, 'baby' family element; or an even higher figure if you have one or more disabled children.

When the Inland Revenue is doing these calculations it must apply the taper in the following order: first to the WTC elements, then to the WTC childcare elements, then to the CTC child elements and finally to the CTC family elements. The practical effect of this is that those payments made to the employee (the non-childcare elements of WTC) are reduced before those made direct to the main carer (the childcare elements of WTC and CTC).

The Tax Credits (Income Thresholds and Determination of Rates) Regulations 2002

4. Changes in your circumstances

Working families tax credit (WFTC) and disabled person's tax credit (DPTC) used to be paid for 26 weeks at a time, regardless of most changes of circumstances. Increases or decreases in your wages did not affect your WFTC or DPTC during the period of your award. CTC and WTC are not like that. Where possible, awards will run for a full April-to-April tax year, but if you fail to meet the qualifying conditions at some point your award should usually end immediately. On the other hand, if your income goes up or down, even very substantially, there is usually no need to notify the Inland Revenue (IR), although it may be advisable to do so. They will be happy to correct any overpayment or underpayment in your award for the current tax year, by means of the award they will make to you for the next tax year.

You *must* report the following changes of circumstances:

- a change to your status as a single person or couple (from December 2005, the latter will include registered same-sex partners);
- you cease to meet the residence conditions (eg you move abroad);
- your childcare costs ending or reducing by £10 a week or more.

You should do so within 3 months of the change occurring, as failure to do this may result in the imposition of a penalty (see Chapter 18(12)).

The effect of changes of circumstances – Your circumstances may change during the course of the year – eg, you may already be in work but then start to meet the conditions for the disability element. Your award will need to be recalculated. This involves looking at the year as being made up of two relevant periods. The IR will calculate the awards for the two periods based on multiples of daily rates, according to the number of days in each period.

A simpler method – which gives results that are accurate enough for practical purposes – is to take each period separately, then proceed as if the maximum credit applied for a whole tax year. Then, having derived the tax credit payable, multiply that figure by the number of days in the period then divide by the number of days in the tax year (usually 365). Do the same for the other period, again assuming that its associated maximum credit applied over a whole year. The total tax credit payable for the year is then the sum of these two adjusted figures.

5. The £2,500 tolerance rule

The £2,500 tolerance rule is applied in the following way.

- If the current year income is greater than the previous year's income by less than £2,500 then the previous year's income is used.
- If the current year income is less than the previous year's income, then the current year's income is used.
- If the current year income is greater than the previous year's income by £2,500 or more then the current year's income less £2,500 is used.

For example, if your income in the previous year was £10,000 but in the current year is £13,000, your income will be treated as if it were only £10,500.

Where you feel that this year's income is likely to vary from that of the previous year, either by being lower or by being more than £2,500 higher, you may ask for a reassessment so that your award is based on the likely income in the current tax year.

The combination of this rule with the different years used for the assessment can have some strange effects.

Example: Bob has had the same full-time job for the last 5 years. Unfortunately, between April 2004 and April 2005 he was incapable of work following a road traffic accident and as a result was receiving only statutory sick pay and then incapacity benefit throughout that year. When he returns to work on 6.4.05, and makes a claim for tax credits, he would get a much higher award than expected, due to the use of his low income for 2004/05. He will be overpaid, and have that overpayment recovered in 2006/07, unless he tells the Inland Revenue that his income for the current year will be higher than that of the previous year so they can reassess his income during the course of the current year on his estimated earnings for 2005/06.

6. Overpayment and underpayment of tax credit

Your initial award of tax credit for any tax year is always based on your income in the previous tax year. It is assumed in the first instance that your income this year will be broadly similar to the previous year. As you progress through the current year, the information you have about your circumstances and your income (which you may or may not have passed to the Inland Revenue) allows a closer approximation to your actual entitlement to be calculated. However, your final entitlement to tax credit can only be calculated after the end of the tax year, at which point full details of your tax situation are known.

The way in which underpayments and overpayments are treated is explained in Box G.4.

G.4 Overpayment and underpayment of tax credit

Overpayments

'In year' overpayments

You may become entitled to much less tax credit during the current year – eg, if your income rises sharply, perhaps because your partner starts work. If you notify the Inland Revenue (IR), they will attempt to reduce the amount paid to you, either by:

- reducing the amount they are paying you from then on, so that they pay you the right amount of tax credit over the course of the whole year; *or*
- not paying you any more tax credit for the rest of the year, if they have already paid you as much as, or more than, you are entitled to. They may also ask you to pay back the extra after the end of the year, once all the relevant information about your income and circumstances is available.

Strictly speaking, these are not necessarily overpayments (as your full entitlement can never be known until the year has actually finished) but rather attempts by the IR to limit *potential* overpayments.

Overpayments at the end of the year

If it becomes apparent at the end of the year that you have been overpaid for the past year (ie 2004/05) the IR will seek to recover the overpayment by:

- reducing your tax credit award for the current year (ie 2005/06). This is their preferred method of recovery; *or*
- asking you to pay back the amount overpaid either by a lump-sum payment or in 12 monthly instalments.

The maximum amounts by which they would reduce your award are:

- 10% if you receive the maximum tax credit award;
- 100% if you receive only the family element of CTC;
- 25% for everyone else.

Are overpayments recoverable?

There is no right of appeal against a decision to recover an overpayment. There is a right of appeal against the underlying decisions about your entitlement on which the overpayment recovery decision was based. If you do appeal, state explicitly that your appeal is about these underlying decisions about your entitlement.

There are two situations where the IR may allow you to repay the overpayment over a longer time period than normal (possibly using top-up payments to extend the payback period), or may decide not to seek to recover the overpayment at all:

- you have been overpaid because of an error on the part of the IR or another government department and it was *'reasonable'* for you to think your award was right (examples of where it would *not* be reasonable for you to think the award was right are where you were paid on the basis of the wrong number of children, or your employer was paying more tax credit to you than the award notice said you should get); *or*
- it would cause hardship to you or your family if you had to pay the tax credit back.

  Hardship will involve considering:
  - your current and future income and essential living expenses;
  - your savings, investments and other assets which you could use over the short to medium term to make the payments (these might make it more appropriate to delay payment rather than not ask for payment at all);
  - your other liabilities – eg mortgage repayments, rent or rent arrears, overpayments of social security benefits or other debts;
  - your previous payment history with the IR and whether you are due to make other payments to them, and how paying the current debt might affect those payments;
  - how long it will take you to pay back the overpayment;
  - whether paying what you owe would result in you not being able to afford essential services, such as gas, electricity or water;
  - whether you have a child or children under 5 or a sick or disabled person in the family whose health could be affected by your paying back the debt, even over an extended period;
  - any other relevant factors.

The effect on income support (IS) and income-based jobseeker's allowance (JSA)

If you have your payment of tax credit reduced or stopped by the IR because of overpayment recovery this may leave you in a very awkward position with these other benefits. This is because you will be treated by the DWP as if you are still getting the right weekly amount of CTC from the IR even though they have either reduced your payment or stopped making payments altogether. At worst, this can leave you living on an income below the normal IS or income-based JSA level. The IR should pay full CTC to people in receipt of IS or income-based JSA even where they were, previously, seeking to pay a lower amount because of overpayment recovery action.

The effect on housing benefit (HB) and council tax benefit (CTB)

What counts for HB and CTB is the amount of tax credit that you actually receive. So, if you are being overpaid tax credit you may receive less HB and/or CTB than you would if you were getting the right amount, but the payment is nevertheless correct. When your tax credit award is lowered, either to recover an overpayment from a previous year or to avoid you being overpaid in the current year, then your HB and/or CTB must be increased to compensate.

Inland Revenue Code of Practice: COP26 – What happens if we have paid you to much tax credit

The Social Security (Working Tax Credit and Child Tax Credit) (Consequential Amendments) Regulations 2003

The Social Security (Working Tax Credit and Child Tax Credit) (Consequential Amendments) (No.3) Regulations 2003

Underpayments

If you are underpaid tax credit, the IR will normally seek to correct this by means of a single payment. If the underpayment comes to light 'in year' (eg because your family income goes down) the payment should correct the amount that you received for that part of the year already passed, and your continuing award will be adjusted to pay the correct weekly amount. If the underpayment comes to light at the end of the year, the payment will correct the amount paid to you for that past year.

The effect on HB and CTB

If you are being underpaid tax credit but are not in pressing need of additional income, you can allow the underpayment to continue until the end of the current tax year, and receive a lump-sum payment that makes up for the accumulated underpayment. You will receive a higher award of HB/CTB in this period because of your low actual income from tax credit. In contrast, if you opt to have the underpayment corrected in the course of the year, then 85% of the additional income is likely to be lost due to reduced HB/CTB payable.

H Care and mobility

This section of the Handbook looks at:

20 Disability living allowance

A. GENERAL POINTS

1. What is disability living allowance?

Disability living allowance (DLA) is a benefit for adults and children with disabilities. It is for people who need help looking after themselves and those who find it difficult to walk or get around. You don't need to have someone looking after you to qualify.

DLA is tax free, not means tested and you don't need to have paid any national insurance contributions. It is paid on top of any earnings or other income you may have. It is almost always paid in full on top of social security benefits or tax credits. DLA is divided into two parts:

- **a care component** – for help with personal care needs, paid at three different levels;
- **a mobility component** – for help with walking difficulties, paid at two levels.

You can be paid either the care component or the mobility component on its own, or both components at the same time. DLA is for you, not for a carer or parent. You can qualify for DLA whether or not you actually have someone helping you. What matters is the effects of your disability and the help you need, not whether you already get that help. If you get DLA, you can spend it on anything you like.

Although DLA can be paid indefinitely, there is an upper age limit for making your first claim. You can only get DLA if you claim before your 65th birthday. Otherwise you claim attendance allowance (AA; see Chapter 21). AA has no mobility component, but the disability tests are the same as for DLA middle and highest rate care components.

You can start off your claim by a free phone call to the Benefit Enquiry Line (BEL): 0800 882200. They will send you a claim-pack and your claim can be backdated to the date of your call. Or, if you need help, they can fill in the form for you over the phone and send the completed form for you to check and sign.

2. Do you qualify for DLA?

To qualify for DLA you must pass a series of non-disability tests and also satisfy at least one of the disability tests. Most of the non-disability tests have exceptions to the standard rules, so off-the-cuff advice may not always be correct.

To qualify for DLA, you must:

- pass at least one of the disability tests (see 9 and 18); *and*
- claim DLA (see 23); *and*
- pass the age test (see 3); *and*
- pass both the backwards and forwards qualifying period tests (see 4); *and*
- pass the residence and presence tests (see Chapter 49(2) and (3)).

The DWP must also be satisfied there is nothing to prevent payment (see 6). If you pass all these tests, you will be entitled to DLA. You will keep your underlying entitlement to DLA even if other rules mean you are not actually paid it.

Box H.1 gives a summary of the non-disability tests. In Box H.6 we suggest sources of further information on DLA and explain the abbreviations used in our references to legislation.

3. Age limits

Lower age limit – There is no lower age limit for DLA care component. But there is an extra disability test for children under 16 (see 9) and you cannot use the 'cooking test' until you reach age 16.

Children can get the higher rate mobility component from age 3 and the lower rate from age 5. The rules for the higher rate are the same as for adults but lower rate mobility also has an extra disability test if you are under 16 (see 18).

Upper age limit – DLA can be paid indefinitely, but you must establish your entitlement by making a successful claim no later than the day before your 65th birthday. You don't need to pass the qualifying period but you must satisfy all the other conditions of entitlement including one of the disability tests no later than the day before your 65th birthday. If you are 65

H.1 The non-disability tests

Qualifying criteria	Care component	Mobility component
Age limits		
■ To make your first claim	From birth to the day before your 65th birthday.	Higher rate from 2 years 9 months to the day before your 65th birthday. Lower rate from 4 years 9 months to the day before your 65th birthday.
■ To be paid	From 3 months old (birth if terminally ill). No upper limit.	From 3 years for higher rate and 5 years for lower rate. No upper limit.
■ Extra tests for children	From birth to the day before your 16th birthday.	For lower rate only, from 4 years 9 months to the day before your 16th birthday.
■ Shorter 'presence in the country' test for babies	Must claim and serve the 3-month qualifying period no later than the day before 6 months old.	Not payable to children under 3.
■ Cooking test	From 16 years to the day before your 65th birthday.	Doesn't apply.
■ Lowest/lower rate	The day before your 65th birthday. From 65 you can keep or renew your lowest rate component or make a repeat claim within one year.	Same as care component.
Qualifying periods		
■ Backwards test	If you're under 65 on the first day of entitlement, you must satisfy the disability tests throughout the 3 months before the award would start. If you're 65 or over – 6 months. No qualifying period if you're terminally ill.	If you're under 65 on the first day of entitlement, you must satisfy the disability tests throughout the 3 months before an award would start. If you're 65 or over and renewing a claim – also 3 months. No qualifying period if you're terminally ill.
■ Forwards test	6 months following first day of entitlement. No forwards test for renewal claims, revisions or supersessions if you're over 65, or for attendance allowance.	6 months following first day of entitlement.
Residence and presence		
■ Standard	Present for 26 out of the last 52 weeks. Present and ordinarily resident, not subject to immigration control.	Same as care component.
■ Babies	Present for 13 out of the last 52 weeks before award if less than 6 months old when claim made and qualifying period served. Present and ordinarily resident, not subject to immigration control.	Not payable to children under 3.
■ Terminal illness	Present and ordinarily resident, not subject to immigration control.	Same as care component.
Other rules		
■ Hospital and special accommodation	Payment may be stopped while in hospital or other special accommodation.	Payment may be stopped while in hospital but is not affected in special accommodation.
■ Prison	Payment suspended while on remand, but arrears paid if you don't get a custodial or suspended sentence.	Same as care component.

H.2 Disability living allowance and other help

DLA acts as a gateway to other types of help. This table gives a list of the rates and components of DLA that entitle you to further help (as long as you pass any other tests there may be for that help).

If you get DLA middle or highest rate care component, you are also eligible for the help available to people receiving only the lowest rate. Similarly, if you get higher rate mobility component, you are also eligible for the help available to people receiving only the lower rate.

'Premiums' are those included in the assessments of income support (IS), income-based jobseeker's allowance (JSA), housing benefit (HB), council tax benefit (CTB) and health benefits. 'Elements' are those included in child tax credit (CTC) and working tax credit (WTC).

Note: The disabled child premium and enhanced disability premium for children are no longer included in new claims for IS and income-based JSA, and are being phased out of existing claims.

Care component

❑ **Lowest rate**

- Disability premium and element
- Disabled child premium
- Qualifying benefit for WTC
- Childcare disregard in HB/CTB
- Childcare element in WTC
- Christmas bonus
- No non-dependant deductions (HB/CTB, IS/JSA housing costs)
- Warm Front Grant
- Parental leave from work (child up to age 17)

❑ **Middle or highest rate**

- Carer's allowance carer test
- Home responsibilities protection
- IS – carer's eligibility
- Carer premium test
- Severe disability premium
- Additional amount for severe disability – guarantee credit of pension credit

❑ **Highest rate**

- Enhanced disability premium
- Severe disability element
- Independent Living Funds
- Personal capability assessment exemption
- Long-term incapacity benefit after 28 weeks

Mobility component

❑ **Lower rate**

- Disability premium and element
- Disabled child premium
- Qualifying benefit for WTC
- Childcare disregard in HB/CTB
- Childcare element in WTC
- Christmas bonus
- Warm Front Grant
- Parental leave from work (child up to age 17)

❑ **Higher rate**

- Exemption from road tax
- Blue Badge
- Motability
- Driving licence at age 16

or over, you cannot claim DLA for the first time unless you count as having made a claim before reaching 65.
Regs 3, Sch 1 DLA Regs; reg 4(1) C&P

Renewal and top-up claims from age 65
If a DLA award ends after you reach 65, you can make a renewal claim within one year of your previous award ending. If you leave it longer than a year, you have to claim attendance allowance (AA), which has no mobility or lower rate care equivalents. You can only re-claim your former rate of mobility component under this concession – you cannot switch rates after 65.

Care component – You can maintain or renew the lowest rate only if you qualified for it before reaching 65. If your care needs lessen after 65, you cannot drop to the lowest rate – you will lose the care component altogether. You can, however, regain the lowest rate if you re-claim within 12 months of your previous award for it ending. If your care needs change after reaching 65, you can switch between the middle and highest rates or move up from the lowest rate, but you must satisfy a 6-month qualifying period.

If you have the mobility component, a change in your care needs after you reach 65 enables your DLA award to be 'superseded'. This means you can claim the care component (at the middle or highest rate), rather than AA, even if you are aged, say, 70. You can still claim the lowest rate of the care component after 65 if you met the qualifying conditions before 65 and have a current mobility award made before 65.
Para 3(2), (3) and para 7 of Sch 1 DLA Regs; CSDLA/388/00

Mobility component – Once you reach 65 you can only stay with the rate you got before you were 65. You cannot move up or down a rate. There is an exception to this rule that allows you to switch to the higher rate, but only if you can show that you met the higher rate conditions before age 65. If you have a current award of the care component, made before you were 65, you can claim the mobility component after your 65th birthday, as long as your mobility difficulties began before you were 65. If your mobility problems are such that you can only satisfy the disability test after your 65th birthday, you cannot get the mobility component.
Paras 1, 5 and 6 of Sch 1 DLA Regs; CSDLA/388/00

4. Qualifying periods

Backwards test

Under 65 – To qualify for DLA you must pass the disability test(s) throughout the 3 months before your claim. You can, however, claim (or ask for the award to be superseded) before the 3 months are up. If your condition starts to get worse before you are 65, you can move up a rate from 3 months afterwards (even if you are over 65 at the end of this qualifying period).
Ss.72(2)(a), 73(9)(a) SSCBA; reg 3, Sch 1 DLA Regs

Over 65 – If your care needs change on or after your 65th birthday, the qualifying period is 6 months, the same as for attendance allowance, not 3 months.

If your mobility gets worse on or after your 65th birthday, you cannot get mobility component for the first time, or switch rates.

Terminal illness – Whatever your age, there is no qualifying period if you are awarded DLA because you are terminally ill (see Box H.4). You will automatically get the highest rate care component, but to get mobility, you have to pass one of the disability tests (see 18) from your date of claim.

Renal dialysis – If you've passed the dialysis test (see 17) during the 3 months before your claim, you have served the qualifying period. Spells dialysing at least twice a week in hospital or as an outpatient getting help from hospital staff always count for the purposes of this qualifying period.

Linked claims – If you re-claim DLA within 2 years of the end of your previous award, the claims are linked. This means if you have a relapse, you don't have to re-serve the qualifying period. You can get DLA as soon as you re-claim, but only at the previous rate and component. If you qualify for a different amount, you will have to serve the qualifying period before it is paid.

If you are over 65, the 6-month qualifying period may apply and you can only have up to one year off DLA (see 3).

Reg 6 DLA Regs

Forwards test

You also have to show that you are likely to satisfy the disability test(s) throughout the 6 months after your claim.

5. How much do you get?

You can get one of the three rates of care component and one of the two rates of mobility component. You'll always get the highest rate to which you are entitled. Each person in your family who qualifies for DLA may claim it. Payment of DLA is affected by some situations (see 6).

DLA acts as a 'passport' for other types of help (see Box H.2).

Care component	per week
Highest rate	£60.60
Middle rate	£40.55
Lowest rate	£16.05

Mobility component	per week
Higher rate	£42.30
Lower rate	£16.05

The disability tests for the care component are explained in 9 to 17 below. The disability tests for the mobility component are explained in 18 to 22.

6. Does anything affect what you get?

Earnings – DLA is not affected by earnings. It is payable whether you are in or out of work, and no matter how much you earn. However, starting work may suggest your care needs or mobility problems have lessened, or you have found a simple way to cut back on the help you need from another person. Your DLA can be superseded because of this, but not just because you have started work. If your care needs or mobility problems are unchanged, you should have little to worry about. You may even have more care needs to enable you to do your job.

Other benefits or help – DLA is usually payable in full on top of any other social security benefit or tax credit. The only exceptions are outlined below.

Constant attendance allowance as part of industrial injuries disablement benefit or war pension overlaps with the care component. You'll be paid the higher of the two. War pensioners' mobility supplement overlaps with mobility component – so you'll get the supplement instead.

DLA is ignored as income for means-tested benefits and tax credits. However, if you are claiming income support (IS) on an 'urgent needs' basis, any DLA is taken into account. In all other cases, however, DLA may trigger extra benefit or tax credit. If you are awarded DLA, check to see if you now qualify for IS, income-based jobseeker's allowance, pension credit, housing benefit, council tax benefit, working tax credit or child tax credit, or higher amounts of any of these benefits. See Box H.2 for how getting DLA may help you qualify for other types of help in cash or kind.

The care component may be taken into account in non-social security means tests, such as in charging for local authority services (discretionary rules) and care in a care home (national rules) – see Chapter 25(6) and Box K.2, Chapter 31. However, the mobility component has specific protection against means testing – it can only ever be taken into account if the law (not policy or practice) governing such a test of means specifically states that the mobility component should count. Always ask for a reference to the exact legal provision under which mobility component is said to count as income.

S.73(14) SSCBA

If you go abroad – See Chapter 50 for details.

Refusing medicals – When you claim DLA, the decision maker can send a DWP approved doctor to visit you to carry out a medical examination. If you refuse to undergo the medical the claim will be decided against you unless you have 'good cause' for your refusal.

S.19 SSA98

You may also be asked to undergo a medical examination if you want your current DLA award to be revised or superseded, or if the decision maker considers it necessary to check it is correct (eg as part of the periodic enquiry process – see 25). In these circumstances, two consecutive failures to undergo a medical examination can result in payment of some or all of your DLA being suspended – but not if you have good cause for your actions. You'll be repaid if the decision maker decides you no longer need to undergo a medical examination, for example if you have been able to supply acceptable alternative evidence. But if payment continues to be suspended for one month or more, your entitlement may end.

S.24 SSA98; regs 19 and 20 D&A Regs

If you go into prison – Payment of DLA is suspended if you go into prison on remand to await trial. If you do not receive a custodial sentence, including a suspended sentence, you'll be paid any arrears of DLA for the time you've spent on remand.

If you go into hospital or special accommodation – Payment of the care component is affected by a period in hospital or special accommodation. Payment of the mobility component is affected only by a period in hospital; it is paid as normal in special accommodation. See 7 and 8.

7. If you go into hospital

Generally, payment of both the care component and the mobility component stops after you've been in hospital for 28 days (for adults) or 84 days (for children under 16).

Payment of benefit starts again from the first benefit pay day (usually a Wednesday) after you leave hospital. If you leave hospital temporarily and expect to return within 28 days, you can be paid your DLA for each day out of hospital (see Chapter 33(9)).

The mobility component can continue to be paid in hospital while you have a Motability agreement in force. Long-stay patients in hospital since before 31.7.95 may be able to keep the mobility component, cut to the lower rate.

If you first claim DLA when you are already in hospital, you cannot be paid until you leave. But you can then be paid for the full 28 (or 84) days if you return to hospital, even if you do so within 28 days.

For more details of how DLA is affected by stays in hospital, see Chapter 33.

Back to hospital within 28 days? – If you are readmitted to hospital, having been at home for 28 days or less since you were last in hospital, the number of days during each hospital stay are added together and payment of DLA stops after a total of 28 (or 84) days.

You count days in hospital from the day after you are admitted to the day before you go home. Neither the day you go in, nor the day you leave count as days in hospital. Box H.3 shows how you can plan a pattern of respite care that enables you to keep your DLA.

Linked spells in special accommodation – For the care component only, if you go into hospital straight from a care home or other special accommodation, or after having been home for 28 days or less, the two periods are added together, and the care component stops after 28 (or 84) days in total (see 8).

8. Special accommodation other than hospitals

Normally you cannot be paid the care component if you live in some types of accommodation, but you should apply for it anyway. Once you establish that you pass the disability tests, you can be paid the care component for any day you are not in special accommodation – eg in your own home or staying with relatives.

The rules on being paid the care component in special accommodation are very complex and this chapter only gives the main points. Chapter 30 gives further details. If you are entitled to DLA care component but are told you will not be paid, or if your DLA stops because of the special accommodation rules, it is worth seeking expert advice. If you receive a form asking about your accommodation and how it is funded, seek advice, as it is often not easy to know how your accommodation should be described.

The mobility component is not affected by stays in special accommodation. The rules below apply only to the care component.

What is special accommodation?

Payment of DLA care component may be affected by stays in the following types of accommodation:

- any home provided under Part III of the National Assistance Act 1948 or Part IV of the Social Work (Scotland) Act 1968 or section 7 of the Mental Health (Scotland) Act 1984;
- any home where *'the cost of [your] accommodation is borne wholly or partly out of public or local funds in pursuance of'* any legislation *'relating to persons under disability or to young persons or to education or training' (including s117 Mental Health Act 1983).*

Reg 9(1) DLA Regs

People who are entitled to DLA care component in special accommodation

See Chapter 30 for more detail, but, in brief, you will be able to receive DLA care component even if you are in special accommodation if:

- you are terminally ill and residing in a hospice, defined as *'a hospital or other institution whose primary function is to provide palliative care for persons... suffering from a progressive disease in its final stages'* (but not an NHS hospital);
- the local authority has accommodated you with someone in a private dwelling and you are under age 18 and accommodated because of your disability or are under age 16 and being looked after by the local authority;
- you are a child living outside the UK and being funded by the Education Act (such as at the Peto Institute Hungary);
- your accommodation is funded by a student grant or loan;
- you are living in a care home and paying the fees in full with or without the help of benefits such as income support or pension credit. However, in Scotland, if you are 65 or over and get free personal care payments from the local authority, you will not be paid DLA care component even if you are otherwise self-funding. If you are self-funding except for nursing care payments, you can be paid DLA care component;
- the local authority is paying your fees only until you are able to repay them in full (eg once you sell your house).

The 4-week concession

If you claim the care component before you are in special accommodation, this can continue for up to 28 days (for adults and children), even if you are not normally entitled to it, as described in the rules above. Payment may stop sooner if you have been in special accommodation within the past 28 days. In this case, the different periods are added together and treated as one stay. So your care component will stop after a total of 28 days. You count a stay in special accommodation from the day after you enter to the day before you leave. Box H.3 shows how you can plan a pattern of respite care that allows you to keep your care component.

H.3 Respite care

As well as this box and Chapter 20(7) and (8), you should read Chapter 30 for the effect on benefits of a stay in a care home, and Chapter 32 for hospital stays.

The linking rule

Payment of both care and mobility components stops after you've been in hospital for 28 days (84 days for children under 16). If you go back into hospital after being at home for 28 days or less, the two (or more) hospital stays are linked. Adding together the number of days in hospital in each linked stay, DLA stops after a total of 28 (or 84) days. You are still paid for days at home.

In the same way, payment of care component stops after you've been in special accommodation for a total of 28 days (adults and children) in one stay, or in linked stays where the gaps at home are 28 days or less. The mobility component is not affected by stays in special accommodation.

If you go into hospital then into special accommodation, or the other way round, payment of care component stops after 28 days, adding together days spent in hospital and in special accommodation. Stays in hospital and special accommodation are linked if they follow on from each other or if you spend 28 days or less at home in between.

If a child under 16 has linked spells in hospital and special accommodation, see 8.

You count a stay in hospital or special accommodation from the day after you enter to the day before you leave.

Careful counting

If you keep a careful count of the days you (or your disabled child) are in hospital or special accommodation, you can establish a pattern of respite care that will allow you to keep the mobility component and/or care component. But even if you can't keep your DLA for all the days in respite care, you can be paid for days at home.

Example: If you have 2 full days of respite care every weekend you can continue like this for 14 weeks (2 x 14 = 28 days). For 14 weekends, you can go into respite care on a Friday and return home on a Monday. Only Saturday and Sunday count as days in hospital or special accommodation – the day you enter and the day you leave count as days at home.

If your respite care is provided in special accommodation, the care component will not be paid for days of respite care (Saturday and Sunday) after the 14 weeks unless you break the link (see below) – although you can be paid for days at home (Monday to Friday). Your mobility component is not affected by a stay in special accommodation so continues to be paid as usual.

If your respite care is provided in hospital, neither the mobility component (unless you have a Motability agreement

If you are not normally entitled to the care component, as described in the rules above, and do not claim it before you go into special accommodation, it is not payable until you leave. Once you leave, you can be paid for the first 28 days after you return to special accommodation, even if you do so within 28 days. This only applies to your first period of payment. After that, any periods with less than 28 days between are added together.

Temporary absences

Once you are entitled to DLA, it can be paid for days you spend away from special accommodation, including the day you leave and the day you return. For example, if you spend a weekend at home with relatives, going home on Friday and returning on Sunday, you will be paid the care component for those 3 days.

Linked spells in hospital and special accommodation

For the care component only, spells in hospital and special accommodation are linked if the gap between them is no more than 28 days. There is no link for the mobility component because payment is not affected when you are in special accommodation.

For adults, the care component stops being paid after a total of 28 days in hospital or special accommodation, or both if you've moved from one to the other with a gap of 28 days or less in between.

The position for children under 16 is more complicated if they have linked spells in both special accommodation and hospital. Payment of the care component for children continues for the first 84 days (12 weeks) in hospital but in special accommodation it stops after 28 days. The following three examples show how the linking rule works for children.

- If you have been in special accommodation (eg residential school) for, say, 6 weeks, return home for a week, and then go into hospital, the care component is payable for your week at home and the first 6 weeks in hospital. This is because you have not yet had a linked spell in hospital or special accommodation of longer than 84 days – so you can be paid for the remainder of the 84 days you spend in hospital.
- If you had been in special accommodation for 12 or more weeks and then went into hospital, the two spells are linked and you will not be paid the care component. You cannot be paid for the 12-week hospital concession because you have already been in either type of accommodation for over 84 days.
- If you have spent 29 days in your own home, you have broken the link with any earlier spells in hospital or special accommodation (see Box H.3). If you go into hospital, you can then be paid for the first 84 days. If you go back to special accommodation you can then be paid for the first 28 days.

B. THE CARE COMPONENT

9. The disability tests

To qualify for DLA care component your care needs must ultimately stem from disability – both physical and mental disabilities may help you qualify. You must need care, supervision or watching over from another person because of your disabilities. You must be *'so severely disabled physically or mentally that ... you require [from another person]':*

during the day

No. 1 *'frequent attention throughout the day in connection with [your] bodily functions' or*

No. 2 *'continual supervision throughout the day in order to avoid substantial danger to [yourself] or others' or*

at night

No. 3 *'prolonged or repeated attention in connection with [your] bodily functions' or*

No. 4 *'in order to avoid substantial danger to [yourself] or others [you require] another person to be awake for a prolonged period or at frequent intervals for the purpose of watching over [you]' or*

part-time day care

No. 5 *'[you require] in connection with [your] bodily functions attention from another person for a significant portion of the day (whether during a single*

in force) nor care component will be paid for respite days after the 14 weeks unless you break the link. You will continue to be paid DLA for days at home.

If a child under 16 is in hospital, you could continue this pattern for 42 weeks (2 x 42 = 84 days), before losing payment of DLA for further days in hospital until you break the link.

Break the link

If you spend 29 days in your own home, you will break the link between respite care stays. The next time you go into respite care in special accommodation, your care component can be paid for another 28 days, in one stay or in linked stays. Similarly, the next time you go into respite care in hospital, your care and mobility component can be paid for another 28 days (84 days for children).

A pattern of respite care interrupted by spells of at least 29 days in your own home will allow you to keep the care and mobility component. Direct payments of DLA into a bank or other account will continue, but you must let the Disability Benefits Unit have details of all dates you enter or leave respite care.

In the example above, you can break the link and at the same time continue to have some respite care. For the next 4 weekends, instead of going into respite care on a Friday and leaving on a Monday, you go in on the Saturday morning and return home on the Sunday evening. Because the day you enter and the day you leave hospital or special accommodation count as days at home, you'll have spent more than 28 days in a row at home and so you'll have broken the link. For the next 14 weekends, you can return to your main Friday to Monday pattern of respite care.

Informing the Disability Benefits Unit

When you first go into respite care, always write to the Disability Benefits Unit (see inside back cover), giving the name and address of the place you are going to, the date you will be entering the home or hospital and the date you will be leaving to return to your own home. If you have planned a specific pattern of respite care in advance, let the Unit have details. Keep a copy of your letter. If there are any changes from your planned pattern of care, write and let the Unit know.

Arranging or keeping to a pattern of respite care that allows you to keep your DLA (by breaking the link every 28 days) will not always be possible. Until that link is broken you will not be entitled to the care component (or mobility component in the case of hospital stays) for any further days spent in respite care from the 29th day onwards. However, you will be entitled for the days spent in your own home. When you tell the Unit the dates you'll be entering and leaving care, the Unit adjusts each payment to your bank or other account as necessary. You are unlikely to wait longer than your next pay day for what you are owed.

period or a number of periods)' or
cooking test
No. 6 *'[you] cannot prepare a cooked main meal for [yourself] if [you have] the ingredients'.*
S.72(1) SSCBA

Highest rate care component – You'll pass the disability test for the £60.60 highest rate if you satisfy:

- either (or both) No. 1 or No. 2 daytime tests; *and*
- either (or both) No. 3 or No. 4 night-time tests.

Basically, your care or supervision needs are spread throughout both the day and the night.

If you are terminally ill, you qualify automatically for the highest rate even if you need no care at all when you claim (see Box H.4 for details).

Middle rate care component – You'll pass the disability test for the £40.55 middle rate if you satisfy:

- either (or both) No. 1 or No. 2 daytime tests; *or*
- either (or both) No. 3 or No. 4 night-time tests.

Basically, your care or supervision needs are spread throughout just the day or just the night.

If you are undergoing dialysis two or more times a week and normally require some help with the dialysis, you may qualify automatically for the middle rate (see 17 for details).

Lowest rate care component – You'll pass the disability test for the £16.05 lowest rate if you satisfy either (or both) the No. 5 or No. 6 'part-time day care' or cooking tests. There is an upper age limit for this rate: you must be under 65 when you first start to satisfy either the No. 5 or No. 6 lowest rate disability tests. There is also a lower age limit: if you are under 16 you cannot use the No. 6 cooking test, but you can use the No. 5 'part-time day care' test.

Children

As well as satisfying any of the No. 1 to No. 5 disability tests, a child or young person under 16 must show that *either:*

- their needs are *'substantially in excess of the normal requirements of persons [their] age'*; or

H.4 Terminal illness

Automatic DLA

If you are considered terminally ill, you don't have to serve the qualifying period to get DLA. Claims identified as being from terminally ill people are given high priority under what the DWP calls the 'Special Rules'. If you are claiming under these, the DWP hopes to send you a decision within 8 working days.

You will qualify automatically for DLA highest rate care component if your death *'can reasonably be expected'* within the next 6 months. If you pass the 'terminal illness' test, you are treated as satisfying the conditions for the highest rate – even if at the time of the claim you don't need nursing-type help from another person. However, to get the mobility component you must pass one of the disability tests (see 18).

Living with a terminal illness, particularly with the shock on first diagnosis, is distressing. Claiming benefits and sorting out any financial problems tend to be the last thing on your mind. In part, claiming DLA is an acknowledgement, if not acceptance, of what is happening to you: and you may not yet be ready to fully face up to that. Unfortunately, DLA cannot be backdated to before the day you actually claimed it. There is no extension of the time limit for claiming to allow time to adjust. All we can advise is to claim as soon as you feel able.

Do note that even though you have a terminal illness, you will fail the test if at the time you claim, your death cannot reasonably be expected within the next 6 months. Discuss things with your doctor to make sure a claim is submitted quickly. If you are turned down, check with your doctor and ask for a revision or lodge an appeal against that decision (see below), or simply make a fresh claim when your situation changes.

How do you claim?

Claim in the normal way (see 23). The claim-pack explains which bits of the claim-form you need to fill in. If you are claiming under the Special Rules, you are asked to send a factual statement (a DS1500 report) from your doctor or consultant to the DWP along with your claim-form. Your doctor should have a supply of DS1500 forms available.

The person who is terminally ill does not have to sign the claim-form. Another person, including their doctor, can claim benefit on their behalf, for example where the terminally ill person is not up to completing the form, or has not yet been told the full nature of their condition. In this box we refer to the terminally ill person as the 'claimant' even though they may not physically make the claim, or even know about the claim. However, payment will be made direct to the claimant.

Hospital – If you are in hospital when you first claim DLA, it cannot be paid until you leave hospital. If you are in special accommodation, you can claim and be paid the mobility component as normal, and in some circumstances you may get the care component. See 7 and 8 for more details.

What happens once you claim?

Once you have claimed, a decision maker decides if you satisfy the test of terminal illness. Decisions are based on the evidence about your clinical condition, diagnosis and treatment, which your doctor or consultant gives in the factual statement. The DS1500 report does not ask about prognosis (ie about your life expectancy). However, the decision maker will refer your case to a doctor for expert advice. That doctor may phone your doctor to clarify any matters.

In some cases your doctor may not feel ready to complete the DS1500 – eg where the diagnosis and future treatment are not yet fully confirmed because one or two other possibilities, with different implications for treatment, have yet to be ruled out. Your doctor can complete the statement based on what is currently known about your condition, and forward complete details when they are available.

If you satisfy the terminal illness test at this first stage, you will be awarded the highest rate care component, normally for the remainder of your life.

If the decision maker considers that you don't satisfy the terminal illness test, based on the information from you and your doctor, a medical examination may be arranged. A DWP doctor will examine you and complete a report. The decision maker will then decide your claim under the terminal illness provisions. If you don't satisfy that test, the decision maker will go on to consider your claim under the ordinary disability tests. If the decision on part or all of your claim is negative, you can ask for a revision or you can appeal (see below).

What if you already get DLA?

In some cases, you will already be getting the lowest or middle rate care component or the mobility component. You don't have to make a separate claim under the terminal illness provisions. Instead, you just write to ask for the award to be superseded on the basis that you now count as terminally ill. You don't have to send in a completed factual statement

- they have *'substantial'* care, supervision or watching-over needs *'which younger persons in normal physical or mental health may also have but which persons of [their] age and in normal physical and mental health would not have'*.

Chapter 35(2) explains how the disability tests apply to children. To get payment from birth, a baby must be terminally ill, in which case the qualifying period, 26-week presence and extra children's tests do not apply. In all other cases, a baby must need substantially more help than a healthy baby. For example, if your baby has severe feeding problems from birth, the qualifying period means that payment can only start from the first pay day on or after the day they reach 3 months old – see 7 if your baby is still in hospital. A shorter (13-week) presence test applies if you are claiming for a baby who is under 6 months old.

The starting point

The starting point for your attention, care, supervision and/or watching-over needs must be that you are *'so severely disabled physically or mentally that [you require]...'*. In most cases this poses no problem.

If you do not have a specific diagnosis of your condition, you may have trouble qualifying. However, your needs may still be taken into account if it is medically accepted that they arise from a condition that is either a physical or mental disability, even if doctors do not know exactly what it is in your case.

Whether or not alcohol or drug misuse is classed as a disability in itself, any mental or physical disability suffered as a result should be assessed in the normal way even if you could control your habit. If you need supervision partly because of excess drinking and partly because of depression, it can all count (CDLA/396/2004). However, attention needs arising solely from intoxication would not generally count (CDLA/ 2408/02).

There is no extra test of the severity of your disability.

from your doctor along with your letter, but it will speed up the decision-making process if you can do so.

If you are successful on this application, the highest rate should be backdated to the date you first counted as terminally ill if you told them within one month. If it has been longer than one month, the highest rate can still be fully backdated if special circumstances caused the delay, so do say in your letter why it has taken you longer (eg you were too ill or distressed to cope).

The legal definition of terminal illness

S.66(2)(a) of the SSCBA provides that you count as being terminally ill at any time *'if at that time [you have] a progressive disease and [your] death in consequence of that disease can reasonably be expected within 6 months'*.

The diagnosis question should be straightforward. Are you suffering from a disease which is a progressive one? Is the disease one which, by its nature, develops and gets worse, perhaps in identifiable stages? Multiple sclerosis, for example, is a progressive disease, even though some people may have long periods of remission, or may never develop the final range of symptoms. Similarly, although AIDS is a syndrome, it counts as a progressive disease because it involves a progressive breakdown of the body's immune system.

It is easily possible to satisfy the diagnosis part of the terminal illness test. What is crucial for qualifying for DLA automatically is the question of prognosis. To pass the prognosis part of the test, the decision maker has to agree that your *'death in consequence of that disease can reasonably be expected within 6 months'*.

There are two aspects to the prognosis test: the connection between the disease and the expected death, and the fact that your death can reasonably be expected within 6 months.

The disease alone doesn't have to be solely responsible for your death. Industrial death benefit, which was abolished in April 1988, had a similar test: death had to be *'as a result of'* an industrial accident or disease. Case law established that as long as death was 'materially accelerated' by the industrial accident or disease, the widow qualified for industrial death benefit even though the immediate cause of death was, for example, pneumonia.

The DLA prognosis test looks forward, rather than backwards. It may be that, given your progressive disease alone, your death could not reasonably be expected within 6 months: but your age or general physical condition may, for example, make respiratory infections more likely. You may be more prone to complications associated with, but not part of, your progressive disease. As long as the progressive disease plays the key role in whether your death can reasonably be expected within 6 months, you should succeed in your claim for automatic DLA. With diseases such as AIDS or motor neurone disease, the progress and nature of the disease itself makes you more vulnerable to other conditions: the connection between the disease and those other conditions is clear.

Note that we use the actual words from the Act. It is important not to translate them into different words as a different form of wording may imply a different test. The statutory test of terminal illness is not a matter of what is possible, or of what is or is not hoped for. Instead, it focuses on expectations of death: if, on all the evidence, your death could reasonably be expected within 6 months, you are entitled to succeed. It is a test of what can reasonably be expected on the evidence, rather than of certainty.

This test does not put an upper limit on life expectancy: it is not a matter of what is the longest period you can reasonably be expected to live. Clearly no one can predict death 6 months ahead to the day, nor even to the month. It is quite possible that your death could reasonably be expected at any time within a period of 5 to 10 months ahead. In this case, the upper limit of your reasonable life expectancy would be 10 months ahead, with death at that stage fairly certain; while 5 months ahead would be the start of the period during which your death could reasonably be expected, rather than just being a possibility.

Appeals

Decisions on whether or not you satisfy the terminal illness test can be revised or appealed in the normal way (see Chapter 58). An existing award can also be superseded. Although the DWP has said it doesn't intend to supersede a terminal illness award just because you have lived for over 6 months, it is also the case that if your prognosis changes so that you no longer count as terminally ill, your award can be superseded.

Harmful medical information – On appeal, if the claimant has not been told about specific medical evidence or advice about their condition or prognosis, and the chair of the appeal tribunal considers that disclosure of that medical advice or evidence to the claimant *'would be harmful to his [or her] health'*, it won't be included in any papers sent to the claimant. If you consider that such evidence could be harmful to the claimant in an appeal, you should clarify this in your appeal letter.

10. What is the 'cooking test'?

This is the No. 6 disability test for the lowest rate care component. You must be aged 16 or over to qualify for the lowest rate on this basis. The upper age limit for starting to qualify for the first time is the day before your 65th birthday. But if you claim before your 65th birthday, the lowest rate can be maintained and renewed.

You have to show that you are *'so severely disabled physically or mentally that... [you] cannot prepare a cooked main meal for [yourself] if [you have] the ingredients'*.
S.72(1)(a)(ii) SSCBA

The cooking test is intended to be a hypothetical or abstract test. It is intended to gauge the level of disability rather than examine your ability to cook or otherwise. The test looks at whether you can carry out all the activities necessary to prepare a cooked main meal without help from another person.

The cooking test covers people whose disabilities mean they cannot cook at all, even if they had help. It also applies to people who don't normally cook, and to those who do cook but cannot prepare the type of cooked main meal at issue or who need some help to carry out the tasks they are capable of.

What does the cooking test involve?

There are a number of different issues involved in the cooking test. The nature of the *'cooked main meal'* which you have to show you *'cannot prepare'* for yourself is crucial. It should be a labour intensive, reasonable, main daily meal, freshly cooked on a traditional cooker. The main daily meal is intended to be a standard meal for just one person, not for the rest of the household.
R(DLA) 2/95

The use of the word 'prepare' in the law puts the emphasis on your ability to prepare all the ingredients ready for cooking. The meal is not intended to be a main meal made up of convenience foods, such as pies and frozen vegetables involving no real preparation.

You *'cannot prepare a cooked main meal for [yourself]'* if you can only do so with some help. The need for any type of help counts – it doesn't have to involve any effort or be at all substantial. But it must be crucial in enabling you to start or carry on with the tasks you are capable of doing by yourself.

What kind of meal is reasonable (eg vegetarian) depends on the community to which you belong. Because this is a hypothetical test, it is irrelevant that you may never wish to cook such a meal or you cannot afford to do so. Nor is it relevant that you prepare, cook and freeze a number of main meals on the days you actually have the help you need (and then defrost and heat them up in the microwave on the other days). The test depends on what you cannot do, without help, if you tried to do it on each day.

If you would be limited to cooking a very narrow range of main meals you should pass the test (CDLA/17329/96).

Intermittent disability – You don't have to show you were unable to cook on every day of the 3 months before your claim and are likely to be unable to cook on every day of the next 6 months. The test is rather about what can be seen as normal for you over a period of time. Taking the ordinary English language meaning of the words, and applying the test to the effects of your disabilities, is it true to say that (over the 9-month period) you *'cannot prepare a cooked main meal...'*?
R(A)2/74; Moyna v Secretary of State for Work and Pensions, 31.7.03(reported in R(DLA)7/03)

The ability to cook a main meal on 4 out of 7 days each week does not mean, in law, that you must fail the test. All depends on the pattern of what you cannot do over the whole of the qualifying period. If you still have difficulties on your good days, that can help tip the balance your way, so explain fully what you cannot do on both your good and your bad days. In practice, if you say on the DLA claim-form that you need help on 1 to 3 days only, your chances of success are much lower.

Reasonableness – The test is one of whether you cannot reasonably be expected to prepare a cooked main meal for yourself. Things like safety, tiredness, pain, breathing difficulties in a hot, steamy kitchen or the time it would take you to do everything may mean that although you can, in fact, prepare a cooked main meal, it is not reasonable to expect you to do so (see R(DLA)1/97). If you cannot stand for long enough, it may be suggested that you could use a stool. Explain why it is not reasonable for you to do the peeling, chopping, waiting for food to cook or other tasks while sitting down (see R(DLA)8/02), eg you might only have the strength and leverage to cut vegetables from a standing position.

Special equipment – The cooking test does not depend on the type of facilities or equipment you have available. The test is satisfied if you cannot perform the tasks necessary to prepare a main meal using normal reasonable facilities and devices (R(DLA)2/95). Whether you could manage by specially adapting the kitchen or making other arrangements is irrelevant. Being able to heat convenience food in a microwave is not relevant. However, if you know how to and do use a microwave to cook main meals with ingredients you prepare yourself, you might not pass the test. If you use a microwave in this way explain any drawbacks, eg can you only cook a narrow range of meals or do ingredients cooked first need to be kept warm and, if so, are you able to use a low oven?

Practice and process

To produce an edible cooked main meal calls for the ability to carry out, by yourself, all the physical and mental actions, tasks and stages involved in the process. If there is any part of the process you are (or would be) unable to carry out by yourself, you'll pass this test – even if you cope (or would cope) well with the rest. See R(S)11/81 for support.

If you have a severe mental disability and therefore you cannot plan ahead or complete complex tasks, you will pass the cooking test. If lack of motivation is caused by, or is a symptom of, a mental disability, so that you cannot begin to prepare a meal or complete the preparations, you could pass the test (CSDLA/80/96).

The process of preparing a cooked main meal includes:

- planning what to prepare for the cooked main meal – eg each type of food, seasoning, and the quantities required. The law says you already have the ingredients for the main meal, so it's debatable whether or not preparation also includes getting them from their usual storage places;
- carrying out all the stages in the correct order and to the required timings;
- washing, peeling and chopping fresh vegetables, meat, etc;
- using taps – eg to fill a saucepan;
- using a cooker – eg lighting the gas, adjusting the heat, opening and closing an oven door;
- putting the food into pans, stirring, tasting, checking whether it's properly cooked;
- lifting and moving full or hot pans on or off a cooker, or bending to lift pans into or out of the oven (explain why it is reasonable for you to want to use the oven – eg to prepare a reasonable variety of suitable meals – or to use a low-level grill);
- draining cooked vegetables from hot pans; *and*
- dishing up your meal.

11. What is 'attention'?

This means active help from another person to do the personal things you cannot do for yourself. It does not matter whether you actually get the help; what counts is the help you need. It must also be help that would need to be given in your presence, not, for example, over the telephone.

To count as 'attention', the help you need because of your disability must be in connection with your 'bodily functions' and it must be 'reasonably required'.

Help with 'bodily functions'

Bodily functions are personal things such as breathing, hearing, seeing, eating, drinking, walking, sitting, sleeping, getting in or out of bed, dressing and undressing, going to the toilet, getting in or out of the bath, washing, shaving, communicating, speech practice, help with medication or treatment, etc. Anything to do with your body and how it works can count.

Indirect or ancillary attention counts but is often forgotten. Think about the beginnings and ends of particular activities. Where there are other tasks involved during the course of attending to a bodily function, these can count if they are done on the spot. For example, if you need help to change bedding because of incontinence, then rinsing out the bedclothes if it is done straight away also counts, as can soothing you back to sleep. If you need help with eating, then cleaning up spills also counts.

Cockburn v CAO, 21.5.97 (reported in R(A)2/98); R(A)2/74; Ramsden v Secretary of State for Work and Pensions, 31.1.03 (reported in R(DLA) 2/03)

If there is some part of an activity you need help with (and you could not carry on without it) that also counts. For example, you may be able to dress yourself, but you cannot get your clothes, or you need to be prompted to dress. It is irrelevant that you can manage most of the activity by yourself. If it takes you a long time to do something, eg getting dressed, you may reasonably require help even though you persevere and eventually manage by yourself.

If you are deaf, the help of an interpreter to communicate counts, as does assistance in developing communication skills. Extra effort attracting your attention may count (R(DLA)1/02). The extra effort involved in two-way communication where one of you is not adequately skilled in sign language, may also be included as 'attention' (R(DLA)3/02).

Domestic duties and other kinds of help

You might need help with things that can't easily be seen as bodily functions, such as reading, guiding, shopping, cooking, housework, etc. But if your disability is such that there is one bodily function that is 'primarily impaired', then whatever activities you need help with in connection with that impaired bodily function can count (as long as it is *'reasonably required'*). For example, in the case of a blind person, the 'primarily impaired' function is seeing. So help reading correspondence or labels, or with guiding – anything you would do for yourself if your sight were not impaired – can count. In this example the help would be attention in connection with the bodily function of seeing, not reading, which is not a bodily function, or walking, which is not itself impaired by loss of sight. Similarly, if you are deaf or paralysed, the primarily impaired function is hearing or movement. Once you have identified the impaired bodily function, think of all the help you need from other people to do things you could do for yourself if you did not have that disability. You don't actually have to be getting help, it is enough that the help is *'reasonably required'* (see below).

Mallinson v Secretary of State for Social Security [1994] (reported in R(A)3/94)

In each case, the help you need must be carried out in your presence and involve some personal contact with you – this can be physical contact or talking or signing. Generally, this rules out domestic tasks such as cooking, shopping and cleaning – they are not themselves bodily functions nor would they normally need to be carried out in your presence. However, while it would not count if someone does the cooking for you, if someone helps you to do the cooking *for yourself*, eg reading labels and recipes, checking cooker settings, this could count if it is reasonably required (see below). You might argue it is reasonable for you to develop or maintain a level of independence. In practice, the DWP has not accepted that help to do domestic tasks counts. But if you need to include such help to meet the required frequency of attention, give details of all the help you need. Try to link the help you need to the bodily function which is impaired – and be prepared to appeal.

There is conflicting case law. To start with, see CDLA/12045/96, about help for a blind person to carry out domestic tasks themself, in which the Commissioner approved CDLA/8167/95 as reflecting the weight of authority.

Disabled parents

Help to care for your child can count as attention. The help must be given to you to enable you to look after the child. For example, lifting a baby so a mother with arthritis can breastfeed counts as attention but undressing a child because the mother cannot manage buttons does not. Waking a deaf parent at night to feed or attend to a child can count. For any help that you need to wash, dress, toilet, feed or play with your child, explain how the help is given to you rather than to the child. The help must be of a close and intimate nature involving you physically or involving talking or signing with you present. You must show that you reasonably need this help to look after your child yourself rather than having someone else do it for you. You could argue, for example, that you need to bond with a baby or that it is reasonable for you to have help to take part in your child's outdoor activities. Parents cannot always persuade the DWP that such help counts for DLA but you are likely to have more success for babies and younger children or for a sick child (see CDLA/5216/98, CDLA/4352/99 and CDLA/16129/96).

'Reasonably required'

The attention you need must be *'reasonably required'* rather than medically required. You may reasonably require more attention than you actually get. For example, if the only help you get is over the telephone, perhaps to encourage you to dress or eat or to check on you, you may well argue that your needs would be more reasonably met by direct help in your presence, or more direct help than is actually available to you. If you are deaf, communication might be easier if you had an interpreter (see R(DLA)3/02). Think about activities you manage only with difficulty or in an unsafe way, even if you don't actually get help from another person.

The test is whether *'the attention is reasonably required to enable [you] as far as reasonably possible to live a normal life'*. This includes social, recreational and cultural activities – what is reasonable depends on your age, interests and other circumstances.

Secretary of State v Fairey (reported in R(A)2/98)

The DLA claim-form asks about the help you need with hobbies, interests and social activities, both indoors and out. Include things you don't do now but would do if you had the help, perhaps things you used to enjoy or things you would like help to be able to do. For each activity explain the help you need from another person with respect to your bodily functions (see above) – eg help getting into outdoor clothes, getting into a car, getting in or out of a chair.

Refusing medical treatment

If you refuse medical treatment that would reduce the help you need from others, you may find this help is consequently not taken into account. In this case you should explain why your refusal is reasonable. You cannot be expected to undergo invasive surgery nor should it count against you if treatment would have unwanted side effects or if a psychiatric condition leads you to avoid treatment (R(DLA)10/02).

During the day

Frequent attention – To pass the No. 1 disability test (see 9 above), you have to show that during the daytime you need this help frequently and throughout the day – during the middle of the day, as well as in the morning and evening. The fact that you can manage most of your bodily functions without help does not mean you fail this test; it depends on the pattern of your accepted care needs.

'Frequent' means *'several times – not once or twice'*, and the pattern of help must be such that, looking at all the facts about your accepted care needs as a whole, it is true to say you need *'frequent attention throughout the day'*. It is difficult to give a clear dividing line between passing the test and not. The best advice is to give as full a picture of your care needs as you can. Describe the help you need, why you need it, and when it is provided. Are your care needs spread throughout the day, or in two or three parts of the day? Is the care provided when you need it or when your carer is available? Would it be better for you if help was provided at other times or for longer?

If your care needs vary because your condition fluctuates over time, give an idea of the pattern of those needs over, say, a month or whatever period of time accurately reflects your circumstances. The decision maker must then focus on what care you need and the pattern of those needs, rather than the length of time it takes to meet your needs and the gaps between the attention.

See R(A)2/80, R(A)4/78, CA/140/85 and 10 above (under 'Intermittent disability')

Significant portion – To pass the No. 5 disability test for the lowest rate (see 9 above), you must show you need help from another person for a *'significant portion of the day'*. That help may be needed all at once, or over a number of occasions. You should pass this test if it would take an hour or so in total to give you the help you need (see CDLA/58/93).

This test for the lowest rate is intended to cover people who, for example, need help only getting up and going to bed but can manage on their own for the rest of the day. But it can also cover anyone whose care needs aren't sufficiently spread out over the whole day to fit the pattern for *'throughout the day'*.

Less than one hour's care, may still count as a significant portion of the day. In deciding this, the position of the carer may be taken into account. If the carer's own life is disrupted by the need to give attention on a considerable number of small occasions in the day, then those periods of providing attention taken together may be significant, even though individually they may be relatively insignificant. Periods of intense, concentrated activity may be more significant than more routine tasks.

(CSDLA/29/94; Ramsden v Secretary of State for Work and Pensions, 31.1.03 reported in R(DLA) 2/03)

Depending on the frequency and pattern of your accepted care needs, it may also be possible to pass the *'frequent attention'* test for the middle rate even though it would take less than an hour in all to give you the help you need. If you need an hour's worth (or less) of help on and off several times over the whole course of the day, the pattern of your care needs should pass the frequent attention test. If the pattern of your care needs isn't clear from the answers in your DLA claim-form, it is worth keeping a diary for a short time to make sure you are not wrongly awarded the lowest rate.

During the night

During the night the help that you need must either be *'prolonged'* (normally at least 20 minutes) or *'repeated'* (needed 2 times or more).

R(A) 2/80, CDLA/5465/2002

There is no fixed time for the start of the night. It depends on when your household closes down for the night. It normally starts when your carer goes to bed and ends when they get up in the morning. Night-time for a disabled child is when the parent is in bed so any attention a parent gives after their child has gone to bed but before the parent's own normal bedtime would be daytime attention. On the other hand, if a parent or carer stays up late or gets up early to attend to you, that should count as night-time attention. If you live alone and keep unusual hours, like getting up at 4.30am, your care needs may count as night-time care between the more usual bedtime hours of 11pm to 7am.

R(A) 4/74, CDLA/2852/02, CDLA/997/03, R(A)1/04 and CDLA/3242/03.

12. What is 'continual supervision'?

Supervision is more or less what it says: you need someone around to prevent any accidents either to yourself, or to other people. The words used are *'continual supervision'*. This means frequent or regular, but not non-stop; you don't need supervision every single minute. The supervision doesn't have to prevent the danger completely, but it must be needed *'in order to effect a real reduction in the risk of harm to the claimant'* (R(A)3/92).

The supervision must be *'reasonably required'*, rather than medically required. For example, you may be mentally alert and know what you should not do without someone on hand to help. Medically speaking, you could supervise yourself. But the question is whether or not you reasonably require supervision from someone else. In practice, supervising yourself might mean that to avoid the risk of danger you would have to do nothing but stay in bed or an armchair. If you would have to restrict your lifestyle in order to supervise yourself without help from someone else, the question is whether or not those restrictions are reasonable. Do they allow you to carry on anything approaching a normal life? If the restrictions on your lifestyle are not reasonable, then you reasonably require help from another person to live a normal life.

The next question is whether you satisfy the rest of the continual supervision test, which has 4 parts (R(A)1/83).

- You must show that your medical condition is such that it may (not will) give rise to substantial danger to yourself or to others. The danger to you could arise from your own actions or from the actions of other people. The danger to others could be wholly unintended (eg if you aren't able to care for a young child safely).
- The substantial danger must not be too remote a possibility. But the fact that an incident may be isolated or infrequent does not rule this out. As well as looking at the chances of the incident happening, the decision maker must look at the likely consequences if it does. If the consequences could be dire, then the frequency with which it is likely to happen becomes less relevant. Explain why a particular risk is reasonably likely in your circumstances.
- You must need supervision from someone else to avoid the substantial danger.
- The supervision must be continual, but the person providing the supervision need not always be alert, awake and active. Standby supervision, and being ready to intervene and help, can also count.

If you suffer from epilepsy and the onset of an attack is unpredictable, with not enough warning for help to arrive or for you to put yourself in a place of safety, then you may qualify for DLA care component: certainly at the middle rate for your daytime supervision needs. This is because of the case of *Moran v Secretary of State for Social Services* (reported in R(A)1/88). The principles in *Moran* also help other people whose needs for supervision and attention are unpredictable, and where the consequences of an unsupervised attack would be grave. It particularly helps those who are mentally alert and can supervise themselves between attacks but not during attacks.

Supervision and falls

If you are mentally alert and sensible, it is sometimes said that you could supervise yourself and so avoid the risk of falling without help from another person. This approach has been ruled too simplistic by R(A)3/89 and R(A)5/90(T).

Decision makers must consider the evidence, properly evaluate the risk of falling in any case, and give sufficient reasons for their conclusions. In particular, it is not enough to say you are sensible. They must identify any precautions you could take and/or any activities you should not do if you are to avoid the risk of falls without help from someone else. It is only if it is *'possible to isolate one or two activities which alone might give rise to a fall, and which could be avoided except for one or two occasions during the course of the day, and [you would] still be left to enjoy a more or less normal life, [that] it would be justifiable to say that continual supervision was not required. Everything will depend upon the facts of the case'* (CA/127/88, para 8). However, there is a close overlap between supervision and attention. Even if your need for help to avoid the risk of falls does not amount to continual supervision, it is possible that particular help could count as attention (see 16).

13. What is 'watching over'?

'Watching over' has its ordinary English language meaning: so it includes needing to have someone else being awake and listening, as well as getting up and checking how you are.

Remember the care component is based on the help or supervision you reasonably need from another person, not the help or supervision you actually get. Your care needs must stem from physical or mental disablement, but it need not be medically essential to have that help or supervision. Rather you should show that, given all the circumstances, the help is reasonably required. Nor do you have to need that level of help every night in the week. It depends on the normal pattern of your needs – 3 or 4 nights a week may be sufficient, perhaps less if the dangers would be very grave.

A *'prolonged period'* is normally at least 20 minutes. It is arguable whether for the 'watching over' test this includes the time immediately before and after you actually need someone watching over you. (Note that the night-time attention test takes this extra time into account – ie the time a carer would take to get out of bed and back to bed after attending to your needs.)

'Frequent intervals' means at least 3 times. But it's worth trying if someone has to check on you twice a night.

Tackle the test in the following way.

- ❑ If you need any active help at night (eg soothing back to sleep, rearranging bedding), state that your night-time care needs are both attention and supervision – you might pass the attention test more easily than the watching-over test.
- ❑ Show how your disability or medical condition is such that it may give rise to substantial danger (as in 12).
- ❑ Outline the nature of the danger(s). Explain the basis for your fears of danger; refer to anything that supports your fears – eg the previous pattern and course of attacks, wandering at night, falls, etc.
- ❑ Think about simpler methods (see 14 below) that may bypass the need to have another person watching over you. Explain fully how and why they haven't worked, or don't or would not work. Are they reasonable in your circumstances?
- ❑ Explain why you cannot avoid the substantial danger without help from another person – eg because of a mental disorder or an inability to administer medication, oxygen, etc during an attack.
- ❑ Relate the danger(s) to the need to have another person awake and watching over you. Do the dangers warrant having another person watching over you for 20 minutes or longer, or to wake up to listen out for you or get up to check on you 2, 3, or more times in the night? On how many nights a week?

Remember the test is based on what you reasonably require, not on what is actually done for you. If you've had a fair number of accidents or incidents at night (or even just one bad accident), that may well suggest that you need more watching-over than you've been getting. If you've had few accidents, etc, the chances are that the watching-over you get is also the watching-over you need.

14. Simpler methods?

It is important to explain why you need particular types of attention or supervision. There may be simpler, more practical ways of meeting your needs. This could mean you don't reasonably (or medically) need as much attention or supervision from another person as you are currently getting. So the decision maker might disregard part of the help you are actually getting. If you can show that you have tried the simpler methods (whatever they may be) and can explain why they are not suitable for your particular circumstances, the decision maker should take the actual help you get into account. In R(A)1/87, the Commissioners said the decision maker should *'explain how his suggestion is practical and compatible with the evidence of [the disabled person's abilities and] agility and with anything resembling normal domestic arrangements...'*. It is clear that a simpler method must also be reasonable.

A typical simpler method is the use of a commode or portable urinal. If you could use one without help, it is often said you don't reasonably require help with trips to the toilet. Doctors often write that you can use a commode without thinking about all the practical issues involved (eg privacy, hand washing, etc) and without thinking about the effect on your morale or general health if trips to the toilet are your only regular exercise. Decision makers must properly consider the practical issues arising from the suggested use of a commode, particularly during the day (CA/156/88). In any case, you might also need help using a commode. Emptying and cleaning out the commode counts as attention if it needs to be done right away (as it generally would be during the day if not necessarily at night) (CSDLA/44/02).

15. Keeping a diary?

Some people won't need to keep a detailed diary of care needs or daily events to support their claims. But for others it could mean the difference between success or failure, or between being awarded different rates.

If your need for attention is unpredictable or changes from day to day, a diary can show exactly how much help had to be given and why. If your condition is getting slowly worse, a diary can help pinpoint the date you began to qualify for a higher rate. It can also help you remember things you would otherwise forget because they are so much a part of your everyday life. If you don't actually get much help, you could note down any incidents or worrying moments when you would have benefited from the help of another person.

If you need continual supervision or watching-over to prevent substantial danger to yourself or others, a diary can show exactly what happened, or what could have happened if someone hadn't been there to stop it.

16. Attention or supervision?

There is often a very close overlap between attention and supervision, and it can be difficult to distinguish between them. Sometimes both can be given at the same time; for example, if you are deaf and don't have much traffic sense, someone walking beside you could be supervising you (ready to stop you walking) and giving attention in connection with hearing (telling you what you need to know to continue walking in safety) (CA/86/87).

Similarly, if you are unsteady on your feet and liable to fall, you might need both supervision and attention when walking. The supervision could be a matter of looking out for any unexpected obstacles or uneven surfacing, and being on hand to catch you if you fell. The attention might involve telling you what is in front of you, or it could be a hand on your arm to steady you.

There are many other possibilities where the help you need can amount to both attention and supervision. It is sensible not to divide the help you need into rigid attention and supervision compartments. Keeping a 24-hour diary, listing all your needs throughout a typical day, may help you think about the types of help that could count as both.

The difference between attention and supervision is important. *'The vital contrast is between activity and a state of passivity coupled with a readiness to intervene'* (R(A)3/94).

With supervision, much of the help is passive, with active supervision (or attention) coming at varying intervals. The object of supervision is to avoid the risk of substantial danger. You need to explain what the danger is and how another person on hand to intervene if necessary reduces the risk of that danger. Depending on how great the risk is and the nature of the danger, the actual situations of potential danger could be quite infrequent.

On the other hand, the attention condition is based only on whether you reasonably need attention in connection with your bodily functions. Instead of showing that the aim of that help is to avoid the risk of substantial danger, you simply have to show that your needs are frequent throughout the day, or prolonged or repeated at night. However, you do need to explain why you need help from another person. For example, if you are incontinent, explain why you reasonably need help dealing with it and cannot or should not have to manage on your own.

If the decision maker does not look at the same needs under both the attention and supervision conditions, you might find you fail both the day attention and supervision conditions. A long gap during the middle of the day might mean that the pattern of help you need does not amount to *'frequent... throughout the day'*. Under the supervision condition, the risk of danger and the situations of potential danger may not be great or frequent enough to warrant continual supervision. Yet if some of the needs which were considered only under the supervision condition could also be taken into account under the attention condition, the combination of needs could well amount to frequent attention throughout the day (and give you the middle rate rather than the lowest rate). This argument only works where some of the supervision also amounts to active attention in connection with any of your bodily functions.

To summarise, attention tends to be active help, while supervision is more passive. Use the DLA claim-form to explain about all your care needs. If you are unsuccessful, or are awarded a lower rate than you think you should get, you can ask for a revision or you can appeal (see 25). In either case, ask that all your needs are considered under both conditions. If you can, list those needs that could count as both attention and supervision.

17. Renal dialysis

Special rules for some kidney patients undergoing renal dialysis help them qualify for the middle rate of care component. Depending on when and where you dialyse, you'll be treated as satisfying the disability tests for the day or for the night. You must show that:

- you undergo renal dialysis 2 or more times a week; *and*
- the dialysis is of a type which normally requires the attendance or supervision of another person during the period of the dialysis; *or*
- because of your particular circumstances (eg age, visual impairment or loss of manual dexterity) during the period of dialysis you require another person to supervise you in order to avoid substantial danger to yourself, or to give you some help with your bodily functions.

Reg 7 DLA regs

Hospital – If you are dialysing as an outpatient and getting help from hospital staff, you won't automatically satisfy the disability tests, but it does help you pass both qualifying periods for DLA (3 months backward test and 6 months forward test – see 4). This is helpful if you alternate between outpatient dialysis and dialysis at home. You'll be treated as satisfying the disability tests for the period you dialyse at home (if this is at least twice a week and you need assistance) even if it is only for a short period. If the help you get as an outpatient is from someone who doesn't work for the hospital, this passes the disability test. Inpatient dialysis counts for both the qualifying period and the disability test, but payment of the care component is affected by a spell in hospital (see 7).

Other types of dialysis – Continuous ambulatory peritoneal dialysis (CAPD), continuous cycle peritoneal dialysis (CCPD) and peritoneal rapid overnight dialysis (PROD) are designed to be carried out without help. You can only be covered by the above rules if your disabilities or frailty mean you need help during the dialysis. If you are fully independent in dialysing you are not covered. But if you need even a small amount of help (eg to change the bag) you should pass the day or night disability test. You don't need to show that attention needed is frequent or supervision required is continual.

C. THE MOBILITY COMPONENT

18. The disability tests

Higher rate

To qualify for the £42.30 higher rate mobility component you must be aged 3 or over. For tests 1, 2 or 3, you must be *'suffering from physical disablement'* (but if it is accepted that you have severe learning disabilities which have a physical cause, you may also qualify). Your *'physical condition as a whole'* must be such that:

No. 1 you are unable to walk (see below); *or*

No. 2 you are virtually unable to walk (see 20); *or*

No. 3 the *'exertion required to walk would constitute a danger to [your] life or would be likely to lead to a serious deterioration in [your] health'* (see below); *or*

S.73(1)(a) SSCBA; reg 12(1)(a) DLA Regs

No. 4 you have no legs or feet (from birth or through amputation) (see 19); *or*

S.73(1)(b), (2)(b) SSCBA; reg 12(1)(b) DLA Regs

No. 5 you are both deaf and blind (see below); *or*

S.73(1)(b), (2)(a) SSCBA; reg 12(2),(3) DLA Regs

No. 6 you are entitled to the highest rate care component and are severely mentally impaired with extremely disruptive and dangerous behavioural problems (see 21).

S.73(1)(c), (3) SSCBA; reg 12(5), (6) DLA Regs

Lower rate

To qualify for the £16.05 lower rate mobility component you must be aged 5 or over. It doesn't matter that you are able to walk but you must be *'so severely disabled physically or mentally that, disregarding any ability [you] may have to use routes which are familiar to [you] on [your] own, [you] cannot take advantage of the faculty out of doors without guidance or supervision from another person most of the time'* (see 22).

S.73(1)(d) SSCBA

Children – There is an extra disability test for the lower rate for children under 16. They must show that either:

- they require *'substantially more guidance or supervision from another person than persons of [their] age in normal physical and mental health would require'*; *or*

- people of their age *'in normal physical and mental health would not require such guidance or supervision'.*

S.73(4)SSCBA

See Chapter 35 for more on DLA for children.

Unable to walk?
Being 'unable to walk' means just that: you cannot take a step by putting one foot in front of the other. If you have one artificial leg, your walking ability is considered when using it. You are unlikely to count as being unable to walk but you may well qualify on the basis that you are virtually unable to walk.

Effects of exertion
For the third disability test for the higher rate it is the exertion needed to walk that must cause the serious problem. How far you can actually walk were you to do so is not relevant. What is relevant is the effect of the effort of walking on your life or health. People with serious lung, chest or heart conditions may qualify in this way; in one case, a man with diabetic ulcers on his feet qualified.

The *'danger'* or *'serious'* deterioration does not have to be immediate, nor does any deterioration have to be long lasting or permanent. If you can only recover from the deterioration in your health by some kind of medical intervention (eg oxygen, drugs) you should explain this on the DLA claim-form. Danger from other causes besides the effort needed to walk (eg being run over) cannot be taken into account.

Deaf and blind
You may qualify for the higher rate if you are blind and also profoundly deaf. You must show that because of those conditions in combination with each other, you are *'unable, without the assistance of another person, to walk to any intended or required destination while out of doors'*. Blind is defined as 100% disablement resulting from loss of vision. This means loss of vision such that you are unable to do any work for which eyesight is essential. Deaf is defined as 80% disablement resulting from loss of hearing (where 100% is absolute deafness). An average hearing loss at 1, 2 and 3 kHz of at least 87dB in each ear counts as 80% disablement. You will be referred to a DWP doctor to assess your hearing loss and loss of vision.

Reg 12(2) DLA Regs; R(DLA)3/95; Sch 2, SS (General Benefits) Regs 1982; Sch 3, Part II, SS (Industrial Injuries) (Prescribed Diseases) Regs 1985

19. Other factors

In a coma – If your condition is such that you cannot *'benefit from enhanced facilities for locomotion'*, you won't be entitled to the mobility component. This really only excludes people who are in a coma or whose medical condition means it is not safe to move them. If you can get out from time to time, even if no one has ever taken you out, you are not excluded from mobility component.

S.73(8) SSCBA

Personal circumstances – The first three disability tests for the higher rate ignore the effects of personal circumstances on your mobility. Where you live (eg on a steep hill or far from the nearest bus stop), your ability to use public transport and the nature of your employment, are all ignored.

Reg 12(1)(a) DLA Regs

Artificial aids and medical treatment – You will automatically qualify under the 4th disability test if you have no legs or feet, regardless of your ability to manage with prostheses. However, the first three disability tests for the higher rate do take into account your walking abilities when using suitable artificial aids such as a walking stick, built up shoe or a prosthesis. If there is an artificial aid or prosthesis which is *'suitable in [your] case'*, and you wouldn't be unable or virtually unable to walk if you used it, you'll fail the test. If you use crutches and can only swing through them, rather than use them to walk with each leg able to bear your weight, then you are unable to walk.

A guide dog does not count as an artificial aid, nor do painkillers. What counts is your walking ability under any painkillers or other medication that you normally take, if it is reasonable to expect you to take it. For example, it may not be reasonable to expect you to carry a bulky nebuliser even though it helps when you get breathless (CDLA/3188/02). If you have refused treatment which might have improved your condition, that cannot be held against you: it is your ability to walk as you are that counts (R(M)1/95).

Reg 12(4) DLA Regs

Terminal illness – Although you are treated as passing the qualifying period for mobility component, you must actually pass one of the disability tests to be paid mobility component from the time you claim it.

20. 'Virtually unable to walk'?

Regulation 12(l)(a)(ii) of the DLA Regulations spells out the factors to be taken into account in deciding whether you are *'virtually unable to walk'*. The test is whether your *'ability to walk out of doors is so limited, as regards:*

- *the distance over which, or*
- *the speed at which, or*
- *the length of time for which, or*
- *the manner in which [you] can make progress on foot without severe discomfort, that [you are] virtually unable to walk'.*

Physical cause
The test of being *'virtually unable to walk'* looks only at physical factors that limit your walking and only at factors that restrict the act of walking outdoors, rather than, for example, where or when you walk outdoors.

People with a severe learning disability who cannot meet the No. 6 test (see 21) may qualify for the higher rate as virtually unable to walk if the interruptions to their walking ability can be shown to be physical in origin (see Box H.5). If you can physically walk but are often unable or afraid to do so, for example, because of mental illness, you may qualify for the lower rate instead (see 22).

CDLA/2822/99 clarifies that, unless there is specific evidence to the contrary, the mobility problems of people with ME are physical in origin and not psychological. Chronic regional pain syndrome should also be accepted as a physical disablement (CDLA/1898/03).

Mobility problems caused by genuine physical pain or physical disability may be included even if the cause of the pain or disability is unknown or is psychological (CDLA/948/00, CDLA/3323/2003). However, the law is not settled on this issue. Other case law says there must be a diagnosis of a physical condition causing the mobility difficulties, at least in part, even if some of the pain is psychological. If you became depressed or anxious partly because of a physical condition, you may qualify even if your mobility difficulties are largely caused by the depression or anxiety, as long as a clear link with the physical condition is accepted (CSDLA/894/01).

Severe discomfort
From the point you start to suffer severe discomfort walking outdoors, any extra distance you walk should be ignored (R(M)1/81 and CM/267/93). For example, you may be able to walk about 20 metres without too much pain or breathlessness, but this discomfort begins to get worse until eventually you are forced to stop. By the time you stop, you may well be in agony. The first question is: at what point do you start to suffer what can be called *'severe discomfort'*? If it is at, say, 40 metres, then any extra walking should be discounted. The second question is whether or not the 40 metres you are

capable of walking *'without severe discomfort'* is *'so limited... that [you are] virtually unable to walk'*.

'Severe discomfort' is subjective; different people have different pain thresholds; and will also show pain in different ways. Severe discomfort does not mean severe pain or distress: *'discomfort is a lesser concomitant [of pain]'*. So severe discomfort is a lesser problem than severe pain, and is far from being excruciating agony – which would cause the most stoic person to stop walking.

Cassinelli v Secretary of State for Social Services (reported in R(M)2/92). This overrules the opposite view taken in R(M)1/91.

The Commissioners (in R(M)1/83) have said severe

H.5 Learning disabilities

If you don't qualify for higher rate mobility component on the basis of 'severe mental impairment' (see 21), you are more than likely to pass the test for the lower rate (see 22). However, some people who are autistic, deaf/blind, or have a learning disability may qualify for higher rate mobility component on the basis of 'virtual inability to walk' (see also 20).

'Virtually unable to walk'?

The need for help to get from one point to another and the purpose of walking are totally irrelevant to the 'virtually unable to walk' test. Instead, this test is tied to physical limitations on a person's ability to put one foot in front of the other and to continue to make progress on foot. These physical limitations can include behavioural problems if they are a reaction to or a result of the person's physical disablement (eg genetic damage in the case of Down's Syndrome or brain damage).

The virtual inability to walk test looks at interruptions in the ability to make progress on foot. These interruptions have been referred to as *'temporary paralysis (as far as walking is concerned)'*. The interruptions must be accepted as physical in origin, and as part of your accepted physical disablement rather than under your direct and conscious control. Thus, being able to put one foot in front of the other does not stop you passing the virtual inability test. You must, however, be able to show that:

- your behavioural problems, which may sometimes include a failure to exercise your powers of walking, stem from a physical disability; *and*
- your walking difficulties, including interruptions in your ability to make progress on foot, happen often enough so that your walking is *'so limited... that [you are] virtually unable to walk'*.

Commissioner's decision R(M)3/86 establishes two parts to the 'virtually unable to walk' test:

- ❑ The decision maker should consider separately the distance, speed, length of time, and manner in which you can make progress on foot (see 20). Any walking achieved only with severe discomfort must be discounted.
- ❑ If the decision maker finds you *'virtually unable to walk'*, they must then decide whether that is attributable to some physical impairment such as brain damage, or to a *'physical disability which prevents the co-ordination of mind and body'*.

If you have had a history of behavioural problems since birth, the decision maker *'should provide very clear reasons for attributing the behavioural problems in question to something other than brain damage'* [or Down's Syndrome etc] (CM/98/89).

What can you do?

- ❑ Provide evidence (from a GP, consultant, etc) to show that:
- the learning disabilities have a physical cause (eg brain damage);
- all the behavioural problems which interrupt outdoor walking stem directly from that physical cause.
- ❑ You can also provide evidence (from a GP, etc) to show it is not appropriate to talk of the person concerned as being able to exercise deliberate and self-conscious choices in the sense of making a *'deliberate election'* to walk or not to walk. The key thing is to get evidence to show that the interruptions in the ability to make progress on foot outdoors are reactions to various stimuli. Those reactions are the result of the brain damage or the genetic damage that caused the learning disabilities, and prevent or interfere with the normal co-ordination of mind and body.
- ❑ You need to be able to give the decision maker a clear picture of the person's normal walking difficulties and the frequency of interruptions in their ability to make independent progress on foot. The idea is to present an objective picture of how the person normally makes, or doesn't make, progress on foot outdoors, without active help from another person.

Focus on walking difficulties

We suggest you do this by trying to carry out a short outdoor walking test. Choose a period of time that you consider will be long enough to get a good impression of the person's walking difficulties, be it one minute or 10 minutes. Ask someone else to take notes if necessary.

For each test:

- ❑ Describe the place where you carry out the test. Mark the starting point. Note the time.
- ❑ Let the person loose. Don't actively intervene to help them walk. A gentle hand on the shoulder or words to help them go in the right direction is OK (to help overcome any fear because they cannot see where they are going). But don't give any physical support or restraint you wouldn't routinely expect to give to a non-disabled person of the same age (so you'll need to be sure the test place you choose is a safe one).
- ❑ Describe exactly what happens. Do they move at all? If yes, then how do they walk? Note what size steps they take; how they lift their legs; the speed of walking; changes in speed and in direction; their balance; and the effect of distractions. This all relates to the manner in which a person walks, and the speed at which a person walks.
- ❑ For each stop or interruption in their walking, note the time, mark the place and measure the distance from the starting point (or from the previous stop).
- ❑ Describe exactly what happened. Why do you think they stopped? Note the time they start to move on again. What made them move on? Or, why do you think they moved on (give all your reasons)?
- ❑ At the end of the period, mark the place they have reached and note the time. How far, in a straight line, is it from their starting point? If they didn't move in a straight line, also measure how far they walked or ran.

Note: If the person's walking ability is also limited by severe discomfort do not continue with the test. As soon as they start to suffer what they, or you, consider to be severe discomfort, note the time and mark the place. Describe the severe discomfort that made them stop. Are there any physical changes in their appearance from when they started walking? Any breathing problems? Any outward and visible signs of their discomfort?

discomfort includes *'pain'* or *'breathlessness'* – factors brought on by the act of walking. It does not include the screaming fits of an autistic child or other factors brought on by resistance to the idea of walking. Normally, severe discomfort has to be brought on by walking, not just by being outside (so that, for example, someone whose skin blistered badly on exposure to sunlight would not qualify), but this does not mean your pain must increase when you walk. If you are already in severe discomfort when you start walking, you can still qualify (R(DLA)4/04).

Distance, speed, time and manner

These 4 factors affect the ability to walk outdoors, and they will often be closely interrelated. There is no set walking distance to mark the difference between success and failure; if there were, there would be little point in the law requiring the decision maker to look also at the speed, time and manner of walking. All of these factors must be considered as well as the question of severe discomfort.

If you are not sure how limited your mobility is, it helps to do a time and motion study on your outdoor walking ability, looking at these 4 points in turn. Walk until you start to feel severe discomfort (if it is safe for you to do so). If you start to feel severe discomfort, record what happens and when in terms of distance and time. This might include factors like pain, dizziness, coughing, spasms, uncontrollable actions or reflexes, breathlessness, angina or asthma attacks. These examples are not exhaustive – record whatever you feel to be severe discomfort. Note how long it takes you to recover before you feel able to walk again without severe discomfort.

If an occupational therapist or physiotherapist has assessed you for equipment and adaptations to your home, or you have been getting therapy from one, they may be to willing to write a report on your outdoor walking ability – either for an appeal tribunal or when you first claim.

The easiest report may be where they confirm they have read your own time and motion study and agree your results are consistent with their own view of the effects of your physical disabilities. It is useless to get a letter simply saying you need mobility component. It gives no help in establishing the extent of your physical walking difficulties, in terms of the legal criteria.

Intermittent walking ability

If your walking ability varies from day to day, you may have difficulty showing that you are virtually unable to walk (including during the two qualifying periods).

It helps to keep an accurate diary. The fact that you can walk on some days might not disqualify you. The question is whether or not the evidence about your walking abilities would allow a decision maker to consider that, looking at your physical condition as a whole, it would be true to say of you that you are virtually unable to walk (including for the duration of the two qualifying periods).

21. Severe mental impairment

This way of qualifying for the higher rate mobility component is aimed at people with severe learning disabilities. If you don't pass this test, you may pass the virtual inability to walk test. Box H.5 looks at how that test applies to people with learning disabilities. If you fail both tests, you will probably pass the disability test for the lower rate (see 22).

To be entitled to higher rate mobility component on the basis of severe mental impairment, you must pass the following tests:

- you must be entitled to highest rate care component (even if it cannot be paid because you live in hospital or special accommodation); *and*
  S.73(3)(c) SSCBA
- you suffer from *'a state of arrested development or incomplete physical development of the brain, which results in severe impairment of intelligence and social functioning'*; *and*
- you *'exhibit disruptive behaviour'* which *'is extreme'*; *and*
- you *'regularly require[s] another person to intervene and physically restrain [you] to prevent [you] causing physical injury to [yourself] or another, or damage to property'*; *and*
- your behaviour *'is so unpredictable that [you require] another person to be present and watching over [you] whenever [you are] awake'*.
  Reg 12(5), (6) DLA Regs

The DWP will normally obtain a specialist's opinion before awarding the higher rate on the basis of severe mental impairment.

'Arrested development or incomplete physical development' must take place before the brain is fully developed, which will be before the age of 30 (R(DLA)2/96). This rules out anyone whose severe behavioural problems start later in life (eg because of a later head injury or a disease such as Alzheimer's). Also ruled out are people whose behavioural problems pass the test in the daytime, but who only get the middle rate care component because they sleep soundly and safely all night. If you are in either of these situations, see Box H.5.

An IQ of 55 or less is generally taken to be *'severe impairment of intelligence'*. But an IQ test is not the only measure of impaired intelligence. Some people, such as those with autism, may do well in abstract intelligence tests but cannot apply their intelligence in a useful way in the real world. For them, an IQ test can give a misleading impression of useful intelligence. So wherever IQ is above 55 or there is no IQ test, the decision maker must consider other evidence, including evidence of impairment of social functioning where that has an effect on useful intelligence. For example, having no sense of danger may indicate a severe impairment of intelligence (CDLA/3215/01).
M(A Child) v CAO, 29.10.99 (reported in R(DLA)1/00)

'Physical restraint' need not involve any force. If all you need to prevent you causing injury or damage is some physical contact, such as a hand on the arm, that is enough (CDLA/2054/98).

You must need watching-over whenever you are awake due to your disruptive behaviour being so unpredictable. Because of this, you might have trouble passing the test if your home or school is structured so that your behaviour is no longer disruptive or so that you can be safely left alone behind closed doors. Emphasise the way in which your behaviour is disruptive despite such a structured environment.

If you think you satisfy each part of this disability test and are turned down, consider asking for a revision or lodging an appeal (see Chapter 58).

22. The lower rate

The lower rate is aimed at people who can walk but cannot generally make use of the ability to do so outside unless accompanied by someone to guide or supervise them. People who are visually impaired or have learning difficulties or mental health problems such as agoraphobia are most likely to qualify. You may qualify if you are deaf and cannot understand spoken or written words sufficiently to seek or follow directions alone. You might also qualify if you have falls, fits or attacks and need someone with you to deal with the consequences. There is an extra test if you are under age the age of 16 (see 18).

Your mobility problems must be due to physical or mental disability. If fear or anxiety prevents you from walking on unfamiliar routes, it must be a symptom of a mental disability.

If your anxiety is connected to your physical condition, but could nevertheless be described as a symptom of mental disability, you may still be able to qualify. For example, a deaf person needing the reassurance of a companion to overcome anxiety about being on unfamiliar routes may qualify if their anxiety is classed as a mental disability.

'Guidance' means directing or leading. It can be physical (eg holding your elbow or putting a hand on your arm) or it can be verbal (eg telling you which turning to take or helping you avoid obstacles). It can also include persuasion or encouragement if you are feeling panicked and too afraid to continue (CDLA/42/94). If you are deaf and cannot read enough to follow road maps or signs and cannot easily understand by lip reading, you may need someone with you to ask for directions or tell you which turnings to take (CDLA/240/94).

'Supervision' can be more difficult, and there have been conflicting Commissioners' decisions on what constitutes supervision for the lower rate mobility component. If you get the middle rate care component for continual supervision to avoid danger you could get the lower rate mobility component because of the same problems, but this is by no means automatic. You still need to explain what supervision you need outdoors and how this enables you to get about. You may well need supervision when out walking to avoid danger but this need not be the reason for supervision or guidance. What is important is that guidance or supervision enables you to overcome your mobility problems, whatever they are, and to take advantage of your ability to walk which you would not otherwise be able to do.

You may find it helpful to consider what purpose your companion serves when you are out walking. If they are simply walking along with you, you are unlikely to qualify even if you feel better by them being there. Supervision means taking a more active role in enabling you to make that journey. They may be watching you for signs of distress, and can encourage or persuade you to continue, or help you return home if necessary. They can be supervising you by looking out for situations you would find upsetting, such as groups of people. If they are aware of why you have difficulties walking outdoors, on the look out for those problems and ready to step in to deal with or distract your attention from them, you are more likely to pass the test.

Give examples of what happens when you walk outside in unfamiliar surroundings. Explain what someone else does to enable you to continue walking. If no one was with you, what would happen? Although any walking you can do on familiar routes is not relevant, it might help to think of why you can manage these trips. What problems would you have in unfamiliar surroundings? If you cannot manage in familiar places either, this is relevant so explain any difficulties you have in routes you know and routes you don't know. If you never actually go out on your own, what is likely to happen if you did? If you never actually go out at all, you might need to argue that the nature of your disability means supervision or guidance could help you get out (CDLA/42/94). However, you would have problems satisfying the test if no amount of help would enable you to go out (CDLA/2364/95).

D. CLAIMS, PAYMENTS & APPEALS

23. How do you claim?

The DLA claim-form is part of the DLA claim-pack: the DLA1, or for children the DLA1 Child. The DWP is testing a shorter claim-form in the area covered by Glasgow Disability Benefits Centre; this might replace the current form, possibly in summer 2005. In other areas, in the meantime, the DLA1 claim-form still has two separate sections. Section 1, the claim-form, asks for personal and general details. Section 2 is the self-assessment questionnaire for the DLA disability tests. There is a page in Section 2 ideally for your doctor or another professional to confirm your statements, but it could also be done by a carer, relative or friend. Your doctor should not charge you for completing this page. Your chances of success will be improved if the doctor, or another professional you name in your application, knows about your practical, day-to-day care needs and mobility difficulties so that they can reply to DWP requests for information with more than just a diagnosis of your condition. Tell them you are claiming DLA and explain your needs, and if you have kept a care diary (see 15) give them a copy.

Don't be put off by the length of the DLA1 – there is a lot of space for your answers. The questions themselves are straightforward but it is important to give as much information as you can and not underestimate the help you need. Think about things you can't do or have trouble with, rather than things you can do. If you don't fill in the form fully or your answers don't give a clear picture of the effects of your disabilities, the DWP may get a factual report from your GP or ask a doctor to examine you.

Try to give accurate answers, rather than guesses. Where the form asks how long something takes, don't guess – time it. Where it asks how far you can walk, measure the distance – most people find it difficult to estimate distances with any accuracy. Where it asks about any equipment you use to help you, remember it is your need for help from another person that counts. Explain any problems you have using the equipment and what help you need from another person to use the equipment, or what help you need despite the equipment (eg getting out of bed to use a commode at night). It is crucial that you explain the help you need from another person, as this is why DLA is paid – not simply because you have a particular condition or disability.

Getting help – Anyone can help you fill in the DLA1. If you would like help from the DWP, you can make a free phone call to the Benefit Enquiry Line (BEL): 0800 882200. BEL staff can complete the forms over the phone with you, then send them to you for you to check, sign and return, or they can answer queries about the questions in the DLA1 – using Minicom if you are deaf or sending you the forms in Braille or large print. Bear in mind, however, that the advice you receive from BEL, though often helpful, is not independent of the DWP.

Many advice and disability organisations can also help and some produce guides to DLA and checklists to help people complete the forms (see Chapter 61(3) for details of our own guides). It is a good idea to keep a copy of your completed form in case you are not happy with the outcome and want to challenge it.

Starting your claim

The best way to start your claim is to ask the DWP for the DLA claim-pack (form DLA1, or DLA1 Child for a child under 16). You can do this by phoning or calling in at any Jobcentre Plus office, ringing BEL (0800 882200), using the postage-paid coupon in the DLA information leaflet DS704, or downloading a claim-form from the DWP website: www.dwp.gov.uk.

If you cannot make the claim yourself, someone else can do it for you. If they sign the form for you, there is space for them to explain why (eg you are too ill to sign).

Renewal claims – If you have been awarded either of the DLA components for a fixed period, the Disability Benefits Unit will write to you up to 6 months before the award ends to invite you to reapply for the fixed-period component(s). You should make sure you return your renewal claim before your current award expires or you could lose benefit. Note, however, that the decision maker may decide to supersede your current award before the expiry date if your renewal claim shows that your circumstances have changed. Your current award could be stopped early, reduced or increased as a result.

Your date of claim

If you write to the DWP or send in the DS704 coupon, DLA can be backdated to the date your letter or coupon reached the DWP. If you phone or visit a Jobcentre Plus office, DLA can be backdated to the date of your call or visit.

A DLA claim-pack issued by the DWP is stamped with the date when you asked for the pack and with a second date 6 weeks later, by which time you should return the completed form. The DWP will also give you a postage-paid envelope addressed to the Disability Benefits Centre that will be handling your initial claim.

As long as you return the completed claim-form within 6 weeks, the date you asked for the pack counts as your date of claim. If you take longer than 6 weeks to return the completed claim-form, explain why at the end of Section 2 of the claim-form. If your delay is reasonable, the time limit can be extended. If not, your date of claim is the day your completed form reaches the DWP.

Advice agencies – If you claim on a DLA1(A) given to you by a Citizens Advice Bureau or other advice agency, your date of claim is the day your completed form reaches the DWP. At present (until the new single-section claim-forms are introduced) if you return only Section 1 of the DLA1(A), DLA can be backdated to the day that section reaches the DWP as long as you return your completed Section 2 within one month. Tick the box provided in Section 1 to show you're doing this, otherwise the DWP will start other follow-up action unnecessarily. Keep a note of the address on the envelope supplied with the claim-pack.

Don't delay – As DLA can only start to be paid from the first pay day on or after your date of claim, you might lose a week or more of benefit if you delay. DLA pay day is normally a Wednesday. If you ask for the claim-pack on a Wednesday, you can be paid from your date of claim. If you ask for it on a Thursday, payment cannot start until the next Wednesday. To avoid these delays, start your claim as soon as you can by ringing BEL: 0800 882200.

Backdating

DLA cannot be backdated to a date earlier than your date of claim. There are only limited situations in which an earlier date can be treated as your date of claim:

- if industrial action has caused postal disruption, the day your claim would have been delivered to a DWP office is treated as your date of claim;
- if the Secretary of State uses her/his discretion to treat anything written as being sufficient in the circumstances to count as a valid claim, the date of that earlier document is treated as your date of claim (see Chapter 57(1)).

24. Who decides your claim?

Claims for DLA are handled first of all by one of the regional Disability Benefits Centres or, in some areas, by the central New Claims Unit. Decisions are made by DWP decision makers, not by doctors. To help make decisions, the DWP, together with the DLA Advisory Board, produce a guide called the *Disability Handbook* (available on our website: www.disabilityalliance.org). This outlines the main care and mobility needs likely to arise in a number of different illnesses and disabling conditions. If your situation doesn't fit neatly within the picture painted by the *Disability Handbook* or if it emphasises the need for medical evidence, the decision maker may ask your own doctor, consultant or other medically qualified person treating you, to complete a factual report. If this in turn does not provide a complete picture, the decision maker can arrange for a DWP approved doctor to visit you at your home and carry out a medical examination in order to prepare a medical report. Such a visit can also be arranged as an alternative to getting in touch with your doctor, consultant etc.

Delays – The DWP aims to give you a decision within 39 working days (ie not including weekends or public holidays) of the day your DLA claim is received. If you are claiming under the 'Special Rules' (see Box H.4) you should get a decision within 8 working days. Compensation may be payable for long delays (see Chapter 60(2) for details).

In any case, if your claim is taking too long, complain to the Customer Services Manager at the Disability Benefits Centre dealing with your claim.

25. What happens after you claim?

Once your claim is decided, you'll be sent a short notification of that decision.

Length of your award – Your DLA award could be for an indefinite period or for a fixed period. You can have one component for a fixed period and one for an indefinite period. If you get both components for a fixed period, these will always end on the same day. The DWP may check your award periodically (see below).

In the past, DLA awards could be given for life but now awards are made for an indefinite period instead. In either case, your award continues for as long as you continue to satisfy the disability tests and other conditions of entitlement. A change in your condition may lead to your DLA award changing (or ending).

If you are not happy with the decision on your claim

Chapter 58 looks at how to challenge a decision. Here we give a brief outline.

You have the right to ask for a revision within one month of the date the decision was sent to you. Or you can ask for an appeal instead – again within one month.

With a revision, a decision maker has another look at your case to see if the decision can be changed. If you ask for a revision, the DWP may ask for more information (eg a factual report or a medical examination) but won't do this in all cases. If some aspects of your claim are not clear, the DWP is more likely to arrange for a short factual report (perhaps from your own doctor) concentrating on just those aspects. If the decision maker does not revise the decision, or does but you are still not satisfied with the outcome, you have another month to appeal.

An appeal is to an independent appeal tribunal. Before your appeal goes ahead, a decision maker will check to see whether the decision can be revised to your advantage. If a decision is revised, you have another month in which to appeal if you are still not happy with the result.

Revision or appeal – You can choose whether to have a revision or an appeal. You should get a quicker decision if you ask for a revision, especially if you can get helpful medical evidence to support your claim. But if you simply ask for the decision to be looked at again, it is unlikely to be changed, particularly if you can't add anything to the information you have already provided.

You may find it difficult to understand why your claim has been refused. The reasons given for the decision are rarely detailed. You should ask for your case papers (see below), which may help you give better information for the revision, but you need to tell the DWP you don't want a decision made until you have had the opportunity to examine the case papers and provide further information. This can add to the time a revision takes but will probably be helpful in ensuring the decision maker has the most relevant information. If you ask for a revision but are not happy with the outcome, you can appeal to a tribunal within one month of that decision.

An appeal takes longer to be determined, and you may be put off by the idea of having to go to a hearing. An appeal can give you more time to examine your case papers and see why your claim was refused. This may help you obtain the most relevant supporting reports from your doctors and carers, and prepare what you want to tell the tribunal about your care and mobility needs. You may also be able to get help with an appeal from your local Citizens Advice Bureau, DIAL or other welfare rights services (see Chapter 59). It is more difficult to appeal against a tribunal decision, which would be your next step if the appeal was unsuccessful, so if you are uncertain about an appeal at the start and feel there is more information you can provide, you should try a revision. You will still have the appeal option if the revision is not successful.

You can dispute any aspect of the decision (eg the rate or length of the award, the starting date, etc) and for any reason. You can ask for a revision by phone but it is best to put it in writing. (If you need to phone, perhaps to avoid missing the deadline, then confirm your call in writing straight away.) The decision letter should make it clear which office to write to and how to phone them. If you want to appeal, ask for form GL24.

Whether you are asking for a revision or an appeal, it is crucial to do so within the one-month time limit, although it is possible to make late applications for appeal or revision where there are special circumstances (see Chapter 58(3)). If you are successful with the revision or appeal, benefit can be fully backdated.

H.6 For more information

In this chapter we refer to legislation on DLA. Here we explain the abbreviations used and suggest other sources of information.

The Acts

SSCBA	Social Security Contributions and Benefits Act 1992
SSA98	Social Security Act 1998
S. or s.	section of an Act
Sch	schedule to an Act
para	paragraph in a schedule

The Regulations

DLA Regs	The Social Security (Disability Living Allowance) Regulations 1991
C&P	The Social Security (Claims and Payments) Regulations 1987
D&A Regs	The Social Security and Child Support (Decisions and Appeals) Regulations 1999
reg	regulation

Case law

See Box R.7, Chapter 58 for information about Commissioners' decisions.

Law and guidance

Social Security Legislation Volume I Non Means Tested Benefits

Social Security Legislation Volume III Administration, Adjudication and the European Dimension, both published by Sweet and Maxwell

Claiming Disability Living Allowance: A self-help guide for disabled people aged 16-64

Claiming Attendance Allowance: A self-help guide for people aged 65 and over with a long-term health problem or disability, both published by Disability Alliance

If the decision was notified more than one month ago or there has been a change of circumstances – To challenge a decision notified more than one month ago, you need to show there are specific grounds – eg:

- there has been a change of circumstances since the decision was made – eg your condition has deteriorated and your need for care or your mobility problems have increased;
- the decision maker didn't know about some relevant fact – eg you missed out some aspect of your care needs or mobility difficulties when you filled in the claim-form.

See Chapter 58, Box R.5 for more details.

Warning: When you challenge a decision, the decision maker may reconsider the whole of your DLA award. Similarly, if you make a top-up claim for one component, you may risk what you already have. If you are happy with the decision on one of the two DLA components, say so in your letter; the decision maker need not consider anything you don't raise in your application. This will not, however, afford cast-iron protection to your existing award.

When can you see your case papers? – Your case papers consist of all the evidence used, including any medical reports, in making the decision. You can ask for copies of your case papers at any stage. If you don't ask for your case papers, they won't be sent to you unless you appeal to a tribunal. It is best to ask for the case papers at the same time as you ask for the revision or lodge the appeal, so you get them as early as possible in the process.

If you haven't kept a copy of your DLA claim-form, or haven't seen any of the other evidence used in your case, you may have missed some obvious mistakes or gaps in the evidence. Once you have identified them through reading through the case papers, get evidence to correct the mistakes or plug the gaps and write a very clear letter to the DWP. Concentrate on explaining how you satisfy the conditions of entitlement rather than, for example, why the evidence from a visiting doctor is inaccurate. By all means point to inaccurate elements of a report, and get further evidence to show it is inaccurate if you can. But then go on to explain what the correct situation is and what this says about your care or mobility needs.

If you are happy with the decision on one component, you may risk it by asking for the other component. In this situation, it is sensible, before you take action, to ask for a copy of your case papers on the basis that you need to be sure that your current award is 'safe'. An experienced adviser may be able to reassure you after looking through the case papers.

If you are challenging a recent decision, take care to stay within the one-month time limit for requesting a revision or an appeal, even if you are still waiting for the case papers to be sent to you.

Periodic checking of awards

Whether you have been awarded DLA for a specific period, indefinitely or for life, you must continue to satisfy all the qualifying rules throughout the award. Although it is up to you to let the DWP know if anything changes which might affect your existing benefit, such as improvements or deterioration in your condition, there is also a system of periodic enquiry to check that DLA awards remain correct throughout their term. Under this process, some people on DLA are asked to give up-to-date information about their circumstances.

Some people are exempt from the process and should not be contacted. If you are in one of the groups below and are contacted by the DWP you should ring the office that sent the letter and tell them you think they have contacted you by mistake. If you are in an exempt group but nonetheless provide the information requested or have a medical, you cannot withdraw it later should your benefit be cut or stopped as a result.

You do not need to have a periodic enquiry if any of the following apply.

- You have a fixed-period award due to end within the next 3 years.
- You get the higher rate mobility component together with either the highest or middle rate care component and you:
  - are aged 65 or over; *or*
  - are paraplegic, tetraplegic, quadriplegic, both deaf and blind, double amputee; *or*
  - have an award that was made before April 1992.
- You get the higher rate mobility component together with the highest rate care component, and have: cystic fibrosis, dementia, haemodialysis, hyperkinetic syndrome, learning difficulties, multiple allergy syndrome, multiple sclerosis, motor neurone disease, neurological disease (including muscular dystrophy), Parkinson's disease, total parenteral nutrition; or are severely mentally impaired (see 21).
- You are terminally ill and being paid under the 'Special Rules' (see Box H.4).

Less than 1% of awards are checked each year, mostly selected at random from groups whose awards the DWP considers are most likely to change, eg those with one component only. If you are selected for a periodic enquiry, you will be sent a DLA300 form. The DLA300 is based on the claim-form so will be familiar to you. You can ask the DWP for copies of the last DLA claim-forms that you filled in, if you have not kept copies, to use as a guide. The DLA300 form must be returned within 3 weeks, although you can ask for a little longer if necessary. It is important you contact the Disability Benefits Unit if you need more time because your benefit can be suspended and eventually terminated if you don't return the form.

Regs 17, 18, 19, 20 D&A Regs

26. How are you paid?

DLA is usually paid once every 4 weeks in arrears direct into your bank, building society or post office card account. The normal pay day for DLA is a Wednesday. If you are terminally ill, DLA is payable once a week.

Appointees – If you cannot manage your own affairs, the DWP can appoint another person to act on your behalf (see Chapter 57(4)). But DLA is your benefit, not your appointee's benefit. If you are under 16, the appointee is usually your mother. If you don't want someone else formally appointed to act for you, but cannot collect your DLA yourself, you can arrange with the bank, building society or post office for someone to do this for you.

27. What if your condition changes?

If your condition gets worse – If you already receive DLA, give the Disability Benefits Unit details of your change of circumstances. Your existing award may be superseded to include a higher rate or a new component. A top-up claim for the component you don't already have doesn't count as a new claim, but rather as a change to your existing award. (See also 25 above under 'If the decision was notified more than one month ago…'.)

If your condition improves – If your need for care or your mobility difficulties lessen, this could mean your rate of DLA should drop. Write to the Disability Benefits Unit to give them details. The decision maker will usually supersede your entitlement.

If your rate of DLA drops (or it ends), but you have a relapse within 2 years, you can regain your former rate of benefit in a linked claim without having to serve the qualifying period again. If you are over 65, you must make your linked claim within a year of your previous award dropping or ending (see 3 and 4 above).

21 Attendance allowance

1. What is attendance allowance?

Attendance allowance (AA) is a tax-free benefit for people aged 65 and over who are physically or mentally disabled and need help with personal care or supervision to remain safe. You do not actually have to be getting any help. It is the help you need that is relevant, not what you get. You can get AA even if you live alone; you do not need to have a carer. AA is not means tested, there are no national insurance contribution tests, and it is paid in addition to other money in most cases (see 3).

In this chapter we give only an outline of AA, because the rules are almost exactly the same as for disability living allowance (DLA – see Chapter 20) care component at the middle or highest rate. Below (see 6), we give the key differences between AA and DLA, and list the parts of Chapter 20 which are also relevant to AA.

2. Do you qualify?

You must meet the following conditions:

- you are aged 65 or over; *and*
- you pass the residence and presence tests (see Chapter 49(2) and (3)); *and*
- you satisfy one of the disability tests and have done so for the last 6 months (see below); *or*
- you are terminally ill (see Box H.4, Chapter 20).

If you have not yet reached your 65th birthday you should claim disability living allowance (DLA) instead.

The disability tests

To pass the disability tests, you must meet at least one of these 4 conditions. You must be *'so severely disabled physically or mentally that... [you require] from another person'*

during the day

- *'frequent attention throughout the day in connection with [your] bodily functions, or*
- *continual supervision throughout the day in order to avoid substantial danger to [yourself] or others' or*

during the night

- *'[you require] from another person prolonged or repeated attention in connection with [your] bodily functions, or*
- *in order to avoid substantial danger to [yourself] or others [you require] another person to be awake for a prolonged period or at frequent intervals for the purpose of watching over [you]'.*

These disability tests are explained in detail in Chapter 20(9) to (16).

Lower or higher rate

The higher rate of £60.60 is for people who need help day and night. So if you meet one of the day conditions and one of the night conditions, you will qualify for the higher rate allowance. The lower rate of £40.55 is for people who need help only during the day or only during the night. So if you meet one of the day conditions or one of the night conditions, you will get the lower rate.

Kidney patients

There are special rules for some kidney patients to help them qualify for AA at the lower rate (see Chapter 20(17)).

Six-month qualifying period

New claim – You must have been in need of care for 6 months before your award can begin, but you can make your claim before the 6 months are up. It does not matter if during these 6 months you could not receive AA in any case – eg if you were in hospital. Make a claim to establish your entitlement, even if you cannot be paid at that time.

Terminal illness – If you are claiming under the terminal illness provisions, you can be paid from the date the decision maker accepts that you satisfy the legal test of terminal illness (see Box H.4). Payment will usually start from the Monday on or after the day your claim is received in a DWP office. You do not have to serve the 6-month qualifying period or pass the 26-week presence test if you count as terminally ill.

Current award – If you already have lower rate AA, you can qualify for the higher rate after you have needed the greater level of attention or supervision for 6 months. You can put in your request before the 6 months are up.

Linked claim – If you previously received AA (or dropped to the lower rate) and have a relapse no more than 2 years from the end of that award, you don't have to re-serve the 6-month qualifying period to regain your former rate of benefit. You still need to claim or ask for your current lower award to be superseded, but you do not have to have needed the help or extra help for 6 months to be paid. For example, you previously received higher rate AA but this was reduced to the lower rate because your condition improved. You have a relapse within 2 years and ask for your award to be superseded to include the higher rate. Your higher rate can be paid from the date you make your request, or from the date of your relapse if you tell the DWP within one month. See Chapter 58 for more details on how to ask for benefit to be changed.

3. Does anything affect what you get?

AA can be paid in addition to almost any other benefit – eg state pension or pension credit (PC).

AA is ignored as income for means-tested benefits, so does not reduce the amount of PC, housing benefit (HB) or council tax benefit (CTB). It may, however, be taken into account in the means test for charging for local authority services, and for local authority-arranged care in a care home (see Chapter 25(6) and Box K.2, Chapter 31).

You will not get AA if you are entitled to disability living allowance (DLA). If you get constant attendance allowance with industrial injuries disablement benefit or war pension, this overlaps with AA and you'll be paid whichever is higher.

Check your benefits – Getting AA can trigger extra help with means-tested benefits. You might qualify for a severe disability premium with your HB or CTB, or a severe disability addition with your PC guarantee credit. If you have not been able to get these benefits before because your income was too high, you might qualify now. Contact The Pension Service and your local authority to make sure they know you are getting AA. See Box H.2 in Chapter 20 for other help available (in this box the highest rate of DLA care component corresponds with the higher rate of AA, and the middle rate of DLA care component corresponds with the lower rate of AA).

Hospital and other special accommodation – If you go into hospital or some types of care home, your AA stops after 4 weeks (see Chapter 20(7) and (8) and Chapter 30(2)).

4. How do you claim?

You can phone the Benefit Enquiry Line (BEL; 0800 882200) and ask for the AA claim-pack (AA1). Your date of claim will usually be the day you phone (see Chapter 20(23)). They can also answer any queries. If you write to the DWP requesting AA, your date of claim will usually be the day your letter reaches the DWP. You can also get a claim-pack from a Citizens Advice Bureau or other advice centre, but, in this case, your date of claim is the date you get the completed form back to the DWP.

If you need help to fill in the form, ring BEL (0800 882200). A DWP adviser can go through the questions with you and complete a form on your behalf, then post it to you so you can check it and sign it. (Bear in mind, however, that their advice, while often helpful, is not independent.)

Backdating – AA cannot be backdated to earlier than the Monday pay day on or after your date of claim. In some limited circumstances an earlier date can be treated as your date of claim (see Chapter 20(23)).

Medical evidence – The claim-form includes a section to be completed by someone who knows you well; this could be your own doctor or another professional involved in your care. Your form may well give the decision maker enough information to make a decision. If not, the decision maker may request a short report from your doctor or another medical person you've named on the form. Try to ensure that this person is fully aware of your care and/or supervision needs; if you have kept a diary of your care needs (see Chapter 20(15)), give them a copy. Alternatively, the decision maker can arrange for a DWP approved doctor to visit you in order to carry out a medical examination.

Length of award – AA may be awarded for a fixed period or indefinitely. If your award is for a fixed period, the Disability Benefits Unit will invite you to make a renewal claim about 4 months before the end of your current award.

How are you paid? – AA is paid to you, not to a carer, and you can spend it as you wish. It is usually payable on a Monday. It is normally paid every 4 weeks in arrears directly into your bank, building society or post office card account.

5. Decisions and appeals

If you are claiming AA for the first time, or after a break, a decision maker based at one of the regional Disability Benefits Centres or, in some areas, at the New Claims Unit in Blackpool, will make the initial decision on every aspect of your claim. If you are making a renewal claim, a decision maker based at the central Disability Benefits Unit (DBU) in Blackpool makes the decision on your claim.

If you are not happy with a decision, you can ask for a revision or lodge an appeal within one month of the date the DWP sends you the decision. The decision letter should make it clear who to write to. If you ask for a revision, a decision maker will reconsider your claim. They can confirm the initial decision, or increase or reduce the rate of your award, or the length of your award. You have a further month to appeal if you are still not happy. If you appeal first, the DWP will look at the decision again in any case and if they do not revise it to your advantage, your appeal will go to an appeal tribunal. Appeal on form GL24.

The one-month time limit to ask for a revision or lodge an appeal can be extended, but only if there are special circumstances for the delay. Otherwise, outside of one month you can ask for the decision to be 'superseded', but only for certain reasons. For example, a change of circumstances such as an increase or decrease in your care needs enables a decision to be superseded. So if your care needs increase, or you no longer need as much help from other people as before, you should write to the central DBU in Blackpool (see inside back cover). The DWP can also decide of their own accord to supersede your award. Chapter 58 gives more details about this, as well as fuller details on the procedures for challenging decisions.

6. DLA or attendance allowance?

You cannot claim disability living allowance (DLA) for the first time after you reach your 65th birthday. Once you are 65, you must claim AA instead. If you already get DLA mobility component, however, you can claim DLA care component (at the middle or highest rate) rather than AA, even if you are aged, say 70.

What are the differences?

The main differences between AA and DLA care component are:

- AA has no £16.05 lower rate for part-time care needs or for the 'cooking test';
- AA has a backwards qualifying period of 6 months in all cases;
- AA has no forwards qualifying period.

What is the same?
The DLA care component, apart from its £16.05 lowest rate (which has no equivalent in AA), is almost exactly the same as AA. The disability tests for the lower and higher rate of AA and for the middle and highest rate of DLA care component are exactly the same, as is the amount payable. Chapter 20 gives full details of DLA and is therefore also relevant to AA. The relevant parts are:
- Chapter 20(6) to (8);
- Chapter 20(9) and (11) to (17) – The disability tests: but only the No. 1, No. 2, No. 3 and No. 4 disability tests apply to AA;
- Chapter 20(23) to (25) and (27);
- Box H.1;
- Box H.3;
- Box H.4.

If you already get DLA
For someone already on DLA whose care needs start to change when they are aged 65 or older, the DLA rules for the care component are, for all practical purposes, the same as for AA. The qualifying period for changing from the lowest rate up to the middle rate, or up to the highest rate, switches from 3 to 6 months. See Chapter 20(4).

If you already get the lowest rate care component you can stay on it after reaching 65, and can make renewal claims (including renewal claims made after a break in entitlement to the lowest rate of up to a year). You can also move up to the middle or highest rate after a supersession if your care needs increase but you cannot drop down to the lowest rate from the middle or highest rate after your 65th birthday. See Chapter 20(3).

22 Help with mobility needs

1. Blue Badge scheme
All Orange Badges under the old Orange Badge scheme have now expired. The new Blue Badge, recognisable throughout the European Union, can be obtained by contacting your social services department. Orange Badges continue to be used on road signs until they are replaced (by January 2010).

The Blue Badge scheme of parking concessions is designed to help people with severe mobility problems, registered blind people and those with severe disabilities in both arms by allowing them to park close to shops, public buildings and other places they may wish to visit.

You should not be wheel-clamped if you are displaying a current badge, although the police may remove your vehicle if it is causing an obstruction.

The badge requires a photo of you. The section showing the date of expiry must be visible from outside the vehicle; displaying the wrong (photo) side can result in a parking ticket.

The scheme allows a vehicle displaying a valid badge in the correct place and driven by a disabled person, or with a disabled person as passenger, to park:
- without charge or time limit at on-street parking meters and in Pay and Display bays;
- without time limit in streets where otherwise waiting is allowed for only limited periods;
- for a maximum of 3 hours in England, Wales and Northern Ireland, or without any time limit in Scotland, on single or double yellow lines.

This is provided the disabled person leaves the vehicle, *and:*
- in England and Wales, a special parking disc is also displayed showing the time of arrival, if parked on yellow lines or in a reserved parking place for badge holders that has a time limit (if you are visiting England or Wales from Scotland or Northern Ireland, ask your local authority for a disc);
- the vehicle is not parked in a bus lane or cycle lane during the lane's hours of operation;
- the vehicle is not parked where there is a ban on loading or unloading; *and*
- all other parking regulations are observed.

Red routes in towns and cities are subject to special controls on stopping, but there is parking provision for badge holders – check signs.

If the disabled person is not, or has not, been in the vehicle, it is an offence to display a Blue Badge – unless the driver is on the way to collect the disabled person or has just dropped them off.

The scheme applies throughout England, Scotland and Wales with the exception of 4 local authorities in Central London which operate their own badge schemes: the City of London; Westminster; Kensington and Chelsea; and Camden. In these areas there is limited recognition, including parking in designated disabled parking bays. Contact Greater London Action on Disability (GLAD), 336 Brixton Road, London SW9 7AA (020 7346 5800) for more details. The *London Blue Badge Parking Guide* (£4.50, from PIE Enterprises, 0870 444 5434) contains lots of advice and excellent maps showing the location of designated bays. Some other local authorities operate their own schemes for certain parking bays or streets.

To qualify for a Blue Badge you must be aged two or over *and:*
- receiving the higher rate mobility component of disability living allowance; *or*
- getting war pensioners' mobility supplement; *or*
- be registered blind; *or*
- drive regularly, and have a severe disability in both arms so that you cannot turn a steering wheel by hand (even if the wheel is fitted with a turning knob); *or*
- have a *'permanent and substantial disability which causes inability to walk or very considerable difficulty in walking'*.

Local authorities can charge a maximum of £2 to issue a badge, but an increase is being considered.

Exemption from congestion charging in Central London is available to Blue Badge holders if they apply to the Congestion Charging Office (for an application form ring 0845 900 1234 or visit www.cclondon.com). This exemption can be used temporarily on any vehicle, including minicabs. Vehicles with an exempt 'Disabled' class tax disc are automatically exempt (this only applies to vehicles registered at DVLA, Swansea). Durham operates a similar scheme and other authorities are considering doing the same. Exemptions for disabled people vary, as the planned national exemption scheme is not yet in operation.

If your local authority refuses to issue a Blue Badge because they do not think you have *'very considerable difficulty in walking'*, you have no formal right of appeal but may reapply for the badge and wait to hear from your local authority after they have contacted your GP. Alternatively, your councillor or local disability group or advice agency might help change their mind. You only have a formal right of appeal (to the Secretary of State for Transport) if you have been denied a badge on grounds of misuse, although a review of the scheme has recommended that an appeal procedure be adopted.

Blue Badge holders visiting certain European countries that provide parking concessions for their own disabled citizens can take advantage of those by displaying their badge. Concessions vary between countries but usually allow for an extension of the time limit where waiting is restricted and an entitlement to parking places reserved for disabled people. You can get full details of concessions and participating countries from the Department for Transport. Ask for their leaflets *European Parking Card For People With Disabilities* and *The Blue Badge Scheme* (020 7944 6100).

A quarterly newsletter and information on the Blue Badge can be obtained from The Blue Badge Network (01384 257001).

2. Exemption from road tax (VED)

Who can get exemption?

All vehicles on the road are liable to Vehicle Excise Duty (VED), better known as road tax. However, exemption from VED (including the £38 first registration fee) for one car is given to two groups of disabled people:

Mobility component – If you get disability living allowance (DLA) higher rate mobility component or war pensioners' mobility supplement, you (or your appointee or someone you choose to nominate in your place) can apply for exemption from VED. Long-stay hospital patients with transitional protection can still get the exemption.

Technically, the vehicle is only exempt while it is being used solely by or for the purposes of the disabled person.

H.7 Mobility checklist

Information on choosing a car

It is important to choose the car and adaptations that are best suited to you. Contact the Forum of Mobility Centres (see below) for practical advice.

Motability

Motability is a charity set up on the initiative of the Government and designed to help people with disabilities use their higher rate mobility component of disability living allowance (DLA) or war pensioner's mobility supplement to buy or hire a car. It offers two types of scheme: a hiring scheme and a hire purchase scheme. Under the hire purchase scheme it is possible to buy an electric wheelchair or a good used car as well as a new car.

People receiving DLA higher rate mobility component (including the parents of children who receive it) or war pensioners' mobility supplement who need adaptations done to their car or help with the initial deposit can apply to Motability for help.

To use any of the schemes your higher rate mobility component must be an indefinite award or a fixed-period award with at least 12 months still to run. The Disability Benefits Unit will pay your mobility component directly to Motability.

You can't renew a Motability agreement if you are in hospital, except under the wheelchair scheme. See Chapter 33.

Full details of these schemes are in booklets available from: Motability, Goodman House, Station Approach, Harlow, Essex CM20 2ET (0845 456 4566).

In some circumstances, Motability can help towards the cost of driving lessons. Write to Motability for details.

Hire purchase agreement on standard cars

There are no controls on hire purchase agreements (although there is consumer protection legislation). It is entirely up to the individual finance house to come to an agreement on terms with the borrower.

Concessions on cars and wheelchairs

Some car companies offer discounts to disabled people, but with increased competition in the retail car market these are less common than in the past. For more information contact the Disabled Drivers' Association, the Disabled Drivers' Motor Club, or the Disabled Living Foundation (see Address List).

The NHS supplies free wheelchairs, and may provide a voucher towards the cost of a more expensive wheelchair of your choice (see Chapter 27(5)).

If you are working, you may be able to get financial help towards a mobility solution through Access to Work – contact them at your local Jobcentre Plus office or the Access to Work Business Centre (01206 288 765).

If you buy a car and are a wheelchair user and need substantial adaptations to the car, you can claim VAT exemption on the purchase price of the vehicle and adaptations, providing the adaptation work is done before you take delivery. There is no VAT to pay on any vehicle adaptation or conversion required for any disabled person to use that vehicle. Contact your local VAT office or ring the Customs and Excise national VAT advice centre (0845 010 9000). Details are also available at: www.hmce.gov.uk.

Concessions on public transport

You can buy a Disabled Person's Railcard which entitles you to one-third off the cost of most train journeys. The scheme is for people getting DLA middle or highest rate care component or higher rate mobility component, attendance allowance, war pensioners' mobility supplement, severe disablement allowance or 80% or more war pension, or who are registered as visually impaired, who are deaf, or who have recurrent attacks of epilepsy.

Train operators also offer some other fare concessions to disabled people.

You can get a leaflet from your local station giving information about how to get a Disabled Person's Railcard, and about fare concessions, access to stations and trains, and travel arrangements. Alternatively, fill in an application form online (www.disabledpersons-railcard.co.uk).

For blind people resident in Scotland, a national travel scheme offers free travel on rail, bus, ferry and underground.

Some local authorities offer concessions to disabled people on local buses. Your social services department can give you details.

Concessions are available on some ferry routes and Eurotunnel for disabled people travelling with a car.

Some toll roads, tunnels and bridges offer limited exemption for disabled people. Contact the Disabled Drivers' Association or the Disabled Drivers' Motor Club (see Address List).

Help with travel to work – see Chapter 16(2).

Assessment services and sources of information

There is a network of accredited mobility centres, members of the Forum of Mobility Centres, which offer professional assessment, advice and recommendations for drivers and passengers with mobility needs. There are other non-accredited centres around the country. For further information regarding Forum Centres ring 08700 434 700. Advice, information and contact details for Mobility Centres can also be found at: www.mobility-centres.org.uk.

What exactly this means has never been defined. The disabled person does not necessarily have to be in the car: instead, it could be being used to do their shopping or running errands. However, the use of an exempt car for purposes totally unconnected with the disabled person is technically illegal. The probability of being prosecuted is low and is only likely to occur where there is flagrant abuse of the exemption (eg where a non-disabled person uses the vehicle to drive to work). The DWP has implied that, where the car is used substantially for the purposes of the disabled person, there is nothing to worry about.

Anyone receiving DLA higher rate mobility component or war pensioners' mobility supplement should automatically be sent a VED exemption form by the office handling the benefit. You can then use the certificate as proof of exemption when applying for a 'tax exempt disc' from the Vehicle Licensing Agency. If you are getting DLA higher rate mobility component and have not been sent an application form, or want guidance on it, write to the Disability Benefits Unit (see inside back cover). If you are getting war pensioners' mobility supplement and have not been sent an exemption form, write to the Veterans Agency (see Chapter 45(7) for the address).

Allow plenty of time when applying for a renewal of the exemption certificate or you may find you need to buy a half-year's tax disc and re-claim any unused whole months when the certificate finally arrives.

If there is a delay in your DLA claim, the exemption will not be backdated.

Passengers getting DLA care component or attendance allowance (AA) – Road tax exemption for passengers getting DLA care component or AA was abolished on 12.10.93. If you were exempt from road tax or applied for help before this date, transitional arrangements allow you to continue getting help under the old scheme. For details of the old scheme, see *Disability Rights Handbook*, 17th edition.

Nominating another person's vehicle

Someone getting DLA higher rate mobility component can nominate another person's vehicle to be exempt from road tax. This may also apply to a company car registered in the name of the company – the person receiving mobility component should nominate the company for exemption. In order to qualify for exemption, the vehicle should be used *'by or for the purposes of'* the disabled person.

The named person who gets the exemption may be changed at any time. For example, if you have nominated someone else for exemption and then get your own car, the exemption can be returned to you.

If you are refused exemption

Even if you have an exemption certificate from the DWP, it is within the discretion of the Vehicle Licensing Agency to refuse to grant exemption from road tax if they think the vehicle will not be used *'solely by or for the purposes of'* the disabled person. They are unlikely to do this unless your intended use of the vehicle would blatantly breach this condition.

If you are refused exemption, there is no formal procedure for appealing. However, you can write, giving full details of why you think you qualify for exemption, the purposes for which the vehicle will be used, etc, to: Driver Vehicle and Licensing Agency, Vehicle Enquiry Unit Centre, Longview Road, Swansea SA99 1BL (0870 240 0010).

Help for carers

This section of the Handbook looks at:

23 Carer's allowance

1. What is carer's allowance?

Carer's allowance (CA) is a benefit for people who regularly spend at least 35 hours a week caring for a severely disabled person. You don't have to be related to, or live with, the disabled person. You can get CA even if you've never worked. You can get CA if you also get attendance allowance (AA) or disability living allowance (DLA), but you must be caring for another person who gets AA or DLA care component at the middle or highest rate.

If you are paid CA, a carer premium of £25.80 will be included in your applicable amount for income support, income-based jobseeker's allowance, housing benefit and/or council tax benefit (see Chapter 4(8)). If you have claimed CA and would have been paid it but for the fact that it overlaps with state pension or another benefit (see 6 below), you also get the carer premium. An equivalent addition to the carer premium is included in the calculation of pension credit (PC) – see Chapter 41(3).

If you are paid CA, the person you are caring for cannot get the severe disability premium included in their applicable amount for means-tested benefits (or the equivalent amount used in PC). Because of this it is not always advantageous to claim CA even if you are eligible. See Chapter 4(7). The person you care for will not lose the severe disability premium (or the PC equivalent) if you are entitled to CA but cannot be paid it because of the overlapping benefits rule.

CA is not means tested and does not depend on past national insurance (NI) contributions, but it is taxable. CA gives you Class 1 NI contribution credits (see Chapter 12(2)) and helps you qualify for the state second pension (see Chapter 42(4)).

2. Do you qualify?

- ❑ You must regularly spend at least 35 hours a week (see below) caring for a person who receives either:
  - disability living allowance (DLA) care component (at the middle or highest rate only); *or*
  - attendance allowance (AA) at either rate; *or*
  - constant attendance allowance (of £49.60 or more) paid with a war pension, industrial disablement pension, workmen's compensation or equivalent benefit.
- ❑ You must be aged 16 or over.
- ❑ You must pass the UK residence and presence tests (see Chapter 49(2) and (3)).
- ❑ You must not be in full-time education. You are treated as being in full-time education if you attend a course for 21 hours or more a week. The 21 hours is the time spent in supervised study. It does not include breaks but can include coursework or homework set by the tutor.
- ❑ If you work, you must not earn more than £82 a week once allowable expenses are deducted (see 5).

CA can continue for up to 8 weeks after the person you look after dies. You must continue to satisfy all the rules other than those related to the care of a disabled person or that person's receipt of a qualifying benefit.

If another person gets CA to look after the same person you look after, you cannot also get CA to look after that person. You can get home responsibilities protection and you may get income support as a carer (but not the carer premium). You and the other carer can decide between you who should claim CA.

You can only get one award of CA, even if you care for more than one person.

If you were aged 65 or over and entitled to CA on 27.10.02 (or invalid care allowance, as it was then called), you can continue to get CA even if you stop caring for 35 hours a week or if the DLA or AA of the person you look after stops or if you start full-time work. You must, however, continue to meet the other CA rules.

Caring for 35 hours a week

If you are caring for more than one person, you can't add together the time you spend caring for each of them. You have to show that for at least 35 hours each week you are caring for one person. If you meet the 35-hours test during part of the year (eg in school holidays) you may qualify for CA during that period.

A CA benefit week runs from the start of Sunday to the end of the following Saturday. The hours of caring in any given week must be 35 hours: you cannot take an average of the hours over a number of weeks. If, for example, you provide care on alternate weekends, you may find it difficult to show that you provide care for 35 hours in any given benefit week, as the care you provide on Saturday will fall within one benefit week and Sunday's care will fall into the next. Time you spend preparing for the visit of the person you care for on the day they arrive, or clearing up after they leave, is part of the time you spend caring – as is collecting them from, or taking them back to, the place where they usually live.

3. How much do you get?

Carer's allowance	per week
For yourself	£45.70
For an adult dependant	£27.30
Extra for dependent children	
(available on claims made before 6.4.03 only)	
For the oldest child	£9.40
For each other child	£11.35

You can get the adult dependant's addition for your wife or husband. To get the addition for an unmarried partner or other adult who lives with you, that adult must look after your child. You cannot get the addition if your partner earns above set limits or receives other specified benefits (see 5 below).

If you are making a fresh claim for CA and want financial help for a dependent child, you should claim child tax credit (see Chapter 18).

4. How do you claim?

Claim on form DS700. You can get this, and a free stamped envelope, from a Jobcentre Plus office or by ringing the free Benefit Enquiry Line: 0800 882200 (0800 220674 in Northern Ireland). You can also claim online at www.dwp.gov.uk.

It is important to submit your claim-form even if the disabled person is waiting to hear whether they have been awarded disability living allowance (DLA) or attendance allowance (AA) – see below.

In areas of the country where Jobcentre Plus is operating, you may be asked to attend a meeting with a personal adviser to discuss work prospects as a condition of receiving benefit (see Box R.1, Chapter 57). You should not be asked to attend an interview if you work for at least 16 hours a week and do not get income support (IS) or if you are aged 60 or over. From October 2005, it is likely that these interviews will become purely voluntary when you claim CA.

Backdating – If you were entitled to CA prior to claiming it, you can ask that it be backdated for up to 3 months.

If the person you care for has claimed DLA or AA but is still waiting for the decision, don't delay claiming CA. AA and DLA are difficult claims to administer and regularly take several months to process. You may need to make two claims for CA to safeguard your entitlement. Your first claim will be refused if no decision has been made on the DLA or AA claim. Once the DLA or AA decision is made, you have 3 months in which to re-claim CA. If you do so, you will be paid from the date of your first claim for CA or the date the DLA or AA award begins if that is later. If entitlement to CA will mean you can start receiving a benefit such as IS because of the award of a carer premium, you should make a claim for this at the same time you claim CA to ensure the IS is also backdated.

What happens next? – You will be sent a written decision on your claim. If you disagree with that decision you have one month in which to dispute it. You can do this either by asking a decision maker in the Carer's Allowance Unit to revise the decision or by lodging an appeal to a tribunal. See Chapter 58 for details.

5. How do earnings affect CA?

You cannot get CA if your net earnings are more than £82 a week (ie after taking off tax, national insurance contributions, half of any contribution you make towards an occupational or personal pension, and any other allowable deductions). This earnings limit increases every year in April. The rules for calculating earnings are the same as those for incapacity benefit dependants' additions (see Chapter 14(5)), except that for CA there is a more generous disregard for care costs: if you pay someone other than a 'close relative' to look after the person you care for or to look after a child aged under 16, these payments are deducted from your earnings. A maximum of half your net earnings can be ignored in this way. A 'close relative' is the parent, parent-in-law, step-parent, son, daughter, son/daughter-in-law, stepson/daughter, brother, sister or partner of either yourself or the person you care for.

If your partner earns more than £27.30, the adult dependant's addition will not be paid. If you are still entitled to any child dependant's addition(s) and your partner earns £170 or more in any week, you will lose an addition for one child in the next week. For each extra £22 earned you lose another child dependant's addition.

Occupational and personal pensions count as earnings for adult and child dependants' additions, but not for the basic rate of CA.

I.1 Caring away from your home

Seek legal advice

If you have to leave your own home in order to care for a disabled or elderly relative or friend, you should seek advice before you go. You may be able to get free legal aid (see Chapter 59); otherwise a Citizens Advice Bureau or housing aid centre is a good starting point.

Housing costs

If you leave your main home temporarily, you remain liable for the housing costs, including the rent or mortgage. If the absence is for 13 weeks or less you can claim help with rent from housing benefit (HB – see Chapter 7) or help with mortgage interest from income support (see Chapter 4(11)), jobseeker's allowance (see Chapter 17(20)) or pension credit (see Chapter 41(3)). This help continues for up to 52 weeks of a temporary absence if the care you provide is medically approved. If you think your absence might be for longer than 13 weeks, you should ask a doctor or other medical professional (eg a nurse) involved in the care of the disabled person to provide a letter approving the care you provide.

HB and help with mortgage interest stop after a continuous absence of 13 or 52 weeks. Regular trips back to your own home (perhaps with the disabled person) can enable you to continue to get benefit beyond these limits. Tell the office dealing with your claim of each visit to your home and keep a record of the dates of these visits. If you leave your home permanently, help with housing costs will stop immediately.

Council tax

If you have left your home empty to normally live elsewhere in order to care for someone, your former home may be exempt from council tax. The person you provide care for must need that care because they are elderly, ill, disabled, have a mental disorder or have a drug or alcohol problem. The empty property must have ceased to be your sole or main residence for the exemption to apply.

If the disabled person's home becomes your sole or main residence, you may be counted as living there for council tax purposes. However, you get a status discount if:

- the person you are caring for is not your child under 18 or your partner;
- they get higher rate attendance allowance, highest rate disability living allowance care component, or the equivalent from the War Pensions or Industrial Injuries schemes; *and*
- you spend at least 35 hours a week on average caring for them.

This means the council tax for the home will be the same as if you were not resident there. See Chapter 8(9).

If you are temporarily absent from your home, the rules for claiming council tax benefit during that absence are the same as those for HB (see above).

Security

If you move to someone else's home to provide them with care, you need to think about what you will do once the need for that care stops. What will happen if your relationship with the cared for person deteriorates? What if they die or go into a care home? What if their mental competence deteriorates and they are no longer able to look after their own affairs?

You should get legal advice about the potential effects of such situations before they happen. For instance, if you have rented out or sold your previous home, do you have a right to remain in the home of the person you look after if they die? You may be able to draw up a legal agreement with that person now, but if their mental state deteriorates establishing a right to remain becomes much more complicated. Do not make assumptions about your rights. Seek advice from an expert. The person you look after will also need legal advice. You should each seek advice separately – your interests will not always be the same.

If you earn over £82 a week and get a means-tested benefit, that benefit may continue even though entitlement to CA (and the carer premium) stops. Earnings of £82 a week or less do not affect CA, but any means-tested benefit you receive may be reduced (see Chapter 5(4)).

6. How do other benefits affect CA?

You cannot be paid CA while you are receiving the same amount or more from the following benefits:

- state pension;
- maternity allowance;
- incapacity benefit;
- unemployability supplement;
- contribution-based jobseeker's allowance;
- widows' benefits and bereavement benefits;
- state training allowance.

This is known as the overlapping benefits rule. If you get less than the basic rate of CA from one of the benefits above, that benefit is paid and topped up with CA to the amount you would get from CA alone. Only the basic rate of these benefits overlap with CA. CA can be paid in addition to any earnings-related or age-related addition to the other benefit.

If your partner receives a dependency addition for you with one of these benefits, the addition cannot be paid if you get the same amount or more from CA. If CA is less than the addition, you receive CA and your partner gets the difference between CA and the standard rate of the dependency addition.

You can get CA at the same time as disability living allowance or attendance allowance.

If the person you look after gets the severe disability premium included in the calculation of a means-tested benefit, this will stop once you get CA. If you cannot be paid CA because of the overlapping benefit rules, the person you care for won't lose the severe disability premium – even if you get a carer premium.

The addition to your CA for an adult dependant won't be paid if your dependant gets an overlapping benefit of £27.30 a week or more.

Severe disablement allowance (SDA) – SDA and CA also overlap. Normally CA is paid in full, topped up with any balance of SDA. You can write and ask for your SDA to be paid in full, if your SDA is the same amount or more than CA. The person you care for is then not excluded from the severe disability premium and you can still claim a carer premium.

7. Carer's allowance and income support

You may be entitled to both CA and income support (IS – see Box B.1, Chapter 3). Because IS is means tested, it is reduced by the amount of your CA. The advantages of claiming CA are outlined in 9. If you are paid CA, the person you care for is excluded from the severe disability premium, but only once CA is actually awarded; arrears of CA do not affect entitlement to the premium (see Chapter 4(7)).

8. Carer's allowance and state pension

If you begin receiving a state pension which is more than CA (not including age- or earnings-related additions), CA will stop. If your state pension is less than CA, state pension is paid and topped up with CA to the basic weekly rate of CA. If all that prevents payment of CA is your state pension, a carer addition (£25.80) is included in the calculation of your pension credit (see Chapter 41(3)), and a carer premium (£25.80) is included in the calculation of housing benefit and council tax benefit (see Chapter 7(25)).

9. Why claim CA?

Your household income might not be greater after claiming CA, since it overlaps with other benefits, but there are advantages to claiming. If you are entitled to CA, even if it can't be paid because of other benefits, you might get:

- a carer premium included in your income support, income-based jobseeker's allowance (JSA), housing benefit, council tax benefit or NHS benefits. The premium is included if you get CA or have an underlying entitlement to CA but receive an overlapping benefit instead (see 6 above). An addition equivalent to the carer premium can be included in the calculation of pension credit;
- national insurance (NI) contribution credits (see Chapter 12(2));
- help to qualify for the state second pension (see Chapter 42(4) under 'Extra state pension');
- a £10 Christmas bonus;
- help towards satisfying the NI contribution conditions for incapacity benefit and JSA (see Chapter 12).

10. Time off from caring

CA rules allow breaks in care of up to 12 weeks in any 26-week period. CA is payable for 12 weeks if you or the person you look after goes into hospital (but see below). Up to 4 of the 12 weeks can be for other temporary breaks in care – eg a holiday or short-term stay in a care home for the person you look after.

If you have had more than the above number of weeks off in the past 26 weeks, you cannot be paid CA for any week in which you do not provide care for at least 35 hours.

Going into hospital – If you are in hospital, your CA will stop after 12 weeks. It may stop sooner if you have been in hospital or had a break in care within the last 26 weeks.

If the person you look after goes into hospital, the 12-weeks-off rule still applies, but in practice your CA may stop sooner. Your CA depends on the disabled person receiving attendance allowance (AA) or disability living allowance (DLA) care component. If they go into hospital and the stay is arranged by the NHS, payment of AA and DLA stops after 4 weeks if they are aged 16 or over, or after 12 weeks for children under 16. Your CA will stop when their AA or DLA stops. If the person can arrange a pattern of respite care that allows them to keep their AA or DLA, CA may continue to be paid (see Box H.3, Chapter 20).

Arranging care breaks – A week off is a week in which you cared for the disabled person for less than 35 hours: so odd days or weekends away are unlikely to affect your CA entitlement. A weekend straddles two CA weeks: a CA week runs from Sunday to Saturday. This means if you arrange respite care from midweek to midweek, you may still care for the required 35 hours both in the week the disabled person goes into respite care and the week they come home. These weeks won't count as weeks off and CA will be paid even though you've had a full week of respite care.

New carers – To get paid CA for breaks in care, new carers must have received benefit for an initial period of 22 weeks. You can include up to 8 weeks of hospital stays in those 22 weeks if you would have cared for the disabled person had they (or you) not been in hospital.

Tell the DWP – Report any of these changes in writing to the Carer's Allowance Unit as soon as possible to avoid having to repay overpaid benefit.

Keep a diary? – If all this seems confusing, keep a diary.

24 Other help for carers

1. Introduction

In this chapter we look at some of the financial and practical help available for carers. Parents of disabled children should also look at Chapter 35. Some of the help depends on you getting carer's allowance (CA – see Chapter 23). See Chapter 8(9) for details of the council tax discount scheme as it affects carers caring in their own home. Other help depends on your own circumstances: whether you have given up work, or your income is low, or you have a disability yourself. The benefits checklist at the front of this Handbook can help you see which benefits you might be entitled to. While CA is the only benefit specifically aimed at carers, others have special provisions that can provide extra money now or may help you claim in the future.

Often your own benefit entitlement is dependent on that of the person you care for, for example on whether they are getting attendance allowance (AA). This is important to remember when you first claim benefit, and whenever there is a change of circumstances that might affect the amount of benefit to which you are entitled. In particular, make sure to tell the CA Unit, the local Jobcentre Plus office and the local authority housing benefit section if the person you care for stops getting AA or the middle or highest rate care component of disability living allowance, or if they go into hospital or a care home. Otherwise you might find you are asked to pay back overpaid benefit. If you care for your disabled child and you get child tax credit make sure you tell the Inland Revenue about any relevant changes.

2. Giving up work

You may qualify for carer's allowance (CA) if you spend at least 35 hours a week caring for someone who gets disability living allowance (DLA) care component at the middle or highest rate or attendance allowance (AA). You are eligible for CA even if you have a partner who is working (see Chapter 23). If you give up work, you may not get CA for the first few weeks because of the way final earnings from work are taken into account.

If your household income and savings are low and you are aged under 60, claim income support. If you have other income or savings, you may be better off claiming contribution-based jobseeker's allowance (JSA) for the first 6 months (see below). If you are over 60, you may be able to claim pension credit (PC) – see 5. If you have dependent children, you may be able to claim child tax credit (Chapter 18). You may also be eligible for housing benefit (HB) and/or council tax benefit (CTB) (see Chapter 7) and help with NHS costs (Chapter 52).

Income support

Income support (IS) is a means-tested benefit for people under 60 who are not expected to sign on as available for work, and is intended to provide for basic living expenses for yourself and for a partner. It can be paid on its own if you (and your partner) have no other income, or it can top up your CA or other income. You normally cannot get IS if you have capital over £8,000. You cannot get IS if you have a partner who works for 24 hours a week or more. See Chapters 3 to 6 for more on IS.

You are eligible for IS if you get CA. You can also get IS if you are *'regularly and substantially engaged in caring for a disabled person'* who gets AA or DLA care component at the middle or highest rate (see Box B.1, Chapter 3); it is possible to get IS under this rule even if the care you provide is for less than 35 hours a week. You can claim IS as a carer for up to 6 months while you are waiting for the AA or DLA of the person that you look after to be processed. If you stop being treated as a carer for IS you continue to be eligible for IS for 8 weeks if you satisfy all of the other IS rules. Otherwise, you may need to claim JSA instead.

Carer premium – If you or your partner get CA, a carer premium of £25.80 a week is included in the assessment for IS (see Chapter 4(8)). You can get a carer premium included if all that prevents the payment of CA is the overlapping benefits rule (see Chapter 23(6)). The carer premium is also included in HB, CTB, income-based JSA and health benefits. An equivalent addition to the carer premium is included in the calculation of PC (see Chapter 41(3)).

Mortgage interest – Normally when you claim IS, there is a 39-week waiting period before mortgage interest is included in your assessment. However, if you are eligible for IS as a carer, 50% of your eligible mortgage interest is included after 8 weeks, and 100% of eligible interest after 26 weeks. If you are considering claiming IS in the near future, but at present your income or capital is too high, it may be worth making your claim now. If your income or savings go down and you qualify for IS on another claim made within 39 weeks, the time limits for the mortgage interest assessment will run from the date of your first claim. See Chapter 4(14).

Jobseeker's allowance

Contribution-based JSA of up to £56.20 a week (but less if you are under 25) is payable for up to 6 months if you have paid enough national insurance (NI) contributions. You are eligible even if you have a partner who is working. The amount you get may be reduced if you have earnings or an occupational pension. It is not affected by other income or savings. You might be better off claiming JSA instead of IS for the first 6 months if you have other household income or savings. CA overlaps with contribution-based JSA – if you claim both you'll be paid JSA, perhaps topped up with CA if that is higher (see Chapter 23(6)).

JSA is for people who are available for, and actively looking for, work. Usually, you are expected to look for a full-time job even though you may have given up work to be a carer. However, if you care for a person who is a close relative or member of your household, you can restrict your availability for work to whatever hours your caring responsibilities allow, subject to a minimum of 16 hours a week. You must show that you have a reasonable chance of finding work despite this restriction. Carers are also allowed to ask for 48 hours' notice before taking up a job offer from the Jobcentre Plus office. See Chapter 17 for more on JSA.

JSA is not payable for up to 26 weeks if you leave your job voluntarily and without 'just cause'. You should not be sanctioned in this way if your caring responsibilities meant that it was no longer reasonable for you to continue working, but you are expected to look for alternatives before giving up work. If possible, talk to your employer about your difficulties to see if there is any alternative to leaving. If your JSA is sanctioned, you can appeal against the sanction itself or against the length of the sanction.

3. Working part time or full time

If you are eligible for income support (IS) as a carer, you are allowed to work without limit on your weekly hours. You can only keep £20 a week of your net earnings (or of your joint earnings if your partner works); anything over that reduces your IS penny for penny (see Chapter 5(4)). You cannot get IS if your partner works for 24 hours or more a week.

The way that earnings are assessed is different for carer's allowance (CA), and it is important to remember that net earnings over £82 a week will stop your entitlement to CA (see Chapter 23(5)). If your net earnings are £82 a week or less, the amount of CA you are paid is not affected.

4. Incapable of work

If you are incapable of work because of disability or ill-health and are under state pension age (60 for women, 65 for men), you may be able to claim incapacity benefit (IB). You should claim even if you have not worked recently, as your entitlement to carer's allowance (CA) can help you pass the national insurance contribution conditions for IB (see 6 below and Chapter 12).

Chapter 11 gives details of the way that incapacity is assessed. Chapter 14(7) gives details of how you claim IB.

After 52 weeks of incapacity a disability premium is included in your income support (IS – see Chapter 4(5)), housing benefit and council tax benefit assessments. Payment of CA usually stops when you get IB because these benefits overlap, but you keep an underlying entitlement. This means you continue to have the carer premium included in your IS assessment. Because your CA is not paid, the person you care for may still get the severe disability premium (see Chapter 4(7)).

5. Over state pension age

If you don't have enough contributions for the full rate of the basic state pension, your state pension can be topped up to £45.70 with carer's allowance (CA). If you were 65 or over and getting CA on 27.10.02, you can continue to get it even if you cease to care for at least 35 hours a week, or the person you care for stops getting attendance allowance (AA) or a qualifying rate of disability living allowance (DLA).

Pension credit (PC) replaces income support (IS) as the means-tested benefit to provide for basic living expenses once you are 60 or over (see Chapter 41). If you claim CA and the only reason it cannot be paid is because your state pension is higher, a 'carer addition' is still included in your PC calculation.

If you are disabled, you may be eligible for DLA or AA even though you are caring for another person (see Chapters 20 and 21). If you and your partner get AA or middle or highest rate DLA care component, or you live alone and get one of these benefits, you may be eligible for an extra amount for severe disability to be included in the PC calculation.

6. National insurance credits

For each week that you get carer's allowance (CA), you get a Class 1 national insurance contribution credit (as long as you have lost, given up, or never had the right to pay reduced-rate contributions). However, if you already get unemployment or incapacity credits for that week, you cannot also get CA credits for that same period. CA Class 1 credits can give you a better deal than these other credits (see Chapter 12(2)). For instance: if you had CA for the 2002/03 and 2003/04 tax years (or would have got CA but for the overlapping benefit rules), your Class 1 credits for those years may mean that if you fall sick in 2005, you'll pass the second contribution condition for incapacity benefit (IB); at the same time, CA entitlement also helps you pass the first contribution condition for IB.

Each tax year in which you have 52 Class 1 credits is a qualifying year for state pension (see Box N.1, Chapter 42).

Home responsibilities protection

If you do not get CA, you might be eligible for home responsibilities protection (HRP). This helps protect your right to a state pension. If you get child benefit for a child under 16 (but see below if your child is 6 or over) or income support (IS) as a carer, you do not have to apply for HRP; it should be recorded automatically. If you do not get CA or IS but you look after someone who gets disability living allowance middle or highest rate care component or attendance allowance, you have to apply for each year you wish to receive the protection. For years from 2002/03 onwards, to get HRP you must apply by the end of the 3rd tax year following the tax year for which you want to claim (see Chapter 43). From April 2003, you can claim the protection for each tax year in which you are a foster parent.

Additional state pension (state second pension)

For each complete tax year in which you get CA or HRP as a carer, you are treated as though you have earned enough to have made full contributions towards the state second pension for that year. If you get HRP because you get child benefit, you only get help towards the state second pension if the child you claim for is under 6 years old (see Chapter 42(4)). If you are a carer and have a child aged 6 or over, you need to claim HRP as a carer to protect your entitlement to the additional pension; child benefit will not provide this protection.

7. Practical help

The person you care for is entitled to an assessment from the local social services department (social work department in Scotland) of their need for services. Social services must also assess your own support needs as a carer and look at your continuing ability to provide care if you ask them to do so (see Chapter 25).

Box J.2 in Chapter 25 gives a checklist of the kind of services that might be available in your area. Your first contact should be the social services department. They should be able to tell you about short-term break options and other practical help. There might be a local carers support group where you can share information with other carers. Contact Carers UK for details of these groups (see Box I.2).

8. If the person you care for dies

As a carer, your own benefit entitlement may depend on the benefits of the person you look after. This is the case if you receive carer's allowance (CA) or income support (IS) for caring for someone. CA stops 8 weeks from the Sunday following the death of the person you cared for. Throughout those 8 weeks you must continue to satisfy all of the conditions for CA not related to caring or payment of a qualifying benefit to the person you cared for. If you were 65 or over and in receipt of CA on 27.10.02, you can continue to get CA indefinitely after the person you cared for has died.

You continue to be eligible for IS with a carer premium and/or to claim IS as a carer for 8 weeks following the death. You continue to be eligible for the additional amount for carers in pension credit for 8 weeks following the death, or indefinitely if you were over 65 and in receipt of CA on 27.10.02.

If you are under 60 you may be expected to sign on as available for work and claim jobseeker's allowance (JSA) from 8 weeks after the death. If you gave up work to be a carer, you may qualify for contribution-based JSA based on national insurance contributions paid when you were working (see Chapter 12(3)). Check first to see if you might be eligible for IS on other grounds, perhaps because you are too ill to look for work or because you are a lone parent.

If you hadn't claimed IS before the death, you may be able to claim it now, either as a carer for up to 8 weeks following the death, or on other grounds after the 8 weeks has ended. Box B.1 in Chapter 3 explains who is eligible for IS.

You may be eligible for bereavement benefits if it is your husband or wife who has died (see Chapter 51).

I.2 For more information

Carers UK (formerly Carers' National Association) provides information and support to carers. It publishes a range of leaflets, free to carers. For a carers' information pack send a large stamped addressed envelope to: 20-25 Glasshouse Yard, London EC1A 4JT (020 7490 8818). For advice, phone the CarersLine (Freephone 0808 808 7777) or visit www.carersuk.org.

Practical help at home

25 Care services

In this chapter we look at:

1. What is community care?

Community care is defined as *'providing the right level of intervention and support to enable people to achieve maximum independence and control over their own lives'*. The objective of the 1993 community care reforms was that fewer people would need to go into care homes because there would be a greater range of care in the community. Although there have been further changes, this is still the main objective. (Chapters 29 to 31 look at care in care homes.)

The first step towards obtaining community care services is an assessment of your needs. Social services currently have the lead role in this but local authorities have a duty to invite the NHS and housing departments to assist in the assessment, where there is a health or housing need. Single assessment processes (called unified assessment in Wales and single shared assessment in Scotland) have been introduced for older people (see 2 and 3 below).

Healthcare and social care

There is no obvious dividing line between a social care need and a healthcare need. Legislation in England, Wales and Scotland allows social services and health bodies to work closely together using pooled budgets and joint commissioning of services. In some areas in England, care trusts combine the functions of health and social services. However, it is important to know if your care is considered to be under the NHS, as most healthcare is free at the point of delivery but people are charged for most social care.

Health bodies may not provide services they consider are not reasonably required. They can take into account their own resources in deciding what services to provide. Local authorities in England and Wales can only provide social care packages. In England (since April 2003) and Wales (since April 2004) the NHS is responsible for meeting the cost of registered nursing care in care homes which provide it, as well as all other reasonably required healthcare.

Intermediate care – Intermediate care services in England ('6 week support for vulnerable people' in Wales) help people leave hospital quicker, or avoid admission, and maximises their independence to resume living at home. It is an intensive service normally lasting no longer than 6 weeks. Although intermediate care covers both health and social care, it should be free (see 6). Support can be provided in your home, housing schemes, day centres, hospitals or rehabilitation centres. Services can include homecare, nursing and intensive rehabilitation. Health and social services should work in partnership to provide these services using a single assessment process and shared protocols. After intermediate care services finish, you should have an assessment to see if you require any ongoing care or health services.

LAC (2001)1; LAC (2003)14, (www.dh.gov.uk) NAFWC 43/02 (www.wales.gov.uk)

Setting eligibility criteria – Following criticism from the Health Ombudsman, local health bodies were asked to review the way they set and apply eligibility criteria for continuing care (see Chapter 29(3)). In England each strategic health authority (SHA) was instructed to ensure that all primary care trusts in its area were using common eligibility criteria by April 2004. Each SHA must publish its policies, plans and eligibility criteria for meeting continuing healthcare needs in its area. The Government has announced that a national framework for eligibility criteria may be introduced in the future. Each local authority in England also has to publish its joint plans for services and must have a long-term care charter, *Better Care, Higher Standards*, publicly available setting out its service standards in health, housing and social services. Scotland and Wales produce similar information.

Delayed discharges – In England, under the Community Care (Delayed Discharges etc) Act 2003 there is an obligation for the NHS and local authorities to work together around discharge arrangements. A duty was placed on the NHS to inform social services of any patient who is likely to require community care services. Social services then have a duty to assess that person, and provide services within certain strict time limits. From January 2004 the local authority has to reimburse an NHS acute trust if a delay in organising a community care assessment (or the setting up of services) is the sole reason that discharge is delayed. You should not be pressured into leaving hospital until suitable care arrangements are in place. If you are returning home, guidance makes it clear that social services must review your case within 2 weeks to ensure the care package is adequate.

LAC (2003)21

The law

There are several Acts, Regulations, Directions and guidance documents going back to the National Assistance Act 1948 that cover community care. Box J.1 gives relevant sections of some of the law. Services for children come under the Children Act 1989 as well as section 2 of the Chronically Sick and Disabled Persons Act 1970. Broadly, children should be able to obtain similar services and have similar systems of appeal as adults. In Scotland, many provisions are similar. The main legislation is found in the Social Work (Scotland) Act 1968, the Children (Scotland) Act 1995 and The Community Care and Health (Scotland) Act 2002, which enabled the Scottish Executive to bring in free personal and nursing care from July 2002 (see 6 and Chapter 29). Although Wales has the same primary legislation as England, detailed policies are developing differently.

2. Where do you go for help?

Go first to the local area office of the social services department, or in Scotland, the social work department. Sometimes NHS

J.1 The law and community care

The duties and powers of statutory authorities (eg health authorities and social services departments) come from several Acts, Regulations and Orders, as interpreted by case law. In following the law, authorities must act in accordance with Directions and mandatory guidance, and take account of other guidance. Details about the law for care home provision are in Box K.1, Chapter 29, but the law on assessments in this box applies equally if you want an assessment of your need for care in a care home.

The main provisions in the various Acts are outlined below. Most of the provisions in Scotland come under different legislation, and although broadly equivalent to the law in England and Wales there are some important differences. Guidance in Wales and Scotland may indicate differing application or interpretation of principles.

Assessments legislation

NHS and Community Care Act 1990

Section 47(1) states ' ...where it appears to a local authority that any person for whom they may provide or arrange for the provision of community care services may be in need of any such services, the authority
(a) shall carry out an assessment of his needs for those services; *and*
(b) having regard to the results of that assessment, shall then decide whether his needs call for the provision by them of any such services.'

Disabled Persons (Services, Consultation and Representation) Act 1986

Section 4 states 'When requested to do so by –
(a) a disabled person [...] *or*
(c) any person who provides care for him [...]
a local authority shall decide whether the needs of the disabled person call for the provision by the authority of any services in accordance with section 2(1) of the 1970 [Chronically Sick and Disabled Persons] Act (provision of welfare services).'

Carers (Recognition and Services) Act 1995

Section 1(1) states '...in any case where –
(a) a local authority carry out an assessment under section 47(1)(a) of the NHS and Community Care Act 1990 of the needs of a person for community care services, *and*
(b) an individual (carer) provides or intends to provide a substantial amount of care on a regular basis for the [...] person, the carer may request the local authority, before they make their decision as to whether the needs of the [...] person call for the provision of any services, to carry out an assessment of his ability to provide and to continue to provide care for the [...] person; and if he makes such a request, the local authority shall carry out such an assessment and shall take into account the results of that assessment in making that decision.'

Carers and Disabled Children Act 2000
(not applicable in Scotland)

Section 1(1) states 'If an individual aged 16 or over ('the carer') –
(a) provides or intends to provide a substantial amount of care on a regular basis for another individual aged 18 or over ('the person cared for'); *and*
(b) asks a local authority to carry out an assessment of his ability to provide and to continue to provide care for the person cared for, the local authority must carry out such an assessment if it is satisfied that the person cared for is someone for whom it may provide or arrange for the provision of community care services.'
Section 2(1) states 'The local authority must consider the assessment and decide –
(a) whether the carer has needs in relation to the care which he provides or intends to provide;
(b) if so, whether they could be satisfied (wholly or partly) by services which the local authority may provide; *and*
(c) if they could be so satisfied, whether or not to provide services to the carer.'

The services must *'help the carer care for the person cared for, and may take the form of physical help or other forms of support'*. Although provided to the carer it may take the form of a service delivered to the cared-for person if both agree and it does not include anything of an intimate nature. Carers can be given vouchers or direct payments.

See Chapter 25(3) for similar provision in the Community Care and Health (Scotland) Act 2002.

Section 1 of the Carers (Equal Opportunities) Act 2004 requires local authorities to inform carers of their right to an assessment.

Children

The assessment of, and provision of services to, children, including disabled children, comes under (as far as most services are concerned) the Children Act 1989 (in Scotland, the Children (Scotland) Act 1995). Assessment of need is undertaken under section 17(2) and Schedule 2 paragraph 3 (section 23 in Scotland). (An assessment under the NHS and Community Care Act 1990 – see above – is also available for services under the NHS Act 1977.) Section 17 (section 22 in Scotland) places on local authorities a general duty to safeguard and promote the welfare of children in need. In meeting this duty they may provide services in kind or in exceptional circumstances, in cash.

Children in need are defined as those who are disabled and those who require the provision of services to achieve a reasonable standard of health or development or to prevent impairment of health or development. 'Disabled' is defined in the same terms as section 29 of the National Assistance Act 1948, below (except for being '18 or over'). In Scotland, section 23 of the 1995 Act allows for the assessment and provision of services not only to children who are disabled but also to any child adversely affected by the disability of another family member. Disabled children are also entitled to all services available under section 2 Chronically Sick & Disabled Persons Act 1970 by virtue of section 28A of that Act.

Providing community care services

Following an assessment, the local authority must decide how it will meet identified needs of the following people:

- provision of residential accommodation to *'persons aged 18 or over who by reason of age, illness, disability or any other circumstances are in need of care and attention which is not otherwise available to them'* – section 21(1)(a) National Assistance Act 1948 (see Chapter 29(3));
- *'persons aged 18 or over who are blind, deaf or dumb or who suffer from mental disorder of any description, and other persons aged 18 or over who are substantially and permanently handicapped by illness, injury, or congenital deformity or such other disabilities as may be prescribed'*. Section 29 National Assistance Act 1948 gives a general provision to promote the welfare of the above people including workshops, suitable work in their own homes or elsewhere, recreational facilities and to give information about services, and keeping a register;
- those above (to whom section 29 National Assistance Act 1948 applies) who are *'ordinarily resident in their area'*. The local authority has a duty, under section 2 Chronically Sick and Disabled Persons Act 1970, to make arrangements for the provision of a range of services. Chapter 25(5) lists these services;
- old people – a general power, under section 45 Health Services and Public Health Act 1968, to promote welfare by providing services;
- *'a person who is suffering from illness, lying in, an expectant*

mother, aged, handicapped as a result of having suffered an illness or by congenital deformity'. Local authorities have a duty, under section 21 and Schedule 8 National Health Service Act 1977, to provide adequate home help and may provide laundry services for households when such help is required owing to the presence of the above. This Schedule also places a duty to provide day and training centres for those with a 'mental disorder';

- *persons who were detained or admitted to hospital under sections 3, 37, 47 or 48 of the Mental Health Act 1983*. Section 117 Mental Health Act 1983 places a duty to provide aftercare services. Section 8 of the Mental Health (Scotland) Act 1984 requires authorities to provide aftercare services for those who have, or have had, a mental disorder, regardless of whether they have been in hospital. The new Mental Health (Care and Treatment) (Scotland) Act 2003 will be implemented in April 2005. This will include provisions placing local authorities under a duty to provide care and support to those who have, or who have had, a mental disorder, as well as services to promote their general well-being and social development;
- in Scotland, the Social Work (Scotland) Act 1968 requires local authorities to make available advice, guidance and assistance to *'persons in need'*. It produces many of the same effects as the legislation above.

Also, Section 2 of the Local Government Act 2000 gives local authorities the power to promote well-being in their area and to provide financial assistance, facilitate activities and provide accommodation.

Registered nursing care contribution

(not applicable in Scotland)

The Health and Social Care Act 2001 (section 49) removes the power of local authorities to provide nursing care by a registered nurse, defined as:

'Any services provided by a registered nurse and involving:
a) the provision of care; *or*
b) the planning, supervision or delegation of the provision of care, other than the services which, having regard to their nature and the circumstance in which they are provided, do not need to be provided by a registered nurse.'

Free personal and nursing care

(only applicable in Scotland)

The Community Care and Health (Scotland) Act 2002 defines the care for which local authorities should not charge. It is defined as:

- 'personal care as defined in section 2(28) of the Regulation of Care (Scotland) Act 2001;
- personal support as so defined;
- whether or not such personal care or personal support, care of the kind for the time being mentioned in schedule 1 to this Act; *or*
- whether or not from a registered nurse, nursing care.'

'Personal care' relates to day-to-day physical tasks and the mental processes related to those tasks. *'Personal support'* means counselling or other help provided as part of a planned programme of care. See Chapter 25(6) for items included in schedule 1 of the Act. The Convention of Scottish Local Authorities (CoSLA) has produced its own guidance on free personal and nursing care.

Charges

Local authorities can charge for domiciliary services. They *'may recover such charge (if any) for it as they consider reasonable'*. If you satisfy your local authority that your *'means are insufficient for it to be reasonably practicable for [you] to pay'* what it has asked, it *'shall not require [you] to pay more for it than it appears to them that it is reasonably practicable for [you] to pay'* (section 17(3) Health and Social Services and Social Security Adjudications Act 1983/section 87 Social Work (Scotland) Act 1968). See Chapter 25(6). There are different rules for charges for services provided under the Children Act 1989 or Children (Scotland) Act 1995.

Those whose domiciliary or residential services are provided under section 117 Mental Health Act 1983 cannot be charged. In Scotland, charges can be made for such 'aftercare' services, although this should not be for personal care provided to a person aged 65 or over. See Chapter 25(6) for details of new Mental Health (Care and Treatment) (Scotland) Act.

Information

Various pieces of legislation lay a duty on authorities to publish information.

- NHS and Community Care Act 1990, section 46(1)(a) and (c) and section 5A of The Social Work Scotland Act (1968)
  'Each local authority
  (a) shall [...] prepare and publish a plan for the provision of community care services in their area.'
- Chronically Sick and Disabled Persons Act 1970, section 1
  '(2) Every [local] authority
  (a) shall cause to be published from time to time [...] general information as to the services provided... under section 29, which are for the time being available in their area; *and*
  (b) shall ensure that any [...] person [...] who uses any other service provided by the authority [...] is informed of any other of those services which in the opinion of the authority is relevant to his needs and of any service provided by any other authority or organisation which in the opinion of the authority is so relevant ...'
- Section 1 of the Carers (Equal Opportunities) Act 2004 requires local authorities to inform carers of their right to an assessment.

Complaints

Section 7 Local Authority Social Services Act 1970 and the Local Authority Social Services (Complaints Procedure) Order 1990/2244 and Directions established the complaints procedures. For Scotland, see SWSG 5/96.

Local authorities have to give appropriate publicity to any procedure established. See Chapter 25(7).

Section 7 gives ministers powers to hold an inquiry into a local authority's exercise of its social services functions, including any breach of its statutory duties. It also gives the Secretary of State 'default powers' to enforce action on a local authority. New social services complaints Regulations are due to be introduced in England in 2005/06 under the Health and Social Care Act 2003.

As well as the specific provisions outlined above, you may complain to the Local Government Ombudsman (see Chapter 60). Judicial review of local authority decisions is also a possibility.

This box gives only basic provisions. If you are challenging a decision about the help you get or need at home or about care in a care home you may find the following useful.

- *Paying for Care Handbook* (Child Poverty Action Group)
- *Community Care and the Law* by Luke Clements (2004, Legal Action Group)
- *Long Term Care for Older People: Law and Financial Planning* by Margaret Richards (2001, Jordons)
- *Community Care Law Reports* (Legal Action Group) – a quarterly digest of case law
- *Encyclopaedia of Social Services and Child Care Law (Volume 3)* (Sweet and Maxwell) – community care legislation including amendments to Acts and Regulations
- *Social Work Law in Scotland* by Mays, Smith and Strachan (W Green & Son)
- *Community Care Practice and the Law* by Michael Mandelstam (2005, Jessica Kingsley)

staff undertake the community care assessment at the request of social services. Care trusts undertaking both health and social care provision are being developed in England. For help with housing, you may be referred to the housing department.

Discuss your needs with your social worker (care manager), if you have one. Otherwise, look up the address of your nearest office in the phone book, under the name of your local authority. For example, look up 'Essex County Council' and find the heading 'Social Services Department, Area Office'. If you outline the type of help you want, they can put you through to the right section and arrange for you to have an assessment. Your health visitor or occupational therapist may also be able to help arrange for the services you need.

See Chapter 26 for help available to buy care at home.

3. Getting an assessment of your needs

If you have difficulty managing at home because of age, illness or disability, you can ask for an assessment of your needs. If it is apparent to the local authority that you might have a need for services, you should not have to ask for it. However, it is not only disabled people who can get a local authority assessment. See Box J.1 for the law on assessments.

The form your assessment takes will largely depend upon the complexity of your needs. However, even if the local authority is unlikely to provide a service because of its resource constraints, you should not be denied an assessment.

R v Bristol City Council ex p Penfold [1998] 1CCLR 315

Assessments for older people – As part of the 'National Framework for Older People', a single assessment process was introduced for older people from April 2004 in England. This aims to ensure that older people receive more appropriate, effective responses to their needs and that health and social care professionals work more closely. Professionals from different agencies can, with your consent, share information to save you being asked the same questions repeatedly. Under the single assessment process there are 4 types of assessment for older people:

- a 'contact assessment' takes basic details and explores whether you have wider health and social care problems;
- an 'overview assessment' is done when your needs are such that various aspects of care need to be explored;
- a 'specialist assessment' explores specific problems by an appropriate member of staff (eg occupational therapists, geriatricians or old age psychiatrists);
- a 'comprehensive assessment' is done if your needs are such that you are likely to be offered intensive or complex support. This may involve a range of different professionals.

You should be encouraged to contribute fully to your assessment.

In Scotland a 'single shared assessment' has been introduced, and 'unified assessments' should be implemented in Wales by June 2005 for older people, and April 2006 for all adult service user groups. There are some differences between these and the single assessment process in England.

LAC (2002)1; HSC 2002/001; NAFWC 09/02; WHC (2002)32; CCD 2/2003; CCD 10/2004

Eligibility criteria guidance – To decide who might receive services, authorities draw up eligibility criteria – ie the circumstances which must be present in any particular case before a person is considered eligible for services. Local authorities publish information about their assessment procedures and their eligibility criteria, and it may be useful to refer to this. Guidance in England, *Fair Access to Care Services*, and in Wales, *Creating a Unified and Fair System for Assessing and Managing Care*, provides a framework for determining eligibility criteria. Scotland introduced a 'Resource Use Measure' (also known as an 'Indicator of Relative Need') in 2003, with the intention of promoting fairer access to resources and equity in resource allocation.

LAC (2002)13; NAFWC 09/02; CCD 9/2002; CCD 10/2004

The assessment result – You should be informed in writing of the result of your assessment and eligibility for services and given a copy of your care plan. If you are not given a written result, you should ask for one. If your needs are urgent, services can be provided before an assessment, which should then be carried out as soon as possible.

Unhappy with the result? – If you are refused an assessment, or feel it has not taken account of your needs, or there is a delay in carrying it out, you can use the complaints procedure (or seek legal advice if it is very urgent) – see 7 below. In England and Wales, practice guidance to *Fair Access to Care Services* makes it clear that the carrying out and completion of a community care assessment should not be contingent on whether or not you can pay for care services, be they provided in a care home or your own home. With respect to services in your own home, a local authority should arrange those services irrespective of resources or capacity, if that is what you are assessed as needing.

Carers

Carers can request that an assessment of their ability to continue providing care be carried out at the same time as the person for whom they are caring is assessed for services. The assessment of the carer should be taken into consideration in the decisions made as a result of the disabled person's assessment. New legislation from April 2005 requires local authorities in England to inform carers of their rights to an assessment and to promote equality of opportunity for carers (Carers (Equal Opportunities) Act 2004). Additional guidance on carers' assessments is being drafted in Wales.

Carers (including, in Scotland, young carers aged under 16) also have a right to be assessed independently. In England and Wales, a carer's assessment may result in services being provided to the person cared for, or additionally, the carer may receive services in their own right. They can choose to receive a direct payment for services they are assessed as needing (see Chapter 26(4)). Local authorities should now be setting up voucher schemes to help carers access short-term breaks. Authorities can charge carers for services provided directly to them. See Box J.1 for more on these rights under the Carers and Disabled Children's Act 2000. Similar provisions are planned in Northern Ireland under the Carers and Direct Payments (Northern Ireland) Act 2002.

The Community Care and Health (Scotland) Act 2002 places a duty on Scottish local authorities to inform carers of their right to an assessment. A carer's assessment can result in additional help being provided to the person cared for. A carer may receive support from the local authority directly (in the form of information, advice or access to other resources) to assist them in their caring role. Guidance makes it clear that Scottish local authorities should not charge carers for support provided to them in their caring role (CCD2/2003).

4. How can you register as disabled?

Anyone whose disability is 'substantial and permanent' can register with their local authority. But you don't have to register to qualify for an assessment or for services. The requirement to keep registers applies only to England and Wales. Therefore this section does not apply to Scotland.

To register, contact the area office of your social services department. They will arrange for someone, usually a social worker or occupational therapist, to visit you and complete a registration form. Registering may not have any immediate benefit, but the more accurately the register reflects the number of disabled people in the community, the better services can be tailored to meet their needs.

Some local authorities automatically register you when you apply for help from them. Some send you a card confirming your registration, others give no written confirmation. All authorities should give you information on services available to disabled people.

5. What help can be provided?

Local authorities have a legal duty to provide certain services. Other services may be provided, but there is no requirement to do so. See Box J.2 for some types of services that may be available. All these services may not be available in your local authority area and the list is not exhaustive.

What are your rights to services?

If you are disabled and you are assessed as needing one of the services listed in section 2 of the Chronically Sick and Disabled Persons Act 1970, your local authority has a duty to make arrangements for the provision of the service. These services are:

- practical help in the home (eg a home help);
- providing, or help in getting, a radio or television or access to a library or similar recreational facilities;
- lectures, games, outings or other recreational facilities outside your home and any help needed to take advantage of educational facilities;
- help with travelling to any of these or similar activities;
- any adaptations (eg a ramp or lift or special equipment) needed in the home *'for greater safety, comfort or convenience'*; this can even include building an extra room on the ground floor;
- holidays;
- meals, either in the home or a local centre;
- a telephone, and any special equipment necessary to use the phone (eg Minicom).

See Box J.1 for the definition of disability and the legal provisions to provide services.

Supporting People services

The Supporting People programme is meant to offer vulnerable people services to improve their quality of life by allowing them to be more independent in the community. This has brought together services that used to be funded from a variety of housing support funds into a locally administered fund. Supporting People provides housing-related services to people living in specialist accommodation (eg supported or sheltered housing) or in their own homes. These services should complement community care and health services. Examples include:

- helping older people remain in their own home as long as they wish to by funding visiting support services;
- continuing to provide services (eg wardens) in sheltered schemes;
- helping young people leaving care prepare for greater independence through training in basic skills such as cooking and hygiene;
- helping people set up home if they are leaving institutions (eg prison) or they have been homeless;
- providing ongoing support for people adjusting to more independent living, if moving into their own home after living in a special housing and support scheme.

Where some housing-related supported services were funded within housing benefits these services are now funded from Supporting People funds. If you receive housing benefit your housing support costs would normally be met by the Supporting People team. Owner occupiers who contracted for housing support services when buying their property (ie for wardens in owner-occupied sheltered housing) and who used to receive payments from income support, jobseeker's allowance or minimum income guarantee for their housing support service charges are now paid an equivalent amount by the local authority. If you have moved to an owner-occupied property with support after April 2003, or were not at that time receiving means-tested benefits, you should now apply to your local authority for an assessment to see if you can get help with costs. If you are receiving care services from social services you would normally only have to undergo one financial assessment. Other housing support services for owner occupiers not in any specific sheltered scheme are developing at local level as Supporting People services are becoming established.

Your needs and local authority resources

Local authorities may wish to refuse or withdraw services because of shortage of resources. They may tighten eligibility criteria defining needs they will meet and services they will provide.

Although a local authority can take its resources into account when setting its eligibility criteria (so the criteria might be tightened when resources are short), if you come within the criteria, and a decision is made that you need services, it cannot use its lack of resources as a reason not to provide the services to meet your assessed need. It cannot take its resources into consideration if you would be left at severe physical risk if services were not provided.

Once services are provided, a local authority may not withdraw or reduce them (whether or not as a result of introducing stricter eligibility criteria) without conducting a review of the community care assessment of the person concerned.

Seek advice (see 7) if you are not getting the services you need because of local authority resources problems. Resources issues are repeatedly coming before the courts, which have been consistent in finding that authorities cannot take resources into account once you have been assessed as needing services.

6. Do you have to pay for your care?

A local authority may charge for domiciliary services (ie services provided at home) and other services in the community (eg day centres), which it either provides or arranges for you. Carers may be charged for services they receive direct. You cannot be charged for services provided by the NHS, eg district nurses. If you are getting intermediate care services (see 1 above) you may not be charged for them for an initial 6-week period. In England, since June 2003 community equipment is free, and minor adaptations which you or your carer are assessed as needing will be provided free by social services, as long as the cost is less than £1,000. (Free-standing equipment does not have a £1,000 cap, although some local authorities have tried to cap equipment at £1,000.) Social services have the discretion to charge for minor adaptations costing over £1,000. In some cases you may be able to get a disabled facilities grant (see Chapter 28). The system for charging for care in a care home is explained in Chapter 31.

LAC(2003)14

Scotland – People in Scotland aged 65 or over are not charged for personal care. The specific amount of free care you will receive is determined by a local authority assessment and there is no set limit to the amount they can provide. Free personal care services may be arranged by the authority, or you can ask for a direct payment (see Chapter 26(4)). Receipt of free personal care while living at home does not adversely affect entitlement to attendance allowance (AA), disability living allowance (DLA) or any other state benefits. Free personal care is defined in the Community Care and Health (Scotland) Act 2002 and includes help with:

- personal assistance – eg help with dressing, getting up and going to bed, using a hoist, help with surgical appliances and manual aids;
- personal hygiene – eg bathing, washing hair, shaving, nail care, oral hygiene;

- continence management – eg toileting, catheter/stoma care, skin care, bed changing, incontinence laundry;
- dealing with problems arising from immobility;
- simple treatments – eg assistance with medication, simple dressings, oxygen therapy and the application of creams and lotions;
- counselling and psychological support including behaviour management and the provision of reminding and safety devices;
- food and diet – eg help with eating, special diets and help with the preparation of food.

Despite the fact that the legal definition of personal care includes *'assisting with the preparation of food'*, guidance issued by the Scottish Executive states that food preparation (other than specialised meals, eg pureed foods) and the provision of meals is not covered. Seek further advice if you are charged for help with meal preparation.

The definition of free personal care covers physical assistance with care and help with the mental processes related to that care – eg helping someone to remember to wash.

Free personal care payments start from the date the assessed service is provided and cannot be backdated (eg to the date of referral or date of assessment). If you are assessed as requiring free personal care but told that you will have to wait before this can be provided, seek further advice. On an admission to hospital, payments continue for 2 weeks.

You may still be charged for shopping, domestic chores or other forms of non-personal care.

Northern Ireland – In Northern Ireland, if you are 75 or over you are not charged for your home help service. The charges for people under 75 are explained in circular HSS1/80, which has been regularly amended.

How much can you be charged?

England and Wales – Local authorities have the power to charge for home care services. Charging policies for domiciliary and day care vary considerably. In England guidance on *Fairer Charging for Other Non-Residential Social Services* (LAC 2001/32) and associated practice guidance lays down a framework as to how local authorities should charge for services.

Similar guidance has been partially implemented in Wales but a decision has been made not to fully implement the guidance around treatment of disability benefits and disability-related costs (NAFWC10/2004). The interim arrangements are that local authorities should follow the income support-plus buffer rules, observe capital limits and ignore earnings. These arrangements will stay in place until free home care for disabled people is implemented in 2005/06.

Local authorities can decide whether or not to charge, and can have policies that are more generous than the guidance. Where there are charges (which is the case in nearly all authorities), each person's circumstances must be considered individually. The local authority should give you written details of how much you will be charged, a breakdown of how this has been worked out, and details of what to do if you

J.2 Checklist of care services

Where to get help

Practical help with caring is available from a number of sources:

- relatives, friends and neighbours;
- private organisations or individuals;
- voluntary organisations;
- local authorities;
- the NHS.

To find out what help is available in your area, first contact your area social services department. If they do not provide a particular service, they should be able to put you in touch with the right organisation. Your area may not have all the services listed below. Authorities have a legal duty to provide information about services available (see Box J.1).

Getting services into the home

Adaptations – see Chapter 28.

Alarm system

Benefits – see Benefits Checklist.

Care Attendant scheme – voluntary schemes with trained helpers to help disabled and older people stay in the community. There may be a local scheme. If not, contact Crossroads (see Address List).

DIAL – see Address List for the nearest Disablement Information and Advice Line (DIAL) group and other sources of telephone advice. They may be able to give you the advice you need, or put you in touch with the right organisation.

Direct payments – by social services departments (social work departments in Scotland; health and social service boards or trusts in Northern Ireland) (see Chapter 26).

District/community nurses – may provide nursing care at home or in a care home, or arrange to supply equipment to help with nursing care, as well as incontinence aids.

Equipment – see Chapter 27.

Good neighbour scheme – less formal than the Care Attendant scheme. Volunteers don't need to be specially trained.

GPs – your general practitioner is the key person in ensuring you get, or are referred to, the services you need. If you are really dissatisfied with your GP you should seriously consider transferring to another doctor.

Health visitors – can provide information and advice on local services and act as a liaison or referral point between disabled people and social services departments. Health visitors automatically visit families with children under 5. They also offer practical advice and support. If you are not in touch with a health visitor, contact one through your local GP, health centre or child health clinic.

Home helps or care workers – can provide a range of practical help in the home – eg domestic tasks, including shopping or personal care tasks such as help with getting up and dressed. Social services (social work departments in Scotland) can provide help with these if they have assessed you as needing this service – see Chapter 25(3).

Home visits – it is possible to arrange a home visit from a chiropodist, dentist, doctor, hairdresser, occupational therapist, optician or a physiotherapist. A Citizens Advice Bureau worker will try to visit you at home if you are housebound and it is not possible to advise you over the phone or by letter.

Hospital after-care schemes – short-term, sometimes intensive, help if you cannot manage when you first leave hospital (see Chapter 25(1)).

Incontinence – see Chapter 27(3).

Independent Living Funds – see Chapter 26.

Intermediate care – intensive therapeutic care aimed at avoiding the need to go into hospital, or to enable you to leave hospital earlier. It usually lasts for up to 6 weeks and may be free (in Wales it is not called intermediate care) – see Chapter 25(1).

Laundry service – see Chapter 27(3).

Library – if you are housebound, you can get home visits from the library service. Check our Address List for organisations such as the National Library for the Blind.

think you cannot afford the charge.

Guidance states that disability-related benefits (defined as the severe disability premium, DLA care component, AA, constant attendance allowance and exceptionally severe disablement allowance) may be taken into account as income. However, where they are, the local authority should assess your disability-related expenditure; policy guidance gives examples of the main types of expenditure. In England, a number of local authorities have decided to allow a set amount for normal disability-related costs in order to avoid intrusive questions; it varies from authority to authority. Local authorities have their own lists of disability-related expenditure but this might not be a comprehensive list and you can ask for a review and for other expenditures to be taken into account. Payments to relatives might be disallowed as disability-related expenditure (*R on the application of Stephenson v Stockton on Tees BC (Admin)*, 7 CCLR December 2004).

If you get higher rate AA or highest rate DLA care component (ie for both daytime and night-time care needs) but you receive only day services, the local authority should not take all of your benefit into account, just the part for daytime care (*R v Coventry City Council ex p Carton*). DLA mobility component should not be taken into account as income (s.73(14) Social Security Contributions and Benefits Act 1992).

Your income should not be reduced below the basic level of income support (IS) (ie personal allowance and appropriate premium(s) – excluding the severe disability premium) through charges, and there should be a buffer of 25% above this level. Earnings are disregarded. If the local authority takes your capital into account, the minimum limit above which you can be charged the full cost of the service should be the same as for care in a care home (£20,500 in England, £21,000 in Wales) and they can use the same tariff income. Local authorities can be more generous if they wish. Only the person receiving the service can be charged and where carers receive services they should be charged following the new guidance. The guidance also states that benefits advice should be provided at the time of the charge assessment, which should include help with advice about entitlement, help with claim-form completion and follow-up action if the user wishes.

Scotland – The Convention of Scottish Local Authorities (CoSLA) has produced its own guidance on charging older people for 'non personal' care services. CoSLA guidance recommends the following.

- Earnings, pensions and social security benefits (except DLA mobility component) should be taken into account as income, and this includes the resources of a partner.
- There is an income disregard of £50.65 for every dependent child you are responsible for.
- Local authority charging should not reduce your income below a threshold of the standard minimum guarantee of pension credit (PC) plus a 16.5% buffer. For 2005/06 this amounts to £128 for a single person and £195 for a couple (figures rounded up).

Meals on wheels – are usually provided from central kitchens and delivered to your home by voluntary helpers.
Occupational therapists – can help you learn or relearn the skills of independent self-care and personal management in all aspects of everyday life. They can also offer advice on, or arrange the provision of, necessary equipment or adaptations to your home.
Odd Job scheme – this could come under a variety of names – often Handy Person scheme. The schemes give practical help with tasks you cannot manage (eg decorating, gardening, etc).
Physiotherapists – provide treatment and advice to relieve pain and help restore and maintain mobility. This includes advice about equipment (perhaps designed by REMAP – see Address List).
Recreational facilities – radio, TV, etc.
Rehabilitation – most district general hospitals have well-equipped rehabilitation departments that can provide a variety of services and techniques to help patients develop their maximum ability. Treatment may also be provided at health centres, at home, or at other suitable centres.
Self-help and socialising – check Address List. You could, for example, join a PHAB club.
Sheltered housing – provides a range of options, from an on-call warden to extra care housing.
Sitting in service – allows your carer time off and may help you get a wider network of friends who can also help.
Sleeping in service – allows your carer a night or weekend away.
Social workers – play a key role in getting services into your home. Sometimes just talking things over with them can help.
Social fund – discretionary one-off payments – see Chapter 10.
Speech and language therapists – cover all forms of communication disorders.
Support for a carer – contact Carers UK (see Address List).
Supporting people services – see Chapter 25(5).
Telephone – if you can't handle and/or read a printed phone book, register for free use of Directory Enquiries (ring 195 for details).
Warm Front (Warm Front Plus) (Warm Deal in Scotland) – provides energy efficiency measures – see Chapter 28(4).

Services away from the home

Adult education
Advice – contact your town hall for a list of local advice centres. See also Chapter 59.
Care homes – can be provided by local authorities, the NHS, private and voluntary organisations (see Chapters 29, 30 and 31).
Day centres – provided by the local authority (or in some cases by voluntary organisations) as places where elderly people or those with disabilities can meet. Meals, chiropody and activities are usually available. If necessary, you can get transport to and from the centre.
Day hospital care – it is possible to stay in hospital during the day but be in your own home at night. This can be done on a regular basis or just in emergencies.
Emergency overnight stay – in hospital or a care home.
Employment schemes – contact social services and/or the disability employment adviser (see Chapter 16(2)).
Holiday/Short-term care – a 'foster' scheme with volunteer families.
Respite or short-stay care – can be in a hospital or a care home. Allows carers a break or holiday and may help you to remain at home longer (see Chapters 20, 30 and 32 for the benefit implications).
Transport – most social services departments (social work departments in Scotland) arrange transport to clubs, day centres and workshops for people with disabilities who are unable to use public transport. The British Red Cross offers a transport and escort service for people unable to use public transport or travel alone. In some areas there are voluntary schemes, such as Dial-a-Ride. Local authority travel-pass schemes may allow you to travel free or at a reduced rate if you are elderly or disabled. From April 2006 pensioners will receive free national bus travel.

- The level of charge is based on a percentage of your excess income. Each local authority is free to determine its own percentage figure.
- Tariff income should be £1 for every £500 from £6,000, but with no upper limit.
- Local authorities should use their powers to abate or waive charges where you would have difficulty paying the assessed charge.
- Local authorities should consider not charging for day care services and for aids and adaptations.

The Scottish Executive has developed guidance on charging for domiciliary care in partnership with CoSLA (CCD 5/2004 and CCD 12/2004).

When can charges not be made?

The local authority cannot charge:

- anyone (family, carer or friend) other than the person using the service. They can only take into account your own income and capital when deciding how much you should pay (although for couples, guidance indicates they can take into account a partner's income and capital if the user has a legal entitlement, or where benefit is paid to one of a couple for both). In Scotland, the CoSLA guidance recommends the assessments of a partner's resources, as both are perceived to benefit from the non-personal care services for which they are being charged;
- the parent or guardian for children's services under the Children Act 1989 (Children (Scotland) Act 1995) if the child is under 16 and the parent or guardian is on IS or receiving any element of child tax credit other than the family element;
- a young person, for services under the Children Act 1989 (Children (Scotland) Act 1995) aged 16-18, on IS or income-based jobseeker's allowance (JSA);
- for intermediate care services (see 1) in England; for '6-week support for vulnerable people' services in Wales, where available. In Scotland people 65 or over can have free home care for up to 4 weeks following a period in hospital either overnight or for surgery as a day patient. It also covers equipment provided during that time. Home care includes meals on wheels, laundry and shopping needed during a period of recovery, and so is wider in definition than personal care;
- in England, for equipment. Minor adaptations less than £1,000 are also free;
- in Scotland, care provided to people 65 or over that comes under the definition of 'personal care' (see 6);
- you, if you have any form of Creutzfeldt-Jakob disease (CJD), as you should be exempt from charges;
- for services provided under section 117 of the Mental Health Act 1983. Under the Mental Health (Scotland) Act 1984, local authorities in Scotland can charge for aftercare services. However, they must not charge for training and occupation (eg day centres) provided for adults with learning disabilities (section 11 of the 84 Act). The new Mental Health (Care and Treatment) (Scotland) Act 2003 is expected to come into force by June 2005, replacing the above provisions and creating new duties on local authorities to provide services to those who have, or who have had, a *'mental disorder'*. There should be no charge for services provided under the provisions of the new Act.

Charges for Supporting People services

The following is a brief outline of the Directions and guidance issued in England for Supporting People services (see 5). It was intended that nobody would be worse off under Supporting People than under previous support services, and consequently there is protection for people who were receiving services at the point of change in April 2003. In Wales, the charging framework follows the English structure. A key difference, however, is that in Wales the Assembly funds some services direct (mostly for younger people) and these will be exempt from charges. Local authorities are responsible for funding services for older people and those which involve community care.

The key points include:

- The following people are not to be charged for Supporting People services:
  - people in receipt of housing benefit (HB);
  - owner occupiers who were receiving housing support-related costs in their IS, JSA or pension credit, who pay their charges to the provider but are paid an equivalent amount from the local authority;
  - people in short-term schemes (aimed at bringing about independent living in less than 2 years);
  - people whose support services are provided under section 117 of the Mental Health Act 1983;
  - in Scotland, people whose housing support services were previously funded by Special Needs Allowance Package (SNAP).
- Tenants who no longer get HB because of Supporting People charges being removed from their rent should be no worse off than they would be if the scheme had not started, for a transitional period until the service is reviewed. The review date is agreed by the local authority with the provider.
- Owner occupiers who since April 2003 no longer get IS, JSA or PC guarantee credit because their support services are no longer included in the calculation will receive an equivalent amount towards their service charges so that they are no worse off for a transitional period.
- Council tenants in 'pooled' accommodation:
  - tenants in council schemes where the support costs were previously pooled may have the support cost separately identified in their rent but will be transitionally protected until the service is reviewed (see above). After the review, each council (local authority landlord) will have its own policy for protecting tenants from what could otherwise be a steep increase in the charge for Supporting People services. Most councils are likely to protect existing tenants from these increases for the life of their tenancy support service;
  - this transitional protection also applies to tenants of services that have been transferred from the local authority to registered social landlords where service charges have been pooled;
  - after the review, regardless of the policy, the landlord will continue to receive full Supporting People grant for each transitionally protected tenant who receives HB and these tenants will therefore not be liable to pay the support charge;
  - new tenants and existing tenants (where they lose transitional protection and are not in receipt of HB) can apply for assistance with the support charge under the local *Fairer Charging* means test.
- Tenants and owner occupiers who receive support services and who are not entitled to HB/IS/JSA/PC may be able to access the local *Fairer Charging* policy for care services, or in Scotland following the CoSLA guidance (see above).
- Where a tenant gets both a care and support service there will probably be a combined assessment of their charge under *Fairer Charging*, unless they receive HB, in which case the support service will be free. In Scotland and Northern Ireland, even if a support service is of a nature which would be free under the charging rules for personal care, it will still attract a charge if this is the only service the person receives.

The guidance states that any framework for charging for support services must avoid 'cliff-edges' whereby new tenants only just above HB could be liable to pay the full cost without any taper. Where there is a joint home care and support charge about to be levied, authorities should use the *Fairer Charging* framework to assess clients. Equally, whenever possible, *Fairer Charging* financial assessments should be used to determine reasonable charges for new tenants who are not covered by the transitional protection provisions. However, it goes on to say that for those who did not get HB prior to April 2003 there is no requirement to reassess them immediately. Also '3-star' and 'excellent' authorities in England have more flexibility in the way they develop their policies.

More details on Supporting People and charges can be found at: for England, www.spkweb.org.uk; for Scotland, www.scotland.gov.uk/housing/supportingpeople/folders.asp.

If you cannot afford to pay the charge

The local authority has a duty to decide how much you can afford to pay and reduce the charge or not charge you at all. It may not withdraw a service because you have failed to pay the charge. This is because the decision to meet a need is separate from, and comes before, any decision to charge for the service. This does not appear to apply, however, to Supporting People services.

The local authority or the provider of housing support services can use debt enforcement proceedings (eg taking someone to court) for the recovery of arrears. If you cannot afford the charge, ask for it to be reduced or waived. For more information on charging, see the materials produced by the Coalition on Charging (see Address List).

Complaints

You can complain about the amount you are being charged and have your case heard by a review panel. Some local authorities have a separate charges complaints procedure, which is shorter than the standard complaints procedure described in 7 below. But in all cases you have the right to go to a complaints panel if you prefer.

7. If you are not satisfied with your care services

Wherever possible, problems should be resolved locally, perhaps with the aid of a local councillor. Social services departments must have a complaints procedure and publicise it. Information regarding the action you can take if you are unhappy about the assessment or the services to be provided should be given at the time of the care assessment and again when you are informed of any charge. A social services complaints officer can provide a copy of the complaints leaflet but it should be easily available from your local office.

Complaints

The local authority complaints procedure in England, Wales and Scotland has three stages: informal problem solving, formal registration, and review.

Informal problem solving – Talk through the problem with the social worker, occupational therapist, home carer or person who is working with you and try to have it put right. If you are still unhappy, go on to the next stage.

Formal registration Write to the Director of Social Services (Social Work in Scotland) or to the complaints officer, set out exactly what your complaint is and ask for it to be registered as a formal complaint. If you need help to write the letter, the social worker or any member of social services can help you, or ask a friend, relative or neighbour.

A complaints officer, who has not had contact with you before, will investigate the complaint. If a complaint is made on behalf of a child, an independent person must be appointed by social services to assist in the investigation of the complaint; Scottish guidance contains no such requirement, although some local authorities have adopted it as good practice. You must get a reply within 28 days of the local authority's receipt of your registered complaint. If this is not the full response to your complaint, you should get an explanation of the current position with a full response within 3 months.

Review – If you cannot resolve a complaint informally or are unhappy with the local authority's full response to your registered complaint, you can ask for the complaint to be heard by a review panel. You must ask for a review within 28 days of the date the authority informs you of the result of their consideration of your complaint.

The review panel consists of three people; one person, the chair, must be independent of the local authority (ie not an elected member or an employee). The complaints hearing must take place within 28 days of the date the local authority received your request for a review. You should be given at least 10 days' notice, in writing, of the time and place of the hearing. You can be accompanied by someone who may speak on your behalf; this person should not be a lawyer acting in their professional capacity.

The review panel must record its recommendations within 24 hours of the hearing and notify you in writing, explaining the reasons for the recommendations. Guidance in Scotland requires a review panel to provide written recommendations within 56 days and *'as soon as reasonably practicable'*.

The local authority has 28 days (in Scotland 42) to decide what action, if any, to take in the light of the review panel's recommendations. The authority's reply should also give reasons for decisions taken. This is particularly important if the decisions differ from the review panel's recommendations. A High Court decision stated that a local authority cannot overrule a review panel's decision without *'substantial reason and without having given (the Panel's) recommendation the weight it required'*.

R v Avon County Council ex p M [1994] 2 CCLR 185

New complaints process

A new local authority complaints process is due to be introduced in England sometime during 2005/06. Draft regulations and guidance indicates it will be a two-stage procedure, described below, but there may be differences in the final guidance. Each authority must appoint a complaints manager.

Handling and consideration by the local authority – Once notified of a complaint, the local authority can try to resolve it through informal means such as discussions with the complainant. After 10 working days (or sooner if the complainant wishes) the complaint must be made formal and put in writing. An investigating officer is appointed to oversee the complaint. The investigation should be completed and a response sent to the complainant within 25 working days, unless extra time is absolutely necessary.

Independent review by the Commission for Social Care Inspection (CSCI) – If the complainant is not happy with the outcome of the local authority investigation, CSCI may decide how best to deal with the matter. Possible actions include: convening a three-person independent review panel; conducting further investigation; referring the matter to the Local Government Ombudsman in agreed circumstances; and taking no further action if review is unlikely to produce a different outcome.

Other steps

You may wish to take your complaint to local councillors or your MP (MSP in Scotland and National Assembly Member in Wales) if you feel it would be helpful for them to know the system is not working for you. If you have exhausted the complaints procedure you can contact the Local Government Ombudsman (in Scotland, the Scottish Public Services Ombudsman) (see Address List). It is also possible to ask the Secretary of State to use her/his default powers.

If it is not possible to resolve your dispute via the complaints procedure you may wish to consider a legal remedy such as judicial review. You can also complain to the local authority's Monitoring Officer (usually the Chief Executive or Borough Solicitor) who is responsible for ensuring that decisions are lawful and procedures correctly followed. It may be useful to contact a national organisation to discuss ways of pursuing your case. You must act quickly. Contact a law centre or the Disability Law Service (see Address List).

26 Buying care

1. Introduction

Local authorities have the main responsibility for directly providing or arranging services for disabled people and others who are assessed as needing them (see Chapter 25). In this chapter we look at some of the cash help available to help pay for care. There are three main sources.

Social security benefits – If you are under 65, you may be able to get disability living allowance care component (see Chapter 20). If you are 65 or over, you may be able to get attendance allowance (see Chapter 21). Carers who spend at least 35 hours a week caring for a severely disabled person may be able to get carer's allowance (see Chapter 23). There are also premiums within income support and pension credit for carers and disabled people (see Chapters 4 and 41).

Independent Living Funds – The two Independent Living Funds (see 2 and 3 below) make cash payments directly to you, which you can use to pay for care to help you live independently in your own home. These are government-funded but independent and discretionary trust funds, governed by a Board of Trustees. A legally binding trust deed sets out the powers and procedures of the Trustees and the eligibility criteria for help from the Funds.

Direct payments – Local authorities have direct payment schemes whereby social services departments (social work departments in Scotland) offer you cash for you to make your own arrangements to meet your assessed needs – see 4 below.

2. Independent Living (Extension) Fund

The role of this fund is to maintain payments made to you under the pre-1993 system. No new applications are accepted. Money from the Extension Fund is wholly ignored when means-tested benefits are being calculated. For details of employment issues, contributions and appeals, see 3 below.

Going into hospital or a care home – Your payments from the Fund may be suspended. However, if you privately employ a carer, an appropriate retainer can be paid for up to 4 weeks to avoid potential disruption to care. The rules are the same as those for the 1993 Fund (see 3 below).

Increases in awards – The Fund may consider increases for people who have *'experienced a significant change in their circumstances'* – eg where total care needs or costs have increased. In these circumstances, the Fund may ask your local authority to review their contribution. The maximum award payable is £715 a week.

3. Independent Living (1993) Fund (ILF)

The Independent Living (1993) Fund (ILF) works in partnership with local authorities to devise joint care packages, which are a combination of services or direct payments from the local authority and cash from the Fund.

Payments are made 4-weekly in arrears and are normally paid into your bank account. Money from the ILF is wholly ignored when means-tested benefits are being calculated and when your local authority assesses your charges for home care services.

Who can get help?

Awards are discretionary, but there are basic guidelines to which the Trustees must have regard. To qualify for help from the ILF you should normally fulfil all of the following conditions. You must:

- be severely disabled to the extent that extensive help with personal care or household duties is needed to maintain an independent life in the community; *and*
- be at least 16 and under 66 years of age; *and*
- be receiving disability living allowance (DLA) highest rate care component; *and*
- be receiving (or it is planned that you will receive) services or cash to a value of at least £200 a week from your local authority (Supporting People services – see Chapter 25(5) – do not count towards this); *and*
- have care needs whose average total cost to the social services department and the 1993 Fund is no more than £715 a week (the maximum payment from the Fund is £420 a week); *and*
- have less than £18,500 savings; *and*
- be living alone or with people who are unable to fully meet your care needs; *and*
- have care needs that are generally stable and expected to be met by the joint care package for the following 6 months. This means that some people who are terminally ill may not be eligible, but each application to the Fund will be looked at on its own merits, according to the criteria. There is no banned list of conditions or diseases.

How to apply for help

If you think you may be eligible for help from the ILF, you should do the following:

- ❑ Ask your local authority social services department for an assessment of your needs, and say you want to apply to the ILF.
- ❑ If the social worker decides the care package you need will involve at least £200 worth of services and/or cash from the local authority, but will not normally cost the ILF and the social services department more than £715 a week in total, they will support your application to the ILF.
- ❑ Once your application has been accepted by the Fund, one of their visiting ILF assessors will visit you and the local authority social worker together. At this visit your care needs can be discussed by all three parties and an agreement reached about the amount and type of care you need.
- ❑ The Fund's social worker will then send in a written report making recommendations about the care package needed.
- ❑ If your application is successful, the Fund will make you a cash award of up to £420 a week. This amount will be paid once the Fund has received details from you of how you will use the money (eg who your care/personal assistants will be or what care agency you will be using). For the care/personal assistants you employ, you must supply their names, addresses, national insurance (NI) numbers and how much you pay them. The Fund is legally required to supply this information, on request, to the Secretary of State. If you have difficulty providing this information you could contact the Fund to discuss the problem.

If you cannot apply to the Fund yourself or manage the money from the ILF, or manage using it to buy part of your care package, someone else can do so on your behalf. Note that the rules for direct payments from the local authority are different (see 4 below).

How much will you have to contribute?

You will always be expected to put at least half of your DLA care component towards the cost of your care. The exact amount will depend on a financial assessment, based on income support (IS) rules (see Chapter 5) – so if you are one of a couple, your capital and income will be counted jointly, except that earnings are always disregarded.

If you get IS or income-based jobseeker's allowance (JSA) – You are expected to contribute any severe disability premium.

If you do not get IS or income-based JSA – The extra amount you are expected to contribute is calculated by working out your income (excluding earnings), and deducting from this any allowances (see below) and the amount you would get if you were on IS (excluding the severe disability premium).

The allowances deducted from your income are based on those for IS but some are more generous. All mortgage payments and endowments are taken into account. Earnings are disregarded. Tariff income is assumed from £11,500.

If you are charged by your local authority at the time of application for the care they are providing, this will be deducted from the amount the ILF will expect you to contribute.

The ILF contribution rules cover the UK, so in Scotland you may be charged by the ILF for personal care. People who are 65 or over and who receive ILF payments can seek advice about whether their local authority would provide them with an equivalent amount of free personal care.

What if you need more care?

If your care needs increase or you need more money, you can apply for an increase in your payments at any time. The Fund may also approach your local authority to ask if they are able to increase their contribution. If your care costs increase, the Fund will not withdraw its commitment even if the combined contribution comes to more than £715. However, the Fund would review its position if costs increase in the first 6 months following your first payment. If appropriate, they will offer you a payment of the maximum amount (£420 a week).

Going into hospital or a care home

If you are admitted to hospital or another type of residential or institutional care, payments from the Fund will be suspended. But payments may continue for up to 4 weeks if they are needed to pay a retainer to directly-employed staff. Your case can be kept open for 13 weeks (or longer at the ILF's discretion) and your payments reinstated if you return to live independently in the community within that time. New provisions have been promised which will allow ILF payments to continue for up to 8 weeks after the death of an ILF claimant or their permanent admission to a care home, in respect of privately employed personal assistants, if the personal assistant does not find other employment during that period. It is not known when these provisions will be introduced.

Employment issues

It is important to check the status of the care/personal assistants who work with you. Each case is different and is judged on its merits by the Inland Revenue (IR). If you employ a worker directly, you should assume you are the employer unless you have checked that they are self-employed. You have all the responsibilities of an employer – eg paying employer's NI contributions, etc. The IR has a simplified way of collecting tax in these situations. If the decision causes any difficulty, you could discuss it with the local tax office. In addition, the Funds have a Helpline for general advice on tax and NI that you can contact through the main ILF phone number (0845 601 8815).

The National Centre for Independent Living has details of books and pamphlets to help people who employ their own care workers, and other support organisations can offer practical assistance to people who employ their own staff through direct payments (see Address List).

Appeals

For complaints about social services, see Chapter 25(7).

If you are dissatisfied with any aspect of how the Funds have dealt with your application, set out your reasons in a letter to the Fund's Chief Executive (see Address List), who will review the case and then may refer it to a subcommittee of the Board of Trustees for a decision.

4. Social services direct payments

Direct payments allow a person who has been assessed as needing services to receive cash to arrange and pay for them. You can have a combination of some services provided directly by social services and others arranged by yourself with direct payments.

Who can have a direct payment?

In England, since 8.4.03, and in Scotland, since 1.6.03, it has been mandatory to make a direct payment to people who fall within the rules below. From 1.11.04 Welsh local authorities have had a duty to offer direct payments to people who fall within these rules; this mandatory duty was extended to all older people from 1.3.05.

To get a direct payment you must be:

- a disabled person (although in Scotland this has been extended to 'any person' aged 65 or over who may require community care services due to infirmity or old age from April 2005); *or*
- a carer (in England and Wales); *and*
- aged 16 or over; *and*
- assessed as needing community care services or services as a carer (as appropriate); *and*
- willing to have payments (you cannot be forced to); *and*
- able to manage payments (alone or with assistance). If you have assistance, you still have the final responsibility for how the money is spent. In Scotland, representatives are able to receive and manage direct payments on behalf of someone incapable of giving consent. Draft guidance suggests this will be limited to attorneys and guardians (under the Adults with Incapacity (Scotland) Act 2000) who have been granted the relevant powers; *and*
- not subject to certain mental health or criminal justice legislation.

Parents and carers – In England and Wales, you can get a direct payment if you are a carer assessed as needing services as a carer. As carers in Scotland do not get services in their own right they cannot get direct payments for themselves. However, see above for the circumstances in which a carer with relevant powers can get a payment on behalf of the person they are caring for. In England, carers are now eligible to receive vouchers for short-term breaks. A similar scheme was piloted in Wales in 2004.

Parents in England, Wales and Scotland can receive direct payments to purchase services for disabled children. Parents who are themselves disabled can use direct payments to purchase children's services. The High Court has ruled that it is lawful to pay an independent trust set up for a user (in this case with trustees composed of the parents and representatives of a disability organisation and the local authority).
R(A and B, X and Y) v East Sussex CC

What can direct payments be used for?

Direct payments can be used to purchase any services which meet your assessed needs. Direct payments cannot be used, however, to purchase care in a care home, apart from periods up to a maximum of 4 weeks (120 days for children) in any one year. Separate periods in a care home of less than 4 weeks are added together towards the maximum only if you are at home for 28 days or less in between.

In Scotland, direct payments cannot be used to pay for services from a spouse or partner or from a close relative living in the same household (although this may be reviewed during 2005). In exceptional circumstances, a local authority can make direct payments to employ close relatives who live elsewhere, or to someone else (but not a close relative) in the same household *'if it is satisfied that that is the most appropriate way of securing the relevant services'*. However, leave has been granted for a judicial review of this issue. In England and Wales direct payments can be used to pay a spouse or relative even if they live with you if the local authority is satisfied that it is necessary to do so.

In Scotland, since 1.6.03, you are able to use a direct payment to purchase services from the local authority. This is not the case in England and Wales.

Guidance to local authorities encourages them to ensure that support for direct payment users is available. Local authorities must check that the money you have been given is spent on the care you have been assessed as needing. They could ask for it to be paid back if it is not used for meeting your assessed care needs.

The National Centre for Independent Living (see Address List) gives advice on direct payments and general advice and information about local independent living organisations if you need individual help. In Scotland, the Direct Payments Scotland Helpline promotes the take-up of direct payments and can tell you about any local direct payment support organisation which can give advice and practical assistance (0131 558 3450 or www.dpscotland.org.uk).

How much are you paid?

Local authorities must make direct payments at a rate equal to their estimate of the reasonable cost of the service to meet your assessed needs and fulfil your legal obligations if you employ your carer/s (eg national insurance payments, employers' liability insurance, holiday and sick pay). If you choose a more expensive way to meet your assessed needs than is *'reasonable'*, you will have to pay the extra cost yourself. For more on employment issues, see 3 above. Payments made will not affect your benefits.

You may be asked to contribute towards the cost of your care. The amount of your contribution will be calculated using the same charging rules as for care arranged by the local authority (see Chapter 25). You will either be paid your direct payment net (with the charge taken off) or gross (where you pay the amount you are assessed to pay in the same way as if you were getting a service).

If you are unhappy with the amount of payment you are offered or any other aspect of the direct payment, you should use the complaints procedure (see Chapter 25(7)).

27 Help with equipment

1. Items for daily living

Under the Chronically Sick and Disabled Persons Act (CSDPA 1970) covering England, Scotland and Wales, local social services (or in Scotland, social work) authorities have a duty in some circumstances to arrange for the provision of equipment or to assist with the carrying out of home adaptations for disabled people. The duty arises when the authority decides you have an 'eligible' need, ie a need the authority has assessed as sufficiently high to qualify for assistance. What is meant by an eligible need varies between authorities.

Once an eligible need has been assessed, the authority has an absolute duty to arrange to meet it in some way within a reasonable period of time. In England and Wales, where specific government guidance has been issued, the assessment should focus explicitly on risks to your independence. Section 2 of the CSDPA 1970 applies directly to England and Wales, and to Scotland by virtue of the Chronically Sick and Disabled Persons (Scotland) Act 1972. (The equivalent legislation in Northern Ireland is the Chronically Sick and Disabled Persons (Northern Ireland) Act 1978, which places a duty on health and social services trusts.)

On request by a disabled person or their carer, a local authority has a duty to make a decision about your possible needs under the 1970 Act or under the 1978 Act in Northern Ireland.

S.4 of the Disabled Persons (Services, Consultation and Representation) Act 1986, for England, Scotland and Wales; and also s.4 of the Disabled Persons (Northern Ireland) Act 1989.

Equipment – The CSDPA 1970 refers to additional facilities for greater safety, comfort or convenience, and to telephones and equipment for using the telephone. It also refers to practical assistance in the home, outings, taking advantage of educational facilities, holidays, etc – all of which could involve a need for equipment.

Home adaptations – The 1970 Act contains a duty to arrange for assistance with the carrying out of works of adaptation to the home. This duty will typically apply to so-called minor adaptations. In practice these are fixtures which affect the fabric of the building but which are easily removable – eg a grab rail. However, this duty may also cover major adaptations which are not (easily) removable and very much more expensive. For example, the major adaptation required may not come within the criteria for provision of a housing grant under housing legislation (see Chapter 28), but may nevertheless come within social services criteria under the CSDPA. Alternatively, a housing grant may not cover the entire cost of the major adaptation, in which case social services must consider whether it has a duty to make up the shortfall or to top up, but not all social services are fully aware of their duties in this respect.

Restrictive policies – Many local authority social services departments have restrictive policies in respect of equipment provision, some of which may be unlawful. For instance, some local authorities say as a matter of policy they don't do certain types of equipment. If applied inflexibly, irrespective of your individual assessed needs, such policies may be unlawful if they result in the local authority not carrying out a proper assessment of your needs. Policies may also be unlawful if they are, in effect, blanket policies that do not allow for exceptions, as they would then fetter the local authority's discretion.

Carers – In England and Wales, under the Carers and Disabled Children Act 2000, social services have a duty to assess informal carers and also a power, but not apparently a duty, to provide services for carers. These services are not defined but could in principle cover equipment and adaptations. Equivalent provisions in Northern Ireland come under the Carers and Direct Payments (Northern Ireland) Act 2002.

The Scottish legislation does not provide explicitly for services to carers. Sections 8 to 11 of the Community Care and Health (Scotland) Act 2002, extend statutory obligations in the Social Work (Scotland) Act 1968 and the Children (Scotland) Act 1995 on local authorities to support carers. Local authorities are required to take account of the contribution of carers, and the views of the person in need and their carer, before deciding what services to provide to a cared-for person.

Charges – Local social services authorities in Wales have a legal power to make charges for equipment but might not exercise it. In England, since June 2003, legislation has prevented social services authorities from charging for equipment provided under the CSDPA or under s.2 of the Carers and Disabled Children Act 2000, or for minor adaptations costing under £1,000 provided under either of those Acts. The £1,000 limit applies only to adaptations. This means equipment must be provided free of charge whatever its cost, and each minor adaptation costing under £1,000 should not be charged for. Guidance says the cost of a minor adaptation is to be calculated in terms of both its purchase and installation expense.

In Scotland, certain equipment must be free because it is classified as coming within free personal care which, under the Community Care and Health (Scotland) Act 2002, applies only to people aged 65 and over. However, what is covered is limited. It includes memory and safety devices, such as personal reminder systems for taking medicine and sound/movement alarms linked to light controls to guide people with dementia to the toilet and to minimise the risks related to wandering at night. It does not include community alarms and other associated devices. In addition, the Scottish Executive has issued guidance stating that frail older people leaving hospital should not be charged for equipment and minor adaptations provided by social services if these are supplied and fitted within a 4-week period following, or immediately prior to, hospital discharge. Otherwise, for most equipment, guidance issued by the Convention of Scottish Local Authorities (CoSLA) recommends that social services should not charge. Alternatively, it considers that if social services wish to charge, they should do so only for small, personal items up to a limit of £20. However, the CoSLA guidance is not binding on Scottish local authorities, and they may not necessarily follow it.

For the charging rules generally, see Chapter 25(6).

Self-assessment – Social services and the NHS increasingly operate self-assessment or self-selection schemes, enabling you to choose some items of equipment yourself. However, your right to have a formal assessment would not be affected.

Direct payments – If certain conditions are met, social services have a duty to make direct payments (see Chapter 26(4)) for equipment as well as for other community care services.

Buying your own equipment

Suitably adapted or specialised equipment is a key factor in enabling someone to live as independently as possible. The range of items is large – so don't buy anything without getting expert advice and, if possible, using the equipment on a trial basis to see if it will work for you. It is particularly important not to be rushed into buying expensive items such as electric scooters, riser/recliner electric wheelchairs, walk-in baths or special beds. These can cost thousands of pounds, and there is evidence of inappropriate, pressurised selling by some salespeople who visit people in their own homes.

For information about VAT relief on equipment for disabled people see the Customs and Excise booklet 701/7/02. If the occupational therapist recommends an item of equipment, ask if there is a centre where you can see the equipment (see Box J.3). Equipment provided by social services is generally considered to be on long-term loan.

Items for daily living include products to make it easier to use the toilet, to wash, dress, use cooking facilities, etc – eg handrails next to the bath and toilet, raised toilet seats, widened doorways or a bathroom on the ground floor.

An occupational therapist in your social services department may be the best person to turn to initially for help. However, all personal and healthcare professionals may be able to give help and advice (eg a social worker, district nurse, health visitor, GP, physiotherapist or a child's school).

2. Healthcare equipment

The NHS, including NHS trusts and primary care trusts, as part of their community health services, may provide healthcare equipment such as special beds, commodes, urinals and continence pads. Some items may serve a dual purpose: for healthcare and for daily living. However, this has meant the NHS and social services sometimes argue about who should provide what – and sometimes neither has provided equipment either at all or at least in timely fashion.

Legally, it is not easy to challenge non-provision of equipment by the NHS if it argues it is short of money. Nevertheless, the NHS should take care not to impose blanket policies on what it will and won't provide. For instance, the Health Service Ombudsman has criticised over-rigid application, by an NHS wheelchair service, of eligibility criteria for the provision of electrically powered wheelchairs.

In the first instance, apply for items via your doctor, district nurse, health visitor, continence adviser, occupational therapist, physiotherapist or social worker. GPs can prescribe equipment on an approved list (a schedule of appliances and devices in the 'Drug Tariff') – including catheters, elastic hosiery, trusses, etc – which have standard prescription charges (see Chapter 52).

An NHS consultant may prescribe equipment necessary for a patient's treatment – eg, walking aids, surgical footwear, leg appliances, artificial breasts, surgical brassieres, wigs and spinal supports. This is free to NHS patients, but the last three items have special prescription charges (if provided for outpatients), and Drug Tariff items for outpatients have standard prescription charges.

Hearing aids are supplied on the prescription of a consultant ear nose and throat surgeon or a consultant in audiological medicine, or patients can be referred by their GP to the audiology department. Hearing aids are supplied on free loan from NHS Hearing Aid Centres. Low-vision aids, including hand magnifiers and more complex appliances, can be prescribed under the NHS through the Hospital Eye

J.3 For more information

Equipment

Contact the Disabled Living Foundation for general information and advice about all types of equipment: 380-384 Harrow Road, London W9 2HU (0845 130 9177; Textphone 020 7432 8009).

Disabled Living Centres and Communication Aids Centres – have a wide range of equipment on show. You can usually try out equipment as well as get advice about what might help you best. Contact the Disabled Living Centres Council for a list of local centres (see Address List).

Ask your doctor, social worker, or health visitor for advice as well. See booklet HB6, *A Practical Guide for Disabled People: Where to Find Information, Services and Equipment,* available from Department of Health, PO Box 777, London SE1 6XH.

See also Age Concern Factsheet 6 *Finding help at home*, and Factsheet 42 *Disability equipment and how to get it* (see Address List).

Contact Disability Alliance's Rights Service for advice on social security matters only: our Rights Workers are not experts on equipment for people with disabilities.

Social services and the NHS

You can get specialist information on all aspects of community care from organisations such as Age Concern, Carers UK, Counsel and Care, Help the Aged, Mind and RADAR (see Address List). They can offer practical suggestions if you haven't been able to resolve the problem locally (see Chapter 25(7) 'Other steps' for some suggestions).

Service. Artificial eyes and orbital prostheses can be supplied on the recommendation of a hospital ophthalmologist.

3. Services to help with incontinence

Incontinence can be costly and causes a lot of extra work. The help available varies from one area to another. It is important to get advice from an NHS continence adviser, GP, practice nurse or physiotherapist to check whether there is treatment that might help. Your need for assistance should be taken into account during a social services community care assessment. There are several types of provision: advice about management of incontinence; treatment (eg drugs, physiotherapy, surgery); supplies and equipment; laundry services; and disposal of waste.

How to get help – The NHS may supply, free of charge, continence aids and equipment to help in nursing sick or disabled people at home and in care homes. These may include the loan of a commode and bed linen, the supply of continence pads, protective pants, inter-liners, disposable draw sheets and bedpans, nappy rolls, etc. It is up to the NHS to decide on the quantity of items, such as pads, and they sometimes decide not to supply any at all. Although this may seem unfair, it is not normally easy to challenge this legally. However, if you are in a care home that provides registered nursing, the NHS should provide free of charge all the incontinence pads you have been assessed as needing, according to guidance from central government (in England and Wales). Protective pants and pads are not available on GP prescription (except in Scotland). If you cannot get an item through the NHS, you can buy it privately from chemists (though the range may be limited) or from specialist mail order firms. Body-worn urinary appliances can be prescribed by GPs, but take the prescription to a chemist or surgical supplier with a skilled fitting service. For more information on aids, equipment and services ring PromoCon (0161 834 2001) or the Continence Foundation (020 7831 9831).

How to obtain a laundry service – If a laundry service is available in your area, it will normally be run by the social services department, probably attached to the home help service. In some areas there is a laundry service run by the NHS while in others there is none, although extra practical help may be given through the home help service. For very severely disabled children, the Family Fund Trust can provide washing machines and/or dryers (see Chapter 35(8)). If you can't cope with the practical problems arising because of incontinence, you may qualify for disability living allowance care component or attendance allowance (see Chapters 20 and 21).

4. Environmental control systems and communication aids

Environmental controls enable people with severe disabilities to operate electrical appliances and equipment from a central control, with switching mechanisms adapted to meet their needs; contact an occupational therapist or your doctor. For more sophisticated equipment, an NHS specialist will assess whether the equipment will help, and if so, arrangements for installation will be made. The equipment is provided on loan and serviced free of charge. Simpler environmental control systems can be provided by local social services authorities, though they are not always aware of their potential obligations in respect of environmental controls and communication aids under s.2 of the CSDPA 1970 (see 1 above).

People with severe difficulties speaking or writing can be helped by a range of communication aids – from charts with pictures to specially adapted computers and electronic voice output devices. These can be provided by the local education authority, schools, or through the Access to Work scheme run through your local Jobcentre Plus office (see Chapter 16(2)), as well as NHS and primary care trusts. If necessary, local speech and language therapists will refer you to a communication aids centre for advice on the most suitable aids.

5. Wheelchairs

Under the NHS, wheelchairs (including electrically powered models) are supplied and maintained free of charge to a disabled person whose need for such a chair is permanent. Any wheelchair on the market may be supplied by NHS wheelchair centres but what will be provided is decided locally, bearing in mind the individual's circumstances and the resources available. In Scotland, criteria are set nationally for electric wheelchairs.

Electrically powered indoor/outdoor wheelchairs can be provided by the NHS if you are severely disabled if it is decided you need one because you are unable to walk or propel an ordinary wheelchair. The NHS locally decides its own eligibility criteria, but this should be within the broad national framework – ie, as well as being unable to propel a manual wheelchair, you should be able to benefit from an improved quality of life and be able to handle the chair safely. If you move to another area but do not meet the criteria there, your wheelchair should in principle not be withdrawn unless there is a good clinical reason for doing so.

Attendant-controlled powered wheelchairs are issued where it would be difficult for the disabled person to be pushed out of doors – eg, where the attendant is aged, the district is hilly, or the person cannot operate an electrically operated indoor/outdoor wheelchair by themselves.

NHS trusts in England have a voucher scheme. Users can add to an NHS voucher their own financial contribution towards a more expensive wheelchair than the NHS would otherwise have provided. You may be unable to use the voucher scheme to get a powered wheelchair. You could use the Motability scheme to buy an electric wheelchair on hire purchase (see Box H.7, Chapter 22).

Anyone who thinks they might need a wheelchair should be referred to their local wheelchair centre for assessment. Your GP, local health centre, physiotherapist or occupational therapy department can tell you where your local wheelchair centre is, or you can ring NHS Direct: 0845 4647.

6. Other sources of equipment

Although social services and the NHS are the main statutory providers of equipment, you can obtain equipment through other channels. The Access to Work scheme, run via your local Jobcentre Plus office, may fund equipment needed for work – eg, a stand-up wheelchair to enable you to use a drawing board (see Chapter 16(2)). Schools or local education authorities can provide equipment needed for education, and education authorities sometimes have an absolute duty to do so where the need is specified in the educational part of a child's statement of special educational needs. The social fund (see Chapter 10) has been used to help people get items ranging from wheelchairs to continence pads. Local and national voluntary organisations (including the Family Fund (Chapter 35(8)) can help by loaning or hiring equipment or providing a grant to buy it (see Box J.3).

28 Housing grants

1. The housing renewal grants system

Local authorities in England and Wales have a general discretionary power to help with improving living conditions. Help can include adaptation or improvement of living conditions by providing a grant, a loan, materials or any other form of assistance.

The local authority can only exercise this general power if it has a published policy setting out the type of assistance it is willing to provide and in what circumstances. Ask your local authority for a copy of its policy. Community equipment, aids and minor adaptations that assist with living at home or aiding daily living and which cost less than £1,000 should be provided free of charge in England.

In Scotland the housing grants system is different (see Box J.4).

2. Disabled facilities grants

A mandatory disabled facilities grant is designed to help meet the cost of adapting a property for the needs of a disabled person.

Who is eligible for a grant?

To be eligible for a disabled facilities grant, you must be:

- an owner occupier; *or*
- a private tenant; *or*
- a landlord with a disabled tenant; *or*
- a local authority tenant; *or*
- a housing association tenant.

Some occupiers of caravans and houseboats are also eligible.

You are treated as disabled if:

- your sight, hearing or speech is substantially impaired; *or*
- you have a mental disorder or impairment of any kind; *or*
- you are physically substantially disabled by illness, injury, impairment present since birth, or otherwise; *or*
- you are registered (or could be registered) disabled with the social services department.

What can you get a grant for?

A grant can be awarded for:

- facilitating a disabled occupant's access to and from the dwelling;
- making the dwelling safe for the disabled occupant and others residing with them;
- facilitating a disabled occupant's access to a room used or usable as the principal family room;
- facilitating a disabled occupant's access to or providing a room used or usable for sleeping in;
- facilitating a disabled occupant's access to or providing a room in which there is a lavatory, bath or shower, and wash-hand basin or facilitating the use of any of these;
- facilitating the preparation and cooking of food by the disabled occupant;
- improving the heating system to meet the disabled occupant's needs, or providing a suitable heating system;
- facilitating a disabled occupant's use of a source of power, light or heat;
- facilitating access and movement around the home to enable the disabled occupant to care for someone dependent on them, who also lives there.

The test of financial resources

Disabled facilities grants are means tested (but not in Northern Ireland if they are made in respect of disabled children). For applications from owner occupiers and tenants, a test of resources is applied to the person with disabilities and their partner, if they have one. This is so even if the disabled person is not the applicant for the grant. For example, a disabled person lives with his brother, who has sole ownership of the property. The brother can apply for a disabled facilities grant to carry out adaptations to his property for the benefit of his brother who has a disability. The test of resources only applies to the brother who has a disability not to the brother who made the application. If the disabled person is a child or young person, the test of resources is applied to the parent(s) or person who has the primary responsibility for their care.

The test of resources is similar, but not identical, to income support (IS) or, if the relevant person is aged 60 or over, pension credit (PC). There are a number of important differences.

- There are no non-dependant deductions.
- If the applicant has dependent children then child allowances and premiums reflecting those used in housing benefit are included (see Chapter 7(25)).
- There is an extra premium (the 'grant premium', sometimes called the 'housing allowance') designed to reflect housing costs, currently £53.79 (or £69.92 for disabled children and young people). This is added to the total applicable amount for every grant application.
- If the applicant is in receipt of IS, income-based jobseeker's allowance or the guarantee credit of PC, the applicable amount is automatically £1 and all their income and capital are disregarded, giving a zero contribution.
- The earnings disregard for disabled people and carers is £15.
- There is no capital cut-off point. The first £6,000 of capital is disregarded. Weekly tariff income is assumed on capital over £6,000.
- There is a system of stepped tapers on 'excess income'.
- The value of personal allowances and premiums are sometimes not uprated at the same time as those for IS or PC.

Working out your contribution

The test of resources is designed to calculate how much, if anything, you can afford to contribute towards the cost of the works. This is done by calculating the value of a notional standard repayment loan you could afford to take out using a proportion of your 'excess income' (see below) to repay the loan. If you have no excess income then your contribution will be zero. Owner-occupiers, including leaseholders, are expected to be able to repay a loan over 10 years; tenants, over 5 years. The higher the amount of excess income the higher the proportion expected to be used towards repaying the notional loan.

Below, we describe how to work out your contribution.

Step 1: Work out your capital

Your own capital, together with your partner's, is taken into account. Certain types of capital are disregarded. The rules are similar to those for IS (see Chapter 5). However, the capital value of the dwelling to which your application relates is disregarded whether or not you live there. The first £6,000 of your capital is ignored. Tariff income of £1 per £250 or part thereof over £6,000 is assumed if the relevant person is aged under 60 and £1 per £500 or part thereof if the relevant person is 60 or over.

Step 2: Work out your income
Your average earnings and other income are based on your income over the 12 months before your application or a shorter period if that gives a more accurate figure. The earnings and income disregards are similar to those for IS (see Chapter 5(4)).

Step 3: Work out your applicable amount
This represents your weekly living needs and those of your partner (see Chapter 4(2) or 41(3)). Add on the grant premium (see above).

Step 4: Work out your excess income
If your income is less than or equal to your applicable amount, you have no excess income. Your contribution is zero. If your income is greater than your applicable amount, the excess income is the difference between the two figures.

Step 5: Work out your contribution
Excess income is apportioned into a maximum of 4 bands and multiplied by the relevant loan generation factor(s). For applications made after 1.4.02 the bands and multipliers are shown below.

The applicable amounts and loan generation factors are usually uprated annually. This uprating does not always coincide with social security April uprating. You may need to ask the local housing authority what the rates are at the time of your application.

Loan generation factors		**owner occupiers**		**tenants**
Band 1	First £47.95	factor	19.97	11.27
Band 2	£47.96 to £95.90	factor	39.94	22.53
Band 3	£95.91 to £191.80	factor	159.76	90.13
Band 4	£191.81 or more	factor	399.41	225.32

The aggregate of Bands 1-4 is the value of the notional loan the applicant is expected to contribute towards the cost of the works.

Example: An applicant who is an owner occupier with an excess income of £100 would calculate their contribution as follows:

Band 1	£47.95	x	19.97	=	£957.56
Band 2	£47.95	x	39.94	=	£1,915.12
Band 3	£4.10	x	159.76	=	£655.01

Applicant's contribution	*£3,527.69*
Total cost of works	£11,000.00
Less applicant's contribution	£3,527.69
Grant amount	*£7,472.31*

Subsequent grants
If an applicant has had to make a contribution to a previous grant on the same dwelling (in the last 10 years for owner occupiers or 5 years for tenants), the value of that contribution is deducted from the assessed contribution on a subsequent grant application. The works under the first grant must have been carried out to the local authority's satisfaction for this offsetting to apply. If the contribution on the earlier grant was more than the cost of the works, leading to a 'nil-grant approval', the value of the works properly carried out can be offset against a subsequent grant contribution.

Applying for a disabled facilities grant
Disabled facilities grants are administered by the local housing authority rather than the social services department where these are different authorities. An application form should be available from the local housing authority. An application must be supported by a certificate stating that the disabled occupant will live in the property for at least 5 years after the works are completed, or a shorter period if there are health or other special reasons.

Approval of a disabled facilities grant
The maximum grant payable under a mandatory disabled facilities grant is £25,000 in England and £30,000 in Wales. Local authorities could provide further assistance for extra costs under their discretionary power (see 3 below).

In order to approve an application for a disabled facilities grant, the local housing authority must be satisfied that the works are both necessary and appropriate for the needs of the disabled person, and reasonable and practicable in relation to the property. In determining whether the works are necessary and appropriate, the local housing authority must consult with the social services department. This is why some local authorities will direct people to the social services department first for an occupational therapy assessment. However, it is important to make a formal application for a grant because the 6-month time limit for the local authority to make a decision only begins from the date of the formal application. They cannot refuse to allow you to make a formal application or refuse to give you an application form.

If you do not get a decision within 6 months of applying, write and ask why and request that a decision be made. Seek legal advice if you still do not get a decision, or if you have been prevented from applying in the first place. Alternatively, you can make a complaint of maladministration to the Local Government Ombudsman (see Chapter 60).

If approved, the adaptations should usually be completed within one year by one of the contractors who supplied an estimate for the application. The local housing authority has a discretion to approve a mandatory grant but to stipulate that it won't be paid for up to 12 months from the date of application. Government guidance says this discretion should only be used sparingly, but it could delay the works being done.

If, after the application for a disabled facilities grant has been approved, the disabled person's circumstances change in some way before the works are completed, the local housing authority has a discretion as to whether to proceed with paying for all, part or none of the works. The local housing authority must take into account all the circumstances of the situation before deciding how to proceed in such a situation.

3. Discretionary power to assist with housing repairs, adaptations and improvements

Major changes to local authority powers to assist with housing repairs, adaptations and improvements were made by the Regulatory Reform (Housing Assistance) (England and Wales) Order 2002, which came into affect on 18.7.02. The Order introduced a new, wide discretionary power to allow authorities to provide financial and other assistance for repair, improvement and adaptation, with limited constraints on the exercise of their discretion.

Scope of the new power
Under the Order, local authorities have the power to set their own conditions for assistance, such as whether to perform a means test and the circumstances under which any financial assistance should be repaid. The power also enables assistance to be given in the form of a grant, a loan, labour, materials, advice or in any combination of these. The power may be used for:

- acquiring accommodation;
- adapting, improving or repairing accommodation;
- demolishing accommodation; *and*
- replacing accommodation that has been demolished.

Local authorities may also take security, including a charge on a person's home.

The Order enables authorities to help people in all tenures, including owner occupiers, tenants and landlords (including companies and registered social landlords).

Grants and loans

The Order extends local authorities' powers to give loans as well as, or instead of, grants. The Government does, however, recognise that loans would not be appropriate in all circumstances – eg for those in severe hardship, or where the individual has no or negative equity in their property. In such cases, the Government believes that grant assistance would be more appropriate.

Protections

Some protections apply in relation to the exercise of the new power. The Order:

- requires that before imposing or enforcing any condition relating to repayment or the making of a contribution, authorities must have regard to the person's ability to afford to make that contribution or repayment;
- requires that authorities must set out in writing the terms and conditions under which the assistance is being given, and satisfy themselves that recipients are aware of any financial commitment they are taking on;
- requires authorities to formulate, publish, have available for inspection and act in accordance with, a policy specifically in relation to housing renewal activities. This policy will set out how they intend to use their new power, to give assistance for housing renewal (see below);
- gives authorities the power to require an applicant to provide information to support their application for assistance (eg proof of ownership, financial details and contractors' estimates) or to prove, after assistance has been given, that they are complying with conditions that the authority has set.

Government guidance

The Office of the Deputy Prime Minister has issued non-statutory guidance to authorities on how to utilise the new discretionary power. It sets out good practice and certain overarching principles, such as the need to be fair, to give priority to the most vulnerable households, to ensure that applicants for loans are properly advised, and to take realistic account of people's ability to contribute towards the cost of works.

The guidance states that the Government would consider that an authority was failing in its duty as a housing enabler if it did not make some provision for assistance. A blanket 'no assistance policy' whether for grants, loans or both, would therefore be unacceptable.

Local authorities are also reminded that they must avoid fettering their discretion to provide assistance. An application for assistance may be legitimately turned down if it falls outside the published policy, but an authority cannot refuse to consider an application, or turn down an application which does not fit the published policy without there being a mechanism in place to determine such cases.

Published policy

The Order legally requires each local housing authority to publish, and act in accordance with, a policy on housing renewal assistance, on which they would be expected to consult service users under their 'Best Value' responsibilities.

The Order specifically provides that no local authority can exercise the new power unless they have:

- adopted a policy for the provision of assistance under the power;

J.4 Grant system in Scotland

Grants for repairs and adaptations to properties in Scotland are available from local authorities to both owners and private tenants. Details of these grants are set out in the Scottish Executive booklet *Housing Grants*, available from local authorities.

The legislation governing the grant system is set out in Part XIII of the Housing (Scotland) Act 1987 as amended by the Housing (Scotland) Act 2001, which introduced the requirement for a test of resources on those receiving grant aid. Grants are, in the main, discretionary awards.

There is a mandatory standard amenity improvement grant available to disabled people. A minimum grant of 50% of the total approved expense is available as of right to a disabled occupant for the provision of an additional standard amenity to meet their particular needs. Standard amenities are:

- a fixed bath or shower with a hot and cold water supply;
- a wash-hand basin with a hot and cold water supply;
- a sink with a hot and cold water supply;
- a toilet.

If your house already has these amenities but they don't meet your needs, you may still get a grant. For example, if you have a toilet upstairs but cannot easily climb up the stairs, you can claim a grant to put in a ground floor toilet.

A discretionary improvement grant, up to an expense limit of £20,000, may also be available for the works and/or adaptations required to make the house suitable for the welfare, accommodation or employment of a disabled person. Although under no obligation to do so, some local authorities may give priority to such applications. If the cost of the works exceeds the set grant limit and the local authority considers there are extraordinary reasons for this, it can apply to the Scottish Executive for an increase in the grant limit.

All houses are subject to the following three conditions for a period of 5 years from payment of the grant:

- the house must only be used as a private dwelling house (although part can be used for another purpose, eg for business); *and*
- the house must not be occupied by the owner or a member of the same family, except as their only or main residence (ie it may not be used as a second or holiday home); *and*
- the house must, as far a possible, be kept in a good state of repair.

There is no bar on a person selling a house following the payment of a grant, but the conditions themselves continue to apply to the property for the remainder of the 5-year period. The local authority would only seek repayment of the grant plus interest if any of the three conditions were breached during the 5 years.

The Warm Deal

To be eligible for £500 worth of home insulation improvements you must be getting one of a list of qualifying benefits. Provision is through approved contractors and includes loft or cavity wall insulation, hot and cold tank and pipe insulation and 4 energy efficient light bulbs.

If you or your partner are aged 60 or over but do not get a qualifying benefit, you can still get a grant of up to £125. People aged 60 or over may be able to get an energy efficiency grant to install central heating and associated insulation works. People aged 80 or over may qualify for an enhanced package of assistance.

For information, ring EAGA Partnership Ltd on 0800 072 0150 (Warm Deal enquiries) or 0800 316 6002 (central heating enquiries).

- given public notice of the adoption of the policy;
- made available for inspection, free of charge, at their principal office at all reasonable times a document that sets out their policy in full; *and*
- made available by post a summary of their policy, on payment of a reasonable charge, if required.

The guidance highlights issues that local authorities need to cover in their policy, such as:

- how their policy links in with their wider housing strategy, linking to health and social care strategies for vulnerable groups and also to wider planning and regeneration strategies;
- how much assistance is available, and in what form;
- who is eligible for assistance, and in what circumstances;
- the form and process for applying for assistance, including applications for assistance outside their policy;
- the circumstances in which a grant or loan must be repaid, and the advice, including financial advice, that is available to help people to access grants and loans;
- complaints procedures;
- service standards such as target times for decisions;
- performance indicators and targets to measure the progress made under the policy; *and*
- provision of a policy implementation plan.

There is no requirement as to how often the policy should be reviewed. However, if an authority wants to change the way it gives assistance or the conditions under which it provides assistance they must ensure their policy clearly allows them to do this. If not, they will need to revise it.

J.5 For more information

The main rules for assistance with repairs, improvements and adaptations are set out in the following statutory provisions:

- The Regulatory Reform (Housing Assistance) (England and Wales) Order 2002;
- The Housing Grants, Construction and Regeneration Act 1996, Part 1;
- The Disabled Facilities Grants and Home Repair Assistance (Maximum Amounts) Order 1996, as amended;
- The Housing Renewal Grants Regulations 1996, as amended.

Guidance is contained in the Office of the Deputy Prime Minister (ODPM) Circular 05/2003, *Housing Renewal* (17.06.03) and *Delivering Housing Adaptations for disabled people: A Good Practice Guide* (November 2004).

The law and guidance are available from The Stationery Office.

The ODPM publishes information on disabled facilities grants and other relevant assistance. Copies should be available from your local authority, a Citizens Advice Bureau, or the ODPM website: www.odpm.gov.uk.

There may be an independent home improvement agency in your area offering advice about grants. Home improvement agencies also help people to apply for grants, obtain other sources of finance to help pay for works, find a good builder, and ensure the works are properly carried out. Ask the local authority if there is one in your area or contact Foundations, the national co-ordinating body (see Address List).

For information about VAT relief on building works, see leaflet 701/7, *VAT Reliefs for People With Disabilities*, available from your local VAT enquiries office (look in the phone book under Customs and Excise).

The guidance states that it is imperative for policy summary documents to be clear and comprehensible to potential applicants. They need to be written in plain English and be available in other relevant languages as well as in Braille and/or taped versions.

4. Energy efficiency grants

England – Under the Warm Front Grants scheme, help towards improvements in insulation, room heating and water heating is available to disabled people and families with children who get a qualifying benefit or tax credit. People aged 60 or over who get a means-tested benefit may be eligible for the more generous Warm Front Plus Grant.

Warm Front provides a maximum grant of £1,500 for installing insulation and improving heating for households using mains gas, solid fuel, oil or off-peak electricity for heating.

You are eligible for Warm Front Plus if you are aged 60 or over and you get pension credit, housing benefit or council tax benefit. This provides up to £2,500 worth of heating improvements, including installation of central heating systems. You can get a leaflet by ringing Freephone 0800 316 2808 or writing to: EAGA Partnership Ltd, Freepost, NEA 12054, Newcastle upon Tyne NE2 1BR.

Wales – The Home Energy Efficiency scheme (HEES) provides a grant of up to £1,500 on a similar basis to Warm Front Grants. HEES Plus provides up to £2,700 for central heating for householders over 60 or disabled and chronically sick and lone parents with children under 16 who are in receipt of a qualifying benefit.

Northern Ireland – The Warm Homes scheme provides a grant of up to £750 to owner occupiers and private tenants who are disabled, over 60 or with children under 16, and who are in receipt of a qualifying benefit. Warm Homes Plus provides up to £2,700 for central heating for householders over 60 in receipt of a qualifying benefit.

5. Alternative housing

Many people prefer to move to a property designed to be accessible for a disabled person rather than have major adaptations to their present home. Even an accessible property may require some adaptations to suit your particular needs. Since October 1999 most new housing must be built to meet the basic access needs of disabled people.

If you are seeking social housing (ie council or housing association properties), contact your local authority and make sure you go on the housing register. It is important to stress your housing requirements. Most housing association properties are allocated via the local authority but some associations operate their own waiting lists, particularly for wheelchair users, so it is worthwhile contacting local housing associations directly.

This section of the Handbook looks at:

Care homes K

A B C D E F G H I J K L M N O P Q R S

29 Help with care home fees

1. Who can get help with care home fees?

If you require help with your care home fees you need to approach local authority social services departments (or social work departments in Scotland). This help will be provided only on the basis of a professional assessment of your needs (see Chapter 25 and Box J.1).

In England and Wales, the NHS is responsible for your registered nursing costs in a home providing nursing care after an assessment of how much care you need by a registered nurse, even if you do not need help with the rest of your fees. You should be assessed by an NHS nurse if you want the NHS to contribute towards your nursing care (see 3 below). In Northern Ireland, payments for nursing costs are made by the Health and Personal Social Services. In Scotland, local authorities will pay a set amount (see 3) for both your nursing and personal care if you are 65 or over; you should only be asked to contribute towards accommodation and living costs. If you are under 65 the local authority will pay a fixed amount towards nursing care only.

If you get help from social services, the amount you pay normally depends on an assessment of your means. Chapter 30 covers the benefits you can receive in a care home and Chapter 31 covers the way local authorities assess how much you should pay if they are helping with funding your place.

The system of needs assessments and charging assessments is the same whether your accommodation is provided in a home managed or owned by a local authority, or in a home managed or owned by a voluntary or private organisation (sometimes described as the independent sector). All come under Part III of the National Assistance Act 1948 if the local authority has provided or arranged the place.

If you enter a care home and don't want or need help with the fees, you should still ask for an assessment of your needs, as the local authority may make other suggestions and could also advise whether the type of home you plan to go into is suitable for your needs, and whether, once your capital is below the capital limit, they will agree to help with the funding.

It is useful to find out what fee level the local authority would be prepared to pay for someone with your needs. You can then compare it to the prices quoted by the homes you visit. Many homes charge people who pay for themselves more than they charge for local authority-funded residents, and some are prepared to put the price down if you later need help from the local authority. This is important if you think you might need local authority funding in the future.

Care in care homes for children aged under 18 is provided under the Children Act 1989 (in Scotland, the Children (Scotland) Act 1995).

Care in hospices is free at the point of use.

Care in care homes must be free of charge for people who have previously been detained in hospital for treatment under certain sections of the Mental Health Act 1983 and who are entitled to aftercare services under section 117 of that Act. In a special report in 2003, and subsequently in its 2003-2004 annual report, the Local Government Ombudsman in 2003 instructed local authorities to identify and reimburse residents who have previously been incorrectly charged for aftercare services.

R v Manchester CC ex p Stennett HoL [2002] 5 CCLR 500; LAC 2000/11

Charges can be made for aftercare services under section 8 of the Mental Health (Scotland) Act 1984 in Scotland, although the charges do not include a set amount for personal care or nursing if you are 65 or over, or for just nursing if you are under 65.

2. Different types of care homes

Care homes are run by a range of providers, and local authorities are able to arrange accommodation in the type of home that most suits your needs. Health bodies as well as local authorities can arrange care in homes that provide nursing. We use the term care home when talking about any of the types of homes listed below. All homes have to be registered as 'fit for the purpose' for the care they intend to provide: in England and Wales under the Care Standards Act 2000 (and the subsequent regulations), in Scotland under the Regulation of Care (Scotland) Act 2001, and in Northern Ireland under the Health and Personal Social Services (Quality and Improvement and Regulation) (NI Order) 2003.

Although all homes that have to be registered are called care homes, some also provide nursing care. There are regulatory bodies in each UK country to ensure homes meet the required standards. Homes must produce a statement of intent, a service users' guide giving details about the home, and a copy of the most recent inspection report. You will also get a statement of terms and conditions (or written contract) describing the services covered by the fee, services not included in the fee, and terms and conditions of occupancy. In England and Wales, homes providing nursing have to itemise separately the costs of accommodation, personal care and nursing.

Homes providing personal care – These can be run by private or voluntary organisations or private individuals. Personal care is not defined, but to trigger the need for registration, it means assistance with bodily functions such as feeding, bathing, toileting, etc. If healthcare is needed it should be provided by the local community health services in the same way as for a person in their own home. Non-physical care such as advice, encouragement and prompting do not trigger a requirement to register. This is so that sheltered housing schemes do not have to be registered. There is no longer a requirement for homes to provide board as well as personal care, although most do. Some local authorities provide care homes, mostly for older people, but they also provide hostels for people with learning disabilities and for those with, or recovering from, a mental illness. Some local authority and independent hostels, which tend to be for younger people, do not provide board as they want to encourage independence. In this case you may count as a 'less dependent resident' (see Chapter 31(3)).

Homes providing nursing care – These may be run by NHS bodies or independent organisations. They provide nursing care as well as personal care, and as part of their registration criteria must have a suitably qualified registered nurse working at the home at all times. Health services such as continence advice, stoma care, physiotherapy, chiropody, specialist feeding equipment, etc should be provided to residents by the NHS, as well as free continence products.

3. How to get help with care home fees

The majority of people who need help to pay for their care get it from the local authority. However, for some people who have high or complex nursing needs the NHS will be responsible for the full cost of their fees in a home providing nursing care. It is also responsible (in England and Wales) for paying for the care you receive from a registered nurse in a home that provides nursing. In Scotland the local authority remains responsible for nursing costs but cannot charge the £65 considered to be the cost of nursing care in Scotland.

NHS responsibilities to fund your care

Continuing NHS healthcare – Care home residents who are fully funded by the NHS do not contribute towards their care home fees but are treated as hospital inpatients for benefits purposes. Eligibility for fully funded NHS care in a care home is established using locally set criteria. Individuals with complex, intense or unpredictable healthcare needs, or whose primary need for accommodation arises from their health needs, should be funded by the NHS. Following the *Coughlan* case (1999), eligibility criteria in many areas were found to be unlawfully restrictive and health authorities were instructed to review their criteria.

R v N and E Devon ex p Coughlan 1999 2 CCLR 285; HSC 2001/015; LAC (2001)18

In 2003 the NHS Ombudsman reported a number of cases where she considered the NHS had been too restrictive and advised health bodies to review their criteria and, if they were found to be too restrictive, to identify patients who should have received funding and recompense them or their estate. The Department of Health has consequently issued advice for local authorities and health bodies to do just this. If you think this may apply to you, contact your local health body or the Ombudsman helpline on 0845 015 4033. Although the cases were in England the reports may equally apply across the UK. In response to the report, each strategic health authority in England was instructed to ensure that all primary care trusts in its area were using common eligibility criteria by April 2004. The Ombudsman issued a follow-up report in December 2004 asking for assurances that the retrospective reviews undertaken were effective, and calling for national eligibility criteria supported by assessment tools, guidance and training, as well as clearer standards of record keeping. The Department of Health has announced that a new national framework for NHS continuing care will be commissioned (Department of Health press release, 2004/0437).

NHS funding for long-term care 20 Feb 2002 (HC399) & Health Service Commissioner – selected Investigations Completed April-Sept 03 (HC119) NHS funding; follow-up report (HC144) Health Service Ombudsman

Assessment for continuing care can be carried out in your home, a care home or more normally in hospital. Continuing care is normally provided within a care home providing nursing care or a hospital but a recent Ombudsman decision has confirmed that it can be provided in someone's own home (*Pointon*, E.22/02-03).

Assessment for continuing NHS care must be undertaken before social services are notified about a patient under the Delayed Discharges Act and patients must be informed of decisions and given a right of review. If a patient asks for a review of a decision on the refusal of NHS-funded care, this should be heard within 14 days. You should be able to remain in hospital until the review is heard and the local authority should not be penalised for this period.

The Continuing Care (NHS responsibilities directions) 2004 and The Delayed Discharges (Continuing Care) Directions 2004

Guidance issued in England in January 2003, *Discharge from hospital: pathway, process and practice*, stresses that local authorities and health authorities need to work closely together for the benefit of patient and carer, who should be fully involved in the hospital discharge process.

Patients being discharged from hospital should be given details of future care options and costs. You can refuse to be discharged into a care home, but cannot insist on staying in hospital.

HSC 2001/015; LAC (2001)18; LAC (2004)20; HSG 95/8; LAC 95/5; SWSG 102/94 (see Box K.1)

Intermediate care (England only) – If your intermediate care (see Chapter 25(1)) has been arranged in a care home, it should be free for up to 6 weeks. In Wales there is a similar system of free services for 6 weeks.

Registered nurse care – Even if you do not qualify for fully funded NHS continuing care, the NHS is responsible in England and Wales for funding the cost of nursing provided by a registered nurse (and in Northern Ireland it is free when provided by the Health and Social Services Department). This is determined by an assessment by a nurse employed by the NHS. If your condition is such that you have complex, intense or unpredictable healthcare needs you should continue to be able to access full funding from the NHS under continuing care. The assessment for fully funded continuing healthcare should precede a determination of your nursing needs.

In England you receive one of three bands depending on your nursing needs: £40, £80 or £129 a week. Where people have nursing care needs lower than the middle band, primary care trusts now have the flexibility to decide any appropriate amount between the lower and the middle band (£40 and £80). There are provisions to pay more than £129 if your nursing needs are very complex. Check that you do not fall within the local criteria for fully funded NHS care (see above), particularly if you fall within the highest nursing band – the eligibility criteria for which are not dissimilar to those for fully funded care. In Wales there is only one band, set at £105 a week (in 2004/05, but subject to annual review). In Northern Ireland the amount is £100. See below for Scotland.

Payment is made to the home, which must either pass it on to you, reduce your fees by that amount or explain how the amount has been taken into account in calculating your fees. You should be given a statement specifying the fees payable for your nursing, personal care and accommodation. If you are being charged for nursing costs already covered by the NHS payment, take this up with the care home manager. If you are unsatisfied with an explanation, you could raise the matter with the primary care trust responsible for the nursing payment.

People who are funded by the local authority also have their nursing costs met by the NHS, but this does not affect the level of charges unless your income is such that the local authority charges meant you were paying for part of your nursing costs.

Your benefits are not affected by receiving free nursing care.

The responsibility of the local authority to fund care

In England and Wales, under s.21(1)(a) of Part III of the National Assistance Act 1948, local authorities have a duty to provide residential care for all those who *'by reason of age, illness, disability, or any other circumstances are in need of care and attention which is not otherwise available to them'*.

Local authorities can meet this duty by providing it in one of their homes or arranging it in an independent sector care home. In Scotland, the duty to provide care home placements is to be found in s.59 of the Social Work (Scotland) Act 1968 and in Northern Ireland in Article 15 of the Health and Social Services (NI) Order 1972.

The local authority must exercise its powers and duties in accordance with directions, and take account of guidance issued by ministers.

Your local authority is expected to give *'support and encouragement'* to people making representations or complaints and so should tell you about, or let you see, relevant directions or guidance. See Box K.1.

Deciding if you need care in a care home

If you think you might need care in a care home, either on a temporary or permanent basis, ask your local authority for a needs assessment (see Chapter 25(3)). Funding will only be given if the local authority thinks that your needs can be best met in a care home. Guidance advises that *'the law does not allow authorities to refuse to undertake an assessment of care needs for anyone on the grounds of the person's financial resources'* – eg because you have capital above the capital limit. They should advise you about what type of care you require, and what services are available.

LAC 98/19 (see Box K.1)

Recently, local authorities have been reluctant, because of lack of funds, to provide expensive packages of care for people to remain in their own homes. It is often cheaper for them to arrange for you to go into a care home. Case law has established that it may be lawful to provide care in a care home rather than meet 24-hour needs at home. However, a recent NHS Ombudsman ruling agreed that a person with dementia should be entitled to constant care at home, and that their psychological needs should have been taken into account in NHS assessments (*Pointon*, published 2.2.04). Some local authorities have a lower ceiling on the amount of care they will provide for older people in their own homes, than that for younger disabled people. This might contravene both the National Service Framework for Older People and the *Fair Access to Care Guidance*, which aim to end age discrimination and ensure equality of access to care across all client groups. See Chapter 25(7) for details of what to do if you disagree with the local authority.

R v Lancashire County Council ex p RADAR and Gilpin 1 CCLR 19

If it is agreed you need care in a care home and you need help with the funding because you cannot afford the fees, the local authority enters into a contract with the home and is

K.1 For more information

The law

- Income Support (General) Regulations 1987 (ISG)
- State Pension Credit Regulations 2002
- Jobseeker's Allowance Regulations 1996 (JSA Regs)
- Health and Social Services and Social Security Adjudication Act 1983 (HASSASSA)
- Mental Health Act 1983/Mental Health (Scotland) Act 1984
- Mental Health (Care and Treatment) (Scotland) Act 2003
- Adults with Incapacity (Scotland) Act 2000
- National Assistance Act 1948 (NAA)/Social Work (Scotland) Act 1968
- National Assistance (Assessment of Resources) Regulations 1992 (AOR)
- National Assistance (Sums for Personal Requirements) Regulations
- National Health Service Act 1977 (NHSA)/National Health Service (Scotland) Act 1978
- National Health Service and Community Care Act 1990 (NHSCCA)
- Health and Social Care Act 2001
- Community Care and Health (Scotland) Act 2002
- Community Care (Delayed Discharges etc) Act 2003

See Box J.1 in Chapter 25 for reference books on community care law. See Box R.7 in Chapter 58 for information on Commissioners' decisions and Box R.9 on where to get access to the law.

Directions, guidance and circulars

These are issued by the appropriate ministers in the devolved governments and have to be followed by local authorities and health bodies. Your local authority or health authority will have copies and they are usually available on the internet.

- **England:** Health Service Directions, Guidance and Circulars (HSGs and HSCs); Local Authority Circulars (LACs) (www.dh.gov.uk)
- **Scotland:** Community Care Circulars (CCDs), previously Social Work Services Group (SWSGs) which are being replaced by Health Department Letters (HDLs), previously Management Executive Letters (MELs), (www.show.scot.nhs.uk/sehd/hdl.asp and www.show.scot.nhs.uk/sehd/ccd.asp or for previous guidance www.scotland.gov.uk/library/swsg/contents.htm)
- **Wales:** National Assembly for Wales Circulars (NAfWCs), previously Welsh Office Circulars (WOCs); Welsh Health Circulars (WHCs)

Challenging decisions

If you are challenging any decisions about residential care, you may find the following particularly useful:

- DMG: *Decision Makers Guide* issued by the DWP for DWP staff (www.dwp.gov.uk)
- CRAG: *Charging for Residential Accommodation Guide* explains the Assessment of Resources Regulations; LAC 2004(25); NAfWC 14/02; HLD 2003/7 with updates and amendments. In Wales, the last amendment was NAFWC 49/04, in November 2004
- LAC 93/7, WOC 25/93, SWSG 11/93: explain which authority you are ordinarily resident in
- LAC 2004(20), WOC 12/93, SWSG 5/93: Choice of Accommodation Direction and guidance CCD 6/2002 explain more expensive accommodation in England and Scotland; in Wales, NAFWC21/2003
- HSC 2001/015, LAC(2001)18, WOC 16/93, MEL(1996)22 and EL 96/8, LAC99/30 and HSC 99/180: NHS responsibilities for meeting continuing care needs (guidance updated in England only)
- LAC(2001)25, CCD7/2002 and CCD13/2004 explain deferred payments in England and Scotland; also covered in NAFWC 21/2003 for Wales
- HSC 2003/06, LAC(2003)7; NAfWC 34/01 explain free nursing care and CCD 4/2002 explains free personal care in Scotland
- LAC(2003)14 explains changes to charging for community equipment and defines intermediate care in England
- LAC(2001)32 Fairer charging for non-residential services in Wales

Further information

Age Concern, Counsel and Care, and Help the Aged are among a number of organisations which produce excellent factsheets covering all aspects of community care. See the Address List at the back of this Handbook.

liable for the full cost of your accommodation and personal care. It will recover from you any contribution you are assessed as having to pay, according to national rules (see Chapter 31). Registered nursing costs are the responsibility of the NHS as described above.

Even if you can pay the fees yourself, this does not necessarily mean the local authority should not arrange your care. If your capital is over the capital limits and you are liable to pay for yourself, a local authority *'must satisfy itself that [you are] able to make [your] own arrangements, or have others who are willing and able to make the arrangements for [you]'*. If you are too frail physically or mentally to make your own contract with the home, and others are not willing or able, the local authority must make the arrangements and charge the full cost.
LAC 98/19 (see Box K.1)

If the local authority hasn't agreed to arrange a place in a care home, it is not responsible for paying the home – you are (unless the authority has an agreement with the home to allow 'direct access' to people in urgent need; or where it retrospectively accepts responsibility).

Scotland
If you are 65 or over and assessed as requiring personal care (see Box J.1) in a care home, you can receive a fixed payment of £145 a week, with a further payment of £65 if you require nursing care (£210 in total). Care home residents who are under 65 can only be considered for a payment of £65 towards their nursing care costs. These payments are made regardless of your income and capital and are issued by the local authority directly to the care home.

You can choose whether or not you want to take up the payments for your care; if you do not, you can continue to make your own arrangements direct with the home. If you access payments, you can also choose whether you want the local authority to contract with the home for just the payments it is making (with you contracting separately with the home for your accommodation and living expenses), or for the local authority to make the contract with the home on your behalf for the whole costs. There may be advantages in the latter arrangement, since the council's standard contract may restrict increases in the care home fees and may also include provisions for monitoring the quality of care.

If you are admitted to hospital the local authority will continue to make payments at the full flat rate for 2 weeks after admission and at 80% for a subsequent month, or until your future placement arrangements are confirmed. You will still need to pay for accommodation and living costs. You may get assistance with these costs, but this will depend on a financial assessment carried out by your local authority (see Chapter 31).

Urgent cases
If your need is urgent, the local authority can arrange for care in a care home without carrying out a formal needs assessment. The assessment should be done as soon as possible. If you urgently need to go into a home providing nursing, the local authority does not have to get the health body's consent beforehand, but should do so as soon as possible. Contact your social services (or social work) department, explain your crisis, and ask for a social worker to visit you urgently. If necessary ask your GP for help when contacting the social services department.

Local authorities deferring provision or funding
Some local authorities, because of their lack of resources, place people on waiting lists for funding after they have been assessed as needing care in a care home. This could mean you have a long wait in hospital or at home (hospital waits may now be less likely, because of the Community Care (Delayed Discharges) Regulations, which make the local authorities liable to reimburse the NHS for causing delays). Other people may already be in a care home but waiting their turn for funding, and so may be running their capital down below the national limits. Some authorities suggest that people may wish to make their own arrangements for care while waiting for local authority funding.

Such waiting lists are arguably unlawful. The local authority may take its resources into account to a limited extent in deciding whether you need care, but it may not do so if you fall within its own eligibility criteria. Once it has decided that you need care in a care home, it has an immediate duty to make some provisions to ensure that you are cared for (subject to the statutory means test – see Chapter 31).
s.21(2A) NAA; See also R v Wigan MBC ex p Tammadge [1998] 1 CCLR 581; R v Kensington & Chelsea RLBC ex p Kujtim [1999] 2 CCLR 340; R v Islington LBC ex p Batantu; MacGregor v South Lanarkshire

The local authority must ignore capital within the upper capital limit when deciding if they need to make arrangements for care in a care home. The value of your own home should not be included in the decision about whether the local authority needs to make the arrangements for you, if you are going to enter into a 'deferred payment agreement' (see Chapter 31(6)). Remember that they disregard the property for the first 12 weeks of a permanent stay. Guidance states that once the local authority has decided you need care and attention which is not otherwise available, it should make arrangements for you *'without undue delay'*. If it is unable to do so, the authority should *'ensure that suitable arrangements are in place to meet the needs of [you and your] carer'*. If you are already in a care home, the local authority should *'step in to take over the arrangements so as to ensure [you are] not forced to use up capital below £18,500' (now £20,500 in England and Northern Ireland, and £21,000 in Wales)*. Guidance in England has strengthened this and local authorities are reminded that *'councils need to ensure that they are in a position to provide Part III accommodation as soon as they are aware that the resident needs it. Once the council is aware of the resident's circumstances, any undue delay in undertaking an assessment and providing accommodation if necessary would mean that the council has not met its statutory obligations. Consequently, the council could be liable to reimburse the resident for any payment he has made for the accommodation which should have been met by the council pursuant to its statutory duties.'*

If you have been placed on a waiting list, seek urgent advice, and see Chapter 25(7) 'Other steps'.
LAC 98/19; SWSG 2/99 LAC (2001)25

You are in a care home and your capital is reaching the capital limit
If you are already in a care home but have not needed help because your capital was above the capital limit, you will need to contact the social services department where the care home is situated when your capital nears the figure set for that year. It will then assess whether you actually need care in a care home, and whether it will meet the cost in that particular home. The help you receive should start from the time your capital reaches the upper capital limit – but see above, 'Local authorities deferring provision or funding'.

Note for couples with joint capital – If you have a joint account in excess of £40,000, it may be worth splitting your account so that you do not have to wait until your joint account is down to this figure. For example, if you have £46,000 in a joint account, your partner will only get help after £5,000 has been paid in fees and your account is down to £41,000. If you split the account so you each have £23,000, help will be available after spending only £2,500 in fees. The example uses the capital limits for England; in Scotland and Wales different amounts will apply.

4. Choice of home

If the local authority decides, after the needs assessment, to offer you a permanent, or respite, place in a care home, it may suggest a particular home or give you advice on homes to choose from. In all cases where a local authority is making the arrangements, you have the right to choose your own care home ('preferred accommodation').

However, if a health body places you in a home providing nursing care and pays the full fee, you do not have the same right to choose a particular home, although the Government has said the health body should take account of patients' wishes. But nor will you be liable to meet any of that home's charges. Although your health body must consent to a local authority placing you in a home providing nursing care, the health body *'would be expected not to interfere with an individual's choice of nursing home'* (HSG 92/54).

Preferred accommodation

If you tell your local authority you want to enter a particular care home, that home is called 'preferred accommodation'. There are legally binding directions and regulations which are intended to ensure that you can exercise a genuine choice over where you live. In reality this choice may be restricted, as described below. 'New Choice of Accommodation' guidance was issued in England in October 2004 as LAC (2004)20. The guidance states there should be a presumption in favour of individuals being able to exercise choice in the care they receive. It states that if a local authority cannot provide a place in your preferred home it must give clear and reasonable justification (in writing) which would relate to the directions on choice. It also states that if a person needs to be placed in another area which is more expensive than their normal costs the local authority should pay more.

If you have preferred accommodation, the local authority must arrange for care in that accommodation, as long as:

- it is suitable in relation to your assessed needs. The guidance clarifies this, stating that the assessment should be individual and that a home should not be deemed suitable for a person just because it satisfies registration for that type of person – there may be other factors. A home may also be suitable even if it does not meet the normal service specification laid down by the local authority;
- it is available. If a place is not available in your preferred home you may have to wait. The local authority should ensure that adequate and suitable care is available while you wait, taking account of your needs and wishes. This care should meet your assessed need and not normally be a hospital bed. If you unreasonably refuse to move to a suitable interim arrangement the local authority can decide that it has reasonably met its statutory duties and may ask you to make your own arrangements. Seek advice if this happens;
- the person in charge of the home is willing to provide a place subject to the authority's usual terms and conditions for such accommodation;
- the accommodation would not cost the authority more than it would usually expect to pay for accommodation for someone with your assessed needs; *and*
- your authority has legal power to make such a placement.

Provisions in the Health and Social Care Act 2001 could make it easier to receive funding from English and Welsh authorities if you choose a care home in Scotland, Northern Ireland, the Isle of Man or the Channel Islands, but regulations have not yet been issued to enable this. Protocols have been developed regarding placements in homes providing nursing care between Wales and England, and Scotland in order to overcome the differences in the NHS payments in England and Wales and the funding structure in Scotland and Northern Ireland. Seek advice for up-to-date information if you plan to move between countries.

More expensive homes

If you have chosen a home which costs more than your local authority would usually expect to pay for someone with your needs, it will nevertheless arrange for your preferred accommodation (given that it satisfies the other conditions above) if a third party is able and willing to meet the shortfall, and to continue doing so for as long as you are likely to be in that care. The new guidance advises that local authorities must ensure that a third party is reasonably able to pay top-up fees for the time you are in the home. These are sometimes referred to as 'third party' contributions. You should not be expected to use your personal expenses allowance of £18.80 (£19.10 in Wales) to help pay for a more expensive home. Neither can you use your own capital or disregarded income to top up the fees, unless you fall within the description below. This was confirmed in *R v E Sussex ex p Ward* 3 CCLR 132. It is permissible, according to the Department of Health, for you to pay for 'extras' which are outside of the care package. As long as you do not feel pressured by the home owner or the local authority, there is no reason why you should not enter into a contract with the home owner for extra services.

Some residents can use their own money to pay for more expensive accommodation. These are people who are either within the period of the 12-week disregard of their property or using the provisions for a 'deferred payment agreement' (see Chapter 31). The Health and Social Care Act 2001 and the Community Care and Health (Scotland) Act 2002 have introduced this to enable people who only receive funding from local authorities for a temporary period and eventually will fund themselves from the proceeds of their home, to go into a home of their choice. People in Scotland who are better off as a result of receiving free personal or nursing care, can use some of their money to pay for a more expensive care home (Additional Payments (Scotland) Regs 2002).

LAC (2004)20; CCD 7/2002 and CCD11/2004

Note that a 'liable relative' (spouse) cannot act as a third party if any maintenance contribution is being paid under s.42 NAA. In Scotland, this restriction does not apply if the local authority is satisfied that the liable relative can sustain both top-up and the maintenance payments(CCD 6/2002).

The local authority cannot use the direction on the Choice of Accommodation or the regulations to set arbitrary ceilings on the amount it will contribute towards care in a care home and to routinely require third parties to make up the difference. Only when a person has expressed a choice of preferred accommodation should the local authority consider a third party top-up arrangement.

The authority must be able to justify its usual cost and show that it is enough to buy a reasonable level of service without contributions from third parties. If the local authority places you in more expensive accommodation because there are no vacancies in 'usual cost' homes, the local authority should meet the additional cost, not a third party. Nor should the local authority seek a top-up payment where an individual's physical, psychological or other needs are such that they can only be met in a more expensive place. This could be because of language, culture, religion or the need to be near family so that regular visits can be made. In some areas it is difficult to find a home that will accept you at the price the local authority is prepared to pay. Homes might say they will accept you quicker if you pay a top-up, but you will have to wait longer if the home is only going to be paid the local authority rate. In these cases you should complain to the local authority. If there are no places at the usual rate then the local authority should place you and be prepared to pay above their rate. Neither you nor a third party should be expected to make a top-up. You should complain if there are too few homes in the area with vacancies at the local authority usual rate, as your choice is therefore restricted. See Chapter 25(7).

Points to note – Guidance in England and Wales makes it clear that the local authority remains responsible for the home's full fees, even though a third party is making a contribution. Local authorities should not encourage homes to make separate arrangements with relatives for top-up payments that are not included in the local authority's contract with the home. If relatives are asked to make a separate payment to the home, you should refer the homeowner to the local authority. Third parties should be aware that they may have to meet the greater share of any subsequent fee increases. Guidance on this is different in Scotland (CCD 6/2002 and CCD 5/2003). This guidance states that the local authority has discretion to collect top-up payments and contract with the care home, or to leave the third party to make top-up payments direct to the care home. In Wales, the Welsh Assembly issued a letter on 8.7.03 reaffirming its guidance on top-up payments as they apply in Wales. Where homes fees rise above the level of the third-party agreement, the local authority should consider the impact of moving the person to a cheaper room or home and take steps where possible so the resident can remain in their current home.

- Third-party payments are treated as your own income in the charging assessment (even if they are made direct to the home).
- These contributions are disregarded as income for income support, pension credit and income-based jobseeker's allowance purposes.
- If the third party stops making a contribution you may have to move to another home. However, you should establish, before that happens, that there are homes in the area at the local authority price that can meet your needs. You should also ask for an assessment of your needs to include an assessment of any psychological or social needs to remain in that home and a risk assessment of any detrimental effects you might face if you had to move. It may be possible to stay in the same home and have the fees met by the local authority if it is part of your assessed need to remain in the home.
- The local authority will not automatically pay an equal share of any increase in the home's fees.
- An increase in your income won't necessarily lessen the need for a third-party contribution; it depends on the result of the charging assessment.
- If the home doesn't keep to its contractual obligations, the local authority may terminate the contract.

What sort of home?
It is very important to choose a home where you think you could be happy and comfortable. Certain standards have to be met because of registration (see 2 above), but services and facilities may vary greatly from home to home. Inspection reports are available on the Commission for Social Care Inspection (CSCI) website: www.csci.org.uk.

Ask your social worker or GP what things to look for and what questions to ask when choosing a place in a care home. They may give you a checklist of questions. Don't take anything for granted. For example, how often will it be possible for you to have a bath? Can you take your favourite armchair with you? Given the increase in home closures, you should try to establish the financial viability of the home, or whether there are any plans to sell it.

You should go and see the home beforehand to make sure you will be comfortable there and get on well with the staff and other residents. You might want to enter the home for a short stay before committing yourself to a permanent stay. You should be given a written contract or statement of terms and conditions if you are being funded by the local authority. Check what the fees cover, what are 'extras', what happens if you are absent from the home, or what period of notice is required. This is especially important if you are making your own contract with the home. If the local authority has made the contract, it is still useful for you to know exactly what is covered. Do not let yourself be rushed into things. See Box K.1 and the Address List for organisations that can support you.

Complaints
All care homes must have a complaints procedure that is accessible and explained to you. Initially you should complain to the manager of the home. Complaints should be responded to within 28 days. The complaints procedure for the home should also make it clear how to complain to the registration body – ie the CSCI in England, the Care Standards Inspectorate for Wales or the Scottish Commission for the Regulation of Care. In Northern Ireland a new body, The Regulation and Improvement Authority, will replace the current body over the next year. If either the NHS or the local authority is involved in any way with your care – ie the NHS is paying for your nursing and you have a complaint about the standards of the nursing, or the local authority has arranged your care and you are unhappy with it – you can also use the NHS or local authority complaints procedures.

30 Benefits in care

In this chapter we look at:

1. What benefits are you entitled to?
If you have moved into a care home (either temporarily or permanently), with or without help from the local authority, the only social security benefits that may be affected are:
- disability living allowance (DLA) care component;
- attendance allowance (AA);
- constant attendance allowance and exceptionally severe disablement allowance;
- income support (IS) and income-based jobseeker's allowance (JSA);
- pension credit (PC);
- housing benefit (HB);
- council tax benefit (CTB).

All other social security benefits can be claimed and paid in the normal way, subject to the standard rules outlined in the rest of this Handbook. It normally makes no difference whether the care home you are in is owned or managed by a local authority, or by a private or voluntary organisation.

NHS-funded care in a care home
If you have moved into a care home you may be eligible for fully funded NHS continuing care to meet the costs of your accommodation and care. In these circumstances you will be treated as if you are in hospital (see Chapter 33).

Following revised guidance on NHS continuing care funding, many residents in care homes that provide nursing have successfully applied for retrospective NHS funding and many are awaiting a decision from the Ombudsman. In these circumstances, any retrospective NHS funding will *not* mean that you have to repay any social security benefits you have received, even though any charge you have paid to the local authority should be refunded to you. This has been made clear in DWP guidance dated May 2004 (DMG Memo Vol

3 08/04).

If you are not eligible for NHS fully funded care in a care home, then you may be entitled to NHS funding for the nursing element of your care – the registered nursing care contribution (RNCC) (see Chapter 29(3)). The RNCC does *not* effect entitlement to social security benefits. This means you are still entitled to receive AA/DLA care component if you are self-funding or if you are only receiving interim funding from the local authority (see 2 below) even though you receive an RNCC.

Regulation 7(5)(f) SS(AA) Regulations and Regulation 9(6)(f) SS(DLA) Regulations

2. Attendance allowance and disability living allowance

Normally you cannot be paid attendance allowance (AA), disability living allowance (DLA) care component, constant attendance allowance or exceptionally severe disablement allowance after the first 4 weeks in a care home (see Chapter 20(8)). However, if you pay the fees for the care home without funding (or only with interim funding) from the local authority, you will be able to keep your AA or DLA care component (see below).

The mobility component is only affected if your stay is in hospital or a similar institution. It is not affected by a stay in a care home, even if you are funded by the local authority.

Chapter 20(8) covers the effect of a stay in 'certain accommodation' (sometimes referred to as 'special accommodation') on DLA care component and AA. See also Box H.3 in Chapter 20.

Paying your own fees

If you are paying your own fees (ie you are a self-funder) there were, prior to 6.10.03, different rules, depending on whether or not you were receiving income support (IS), income-based jobseeker's allowance (JSA), pension credit (PC) or housing benefit (HB), and whether or not you were in a care home independently of any contract between the care home and the local authority.

These complex rules no longer exist. The only criteria determining whether you are self-funding, and therefore able to keep your AA/DLA care component, is that you do not receive any financial help (or you only receive financial help on an interim basis (see Chapter 31(6)) from the local authority towards the cost of the care home fees. This means that being in receipt of IS/income-based JSA/PC/HB no longer prevents the payment of AA/DLA care component, even where the local authority has contracted for your accommodation at full cost to you. There is no longer a loophole. This change was brought into effect by the removal of:

- the restriction on the payment of AA/DLA care component where the cost of your accommodation may be borne by the local authority; *and*
- the restriction on the payment of AA/DLA care component to a self-funding person where IS/income-based JSA/PC/HB were in payment.

In Scotland, from July 2002, if you are 65 or over you will not be entitled to AA or DLA care component if you are receiving help from the local authority with the cost of your care under the 'free personal care' arrangements. If you are under 65, you will still be paid DLA care component if the only help you get is for 'free nursing care'.

If your fees are currently being met by a local authority, a Commissioner's decision (CA/2937/97) has confirmed that you are treated as though you are paying the full fee provided it is clear you will eventually be paying back the local authority in full – ie you are a retrospective self-funder. Although normally you would not be able to get AA or DLA care component if the local authority was paying the fees, in this case you can. This is most likely to apply if you are in the process of selling your home or have a deferred payment agreement with the local authority (see Chapter 31(6)).

If you are selling your home but it is uncertain whether the proceeds from the sale will be enough to mean that you will have to pay back the local authority in full, seek expert advice, as the law on this is still not clear.

Direct payments

Local authorities can give you direct payments for you to arrange your own care at home, and you can also use the money to buy up to 4 weeks respite care in any one year (see Chapter 26(4)). AA and DLA care component, therefore, will not normally be affected. But, if you need another period of care or hospital treatment within the linking period (see Chapter 20(7 and 8)), your AA or DLA care component could be affected.

Example: You use your direct payment to buy 4 weeks in a care home, then 2 weeks later your carer falls ill, so you return to the care home. This time your stay is funded by the local authority under a contract with the home. Your AA or DLA care component is affected immediately as it links with a period when your care was being funded by local authority money because you were using the payment from the local authority to buy your respite care.

3. Housing benefit

Registered care homes

You cannot get housing benefit (HB) for the costs of a registered care home. See below for help with meeting the costs of your own home.

Homes that do not need to register

If you live in a care home (eg a hostel) that does not provide personal care but only advice, support and encouragement (and so does not have to register), you may be able to receive HB to help meet the cost of your rent. If you get HB you will also be entitled to free Supporting People services, which include advice, support and encouragement (see Chapter 25(5)).

Some homes that were not required to register before April 2002, and where residents were able to claim HB, may now have to register as care homes under the Care Standards Act 2000 (Regulation of Care (Scotland) Act 2001). If they do, you may no longer be able to claim HB. You should therefore have any contribution reassessed by the local authority (see Chapter 31).

Help with meeting the costs of your own home

If you go into a care home for a temporary stay or for respite care, you can continue to receive HB – or help to cover mortgage interest payments with income support (IS), income-based jobseeker's allowance (JSA), or the guarantee credit of pension credit (PC) – for up to 52 weeks, as long as it is clear that:

- your stay is not likely to last longer than this;
- you intend to return to your own home; *and*
- you have not rented out where you normally live to someone else.

However, if you go into a care home for a trial period with a view to a permanent admission, HB (or IS/income-based JSA/PC mortgage interest) is only paid for up to 13 weeks (see Chapter 7(6)).

Until recently, if you went into a care home for a temporary or trial period stay and you subsequently decided to become a permanent resident, HB ceased from the date you decided you were not returning to your home in the community. This caused a problem where you were required to give notice of termination of tenancy as you remained liable for the rent during this period. However, following a recent Commissioner's decision (CH/4546/2002), the Housing

Benefit (General) Regulations 1987 have been amended from 4.10.04. Now, if you move to a care home from a home where you remain liable for the rent (eg because a notice period for the termination of the tenancy is being served), you are to be treated as occupying your former home for up to 4 weeks, as long as that liability could not reasonably have been avoided. Hence, HB can be paid on your former home for that period.

4. Council tax benefit

You can get council tax benefit (CTB) only if you are liable to pay council tax. Your former home is exempt from council tax if it is unoccupied *and* you are now solely or mainly resident in any type of care home. Before this is the case, your former home, even though it may be unoccupied, will still be treated as your 'sole or main' home and you can get CTB in the normal way (see Chapter 7(11)).

5. IS/income-based JSA

Capital limits in care homes

For all types of registered care homes mentioned in this section of the Handbook, if you are a permanent resident aged under 60, you can claim income support (IS) or income-based jobseeker's allowance (JSA) if your capital is £16,000 or less. Tariff income of £1 for every £250 or part thereof only starts at £10,000 (see Box B.2, Chapter 5).

If you know you want to stay in a care home, your admission can be permanent from the start. Most local authorities, however, prefer you to have a trial period to see if you like it. During a trial period (and for temporary stays), the IS and income-based JSA capital limit is £8,000. This only goes up to £16,000 when your stay is permanent. You are still considered to be a permanent resident if you are temporarily absent from the care home for up to 13 weeks.

You can get help from the local authority if your capital is no more than the capital limit for your country (see Box K.2) regardless of whether your stay is temporary or permanent. However, in Scotland you get free personal care regardless of the level of your capital. Chapter 5(11 and 12) looks at how capital is valued and what can be disregarded. The value of your own home is disregarded during a temporary stay in a care home.

IS/income-based JSA in care homes

If you are a resident in a care home and you are over 16 and under 60, your IS or income-based JSA is worked out in the standard way by adding together:

- your personal allowance; *and*
- any premiums to which you are entitled (which can include severe disability premium (SDP) while disability living allowance (DLA) care component is payable).

Even if you are not entitled to IS or income-based JSA in your own home, you may be entitled when you go into a care home.

Temporary admission (single person) – If you go into a care home for a temporary period, the amount of IS or income-based JSA you receive will usually not change. However, if the severe disability premium and the enhanced disability premium (if applicable) are included in the calculation, they will no longer be included where DLA care component has ceased.

Temporary admission (couple) – If one of you goes into a care home or if you both go into different rooms in the same care home or into different care homes for a temporary period, for IS or income-based JSA purposes you will still be assessed as a couple, but you will each get the appropriate single person rate in your applicable amount if this amount is more than the couple rate. If the appropriate single person rate is the greater amount, the person at home (or in a different room in the same care home or in a different care home) will get a single rate personal allowance plus premiums and any housing costs, and the person in care will get a single rate personal allowance plus any appropriate premiums at the single rate amount. These are then added together, and your combined income is taken from this figure to give the amount of IS or income-based JSA to be paid to the claimant.

If you both go together into the same room in the care home, then you will receive the couple rate of IS or income-based JSA plus any appropriate premiums. Housing benefit (HB)/council tax benefit (CTB) will continue to be paid for your housing costs at home.

SDP and temporary admissions – There is often confusion about the SDP where one of a couple goes into a care home for a temporary period. If carer's allowance (CA) is paid to a carer, SDP will not be paid. However, in other circumstances, a recent Commissioner's Decision CIS/1544/2001 held that the SDP should be included in the calculation of IS or income-based JSA for each qualifying person, even where a partner in the community may have prevented its inclusion previously. The *Decision Makers Guide* (DMG Vol 4, 23231-33) was amended in November 2002 to reflect the Commissioner's Decision.

In practice, SDP is often left out of the calculation for both temporary and permanent admissions, and if you are being assessed by the local authority you do not see any benefit from the extra money anyway. In this case, the main thing you need to check is that the local authority is not assuming you are getting SDP and therefore including it in the calculation of your charge, even if you are not being paid it.

Some authorities do not assess the charge for temporary stays and charge a flat rate instead. Where this is the case, if no one receives CA for looking after you and the DWP has not included SDP as part of their calculation, seek advice, since any additional benefit you receive will not be taken away in social services charges.

Permanent admission (single person) – If you are a single person going into a care home on a permanent basis, the amount of any IS or income-based JSA will usually only change in the following circumstances.

- If you have capital between the £3,000 and £8,000 capital limits, there will be a reduction in the tariff income (and therefore an increase in IS or income-based JSA) applied because of the different capital limits for permanent residents in a care home (see above).
- If you were not entitled to IS or income-based JSA previously because your capital was more than the £8,000 capital limit, you may become entitled when you enter a care home permanently because of the higher capital limit of £16,000.
- If you are a single person and you have a carer in receipt of CA or you are living with a non-dependant in the community you may become entitled to, or there may be an increase in, the amount of IS or income-based JSA payable when you enter a care home permanently. This is because CA will no longer be payable to a carer and the non-dependant will no longer count as a non-dependant. Therefore, the SDP will be included in the IS/income-based JSA calculation for any period where attendance allowance/DLA care component remains in payment.

Note: If the SDP and the enhanced disability premium (if applicable) were included in the calculation of IS when you were in the community they will no longer be included where the payment of DLA care component has ceased.

Permanent admission (couple) – If you are one of a couple permanently in a care home, each of you will be treated as separate single claimants. Any jointly-owned capital will be split, and the IS or income-based JSA calculation should be based solely on each of your individual capital and income. See Chapter 29(3) for information about joint capital. If you both enter the same care home you may still be assessed by the DWP as a couple, although case law (R(IS)1/99) has now established that most people should be assessed as separate individuals even if they share a room. Seek advice if you are treated as a couple in this situation.

6. IS/income-based JSA and maintenance

Liable relatives – The income and capital of the non-resident spouse cannot be taken into account in determining a permanent resident's claim to income support (IS) or income-based jobseeker's allowance (JSA). However, a husband and wife are each liable to maintain the other and the non-resident spouse can be asked to make a contribution. The non-resident should not feel pressured into paying more than they can reasonably afford given their actual resources and expenses. Unless the DWP obtains a court order, payment is voluntary. In practice, legal proceedings are rarely undertaken, although the DWP may put pressure on the non-resident spouse to make 'voluntary' payments. Normally, any payment made by the non-resident spouse is taken into account as the resident spouse's income. But if you are receiving a payment to help meet the costs of more expensive 'preferred' accommodation (see Chapter 29(4)), IS and income-based JSA ignore these payments.

Note: These liable relative rules do not apply to pension credit.

7. Pension credit

Capital limits in care homes

Capital under £6,000 for temporary (or trial period) residents, or £10,000 for permanent residents, does not attract any assumed or tariff income. You are still considered to be a permanent resident if you are temporarily absent from the care home for up to 52 weeks. Tariff income on capital above £6,000 (or £10,000) is £1 a week for every £500 or part thereof. There is no upper capital limit. See also 'Capital limits in care homes' in 5 above for information common to both income support (IS) and pension credit (PC).

PC in care homes

If you are a resident in a care home and you are aged 60 or over, your guarantee credit element of PC is worked out in the usual way, by adding together your standard minimum guarantee and any additional amounts to which you are entitled (which can include the severe disability additional amount while disability living allowance (DLA) care component or attendance allowance (AA) is payable). The savings credit element of PC is also worked out in the usual way. See Chapter 41.

For both elements there will normally be a specified 'assessed income period' of 5 years or less. During a typical 5-year award period, certain elements of your income are treated as constant with deemed annual increases built in. It is not a fixed award, as the deemed increases will alter the amount of the award from year to year. This will mean that, usually, if you are going temporarily into a care home there will be no need to notify the DWP. However, if you are in receipt of AA or DLA care component you will still need to inform the Disability Benefits Unit (see inside back cover) if your temporary stay will be for more than 28 days (or less if you have been in hospital or a care home within the previous 29 days, as this period will be linked – see Chapter 20(8) and Box H.3). If you are going into a care home on a permanent basis, any assessed income period will end and therefore you will need to inform the DWP.

Temporary admission (single person) – The rules are the same as for IS, ie there will usually be no change in the amount of PC you receive, except that the severe disability additional amount will no longer be included in the calculation of PC where AA (or DLA care component) has ceased.

Temporary admission (couple) – The PC rules for one or both of you going into a care home on a temporary basis are significantly different from the IS rules. Unlike for IS, there is no provision for the treatment of couples as two single people in terms of the appropriate minimum guarantee where one is going into a care home on a temporary basis. This means that the amount of PC payable will usually be the same as the amount payable when you were both in the community.

However, if the severe disability additional amount is included in the calculation at the single or couple rate, it will no longer be included where AA or DLA care component in payment to the resident has been suspended. This is the case even where your partner is in the community and in receipt of AA or DLA care component themselves. This is because you, as the resident, are treated as still being in the household and not disregarded for the purposes of qualifying for the severe disability additional amount.

A similar situation occurs when one of a couple is temporarily in hospital, but the PC regulations provide for this by allowing a single severe disability additional amount to continue in payment for the partner at home. It is likely that an amendment to the PC regulations will be laid in due course which will create the same provision for one of a couple temporarily in a care home.

The treatment of couples as couples for PC appropriate minimum guarantee purposes in these circumstances instead of as single people (as they are for IS) also has problematic knock-on effects for local authority charging (see Chapter 31).

Permanent admission (single person) – If you are a single person going into a care home on a permanent basis, the amount of any PC will usually only change in the following circumstances.

- If you have capital between £6,000 and £10,000 then there will be an increase in the amount of PC payable, as there will no longer be a tariff income applied, due to the increased lower capital limit in a care home of £10,000.
- If you have capital over the £10,000 lower capital limit for care homes, then there will be a reduction in the amount of tariff income applied (and therefore an increase in PC) due to the increased lower capital limit from £6,000 to £10,000 in a care home.
- If you are a single person living with a non-dependant in the community or you had a carer in receipt of carer's allowance then you may become entitled to PC, or there may be an increase in the amount of PC, due to the severe disability additional amount being included in the appropriate minimum guarantee for any period that AA or DLA care component remains in payment.

Note: If the severe disability additional amount was included in the calculation of PC when you were in the community, it will no longer be included where the payment of AA/DLA care component has ceased.

Permanent admission (couple) – If you are one of a couple permanently in a care home, each of you will be treated as separate single claimants. Any jointly owned capital will be split, and the PC calculation should be based solely on each of your individual capital and income (see Chapter 29(3) for information about joint capital). If you both enter the same care home you may still be assessed by the DWP as a couple, although case law (R(IS)1/99) has now established that most people should be assessed as individuals even if they share a room. Seek advice if you are treated as a couple in this situation.

8. Special help for war pensioners

Some war pensioners may qualify for help in getting their fees paid by the Veterans Agency. It can cover nursing home fees and respite breaks. The help from war pensions is not means tested. For more information see Chapter 45(11).

31 Charging for care

1. The legal basis of the financial assessment

Section 22(1) of the National Assistance Act 1948 (NAA) provides for the local authority to charge you for the accommodation they provide, whether in a care home owned by a local authority or in an independent care home.

The local authority must provide care in care homes for those who need it unless it is *'otherwise available to them'*. The Health and Social Care Act 2001 and its subsequent regulations reaffirm that a local authority cannot say that accommodation is *'otherwise available'* because of your capital if you have less than the upper capital limit for your country (see Box K.2). Following the *Robertson v Fife* House of Lords case (25.7.02) it has been made clear that the provision of services to a person who is assessed as being in need of them is not related to the ability of the person to meet the costs.

The Health and Social Care Act also has provisions which make it clear that if you are entering into a deferred payments agreement (see 6 below) your former home is not included by the local authority in deciding whether accommodation is otherwise available. Comparable provisions for Scotland are in the Community Care and Health (Scotland) Act 2002.

The local authority has to fix a standard rate for the accommodation. The standard rate for local authority care homes is the full cost to the authority of providing your place in that accommodation. The standard rate for independent care homes is the gross cost to the local authority of providing or paying for your place in that accommodation under a contract with the independent care home.

If your income or capital is sufficient for you to pay the standard rate, you can still, in some circumstances, have the local authority make the arrangements for you but you will be assessed to pay the full cost less any registered nursing care contribution (RNCC) from the NHS for nursing provided (see Chapter 29(3)).

If you cannot pay the standard rate, the local authority must assess your ability to pay under national rules and calculate what lower amount to charge you. The basis of that assessment is in the National Assistance (Assessment of Resources) Regulations 1992 (AOR), as amended. These regulations are explained in the *Charging for Residential Accommodation Guide* (CRAG). Local authorities must take account of the CRAG because it is statutory guidance issued by the Secretary of State. It is updated and amended and circulars are issued with each amendment. There are separate guides for England, Wales and Scotland (see Box K.1).

The amount you can keep for your personal expenses depends on the National Assistance (Sums for Personal Requirements) Regulations, which set a rate each year. The proposed rate for 2005/6 is £18.80 (£19.10 in Wales). Section 22(4) of the NAA also gives the local authority discretion to allow a higher amount (see 5 below).

Capital

If you are in a care home (whether your stay is permanent or temporary – see Box K.2 for definitions) and your savings are over the capital limit for your country (see Box K.2), you will have to pay the standard rate for your accommodation until your capital drops to these limits or less. Some items of capital are ignored or disregarded in the assessment. These are listed in Schedule 4 of the Assessment of Resources Regulations (see Box K.2 and 6 below).

If you have capital over the lower capital limit for your country a tariff income is assumed (see Box K.2).

See Box K.2 and 6 below for information about how your property is treated.

Income

In general, assume all income counts unless it, or a part of it, is specifically ignored under Schedules 2 or 3 of the Assessment of Resources Regulations (see Box K.2). The 'income disregards' are very similar to those for income support (IS) (see Chapter 5). Note that pension credit, IS or income-based jobseeker's allowance are taken into account as income by the local authority (except for any element for housing costs and the savings disregard applied to the savings credit element of pension credit – see Box K.2).

2. Key points

- The local authority does not have to carry out a charging assessment for the first 8 weeks of a temporary stay in care; they can charge what is reasonable.
- If you count as a 'less dependent resident', the local authority can ignore the whole of the charging assessment if that is reasonable in your situation (see 3 below).
- If you are a temporary resident in the care home, the charging assessment is slightly different in order to allow for your costs at home (see 7 below).
- If you are one of a couple, the law does not allow a joint charging assessment; only the resident's own income and capital affects the assessment. However, see 4 below for when the non-resident partner is the claimant of benefit paid in respect of both members of the couple.
- Whatever your source(s) of income, you'll generally be left with no less than the personal expenses allowance (PEA) of £18.80 a week (£19.10 in Wales). Except for any income ignored in the assessment, which, since October 2003 has included a savings disregard in certain circumstances where you are aged 65 or over (see Box K.2), the rest of your income goes towards meeting the standard rate for your accommodation.
- Any difference between what you pay and the standard rate is met by the local authority, which is liable for the full cost of the fees (although see Chapter 29(4) if you have chosen more expensive accommodation than the local authority thinks you need).
- If the application of the law affects you unfairly, urge the local authority to use its discretion in s.22(4) National Assistance Act to correct that unfairness by letting you keep more than £18.80 (£19.10 in Wales) a week of your income for your PEA (see 5 below).
- The assessment is largely based on income support (IS) rules but there are some important differences, and the local authority has some more discretion (see Box K.2).
- In England and Wales only, if your accommodation is provided as part of your aftercare package under section 117 of the Mental Health Act 1983, you should not be charged for your accommodation. The House of Lords has now confirmed previous judgments in the lower courts that there is no power to charge for s117 costs. Guidance following the earlier judgments (*R v Richmond upon Thames LBC ex p Watson* [1999] 2 CCLR 402), told local authorities which were still charging that they must stop immediately (LAC 2000/3). You should seek urgent advice if you are being charged or have been charged in the past and have not received a refund. If you receive aftercare

under s117 you will still be entitled to benefits, including IS and pension credit, in the normal way. However, disability living allowance (DLA) care component and attendance allowance (AA) are not likely to be payable, as case law (CDLA/870/2004) now suggests that s117 of the Mental Health Act is an *'enactment relating to persons under disability'* (even though it is not specified as such in Appendix 1 to Chapter 61 of the *Decision Makers Guide*) for the purposes of defining those people in *'certain accommodation'* for whom DLA care or AA is not payable.

❑ Note that the draft Mental Health Bill in England proposes a limitation of 6 weeks on the period of free aftercare.

3. Less dependent residents

If you count as a *'less dependent resident'* (CRAG para 2.008 defines who should be treated as less dependent) the local authority has complete discretion to ignore the whole of the charging assessment if that is *'reasonable in the circumstances'*. This is because it has been recognised that to live as independently as possible you will need to be left with more than the personal expenses allowance (CRAG para 2.007).

4. Couples

Couples and maintenance

The local authority has no power under the National Assistance Act (NAA) to assess couples jointly. The financial assessment should be of the income and assets of the resident only (including any entitlement to pension credit (PC), income support (IS) or income-based jobseeker's allowance). The spouse remaining at home has no obligation to fill in any sections of the assessment form asking about their income and assets. Indeed, the guidance underlines this and states *'local authorities should not use assessment forms for the resident which require information about the means of the spouse'* (CRAG para 11.005). What the local authority can currently do is approach the spouse (but not an unmarried partner, who has no liability) and inform them of their duty as a 'liable relative' under s.42 of the NAA to maintain their spouse.

Liable relatives – The spouse can voluntarily agree a 'reasonable' amount to pay in support of the resident in the care home. There are no guidelines as to what counts as reasonable. Ultimately it is only a court which can set an amount (if any) a liable relative should pay. Seek advice if you are in this position. Guidance was issued in 2002 on how to approach liable relative payments (CRAG paras 11.005A to 11.006A). The DWP has similar rules about liable relatives (see Chapter 30(6)) although they do not apply in respect of PC.

Note: In the *'proposed changes to residential care charges from 5.4.04'* the Department of Health stated that it is was planning to repeal the liable relatives rules at the earliest opportunity. In Scotland, the Scottish Executive has also stated an intention to repeal this rule from Scottish charging at the earliest legislative opportunity. In the interim, Scottish Executive guidance encourages local authorities to use their discretion not to apply the liable relatives rule.

Benefit paid to non-resident partners in respect of couples

If you are one of a couple going temporarily into a care home and your partner is the claimant of IS or PC in respect of both of you, guidance states that *'it would be reasonable to expect the partner receiving the IS/PC to contribute to the charge for accommodation for the other partner a sum equivalent to the IS/PC payable for that partner'* (CRAG para 4.005).

The issue that arises for local authorities is what constitutes a reasonable amount. For couples in receipt of IS, the situation is quite straightforward, as, in most cases, the applicable amount in these circumstances is usually calculated using two single persons' applicable amounts added together (see Chapter 30(5)), which can be apportioned easily to find out the amount paid in respect of the resident. However, for couples in receipt of PC, the situation is complicated by the fact that PC is calculated using the couple appropriate minimum guarantee (see Chapter 30(7)).

The same apportionment issue arises for local authorities when they are deciding how much to increase the personal expenses by to allow an amount for the partner in the community when it is the resident who is the claimant of PC for both members of the couple. The most common approaches by local authorities to this issue are discussed in 5 below.

5. The personal expenses allowance

You will get the same £18.80 (£19.10 in Wales) personal expenses allowance (PEA) whether you are in a local authority or independent care home on a temporary or permanent basis. It is intended that your PEA should be spent as you wish on personal items. Neither the care home nor the local authority have authority to require you to spend your PEA in any particular way.

If you aren't able to manage your PEA because of ill-health, the local authority may (subject to your agreement, or that of your personal representative) deposit it in a bank account on your behalf, and use it to provide for your smaller needs. Any money that is unspent on your death will form part of your estate.

CRAG guidance reminds local authorities that the PEA should not be used for care that is contracted for because it has been assessed, by the local authority or the NHS, as needed. Continence supplies and chiropody should be fully reflected in the care plan.

Increasing the PEA

The local authority has discretion, under s.22(4) NAA, to allow more PEA in 'special circumstances'. This discretion can be used if you need to keep more of your income in order to lead a more independent life or to pursue a hobby that is important to you. Guidance (LAC 97/5) also reminds local authorities that where a resident is temporarily absent there is the discretion to vary the PEA to enable the resident to have more money while staying with family or friends.

If you are one of a couple, the PEA may be increased so that you can help support your partner at home, perhaps because you are not married and so cannot have half of your personal or occupational pension disregarded, or because, as the resident, you are in receipt of income support (IS) or pension credit (PC) paid in respect of both of you (CRAG 5.005). Basically, the local authority should not require a charge that would leave your partner without enough money to live on; however, the local authority could consider being on IS/PC as 'having enough to live on'.

If you are one of a couple going temporarily into a care home and you are the claimant of IS in respect of both of you, then the local authority usually has a straightforward task of apportioning the IS according to your individual incomes because IS is usually calculated using two single persons' applicable amounts added together (see Chapter 30(5)). However, if you are one of a couple going temporarily into a care home and you are the claimant of PC in respect of both of you then the position is far less straightforward because PC is calculated using the couple appropriate minimum guarantee rather than two single persons' appropriate minimum guarantees added together (see Chapter 30(7)). This means that local authorities have to decide how they carry out an apportionment. In most cases, it seems that as a starting point local authorities are either:

- dividing the couple rate standard minimum guarantee equally (ie £167.05 divided by 2 = £83.53) and adding any

K.2 Capital and income

General

The local authority assessment of capital and income under the National Assistance (Assessment of Resources) Regulations 1992 (AOR) is closely based on the assessment for income support (IS) (see Chapter 5). We note the key differences below. Abbreviations used are listed in Box K.1.

Capital limits

For local authority charging purposes these are:

- in England, £20,500 upper limit, and £12,500 lower limit for tariff income purposes; in Scotland, £19,500 and £12,000; and Wales £21,000 and £14,750 – for both temporary and permanent residents.

For IS, the capital limits are:

- £8,000 upper limit and £3,000 lower limit (for tariff income) for temporary residents;
- £16,000 upper limit and £10,000 lower limit (for tariff income) for permanent residents.

For pension credit (PC), the capital limits are:

- no upper limit for temporary or permanent residents;
- £6,000 lower limit (for tariff income) for temporary residents;
- £10,000 lower limit (for tariff income) for permanent residents.

Note: The tariff income for local authority charging purposes and IS purposes is calculated using £1 a week for every £250 or part thereof in excess of the lower limits. For PC purposes, it is £1 a week for every £500 or part thereof in excess of the lower limits.

Arrears of benefits

There is a 52-week limit on the disregard of arrears of some benefits for charging assessments. For IS, income-based jobseeker's allowance (JSA) and PC, this period is extended in certain circumstances (see Chapter 5(12)).

Your home

See also Chapter 31(6). If you are a 'temporary resident', the value of 'one dwelling' is ignored if:

- you intend to return to live in it as your home; *and*
- it is still available to you; *or*
- your property is up for sale and you intend to use the proceeds to buy a more suitable property to return to.

You count as a **temporary resident** if your stay is unlikely to last more than 52 weeks or *'in exceptional circumstances (is) unlikely substantially to exceed that period'*. If you are not sure of your long-term plans, it is usually best to say you intend to return to your own home. However, if you are one of a couple going into a care home on a trial basis with a view to a permanent stay, then for PC purposes you will still be treated as a couple, whereas if you are one of a couple going permanently into a care home, you will be treated as two single people and any PC entitlement will be paid to each of you based on your individual resources. Therefore, it may be financially beneficial in these circumstances to be permanent from the day of entering the care home (see Chapter 31(4 and 5)).

You count as a **permanent resident** if the agreed intention is for you to remain in a care home.

The local authority has discretion, not found in IS/PC, to disregard the value *'of any premises occupied in whole or in part by a third party where the local authority considers it would be reasonable to disregard the value of those premises'* (para 18, Sch 4 AOR). Examples are given where a carer has given up their own home in order to care, or the person remaining is an elderly companion of the resident (CRAG para 7.007), but the examples are not exhaustive. If you think a disregard should apply to your property, and it has not been, use the complaints procedure (see Chapter 25(7)).

While your home is up for sale

If you are a permanent resident, one important difference is the way your home is treated. Unlike IS/PC, when your old home is up for sale the local authority does not ignore the value for 26 weeks or longer where reasonable. It counts as capital from the 13th week after you have become a permanent resident, and although the local authority may help towards your care home fees while your home is up for sale, you will have to pay back the full amount once your old home is sold. See also Chapter 31(6) for information about deferred payment agreements.

If you jointly own property

It is only *your* actual interest which is to be valued. It is recognised that it might be hard to find a willing buyer for a part-share in a property (CRAG 7.012). A recent Ombudsman decision concerning Lincolnshire County Council (03/C/9384 – 28.6.04) makes it clear that a local authority should deal with the question of the valuation of a property in accordance with the guidance and without delay. Seek advice if you disagree with how your share is valued. IS has used a 'deemed' share based on the number of owners rather than the actual share in the property (see Chapter 5(11)).

If you jointly own a property with a spouse who decides to sell in order to move (eg to a smaller house), then you can give them some of your share of the proceeds to help buy the new home. The local authority shouldn't consider this as deprivation of your capital (CRAG 6.063).

Jointly-owned capital

If you jointly own capital (other than property) with your partner (or any other person), the local authority will divide it into equal shares in the charging assessment, regardless of what your actual share is. This applies whether you are a temporary or permanent resident, unlike the DWP rules for couples, which count your capital together until you become a permanent resident, when they divide your capital.

Personal possessions

The value of these is ignored unless you acquired them with the intention of reducing your capital in order to satisfy a local authority that you are unable to pay for your accommodation at the standard rate or to reduce the rate at which you would otherwise be liable to pay for your accommodation (para 8, Sch 4 AOR).

Deprivation of capital

The notional capital rules described in Chapter 5(15) are not mandatory for local authorities. They have discretion not to apply reg 25(1) of the AOR Regs. If they do apply reg 25(1), the rules are similar to the IS rules. However, the local authority can decide that property has been disposed of in order to reduce the residential charge without having to decide that the resident knew of the capital limit or anticipated the need to enter a care home.

Yule v South Lanarkshire Council 2000 SLT1249

Another case has held, however, that the local authority must take account of the resident's 'subjective purpose' in disposing of the property and give reasons for accepting or rejecting any evidence provided by the resident.

R on the application of the personal representatives of Beeson and Dorset County Council and the Secretary of State for Health 2001

The local authority 'diminishing notional capital' rule

reduces your notional capital on a weekly basis. It is reduced by the difference between the charge you are currently paying and the charge you would have paid if the local authority had not taken 'notional capital' into account (reg 26 AOR).

The 6-month rule

Section 21 HASSASSA is the source of the '6-month rule'. It is separate from the 'deprivation of capital' rule in reg 25, AOR Regs. Even if s.21 HASSASSA does not apply, the local authority may nevertheless take the value of the transferred asset into account under reg 25.

Section 21 HASSASSA may be applied if:

- you transferred cash or any other asset, which would have affected the charging assessment, to someone else; *and*
- you did this *'knowingly and with the intention of avoiding charges for the accommodation'; and either*
- you transferred the asset 6 months or less before the day the local authority has arranged a placement in a care home; *or*
- you transferred the asset while you were being funded by the local authority in a care home; *and either*
- you were not paid anything, or given anything, in return for the transfer; *or*
- you were paid, or given something, less than the value of the asset in return for the transfer.

Where a resident is self-funding in an independent sector home, has not been assessed nor had their placement arranged by a local authority, the 6-month rule only applies if the local authority takes over the arrangements within that time (CRAG, Annex D(2.1)).

If s.21 HASSASSA applies, the person to whom you transferred the asset is *'liable to pay ... the difference between the amount assessed as due to be paid for the (residential) accommodation... and the amount (which you are paying)'*. In this case, the local authority has a choice. It may:

- use reg 25 to base the charging assessment on the amount of 'notional capital' you gave away, as well as on your actual capital and income; *or*
- if you cannot pay the assessed charge, it may use s.21 HASSASSA to transfer the liability for the part of the charges assessed as a result of the notional capital from you to the person(s) to whom you transferred the asset, up to the value of the transferred asset.

Some people mistakenly think that if they have given away assets more than 6 months before entering a care home it cannot affect the amount they would have to pay for a care home. However, if a significant purpose of giving away an asset was to get help, or more help, from the local authority with the cost of a care home, the deprivation of capital rule may be applied – even if the transfer took place over 6 months before. Obviously, if you have given away something which would not have affected the charging assessment at all, the deprivation of capital rule cannot apply, nor can s.21 HASSASSA.

If the local authority refuses to arrange a place for you in a care home because the asset you gave away, together with other savings, was worth more than the capital limit in your country (see above), seek urgent advice.

See also Robertson v Fife Council (25.7.02)

Charitable and third party payments

These are described in Chapter 5(7 and 9). Regs 42 and 51, ISG apply to the local authority's charging assessment. However, such a payment, of income or of capital, will be taken into account if it is for *'any item which was taken into account when the standard rate was fixed for the accommodation provided'* (regs 17 and 25, Sch 3, para 10(2), AOR). If a third party is making a payment to meet the shortfall for more expensive accommodation, that payment is always taken fully into account as your income by the local authority, but not by the DWP for social security benefits.

Income

- ❑ Attendance allowance and disability living allowance (DLA) care component are only disregarded if you are a 'temporary resident' – see above (para 6 Sch 3 AOR).
- ❑ DLA mobility component is disregarded as for income support (IS) and pension credit (PC).
- ❑ IS, PC and income-based jobseeker's allowance (JSA) are taken fully into account but payments in these benefits made towards housing costs (eg payments toward mortgage interest) are disregarded (Sch 3 AOR). See below for the savings disregard applied to the savings credit element of PC.
- ❑ Housing benefit and council tax benefit being paid in relation to your usual home will be disregarded.
- ❑ Supporting People payments are disregarded.
- ❑ Housing costs – the local authority can disregard any payments you are making towards your housing costs as a temporary resident (see Chapter 31(7)).
- ❑ Contributory benefits dependants' additions have been abolished since April 2003 but existing claims will be protected. If you get a child or adult dependant's addition (eg as part of your incapacity benefit or state pension), it is disregarded if it is paid to the person for whom it is intended (para 28B Sch 3 AOR).
- ❑ Working tax credit is taken fully into account.
- ❑ Child tax credit is disregarded.
- ❑ Child support maintenance payments, child benefit and guardian's allowance are disregarded (unless the child is in the accommodation with you).
- ❑ If you have a spouse with whom you are not residing, half your personal or occupational pension or payment from a retirement annuity contract will be disregarded if you pass at least this amount to your spouse. If you pass nothing or less than half, there is no disregard. The disregard is for both temporary and permanent residents. (The IS/PC and income-based JSA rules do not have a similar disregard.)

Savings disregard

Since the introduction of pension credit (PC), the Department of Health has applied a savings disregard for residents aged 65 or over (NA(AOR)(A)(NO2) (England) Regulations 2003 and similar provisions in Scotland and Wales).

The savings disregard applies in the following ways. At the time of writing, the amounts stated are the proposed amounts for 2005/06.

- ❑ If you are a resident in receipt of the savings credit element of PC with pre-PC qualifying income of between £82.05 (basic state pension) and £109.45 (standard minimum guarantee) a week (or between £131.20 and £167.05 for couples) you will have a disregard of an amount equal to the savings credit award or £4.85 a week (£7.20 for couples), whichever is less.
- ❑ If you are a resident in receipt of the savings credit element of PC with pre-PC qualifying income in excess of £109.45 a week (£167.05 for couples) you will have a disregard of £4.85 a week (£7.20 for couples).
- ❑ If you are a resident who is not in receipt of the savings credit element of PC because, although you have qualifying income, your total income is in excess of £150.55 a week (£220.82 for couples), you will have a disregard of £4.85 a week (£7.20 for couples).

additional amount included in the appropriate minimum guarantee to the amount for the person for whom it is paid. Then they deduct any assessable income received by the partner in order to reach an amount by which to vary the PEA; *or*

- allowing the amount that would be paid by way of the guarantee element of PC to the partner as if they were a single person and varying the PEA by this amount.

These different approaches produce significant variations across the country in the amounts allowed in charging assessments for partners in the community. If the amount allowed for your partner leaves them without enough money to live on, you should seek advice with a view to using the complaints procedure (see Chapter 25(7)).

6. Treating your home as capital

The value of your previous home will be ignored when the local authority assesses your resources:

- if you are temporarily resident in a care home; *or*
- for the first 12 weeks of a permanent stay in a care home; *or*
- if the home is occupied by your spouse or partner (unless you are estranged or divorced from them); *or*
- if your home is occupied by your estranged or divorced partner and they are a lone parent with a dependent child; *or*
- if the home is occupied by a relative of yours or a relative of a member of your family who is:
  - aged 60 or over; *or*
  - incapacitated; *or*
  - aged under 16 and a child for whom you are liable to maintain.

A 'relative' is your parent, parent-in-law, son, daughter, son/daughter-in-law, step-parent, stepson/daughter, brother, sister, or the partner of any of the above, grandparent, grandchild, uncle, aunt, nephew or niece. 'Incapacitated' is not defined but guidance says you count as incapacitated if you get incapacity benefit, severe disablement allowance, disability living allowance (DLA), attendance allowance (AA) or constant attendance allowance, or you would satisfy incapacity conditions for any of these.

The local authority also has discretion to ignore the value of the property if anyone else lives there. Box K.2 gives the legal basis for this discretion and explains when it is likely to be used.

If your home is taken into account, its value will be based on the current selling price, less any debts (such as a mortgage) charged on it, and less 10% in recognition of the expenses that would be incurred in selling it. Its value should be reassessed periodically. The capital value of your home is assessed in this way until it is sold and added to any other capital you have; the local authority may help towards your fees while your home is being sold. Seek advice if you are refused help with funding pending the sale of your home if the local authority has assessed you as needing care in a care home. Once your home is sold, the actual capital realised less any debts and the actual expenses involved in the sale are taken into account (CRAG 6.011a and 6.015).

The local authority can't make you sell your home to pay the assessed charge for your accommodation, other than through the courts. But s.22 HASSASSA 1983 and s.23 for Scotland (see Box K.1, Chapter 29) allow the authority to place a legal charge on the property so that it can recover any outstanding debts when the property is eventually sold; if the property is jointly owned, the local authority is advised to put a caution on it, which has a similar effect (CRAG Annex D(3.5) – this annex does not apply to Scotland). But see Box K.2 for the valuation of jointly owned property.

The value of any other property you own will usually be taken into account as capital.

Deferred payment agreements

Deferred payment agreements are available to people in care homes who do not wish to sell their home (for whatever reason), or who face a delay in selling it, and have:

- less than the upper capital limit in England and Wales and the lower capital limit in Scotland (disregarding the value of their home); *and*
- insufficient income to meet the cost of their placement.

The scheme allows the local authority to enter into a written agreement with the resident whereby:

- the local authority places a legal charge on the resident's property, or in Scotland has a standard security granted in the agreement;
- the local authority contracts to pay the full fees of the placement to the home;
- the resident is assessed to pay a weekly charge to the authority based on their weekly income (less the PEA); *and*
- payment by the resident of the balance of the weekly cost of the placement is deferred until the resident dies or the property is sold.

Local authorities have discretion as to whether to enter into an agreement in individual cases.

Guidance to local authorities about operating the scheme is set out in LAC (2001)25 (see Box K.1). It says that caution should be exercised where there is an outstanding mortgage on the property or the amount of the deferred payment is very high. If the local authority refuses to enter into an agreement it should put the refusal in writing. You should use the complaints procedure if you wish to challenge the decision (see Chapter 25(7)).

Further guidance (LAC (2002)15) (England only) was issued in October 2002 as a number of local authorities had only made limited use of the power to make deferred payments. A draft model legal agreement for creating a legal charge for deferred payment agreements has been revised and is available on the CRAG website (www.dh.gov.uk/policyandguidance/organisationpolicy/financeandplanning/residentialcare/fs/en). In Scotland, guidance is contained in Circular No. 13/2004 (available at www.show.scot.nhs.uk/sehd/ccd.asp). In Wales, guidance is contained in NAFWC 21/2003 (available at www.wales.gov.uk/subisocialpolicy/content/circulars/crag/crag16-e.pdf).

Points to note:

- ❑ Deferred payments should not be used if the value of your home should be disregarded under the Assessment of Resources Regulations (see Box K.2).
- ❑ Residents should be given full information about the scheme and advised to seek independent financial advice before entering an agreement.
- ❑ If you enter into an agreement you may have to pay for land registry searches and other legal expenses relating to placing a legal charge on your property.
- ❑ Local authorities can charge interest on the debt from 56 days after your death or after you terminate the agreement.
- ❑ Local authorities can still use s.22 HASSASSA 1983 to place a legal charge (charging order in Scotland) on your property. However, according to the guidance in LAC(2002)15, this provision should only be used where residents are unwilling to pay their assessed contribution and a debt arises (para 7.019 CRAG). If the local authority uses its ordinary debt recovery powers to put a charge on your property, s.24 HASSASSA places a duty on the authority to charge reasonable interest on the sum owed after the day of death. Before then the authority cannot charge you interest.
- ❑ In certain situations you can change from being subject to the provisions of s.22 HASSASSA 1983 to having a deferred payment agreement.

- ❑ Local authorities have the discretion to make allowances for ongoing expenses relating to the property but this may increase the debt repayable when the property is sold.
- ❑ If you enter a deferred payment agreement you should note the following effects on your benefit entitlement:
- ■ if you are under 60, you will not be entitled to income support (IS) while the property is not up for sale if your interest in the property is worth more than £16,000. If you are aged 60 or over it is also unlikely that you will be entitled to pension credit (PC) if your house is not up for sale, as the tariff income applied on capital above £10,000 is likely to mean that your income will exceed your appropriate minimum guarantee. This means the total debt re-payable to the local authority at the end will be greater. However, for those whose property is at the lower end of the market it is worth checking to see if you could still get the guarantee credit of PC or if it affects your PC savings credit;
- ■ you will retain your entitlement to AA or the DLA care component during a deferred payment agreement because you will be treated as a self-funder as long as it is clear you will eventually pay back the local authority in full. This is the case even if you get IS/PC with the severe disability premium (or PC equivalent) during this period. In Scotland this will not apply if you are 65 or over and receiving free personal care (see Chapter 30(2)).

It is important to ensure that you receive all the benefits you are entitled to during the period of the deferred payment agreement, as this will help reduce the debt to the local authority.

Deprivation of capital

If you have given away any assets, such as your former home, or sold them for less than they are worth in order to avoid or lessen the charge, the local authority may take their value into account in the charging assessment (see Box K.2 for more details).

7. Meeting the costs of your own home

If you are a 'temporary resident' (see Box K.2), the local authority can disregard payments you are making towards *'any housing costs... including any fuel charges, which are included in the rent of a dwelling to which (you) intend to return... to the extent that the local authority considers it reasonable in the circumstances to do so'* (Sch 3 para 27 AOR).

CRAG gives a list of examples including service charges, insurance premiums, water rates, standard charges for fuel and any rent or mortgage payments not covered by housing benefit (HB), income support (IS), income-based jobseeker's allowance (JSA), pension credit (PC) or Supporting People payments (CRAG para 3.011 and para 3.012).

If no one is left living in your home and you have entered a care home for a short period, see Chapter 7(6); Chapter 8 covers the council tax. See also Chapter 30(3 and 4).

After 52 weeks, or 13 weeks in the case of a trial period, and as soon as it is clear that your stay in the home is permanent, you will be excluded from HB, IS/JSA and PC housing costs. Yet your liability to pay rent and/or a mortgage in respect of your former home continues until you have terminated your tenancy or sold your home. In this case, you may be able to ask your local authority to vary your personal expenses allowance to help you meet these ongoing costs now you are a permanent resident. If you have given notice on your tenancy in the community, you will be able to continue to claim HB for up to 4 weeks (see Chapter 30(3)).

If your former home is vacant, and you are a permanent resident you should not have to pay council tax.

If your partner, children or relatives continue to live in your home, the help they can receive for their housing costs depends on their circumstances. If they are paying the housing costs, even though you are the person liable for them, they can claim HB, IS or PC housing costs instead of you.

8. What happens if you move out?

When you move out of a care home, you will be entitled to social security benefits in the usual way.

If you are entitled to income support, income-based jobseeker's allowance or pension credit once you move from a care home into unfurnished or partly furnished accommodation, you may get a social fund community care grant (see Chapter 10).

Your local social services department will be able to advise you on local authority benefits and services that are available in your area (see Chapters 25 and 27 for details).

If you go away from your care home on a temporary basis, your local authority can use its discretion to vary the personal expenses allowance to enable you to have more money while away. You may also be able to claim disability living allowance care component or attendance allowance for periods away from the care home. Chapter 30 covers the effect on benefits of stays in, and absences from, care homes.

L Hospital

This section of the Handbook looks at:

32 Going into hospital

1. What should you do beforehand?

Stays in hospital can affect benefits. Chapter 33 provides details. Three of the principle disability benefits – attendance allowance (AA), disability living allowance (DLA) and carer's allowance (CA) – can be stopped after a just a few weeks in hospital (see Chapter 33(6)); so can child benefit. In turn, this can affect your entitlement to income support, housing benefit (HB), council tax benefit (CTB) and pension credit (see Box L.1). Consequently, you should let the DWP know if you or a dependant are admitted to hospital. If you get CA, you must tell the DWP if the person you are looking after is admitted. If you get HB or CTB, and a spell in hospital results in AA, DLA, CA or child benefit being stopped, you also need to tell the local authority.

Write to the office(s) dealing with your benefits to let them know the date you expect to be admitted to hospital and how long you are likely to stay. You should still report your actual admission or tell the office(s) if it is cancelled or postponed. It is sensible to do this beforehand, but do not worry if you have been unable to. Do it as soon as you can.

Medical certificates – If you need sick notes to get benefit when in hospital, ask the sister or charge nurse for one.

Hospital or similar institution? – Benefits are affected in the same way by a stay in a 'similar institution' to a hospital. This is not defined in legislation, although you must receive inpatient medical treatment or professional nursing care in the home under specified NHS legislation. For example, if your stay in a care home is arranged and paid for by the health authority, this will count. You are not considered to be staying in a hospital or similar institution if the only contribution from the NHS is towards nursing care under the Health and Social Care Act 2001 in England and Wales or the Community Care and Health (Scotland) Act in Scotland.

Reg 2(2), SS (Hospital In-Patients) Regulations; White v CAO, TLR 2.8.93; Botchett v CAO, TLR 8.5.96 (discussed in footnotes to reg 21 IS (General) Regs in Volume II, Social Security Legislation 2004 – see Box R.9); CDLA/7980/95

Private patients – If you are a private patient paying the whole cost of accommodation and non-medical services in hospital, you are not deemed to be an inpatient and therefore the normal rules of benefit entitlement apply, not those described in this or the next chapter.

2. Hospital fares

You may be able to get help with fares or other travel expenses for yourself (and for someone who has to go with you if you are incapable of getting to the hospital or treatment centre on your own), if you:

- (or your partner) are getting income support (IS), income-based jobseeker's allowance (JSA) or pension credit (PC) guarantee credit; *or*
- are aged under 16 (or under 19 and in full-time education); *or*
- (or your partner) are getting working tax credit (WTC) and child tax credit (CTC); *or*
- are getting WTC with any disability element; *or*
- are getting CTC but are not eligible for WTC and your gross annual income is below £15,050; *or*
- are covered by the low-income scheme (see Chapter 52(5)). If your income is above the low-income level but would fall below it if you paid the fares, you may still be eligible for help with part of the cost; *or*
- are aged 16 or 17 and supported by a local authority because you have recently left local authority care; *or*
- (or a member of your family) are an asylum seeker who gets support under the National Asylum Support System or a local authority; *or*
- permanently reside in a care home paid for wholly or partly by the local authority; *or*
- are a war disablement pensioner (being treated for your pensionable disability); *or*
- live in the Isles of Scilly or the Scottish Islands and Highlands; *or*
- are a patient at a genito-urinary medicine clinic more than 15 miles from your home (or more than 5 miles if you need to attend weekly); *or*
- are getting NHS treatment abroad.

Parents – If your child has to go into hospital or attend on a regular basis, you may claim help with travel expenses to accompany your child to and from the hospital.

Inpatients sent home on short leave – If you are sent home as part of your treatment, or for the hospital's convenience, your fares are regarded as part of your treatment costs and should be met by the hospital and not under the hospital travel expenses means-tested scheme.

If you are sent home on short leave for any reason, you will get your full benefit entitlement (including disability living allowance and attendance allowance) if you notify the DWP. This is worked out on a daily basis (see Chapter 33(9)).

How to claim the cost of fares

The hospital will refund your fares if you produce proof of your entitlement (eg your benefit award letter or tax credit exemption certificate). If you have already claimed on low-income grounds, show your HC2 certificate (full entitlement) or your HC3 certificate (partial entitlement).

If you haven't yet claimed on low-income grounds, ask the hospital or DWP for form HC5 to claim a refund, and form HC1 to establish your entitlement to full or partial help. Ask the hospital to fill in their part of the HC5, then fill in the rest of the HC5 and the HC1 and send both forms to the address given on the forms. The HC5 must be returned within 3 months of paying your fares.

What travel expenses can be covered?

The law allows help with *'the cost of travelling by the cheapest means of transport available'*. Normally this means the cost of second-class public transport. If public transport is available but you go by car, your fuel costs can be covered up to the amount of the second-class fare. If you are unable to use public transport because of a physical disability or it is not available, and you go by car or taxi, your fuel costs or fares will be covered. You should get agreement from the hospital first. The travel costs of an escort can also be met, if you need to be accompanied for medical reasons.

If you are travelling overseas for NHS treatment you are covered under the same rules, subject to the health authority's agreement to the mode of transport.

Partial help with fares – The amount shown on an HC3 certificate for partial help is the amount you are expected to be able to pay for travel expenses in any one week (from Sunday to the following Saturday). If your actual hospital travel expenses in any particular week covered by that HC3 certificate are higher, the excess is refunded. This helps if you have to travel long distances to hospital – as long as your capital is no more than £8,000 (aged under 60) or £12,250 (if you or your partner are aged 60 or over) or £20,500 (if you live in a care home). Your income could be well above your requirements, yet it would still be worthwhile claiming help. For example, if your excess income figure shown on the HC3 certificate is £44, but your travel expenses to and from hospital in a particular week are £64, you could have £20 of your expenses refunded.

The 'expenses within one week' rule also helps if you have to make several visits to the same, or to different, hospitals within the same week. Ask the hospital fares office for details of the arrangements for dealing with several visits within the same week.

Visitors' hospital fares – If you are on IS, income-based JSA or the guarantee credit of PC, you may be able to get a community care grant from the social fund to assist you or a member of your family with travel expenses in the UK (including overnight accommodation charges) – see Chapter 10.

War pensioners – If you attend hospital for treatment for your war disablement, you can get a wider range of expenses regardless of your income. Write to the Veterans Agency, Norcoss, Thornton-Cleveleys FY5 3WP.

Other sources of help – Other possible sources of help with travel expenses for patients and visitors include hospital endowment funds, education departments, social services departments, the Family Fund (see Chapter 35(8)) and various charities. For advice about these, contact a hospital social worker or an advice centre. Further information is available on the Department of Health website: www.doh.gov.uk/hospitaltravelcosts.

33 Benefits in hospital

1. What happens to your income support or pension credit?

If you go into hospital, income support (IS) and pension credit can sometimes continue to be paid indefinitely without being reduced. However, if benefits such as disability living allowance, attendance allowance or carer's allowance are withdrawn, this will affect the amount of benefit you receive. See Box L.1.

IS can continue to be paid during a temporary absence abroad for the purpose of receiving NHS hospital treatment (see Chapter 50(4)).

2. What happens to your jobseeker's allowance?

You cannot normally claim jobseeker's allowance (JSA) while you are in hospital because you will not be deemed capable of work or able to satisfy the labour market conditions. However, if you are already receiving JSA when you go into hospital, you can be treated as being capable of, available for, and actively seeking work for up to 2 weeks. You can do this twice within any 12 months of the same jobseeking period (see Chapter 17(8)). When your JSA stops, you should claim incapacity benefit and income support.

JSA can continue to be paid during a temporary absence abroad for the purpose of receiving NHS hospital treatment (see Chapter 50(6)).

3. What happens to your housing benefit and council tax benefit?

If you get housing benefit or council tax benefit, the applicable amount may change during a spell in hospital as a consequence of the withdrawal of benefits such as disability living allowance, attendance allowance or carer's allowance. The rules are similar to the income support/pension credit rules (see Box L.1).

4. What about tax credits?

Child tax credit and working tax credit (WTC) are not automatically affected by a stay in hospital. However, if you cease to be treated as employed because of a stay in hospital you would no longer qualify for WTC, and if your other income changes this may affect the level of your award. Inform the Inland Revenue of your change of circumstances to avoid unnecessary underpayment or overpayment (see Chapter 19(5)).

5. What about SSP and SMP?

Going into hospital does not affect entitlement to statutory sick pay (SSP) or statutory maternity pay (SMP).

6. What happens to non-means-tested benefits?

Most non-means-tested benefits continue to be paid indefinitely if you entered hospital after April 2005. If you went into hospital before April 2005 your benefits will be 'downrated' once you have been in hospital for 52 weeks (see 7).

Exceptions apply, however, to attendance allowance (AA), disability living allowance (DLA) and carer's allowance (CA), as well as to child benefit, guardian's allowance and any child dependant's addition that may still be payable with other benefits. They are treated in the following way.

During the first 4 weeks

There is normally no change, except in the following cases.

If you are discharged from hospital but re-admitted within 28 days, the periods in hospital are added together to calculate the date from which your benefit is to be adjusted. If you have come from a local authority owned or managed care home, you may find your benefit reduced straight away because of the 28-day linking rule (see Box L.1).

War disablement pension can often be increased when you go into hospital, if the treatment is for the war injury. See Veterans Agency Leaflet 2.

Jobseeker's allowance can be paid for up to 2 weeks (see 2).

After 4 weeks

AA and DLA for adults stop. See below if you have a Motability agreement.

CA will stop if the person you are caring for has been in hospital for 4 weeks and their AA or DLA care component has stopped.

AA or DLA care component and your carer's CA will stop before the 4 weeks is up if you had been in hospital or any other special accommodation in the 28 days before you were admitted to hospital. DLA mobility component will stop before the end of 4 weeks only if you'd been in hospital in the 28 days before this hospital stay.

If you claim DLA or AA when you are already in hospital, it cannot be paid until you leave.

See Chapter 20(7) and (8) for more on DLA.

Constant attendance allowance (payable in the War

L.1 What happens to income support, council tax benefit, housing benefit and pension credit?

Though these benefits may continue to be paid throughout the period of your stay in hospital, they can be reduced depending on your circumstances.

Stage 1 – from the 1st day

There is normally no cut in your income support (IS), housing benefit (HB) or council tax benefit (CTB) applicable amounts or your pension credit (PC) appropriate amount during your first 4 weeks in hospital. However, the reduction could come sooner if you are affected by the 28-day linking rule.

The 28-day linking rule – If you are discharged from hospital but are re-admitted within 28 days, the periods in hospital are added together to calculate the date from which your benefit is to be adjusted.

To count the days in between hospital stays, start with the day after you leave hospital. The day you leave counts as a day in hospital. End with the day you return – this counts as a day at home.

The linking rule does not apply to the questions of whether or not you can still be treated as occupying your home, or whether or not you still count as members of the same household.

A day at home means the rules on these matters have to be applied afresh once you return to hospital.

Extra benefit – IS does not increase if either you or your partner go into lodgings to be near the member of your family who is in hospital. Instead, you may have to look to the social fund for help (see Chapter 10). You may qualify for the severe disability premium temporarily while your carer or another non-dependant is in hospital. See Chapter 4(7).

Stage 2 – from the 29th day

After 4 weeks in hospital, attendance allowance (AA), disability living allowance (DLA) care component and (in most cases) DLA mobility component for an adult are withdrawn. If you had been in hospital (or for AA or the care component, other special accommodation) during the 28 days before your current spell in hospital, these periods will be added together and benefit will be withdrawn after the combined total of 4 weeks in hospital (see Chapter 20(7) and (8)).

Once AA or DLA care component stops, the severe disability premium (or equivalent PC addition) is withdrawn. However, if you have a partner and both of you had been getting AA or DLA care component, you keep the premium even after the AA or DLA care component stops, but at the single rate of £45.50.

A carer premium (or equivalent PC addition) may be withdrawn at stages 2, 3 or 4 depending on your situation. In general, it is withdrawn 8 weeks after carer's allowance (CA) goes, or, if your CA is overlapped by another benefit, after AA or DLA care component stops (see Chapter 23(10)).

If you are entitled to an amount of IS only because of the inclusion of a severe disability premium in your applicable amount, the withdrawal of this payment at the 4-week stage means the loss of IS. The same applies in the case of the withdrawal of an addition for a severely disabled person in the guarantee credit of PC. In both cases you would have to make a fresh claim for HB and CTB. Apply directly to your local authority.

Stage 3 – from the 85th day

After 12 weeks in hospital, there is a change if the patient is a dependent child. DLA for the child is withdrawn. If you are still receiving an allowance for them in your IS, this is cut to £16.40. There is no change to the HB/CTB allowance for that child. A disabled child premium or enhanced disability premium for a child based on DLA is not withdrawn until the child ceases to count as a dependant.

Stage 4 – after 52 weeks

If you go into hospital in April 2005 or later you can continue to receive state pension, IS, PC, incapacity benefit (IB) and severe disablement allowance for the entire duration of your stay in hospital. This is because of new rules announced in the 2005 Budget, which will come into effect from April 2006. The position is less clear with regard to HB and CTB.

If you went into hospital before April 2005 your benefits will be affected after 52 weeks in hospital. IS, PC, HB and CTB are generally downrated. At the same time, non-means-tested benefits such as state pension, IB and widows' and bereavement benefits are also downrated. You could find that as a consequence you may now actually become entitled to IS or PC if you weren't before, or that they will have to be recalculated in your favour.

IS/HB/CTB – for those who entered hospital prior to April 2005

Single claimant – Your IS personal allowance is cut to £16.40 a week. All premiums are withdrawn.

Lone parent – Your IS personal allowance is cut to £20.50. If you have retained entitlement to them, you will still qualify for any allowances for dependent children, the family premium, disabled child premiums and enhanced disability premiums for children. All other premiums are withdrawn.

Couples – If you are one of a couple, and you or your partner have been in hospital for over 52 weeks, you will be treated as separate claimants. This may have happened sooner if it had become clear that you or your partner would not be able to return home or would be in hospital for substantially longer than 52 weeks.

Once you are treated as separate claimants, the patient's IS personal allowance will be cut to £16.49. The partner at home can then qualify for benefit in the normal way, but as a single claimant or lone parent.

Housing costs – Once you have been away from your own home continuously for 52 weeks, you can no longer be treated as occupying it as your home. IS housing costs will stop if you count as a single claimant. Your HB entitlement will also stop.

Child – Once a child has been in hospital for 52 weeks you continue to have any £16.40 allowance included in your IS assessment for as long as you keep visiting the child. But the child will be excluded from the HB assessment.

Treatment abroad – Special rules apply for patients receiving NHS hospital treatment abroad (see Chapter 50(4)).

Pension credit

The guarantee credit of PC is downrated in a similar fashion to IS. The savings credit element is not itself downrated as such, but the amount may still change once the additions in the appropriate amount of the guarantee credit are withdrawn or when you are no longer treated as a couple.

Pensions and Industrial Injuries schemes) and war pensioners' severe disablement occupational allowance stop.

Motability – If you have a Motability agreement in force when you go into hospital, DLA mobility component continues to be paid to Motability for the full term of the agreement. Any balance that would otherwise be paid to you stops after 28 days.

You cannot begin or renew a Motability agreement while you are in hospital. An exception allows the renewal of agreements under the Motability wheelchair scheme provided the new agreement is entered into the day after the old one ends. Note that the mobility component will be paid if you renew a Motability agreement during a temporary absence from hospital.

After 12 weeks

Child in hospital – Child benefit or guardian's allowance are paid for the first 12 weeks if your child or a child you care for goes into hospital. After 12 weeks you can continue to get these benefits for a child in hospital only if you are regularly spending money on the child's behalf (eg on clothing, pocket money, magazines). If you continue to get child benefit you will continue to get any child dependant's addition that may still be payable with other benefits (such as incapacity benefit), otherwise this will also end.

DLA care component and mobility component for a child under 16 stop after 12 weeks in hospital. DLA care component may stop before the 12 weeks is up if your child had been in hospital or any other special accommodation in the 28 days before this hospital stay. DLA mobility component will stop before the end of 12 weeks only if your child had been in hospital in the 28 days before this hospital stay. See Chapter 20(7) and (8) for more details. If there is a Motability agreement in force, the mobility component continues to be paid to Motability (see above).

If you or your partner are in hospital – Child benefit normally continues to be paid.

CA stops after the carer has been in hospital for 12 weeks (but it may stop sooner – see Chapter 23(10)).

7. What happens after one year?

New rules announced in the March 2005 Budget will have a substantial effect on the benefits of long-stay hospital patients. Previously, most benefits would be reduced or downrated after a period of 52 weeks in hospital. As a consequence of the new rules, if you enter hospital in April 2005 or after, you will continue to receive your full entitlement to state pension, incapacity benefit (IB) and severe disablement allowance (SDA) for an indefinite period (as long as you continue to satisfy the other conditions of entitlement to these benefits). Income support (IS) can also be paid for an indefinite period (again, as long as the other conditions of entitlement are met), though the rate may be affected by the withdrawal of benefits such as disability living allowance (see Box L.1).

It is expected that the new rules will also provide for pension credit (PC), industrial injuries' unemployability supplement, widows' and bereavement benefits to continue to be paid for indefinite periods in hospital.

The position is less clear with regard to housing benefit (HB) and council tax benefit (CTB).

What if you went into hospital before April 2005?

After you have been in hospital for 52 weeks any state pension, IB, SDA, industrial injuries' unemployability supplement, widows' and bereavement benefits you receive will be reduced to a flat rate of £16.40 a week. The reduction cannot apply to any day that does not count as a day in hospital; you will be entitled to full pro rata benefit for days of absence on leave (see 9 below). If you have a dependent wife or husband in hospital, the weekly rate of state pension, IB or SDA paid to you for them is reduced to £16.40 a week. The way that IS and PC are treated is covered in Box L.1.

Who cannot get the £16.40 allowance? – You can be paid less than £16.40, or nothing at all, if you have been in hospital for more than 52 weeks *and*:

- you cannot act for yourself and your benefit is paid to the hospital authorities (either as the appointee or on the appointee's request); *and*
- the medical officer in charge of you certifies that you are unable to use part or all of the allowance, which is intended to provide for personal comfort or enjoyment. The medical officer must state the amount (if any) that can be used by you or on your behalf. The medical officer has absolute discretion over how much money you get or whether you get any at all, either directly or in the form of comforts.

A similar rule applies to IS, with the proviso that the decision maker can award benefit if they consider it reasonable *'having regard to the views of the hospital staff and the patient's relatives if available as to the amount necessary for [the patient's] personal use'*.

Housing costs – Once you have been in hospital for 52 weeks, if you have no dependants living in your home, you can no longer receive IS or PC housing costs. Nor can you get HB or CTB. The maximum period of absence in one stretch during which IS or PC housing costs and HB/CTB can be paid is 52 weeks. If you have dependants or other people living in your home, their right to benefit depends on their own circumstances. If you are one of a couple and have been in hospital for 52 weeks, you and your partner are treated as separate claimants.

8. What extra help can you get?

When your income is reduced during a spell in hospital, you may become eligible for income support (see Box L.1 and Chapter 3), pension credit (see Chapter 41), housing benefit and/or council tax benefit (see Box L.1 and Chapter 7).

9. What about when you leave hospital?

Whether or not any benefit has been changed or stopped while you or a dependant have been in hospital, make sure you inform your local Jobcentre Plus office and also the local authority if you are getting housing benefit or council tax benefit, as soon as you know the date you or your dependant are coming home. You should still report your actual date of discharge, or tell the appropriate office if it is cancelled or postponed.

Temporary absence from hospital

If you or a dependant spend a few days at home – perhaps for a trial run, or if you are in and out of hospital on a regular pattern – tell your local Jobcentre Plus office and ask them to pay the full amount of benefit for the days at home (see below for what counts as a day at home). Get a note from the hospital to say how many days you have at home.

Can your carer get carer's allowance (CA)? – If you go home regularly each weekend and receive attendance allowance (AA) or disability living allowance (DLA) care component (at the middle or highest rate), your carer might

L.2 For more information

The following leaflets are free:

- GL 12 *Going into Hospital?* and
- HC 11 *Help With Health Costs*, both available from local DWP offices; *and*
- VA Leaflet 2 *Notes for people getting a War Pension living in the United Kingdom*, from your local War Pensioners' Welfare Office.

A B C D E F G H I J K L M N O P Q R S

qualify for the full rate of CA. This is because CA is a weekly benefit and is never paid on a daily basis. See Chapter 23(2) to check whether your carer can meet the 35 hours a week caring test.

DLA and AA – These are adjusted on a daily basis where you are expected to return to hospital within 28 days. AA and DLA care component (but not mobility component) are also adjusted on a daily basis where you are expected to return to a care home within 28 days (see below).

If you are not expected to return to hospital within the appropriate time limit, and when you are finally discharged from hospital, full benefit resumes from the first pay day.

Are you expected to return within 28 days? – Payment at a daily rate depends on what is expected on the day you are discharged from hospital. What happens after you leave does not affect what was originally expected.

The daily rate provisions do not apply if, on the day of discharge, you were not expected to return to hospital within 28 days. Nor can they apply even if you return to hospital within that period. If you have been out of hospital for 28 days or less, your current spell in hospital links with the previous spell. When you go back to hospital you'll have the remainder of your 4 weeks, or 12 weeks (for DLA for a child), at full-rate benefit. If your benefit had been adjusted (downrated or withdrawn) during the previous spell in hospital, it will be adjusted again. However, as the daily rate provisions do not apply, your benefit can be adjusted only from the first pay day after the day you were readmitted to hospital. If you have had 29 or more days out of hospital (or out of other special accommodation for AA and DLA care component) the separate spells are not linked together. So your benefit won't be adjusted until the pay day after 4 weeks, or after 12 weeks (for DLA for a child).

The daily rate provisions cease to apply once you have been out of hospital for 28 days, or for AA and DLA care component if you've been out of hospital or other special accommodation for 28 days.

What days can you claim for?

You can get full benefit paid on a daily basis for each whole day spent out of hospital. If you stay in hospital as an inpatient throughout a complete 24-hour period, you count for benefit purposes as being in hospital on that day unless you are paying a charge which is designed to cover the whole cost of your accommodation or non-treatment services.

The day you leave or return to hospital – For DLA and AA, both the day you are admitted or return to hospital and the day you are discharged or leave hospital count as days out of hospital. You can be paid for both of those days as well as whole days out of hospital.

For all other benefits:

- the day you are admitted is treated as a day *out* of hospital;
- the day you are discharged is treated as a day *in* hospital.

Absence during the day – The regulations don't state whether or not you count as being in hospital if you are away for part of the day, and case law is conflicting. You cannot be paid DLA or AA for days when you are an inpatient for part of the day even if you are away from hospital for some of the day (CDLA/11099/95). For other benefits, the position is not so clear. One decision, CS/249/89, held that a person could only be regarded as an inpatient if they were in hospital 24 hours a day. So if you return to sleep at night in hospital but are absent in the daytime, you might be entitled to full benefit for that day. However, other decisions have held otherwise. A tribunal is entitled to follow whichever decision it prefers.

There are a number of relevant decisions including CSS/617/97, R(IS)8/96, CIS/192/91, R(S)4/84, R(S)1/66, R(S)8/51, R(S)9/52.

What if you have missed out on benefit?

For most benefits, you have 3 months in which to claim. However, for IS you must have special reasons if there is any delay in your claim (eg you didn't have help to make your claim earlier – see Chapter 57(3)) otherwise you will only be paid from the day you claim. A claim for DLA or AA cannot be backdated.

If you've been getting a reduced rate of any benefit while in hospital, you should tell your local Jobcentre Plus office that you have been out of hospital. Similarly, if you are entitled to DLA or AA, contact the Disability Benefits Unit in Blackpool (see inside back cover) and tell them when and for how long you were out of hospital so that you can be paid for the days at home. It is important to notify the right office within one month of coming out of hospital to ensure you are paid the full rates for each day at home – any later and you will have to show you have special reasons for the delay in telling them of your change in circumstances (see Chapter 58(5)).

Permanently out of hospital

In general, you should get the benefit you were getting before you went to hospital at the normal rate. If you go from hospital into a care home, see Chapter 30.

If you did not draw any benefit before you went into hospital and have no entitlement to contributory benefits, look at the chapters on income support and pension credit, and if you are aged under 20, incapacity benefit. Once you leave hospital, all the normal rules for these benefits will apply to you. Chapter 10 covers the discretionary social fund. If you have been in hospital for an extended period you may get a community care grant to help establish yourself in the community.

10. Discharged before you're ready?

If acute nursing care in hospital is no longer essential for you, the hospital will clearly wish to discharge you. It may be impossible for you to return home without support services in place. In some cases you may even count as homeless. Get advice. Before being discharged, your care needs should have been assessed. However, don't agree to a discharge unless you are happy with the arrangements for continuing care and support as set out in your care plan (see Chapter 25(3)). Don't agree to move to a care home unless you are absolutely clear about how, and for how long, the full cost will be met. See Chapters 25 to 31 for more details about care at home and in care homes.

This section of the Handbook looks at:

Children and young people

M

A B C D E F G H I J K L M N O P Q R S

34 Maternity and parental rights

1. Help with health costs

You are entitled to free prescriptions and dental treatment if you are pregnant or have had a baby in the previous 12 months and you have a maternity exemption certificate. Ask your doctor, midwife or health visitor for an FW8 application form on which to apply. If you or your partner get income support (IS), income-based jobseeker's allowance (JSA) or pension credit (guarantee credit), you are entitled to milk tokens for yourself as part of your claim. Inform your local Jobcentre Plus office that you are pregnant.

You qualify for free vitamins through your antenatal clinic, or on prescription if necessary, while you are pregnant or breastfeeding. If you are on IS or income-based JSA you should continue to get milk tokens and vitamins for your child until they are 5 (unless you stop claiming the benefits). If you are getting child tax credit you will be able to get milk tokens and vitamins if you do not work more than 16 hours a week and your family's gross annual income is less than £13,910.

Anyone who attends a maternity, child healthcare or baby clinic can buy dried milk for their baby at a reduced price through the clinic.

2. Maternity leave

Any woman working while she is pregnant is entitled to 26 weeks 'ordinary maternity leave' (OML). Women who have worked for the same employer for at least 26 weeks by the 15th week before the baby is due qualify for 26 weeks 'additional maternity leave' from the end of OML. For both types of leave you must fulfil strict notification requirements, including letting your employer know you are pregnant and telling them, by the end of the 15th week before your baby is due, when you want to take your maternity leave.

Parental leave – Parents who have worked for one year are entitled to 13 weeks' parental leave, which can be taken up until the child's 5th birthday. If your child gets disability living allowance you can take 18 weeks' leave up until their 18th birthday. See Box M.1 for more information.

Time off for antenatal care – Every pregnant employee is entitled to time off with pay to keep antenatal appointments made on the advice of a doctor, midwife or health visitor.

3. Statutory maternity pay

You may be able to get statutory maternity pay (SMP) when you stop work to have your baby. You will not have to repay it if you do not return to work. You qualify if:

- you have worked for the same employer for at least 26 weeks into the 15th week (the 'qualifying week') before the week the baby is due – ie when you are 26 weeks pregnant (a 'week' starts on Sunday and runs to the end of the following Saturday); *and*
- you are still in your job in the qualifying week (it doesn't matter if you are off work sick or on holiday); *and*
- your average earnings are at least £82 a week; *and*
- you give your employer the right notice (see below).

How much do you get?

SMP is paid by your employer for up to a maximum of 26 weeks. For the first 6 weeks you get 90% of your average weekly earnings (with no upper limit). The average is calculated from your gross earnings in the 8 weeks, if weekly paid, or 2 months, if monthly paid, before the end of the 15th week before the baby is due. If a pay rise is awarded for the whole or any part of this period, your employer must recalculate your normal weekly earnings to include the pay rise and pay arrears of SMP to you.

ECJ Alabaster and Woolwich plc, Secretary of State for Social Security (C-147/02).

The remaining 20 weeks are paid at the standard rate of £106, or 90% of your average weekly earnings if this calculation results in a figure that is less than £106.

You may have to pay tax and national insurance contributions out of your SMP.

When is it paid?

SMP can start from the 11th week before the baby is due. You decide when you stop work and start your maternity pay period. You can work up until the baby's birth. If your baby is born early (ie prior to the 11th week before it is due), your SMP will start the day after the birth. See 8 below if you are off work with a pregnancy-related illness.

You should write to your employer at least 28 days before you plan to stop work, asking for SMP. If you have not already done so, send them your maternity certificate (form MAT B1), which your doctor or midwife will give you when you are about 21 weeks pregnant. Tell your employer as soon as is reasonably practicable if your baby is born early.

If you are not eligible for SMP, your employer should give you form SMP1 within 7 days. You may be eligible for maternity allowance (see 4 below).

SMP works in a similar way to statutory sick pay (see Chapter 13), so you have the right to ask your employer for a written statement about your SMP position. If you disagree, you can refer your case to the Inland Revenue Statutory Payments Team (tel. 0115 974 0000) for a decision. If the Inland Revenue decides against you, you can appeal to the Tax Commissioners. Your employer can also appeal.

See Box M.1 for where to get more information on SMP.

4. Maternity allowance

If you cannot get statutory maternity pay, you may qualify for tax-free maternity allowance (MA).

To qualify, you must have worked, either employed or self-employed, in at least 26 of the 66 weeks before the week in which the baby is due, and earned an average of at least £30 a week for 13 of these weeks. MA is £106 a week, or 90% of your average weekly earnings if they total less than £106.

Add together all your earnings received in any 13 of the 66 weeks before your baby is due, then divide by 13 to work out your average weekly wage. Earnings in different jobs and from a mixture of employed and self-employed work can be added together. If you have paid 13 Class 2 national insurance contributions you will be treated as having earnings sufficient to result in the payment of MA at £106 a week. You will be treated as having earnings of £30 for any week in which you are covered by a certificate of small earnings exception.

When is it paid?
MA is paid for up to 26 weeks and can start from 11 weeks before the expected week of childbirth. If you are employed or self-employed, you may delay the start of your MA up until the baby's birth (but see 8 below if you are off work with a pregnancy-related illness). However, if you are not employed, your MA will start from the 11th week before the expected week of childbirth.

How do you claim?
Fill in form MA1 and send it to your local Jobcentre Plus office together with your maternity certificate (MAT B1) and form SMP1 if you have it. You can get MA1 from the DWP, your antenatal clinic, or the DWP website: www.dwp.gov.uk/advisers/claimforms/ma1.pdf. Send in form MA1 as soon as you can after you are 26 weeks pregnant. Don't delay because you are waiting for MAT B1 or SMP1. You can send them later. If you claim more than 3 months after the start of your MA period you may lose money. If you are not entitled to MA, the DWP should check if you can get incapacity benefit instead (see 8).

5. Statutory paternity leave

Statutory paternity leave is one or 2 weeks leave from work, to be taken within 56 days of the birth or of the due date, if the baby is born early, for fathers or partners of the mother (including same-sex partners) to support the mother or care for the baby. You can get statutory paternity leave if you have worked for the same employer for at least 26 weeks by the 15th week before the baby is due and are still employed when the baby is born. It is important to give the correct notice for leave – you should tell your employer you plan to take paternity leave by the end of the 15th week before the week your baby is due, or if this isn't possible, as soon as reasonably practicable. You can use form SC3 to notify your employer.

M.1 For more information

Pregnancy and parenthood
Useful guides include:

- *Maternity Leave (PL507), Paternity Leave and Pay (PL514), Adoptive Parents (PL515), Parental Leave (PL509 Rev 1)* in English, Welsh and other languages including Arabic, Urdu, Vietnamese, Greek and Somali from the Department of Trade and Industry website: www.dti.gov.uk/workingparents.
- *Babies and Children* (BC1) from the DWP.
- *E15 and E15 supplement – Pay and time off for parents* from the Inland Revenue.

The Maternity Alliance can advise on benefits, employment rights and practical support from social services and health services (see Address List).

Disabled parents can get information from Disability, Pregnancy and Parenthood International and support from the Disabled Parents Network (see Address List).

Education
Special Education Handbook – £12 (plus £2 p&p) from the Advisory Centre for Education (ACE), 1c Aberdeen Studios, 22 Highbury Grove, London N5 2DQ. For advice on special educational needs, ring the free ACE helpline: 0808 800 5793.
England – *Special Educational Needs: A Guide for Parents,* a free guide to provision in England published by the Department for Education and Skills (also in Braille). Available from DfES Publications, PO Box 5050, Sudbury, Suffolk CO10 6ZQ (0845 602 2260) or from General Teaching Council, Whittington House, 19-30 Alfred Place, London WC1E 7EA (0870 001 0308).
Scotland – For advice and the *Parent's Guide to Special Educational Needs,* contact Enquire: 0845 123 2303.
Wales – *Information for parents and carers of children and young people who may have special educational needs,* a free guide available from the National Assembly Education Department: 029 2082 6078.

6. Statutory paternity pay

You can get statutory paternity pay (SPP) if you have worked for the same employer for at least 26 weeks by the 15th week before the baby is due and have average earnings of at least £82 a week. It is paid by employers for up to 2 weeks at a rate of £106 a week, or 90% of your average earnings if they total less than £106.

You must give your employer at least 28 days (or as soon as reasonably practicable) notice of the date you want your SPP to start. You can use form SC3 to notify your employer.

If you can't get SPP your employer must give you form SPP1 explaining why you don't qualify. You may be able to claim income support during paternity leave (see Box B.1, Chapter 3).

7. Rights for adoptive parents

You have a right to 26 weeks paid 'ordinary' adoption leave with a further 26 weeks unpaid 'additional' adoption leave if you have worked for the same employer for at least 26 weeks by the week in which you are notified of being matched with a child for adoption. A couple adopting jointly can choose who takes adoption leave and who takes paternity leave. Statutory adoption pay (SAP) is at a flat rate of £106, or 90% of your average earnings for 26 weeks (whichever is less). To qualify for SAP you must also have average earnings of at least £82 a week.

Adoptive parents can also get parental leave.

8. Unable to work due to sickness or disability?

If you are employed, you may be able to get statutory sick pay (SSP) – see Chapter 13. If you can't get SSP, you may be able to get incapacity benefit (IB) – see Chapter 14. IB is for people who are unable to work through sickness or disability. For most people, entitlement depends on having paid enough national insurance (NI) contributions.

If you are entitled to SMP or maternity allowance
You can stay on SSP or lower rate short-term IB (this is paid for the first 28 weeks of incapacity) up until the date of the baby's birth, or the date you are due to start your maternity leave. But if you have a pregnancy-related illness in the last 4 weeks before the week the baby is due, your statutory maternity pay (SMP) or maternity allowance (MA) starts automatically.
SMP – Once your SMP begins, any SSP or lower rate short-term IB stops. If you were getting higher rate short-term, or long-term, IB and went onto SMP, you can stay on IB as well. The amount you get is reduced by the amount of SMP you receive, so it could be overlapped completely.
MA – You can claim or continue to receive IB (at any rate) while you are on MA. They overlap, so you are paid whichever is higher. You don't have to pass any tests of incapacity to show you are incapable of work while you are entitled to MA.

The time you spend on MA counts towards working out when you are due to move to the next rate of IB, so you could become entitled to higher rate short-term IB if you were on the lower rate before your MA started.

If you are not entitled to SMP or MA

If you pass the NI contribution conditions (although some people don't need contributions – see Chapter 14), you may be entitled to IB from 6 weeks before the baby is due, up to 2 weeks after the birth. You need your MAT B1 but not medical certificates; nor do you have to pass any incapacity tests.

You may be able to get IB outside of these weeks, but you must usually pass the 'own occupation test' or 'personal capability assessment' to prove you are unable to work, as well as all the usual conditions for benefit (see Chapters 11 and 14). You do not have to pass these tests at any time during your pregnancy if there is a serious risk to you or the baby because of pregnancy unless you stop work, or there would be if you tried to work (see Chapter 11(4)).

9. Sure Start maternity grant

If you get income support, income-based jobseeker's allowance, pension credit, child tax credit paid at a rate which exceeds the family element (see Chapter 19(2)), or working tax credit where there is a disability or severe disability element included in the award, you may qualify for the £500 Sure Start maternity grant from the social fund (see Chapter 9).

10. When the baby is born

Claim child benefit (see Chapter 36).

A new baby may entitle you to child tax credit for the first time. If you are already getting this your entitlement will increase from the date of birth if you notify the Inland Revenue within 3 months. See Chapter 18.

Tell your local Jobcentre Plus office and local authority housing benefit section. A new baby may mean you can get more help, or qualify for the first time for income support, income-based jobseeker's allowance, housing benefit or council tax benefit.

Your baby automatically qualifies for free prescriptions.

You have 6 weeks to register your baby's birth. When you register the birth, the registrar will give you form FP58 (EC58 in Scotland). You need to complete this and send it to your GP so your baby can get an NHS card.

You have 3 months from the date of birth, adoption or parental order (granted following surrogacy) in which to claim a Sure Start maternity grant (see Chapter 9). If you are adopting, your baby must be aged under 12 months at the date of claim. It may be possible to get a grant or loan from the discretionary social fund (see Chapter 10).

35 Disabled children

1. What help can you claim?

If your child is disabled, you may be entitled to benefits or services that are described in other chapters in this Handbook. Your right to some benefits or services will depend only on the effect of your child's disability. Your right to others will depend on your own financial, or other, circumstances. The benefits checklist on pages 4-5 is a quick guide to the help available. In this chapter we highlight some of the specific help for disabled children.

For further information on benefits and services for children with disabilities ring the Contact a Family Helpline (Freephone 0808 808 3555).

From birth

You can register your child with the social services department. You can also apply to your local education authority (LEA) for an assessment of your child's special needs.

If your child is registered as blind you may get:

- a disabled child premium in the assessment of your housing benefit (HB), council tax benefit (CTB) and health benefits and a disabled child element with your child tax credit (CTC);
- a 50% reduction on your TV licence if you transfer the licence into the child's name.

You may be able to get help from the Family Fund with some of the extra costs arising from a child's disability (see 8 below).

If you get income support (IS), income-based jobseeker's allowance (JSA) or pension credit you may be able to get a community care grant from the social fund (see Chapter 10). Often the needs of disabled children are given a high priority.

You may get help with adaptations in the home (see Chapter 28).

You can get free milk tokens if you are an expectant mother or have a child under 5 years old and get IS, income-based JSA or CTC (if you do not work more than 16 hours a week and your family income is below £13,910). This is part of the Welfare Food Scheme, which is soon to be replaced by Healthy Start, which offers fixed face-value vouchers for a range of foods including fresh fruit, vegetables and liquid/infant formula milk.

From age 13 weeks

You can be paid the care component of disability living allowance (DLA) for your baby from when they are 3 months old – claim any time beforehand. See 2 below and Chapter 20. If your baby is terminally ill (Box H.4, Chapter 20 explains the legal definition), they qualify automatically for the highest rate care component and payment can begin as soon as you claim DLA after the birth. If your child has a terminal illness, you may get early access to their Child Trust Fund (see Chapter 36(7)) to buy things they need.

If your baby is awarded DLA, you may get a disabled child premium included in the assessment of your HB, CTB, and health benefits, or a disabled child element included in the assessment of your CTC. If DLA highest rate care component is awarded, an enhanced disability premium (or for CTC, a severely disabled child element) will also be included in the assessment.

If your baby is awarded DLA middle or highest rate care component you may get carer's allowance (see Chapter 23).

From 2 years

You can now be paid or claim:

- vaccine damage payment (see Chapter 47);
- a Blue Badge (see Chapter 22);
- a special educational needs assessment – an LEA in England and Wales has a duty to identify any child who may have special educational needs. You can ask them to assess your child. If they give you a statement of your child's special educational needs, the LEA should consider reviewing this every 6 months. However, it must be reviewed at least annually. In Scotland, there are similar provisions. See Box M.1 for more information.

From 3 years

A disabled child can be paid DLA higher rate mobility component (see 2 below and Chapter 20(18)). Claim from 3 months beforehand. The higher rate mobility component can give access to leasing or purchasing a car through the Motability scheme (see Box H.7, Chapter 22).

You can apply for road tax exemption if your child gets higher rate mobility component (see Chapter 22).

From 5 years

A disabled child can be awarded DLA lower rate mobility

component. Claim from 3 months beforehand. It is often awarded to children with learning disabilities or who are blind or deaf, but any disabled child who needs extra supervision or guidance outdoors on unfamiliar routes may qualify (see Chapter 20(18)).

Free milk stops once a child reaches the age of 5. If your child is not registered at school because of their disability, they can continue to receive free milk until they are 16, although this concession is likely to be scrapped when the Healthy Start scheme is introduced (see above). In Wales free school milk is available to all children at Key Stage 1. In England and Scotland schools are not obliged to provide milk, and practice varies: where schools provide milk they cannot charge parents who are in receipt of IS or income-based JSA.

If you get IS, income-based JSA, CTC (if you do not work more than 16 hours a week and your family income is below £13,910) or support under the Immigration and Asylum Act 1999, you are entitled to free school meals for each child attending school. You may be able to get a discretionary school clothing grant from the LEA.

If your child has to travel more than two miles to school, the travel is free. For a disabled child, you may get help even if travel to school is less than two miles. Also, LEAs have discretion to help meet a parent's travel costs where a child boards in a grant-maintained special school which is some distance from the family home.

If your child gets DLA, you can take any remaining parental leave from work up until their 18th birthday (the maximum parental leave you can take for a disabled child is 18 weeks).

From 8 years
If your child has to travel more than 3 miles to school, travel is free.

From 12 years
If your child has a statement of special educational needs from the LEA, the annual Year 9 review must include a Transition Plan.

From 16 years
At 16, your child can claim social security benefits in their own right (see Chapter 37) and can qualify for the lowest rate of the DLA care component on the basis of the 'cooking test' (see Chapter 20 (9) and (10)). If your child stays on at school or college after 16, they may qualify for an educational maintenance allowance.

2. Disability living allowance for children

Disability living allowance (DLA) provides help towards the extra costs of bringing up a severely disabled child. It is paid on top of almost any other income you may have and gives you access to other kinds of help. There are two parts to DLA:

- **a care component** – for children needing a lot of extra personal care, supervision or watching over because of their disability. This is paid at 3 different rates. It can be paid from the age of 3 months, or from birth for a terminally ill baby;
- **a mobility component** – a higher rate for children aged 3 or over who cannot walk or have severe walking difficulties and a lower rate for children aged 5 or over who can walk but who need extra guidance or supervision on unfamiliar routes outdoors. The higher rate may also be paid to children getting the highest rate care component who are severely mentally impaired with extremely disruptive behaviour and to deaf-blind children. The lower rate mobility component has an extra disability test for children under 16 (see below).

Chapter 20 deals with the main rules for DLA.

DLA care component
This is payable from when your child is 3 months old if they need much more help than a non-disabled child of the same age (or from birth if your baby is terminally ill). Chapter 20 covers the DLA disability tests and other rules. The following issues are specific to children.

The *Disability Handbook* (a DWP guide – see Box R.9 in Chapter 58) gives guidance to decision makers about the care needs of children, both generally and in relation to specific disabilities. It points out that all young babies require extensive care and that mobility inevitably leads to increased supervision needs. Thus, even though your child may have had a specific disability or condition diagnosed, they will not necessarily qualify for DLA care component at that stage. What counts for the care component is the practical effect of that disability in terms of the child's needs for personal care, supervision or watching over.

Extra care or supervision needs – For a child under 16, such requirements must also be *'substantially in excess'* of what is normally required by a child of the same age, or the child must have substantial needs that non-disabled children of the same age would not have. This extra test does not apply to children who are terminally ill.

Such needs might be 'in excess' of the care and supervision required by a non-disabled child because they are more frequent or take longer to attend to, or the child might need a greater quality or degree of attention or supervision. For example, a child who needs to be fed has needs in excess of a non-disabled child of the same age who just needs food cut up, even though both might need attention for the same length of time during meal times. However, the *Disability Handbook* takes a different approach, emphasising the amount of attention given in addition to a normal care routine for a child of that age. It advises that attention differing in kind from that given to a non-disabled child of the same age does not necessarily involve a greater amount of attention. The difference could be important particularly for younger children. If you need to appeal, use Commissioner's decision CA/92/92 for support (see Box R.7, Chapter 58).

When comparing a child's need for supervision, the focus is on the quality or degree of supervision required compared to a non-disabled child. For example, a disabled child might need someone actually watching over them, whereas a non-disabled child of the same age might also need someone around but it would be enough if they were in another room.

The extra test demands a comparison between your child and other non-disabled children of the same age. Children obviously vary greatly so comparison is made with an 'average' child. Your child's needs are 'substantially' greater if they are outside the range of attention or supervision normally required by the 'average' child, even though a particularly needy or difficult child might need the same level of attention or supervision. You might find it useful to compare your child's needs with those of school friends or brothers and sisters at that age.

Under 1s – The guidance in the *Disability Handbook* essentially rests on the incidence of non-standard interventions or actions the child requires because of their disability. For example, all babies require feeding, but if your baby has severe feeding problems or requires feeding by tube into the stomach or vein, they are likely to qualify for the care component.

Babies with disabilities involving or requiring the following types of actions or interventions are also likely to qualify: regular mechanical suction; regular administration of oxygen; tracheotomy; dealing with a gastrostomy, ileostomy, jejunostomy, colostomy, or nephrostomy. Babies are likely to qualify if they have: severe hearing or vision impairment; severe multiple disabilities; frequent losses of consciousness associated with severe fits secondary to asphyxia at birth or to rare metabolic disease; renal failure; cystic fibrosis; asthma; cerebral palsy; or if they are extremely premature.

Under 2s – If your child is not mobile, while that actually reduces their supervision needs, it may increase other needs or lead to other needs at a later stage (eg if you routinely have to carry your one- to 2-year-old from room to room).

Further examples are given in the *Disability Handbook* of children whose care needs may increase from age one. Likely to qualify are:

- children with brittle bones or haemophilia at risk of fractures or haemorrhage from bumps and falls;
- mobile children with hearing or visual problems who cannot respond to a warning shout or see a potential danger;
- children with cerebral palsy with impeded mobility who need their parents to change their position frequently to reduce the risk of postural deformity;
- children with severe learning disabilities who need extra stimulation to maximise their potential, or who eat undesirable substances or mutilate themselves.

Developmental delay may mean a child needs a continued level of attention more appropriate to a younger child. The guidance in the *Disability Handbook* gives a chart of 'normal' development in children up to the age of 6 as a comparison.

The guidance does not provide exhaustive advice. For example, it does not mention the care needs created by severe eczema/ichthyosiform erythroderma and similar skin conditions. These can sometimes involve a substantial amount of extra care – eg frequent bathing, nappy changing, applying preparations and dressings, and comforting a child whose sleep is disturbed.

If your child qualifies for the care component and it seems the condition(s) giving rise to a need for help are likely to continue, the decision maker may well make an award until the 6th birthday to avoid undue stress on parents and enable the child's care needs to be re-assessed after the end of the first year at school. An award for a very severely disabled child with considerable and lasting care needs can be indefinite.

DLA mobility component

Lower rate – The lower rate mobility component can start from age 5. It is for people who can walk but who need someone with them to guide or supervise them most of the time when they are using unfamiliar routes. It is particularly aimed at people with visual impairments or learning disabilities, but others can qualify. For example, a hearing-impaired child may need such guidance or supervision.

Children under 16 must show they need *'substantially more'* guidance or supervision than a child of the same age would require, or show that a child of the same age would not require such guidance or supervision. Although most young children need guidance or supervision in unfamiliar places, what matters is the nature and extent of your child's needs compared with another child of the same age.

For example, if a child lacks awareness of danger from traffic and other outdoor hazards, or could not give their name and address if they got lost, or would become more disorientated or distressed than a child of the same age without a disability, all these might suggest a need for guidance or supervision beyond that normally required. A deaf child might need someone within reach watching out for them because they can't hear warnings or dangers (CDLA/2268/99). A non-disabled child might not need such close supervision.

Higher rate – The higher rate mobility component can start from age 3. It is principally aimed at those who cannot walk or are virtually unable to walk. Deaf-blind children may also qualify. There is no extra test for children to get the higher rate. See Chapter 20(18).

Children with learning disabilities who get the highest rate care component might also qualify if their behaviour is extremely disruptive because of arrested or incomplete brain development (see Chapter 20(21)). However, if they don't get highest rate care component, they might still pass the 'virtually unable to walk' test. Box H.5 in Chapter 20 explains how that test applies to children with learning disabilities.

Some disabled children might qualify for the higher rate at age 3 because of late development (eg in a child with learning disabilities or sensory impairments). They may, however, move down to the lower rate as their walking ability improves but they need extra guidance or supervision.

Refused DLA?

If your child is refused DLA or awarded a lower rate than you expected, you should consider asking for a revision. Even if you are not successful, you will get written reasons for that decision. These reasons may give you a clear picture of why the current claim failed, and may also give you some idea of the type of changes that might lead to entitlement in the future. If your child does not qualify now, they may well qualify at a later stage in childhood. If, however, you feel that your child does qualify now, you should consider lodging an appeal. Revisions and appeals are covered in Chapters 20(25) and 58.

3. Carer's allowance

If your child gets the middle or highest rate of disability living allowance care component, you may get carer's allowance (CA) for looking after them (see Chapter 23). CA is not means tested, but if you are working you must not earn more than £82 a week (after any deductions for certain allowable expenses).

If you are on a low income and entitled to CA (even if it cannot be paid because you receive another benefit), you may get a carer premium included in the assessment of your income support, income-based jobseeker's allowance, housing benefit or council tax benefit (see 4 and Chapter 4(8)), or a carer addition included in your pension credit assessment.

4. Low income benefits

Income support (IS) and income-based jobseeker's allowance (JSA)

You may be entitled to IS if your income is less than your 'applicable amount' (a set amount representing your weekly living needs) and your savings are no more than £8,000. See Chapter 4.

You are eligible for IS if you are under 60 and care for a child who gets the middle or highest rate of disability living allowance (DLA) care component or you are a lone parent with a child under 16 (see Box B.1, Chapter 3). Normally, you cannot claim IS if you work 16 hours or more a week, but this restriction does not apply if you are eligible for IS as a carer. However, your partner must not be working 24 hours a week or more.

If you are not eligible for IS, you may get income-based JSA (see Chapter 17). If you are aged 60 or over you will need to claim pension credit (PC) instead (see Chapter 41).

Carer premium – If you or your partner are entitled to carer's allowance (CA), a carer premium is included in the assessment (see Chapter 4(8)).

Pension credit

If you are aged 60 or over you may be eligible for PC. The assessment of PC includes a carer addition for those entitled to CA (see Chapter 41(3)).

5. Tax credits

Child tax credit (CTC) – is an income-related payment for people responsible for children whether they are in work or out of work. It has replaced the support for children found previously in a range of benefits, including IS and JSA. Parents already getting income support (IS) or jobseeker's allowance (JSA) by April 2004 have continued receiving support for their children through those benefits. However, they will be moved onto CTC at some point after April 2005.

A disabled child element is included in the CTC assessment for each child who is registered as blind or gets disability living allowance (DLA) (see Chapter 18(4)). A severely disabled child element is included on top of the disabled child element for each child who gets DLA highest rate care component. See Chapter 18 for details of how to claim.

Working tax credit (WTC) – provides financial support for people in (relatively) low-paid work. If you have a dependent child you need to be working for 16 or more hours a week. You claim on the same form as CTC. See Chapter 18.

6. Help with housing costs

If you rent your home, you may get housing benefit (HB) to help pay the rent (see Chapter 7), whether or not you are working. You may get council tax benefit (CTB) to help pay the council tax (see Chapter 7(10)). In each case your savings must be no more than £16,000 (unless you receive the guarantee credit of pension credit).

The assessment for HB or CTB will include:

- a disabled child premium for each child who is registered as blind or who gets disability living allowance (DLA) at any rate;
- an enhanced disability premium for each child who gets DLA highest rate care component;
- a carer premium if you or your partner are entitled to carer's allowance.

You may get a reduction in your council tax bill through the Disability Reduction scheme if your child uses a wheelchair indoors or needs an extra room because of their disability (see Chapter 8(8)). There is no test of income and capital.

Income support, income-based jobseeker's allowance and the guarantee credit of pension credit can all include help with mortgage interest payments and interest on a loan used to adapt your home for the special needs of your disabled child (see Chapter 4(12)). If you need adaptations in the home, check first to see if you can get help from social services (Chapter 25) or a disabled facilities grant from your local housing authority (Chapter 28).

7. Child support

If you do not live with the other parent of your child, the Child Support Agency may require you to apply for child support maintenance when you claim income support or income-based jobseeker's allowance. Maintenance is assessed according to a fixed formula but variations may be allowed where there are extra costs arising from a disability or long-term illness. If your child is disabled, it may be possible to top up a maintenance award through the courts. The way maintenance is worked out is currently being reformed. For details on how maintenance payments affect benefits see Chapter 5(8).

8. The Family Fund

The purpose of the Family Fund is to ease the stress on families arising from the day-to-day care of a severely disabled child under 16 by providing grants and information. It is an independent charity financed by the Government.

Do you qualify?

Any family caring at home for a severely disabled child under the age of 16 may apply for help from the Fund. The Fund is discretionary but works within general guidelines agreed with the Department of Health, and your financial circumstances will be taken into account. You cannot get help for a child who is in the care of a local authority.

What kind of help is there?

The Family Fund cannot give help with items that should be available from your health or local authority but it can complement their support. It can help with:

- holidays or leisure activities for the whole family;
- a washing machine or tumble dryer if a child causes extra washing;
- bedding and clothing if there is extra wear and tear;
- transport expenses if the child does not get higher rate disability living allowance (DLA) mobility component but has difficulty getting around;
- driving lessons for the child's main carer;
- play equipment related to the child's special needs.

The Fund will also consider other things related to the care of the child.

Applying to the Family Fund

You can get an application form from the Family Fund, PO Box 50, York YO1 9ZX (0845 130 4542), or apply online: www.familyfundtrust.org.uk.

The Fund may ask one of their visitors to arrange to see you if it is the first time you've applied. The visitor will discuss your application with you in greater detail.

If you wish to appeal against a decision or make a complaint, you can write to the Chief Executive.

36 Child benefit

1. Who gets it?

You can get child benefit if you are responsible for a dependent child and you pass the residence and presence tests (see Chapter 49(2) and (3)). There is no lower age limit for the child when claiming child benefit. It is tax free and does not depend on your income or savings or whether you stay at home with the child. You do not have to be the parent. Child benefit is administered by the Inland Revenue.

A 'dependent child' is a child or young person under the age of 16, or under the age of 19 and in full-time, non-advanced education – ie, more than 12 hours a week at school or college. You cannot count homework, private study, unsupervised study or meal breaks towards the 12 hours and the education can only be up to and including A-level, NVQ level 3 or equivalent. If the young person themselves becomes entitled to benefit, for example, income support (IS) or incapacity benefit (IB) or to a training allowance, you cannot get child benefit for them.

It is intended that from April 2006 child benefit will also be extended to anyone responsible for young people aged 16 to 19 in unwaged work-based learning and 19-year-olds completing certain courses of education or training.

When your child leaves school?

If your child is in paid work for more than 24 hours a week, you cannot get child benefit for them. However, until the terminal date (see below), if the young person stops work or leaves the training course, you have retained your entitlement to the benefit as long as the other conditions are satisfied. This is sometimes known as an 'underlying entitlement' and you can write to the Child Benefit Office in Newcastle (see Address List), telling them about the change and receive the benefit again. Keep a copy of the letter.

If your child has left school or college and is not entitled to no-contribution IB, IS or income-based jobseeker's allowance (JSA), you will continue to be entitled to child benefit for that child until the 'terminal date'. This is the first Monday after the end of the school holiday following the school leaving date (ie the first Monday in January, or the Monday after

Easter Monday, or the first Monday in September).

Once your child reaches the terminal date, you may continue to be entitled to child benefit during what is called the 'child benefit extension period' (CBEP). The CBEP starts from the terminal date for your child. It lasts for 16 or 17 weeks for summer school or college leavers, or 12 weeks for those who leave at Easter or Christmas.

To be entitled to child benefit during the CBEP you:

- must write and ask for benefit to continue; *and*
- must have been entitled to child benefit before the CBEP began because your child was still in full-time education or was in the holiday period up to the terminal date.

Your child must be:

- under 18 and not in (or treated as in) full-time education; *and*
- registered at a Careers Office or Connexions Service for work or training; *and*
- not on a relevant training course, eg Work-Based Learning for Young People, for which a training allowance is paid; *and*
- not working for 24 hours or more a week; *and*
- not entitled to IS, income-based JSA or no-contribution IB.

If your child stops work or leaves training during the CBEP, child benefit is again payable until the end of the CBEP if you and your child pass the other tests.

Other conditions

You can't get child benefit if the child is on a course of education higher than A level or is an employed trainee sponsored by an employer or a Learning and Skills Council.

You may not be able to get child benefit if:

- your child is in local authority care for more than 8 weeks, unless the child regularly stays with you for at least one day each week (midnight to midnight). But you can get child benefit if your child is home for 7 consecutive days plus an extra one week's benefit if they are at home for at least one day at the end of that 7 days;
- you get an allowance as a foster carer to a child placed with you by a local authority or voluntary organisation;
- the child is married.

2. How much do you get?

Child benefit	per week
Only/eldest qualifying child	£17.00
Each other child	£11.40

If you have been getting the old lone parent rate of child benefit since before it was abolished on 6.7.98, you continue to get it (at £17.55 a week) instead of the higher rate for the only/eldest child. You can only apply for the lone parent rate now if you were getting child benefit on 5.7.98 and you:

- apply for the lone parent rate within one month of income support (IS) or jobseeker's allowance (JSA) ending when you begin paid employment. Your IS or JSA must have included the lone parent rate of the family premium or a disability premium or any pensioner premium, provided that since 5.4.98 you have been, and still are, a lone parent; *or*
- are a lone parent getting one of the following benefits on 5.7.98: child dependant's addition with either carer's allowance, state pension, widowed mother's allowance, widowed parent's allowance, widow's allowance or unemployability supplement, or a child's special allowance or child allowance under the old industrial death benefit scheme; and you apply for the lone parent rate within one month of the other benefit stopping.

Does anything affect what you get?

Child benefit is counted in full as income when your resources are calculated for entitlement to housing benefit and council tax benefit, but is ignored when calculating entitlement to IS, income-based JSA, working tax credit and child tax credit.

Child dependants' additions – If you are still entitled to a child dependant's addition with another benefit the addition is reduced to £9.40 if you get the higher £17 rate of child benefit for that child. The extra amount in the lone parent rate also overlaps with child dependants' additions.

3. Who should claim it?

The person responsible for the child must make the claim. This person must be living with the child or be contributing at least the rate of child benefit for the child's support.

People who get child benefit are entitled to home responsibilities protection (see Chapter 43). This can protect the amount of state pension you may get when you retire. So if your national insurance contribution record is affected because you are bringing up children, it is important that you claim child benefit. More than one person can be entitled to child benefit for the same child or young person, but only one person can be paid.

4. How do you claim?

Just after your baby is born you should receive an information pack, sometimes called a Bounty Pack, containing a child benefit claim-pack. If you don't receive one, you can get one from your local Jobcentre Plus office. Ask for a CH2 form.

You will be asked to send the birth or adoption certificate with the form, but do not wait. You can send certificates later. If you live in Great Britain send everything to the Child Benefit Office (GB), PO Box 1, Newcastle upon Tyne NE88 1AA. If you live in Northern Ireland, send everything to the Child Benefit Office (NI), Windsor House, 9-15 Bedford Street, Belfast, BT2 7UW. You can also apply online at: https://esd.dwp.gov.uk/dwp/index.jsp.

Don't delay making your claim. It can only be backdated for 3 months from the date the Inland Revenue receives it.

5. What happens after you claim?

The birth or adoption certificate will be returned to you within a short time and you will be sent a written decision on your claim. Benefit is normally paid 4-weekly in arrears, unless you get the lone parent rate of child benefit or if 4-weekly payments make it difficult to manage your money. You must write to the Inland Revenue to say why you want weekly payments. You have the choice of payment direct into a bank or building society account or into a post office card account (see Chapter 57(5)).

If your claim isn't successful or is stopped later you can appeal against the decision (see Chapter 58).

6. Guardian's allowance

This is a tax-free benefit for anyone looking after children who are effectively orphans. You can get guardian's allowance if you are responsible for a child who is not your birth or adopted child and both parents of the child are dead, or one is dead and the other is:

- unknown with respect to their whereabouts; *or*
- divorced and liable for neither custody or maintenance of the child; *or*
- serving a prison sentence of more than 2 years from the date the other parent dies; *or*
- detained in a hospital under certain sections of the Mental Health Act 1983.

The benefit is worth £12.20 a week and does not depend on your income or savings or whether you have paid national insurance contributions. Claim on form BG1 and send it to the Guardian's Allowance Unit at the Child Benefit Office.

7. Child Trust Fund

The Government has introduced a long-term savings and investment account called the Child Trust Fund (CTF). The aim is to make sure every child has savings at the age of 18, to encourage the habit and teach the benefits of saving, and to help children understand personal finance.

Who is eligible? – Every child born on or after 1.9.02 is eligible for the CTF, provided:

- you receive child benefit for them; *and*
- they live in the UK; *and*
- they are not subject to immigration controls.

The children of Crown servants, including the Armed Forces, posted abroad, qualify because they are treated as being in the UK.

How much does your child get? – You will be sent a voucher for £250 to start the account. Children in families receiving child tax credit, with a household income below £13,910, will receive an additional £250.

A further payment (amount not yet known) will be made when your child is 7.

Other features – Parents can choose the type of account they want for their child. Families and friends can contribute to the CTF up to a maximum of £1,200 each year. The fund and any income or gain is tax free. Money cannot be taken out of the account until the child turns 18. Only the 18-year-old can withdraw the money and they will have full control of how to use it.

37 Young disabled people

1. Becoming a claimant

Once you reach 16, you can claim income maintenance benefits in your own right, even though you may still be at school. Most 16- and 17-year-olds are not eligible for income support (IS), but many severely disabled 16- and 17-year-olds do qualify for it. This chapter gives a brief sketch of the IS rules (see Chapter 3 for full details).

Appointee or agent?

Disability living allowance (DLA) is a personal benefit. Although someone will have acted as your appointee, you were the DLA claimant. At 16, the need for an appointee will be reviewed. If you are able to act for yourself, your parent's appointment to act for you will end. If you are mentally capable of handling your own affairs, but physically unable to manage them, you can nominate someone to act as agent in order to collect benefit payments. Ask the DWP for details.

If you continue to need an appointee, that appointment will be for all social security benefits, rather than restricted to only DLA.

Disability living allowance

DLA may be awarded for any period from 6 months or longer, or it can be awarded indefinitely. It should only stop at your 16th birthday if the decision maker thinks a renewal claim would be necessary to reconsider your care and/or mobility needs.

DLA care component and the lower rate mobility component each have an extra test for children under 16. This ends on your 16th birthday when you no longer have to show that your care, supervision, and/or guidance needs are much greater than those of a non-disabled person.

If you have to make a renewal claim at 16, be careful. Some people have lost benefit even though the disability tests become easier at 16. Don't assume that you will automatically continue to get the same rate as before. Read Chapter 20 again before you fill in the claim-form.

Late claims

If you miss claiming incapacity benefit (IB) or IS from your 16th birthday, you may get some arrears of benefit. To get up to 3 months arrears of IS, you (or your parent if they are the appointee) must have 'special reasons' for a delayed claim (see Chapter 57(3)). A claim for IB can be backdated automatically for 3 months.

2. Incapacity benefit

Incapacity benefit (IB) can be paid from your 16th birthday. Entitlement depends on passing an incapacity for work test called the 'personal capability assessment' or having a condition that exempts you from the test (eg you are exempt if you have severe learning disabilities, are registered blind or get disability living allowance (DLA) highest rate care component). Chapter 11 explains this test.

The amount of benefit goes up in stages over the first year of the claim. For the first 28 weeks IB is paid at a short-term lower rate of £57.65 a week, for the next 24 weeks at a short-term higher rate of £68.20 a week, then from 52 weeks at a long-term rate of £76.45 a week with an extra age addition of £16.05 a week. But if you get DLA highest rate care component or are terminally ill, the long-term rate is paid early, after the first 28 weeks.

If you are aged under 20 (or under 25 in some cases if you have been in education or training) you can claim 'no-contribution' IB under special rules without having paid any national insurance (NI) contributions. After that age, your ability to claim depends on passing NI contribution conditions. Chapter 14 gives full details.

3. 'Normal' schooling and incapacity benefit

If you are under 19 and still at school or in full-time education, your entitlement to incapacity benefit (IB) under the special rules also depends on the type and hours of schooling received.

You must still meet the basic conditions of entitlement (see Chapter 14) – eg pass the personal capability assessment, unless exempt.

You can get IB as long as you attend classes or periods of supervised study adding up to less than 21 hours a week. Lunch breaks, breaks between lessons, free periods, and periods of private (unsupervised) study or homework do not count. If you attend classes for less than 21 hours, the type of education you receive and the school you attend make no difference to IB.

If you attend classes for 21 hours or more each week, you may still qualify for IB if the extra hours of classes would not be *'suitable for persons of the same age and sex who do not suffer from a physical or mental disability'*. A Commissioner's decision (R(S)2/87) looks at this definition: it establishes that the methods of teaching may make a course unsuitable for a non-disabled person. This is a key decision for deaf or blind teenagers, as well as those who have other verbal or written communication difficulties.

When adding up the hours of instruction, ignore the time spent on any course that would not routinely be followed by a non-disabled person of the same age or sex. You are looking at what is taught and how it is taught. If special teaching (eg speech practice) or special methods (eg use of Braille texts) are integrated into all lessons, you don't have to quantify the non-suitable hours precisely. It is enough if the balance of probabilities shows that any suitable hours are less than 21 a week.

If you are a teenager with learning disabilities whose mental age is well below your physical age, it is probable that the whole of your course would not be suitable for a non-disabled person of the same age.

In other cases (and where you are in an integrated class with non-disabled pupils of the same age), you may have to look more closely at the nature of the course. For example, if you are a teenager who is deaf and you consequently have to receive extra hours of English and mathematics, those extra hours are only necessary because of your deafness – so the extra hours should be ignored. The point is that you wouldn't expect to find a non-disabled 16-year-old of the same general intelligence doing those extra hours of English and maths.

The fact that you are following a GCSE course does not automatically mean the course is suitable for a non-disabled teenager. The methods of teaching may make it unsuitable, or the particular course may be spread over, say, 2 or 3 years, whereas normally it would take one or 2 years or would be taught in that way to a slightly younger age group.

If you are not be able to qualify for IB, you might meet the easier qualifying test for income support.

4. Income support

At 16, you can claim income support (IS) in your own right as a disabled person, whether you are at home, at school, or attending a training centre (see Chapter 3(4 and 5) for details).

If you are a 16-, 17- or 18-year-old still at school, you only have to show that because of your mental or physical disability you would be unlikely to get a job within the next year if you left school and signed on for work. You do not have to prove you are incapable of work.

However, if you have left school, you do have to show that you are incapable of work. This is assessed under the 'own occupation test' or 'personal capability assessment' unless you are exempt (see Chapter 11).

At 16, if you live with your parents or at a boarding school, you will usually qualify for an IS personal allowance of £33.85. However, if you qualify for the disability premium of £23.95, you will be entitled to a higher personal allowance of £44.50. This brings your IS applicable amount up to £68.45 a week. This is usually higher than incapacity benefit (IB) during the first year of IB entitlement. IB pays more than IS once you move onto the long-term rate combined with the age-related addition, which together come to £92.50. This will happen after 52 weeks of entitlement (or 28 weeks if you get disability living allowance (DLA) highest rate care component or are terminally ill).

You will qualify for a disability premium if you get DLA, are registered blind or have been incapable of work for 52 weeks (see Chapter 4(5)). These weeks can fall before your 16th birthday, so IS including a disability premium could begin from your 16th birthday.

An enhanced disability premium of £11.70 is included in the IS assessment, and can be added on top of a disability premium, if you get DLA highest rate care component.

Capital

Once you reach 16, the rules about capital change if you make a claim for IS in your own right. If you have over £3,000, a tariff income is assumed (see Box B.2, Chapter 5). However, capital in a trust fund set up from a payment made because of a personal or criminal injury to you is disregarded indefinitely (see Chapter 5(12)). The capital limits are higher if you are living in a care home (see Chapter 30(5)).

5. IS or incapacity benefit? Or both?

If your capital is above the income support (IS) limit of £8,000 (£16,000 if you live in a care home), you can only claim incapacity benefit (IB). If you are still at school, the hours and type of education you receive may rule out IB, even though it makes no difference to your IS entitlement.

The best advice is to claim both IS and IB when you reach 16. If you do not get disability living allowance and are not registered blind, include with the IS claim, if you can, a backdated medical certificate from your GP covering the last 52 weeks. If the IS assessment includes the £23.95 disability premium, the total IS applicable amount will come to £68.45, so you can get £10.80 IS a week to top up the £57.65 from the short-term lower rate of IB. After 28 weeks you can get 25 pence IS a week to top up the short-term higher rate of £68.20. IS will be £11.70 higher still if it includes the enhanced disability premium.

Usually after you have been getting IB for a year, you will no longer qualify for IS. Only those who qualify for higher amounts of IS can continue to get it on top of the long-term rate of IB.

6. Child benefit

If you are between the ages of 16 and 19 and are receiving incapacity benefit (IB) or income support (IS), your parents cannot claim child benefit for you as well, even though you may still be at school. When you are awarded IB or IS, any arrears will be reduced to take account of any child benefit your parents have received for you for the same period.

38 Financing studies

1. Grants and loans

Financial support for students in higher education is mainly in the form of means-tested contributions for tuition fees, means-tested loans for living expenses, and supplementary grants for students in particular circumstances. See Box M.3 for where to find more information.

What you are entitled to depends not only on what part of the UK you are studying in, but also where you are from. For student support, contact the following:

- your local education authority if you live in England or Wales;
- the Student Awards Agency for Scotland (SAAS) if you live in Scotland;
- your Education and Library Board (ELB) if you live in Northern Ireland.

Fees

Students from England, Wales or Northern Ireland following a full-time publicly funded higher education course anywhere in the UK may have to contribute towards tuition fees. For the academic year 2005/06 the contribution is up to £1,175. If you are aged under 25, the level of contribution depends on your income and that of your parents. If the parent you live with has remarried or is living with someone, the income of their new spouse or partner will also be taken into account. If you are a mature student, you will be assessed on your own income, and that of your spouse, civil partner or cohabiting partner if you have one.

Students from Scotland studying in Scotland on their first higher education course are exempt from paying tuition fees. Instead, they pay a graduate endowment once they have graduated, which can be added to their student loan debt. However, students who have received disabled students' allowances in higher education will not have to pay this endowment. If you are from Scotland and studying elsewhere in the UK, you follow the same rules as students from England, Wales and Northern Ireland.

Note: From September 2006, universities and colleges will be able to charge up to £3,000 a year for their courses. Amounts charged will vary between courses, universities and colleges. Grants of up to £2,700, depending on your household's income, will be available. Bursaries will be available to those in receipt of the maintenance grant. Variable fees will not apply to students who are studying in Scotland or in Wales (to date there is not a decision whether to introduce variable fees or not in Northern Ireland).

Full-time loan

You can apply for a student loan if you are a full-time student from the UK and under 50 years of age (or between 50 and 54 and can show that you intend to enter employment after the course has finished). You only start to pay back the loan once you reach a certain salary level.

There are two parts to the loan. All students meeting the age criteria can apply for the first part. The second part depends on your income. The amount of loan you receive also varies according to where you live and study.

Higher education grant

Full-time undergraduate students in England and Wales who started their course in September 2004 or later can apply for a higher education grant of up to £1,000. It is means tested and only students from low-income families will get the full amount. Welsh students may also be eligible for an additional 'assembly learning grant'; apply to your LEA. In Scotland and Northern Ireland, separate bursaries are available – contact the SAAS or ELB for further details.

M.2 Rates of grants and loans (2005/06)

Disabled students' allowance (DSA)

The figures shown are the maximum in each case for disability-related costs of study.

Major items of specialist equipment	£4,680 per course
Non-medical helper	
Full-time course	£11,840 a year
Part-time course	£8,885 a year
General/Other expenditure	
Full-time course	£1,565 a year
Part-time course	£1,170 a year

Travel

Extra travel costs incurred as a result of disability, not normally for everyday travel costs; no maximum amount

Postgraduate (maximum DSA) £5,640 a year

For postgraduate courses there is one allowance for all costs. PGCE/ITT courses are eligible for DSAs at undergraduate rates. Most Research Council funded study includes DSAs at undergraduate rates.

Student loans

Place of residence	Full year	Final year
Parental home	£3,320	£2,900
London	£5,175	£4,490
Elsewhere	£4,195	£3,645

Part-time grants

A variable grant, payable at one of 3 rates: for a course studied at between 50-59% of the speed of a full-time course, the maximum is £590; for 60-74%, £710; for 75% plus, £885. A non-repayable grant of up to £250 can help meet the costs of books, and travel and course expenditure. Both of these grants are available to students from lower-income households who are studying the equivalent of at least 50% of a full-time course.

Part-time grant

Part-time students from England, Wales and Northern Ireland on courses involving at least half the hours (50%) of a full-time course and who are on low incomes can apply for a means-tested fee grant and course grant to help with course expenses, books and travel. For 2005/06 entry, the maximum fee grant is £885 and the maximum course grant is £250 a year. Part-time students from Scotland and studying in Scotland can apply for a part-time loan from SAAS to cover study-related costs such as travel or books. See Box M.2 for amounts.

Access to Learning Fund/Hardship Fund/Support Fund

In England the Access to Learning Fund is administered by the educational institution; in Scotland it is known as Hardship Funds, in Northern Ireland the Support Fund, and in Wales the Financial Contingency Funds Scheme operates a similar scheme.

Each institution administers these funds, which are available to students experiencing financial hardship. In England and Wales, priority is given to mature students, disabled students, final year students and care leavers over the age of 18. In Northern Ireland and Scotland, it is up to the individual university how the funds are distributed. Contact the student support officer responsible for financial advice to obtain an application form.

Supplementary grants

If you are studying on a designated course and meet the residency criteria, you may be eligible for supplementary grants including:

- disabled students' allowance (DSA) – see below;
- parents' learning allowance and childcare grant – for full-time students with dependent children;
- adult dependants' grant;
- travel costs (if you have additional travel costs because you must attend a clinical placement in the UK as part of your full-time course in medicine or dentistry or a college or university outside the UK as part of your course, or for Scottish students general travel costs above a certain amount);
- care leavers' grant.

Dependants' grants and grants for students with child dependants are means tested but DSA, care leavers' grant and travel costs are not. While previous study may prevent you getting help with tuition fees and the higher education grant, it does not affect entitlement to supplementary grants. Apply to the LEA or SAAS.

Disabled students' allowance (DSA) – DSA is not means tested. It is for any additional disability-related costs of study – covering specialist equipment, non-medical helpers and general or other expenditure. Full- or part-time postgraduates in the UK can get DSA if they do not receive an award from the Research Councils (or similar organisation), which provide support equivalent to DSA. For rates, see Box M.2.

In order to receive DSA, you will require a needs assessment. Your awarding authority will advise on the process for this. The needs assessment will identify what extra study-related needs you will have because of your disability.

For more information see Box M.3, and ask the LEA for the leaflet *Bridging the Gap*.

Other help for students

Other sources of financial support may be available to those in higher or further education, including:

NHS bursaries – These are for NHS-funded places on health professional courses.

Postgraduate courses – Financial support may be available from a range of sources (eg from the Research Councils, your university or charitable trusts), depending on the subject you intend to study.

Career Development Loans – For vocational courses, there is the Government-sponsored Career Development Loan offered by banks. Amounts vary from £300 to £8,000.

Charities and trusts – Trusts will not usually provide you with your main source of finance for a full-time course, but they may give you a top-up or pay for a special need. Some trusts give small grants or loans to students with disabilities who are in particular difficulty. See Box M.3 for more information.

2. Students and benefits

Chapter 37 looks at the position of disabled teenagers under 19 who are at school or doing non-advanced courses. Here we look at the position of disabled students who are under 19 but on an advanced course, or over 19 and in full-time education (advanced or non-advanced) and also at provisions for unemployed people and those receiving pension credit (see 4).

3. Income support

Chapter 3 deals with the main rules for income support (IS). If you are one of a couple and your partner is not also a student, they may be eligible for IS in the normal way.

Part-time study – If you are eligible for IS under the usual rules (see Box B.1, Chapter 3) you can study part time while claiming IS.

Full-time course – You are eligible for IS during term time and all vacations if:

- you are a disabled student; *and*
  - your applicable amount includes a disability premium; *or*
  - your applicable amount includes a severe disability premium; *or*
  - you have been incapable of work (or entitled to statutory sick pay) for 28 weeks (2 or more periods of incapacity can be added together provided they are no more than 8 weeks apart). Chapter 11 has details about how incapacity for work is assessed; *or*
  - you are claiming disabled students' allowance (DSA) because of deafness;
- you are a lone parent whose youngest child is under 16;
- you are a refugee on a course learning English;
- you have limited leave in the UK subject to 'no recourse to public funds' and have a temporary problem in getting funds from your usual source.

Student couples with a child, if eligible for IS under the ordinary rules, can get IS in the long vacations. Alternatively, one of the couple may be able to claim jobseeker's allowance, providing they are available for work.

Whether your course is full- or part-time usually depends on how it is classed by the institution. However, if you are on a course of government-funded further education in England or Wales it is full-time if it involves more than 16 guided learning hours a week. In Scotland, it is still full-time if structured learning packages make up the hours to over 16 a week, up to a maximum of 21 hours a week.

How does your grant or loan affect IS?

Student loans – If you are eligible for a student loan, the maximum available is taken into account as income in the IS assessment, whatever amount you actually borrow. If you don't apply for a loan, the decision maker will still take into account the maximum loan you could have got if you had applied, assuming no means-tested deduction from the loan. Where the parents or partner of a disabled student are unable or unwilling to meet their contribution to a loan or grant in full, only the actual contribution is taken into account.

When your IS is worked out, £10 a week of your loan is ignored as well as:

- £275 a year for travel costs from a loan (2004/05 rates);
- £343 a year for books and equipment from a loan (2004/05 rates). However, if you receive any grant that specifically includes an amount for books and equipment, the amount you actually receive is disregarded from your grant income.

If you are not eligible for a loan the deduction for travel, books and equipment is made from any grant income instead.

To work out the weekly income to take into account, the loan is divided over the weeks from the start of the first benefit week in September, or at the start of the autumn term if that is earlier, until the end of the last benefit week in June, or, in the final year, until the end of your course. If you stop being a full-time student before the end of your course, any loan may continue to be taken into account but without any disregard, whether or not you repay all or part of it.

Grants – The following grants are ignored in the assessment:

- any grant for tuition and examination fees;
- disabled students' allowance;
- any amount intended for the maintenance or childcare costs of a dependent child;
- the higher education grant;
- any grant for travel costs;
- any grant for maintaining a second home (less any housing benefit payable);
- any grant for books and equipment.

In general, grants that cannot be ignored are taken into account over the period for which they are payable (eg a care leavers' grant during the weeks of the long vacation). An adult dependants' grant is taken into account over the same period as a student loan. If you stop being a student before the end of your course, any grant which has to be repaid continues to be taken into account as income until you've repaid it in full or until the end of the term or vacation when you left the course.

Access and Hardship Funds – Access to Learning Funds, Hardship Funds and Support Funds are paid to students experiencing financial hardship. The rules concerning these payments differ according to how the funds are to be used.

- ❑ If the payment is intended to cover a one-off cost (eg for fuel, debts, books or special equipment) it will count as capital and will only affect your claim if your capital exceeds £3,000 (see Box B.2, Chapter 5). If the payment is for everyday living expenses (eg food; see Chapter 5(7)) it will count as capital but this will be ignored for 52 weeks. This capital will only affect your claim if the funds have not been used by the end of the 52-week period.
- ❑ If the payment is to be used on an ongoing basis and is paid as a lump sum or in instalments, it will count as income. This income will be disregarded in full unless the payment is for everyday living expenses. In this case £20 a week will be disregarded.
- ❑ If the payments are intended to bridge the gap before starting a course or receiving the student loan, they will be ignored completely even if they are intended to cover everyday living expenses.

Voluntary or charitable payments – One-off or irregular payments are treated as capital. Regular payments are treated as income but are ignored completely if they are not for everyday living expenses (see Chapter 5(7)). Otherwise up to £20 a week is ignored as income (subject to an overall £20 maximum if you also have a student loan or access fund payment, see above).

Career Development Loans – The part of the Career Development Loan intended to cover fees or examination costs is disregarded when calculating income. Amounts specifically intended to meet everyday living expenses are taken into account. These parts of the loan are divided over the number of weeks of study for which the loan was paid.

4. Other benefits

Housing benefit (HB)

Most students attending a full-time course are excluded from HB throughout the year(s) until the course finally ends. However, you can claim HB if you are in any of these groups:

- You get income support (IS) or income-based jobseeker's allowance (JSA) as a full-time student.
- You qualify for disabled students' allowance because of deafness.
- You are a lone parent or a pensioner.
- You qualify for a disability premium or severe disability premium, or you have been incapable of work (or entitled to statutory sick pay (SSP)) for 28 weeks (2 or more periods of incapacity can be added together if they are no more than 8 weeks apart).
- You are one of a couple and your partner is not a student. Your partner can claim HB (the student rules will apply to your income).
- You are one of a couple, your partner is also a student and you have a dependent child. You will be eligible for HB throughout the course (not just in the long vacations as for JSA and IS).
- You can get HB temporarily while waiting to return to your course after an agreed break because you were ill or had to care for someone. You can get HB once you have recovered or your caring responsibilities have ended until either the date you return to your course or the date your education establishment has agreed that you can return to your course, whichever is earlier, but only for a maximum period of one year and providing you are not eligible for a student loan or grant during this time.
- You are under 19 and a full-time student on a non-advanced course.

New regulations mean certain full-time students, including disabled students, living in accommodation provided by their educational establishment are eligible for HB. Part-time students renting accommodation from their educational establishment may also benefit from the new regulations, but only if they would be eligible for HB if they were a full-time student.

Students on IS – If you are on IS, occupying your dwelling as your home, and liable to pay rent for it, your HB is worked out in the normal way (see Chapter 7).

Other students – If you don't get IS, your HB is worked out normally but is also subject to special rules for the treatment of a student loan and grant income. The treatment of income is much the same as under IS (but all students, including disabled students, are assumed to receive the full assessed parental contribution towards their loan).

If you have a partner and have to live in two separate homes while you are on the course, you can get HB for both homes only if you are eligible for HB as a student.

Non-dependant deductions – See below.

Council tax benefit

If the only adult residents in your home are students you will not be liable to pay council tax, as your home is an exempt dwelling (see Box C.5, Chapter 8). If students live with non-students, the students are disregarded for council tax purposes,

M.3 For more information

Careers help

Connexions is the advice and guidance service for all young people aged 13-19 (or up to 25 for anyone with a disability). The Connexions personal adviser can support young people in school, college, post-16 education, work-based learning, employment, and those not in education, training or employment.

If you have left school, you could contact the nearest college (get the address from your library or Learn Direct 0800 100 900), and ask for an interview with the college co-ordinator for special needs to discuss the courses on offer and how the college might help if you have particular needs (eg access, special equipment, tutorial help).

If you left school some time ago, or have become disabled since leaving school, contact the disability employment adviser at the Jobcentre Plus office about further education and training. If you are over 20 and live in England you may get help and advice from your local Next Step centre (www.nextstep.org.uk).

Information for students with disabilities

Guides and information booklets, including guides to financial assistance for students with disabilities in further or higher education, and on applying for DSA, are published by Skill (www.skill.org.uk; or see Address List).

The RNIB can offer advice and assistance to visually impaired students. For details of student support services ring their helpline (0845 766 9999).

Student grants and loans

For copies of government guides to student grants and loans, contact:

- in England and Wales: local education authorities, or DfES Information Line (0800 731 9133; Textphone 0800 328 8988; www.dfes.gov.uk/studentsupport);
- Scotland: Student Awards Agency for Scotland, Gyleview House, 3 Redheughs Rigg, Edinburgh EH12 9HH (0845 111 1711; www.student-support-saas.gov.uk);
- Northern Ireland: Department for Employment and Learning (DEL), Adelaide House, 39-49 Adelaide Street, Belfast BT2 8FD (028 9025 7728; www.delni.gov.uk).

For information on payment of student loans, contact: The Student Loans Company, 100 Bothwell Street, Glasgow G2 7JD (0800 405010; Minicom 0800 085 3950; www.slc.co.uk).

For information on Career Development Loans: 0800 585505 or www.lifelonglearning.co.uk/cdl/index.

For information on Access to Learning Funds, ask your student union, personal tutor or welfare office.

Students, student support and benefits

For detailed information on entitlement to benefits and tax credits, and the treatment of student income in the calculation of benefits and tax credits, see *Student Support and Benefits Handbook 2004/05* and *Benefits for Students in Scotland Handbook* (Child Poverty Action Group).

Charities and trusts

There are a number of reference books, which should be available through public libraries, including:

- *Educational Grants Directory* (Directory of Social Change)
- *The Grants Register* (Macmillan)

The Students Awards Agency for Scotland maintains a Register of Educational Endowments covering education trusts set up in Scotland.

Funding from Charitable Trusts, an information booklet published by Skill (see above), has a list of grant-making trusts and advice on applying.

which may help towards a discount (see Chapter 8(9)).

If you're not liable to pay council tax, you cannot get council tax benefit (CTB) in any case. Even if you are liable to pay council tax, you may not qualify for Main CTB (see Chapter 7(11)), as only some full-time students are eligible. If you would be eligible for HB as a student (see above) you will also be eligible for Main CTB. Your income is worked out in the same way as for HB.

Second adult rebate – Students who are liable to pay council tax can claim second adult rebate even if they are excluded from Main CTB. It is worked out in the standard way – see Chapter 7(27).

Non-dependant deductions – If you are a full-time student living in someone else's home as a non-dependant, no deduction is made from the householder's CTB during your whole period of study, including the summer vacation. For CTB purposes, there is no deduction even if you get a job during the long vacation. However, for HB, if you get a job (for 16 or more hours a week) during the summer vacation, a non-dependant deduction will be applied.

Jobseeker's allowance (JSA)

General rules – Students attending a full-time course are normally excluded from JSA until the end of the course, or until they abandon it or are dismissed from it. However, if you have a partner who is also a student and you have a dependent child, you can get JSA during the long vacation as long as you are available for work.

You can also get JSA temporarily while you are waiting to return to your course after an agreed break because you were ill or because you had to care for someone. You can claim JSA once you have recovered or your caring responsibilities have ended until either the date you go back to your course or the date your education establishment has agreed that you can go back, whichever is earlier, but only for a maximum period of one year and providing you are not eligible for a student loan or grant during this time.

Employment-related course – If you are aged 25 or over and have been claiming JSA for at least 2 years (or receiving national insurance (NI) contribution credits for unemployment or for people aged 60 or over), you may be able to go on a full-time employment-related course of a year or less and stay on JSA. The employment officer at the Jobcentre Plus office decides whether the course qualifies. Note that benefit could be sanctioned for 2 weeks if you leave the course after the first 4 weeks without good cause, unless it was not suitable for you.

Part-time study – You can study part-time and get income-based or contribution-based JSA if your course or training takes place outside of the hours you are required to be available for work. These times are usually recorded in your jobseeker's agreement. But if the course overlaps with the hours in which you must be available for work, you can still get JSA for part-time study if you are:

- willing and able to rearrange the hours of your course immediately to take up employment; *or*
- willing and able to give up the course if a job becomes available.

Special rules apply if the Jobcentre Plus office has agreed you can restrict the hours you are available for work. If the hours you are studying overlap with the hours you are required to be available for work the overlap will be ignored if:

- for the whole 3 months before you started the course you were on Work-Based Learning for Young People, or getting JSA, incapacity benefit (IB), or SSP, or getting IS on the grounds of incapacity for work; *or*
- in the 6 months before you started the course you met the above condition for a total of 3 months, as long as for the rest of the time you were in full-time work, or earning too much to get any of those benefits.

If you meet these conditions, your studies are ignored when deciding if you are available for work.

Pension credit (PC)

If you are a student aged 60 or over (or have a partner aged 60 or over) you (or your partner) may be eligible for PC, IS or JSA. Because income from student financial support is treated more generously under PC, you should check to see if you would be better off if you (or your partner) claimed PC instead of IS or JSA. If you or your partner receive PC, the more generous rules for calculating HB and CTB may also apply.

Incapacity benefit and severe disablement allowance (SDA)

In general, IB is payable during term time as well as vacations and is not paid at a reduced rate because of any grant or loan you receive. However, if you are under 19 you may be caught by the full-time education exclusion (see Chapter 37(3)).

Normally, the age limit for claiming no-contribution IB is 20. There is an exception allowing claims to be made until age 25 if you have been on a course from at least 3 months before your 20th birthday (see Chapter 14(3)). If you satisfy the NI contribution conditions for IB, you can claim whatever your age, and entitlement is not affected by your studies.

Note: To be entitled to IB you must be accepted as incapable of work, assessed under the 'personal capability assessment' (PCA) unless you are in an exempt group. In assessing your ability to carry out the range of activities in the PCA, the DWP will look at how you manage in your daily life, including the time you are attending your course (see Chapter 11). When beginning study you must declare this as a change of circumstances. This may trigger a review of your benefit, but does not necessarily mean you will lose it.

SDA was abolished from 6.4.01, but existing claimants continue to receive it. SDA is payable throughout the year and is paid in addition to a grant or loan.

Disability living allowance (DLA)

DLA can be paid over and above any grant, loan, disabled students' allowance (DSA) or IS. If your college provides care and assistance for you, the college authorities may claim some or all of the DLA care component from you towards their costs. If you are living in a residential college, your care component will stop for the time you are there, if it counts as 'special accommodation' (see Chapter 20(8)).

Students in higher education who require help with personal care can claim DSA to cover the cost of non-medical helpers (see 1 and Box M.2). Your DSA will only fund academic helpers without whom you would be unable to follow the course. For basic personal care needs that arise whether or not you are on the course, you should apply for financial assistance from the social services department in your home area and use, for example, a Community Service Volunteer.

N Retirement

This section of the Handbook looks at:

39 Early retirement

1. Introduction

For some people with disabilities, the prospect of working into their 50s and 60s may not be a realistic one. Those with progressive disabilities or illnesses may be unable to continue working or may not be able to continue in their normal job. For others, the efforts involved in going to work may get more difficult as they become older. Consequently, some people have to retire early and it is important they know about the financial help available to them.

However, if you are ill or disabled and you feel you are being discriminated against at work or being pressured to retire early when you don't wish to, see Chapter 55 for information about your rights under the Disability Discrimination Act.

2. Still able to work

If you are not incapable of work, you may be regarded as unemployed for benefit purposes should you give up work before state pension age. This may arise where your firm has a compulsory retirement age below state pension age, or you feel your job is too much for you and you cannot find one nearer home or easier to cope with. In both cases, you may be able to claim jobseeker's allowance (JSA). Read Chapter 17, and note the following points.

- ❑ You must be available for and actively seeking work and have entered into a jobseeker's agreement.
- ❑ Benefit is 'sanctioned', ie is not payable, for up to 26 weeks if you leave your job voluntarily and *'without just cause'*. Those who are compulsorily retired or who have taken voluntary redundancy cannot be sanctioned. However, voluntary early retirement may lead to non-payment of benefit for up to 26 weeks – unless health problems were your main reason for taking, or asking for, early retirement.

It is crucial to seek advice before taking early retirement. You should appeal against any decision to apply a benefit sanction and also against the length of the sanction.

The maximum length of time for which benefit is not payable is 26 weeks. Even if a sanction is applied, appeal tribunals can decide on a shorter period – the minimum is one week. See also Chapter 17(9).

Contribution-based JSA, which is paid for up to 6 months, is £56.20 a week if you are aged 25 or over. If you have an occupational or personal pension of more than £50 a week, your JSA will be reduced by the amount your pension exceeds £50. Entitlement to income-based JSA depends on your income, savings and other circumstances.

3. Occupational pensions and early retirement

An occupational pension may be paid to someone under the normal retirement age in their job if the scheme provides for an early pension on grounds of 'incapacity'. Under some pension schemes, the pension payable is based both on the employee's actual service to date and on their potential service up to the normal retirement age for that particular firm's pension scheme. There may, or may not, be an actuarial reduction.

Ask your employer, personnel officer or trade union what your firm is offering you.

4. State benefits and ill-health

You can claim incapacity benefit (IB) if you are incapable of work, provided you satisfy the contribution conditions. If you have an employer, you should first qualify for statutory sick pay (SSP) for up to 28 weeks (see Chapter 13). You can continue to receive IB until you reach state pension age or until your condition improves enough for you to be considered fit enough to work again.

If you have an occupational or personal pension of more than £85 a week, this may reduce the amount of IB you get. However, people receiving IB before 6.4.01 and new claimants receiving disability living allowance highest rate care component will not have their IB reduced. For other claimants, IB will be reduced by 50 pence for every pound of private pension over £85 a week. See Chapter 14(5) for more details.

For full details of SSP, IB and the meaning of 'incapacity for work' see Chapters 11, 13 and 14.

40 Benefits in retirement

1. What benefits can you get?

State pension age is 60 for women and 65 for men (but see Chapter 42(2) for future changes to equalise state pension ages). Once you reach that age, and not before, you can claim state pension. State pension is dealt with in Chapter 42. This chapter looks at other benefits you may be able to get at state pension age. Sometimes you will need to decide whether to draw state pension or receive another benefit instead. Other benefits, such as attendance allowance and pension credit, can be paid in addition to state pension.

2. What if you go on working?

You can claim state pension at state pension age whether or not you go on working. Chapter 42 explains more about state pension.

If you put off claiming state pension, you may be able to earn extra pension or, following changes introduced in April 2005, receive a one-off taxable lump-sum payment (see Chapter 42(4)).

If you work at any time after state pension age you will not have to pay national insurance contributions. You will need to give your employer a Certificate of Age Exception. If you make a claim for state pension shortly before state pension age, you can ask for the certificate by ticking the box on the claim-form. Otherwise you can get the certificate by writing to or ringing the National Insurance Contributions Office (see inside back cover).

Statutory sick pay – If you are employed and earning £82 a week or more, you should claim statutory sick pay (SSP) from your employer if you are sick for at least 4 days in a row. You are not entitled to SSP once you've reached the age of 65 (men and women). But if you reach 65 while you are getting SSP, your benefit will continue until the end of that period of entitlement.

3. Incapacity benefit

If you are receiving long-term incapacity benefit (IB) this will stop when you reach state pension age. (Under previous rules it could be paid for 5 years after state pension age, but this is no longer possible.)

Short-term incapacity benefit

If you are getting short-term IB when you reach state pension age it can continue to be paid. The full basic lower rate of short-term IB for people over state pension age is £73.35 for the first 28 weeks of incapacity. The higher rate is £76.45 a week after the first 28 weeks of incapacity. You will receive less if you do not have sufficient qualifying years for a full basic state pension. You may also receive any additional state pension or graduated retirement benefit to which you would be entitled with your state pension.

Short-term IB can be paid for up to a year of incapacity – either continuously or in linked periods of incapacity where the gaps are no more than 8 weeks (or 52 weeks if you are a 'welfare to work beneficiary' – see Chapter 15(12)).

In deciding whether to draw state pension or continue to receive short-term IB, you should note that the full basic state pension is higher than the basic rate of IB, and any personal or occupational pension above £85 a week will reduce IB but will not affect state pension. Also, state pension, but not IB, counts as qualifying income for the savings element of pension credit (see Chapter 41(4)). On the other hand, state pension is taxable, but short-term IB is tax free for the first 28 weeks.

Once your short-term IB has run out and you are over state pension age, you cannot go onto long-term IB.

As long as your incapacity for work began before state pension age, you can make a claim up to 3 months after the day before your 60th (women) or 65th (men) birthday. You must be able to pass all the qualifying conditions for the earlier period and you'll need a backdated medical certificate.

If you are getting long-term IB, it stops as soon as you reach state pension age. You cannot go back to claiming short-term IB.

See Chapter 14 for more details on IB.

Increases for dependants

If you are receiving IB you may be entitled to an addition for your husband or wife once they (not you) reach the age of 60. (Before age 60, you can only get an addition for your partner if you have a dependent child.) However, if they have earnings or are in receipt of state pension or certain other benefits you may not get the addition. See Chapter 14(4) for more information.

4. Carer's allowance

There is no upper age limit for claiming carer's allowance (CA), previously called invalid care allowance (ICA). You must, however, satisfy the usual conditions of entitlement to CA (see Chapter 23).

If you are entitled to CA after state pension age you may not appear to be better off due to the overlapping benefit rules. CA overlaps with state pension, so once you reach state pension age and draw your pension, CA can only continue to be paid if your state pension is less than £45.70 a week (the rate of CA). You can be paid CA on its own, or as a top-up to state pension. However, even if your CA is overlapped, it is often well worth claiming because it can increase your income from pension credit (PC), housing benefit (HB) and/ or council tax benefit (CTB) through the carer premium or carer addition (see below).

If you were 65 or over and in receipt of ICA on 27.10.02, your CA continues even if you no longer care for a disabled person or you start earning over £82 a week. Otherwise you must continue to satisfy the conditions for CA in order to receive it after the age of 65.

Carer addition and carer premium – While you receive CA, or would receive it but for the overlapping benefit rules, your 'appropriate minimum guarantee' for PC includes a carer addition of £25.80, or your 'applicable amount' for HB and CTB includes a carer premium of the same amount. This means that you may start receiving higher levels of these benefits when you are awarded CA or you may become entitled to benefit for the first time.

As explained above, if you were aged 65 or over and receiving ICA on 27.10.02 you can continue to get CA – and thus the carer addition or premium – even if you are no longer caring for the disabled person.

The carer addition or premium continues for 8 weeks after your CA ceases – eg where the disabled person's attendance allowance (AA) or disability living allowance (DLA) is withdrawn after 4 weeks in hospital. If the disabled person regains AA or DLA care component at the middle or highest rate, your carer addition or premium should resume.

5. Severe disablement allowance

Severe disablement allowance (SDA) was abolished for new claimants from 6.4.01 onwards, so the information here only applies to people entitled to it before that date. For more information about SDA, see Box E.9 in Chapter 14.

SDA overlaps with state pension. But, if you don't qualify for state pension, or it is lower than SDA, your state pension can be topped up to your full SDA entitlement, including any age-related addition. On the other hand, you can put off claiming state pension and keep your tax-free SDA. If you would be due to pay tax on your state pension, you may be better off doing this in some situations even if your pension is a bit higher than your SDA. But note that state pension, but not SDA, counts as qualifying income for the savings element of pension credit (see Chapter 41(4)).

Once you reach 65 you continue to get SDA even if you are no longer incapable of work or 80% disabled, provided you were entitled to SDA immediately before your 65th birthday. You no longer need to send in doctor's statements.

6. Attendance allowance

Attendance allowance (AA) is a benefit for ill or disabled people aged 65 or older. There is no upper age limit. Many older people fail to claim AA. Some people do not realise that it is tax free, not means tested, and can be paid on top of state pension or pension credit. Others put their problems down to 'old age' rather than disability. See Chapter 21 for full details.

7. Disability living allowance

If you are 65 or over you cannot start to receive disability living allowance (DLA). However, if you were getting DLA before you reached 65, you continue to be eligible for DLA provided you continue to satisfy the other conditions. See Chapter 20.

If you are a war pensioner, see Chapter 45. There is no upper age limit for war pensioners' mobility supplement.

8. Pension credit

Pension credit (PC) replaced income support on 6.10.03 for people aged 60 and over. PC has two elements: the guarantee credit and the savings credit. There is no upper capital limit, but savings over £6,000 (or £10,000 if you live in a care home) will be taken into account.

If your income is not more than about £109.45 a week for a single person or £167.05 for a couple, you may be entitled to PC guarantee credit to top up your income to this level.

If you are disabled, or you are entitled to carer's allowance, or you have certain housing costs, you may be able to have more income and still be entitled to PC guarantee credit.

The savings credit is for people aged 65 or over and can provide additional money to those who have modest savings. For more information on PC see Chapter 41.

9. Housing benefit and council tax benefit

You may be entitled to help with all or part of your rent and/or council tax through housing benefit (HB) and/or council tax benefit (CTB).

If you apply for pension credit (PC) you will also be asked if you want to claim these benefits. If you are not entitled to PC, you may still be eligible for HB and/or CTB. In this case claim directly from the local authority, not the DWP. See Chapter 7 for full details.

10. Other benefits

Most people aged 60 and over will be entitled to a winter fuel payment (Chapter 9). There is a higher level of winter fuel payment for people aged 80 or over. In winter 2005/06 there are additional payments for people aged 65 or over to help cover living expenses, such as the council tax (see Chapter 8(11)).

There are also other forms of help you may be able to get, such as grants or loans from the social fund (Chapters 9 and 10) or help towards NHS health costs (Chapter 52).

11. Equal treatment

The principle of equal treatment in European Community law is that men and women should be treated equally. However, Council Directive 79/7/EEC on the progressive implementation of equal treatment in social security matters excludes from its scope the age at which old age or retirement pensions are granted and also *'the possible consequences thereof for other benefits'*.

Because 'retirement pensions' are excluded, the current difference in state pension ages for men and women is lawful, as are overlapping benefit rules whereby a non-contributory benefit such as carer's allowance is reduced by the amount of any state pension payable.

A number of successful test cases have led to changes in the law to treat men and women equally (eg within invalid care allowance – now carer's allowance). However, the European Court of Justice has ruled that the unequal treatment within invalidity benefit (replaced by incapacity benefit) and reduced earnings allowance was lawful. While this has had the effect of limiting the scope for future challenges to discrimination in other benefits under European Community law, the Human Rights Act 1998, which came into force from 2.10.00, presents new possibilities that are yet to be tested in the courts. In any case, if you find that you receive less benefit than someone of the opposite sex who is the same age, you may wish to seek advice about your position.

41 Pension credit

In this chapter we look at: page

1. What is pension credit?

Pension credit (PC) is the commonly used name for state pension credit, a means-tested benefit for people aged 60 and over which started on 6.10.03. PC has two elements: the 'guarantee credit' which replaced income support (IS) for people aged 60 and over; and the 'savings credit' for people aged 65 and over, which is intended to provide extra money for people who have modest savings.

- **Guarantee credit** – if your income is below a certain level, known as the 'appropriate minimum guarantee', the guarantee credit makes up the difference.
- **Savings credit** can be paid if you or your partner are over 65. See 4 below for how the savings credit is calculated.

PC can meet mortgage interest payments and other housing costs. You may get housing benefit (HB) and council tax benefit (CTB) to help with rent and council tax. If you get the guarantee credit, you will be passported to full HB/CTB and may also be entitled to help with health costs such as free dental treatment (see Chapter 52) and help with hospital fares (see Chapter 32). If you receive either or both parts of the credit you may get help from the social fund (see Chapters 9 and 10) and energy efficiency grants (see Chapter 28).

2. Who can claim pension credit?

To claim PC you must be aged 60 or over. If you have a partner, they can be younger. Only one member of a couple can claim. You must be present in Great Britain (GB), habitually resident and not subject to immigration control (see Chapter 49(2 & 3)). PC can be paid for the first 4 or 8 weeks of a temporary absence from GB (see Chapter 50(5)). There is no limit on the number of hours you can work, although most earnings are taken into account (see 5 below). There is no capital limit for PC, but any capital over £6,000 will be counted as generating income (see 6 below).

3. Calculating your guarantee credit

Guarantee credit is calculated by comparing your 'appropriate minimum guarantee' with your income (see 5 below for how income is calculated). Your appropriate minimum guarantee always includes a 'standard minimum guarantee' which is:

Standard minimum guarantee	per week
Single claimant	£109.45
Couples	£167.05

In addition, your appropriate minimum guarantee can include:

- an additional amount for severe disability of £45.50 a week for a single person or couple where one partner qualifies, or £91 for a couple where both partners qualify. The rules for this addition are the same as those for the IS severe disability premium (see Chapter 4(7));

- an additional amount for carers of £25.80, worked out in the same way as the IS carer premium (see Chapter 4(8));
- an amount for any eligible housing costs such as mortgage interest (see Chapter 4(11));
- a 'transitional' extra amount if you were getting IS or income-based jobseeker's allowance immediately before you started to get PC, and they were payable at a higher rate than the PC.

PC does not include any amounts for children. If you have children, claim child tax credit (see Chapter 18).

Your income, as calculated in 5 below, is compared to your appropriate minimum guarantee. If your income is less, the difference is paid as your guarantee credit.

Example: Rashida is single and her only income is state pension of £82.05 a week. Her guarantee credit is worked out as follows:

Appropriate minimum guarantee	£109.45
Less income	£82.05
Guarantee credit	*£27.40*

4. Calculating your savings credit

Savings credit may be paid if you or your partner are 65 or over and have 'qualifying income' above your 'savings credit threshold'.

Savings credit thresholds	**per week**
Single person	£82.05
Couple	£131.20

Some people will receive savings credit in addition to guarantee credit; others will receive only savings credit. The maximum amount of savings credit payable is £16.44 a week for a single person and £21.51 for a couple.

The calculation is as follows:

Step 1: Work out your total income
This is the same figure used in the guarantee credit calculation (see 5 below for how income is calculated).

Step 2: Work your appropriate minimum guarantee
Again this is the figure used for guarantee credit (see 3 above).

Step 3: Work out your 'qualifying income'
This is your total income used to calculate guarantee credit but excluding working tax credit, incapacity benefit, contribution-based jobseeker's allowance, severe disablement allowance, maternity allowance or maintenance payments made by a spouse or former spouse.

Step 4: Compare the 'savings credit threshold' with your qualifying income
If your qualifying income is the same as or less than the savings credit threshold (see above) you will not be entitled to savings credit. If your qualifying income is more than the threshold make a note of the difference and proceed to Step 5.

Step 5: Calculate 60% of the difference from step 4
Work out 60% of the difference between the savings credit threshold and your qualifying income. If the result is more than the maximum savings credit figure of £16.44 for a single person (or £21.51 for a couple), use the relevant maximum savings credit figure instead.

Step 6: Calculate the savings credit

- ❑ If your total income is the same as or less than your appropriate minimum guarantee, your savings credit will be the figure you arrived at in Step 5.
- ❑ If your total income is more than your appropriate minimum guarantee, you must work out 40% of the difference between your total income and your appropriate minimum guarantee. You then deduct this 40% figure from the amount you arrived at in Step 5.

Example: Paul is a single claimant with a state pension (basic and additional) of £90 a week and an occupational pension of £43.65 a week. Using the steps above, the calculation is as follows:

Step 1: Paul's total income is:

State pension	£90.00
Plus occupational pension	£43.65
Total income	*£133.65*

Step 2: His appropriate minimum guarantee is £109.45 – he does not qualify for any of the 'additional amounts'. His income is above this amount so he does not qualify for guarantee credit.

Step 3: All his income is qualifying income so his qualifying income is also £133.65.

Step 4: He compares his qualifying income with the savings credit threshold. It is higher so he works out the amount by which his qualifying income is above the threshold:

Qualifying income	£133.65
Less Paul's savings credit threshold	£82.05
Difference equals	*£51.60*

Step 5: He works out 60% of the difference:

£51.60 x 60% =	£30.96

This is more than the maximum savings credit of £16.44 for a single claimant, so for the next step he uses that figure of £16.44.

Step 6: His total income is more than his appropriate minimum guarantee – the difference is:

Paul's total income	£133.65
Less appropriate minimum guarantee	£109.45
Difference equals	*£24.20*

He works out 40% of this difference, which comes to £9.68. He takes this figure from the maximum savings credit (the result of step 5):

Maximum savings credit	£16.44
Less	£9.68
Savings credit	*£6.76*

Not sure if you are entitled to savings credit?
The calculation for savings credit is quite complicated and if you are not sure whether you qualify, you should apply anyway.

You can find more information and examples of the calculation in the DWP *Guide to Pension Credit* (PC10S). You could get advice from The Pension Service or a local advice agency about your likely entitlement, or look at the PC calculator on The Pension Service website: www.thepensionservice.gov.uk.

5. Income

You need to add up your income to work out any entitlement to PC. Some types of income, including state and private pensions are counted in full; some types of income are fully disregarded and others are partially disregarded. If you have a source of income not covered here, check with The Pension Service to see how it is treated. In general, income is calculated in a similar way to income support (IS) for younger people, but there are differences.

Income is assessed after deduction of income tax and, in the case of people with earnings, after deduction of national insurance (NI) contributions and half of any contribution made to a private pension. Income is assessed on a weekly basis so if you have income paid for other periods it is divided into weekly amounts. For a couple, the income of both partners is added together.

Income generally counted in full – The following types of income are counted in full:

- state pensions;
- occupational and private pensions;
- annuities;
- retirement annuity contracts;

- regular payments from an equity release scheme;
- war disablement and war widow's/widower's pensions (but see below for disregards);
- other types of pensions including civil list pensions and those paid to victims of Nazi persecution (but see below for partial disregards);
- most social security benefits (except those listed below);
- earnings (but see below for partial disregards);
- working tax credit;
- payments from boarders, lodgers or sub-tenants (but see below for partial disregards);
- regular payments from trust funds in most circumstances – but see below;
- payments from a spouse or former spouse;
- 'deemed income' from capital over £6,000 (see 6 below).

Disregarded income – Forms of income that are completely disregarded include:

- attendance allowance and disability living allowance (and their equivalents in the War Pensions and Industrial Injuries schemes);
- housing benefit and council tax benefit;
- Christmas bonus;
- social fund payments including the winter fuel payment;
- bereavement payment;
- child benefit, child tax credit, guardian's allowance and child special allowance;
- increases for dependent children paid with certain other benefits;
- charitable and voluntary payments (except for voluntary payments from a spouse or former spouse, which are counted in full);
- payments, other than social security benefits or war pensions, paid as a result of a personal injury that you or your partner receive;
- actual income from capital;
- war widow's/widower's supplementary pension;
- exceptionally severe disablement allowance and severe disablement occupational allowance paid with war disablement pensions;
- payments from your local authority social services department for personal care; *and*
- any other types of income that are not specified in the legislation as being counted.

Partially disregarded income – Forms of weekly income that are partially disregarded include:

- £5 of your earnings from work if you are single or £10 if you are a couple. A higher £20 disregard applies in some situations, eg for some disabled people or carers. The rules are similar to those for IS (see Chapter 5(4)), but there are minor differences; for details contact an advice centre or The Pension Service;
- £10 of the total of any income from a war widow's/widower's pension, war disablement pension, a guaranteed income payment made under the new Armed Forces and Reserve Forces Compensation scheme, or pension paid for victims of Nazi persecution or widowed parents/mother's allowance;
- £20 payment from a tenant, sub-tenant or boarder and, in the case of a boarder half of any payment above £20 is also disregarded. The disregard applies to each tenant and/or boarder making payments.

If you have used the equity in your home to buy an annuity, any part of the income that is being used to pay the interest on the loan is disregarded.

Income from trust funds

This will be ignored if the trust fund was set up from a lump sum received for a personal injury. In other situations, trust fund income is generally taken into account, but there are some exceptions for discretionary payments.

Notional income

In some cases you can be treated as having income that you are not actually receiving and this is known as notional income. This will apply if there is income available that you have chosen not to take – for example, if you have not claimed your state pension or not drawn a personal or occupational pension that you are entitled to. You may also be assessed as having notional income if you have given up the right to an income you could have received.

6. Capital

Capital includes any savings, investments, land and property you own. If you have capital of £6,000 (£10,000 if you live in a care home) or less, this will not affect your PC. There is no upper capital limit for PC but if you have capital of more than £6,000 (£10,000 in a care home) you will be counted as having an extra £1 a week income for every £500 (or part of £500) over this limit. In PC this is officially called 'deemed income' while for other benefits the term is 'tariff income' (or sometimes 'assumed income'). For example, if you do not live in a care home and you have savings of £7,050 you will be deemed to have an income of £3 a week from that capital; if you have savings of £15,300 you will have a deemed income of £19 a week. If you have a partner your capital is assessed together, but the amount that is disregarded (see below) is still the same.

Most forms of capital are taken into account including: cash, bank and building society savings, National Savings accounts and certificates, stocks and shares, premium bonds, income bonds and property (other than your home). However, some types of capital are disregarded as explained below.

How capital is valued

Your capital is generally valued at its current market or surrender value, less 10% if there would be costs involved in selling and less any debt secured on the property.

Jointly owned capital – If you own capital jointly with other people you would normally all be assessed as having an equal share. See Chapter 5(11) for more about valuation of jointly owned property for income support (IS); the position is likely to be similar for PC.

Disregarded capital

In working out your deemed income from capital, the following types of capital are disregarded indefinitely or for a certain period of time.

❑ **Your home and property**

- the value of your home;
- the value of any property occupied by person who is a close relative (see Chapter 4(7)), grandparent, grandchild, uncle, aunt, nephew or niece of yourself or your partner, if they are aged 60 or over or 'incapacitated'. The value will also be disregarded if your partner or former partner lives there and you are not estranged or divorced (eg if you have moved to a care home);
- the value of a property for up to 26 weeks (or longer in some circumstances) if: you have acquired it and plan to live there; you are trying to sell it; you are carrying out essential repairs or alterations in order to live there; or you are taking legal action so you can live there;
- the value of your former home if you left because of divorce or estrangement, for 26 weeks (or indefinitely if your former partner lives there and is a lone parent);
- the following types of capital received for specific purposes are ignored for up to a year (or until an assessed income period ends if that is longer – see 9 below): money received, for example from the sale of a property, that is earmarked to buy a new home; money from an insurance policy that is to be used for repair or replacement; or money such as a loan or grant to pay for essential repairs

or improvements.

❑ **Other disregards**

- personal possessions;
- the surrender value of a life insurance policy (although if this matures or is cashed in, the money you receive will count as part of your capital);
- the right to receive income from an occupational pension, personal pension or retirement annuity contract;
- the value of a pre-paid funeral;
- the £10,000 ex-gratia payment made to Far Eastern Prisoners of War or their widows/ers;
- Second World War Compensation Payments – eg for forced labour or lost property.

From July 2005 a lump-sum payment made because you deferred drawing your state pension for at least a year will be disregarded.

Personal injury payments and trust funds

If you or your partner received a lump-sum payment because of a personal injury, an amount of capital equal to the money you received will be disregarded. If you used the money to set up a trust fund, the value of this trust will be ignored.

Payments from special trusts such as the Macfarlane Trust or the Eileen Trust are also disregarded indefinitely or for a certain period. The rules are the same as for IS (see Chapter 5(12)).

Arrears of benefits

Arrears (or ex-gratia payments) of the following benefits are ignored for 52 weeks after you get them or until the end of your assessed income period (if you have one and it is longer): attendance allowance, disability living allowance, housing benefit, council tax benefit, IS, income-based jobseeker's allowance, PC, war widow's supplementary pensions, constant attendance allowance and exceptionally severe disablement allowance (paid under the War Pensions or Industrial Injuries schemes), child tax credit, child benefit and social fund payments. If the amount of arrears or compensation is £5,000 or more and it is paid because of official error, and you receive the payments while you are getting PC, it will be ignored for as long as you continue to receive PC. Payments under Supporting People services are treated in the same way as arrears of benefits.

Notional capital

If you have 'deprived' yourself of capital in order to get PC or to increase the amount you receive then you will be treated as still having that capital and this is known as 'notional capital'. This might occur if you gave money away to a relative in order to get more PC. However, you will not be assessed as having notional capital if you used your savings to repay or reduce a debt or to buy goods or services that are 'reasonable' given your circumstances. The DWP guide to PC (PC10S) gives the example that a decision maker might consider replacing a car to be reasonable but not buying a Rolls Royce. Any notional capital you are treated as having will reduce over time in line with the rules for IS (see Chapter 5(15)).

7. How to claim

You can make a claim in a variety of ways. You can ring The Pension Service application line: Freephone 0800 99 1234 (you will be asked questions over the phone and then the application form will be sent to you to check and sign). You can also ring that number to get a form sent to you. You can write to: Freepost NAT 3780, PO Box 457, Mexborough S64 9ZZ. You can also send the tear-off coupon in leaflet PC1L *Pension Credit*, available from post offices. Alternatively, an advice agency or local Pension Service staff can help you fill in the form on a face-to-face basis – either at an advice session or through a home visit.

8. Backdating and advance claims

Normally, your PC will run from the date on which your written claim is received at the relevant office, or the date of a claim by phone or in person (including someone acting on your behalf) which is subsequently confirmed by a signed statement. However, your claim can be backdated for up to 12 months provided you met the qualifying conditions throughout that period.

If you will become eligible for PC in the future, for instance because your 60th or 65th birthday is coming up or you are about to have a drop in income, you can make a claim up to 4 months in advance of this change.

9. The assessed income period and change of circumstances

When you claim PC, The Pension Service will decide whether you are entitled to guarantee credit, savings credit or both. If you or your partner are 65 or over the decision maker may also set an 'assessed income period' (AIP) of up to 5 years (this was 7 years at the start of the scheme). Unless there are likely to be changes in the next 12 months which will affect your 'retirement provision' (see below), the AIP will normally be the maximum allowed.

For the rest of the AIP you do not have to inform The Pension Service of any changes in your retirement provision. Your retirement provision refers to any of the following that either you or your partner may possess or receive:

- capital;
- state pensions;
- other pensions including an occupational, personal or stakeholder pension scheme, an overseas pension arrangement, and a pension paid from the civil list;
- regular payments from an equity release scheme;
- retirement annuity contracts or other annuities.

Changes in your state pension will automatically be taken into account during the AIP. So when you qualify for an age addition on your 80th birthday, or when your state pension is uprated, your PC will be reduced accordingly. Adjustments will also be made automatically, where appropriate, to other pensions or annuity income. For example, if your occupational pension increases each April in line with inflation, this will be taken into account. In order for this to happen, you may be asked about any regular changes to your pensions when you apply for PC.

Other changes to your retirement provision will be ignored for the rest of the AIP. For example, if you inherit some capital or win money from Premium Bonds you will not need to inform The Pension Service. Any increase in capital or other retirement provision will only be taken into account when your AIP ends. On the other hand, if your retirement provision falls (eg your capital goes down) so that you are entitled to more PC, you can ask for a supersession of your award (see Chapter 58, Box R.5). The Pension Service will then reassess your retirement provision and if this is less than the figure they have been using your PC may increase.

During an AIP you must still report other changes in circumstances that may affect your benefit, including a change in earnings, moving home, a change in family circumstances or a period in hospital (see Chapter 33(1)).

Your AIP will end if:

- you marry or get a new partner;
- you separate from your partner;
- you or your partner become 65;
- you no longer satisfy the entitlement conditions for PC;
- part of your retirement provision stops being paid temporarily or the amount being paid is less than the amount due and you ask for your PC to be recalculated;
- you are single and are provided with accommodation in a care home permanently.

If a supersession results in the end of your AIP, PC changes from the day following the end of the period.

If you are not given an AIP, you will need to report all changes of circumstances that could affect your benefits entitlement including changes in pensions and savings. When you receive an award of PC you will be advised which changes must be reported.

10. How PC is paid

PC is normally paid weekly in advance. But if the weekly amount of PC you are due is less than £1, payments may be made at intervals of up to 13 weeks in arrears. If the weekly amount is less than 10p no PC will be paid unless it can be paid with another benefit. PC is normally paid on Mondays, or on the day you are paid state pension, if that is different. See Chapter 57(5) for more about benefit payments.

11. Decisions and appeals.

Decisions on your PC claim are made by DWP decision makers based at The Pension Service (see Chapter 2). The rules for decisions and appeals are the same as for other DWP benefits (see Chapter 58).

42 State pension

1. State pension

The two main categories of state pension are contributory and are known as Category A and B pensions. Category A pensions are normally based on your own national insurance contribution record. Category B pensions are payable only to married women, widows and some widowers and are based on their spouse's contribution record.

Category D pensions are non-contributory and only payable to people aged 80 or over.

All categories of state pension are taxable.

For more details, see leaflets RM1 *Retirement* and NP46 *A Guide to State Pensions.*

2. When can you get a state pension?

You can get a state pension if you've reached state pension age (currently 60 for women, 65 for men – see below), you meet the contribution conditions and have made a claim. You can claim at any time from 4 months before state pension age. Normally, for Category A pensions, you yourself must have met the contribution conditions. You can receive a reduced-rate basic state pension if you have met the conditions to give you a state pension of at least 25% of the standard rate, ie you must have paid or have been credited with enough contributions to make at least a quarter of the years in your 'working life' count as 'qualifying years' (see Box N.1). For Category B pensions, your spouse must have met these contribution conditions.

If you do not draw your state pension at 60 (women) or 65 (men) you may get extra state pension or, following rules introduced in April 2005, a one-off taxable lump-sum payment when you do start to claim (see 4).

Changes to state pension age – The Pensions Act 1995 introduces an equal state pension age of 65 for both men and women. This change will be phased in between 2010 and 2020. Women born on or before 5.4.50 will get their state pension at age 60, while those born on or after 6.4.55 will not be able to receive a state pension until they are 65. Those born between these dates will be able to claim their state pension between 60 and 65, depending on their date of birth.

3. Working and the state pension

Any earnings you receive after reaching state pension age do not reduce your state pension. If you carry on working and do not draw your pension you may earn extra state pension or a one-off lump sum (see 4 below). If you have already claimed state pension, you can give up your claim in order to earn extra state pension. You can only give up a state pension once, and cannot backdate that choice.

There is an earnings limit for an addition for a wife or other adult dependant (see 4 below).

4. Contributory state pensions

Category A pension

This is normally based on your own national insurance (NI) contribution record. But some widows and widowers can get a state pension even if they have not met the contribution conditions, as long as they were getting incapacity benefit (IB) just before reaching state pension age. Other widows, widowers and divorced people may be able to use the contribution record of their former spouse to help them qualify (see leaflets NP45 and NP46).

If you have met the contribution conditions in full, you can receive a basic state pension as follows:

Basic state pension	per week
For yourself	£82.05
For an adult dependant	£49.15
For the first dependent child (tax free)*	£9.40
For each other dependent child (tax free)*	£11.35

* on claims made prior to 6.4.03

An adult dependant can be a wife or someone looking after your dependent child, or in limited circumstances, a husband. The age of an adult dependant makes no difference.

If they are working, the increase won't be paid if they earn more in any week than their earnings limit (occupational and personal pensions count as earnings here). The earnings limit for an adult dependant is £56.20 if the dependant lives with you, and £49.15 if you do not live together (except in the case of a person looking after your children who does not live with you, where there is no earnings limit).

If your partner receives income maintenance benefits (eg severe disablement allowance – SDA – or IB) those benefits will reduce or cancel out a dependant's increase to your state pension.

A woman can only receive an increase for her husband if, immediately before drawing a state pension, she was receiving an increase for him with IB.

Increases for dependent children are not payable on new claims for state pension from 6.4.03. If you have dependent children, you should claim child tax credit at the same time that you claim state pension (see Chapter 18).

Category B pension

This is payable mainly to women over state pension age who are, or have been, married, but also to some widowers. It is based on the contribution record of your spouse or former spouse. If they had not fully met the contribution conditions, you will receive a reduced-rate state pension.

Married women – If your husband has met the contribution conditions, both of you are over state pension age, and he has claimed his own state pension, you can claim a Category

N.1 State pension – the qualifying conditions

Your entitlement to a basic state pension depends on three factors:

- your national insurance (NI) contributions;
- your qualifying years;
- your working life.

In order to qualify for basic state pension you must meet two conditions.

- ❑ In at least one tax year since 6.4.75 you must have actually paid contributions on earnings equivalent to 52 times (50 times from 6.4.75 to 5.4.78) the lower earnings limit for that year; or have paid 50 flat-rate contributions at any time before 6.4.75.
- ❑ You must also have paid or have been credited with enough contributions to make at least a quarter of the years in your 'working life' count as 'qualifying years'.

National insurance contributions

From 1948 contributions were paid at a flat rate. Between 1961 and 1975 there was a system of graduated contributions, which were paid by some people in addition to flat-rate contributions. Graduated contributions were paid as a percentage of earnings between specified limits and earned people entitlement to graduated retirement benefit.

Since 1975 employees pay Class 1 contributions as a percentage of gross earnings, collected with income tax. You can also be credited with contributions. For example, you will normally be credited with a contribution for any week in which you are unemployed and signing on as available for work or in which you are incapable of work. These credits help you pass the contribution condition for a basic state pension. Your record can also be protected by home responsibilities protection (see Chapter 43).

For state pension purposes only, you may also be entitled to credits for the tax years of your 16th, 17th and 18th birthdays. Class 1 (employee), Class 2 (self-employed) and Class 3 (voluntary) contributions can all count towards your entitlement to a state pension.

Chapter 12 gives more details about contributions and contribution credits.

Your qualifying years

A 'qualifying year' is a tax year in which you have paid or been credited with enough contributions for a state pension.

In the old scheme, qualifying years were worked out by adding up all your stamps and dividing them by 50.

Under the current scheme, a qualifying year is one in which you have paid or been credited with contributions on earnings equivalent to 52 times the lower earnings limit for the year.

In the year April 2005 to April 2006, the lower earnings limit is £82 a week. However, people will only start to pay contributions on earnings above a higher level of £94 a week, the 'primary threshold'. Although they will not be paying contributions, people with earnings between £82 and £94 will still be building up entitlement to a state pension and other contributory benefits. When we refer in this book to people who have 'paid contributions' we are also including those in this position who are treated in the same way as those paying contributions.

For self-employed people and those paying voluntary contributions, the test is the number of flat-rate contributions, as it was under the old scheme, but divided by 52.

Working life

Your 'working life' is the period on which your contribution record is based. This is normally from the start of the tax year in which you became 16 to the last full tax year before you became 65 (for men) or 60 (for women).

Working life is therefore normally 44 years for a woman and 49 years for a man. But if you were already over 16 when the NI scheme started in 1948, your working life may be shorter. Contact The Pension Service for information. (Working life for women will increase as women's state pension age increases from 2010 onwards.)

To get a full basic state pension, about 9 out of every 10 years in your working life must be qualifying years. Women with a working life of 44 years need 39 qualifying years for a full basic state pension and men with a working life of 49 years need 44 qualifying years.

If you do not have enough qualifying years to get a full state pension, you will get a reduced pension as long as you have at least a quarter of the qualifying years you would need for a full pension.

Working out your state pension

In most cases, you won't need to work out your entitlement to a state pension. All your records should be on the computer in Newcastle, so all you have to do is to make sure that you put in a claim.

In a few cases it may be important to work out your state pension entitlement. For example, you may have worked for an employer and had full contributions deducted but find that you don't get a full state pension. This could be because one of your employers may not have paid over all your contributions – perhaps because of a bankruptcy.

If you think you are entitled to a different state pension, get in touch with The Pension Service immediately. They will check your contribution records and investigate any deficiencies.

You can also check the calculation yourself. If you reach a different figure and can show that you did not connive with your ex-employer in avoiding paying the contributions, the Inland Revenue (IR) can accept those contributions you had deducted from your pay as if they had been paid over at the right time. This power covers all contributory benefits. If you have not kept all your pay slips, or a good proportion of them, you may find that the IR will already have enough details.

A more normal example of needing to work out your potential entitlement to a state pension is if you are a married woman deciding whether or not to give up your existing right to pay the reduced-rate married woman's contribution.

State pension forecasts

To check your contribution record, you can ask for a state pension forecast if you are over 4 months away from your 60th birthday (women) or 65th birthday (men).

The forecast will give you your current state pension entitlement based on the records held by the IR. It should allow you (with some help if necessary) to make the right decisions about your future contribution position.

To get a forecast contact your local Jobcentre Plus office and ask for form BR19 or ring the State Pension Forecasting Team on 0845 300 0168.

B pension of up to £49.15. If he has a reduced contribution record, you will receive a proportionally reduced state pension. Your earnings received after you reach state pension age do not affect your state pension.

Widows and widowers – See DWP leaflet NP45 for details. If you qualify for a full Category B pension, you will get £82.05 a week.

Category A and Category B pensions overlap. So if, for example, you are a married woman with a basic state pension of £30 on your own contributions, you cannot receive this in addition to £49.15 Category B pension based on your husband's contributions. Instead, your state pension will be topped up to £49.15 using your husband's contributions.

Other state pension payments

Your Category A or B pension may also include:

Additional state pension – From 1978 to April 2002 additional state pension was built up under the state earnings-related pension scheme (SERPS). But from April 2002 the state second pension (S2P) replaced SERPS. If you are an employee with earnings over a certain level you will be contributing to the additional state pension unless you are contracted out of S2P and paying into a contracted out occupational pension or an appropriate personal pension or stakeholder pension (see Box N.2). Under S2P, some people who do not have earnings will be credited into the additional state pension.

To calculate your additional state pension, your earnings each year are added together (up to the upper-earnings limit, currently £630 a week) from April 1978 up to the April before you reach state pension age. The DWP then takes away the qualifying level of earnings for the basic state pension (£82 a week in 2005/06). This leaves a surplus of earnings for each year, which are then re-valued in line with increases in average earnings.

The original formula provided a state pension based on 25% of earnings between the specified levels. However, changes were introduced to phase in, between 1999 and 2009, a reduction in the amount of additional state pension people receive. The main aim of these changes was to reduce the maximum level of SERPS from 25% of earnings to 20% for people reaching state pension age from 2009 onwards (with some protection for years up to 1987/88). However, under S2P the amount of additional state pension someone earns is calculated in a different way. At present, S2P is related to earnings (although it may change to be a flat-rate state pension in the future). However, until that happens, everyone paying into S2P will be building up at least as much state pension as under SERPS, and anyone earning less than around £27,800 will be building up a higher state pension than under SERPS.

Certain disabled people, carers and people with low earnings will be credited into S2P. In 2004/05 people with annual qualifying earnings of at least £4,264 but less than £12,100 will be credited into S2P as though they have earnings of £12,100. You will also be treated as having earnings of £12,100 if, throughout the year, you:

- are paid carer's allowance, or would be paid it but for overlapping benefit rules; *or*
- are paid the long-term rate of IB, or would be paid it but for overlapping benefit rules or because you do not fulfil the contribution conditions; *or*
- are paid SDA (Note: Credits for disabled people getting SDA and IB will be subject to them having paid a certain number of years of contributions on retirement); *or*
- can get home responsibilities protection (HRP – see Chapter 43) because you are looking after a disabled person or a child under the age of 6. In most cases you will automatically be credited into S2P but some people need to claim HRP as explained in Chapter 43, and from 2002/03 onwards you must do this by the end of the third year following the one year for which you are claiming HRP.

For more details about the additional state pension see leaflet NP46.

For additional state pension earned up to 5.4.97, if you were contracted out of SERPS and were a member of a company salary-related scheme, all or part of your 'additional' pension will be paid, as a *'guaranteed minimum pension'* (GMP), via your employer. In this case, your state pension will include any increases needed to increase your GMP in line with inflation. For GMPs accruing after 6.4.88, the employer pays the first 3% of inflation proofing.

If you were contracted out of SERPS and belonged to your company's money purchase scheme or a personal pension scheme, you will receive a pension based on the value of the fund built up (through contributions and the investment return on these). The part of the fund which is intended to replace SERPS is known as your 'protected rights'. There is no GMP as such, but your additional state pension will be reduced by an amount which may be more or less than the pension provided by your scheme.

Since 6.4.97 there has not been a link between SERPS/S2P and contracted-out pension schemes. Instead of providing a GMP, a contracted-out salary-related scheme has to satisfy an overall test of quality. For contributions made from 6.4.97 your state pension will no longer be calculated by making a deduction from your additional state pension to take into account the time you have been in a contracted-out scheme. You will either receive an additional state pension or, if you are contracted out, an occupational or personal pension based on the scheme's rules.

Note that an additional state pension can be paid on its own if you aren't entitled to any basic state pension. It is also payable with long-term IB – but only for people who previously received invalidity benefit and are covered by the transitional rules – and with the widowed parent's allowance or widow's pension.

Widows and widowers may be able to inherit part or all of their spouse's SERPS and half of their S2P as part of their state pensions. Contact The Pension Service or see DWP guide NP46 for more information.

Graduated retirement benefit – This is based on graduated contributions made between April 1961 and April 1975. However, levels of payment are low – typically only £2 or £3 a week. Graduated retirement benefit can be paid on its own.

Invalidity addition – This may be paid if, within 8 weeks before reaching state pension age (or 52 weeks if you are a 'welfare to work beneficiary' – see Chapter 15(12)), you were receiving:

- an invalidity allowance with your invalidity benefit; *or*
- transitional invalidity allowance with IB; *or*
- an age addition with long-term IB.

Provided you get some additional state pension, you can get this even if you don't get any basic state pension. It is paid at the same rate as your invalidity allowance or age addition but is offset against an additional state pension or contracted out deduction.

Increments for deferring retirement – New rules were introduced in April 2005 to provide greater incentives for people who put off (or 'defer') claiming their state pension. If you put off drawing your pension for at least 7 weeks before April 2005, your state pension (including graduated retirement benefit and additional state pension) will be increased by 1% for each 7 weeks that you deferred drawing your pension. Before April 2005 you could only defer your pension for up to 5 years.

For periods of deferment after 6.4.05, your pension is increased by 1% for each 5 weeks that you put off drawing your pension, as long as you defer it for at least 5 weeks. Alternatively, if you defer your pension for at least 12 consecutive months, instead of an increased pension you can receive a one-off taxable lump sum based on the amount of pension you would have received plus interest. (This lump sum will be disregarded for income-related benefits such as pension credit.) If you defer for less than a year you will not receive interest payments but if you choose you can have your backdated pension paid as a lump sum. Under the new rules you can defer your pension and receive extra pension or a lump sum for as long as you wish – there is no longer a 5-year limit.

You cannot clock-up extra state pension by keeping another income maintenance benefit, such as widow's pension, after state pension age. An addition for an adult dependant won't be increased if you defer claiming state pension. However, a Category B pension may be increased, but not in respect of any period during which a wife receives any state pension or graduated retirement benefit based on her own contributions.

For more information about putting off your pension and things to take into account when considering your best option, see DWP leaflet SPD1 *Your state pension choice – pension now or extra later: a guide to state pension deferral.*

Age addition – This is 25p for people aged 80 or over.

5. Non-contributory state pension

Category D pensions

This is non-contributory and is paid at £49.15 a week to people who do not have a contributory state pension. Someone who has a contributory state pension of less than £49.15 can receive a Category D pension to top up their state pension to a total of £49.15. To qualify you must be aged 80 or over and satisfy certain residency conditions. To claim, ask The Pension Service for form BR 2488.

6. How do you claim state pension?

Normally The Pension Service sends you a claim-pack about 4 months before you reach 60 (women) or 65 (men). This will give you three options. You can ring 0845 300 1084 to make a claim over the phone; ring that number to be sent a claim-form; or send in a tear-off slip to get the claim-form. Although normally you will be automatically contacted about your state

N.2 Private pensions and further information

Pension options

In addition to building up a basic state pension, employees earning more than the lower earnings limit (£82 a week from April 2005) will normally be building up additional pension through the state second pension (S2P) (see Chapter 42(4)) unless they have 'contracted out' and joined their employers' occupational pension scheme or a personal pension instead. If you contract out of the state scheme through your employer's occupational pension, both you and your employer will pay a lower rate of national insurance (NI). If you contract out with an appropriate personal pension or a stakeholder pension (a type of personal pension which meets certain conditions) the Inland Revenue will pay a rebate of your NI contributions to your scheme provider. Some occupational pension schemes are not contracted out of S2P, so you can build up entitlement to both types of pension; it is also possible to contribute to other types of pensions, such as a stakeholder pension, and still be in S2P. If you are self-employed you cannot build up S2P or join an occupational pension, but you could pay into a personal pension.

The best way of building up a second pension is often to join an occupational pension scheme if your employer runs one. Your employer will provide details of the terms and conditions. You can get general information about your pension options from sources such as DWP pension leaflets and other publications including Age Concern's book *Your Guide to Pensions*. However, in some cases you may need to seek professional pensions advice, especially if you are not sure whether to contract out of S2P or not.

Private pensions and social security benefits

A private pension will be counted as income for means-tested benefits such as income support, income-based jobseeker's allowance (JSA), housing benefit or council tax benefit. It is also counted as income for pension credit, although it may help you qualify for savings credit. It will not normally affect your entitlement to non-means-tested benefits. However, an occupational or personal pension over certain levels may affect incapacity benefit or contribution-based JSA and a private pension counts as earnings if your partner is claiming an increase for you as an adult dependant, or if they are claiming an increase for a child dependant. More information is given in the appropriate sections of this Handbook.

Problems with occupational, personal and stakeholder pensions

If you are a member of an occupational pension scheme or have a personal or stakeholder pension and you have a problem with your pension, ask your pension provider for details of their internal disputes procedure.

If you are not satisfied with the response or need further help or advice you can contact the Pensions Advisory Service (Helpline 0845 601 2923). They can give general information or individual advice about pension problems and may be able to help resolve the problem by taking up your case and negotiating with your provider. If the Pensions Advisory Service cannot solve your problem, they may recommend that you take your complaint to the Pensions Ombudsman.

The Pensions Advisory Service and the Pensions Ombudsman are both based at 11 Belgrave Road, London SW1V 1RB.

In April 2005 The Pensions Regulator replaced the Occupational Pensions Regulatory Authority (OPRA) as the body that regulates pension schemes. It is based at Invicta House, Trafalgar Place, Trafalgar Street, Brighton BN1 4DW (01273 627 600).

The Pension Tracing Service (formerly called Pension Schemes Registry) provides a free tracing service for people who want to contact a scheme in which they may have pension rights but do not know the contact address: The Pension Tracing Service, The Pension Service, Whitley Road, Newcastle upon Tyne NE98 1BA (0845 600 2537).

DWP leaflets

The following DWP guides give general information about different types of pensions:

PM 1 *A Guide to your Pension Options*
PM 2 *State Pensions – Your Guide*
PM 3 *Occupational Pensions – Your Guide*
PM 4 *Personal Pensions – Your Guide*
PM 5 *Pensions for the Self-Employed – Your Guide*
PM 6 *Pensions for Women – Your Guide*
PM 7 *Contracted-Out Pensions – Your Guide*
PM 8 *Stakeholder Pensions – Your Guide*
PM 9 *State Pensions for Parents and Carers – Your Guide*
NP 46 *A Guide to State Pensions*

These can be obtained by ringing 0845 731 3233 or Textphone 0845 604 0210, or by downloading from www.thepensionservice.gov.uk/resource_centre/downloads.asp#guides.

pension, this does not always happen. The Pension Service may not have your current address, especially if you have not worked for some time. If you haven't received the claim-pack by 3 months before your 60th/65th birthday ring 0845 300 1084 or contact your local Jobcentre Plus office to get a pack. (This number is only for making a claim. Staff will not be able to provide general information about pensions or help if you are more than 4 months away from state pension age.)

If you do not draw your pension when you reach state pension age and you claim on or before 6.7.05, you can only get up to 3 months back payment. If you claim on or after 7.7.05 and before 6.4.06, your pension can be backdated to 6.4.05. From 6.4.06, state pension can be backdated for up to 12 months. Instead of receiving backdated pension you may prefer to receive an increased pension (see 4 above). If you have deferred your state pension you should contact The Pension Service up to 4 months before you do wish to draw it. If you have already started to draw your state pension but wish to give it up in order to gain increases or a lump sum, contact The Pension Service. You can only give up your state pension once and you cannot backdate this choice.

State pension can only start from a pay day, which is normally Monday for people who start to draw their state pension now. You cannot receive any state pension for days before your first pay day, even if you have reached state pension age.

7. How is state pension paid?

State pension is normally paid directly into a post office, bank or building society account. You can choose to receive it weekly in advance or in arrears every 4 or 13 weeks. If payment into an account is not suitable for you or you do not provide account details, your state pension will be sent by cheque through the post each week. It is no longer possible to receive your state pension using an order book. See Chapter 57(5) for more on payments.

If your state pension is £5 or less a week, it will normally be paid in a lump sum along with your £10 Christmas bonus.

43 Home responsibilities protection

1. What is home responsibilities protection?

Home responsibilities protection (HRP) aims to protect your basic state pension rights (and bereavement benefits) when you are not paying national insurance contributions because you are looking after someone who is sick or disabled for a whole tax year and are not getting a benefit, such as carer's allowance (invalid care allowance before April 2003), which credits you with contributions. This scheme first began in April 1978, so only the tax years after that time can be covered by HRP. HRP is not a contribution credit and does not make up a deficiency in a person's contribution record.

HRP is intended to help you satisfy the second condition for the full basic state pension (see Box N.1), which is that 9 out of every 10 years in your working life must be qualifying years. The total number of years in which you were awarded HRP will be deducted from the number of qualifying years you normally need for a full basic state pension. HRP cannot reduce the required number of qualifying years to less than 20.

2. Do you qualify?

You will qualify for HRP if throughout a complete tax year:

- you spend at least 35 hours a week looking after someone who gets attendance allowance, disability living allowance care component at the middle or highest rate, or constant attendance allowance, for 48 or more weeks in the year (52 weeks for tax years before 6.4.88); *or*
- you get income support and are not required to register for work because you are looking after a sick or disabled person; *or*
- you are paid child benefit for a child under 16; *or*
- you are a foster carer (for tax years 2003/04 onwards).

3. Does anything affect the provision of HRP?

Work – Work makes no practical difference. If you qualify for HRP, you will get it if you have not paid or been treated as having paid enough national insurance (NI) contributions that tax year to count for state pension.

Change of circumstances – If any one of the conditions in 2 (above) covers you for only part of the year but another covers you for the rest of the same year, you can apply for HRP. But, if you meet the qualifying conditions for only part of that year, you will not get HRP for that year.

Married women and widows – If you are still liable to pay the reduced-rate contribution at any time during a tax year, you cannot get HRP for that tax year. You can change to paying full NI contributions from the start of the next tax week after you notify the DWP. But this will make no difference to your HRP position until the start of the next tax year after you change to full liability.

After you have spent 2 consecutive tax years without paying a reduced-rate Class 1 contribution (and were not self-employed), your right to pay reduced contributions will end at the end of the second tax year in any case. If you are likely to spend more than 2 tax years out of the employment field, it may be worth switching to full NI liability.

4. How do you apply?

If you are a man or a woman getting child benefit and your name is the first or only name on the order book or on letters about child benefit, or you are getting income support and are not required to register for work because you are looking after a sick or disabled person, you do not have to apply. Your HRP should be recorded automatically (you can check with your local Jobcentre Plus office that this is happening).

If you are the parent whose national insurance (NI) contributions record is affected, it is important to be the one claiming child benefit. Contact the Child Benefit Office if you wish to change to become the claimant. For tax years from 2004/05 onwards you will be treated as having entitlement to child benefit where payment has been transferred to you by a 'higher priority claimant' in the first 3 months of the tax year (and child benefit would have been payable to you but for the fact that it was still being paid to that other claimant).

If you are looking after someone who is getting disability living allowance care component at the middle or highest rate, attendance allowance or constant attendance allowance, you are a foster carer or if you are covered partly by one of the general conditions and partly by another, you will have to apply for each tax year you need HRP. But note that if you get carer's allowance (and haven't kept your right to pay reduced-rate contributions – see 3), you will be credited automatically with NI contributions and may not need HRP.

To apply, just complete the form in leaflet CF411. You can get this from your local Jobcentre Plus or Inland Revenue office. For tax years up to 2001/02, if HRP has not been awarded automatically, you can apply at any time, but from tax year 2002/03 onwards you need to notify the DWP by the end of the third year following the year for which you are claiming HRP.

This section of the Handbook looks at:

Special compensation schemes

O

44 Industrial Injuries scheme

1. Who is covered by the scheme?

The Industrial Injuries scheme provides no-fault tax-free benefit for an employee who *'suffers personal injury caused after 4.7.48 by accident arising out of and in the course of'* work, or who contracts a prescribed disease or a prescribed injury while working.

S.94 Social Security Contributions and Benefits Act 1992 for accidents; ss.108–110 for prescribed diseases

You are covered by the Industrial Injuries scheme if you are working for an employer. It doesn't matter if you don't earn enough to pay national insurance (NI) contributions, or if you are too old or too young to pay them – eg a 14-year-old paper boy could be covered. Nor does it matter if the accident happens on your first day at work. What counts is that you are gainfully employed under a contract of service, or as an office-holder with earnings that would be taxable under Schedule E. If you are genuinely self-employed you will not be covered unless the accident happens while you are doing specified types of voluntary work, eg a special constable.

You are covered by the Industrial Injuries scheme if your accident occurred outside the UK if your employer was paying NI contributions for you while you were working abroad or if you were working in a European Community country or Norway or on the continental shelf of the UK, or as a mariner or airman, or as a volunteer development worker who continued to pay UK contributions.

Apprentices who are not 'gainfully employed' are covered by the scheme. But if you are a non-employed trainee on either a youth or adult training scheme you are covered by a special scheme instead. Benefits are equivalent to those paid under the Industrial Injuries scheme. For more information ring 01977 464111 and ask for the analogous Industrial Injuries section.

If there is any doubt over your status as an employed earner, your case is decided by an officer of the Inland Revenue with a right of appeal to the Tax Commissioners. It may be possible to show that you were an employee for benefit purposes (despite the tax and NI arrangements) if the real relationship between you and the contractor is that of an employee and employer. This applies in particular to building workers who are very often categorised as self-employed; it may well be decided that you are in fact an employed earner. Your trade union may be able to advise you.

2. Industrial accidents

If you have an accident at work you should report the details as soon as possible to your employer. Enter them in the accident book (one must be kept at any workplace where 10 or more people usually work). Do this even if things don't seem serious at first. A cut can turn septic. A pain in the stomach can turn out to be a hernia. If you think the accident might have some ill-effect in future, apply to the DWP for a declaration that you have had an industrial accident. You can get the application form (BI95) from your local Jobcentre Plus office.

In most cases it will be clear that an 'accident' has happened and that it was 'industrial', but case law has expanded these concepts to include less obvious situations. For example, a conversation or verbal harassment could constitute an accident. Box O.1 looks at these issues in more detail and at some of the problems that can arise.

If you are in any doubt about whether you are covered by the Industrial Injuries scheme you should apply for an 'accident declaration' and claim benefit anyway. The case law is complex so always get advice if you are turned down.

If your accident occurred before 5.7.48 see DWP booklet DB1, *A guide to Industrial Injuries Benefits*, which gives details of the Workmen's Compensation scheme.

3. Prescribed industrial diseases

Benefit can be paid for around 60 different diseases or conditions which are prescribed as being risks of particular occupations and not risks common to the general population. These are listed in the DWP guide DB1 along with the types of occupations you must have worked in to qualify for benefit.

Provided you have worked in the relevant occupation at some time since 5.7.48, it does not matter if the disease started earlier; the date of onset can be treated as 5.7.48 (CI/17220/96). If your relevant occupation finished before 5.7.48, you may be covered instead by the Pneumoconiosis, Byssinosis and Miscellaneous Diseases Benefit scheme or the Workmen's Compensation scheme. Booklet DB1 has details.

It is up to you to claim benefit for a prescribed disease. If you have any reason to suspect that your illness is related to your work, you must ask the DWP and your doctor for advice. If you do not, you may lose benefit. For example, few secretaries realise that they may be covered by prescribed disease A4 if they experience cramp of the hand or forearm. Similarly, welders or hairdressers with hay fever symptoms may have a claim for prescribed disease D4, allergic rhinitis.

If your disability arises from a non-listed condition that was contracted at work, you may still be able to claim under the 'accident' provisions. Case law has shown that the 'catching' of the condition can be accepted as an industrial accident; such cases include a nursery nurse who contracted poliomyelitis from an infected child (CI/159/50) and a tinner whose frequent burns on the hands caused cysts (R(I)24/54).

4. Common law compensation

In addition to a claim for benefit under the Industrial Injuries scheme you may have a civil claim for personal injury against your employer. With industrial diseases this could apply even if you did the job years ago or the employer has ceased trading; in some cases an award can be significantly more than can be claimed in benefits. You may also claim for non-listed conditions. Normally, your employer has to be partly at fault, but for some industrial diseases (eg deafness) there are no-fault compensation schemes that have been negotiated between unions and employers. The time limit for filing civil claims is 3 years from the date of the accident. For diseases, the 3 years start from the date you became aware that your disease or condition was caused by work.

You will need a solicitor. Your union may help or you can contact The Accident Line (see Box O.4). While many solicitors deal with personal injury claims, it is important to choose a solicitor who specialises in your specific condition, particularly if you have an asbestos-related disease. An advice centre may be able to advise you, or you could try the Community Legal Service website: www.clsdirect.org.uk.

For information about the way in which benefits are affected by compensation payments, see Chapter 48 and Chapter 5(12).

For certain dust diseases including mesothelioma, asbestosis and pneumoconiosis, a lump-sum payment can be claimed under the Pneumoconiosis etc (Workers' Compensation) Act 1979, when a civil compensation claim may not be possible because the employer is no longer in business. If in doubt, claim anyway. Negligence need not be proved and payment is made in full without recovery of DWP benefits paid. You should make a claim under the Act at the same time as you claim industrial injuries disablement benefit (IIDB). Any payment made will be based on your age and the DWP percentage assessment of your disablement for IIDB purposes, but do not wait for an assessment before claiming under the Act. Posthumous claims can be made by dependants but any payment made is substantially less than is paid if the sufferer makes the initial claim. For claim-forms and more information ring free on 0800 279 2322.

There are special schemes in particular industries, eg mining and the NHS. Trade unions should be able to advise their members on these, as well as on benefits and other types of compensation. Various schemes created by agreements between British Coal and mining unions are now administered by the Department of Trade and Industry. For more information, contact DTI Coal Liabilities Unit, 1 Victoria Street, London SW1H 0ET.

5. What benefits can you claim?

Statutory sick pay or incapacity benefit

If you are employed but incapable of work, you should claim statutory sick pay (SSP) from your employer (see Chapter 13). If you are not entitled to SSP, you can claim incapacity benefit if you have paid enough national insurance contributions (see Chapter 14).

The provision for claiming no-contribution sickness benefit on the grounds of industrial accident or disease was abolished in April 1995 (see Box E.10, Chapter 14).

O.1 Accidents at work – principles of entitlement

What is an accident?

You must first show that an 'accident' has occurred. While this is usually clear cut, there are situations where it may not be immediately obvious. In CI/2414/98, for example, a conversation with a colleague causing the claimant to suffer stress and depression was accepted as an accident and the opinion given that words alone such as *'verbal sexual harassment at work [could] amount to an accident or series of accidents as might misinformation designed to shock or causing shock'*.

In most cases an accident will involve an unexpected event. In *CAO v Faulds* (appendix to R(I)1/00), the claimant was a fireman suffering post-traumatic stress disorder after attending a series of horrific incidents. The House of Lords rejected the argument that attending such incidents was the job for which he had been trained and so could not constitute 'accidents' to him, and decided that an accident need not be an unexpected event but that the sustaining of an *unexpected* personal injury caused by an *expected* event or incident may itself amount to an accident.

Accident or process?

Problems can arise where the injury developed relatively slowly through the normal course of work. This is called injury by 'process'. If your injury developed as a result of a continuous process at work you will not be entitled to industrial injuries benefits, unless your injury is listed as one of the prescribed industrial diseases.

However, Commissioners tend to recognise that an industrial accident has happened where an injury can be shown to be the cumulative result of a series of accidental injuries. A series of small incidents, each of which is separate and identifiable, that were slightly out of the ordinary can be enough to count as 'accidents'. But each one must have led to some physiological or pathological change for the worse. For example, in R(I)43/55 the claimant developed a psychoneurotic condition and skin disorder. He had been working near a machine that irregularly produced loud explosive reports. Any one of them could have been the start of a major explosion. It was held that each explosion was an 'accident' with a cumulative effect on his condition.

If a process has only been going on for a short time, or you have just started a new job or have had a change in working conditions, it may be easier to show you have suffered injury by accident, but each case will be a matter of fact and degree.

What about other causes of injury?

If you have a condition that predisposes you to certain injuries you can still be covered by the scheme but some aspect of your employment must have caused the injury. Your claim will fail if it was pure coincidence that you had the heart attack, strain, fit, etc at work rather than somewhere else.

For example, an asthma sufferer had an acute asthma attack due to fumes from a fire at work. He was covered, as it was probable that he would not have had that attack if it had not been for the fire at work.

But this is not always clear cut. In R(I)6/82, it was confirmed that, even if an accident happens out of the blue, it will count as an 'industrial' one if the activity you are doing represents a special danger to you because of something in yourself or you are also injured because of coming into contact with the employer's plant or premises (eg by falling on to the floor).

Industrial injuries disablement benefit

Industrial injuries disablement benefit (IIDB) is paid to compensate those who have suffered disablement from a *'loss of physical or mental faculty'* caused by an industrial accident or prescribed disease (see Box 0.2). Your employer does not have to be at fault in any way for you to get benefit.

You can claim whether or not you are incapable of work or have had any drop in earnings. Benefit is payable from 15 weeks after the date of the accident or the onset of the disease if your disablement is assessed at 14% or more. For some prescribed chest diseases you can get benefit if the assessment is from 1% to 13%. For occupational deafness you can only get benefit if your disablement is 20% or more.

If you are claiming for a prescribed disease, the date of onset should be the date the disease started, not the date of claim. As benefit is only payable 15 weeks after this date, you should check this and challenge it if necessary. However, for occupational deafness, the law says that the date of onset must be the date a successful claim was made, and payment can start from that day. There is no 15-week waiting period for people with prescribed disease D3, diffuse mesothelioma.

Reduced earnings allowance

Reduced earnings allowance (REA) replaced special hardship allowance from 1.10.86. REA itself was abolished on 1.10.90, but only for accidents or diseases occurring after that date. So if your accident or the onset of a prescribed disease (which must be listed before 10.10.94) occurred before 1.10.90, you can still claim REA and there is no upper age limit. See 14 for more details.

Retirement allowance

Retirement allowance (RA) replaces REA if you are already getting at least £2 a week REA and are not in regular employment when you reach state pension age. See 15 for more details.

IIDB, REA and RA are all tax free and paid on top of any earnings or other non-means-tested benefits you may receive.

Industrial death benefit

Industrial death benefit is now only payable where the death occurred before 11.4.88. Those widowed on or after 11.4.88 as a result of an industrial accident or prescribed disease are entitled to widows' benefits and, since 9.4.01, bereavement benefits, without having to satisfy any contribution conditions (see Chapter 51).

6. How do you claim industrial injuries disablement benefit (IIDB)?

You should get form BI100A for an accident; BI100(Pn) for pneumoconiosis, byssinosis or an asbestos-related disease; BI100(OD) for occupational deafness; BI100(OA) for occupational asthma; BI100C for chronic bronchitis and emphysema in underground coal miners; BI100E for allergic rhinitis; or BI100B for any of the other prescribed industrial diseases.

You have 3 months from the first day you were entitled to benefit (15 weeks after the accident/accepted date of onset of the disease) in which to make your claim. If you claim after this, benefit cannot be backdated more than 3 months even if you have a good reason for not claiming earlier.

There are special time limits for the following prescribed diseases.

- **Occupational deafness** – To qualify, you must have worked in one or more of the listed jobs as an employed earner for a total of at least 10 years, and have a hearing loss of at least 50db in each ear, due, in the case of at least

Is it an 'industrial' accident?

To count as an 'industrial' accident, it must have arisen *out of* and *in the course* of employment. The difference between these phrases is clearly shown in *CAO v Rhodes* (appendix to R(I)1/99). Here, a Benefits Agency worker was assaulted by a neighbour whom she had reported for undeclared earnings. As the worker was at home on sick leave, she was found to have had an accident *out of* her employment but not *in the course* of it. Had she been working at home on the day, the outcome might have been different.

If your accident happens during an early arrival, late stay or permitted break on the employer's premises you would probably be covered. But if you had got in early or overstayed the break purely for your own purposes (eg to have a game of snooker), you would have taken yourself outside the course of your employment.

Travelling to and from work

In the main, you are not covered if you have an accident while travelling to or from your regular workplace but you may be covered while travelling in the employer's time to an irregular workplace so that your journey can be accepted as having formed part of the work you were employed to do (see R(I)// 85). One important (but not conclusive) factor is whether you were being paid for the time spent on the journey or were able to claim overtime or time off in lieu for it. You will usually be covered if you are in transport provided by your employer. You will not be covered if your journey is for your own purposes, unconnected with your work (unless it is reasonably incidental to it).

Peripatetic workers, such as home-helps, are normally accepted as covered when travelling between jobs but not when travelling to the first or from the last job.

'Emergencies'

If you have an accident while responding to an emergency, you will be covered if what you did was reasonably incidental to your normal duties and was a sensible reaction to the emergency. Besides the obvious emergencies of fire and flood, unexpected occurrences can also count.

In one case, a lorry driver delivering bricks helped move a concrete mixer out of the way and was injured. He was covered as, even though that was not a normal part of his duties, it was reasonably incidental to his work and it was in his employer's interests for him to complete his delivery quickly.

Accidents treated as 'industrial'

Some accidents can be 'treated as' arising out of work. If you have broken any rules but what you have done is for the purposes of, and in connection with, your employer's business, you will be covered if you have an accident. You may have problems if what you have done is not part of your job, but if you can show that your employer would not automatically have stopped you doing the activity in question you might succeed. You must also show that it was in your employer's interests.

If you have an accident during work because of someone else's misconduct, negligence or skylarking, you will be covered if you can show that you did not contribute directly or indirectly to the accident. You will also be covered if, during the course of your work, you are struck by any object or by lightning.

one ear, to occupational noise. If you qualify you will be paid from the date your claim is received in a DWP office – and that date must be within 5 years of the last day you worked in one of the jobs prescribed (see below under 'Occupational asthma'). There is no backdating of claims.

The Court of Appeal, in McKiernon v Secretary of State [1989], held that the 5-year time limit was not valid in law. However, the law was changed to make the time limit valid retrospectively.

- **Occupational asthma** – You cannot get IIDB for occupational asthma if you stopped working in the prescribed job more than 10 years before your date of claim. But this 10-year limit does not apply if you have asthma because of an industrial accident and have been awarded IIDB for life or for a period which includes your date of claim. Since 10.7.00, for the purposes of satisfying the 10-year limit (and the 5-year limit for occupational deafness), only employed earners' employment counts. If you are outside these time limits, a return to a listed occupation for just one day would start the period running again.
- **Chronic bronchitis and emphysema** – To qualify you must have worked underground in a coal mine for a total of 20 years (this includes periods of sickness absence) and have a defined reduction in lung capacity. In April 1997 the medical conditions were modified, so if your claim was refused under the old rules you should reapply.

7. How is your claim decided?

Since 5.7.99, all decisions, including medical issues such as diagnosis and degree of disablement, are made by the

O.2 How is disablement assessed?

The legislation uses three different terms when considering disablement questions. These are:

- loss of faculty;
- disability;
- disablement.

They are each used as different concepts and must not be confused. They are not defined in the law but have been considered by the Social Security Commissioners, particularly in R(I)1/81.

Loss of faculty

A 'loss of faculty' is any pathological condition or any loss (including a reduction) of the normal physical or mental function of an organ or part of the body. This does include disfigurement, even though there may not actually be any loss of faculty. For industrial injuries disablement benefit (IIDB), the loss of faculty must be caused by an industrial accident or prescribed disease.

A loss of faculty is not itself a disability. It is the starting point for the assessment of disablement. It is a condition that is either an actual cause of one or more disabilities or a potential cause of disability. For example, the loss of one kidney is a 'loss of faculty'. If the other kidney works normally, you may not notice any problems. But you will have lost your back-up kidney, so this is a potential cause of disability in the future. Appeal tribunals have assessed the loss of one kidney (the other functioning properly) at between 5% to 10%.

Disability

A 'disability' means an inability to perform a bodily or mental process. This can be a complete inability to do something (eg walking), or it can be a partial inability to do something (eg you can lift light weights but not heavy ones). The disability must result from the relevant 'loss of faculty' to count for IIDB. Note that the availability of artificial aids may reduce the actual disability. The only reported Commissioners' decisions on this, R(1)7/67 and R(1)7/63, concerned spectacles.

Disablement

'Disablement' is the sum total of all the separate disabilities you may experience. It represents your overall inability to perform the 'normal' activities of life – the loss of your health, strength and power to enjoy a 'normal' life. There is a complete scale of assessment from 1 to 100% disablement. Every case is decided individually, so it is possible to give only general guidelines. Some types of disability have a fixed percentage, which can be increased or decreased depending on the circumstances of the case. These 'scheduled assessments' are listed in Box O.3. Other disabilities are assessed in relation to this list.

What is taken into account?

The assessment is done by comparing your condition (all your disabilities due to the relevant loss of faculty) with that of a person of the same age and sex whose physical and mental condition is 'normal'. The decision maker, or in practice the DWP doctor who assesses you, also has to make judgements about what is normal for someone of your age and sex. For example, how much hearing loss is normal for a man of 50? At what age does it become normal to lose teeth and wear false teeth?

If your condition differed from normal prior to the accident and therefore the industrial injury is more disabling than it would otherwise be, the assessment may be increased to take account of this. For example, decision makers *'are entitled to increase the disablement percentage to take account of the fact that, when disaster struck, he was blind. They are not entitled to compensate him for the blindness itself, but they are entitled to take account of the fact that a particular happening to a blind man, or somebody suffering from some other disability, may be more serious of itself than it would be in the case of a man who suffered from no disability'* (*Murrell v Secretary of State for Social Security* (appendix to R(I)3/84)).

The decision maker also has to consider how your condition affects you, rather than just considering what is generally true of people with your condition or taking the same drugs. Inconvenience, genuine embarrassment, anxiety, or depression can all increase the assessment.

If your disablement also has a mental element, R(I)4/94 provides a useful summary of the ways in which that might affect the assessment of disablement. R(I)13/75 discusses the differences between hysteria, malingering and functional overlay. See also CSI/1180/01 and CI/1756/02.

There have been a number of cases involving stress-related conditions, which are particularly difficult to assess in relation to the schedule. CI/1307/99 is useful in this respect, the Commissioner using the tariffs for facial disfigurement and loss of sight as bearing the closest comparison in that they interfere with interpersonal communications.

The fact of your loss of earning power, or incapacity for work, cannot be taken into account in the assessment. Nor can the fact that your disabilities may lead to extra expenses. But the disabilities that lead to incapacity for work (or extra expenses) are taken into account, along with disabilities that do not affect your working capacity at all.

The assessment doesn't just depend on your condition on the day (or time of day) you are examined. If your condition varies, the doctor will work out an average assessment taking into account your good and bad spells. It is arguable that any loss of life expectancy can also be taken into account, as well as the effect of your knowledge of the nature of your disability on your life.

Secretary of State – in practice a DWP decision maker acting on behalf of the Secretary of State. As decision makers are not medically trained they invariably adopt the DWP doctor's opinion on medical questions, so in practice there is little difference from the previous system when such decisions were made by adjudicating medical authorities and medical appeal tribunals.

However, one important effect of the 5.7.99 changes was highlighted in CI/1307/99, where the Commissioner replaced a medical appeal tribunal percentage assessment of disablement with his own, thereby establishing the principle that the degree of disablement is a legal rather than medical matter. He also attempted to set some objective standards to explain his assessment by reference to the listed percentages in Schedule 2 (see Box O.3).

This was taken further in CI/499/00, and more recently in CI/1199/02, and means that future tribunals will need to explain their assessments in some similarly objective way (see Box O.2 for details).

Accident cases

The decision maker decides whether you have had an industrial accident and if so, whether it arose out of and in the course of your work. If the decision is in your favour, you will be asked to go for a medical examination.

You will be examined by one (or possibly two) DWP doctors. They will provide the decision maker with a report giving an opinion on whether you have a loss of faculty as a result of the accident and, if so, the extent to which that loss of faculty leads to disablement and the period over which it is

Scheduled and non-scheduled assessments

The scheduled assessments, listed in Box O.3, are fixed on the assumption that your condition has stabilised and there are no added complications. Other disabilities are assessed accordingly.

If your disability is not in the schedule, the decision maker *'may have such regard as may be appropriate to the prescribed degrees of disablement'*. They should try to assess your disabilities so that your percentage assessment looks right in relation to the scheduled assessments.

When you look at the schedule, remember that 100% is not total and absolute disablement. It is just the legal maximum assessment. If the scale could go higher, some people would be assessed as 200% disabled – or more.

The schedule says that if you are totally deaf, or severely facially disfigured, the fixed assessment is 100%.

If you have had either arm amputated just below the shoulder, you will be assessed at 80% – even if you cope perfectly well. If the amputation has not yet stabilised, or there are other complications with it, a higher assessment can be made.

If you cannot use one arm at all, you may well be assessed at 80% – as if you had actually lost your arm. CI/1199/02 usefully illustrates this point in relation to vibration white finger (PD A11).

Several conditions

Four different disabilities due to the same accident or prescribed disease may be each assessed as causing 10% disablement, but the assessment will not always be the total of 40%. This is because the interaction of different conditions in one person may be far more disabling – so the final assessment could well be higher. If you have several of the minor scheduled conditions, the total percentage assessment could be less or more than the actual total of the percentages for each of the scheduled conditions. The doctor will give their opinion on what is the appropriate assessment for you – given your age, sex and physical and mental condition as a whole. So even for the scheduled assessments, the doctor may increase (or decrease) the percentage(s) if that is reasonable in a particular case.

Pre-existing condition

If your disability has some other cause, you may have problems – eg where a previous back injury is followed by an industrial injury to your back. However, your percentage assessment should only be cut, or offset, if there is evidence that a pre-existing condition would have led to a degree of disablement even if the accident had not happened. If there is no evidence for this, the offset should not be made. R(I)1/81 explains the concepts fully.

If an offset is justified, the net assessment (ie after the offset) should reflect any greater disablement because of the interaction between the two (or more) causes of the same disability. Note that a pre-existing condition may cause disablement later. Although the disablement you would have had from that pre-existing condition alone cannot be taken into account, its interaction with the effects of the industrial injury may lead to greater disablement. This could justify a request for a supersession on the grounds of a change of circumstances (see 10).

Conditions arising afterwards

If a condition is 'directly attributable' to the industrial accident or disease, it is assessable in the normal way. If it is not 'directly attributable', but is also a cause of the same disability, then whether or not any greater disablement can be taken into account depends on the percentage assessment for the industrial accident or disease. If the disablement resulting from the industrial accident is assessed at 11% or more, that assessment can be increased to reflect the extent to which the industrial injury is worsened because of the later condition. This can be done at the time of the assessment, or later on an application for a supersession. Note that in reaching the 11% benchmark, account is taken of any greater disablement because of the interaction with a pre-existing condition that is also an effective cause of the disability.

The 11% rule does not apply where one is considering the interaction between two or more industrial accidents or diseases (see R(I)3/91).

The medical report completed by the DWP doctor provides a useful guide to the methods of assessment where there is more than one cause of the same disability and where the interaction of another condition causes greater disability.

The Medical Assessment Framework

Guidance on assessing disablement given to examining doctors (and decision makers) includes the Medical Assessment Framework (MAF), which has now been made public. It contains a 'rough guide' to the level of assessments giving examples which seem to confuse 'disablement' with 'loss of faculty' and could explain why percentages for certain conditions can seem unaccountably low – eg no back conditions seem to merit an assessment of more than 30%.

References to the MAF now appear in tribunal papers. In CI/499/00 the Commissioner warns that the guide *'must not be used in substitution for the legal test'*. He adds that not explaining how an assessment percentage was reached will be an error of law and usefully goes on to describe ways this might be done, including by reference to the list in Schedule 2 (see Box O.3), the practice used in CI/1307/99 (see 7). The MAF is available on our website: www.disabilityalliance.org/links.htm.

likely to last. The percentage assessment of your disablement can cover a past period as well as a forward one.

The decision maker will then decide your claim based on this medical report as well as any other available evidence, such as a letter from your GP. In practice they will normally adopt the DWP doctor's opinion.

Prescribed industrial diseases

The decision maker will decide whether you have worked in one of the occupations prescribed for your particular disease or condition and whether it was caused by that occupation. For many prescribed diseases there is a presumption in law that, unless the contrary can be proved, your condition was caused by your job if you were working in the listed occupation on the date of onset or within one month of that date. If it is decided that you don't satisfy these employment conditions, your claim will be refused. You have the right to appeal against this decision within one month.

0.3 Listed conditions

Prescribed degrees of disablement

Description of injury	Degree
Loss of both hands or amputation at higher sites	100%
Loss of a hand and a foot	100%
Double amputation through leg or thigh, or amputation through leg or thigh on one side and loss of other foot	100%
Loss of sight to such an extent as to render the claimant unable to perform any work for which eyesight is essential	100%
Very severe facial disfiguration	100%
Absolute deafness	100%
Forequarter or hindquarter amputation	100%
Amputation cases – upper limbs (either arm)	
Amputation through shoulder joint	90%
Amputation below shoulder with stump less than 20.5 centimetres from tip of acromion	80%
Amputation from 20.5 centimetres from tip of acromion to less than 11.5 centimetres below tip of olecranon	70%
Loss of a hand or of the thumb and four fingersof one hand or amputation from 11.5 centimetres below tip of olecranon	60%
Loss of thumb	30%
Loss of thumb and its metacarpal bone	40%
Loss of four fingers of one hand	50%
Loss of three fingers of one hand	30%
Loss of two fingers of one hand	20%
Loss of terminal phalanx of thumb	20%
Amputation cases – lower limbs	
Amputation of both feet resulting in end-bearing stumps	90%
Amputation through both feet proximal to the metatarso-phalangeal joint	80%
Loss of all toes of both feet through the metatarso-phalangeal joint	40%
Loss of all toes of both feet proximal to the proximal inter-phalangeal joint	30%
Loss of all toes of both feet distal to the proximal inter-phalangeal joint	20%
Amputation at hip	90%
Amputation below hip with stump not exceeding 13 centimetres in length measured from tip of great trochanter	80%
Amputation below hip and above knee with stump exceeding 13 centimetres in length measured from tip of great trochanter, or at knee not resulting in end-bearing stump	70%
Amputation at knee resulting in end-bearing stump or below knee with stump not exceeding 9 centimetres	60%
Amputation below knee with stump exceeding 9 centimetres but not exceeding 13 centimetres	50%
Amputation below knee with stump exceeding 13 centimetres	40%
Amputation of one foot resulting in end-bearing stump	30%
Amputation through one foot proximal to the metatarso-phalangeal joint	30%
Loss of all toes of one foot through the metatarso-phalangeal joint	20%
Other injuries	
Loss of one eye, without complications, the other being normal	40%
Loss of vision of one eye, without complications or disfigurement of the eyeball, the other being normal	30%
Loss of fingers of right or left hand	
❑ **Index finger:**	
Whole	14%
Two phalanges	11%
One phalanx	9%
Guillotine amputation of tip without loss of bone	5%
❑ **Middle finger:**	
Whole	12%
Two phalanges	9%
One phalanx	7%
Guillotine amputation of tip without loss of bone	4%
❑ **Ring or little finger:**	
Whole	7%
Two phalanges	6%
One phalanx	5%
Guillotine amputation of tip without loss of bone	2%
Loss of toes of right or left foot	
❑ **Great toe:**	
Through metatarso-phalangeal joint	14%
Part, with some loss of bone	3%
❑ **Any other toe:**	
Through metatarso-phalangeal joint	3%
Part, with some loss of bone	1%
❑ **Two toes of one foot, excluding great toe:**	
Through metatarso-phalangeal joint	5%
Part, with some loss of bone	2%
❑ **Three toes of one foot, excluding great toe:**	
Through metatarso-phalangeal joint	6%
Part, with some loss of bone	3%
❑ **Four toes of one foot, excluding great toe:**	
Through metatarso-phalangeal joint	9%
Part, with some loss of bone	3%

Schedule 2, Social Security (General Benefit) Regs 1982

If the decision maker decides that you do satisfy the employment conditions, you will be asked to go for a medical examination by one (or possibly two) DWP doctors. They will send a report to the decision maker giving their opinion on whether you have the prescribed disease; any resulting loss of faculty; the level and period of your disablement; the date of onset; and whether your disease is due to your employment. The doctor(s) can obtain reports from your hospital consultant and GP if necessary. Although in deciding your claim the decision maker has to take into account all the available evidence, they will normally adopt the DWP doctor's opinion.

If you are claiming for certain asbestos-related diseases or some prescribed cancers, your claim will be fast-tracked and you will be sent for a medical examination while the employment questions are being considered. If you are suffering from diffuse mesothelioma (PD D3), a medical examination may not be necessary if confirmation of your diagnosis is provided by your consultant, GP, or specialist nurse. This is because since 29.7.02, providing you meet the employment conditions, you are automatically assessed as 100% disabled once diagnosis is confirmed.

For some prescribed diseases you may be asked to have a particular test before being sent for a medical examination. For pneumoconiosis this involves a chest X-ray; for occupational deafness a hearing test; and for chronic bronchitis and emphysema a breathing test. If the results of these tests show that you meet the particular criteria for these conditions you will be sent for a medical examination. If not, your claim will be disallowed. You have one month to appeal against a disallowance.

If you have had (or have) industrial injuries disablement benefit for the same disease, the decision maker may need to decide whether there has been a worsening of your condition or whether you have contracted the disease afresh. This is known as the recrudescence question.

As the questions to be decided on your claim are often complex, you should always try to get advice and help with an appeal if your claim is turned down at whatever stage. See Chapters 58 and 59.

How disablement is assessed

When you attend a medical examination, the DWP doctor(s) will give an opinion on the extent and likely duration of your disablement and must consider all the disabilities resulting from the accident or disease, including the worsening of pre-existing conditions. They will assess the disablement resulting from any 'loss of faculty' by comparing your condition with that of a healthy person of the same age and sex. For this purpose, your job and other personal circumstances do not matter. See Box O.2 for details on the principles of assessment.

The decision maker can make a 'provisional' or a 'final' assessment. A provisional assessment is reviewed towards the end of a set period and reassessed, so if your condition is taking time to stabilise, you may have a series of provisional assessments. But, if your disablement is less than 14% and it looks unlikely that the current assessment can be added to any other assessments to reach the 14% minimum for payment, a final assessment will be made instead. A 'final' assessment may be for life if your disablement is considered permanent and unlikely to change appreciably, or for a fixed and limited period. In the latter case, the decision maker is effectively saying you will no longer be affected by the accident or disease after that date. This is not the same as saying there is no longer any disablement but that the causative link has then been broken.

Reduced earnings allowance (REA) is only payable during the period of a disablement assessment of at least 1%. If your assessment is a final one for a limited period, REA cannot be paid beyond that period. To safeguard your award of REA you can either appeal against the period of the assessment or you can wait until near the end of the assessment period and ask for the decision to be superseded, on the grounds of a change of circumstances (see 10). As either option could result in a nil assessment you might decide to wait. But, to be safe, you should apply for a supersession before your final assessment ends because if there is a break of even one day between assessment periods you could lose your REA for good (see 14).

8. How much do you get?

Lump-sum gratuities – pre-1.10.86 claims

If you claimed industrial injuries disablement benefit (IIDB) before 1.10.86 and your disablement was assessed at 1% to 19%, you were paid a lump-sum gratuity (unless you were claiming for certain chest diseases for which a pension was paid). The amount of gratuity paid depended on the percentage and duration of your assessment; if it was 20% or over, you were paid a weekly pension as now.

If you were entitled to special hardship allowance (SHA), you could choose to have the IIDB paid as a weekly pension on top instead of as a lump sum. This is no longer possible, but an existing pension in lieu of a gratuity can continue (if you remain entitled to reduced earnings allowance, which replaced SHA) until the end of the period of your assessment.

A gratuity for a final life assessment lasts for 7 years (R(I)11/67) when deciding if any offset is appropriate against a further award for a subsequent accident or disease or an increase in the original assessment. (For an example of how this works in practice, see *Disability Rights Handbook* 23rd edition, p151.)

Weekly pension – claims after 1.10.86

Since 1.10.86, you can get benefit only if your total disablement is assessed at 14% or more, or at least 1% for pneumoconiosis and byssinosis.

Benefit is paid as a weekly pension. Assessments of 14-19% disablement are paid at the 20% rate. Assessments of 24% (or 44% etc) are rounded down and paid at the 20% rate (or 40% etc). Assessments of 25% (or 45% etc) are rounded up and paid at the 30% rate (or 50%, etc). For pneumoconiosis and byssinosis, assessments of 1-10% are paid at the 10% rate and assessments of 11-24% are paid at the 20% rate.

Anyone diagnosed as having pneumoconiosis (PD D1) is automatically treated as at least 1% disabled and therefore entitled to benefit. As it appears (from R(I)1/96) that the DWP may have treated such claims incorrectly in the past, you should contact them if you have had a claim for pneumoconiosis turned down. Benefit can be paid back to 25.8.94 if appropriate and compensation paid for official error. See DWP leaflet PNEU1 for more details.

Percentages and amounts

20%	£24.76	**50%**	£61.90	**80%**	£99.04
30%	£37.14	**60%**	£74.28	**90%**	£111.42
40%	£49.52	**70%**	£86.66	**100%**	£123.80

Note: Lower rates apply to under-18s without dependants.

Aggregation of assessments

Disablement assessments for more than one industrial injury or disease can be added together, or aggregated, if the assessment periods overlap. This can help you reach the minimum payment figure of 14% during a common core period and so makes it worth claiming IIDB for even 'minor' injuries.

It has always been possible to aggregate a provisional assessment on a pre-1.10.86 claim with assessments for any subsequent accidents or diseases but not a pre-86 assessment for which you had had a final life award and been paid a lump-sum gratuity. Case law (R(I)3/00 relying on CI/522/93 and R(I)11/67) now makes this possible. Decision makers will only aggregate if you have at least one assessment that has been made after 1.10.86. So, for example, they would refuse to aggregate two pre-86 life awards of 11% and 9% but would aggregate them if either award was increased after 1.10.86, or a successful claim for a further accident/disease was made after 1.10.86, even if it actually occurred before this date. See CI/1532/02 and R(I)4/03.

Aggregation is a very complex area of law so anyone who has had a gratuity in the past and thinks this percentage assessment may not be being aggregated with any further assessment(s) should ask the DWP to supersede any previous decision and award them a weekly pension, if this brings them to at least 14%, or to increase their existing pension to take account of the earlier assessment. Decision makers are advised to revise on the grounds of official error or supersede if the decision was made after 24.7.95. Arrears cannot be paid back to a date earlier than 24.7.95, the date of CI/522/93 (see R(I)1/03). Decision makers should also consider compensation under their financial redress for maladministration scheme (see Chapter 60(2)) but may need to be prompted. Assessments of under 20% for occupational deafness cannot be aggregated. The special rules that apply to assessments for pneumoconiosis and byssinosis mean that aggregation is only carried out if it is to your advantage.

9. How do you appeal?

You have the right of appeal to an appeal tribunal against the Secretary of State's decision on your claim. You have one month from the date the decision was sent to you. To appeal, you should fill in the form in DWP leaflet GL24. You should give as much detail as possible as to why you disagree with the decision. As industrial injuries benefits are complex, you may need expert advice – your trade union or a local advice centre may help.

As an alternative to an appeal, you can ask the DWP to look at your claim again; this is called a revision. However, in cases where a medical question is involved, the decision maker is unlikely to change the original decision based on the DWP doctor's report even if you provide your own medical evidence to support your claim. As the time limit for appeal is now so restricted, it may be safer to appeal straight away. (See Chapter 58 for full details of the dispute procedure.)

10. If your condition gets worse

Since 5.7.99, to increase your assessment or extend the period it covers you must ask for a supersession on the grounds of a change in circumstances and, as a result, your claim will be looked at afresh. Any new assessment could be lower rather than higher. It could even be reduced to nil, which could then also involve a loss of reduced earnings allowance, although retirement allowance is not affected as it is awarded for life and not linked with any disablement assessment.

Try to get advice before applying; you should be particularly careful if you have now developed arthritis or spondylosis. This can often lead to your disability being assessed as 'constitutional' and not due to the effects of your injury or prescribed disease. To ask for your claim to be looked at again on the grounds of a change of circumstances, get form BI168 from your local Jobcentre Plus office.

Payment and aggregation of assessments following a supersession

If your request for an increased assessment is successful and the new percentage is 14% or more, you will get a pension, even if the actual increase in the assessment is only 1%. If you had been paid a gratuity for that injury in the past, as this is likely to be more than 7 years ago, no offset will be appropriate (see 8).

If your assessment is increased but remains under 14% you will not get benefit unless you can aggregate that percentage with any other current assessment(s). In this case, the whole percentage assessment becomes available for aggregation, not just the actual increase in percentage gained. This can be added to any current assessments you may have, including any final life assessments for which you received a lump-sum gratuity.

However, the position is slightly different if you are currently getting a pension in lieu of a gratuity for the original assessment. In this case, your right to a pension in lieu will end and you will receive the balance (if any) of the original gratuity, plus the appropriate gratuity for the increase in the percentage assessment or period. Or, if your disablement is assessed at 14% or more, you will receive a pension at the appropriate rate.

11. Extra allowances

The following additional allowances can be paid:

Additional allowances	per week
Constant attendance allowance	
– part time	£24.80
– normal maximum	£49.60
– intermediate rate	£74.40
– exceptionally severe cases	£99.20
Exceptionally severe disablement allowance	£49.60
Unemployability supplement*	£76.45
(earnings limit £4,056 pa)	

*This was abolished from 6.4.87 for new claims and is only payable to existing claimants

12. Constant attendance allowance

Constant attendance allowance is automatically considered when your disablement assessment totals 95% or more. Your need for care and attention must be as a result of an industrial accident/disease. If you think this has been missed, claim on form BI104, available from your local Jobcentre Plus office. If you receive disability living allowance (care component) or attendance allowance, this will be reduced by the amount of any constant attendance allowance you receive.

There is no right of appeal if your claim is refused, but you can ask for the decision to be looked at again if you feel some facts were not taken into account.

13. Exceptionally severe disablement allowance

This is automatically considered if you qualify for one of the two higher rates of constant attendance allowance. However, your need for that level of attendance must be likely to be permanent. Again, there is no right of appeal if your claim is refused. For more details of this and constant attendance allowance, see DWP booklet DB1.

14. Reduced earnings allowance

You can claim reduced earnings allowance (REA) if your accident happened before 1.10.90 or your disease started before 1.10.90, provided the disease (or the extension to the prescribed disease category) was added to the prescribed list before 10.10.94. REA will not be paid for newly prescribed diseases or extensions to those already listed.

Since 7.4.97, a claim for REA cannot be backdated for more than 3 months. Before this date benefit could be backdated for 'good cause' – see *Disability Rights Handbook* 26th edition.

You must claim REA separately from industrial injuries disablement benefit (IIDB). Get claim-form BI103 from your local Jobcentre Plus office. It is possible to have more than one award of REA if you have had more than one industrial accident or disease. This was confirmed on 30.7.01 by the Court of Appeal (*Hagan*) (R(I)2/02). However, you cannot be paid more than the equivalent of 140% disablement when your IIDB and any REA awards are added together.

Once you have made a successful claim for REA, you can make renewal claims, subject to the usual rules. But if you were entitled to REA immediately before 1.10.90 (ie on 30.9.90), a break in entitlement of just one day after this date may mean you lose REA for good.

If you are getting REA when you reach state pension age and are not in regular employment, your REA will be replaced by retirement allowance (RA), paid at a lower rate (see 15). However, there is at present a loophole in the law which allows anyone claiming REA for the first time *after* state pension age, to be paid REA at normal rates without ever having this converted to RA. So, if you are nearing state pension age, it may be to your advantage to delay your claim until you are over 3 months past state pension age. In this way, your claim cannot be backdated prior to state pension age and any REA awarded can therefore continue to be paid indefinitely.

Who qualifies for REA?

To qualify for REA you must have a current assessment of at least 1% in respect of an accident or disease that occurred before 1.10.90 (see above). You must also be unable to return to your regular occupation or to do work of an equivalent standard because of the effects of the disablement caused by your accident or disease.

The broad aim is to make up the difference between what you are capable of earning, as a result of the injury or disease, in any suitable alternative employment and what you would have been likely to earn now in your regular job if you had not had the accident or disease and were still in it. There are two ways of qualifying for REA.

- ❑ **Under the continuous condition** – You must have been incapable of following both your *'regular occupation'* and any *'employment of an equivalent standard which is suitable in [your] case'* ever since 90 days after your accident happened or your disease began.
- ❑ **Under the permanent condition** – It is enough if you are now *'incapable, and likely to remain permanently incapable, of following [your] regular occupation'* and also incapable of any *'employment of an equivalent standard ...'*

Sch 7, para 11(1)(b) Social Security Contributions and Benefits Act 1992

Earnings

On a first claim, your pre- and post-accident earnings are individually assessed. On subsequent claims for the same accident or disease, revisions may be linked to the general movement in earnings of broad occupational groups, depending on how the law applies to your situation.

Broadly, if your post-accident earnings are less than your pre-accident earnings would be now, the difference is made up by REA, subject to the maximum payment of £49.52. This comparison may be totally hypothetical – eg if your regular job no longer exists and disabilities that cannot be taken into account in the REA assessment make you incapable of any work. If you are unable to do any work because of the accident or disease you should get the maximum amount of REA, even if you are still being paid full wages from your employer.

Tackling appeals

Case law on REA, much of which originally applied to the earlier special hardship allowance, is complex and extensive. For example, there may be arguments over what your 'regular' occupation is, particularly if your accident happened during lower-paid 'stop gap' work; or you may argue that your reasonable prospects of advancement should be taken into account. If your claim is turned down or you do not get maximum REA, do not give up without first taking expert advice. As well as depending on case law, your claim may rest on a mass of detailed facts, as well as medical evidence. It is quite possible that the decision maker made a decision in ignorance of some of the relevant facts.

You have a right of appeal against the refusal of REA, or against the amount awarded. See Chapter 58 for details.

No percentage assessment?

To get REA, you must have a current disablement assessment of at least 1%. You also need to be sure that the loss of faculty identified by the DWP doctor in their report covers all the disabilities created by the industrial accident/disease and is sufficient to contribute materially to your being incapable of following your regular occupation.

The DWP doctor gives their opinion on the link between the accepted loss of faculty and your inability to follow your regular occupation. The decision maker is not bound to accept this but in practice usually does.

If you don't have a current percentage assessment or the loss of faculty needs to be more broadly identified, you have to tackle that side of things first by appealing, or by seeking a revision or supersession. An appeal may be the best bet if you need to broaden the loss of faculty. If you are out of time, make a late appeal (see Chapter 58(7)). In a separate letter, ask for a revision or supersession. If you are trying to cover a gap in your assessment period to re-qualify for REA, a late appeal may be a better option because of the restricted backdating on supersession.

Since 20.5.02, if the decision on your disablement assessment is revised or changed at appeal, the decision maker can go on to revise the decision on your REA if this is to your advantage. This precludes the need for a separate appeal on the REA question (see Chapter 58, Box R.5).

15. Retirement allowance

Retirement allowance (RA) is a maximum of £12.38 a week or a minimum of 50p a week. It is the lower of 10% of the maximum rate of disablement benefit, or 25% of the reduced earnings allowance (REA) you received immediately before reaching state pension age (60 for women, 65 for men) or ceasing regular employment, if that was later. In practice, if you had maximum REA, your RA would be £12.38. If you had already retired and claimed your state pension before 10.4.89, you don't get RA, but your REA is frozen for life.

RA is payable for life and the link with any percentage assessment is broken. It is only payable if you are transferring from REA. If you want to stay on REA when you reach state

O.4 For more information

Industrial injury

For reference use *Social Security: Legislation 2004 Volumes I* and *III* (published annually by Sweet & Maxwell) and *The Law of Social Security* by Wikeley, Ogus and Barendt (Butterworths). *Compensation for Industrial Injury* by R Lewis (1987, published by Professional Books Ltd/Butterworths; out of print but may be available in large libraries) is useful for case law prior to 1987. The DWP produces a technical guide for advisers – DB1 *A Guide to Industrial Injuries Benefits.*

Accident Line – If you have been injured in an accident or have an industrial disease, you can arrange a free legal consultation with a local solicitor specialising in personal injury claims by ringing The Accident Line on Freephone 0500 192939 (England and Wales).

pension age, you can only do so while you remain in regular employment (see below). However, if you are approaching state pension age and have not yet claimed REA, you should consider delaying your claim in order to keep it indefinitely (see 14).

RA replaces REA if, when you have reached state pension age (60 for women, 65 for men), you give up regular employment and on the day before you give up that employment your award(s) of REA add up to at least £2 a week. If you stopped work before reaching state pension age you are treated as giving up regular employment in the week you reach state pension age. If you continue regular employment after state pension age your REA will be replaced by RA when you stop work.

Regular employment – Since 24.3.96, this is defined as gainful employment under a contract of service that requires you to work for an average of at least 10 hours a week over any 5-week period (not counting any week of permitted absence such as leave or sickness), or gainful employment (which may be self-employment) that you undertake for an average of at least 10 hours a week over any 5-week period.

Challenges to the March 1996 legislation lost at the Court of Appeal (Plummer and Hammond) in December 1998, and in May 2000 the European Court (Hepple and others) found that the different cut-off ages for men and women on REA were lawful. (However, Hepple is currently being pursued through the European Court of Human Rights on the discrimination point.)

45 War disablement pension

1. The War Pensions scheme

From 6.4.05 the Veterans Agency (VA) has introduced the new Armed Forces Compensation scheme (AFCS), which will replace the existing War Pensions scheme (WPS) and the Armed Forces Pensions scheme (AFPS) for injuries, illnesses or deaths caused on or after 6.4.05. The War Pensions scheme will remain in place for those who already had awards made under it by 5.4.05, and to new claimants whose injury, ill-health or bereavement was caused by service before 6.4.05. We cover the AFCS in detail in a new factsheet. For a copy, send a stamped addressed envelope to the Disability Alliance (see back cover for our address), and ask for Factsheet F20. The factsheet is also downloadable from our website: www.disabilityalliance.org.

The existing WPS is administered by the VA, part of the Ministry of Defence, and is primarily intended to provide benefits for disablement caused or made worse by service in HM Armed Forces. It is much wider in scope than the Industrial Injuries scheme; there is no list of prescribed diseases, jobs or substances. You can claim for any medical condition whatsoever providing you can show a link between that condition and your service. You do not have to have been involved in a war or been on active service when the injury or condition was caused. You could have been injured simply playing organised sport on the base or suffered an illness during service which has done permanent damage (eg an ear infection causing some hearing loss). Or you could have an existing condition that has been made worse by service. Although most pensions are paid for physical injuries, claims for mental and psychological conditions such as schizophrenia and post-traumatic stress disorder can now be accepted, if conditions for entitlement are met. Conditions such as multiple sclerosis, Menière's disease, Hodgkin's disease, diabetes mellitus, certain cases of gastritis and peptic ulcers and heart disease in lower limb amputees can also be accepted. So, if you have claimed for one of these conditions in the past and been refused, you should claim again now.

Civilians and some other groups are covered by the scheme but only for certain physical injuries (see below).

2. Who can claim?

You can claim for any present disablement resulting from:

- an injury or condition caused or made worse by service in HM Armed Forces at any time. This includes service in the Home Guard, Nursing and Auxiliary Services, the UDR from 31.3.70, the Territorial Army, and Cadets (certain cadets are covered by a similar but separate Ministry of Defence scheme);
- a physical injury or disease sustained as a civilian during World War 2 either as a result of enemy action or action in combating the enemy;
- a physical injury or disease sustained while carrying out duties as a Civil Defence Volunteer in World War 2;
- an injury or condition caused or made worse by service during World War 2 in the Polish Forces under British Command or while serving in the Polish Resettlement Forces;
- certain injuries or illnesses sustained while serving in the Naval Auxiliary Services, Coastguard or Merchant Navy in the 1st or 2nd World War, or conflicts in the Gulf, Falklands, Suez or Korea; or while being held prisoner.

If you are a dependant of someone whose death has been caused or 'substantially hastened' by service in HM Forces you can also claim a war pension (see 8 below).

3. How much can you get?

War disablement pension – The basic disablement pension depends on your degree of disability, assessed on a percentage basis as in the Industrial Injuries scheme (see Box O.2, Chapter 44). If your assessment is 20% or more, a weekly pension is paid. If it is less than 20%, you get a one-off lump-sum gratuity unless your claim is for noise-induced sensorineural hearing loss (see below).

War disablement pensions are tax free. The maximum pension at the 100% rate is £131.30 a week. See Veterans Agency (VA) Leaflet 9 for the full range of rates payable.

Hearing loss – When your claim is for noise-induced sensorineural hearing loss and your assessment is less than 20%, no gratuity is paid. No account is taken of any related condition, such as tinnitus.

If your hearing loss alone is assessed as at least 20%, any additional disability can be added on to increase the percentage you get. To get 20%, your average hearing loss must be 50dB or more in each ear.

A gratuity can still be paid for hearing loss due to other causes such as bomb blast, ear infections or the effects of ototoxic drugs used to treat other conditions linked with service.

Supplementary allowances – Tax-free supplementary allowances can be paid on top of a basic war disablement pension or gratuity. Some allowances you have to claim, others are paid automatically (see 4 and 5 below and VA Leaflet 2).

4. Allowances you have to claim

War pensioners' mobility supplement – To qualify, your walking difficulty must be caused wholly or mainly by your pensioned disablement, which must be assessed at 40% or more. The other qualifying conditions are similar to those for disability living allowance (DLA) higher rate mobility component (see Chapter 20(18)) except there is no special category for severe mental impairment.

War pensioners' mobility supplement cannot be paid at the same time as DLA mobility component but is paid at the higher rate of £47.25 a week. There is no upper age limit for claiming.

When claiming, you can choose to attend a medical

examination or fill in a self-assessment claim-pack. Your disability must be expected to last at least 6 months from when you claim but, unlike DLA, you do not have to meet a 3-month qualifying period prior to this.

Constant attendance allowance – This is paid if your pensioned disablement is assessed at 80% or more and you consequently need a lot of personal care and attention, or supervision. It is paid at 4 different rates:

- part-day – £24.80;
- full day – £49.60;
- intermediate – £74.40;
- exceptional – £99.20.

Regulations specify the level of care needed for each rate to be payable. If, because of your pensioned disablement, you are terminally ill, you will get the exceptional rate.

Constant attendance allowance overlaps with ordinary attendance allowance and DLA care component. If you qualify for both you will be paid the higher amount. When claiming, you can choose to have a medical examination or fill in a self-assessment claim-pack.

Unemployability supplement – This is similar to incapacity benefit (IB) in the social security scheme and is paid if your pensioned disablement is assessed at 60% or more and you are likely to be permanently unable to work because of your war pensioned disablement. You must be under age 65 when you claim, but once awarded it can continue to be paid after age 65.

You cannot get unemployability supplement at the same time as IB or basic state pension, but any earnings-related or graduated pension is paid separately by the DWP on top. Unemployability supplement is £81.15 a week and you can claim extra for dependants. A child allowance stops at age 16 so you need to reclaim it if your child is continuing in full-time education. An invalidity allowance may be paid on top; there are three rates depending on your age when you first became permanently incapable of work: £5.15, £10.30 and £16.05.

Allowance for lowered standard of occupation – This is similar to reduced earnings allowance in the Industrial Injuries scheme and is paid up to the same rate of £49.52 a week. It is paid if your pensioned disablement is assessed at 40% or more and you are unable to follow your regular occupation or do work of an equivalent standard because of your war pensioned disablement. You must be under age 65 when you claim, but once awarded it can be paid after age 65. This allowance plus your basic war pension cannot add up to more than the 100% rate pension.

You cannot get unemployability supplement at the same time but you can keep your state pension or IB, so this allowance could be a better option if you later meet the conditions for unemployability supplement as well. State pension and long-term IB are both taxable.

Clothing allowance – This is £169 a year and is paid if your pensioned disablement is assessed at 20% or more and causes exceptional wear and tear to your clothing – eg because of incontinence or the use of an artificial limb.

Treatment allowance – To qualify, you must suffer actual loss of earnings due to having treatment at home or in hospital because of your pensioned disablement. Treatment allowance is paid to top up your current percentage (whether you have a pension or gratuity) to the 100% rate of the basic pension. Claim immediately treatment starts, as no payment is made for days before you claim unless illness or disability prevented you claiming earlier.

Rent allowance – If you are getting a war widow(er)'s pension *and* a child allowance, you can claim up to £37.55 a week rent allowance towards your accommodation costs (rent, mortgage, council tax and water rates). This can continue for 26 weeks after the child's allowance stops.

5. Allowances that are paid automatically

Exceptionally severe disablement allowance – This is paid if you get constant attendance allowance at either of the two highest rates on a permanent basis. It is £49.60 a week.

Severe disablement occupational allowance – This is paid if you get either of the two highest rates of constant attendance allowance but you are nevertheless normally in employment. It is £24.80 a week. You cannot get it as well as certain social security benefits, eg state pension, incapacity benefit, severe disablement allowance and carer's allowance.

Comforts allowance – This is paid if you get unemployability supplement and/or constant attendance allowance, at two rates: £10.60 or £21.20 a week.

Age allowance – This is paid at age 65 if your disablement is assessed at 40% or more. The amount depends on your degree of disablement, and it varies between £8.80 and £27 a week.

6. Does anything affect what you get?

A basic war disablement pension is not affected by earnings or by any non-means-tested social security benefit, with the exception of industrial injuries disablement benefit for the same disablement.

The supplementary allowances, however, can affect the payment of similar benefits available under the social security scheme. For example, constant attendance allowance normally overlaps with ordinary attendance allowance and disability living allowance care component, so you cannot get both in full.

You cannot get full allowances for dependants payable with non-means-tested social security benefits as well as those payable with unemployability supplement. But the total paid will be the higher of the two.

For means-tested benefits such as income support, £10 a week of a war disablement pension is not treated as income. Certain supplementary allowances are ignored in full, these are: constant attendance allowance, exceptionally severe disablement allowance, severe disablement occupational allowance and war pensioners' mobility supplement. So it is important to give a breakdown of how your war pension is made up when claiming means-tested benefits. Your local authority may ignore more than £10 for claims to housing and council tax benefit under a local scheme.

If you enter hospital, basic war pension is unaffected but some supplementary allowances are (see Chapter 33).

7. How do you claim?

You can get a claim-form by ringing the Veterans Helpline on 0800 169 2277, by writing to the Veterans Agency, Norcoss, Thornton-Cleveleys FY5 3WP, or by contacting your local War Pensioners' Welfare Office (addresses in VA Leaflet 1). Claim-forms are available on the Veterans Agency (VA) website: www.veteransagency.mod.uk. Make sure you complete and return the claim-form within 3 months or you could lose benefit.

If you claim by telephone, your service and medical details will be taken so the VA can obtain your service records while

O.5 Far East prisoners of war

Tax-free lump-sum payments of £10,000 can be claimed by former prisoners of the Japanese during World War 2, or by their widows or widowers. Former members of the forces, civilians and some members of the colonial forces are included. The payment is disregarded indefinitely for means-tested benefits and there is no time limit for claiming. For more details and a claim-form ring the Veterans Helpline on 0800 169 2277.

they are waiting for you to complete and return the claim-form, so speeding up a decision on your claim.

When to claim?
Under the existing War Pensions scheme you cannot claim for a war disablement pension if you are still serving in the Forces. For ex-service personnel, there is no time limit for making a claim but any award is normally only paid from the date of your claim.

Backdating is restricted to a maximum of 3 years in a prescribed list of circumstances. These are:

- you have been unable to claim earlier due to ill-health or disability;
- there has been a change in medical opinion;
- documents that were previously classified become available; *or*
- the Ministry of Defence HQ has failed to forward papers to the VA where someone has been invalided out of or died in service.

In cases of official error, full backdating is still possible. Since 9.4.01, there is a right of appeal if backdating is refused.

It is in your interest to claim quickly. If your claim is made within 7 years of leaving the Forces it is easier to have it accepted, as the onus is on the VA to prove that your disability is not linked to your service. After 7 years, the burden of proof shifts to you to prove your claim. For example, a person contracting multiple sclerosis within 7 years of discharge from the Forces was awarded a war disablement pension because the cause of this condition is unknown, and so the VA was unable to prove that it was not linked to their service.

Whenever your claim is made, the legislation states that the benefit of any reasonable doubt should always be given to the claimant.

In the past, the VA refused claims where a claimant had no corroborative evidence. The High Court (*Secretary of State for Social Security v Mitchell, Wilson & Bennett, 17.10.97*) decided this was unlawful and that any evidence, including the claimant's own word, should be considered when making a decision. If your claim was turned down for this reason in the past you should get independent advice.

For civilians, there is a 3-month time limit from the date of the injury for making claims. The VA used to waive this limit but will now only consider claims that are technically out of time if you provide independent supporting evidence. The types of evidence they will accept are listed on the claim-form. If your claim is refused because of this, you should get independent advice.

If you are invalided from the Forces or die in service, your service medical records should be sent automatically to the VA for an award to be considered.

O.6 For more information

The main legislation covering the War Pensions scheme is contained in The Naval, Military and Air Forces Etc (Disablement and Death) Service Pensions Order 1983, SI 1983/883 (as amended most recently by SI 2004/708), available from The Stationery Office, Tel 0870 600 5522 or visit: www.tso.co.uk. Civilians and merchant seamen are covered by SI 1983/686 and SI 1964/2058 respectively.

Veterans Helpline – 0800 169 2277
Call the Helpline for queries about your claim or the War Pensions scheme and to get claim-forms and leaflets. Their leaflets are also available on the Veteran's Agency website: www.veteransagency.mod.uk

What happens after you claim?
The VA will check your service records, if appropriate, to decide if you come within the scheme. If you do, the cause and the degree of your disability will be decided by the VA doctors, after medical evidence has been obtained.

8. War widows, widowers and other dependants

Since 8.4.02, widowers have been able to claim a pension on the same basis as widows. A war widow(er)'s pension can be paid if:

- your spouse's death was due to, or substantially hastened by, an illness or injury for which they were either getting a war disablement pension or to which they would have been entitled had they claimed; *or*
- they were getting constant attendance allowance at any rate, or would have been had they not been in hospital; *or*
- since 7.4.97, they were getting unemployability supplement at the time of death and their pensionable disablement was at least 80%.

In some circumstances an unmarried partner can also qualify.

If your late spouse was getting a war disablement pension when they died you will not be awarded a war widow(er)'s pension automatically – you have to apply. However, if they were getting constant attendance allowance or unemployability supplement prior to their death, a temporary widow(er)'s allowance is paid automatically for the first 26 weeks. This is normally paid at the same rate as that paid to the spouse before their death.

You cannot be paid a war widow(er)'s pension as well as a national insurance (NI) bereavement benefit or widow's pension, but a war widow(er)'s pension is tax free and normally paid at a higher rate. You can also get benefits based on your own NI contributions, such as state pension or incapacity benefit, on top.

A war widow(er)'s pension is currently £99.50 a week, and for an unmarried dependant who lived as a spouse £97.15 a week.

A supplementary pension of £64.62 a week is paid on top of a war widow(er)'s pension if your late spouse's service ended before 31.3.73. This is totally disregarded for means-tested benefits.

Extra allowances that widow(er)'s can claim include age allowances of £11.40, £21.80 or £32.35, and child allowances (for details see VA Leaflet 2).

Before April 2002, widowers could claim a pension only if they met extra conditions, including being *'incapable of self support'*. So if you have had a claim refused in the past because you did not meet the 'extra conditions', you should reclaim immediately.

You may be able to claim help with funeral costs (see 11).

9. Reviews

Decisions on war disablement pensions are made by officials acting on behalf of the Secretary of State. Regulations state that most decisions can be reviewed *'at any time, on any ground'*.

This applies when you request a review because you are unhappy with a decision (eg your claim has been refused or you disagree with the level of assessment) or because your circumstances have changed since the decision was made (eg your condition has got worse).

However, the Veterans Agency (VA) will only review the decision if you give substantive reasons for your request, although you do not have to provide corroborative evidence. If the VA believes you have not given substantive reasons they can refuse to review and there is no right of appeal against such a refusal. If this happens seek independent advice.

If the VA carries out a review, any new decision, even if it remains the same, will carry a fresh right of appeal. If the review is in your favour, you will normally be paid from the date of your review request.

If you are requesting a review on the grounds that your condition has deteriorated, you should be aware that your assessment could be reduced as well as increased. This is particularly worth bearing in mind if your pensioned condition is noise-induced hearing loss, where you cannot get an increase in your assessment anyway because of the restrictive approach now used to assess these claims.

If you are unhappy with a decision, it may be better to appeal straight away rather than ask for a review. In any case, when you appeal, the VA will look at your case again to check if their decision was correct and so could change it, making a tribunal hearing unnecessary.

10. Appeals

Appeal rights apply to most decisions about war pensions made on or after 9.4.01. Appeals can be made against decisions relating to service prior to 3.9.39, to most supplementary allowances and to funeral expenses. You can appeal against the refusal of an award, the level of award, the date from which the award runs and any changes to the amount or period of the award.

It is important that you get help with an appeal or a review. Some ex-service organisations like the Royal British Legion can help prepare your case and represent you at the tribunal. Alternatively, an advice centre may be able to help.

Your appeal is to the Pensions Appeal Tribunal (PAT), an independent body set up by the Lord Chancellor's Department, and not part of The Appeals Service. The tribunal must have a legally qualified member and normally has a doctor but does not need to have a member of the same sex and service background as you. If you are challenging the level of your assessment, a medical examination may be carried out.

As with social security tribunals, the PAT will not need to consider issues not raised at the hearing and will only be able to consider circumstances up to the date of the decision.

Appeals to a PAT take considerably longer to be heard than social security tribunals. It can be up to two years before the papers (known as a 'statement of case') are prepared and a date of hearing set. Any further appeal against a PAT decision is only possible on a point of law to the Social Security Commissioners (known in this case as the Pensions Appeal Commissioners). For more on appeals to the Commissioners, see Chapter 58(18).

There is a 6-month time limit in which to appeal against a Veterans Agency decision, except in the case of an interim assessment, when it is 3 months. Late appeals can be made up to 12 months after this period if the delay is due to the serious illness or death of the claimant, their spouse or a dependant; the disruption of normal postal services; the failure to notify the claimant of the decision; or exceptional circumstances applying to the claimant. The PAT decides whether your appeal is in time or whether a late appeal can be accepted and must give written reasons for its decision.

11. Extra help you can get

Funeral costs

If death was due to a condition caused by service or the person died while being treated in hospital for their pensioned disablement, whatever the cause of death, a grant can be claimed to help with funeral costs. Where the funeral took place on or after 12.4.04, a grant up to a maximum of £1,400 can be claimed. Unlike a grant from the social fund, the financial circumstances of the person making the claim are ignored. There is no means test and any payment made is not recoverable from the deceased's estate.

Regulations now specify the type of costs that can be allowed. There is a right of appeal if you are turned down. A claim must be made within 3 months of the funeral.

Other help

You can apply to the Veterans Agency (VA) for any of the following services or appliances as long as you need them wholly or mainly because of your pensioned condition and they are not available free from the NHS or social services. There is no means test and no charge but you must apply before arranging or purchasing any treatment or appliance, as refunds are not normally made. These provisions are discretionary so there is no right of appeal if you are refused. You can ask your local War Pensioners' Welfare Manager to visit and discuss any of these services and appliances with you and help you apply.

Hospital treatment expenses – Payment can be made for travel costs, subsistence or loss of earnings incurred when attending hospital (or similar centre) for treatment. Some visitors to a war pensioner who has been in hospital for over 12 months can also get help with travel costs.

Private treatment – Payment can be made for approved treatment not available free on the NHS.

Priority treatment – War pensioners are entitled to priority NHS treatment for their pensioned disablement. If you have problems, contact the Veterans Helpline.

NHS charges – War pensioners are exempt from NHS prescription charges if they are required for pensionable conditions.

Chiropody – Fees can be paid if your health authority cannot provide free treatment.

Appliances – Various items, such as orthopaedic chairs, spectacles, corsets and dental treatment can be paid for if not available free through other agencies.

Home adaptation grant – Up to £750 can be allowed for small adaptations (eg a stair lift) in addition to any grant payable by the local authority.

Care home fees (for skilled nursing care) – If you need 24-hour skilled nursing care because of your pensioned disability, the VA may pay care home fees. The care home must be registered under the Registered Homes Act.

Short-term breaks (convalescence) – You can claim care home fees for up to a maximum of 4 weeks a year to enable you to have a short-term break. But if you have recently been discharged from hospital or are recovering from an operation the VA is unlikely to pay, as they consider this to be an NHS responsibility.

Respite breaks – In some circumstances you can claim the cost of care home fees in order to give your carer a break. Your carer has to provide medical evidence that a break is needed.

46 Criminal injuries compensation

1. Who can claim?

You can claim compensation from the Criminal Injuries Compensation Authority if you suffer personal injury directly resulting from a crime of violence in Great Britain (GB), or on a British vessel, aircraft or hovercraft, or in a lighthouse off the coast of GB, or within 500 metres of an installation in any part of the seas around GB over which Britain exercises control.

A crime of violence includes child abuse, and personal injury might include physical injury, mental injury, disease, or pregnancy or sexually transmitted diseases contracted as a result of rape.

You can also claim compensation if you are injured when trying to stop someone from committing a crime, or trying to stop a suspected criminal, or helping the police to do so. In this case, if the injury is accidental, you must have been taking a justifiable, exceptional risk.

You can claim compensation even if your attacker is immune from prosecution under the law, for example because of mental illness.

If the injury was caused by a traffic accident, it is only covered if the driver of the vehicle deliberately drove it at you in an attempt to injure you.

Compensation can be reduced or withheld unless the Criminal Injuries Compensation Authority is satisfied that:

- you took all reasonable steps to inform the police or, in limited circumstances, another appropriate authority, of the incident, and co-operated fully in their investigations;
- you have given the Authority all reasonable assistance, eg by providing information;
- your *'conduct ... before, during or after the incident giving rise to the application'* does not make it *'inappropriate that a full award or any award at all be made'*. If you have a criminal record, or if you in any way contributed to the attack, compensation may be reduced or refused.

Violence within the family – If you and your attacker were living together as members of the same family, you can apply for compensation provided that:

- you were injured on or after 1.10.79;
- your attacker has been prosecuted (unless there are good reasons why this has not been done);
- you and your attacker have stopped living together, except in the case of child victims – although a full explanation will be required in this case, and the attacker must not be likely to benefit from a compensation award.

A man and woman who aren't married but who are living together as husband and wife, are treated as members of the same family under this scheme.

Sexual offences – The Authority looks with particular care at all claims in respect of sexual or other offences which arise out of a sexual relationship, especially if there has been any delay in submitting the application. Compensation will not be payable unless the Authority is satisfied that the attacker will not benefit from the award.

2. How do you claim?

Apply as soon as possible after the incident. You can get the appropriate claim-form from the Criminal Injuries Compensation Authority (see Box O.7). You can apply for compensation if your attacker is unknown or has not yet been arrested.

All applications must be made to the Authority within 2 years of the date of the injury, although they can accept late applications in exceptional circumstances if it is in the interests of justice to do so. The Authority is sympathetic to late claims made in respect of children and young people (under age 18) or people with learning difficulties, and may waive the time limit. Claims in respect of child abuse should therefore be made even if the injuries occurred over 2 years ago. Send a covering letter explaining the delay. Applications for children should normally be made by a person with parental responsibility for the child.

O.7 For more information

The Criminal Injuries Compensation Authority publishes a general guide to the Criminal Injuries Compensation scheme. You can get this guide, and any claim-forms you need, free from: Criminal Injuries Compensation Authority, Tay House, 300 Bath Street, Glasgow G2 4LN (Freephone 0800 358 3601).

Traffic accidents

If you are the victim of an uninsured or untraced motorist, there is a different scheme for compensation for personal injuries. This is run by the Motor Insurers' Bureau (MIB), a company established by motor insurers, which has agreements with the Government to provide that compensation. Compensation is worked out in the same way as common law damages. If the driver cannot be traced, you must report the accident to the police within 14 days or as soon as reasonably practicable and you must apply to the MIB within 3 years of the accident, but generally you should act quickly. For details, contact: Motor Insurers' Bureau, Linford Wood House, 6–12 Capital Drive, Linford Wood, Milton Keynes MK14 6XT (tel 0190 883 0001).

3. How much do you get?

Compensation is made up of several possible elements.

- ❑ **For the injury itself** – A fixed sum assessed by reference to a tariff that groups together injuries of comparable severity and allocates a sum of compensation to them. The Authority will obtain a medical report on you, and will decide where in the tariff your injury features. This 'tariff of injuries' is included in the guide available from the Authority (see Box O.7).
- ❑ **Loss of earnings** – No compensation is paid for the first 28 weeks of lost earnings. Any loss of earnings and/or earning potential beyond that will be compensated, subject to certain limits. Loss of pension rights may also be compensated.
- ❑ **Special expenses** – Examples of these include care costs, or equipment such as a wheelchair, or towards expenses for medical, dental or optical treatment. To qualify, you must have suffered from the injury for at least 28 weeks and if so, the award will be backdated to the date of injury.

Compensation if the victim has died

If someone has died as a result of a criminal injury, an amount for funeral expenses will be paid, and compensation may be paid to their family.

Funeral expenses – The Authority only pays an amount it considers reasonable. The religious and cultural background of the victim and their family will be taken into account in deciding what is reasonable. Whoever has paid for the funeral of a victim of a crime of violence may claim.

Fatal injury award – A relative of someone who has died as a result of violence can claim a flat-rate fatal injury award of £11,000 for one claimant, or £5,500 each for two or more claimants.

The only people who can claim this award are the husband or wife; an unmarried partner (including partners of the same sex) who had been living with the deceased for at least 2 years; a parent; a son or daughter.

Dependency award – If a relative was financially dependent on the deceased for their living expenses, an award will be made to reflect the extent of financial dependency, subject to a maximum amount. Close relatives (parents, children and partners) can claim, as for the fatal injury award above, and also former wives or husbands if they were being financially supported by the deceased.

Loss of a parent – In the case of an application on behalf of a child under 18, a payment of £2,000 a year will be made to the child in respect of the death of their parent, to reflect the extent the child was dependent on the parent in ways other than financially, eg caring for the child.

Compensation recovery

Your award may be reduced in some cases to take account of other payments received.

- ❑ **Social security benefits and insurance payments** – Benefits received or insurance payments for the same event are deducted in full from an award for loss of earnings, special expenses or a dependency award. Any award which is tariff based is not affected (eg for the injury itself or a fatal injury award).

- **Occupational pensions** – Any loss of earnings or dependency award will be reduced to take account of an occupational pension payable as a result of the injury or death. Pension rights from payments made only by the victim or dependant are disregarded.
- **Compensation from the courts** – The full amount of any compensation payment for personal injury or damages made by a civil or criminal court in respect of the same injury is deducted from any award under the Criminal Injuries Compensation scheme.

4. How is your claim decided?

The Authority's staff will look at your claim to check that the information you have given is correct. On the claim-form, you are asked to give them authority to contact the police, your doctor, employer, or anyone else relevant, to obtain confirmation of the incident, your injuries, loss of earnings, etc. They may ask you for other details. All these enquiries are made in strict confidence. In some cases, you might be asked to undergo a medical examination by a doctor chosen by the Authority.

After gathering this information, the Authority's staff will decide if you come within the scheme, and, if so, will assess the amount of compensation.

You will be sent a written decision. You must reply in writing and accept the decision before any payment is made. Where the award has been reduced or disallowed, you will be given reasons.

5. If you don't agree with the decision

If you are not happy with the decision, you can apply, in writing, for a review. The Authority must receive your request within 90 days of the date of the letter notifying you of the decision. Your application must be supported by reasons, together with any additional evidence. If you haven't had help with your claim, it is important to get advice to make sure you have included all the relevant information. Contact your local Victim Support scheme for help.

If you ask for an extension, it must be received by the Authority within 90 days. This 90-day time limit can be extended if you can show good reason for applying late or if it is in the interests of justice to do so.

After the review, if you are still dissatisfied with the decision, you can appeal to an independent body, the Criminal Injuries Compensation Appeals Panel. The Appeals Panel must receive your appeal within 90 days of the date of the letter notifying you of the outcome of the review.

Your appeal will be screened by an adjudicator who may decide to refer your case to an oral hearing. You will get at least 21 days' notice of the hearing. You can bring a friend or a legal adviser to represent you.

Both reviews and appeals involve a full reconsideration of eligibility and the amount of the award, and could result in loss of an award or a reduced award.

6. If your condition changes

The Authority can re-open your case if your condition has deteriorated to the extent that the original assessment is unjust given your present condition. It can also re-open a case where a person has since died as a result of the injury. If you apply more than 2 years after the original decision, it is important to give as much information and medical evidence as you can with your application. The Authority will only consider it if it has enough evidence without needing to make extensive enquiries.

47 Vaccine damage payments

1. What is this scheme?

The scheme provides a tax-free lump sum of £100,000 for a person who is (or was immediately before death) severely disabled as a result of vaccination against specific diseases. It is described in leaflet HB3 *Vaccine damage payments* (see 4 below).

2. Who qualifies?

Payments can be made to a person who has been severely disabled as a result of vaccination against diphtheria, tetanus, pertussis (whooping cough), poliomyelitis, measles, rubella (German measles), mumps, tuberculosis, meningococcal group C (meningitis C), haemophilus influenzae-type B (Hib) or smallpox (vaccination up to August 1971). Claims can be made on the basis of combination vaccines for diphtheria, tetanus and pertussis (DTP), measles and rubella (MR), measles, mumps and rubella (MMR), and the new five-in-one vaccine.

People damaged before birth as a result of vaccinations given to their mothers during pregnancy are included in the scheme, as are those who have contracted polio through contact with another person who was vaccinated against it using an orally-administered vaccine. The claimant must also satisfy the following conditions.

- The vaccination must have been carried out in the UK or Isle of Man (except for serving members of the forces and their immediate families vaccinated outside the UK as part of service medical facilities, who are treated as if vaccinated in England).
- The vaccination must have been carried out either when the claimant was under 18 (except for rubella, poliomyelitis and meningococcal group C) or at a time of an outbreak of the disease within the UK or Isle of Man.
- The claimant must also be over the age of two on the date of the claim, or, if they have died, they must have died after 9.5.78 and have been over the age of two.
- The claim can be made at any time before the claimant's 21st birthday, or, if they have died, the date on which they would have attained that age, or up to 6 years after the date of the vaccination, whichever date is later. There were stricter age-limit rules prior to 16.6.02. If a claim was turned down prior to this date under the stricter rules, or was not made following advice with respect to those rules, see 5 below.
- In the case of someone who contracted polio through contact with another person who was vaccinated against it, they must have been *'in close physical contact'* with the other person during the period of 60 days which began on the 4th day after the vaccination. They must also have been *'looking after'* the vaccinated person or been looked after jointly with them.

3. What is 'severe disablement'?

A person is considered to be severely disabled if the disablement due to vaccination damage is assessed at 60% or more. Prior to 16.6.02 the disablement had to be assessed at 80% or more. If a claim was turned down prior to this date under the stricter rules, or was not made following advice with respect to those rules, see 5 below. Disablement is assessed in the same way as for industrial injuries disablement benefit (see Box O.2, Chapter 44).

4. How do you claim?

Get leaflet HB3 and a claim-form by writing to the Vaccine

Damage Payments Unit, Palatine House, Lancaster Road, Preston PR1 1HB (01772 899 944). You can also download the claim-form from the DWP website: www.dwp.gov.uk.

Don't delay in claiming. If you already have supporting medical evidence send a copy with the claim. Otherwise, the Vaccine Damage Payments Unit will obtain medical evidence on your behalf. If the disabled person is under 18, the claim should be made by the parents or guardian.

5. What if you are refused?

If your claim is refused, you will be sent a written decision with reasons. If you disagree with this decision, you can ask the Secretary of State to consider a reversal of the decision or you can appeal to an appeal tribunal. There is no time limit for making your appeal.

The appeal tribunal is made up of a lawyer chairperson and one or two doctors. At the hearing you may be represented by another person, and you may call and question witnesses. You can get legal advice under the Legal Aid scheme for the work leading up to the hearing (see Chapter 59), although the scheme doesn't cover representation at the hearing itself. Before the hearing, you will be able to study the evidence on which the refusal was based. The tribunal's decision will be given to you on the day of the hearing or sent to you shortly afterwards.

If you want the Secretary of State to consider a reversal of their decision, or the decision of an appeal tribunal, you should write to the Vaccine Damage Payments Unit requesting a reversal, giving reasons why you think the decision is wrong, within 6 years of the date you were notified of the original decision or within 2 years of the date you were notified of the appeal tribunal decision, if that is later. You may provide new evidence in support of your request.

If the Secretary of State has made a payment, the decision can be reconsidered at any time where he or she has reason to believe that there was a misrepresentation or non-disclosure of relevant information.

If you previously claimed but were disallowed because of a failure to satisfy either the time limit or disability threshold rules that applied before 16.6.02, you will be able to have the claim reconsidered if the new rules, which came into force from 16.6.02, are now satisfied. Similarly, if you were advised not to claim because of the earlier time limits or disability threshold rules, then your case might be looked at again. A further claim in such circumstances should be made before 16.6.05. If you think any of these situations apply to you contact the Vaccine Damage Payments Unit.

6. Does it affect other benefits?

The capital value of a vaccine damage payment held in a trust fund is ignored for the purposes of income support, income-based jobseeker's allowance, council tax benefit and housing benefit. If the payment is not held in a trust fund, its capital value will be taken fully into account.

Any payments made out of the trust fund to or for the disabled person may be treated as income or capital depending on how often the payments are made.

- ❑ Regular payments will be ignored provided that payments are intended and used for items other than everyday living expenses of food, ordinary clothing and footwear, household fuel, housing costs covered by benefit, council tax or water charges.
- ❑ Up to £20 a week of regular payments that are intended and used for these everyday living expenses will be ignored. However, where a £10 disregard has already been allowed on other income, eg war widow's pension, only £10 of the regular payment can be ignored.
- ❑ Payments made to a third party (eg a shop) or payments required to be made under the terms of the trust to a third party will be completely ignored, provided that the payments are not used for everyday living expenses.

Other lump-sum payments will be treated as capital and will reduce benefit if the payments bring the total capital above the lower capital limit (see Box B.2, Chapter 5).

48 Compensation recovery

1. Compensation recovery

If, as a result of an accident, injury or disease, you claim compensation, the 'compensator' (the person who caused the accident, injury or disease, or more commonly, their insurer) is liable to pay damages to you and to repay benefits to the DWP via the Compensation Recovery Unit (CRU).

Social Security (Recovery of Benefits) Act 1997

It is not the actual benefits that are recovered, but an amount equivalent to the total amount of recoverable benefits paid as a result of your accident, injury or disease. In certain circumstances it will be possible for the compensator to deduct some or all of the amount they have to repay to the DWP from the gross compensation award, a practice known as 'offsetting'. Not all social security benefits are recoverable, as some are paid for reasons that may have no connection to the compensation claim. Recoverable benefits are listed in 2 below.

Social security benefits are not paid in respect of pain, suffering, personal inconvenience and so on, and therefore no offsetting can be made against the general damages element of your compensation award. If your compensation award is only made up of such damages, the compensator will have to bear the full cost of paying your compensation and repaying benefits to the DWP.

In cases involving accidents and injuries, benefits are recoverable from the day following the accident or injury for a period of 5 years or up to the date the claim is settled, whichever is earlier. In disease cases, the 5-year recovery period begins on the date on which a recoverable benefit is first claimed as a consequence of the disease.

The certificate of recoverable benefits

Before a compensation payment is made, the compensator must request a 'certificate of recoverable benefits' (CRB) from the CRU. The CRU will issue a CRB to the compensator (or their insurer) and send a copy to you (or your solicitor), so that both parties can estimate the extent of any potential offsetting. Since offsetting can greatly affect the size of the net compensation award both sides should take it into account when conducting negotiations.

CRBs are valid for a minimum period of 16 weeks. If the compensator does not have a CRB to cover the date the award is settled, the CRU has the power to issue a one-day CRB showing the amount of recoverable social security benefits that were due at the actual time of settlement. When this happens, the compensator will have lost the opportunity to make a full offset against the compensation award.

You and the compensator have the right to request a review of a CRB at any time if either of you believe that the calculation of the certificate is incorrect or that benefits which were not paid as a consequence of the accident, injury or disease have been included. However, an appeal against a CRB can be made only after the full amount of recoverable benefit has been repaid to the CRU. See 4 below for details on appeals.

2. Benefits which can be recovered

Compensation can be reduced to take account of benefits paid in respect of the following:

- **loss of earnings** – disability working allowance,

industrial injuries disablement benefit, incapacity benefit (IB), income support (IS), invalidity benefit, jobseeker's allowance, reduced earnings allowance, severe disablement allowance, sickness benefit, statutory sick pay (before 6.4.94), unemployment benefit, unemployability supplement;

- **cost of care** – attendance allowance, disability living allowance (DLA) care component, constant attendance allowance, exceptionally severe disablement allowance;
- **loss of mobility** – DLA mobility component, mobility allowance.

In making an order for a compensation payment, the court must specify how much is to be awarded under each of these three headings.

Offsetting – an example: An award of compensation is agreed:

Compensation award:	*£100,000*
broken down as:	
General damages	£40,000
Loss of earnings	£30,000
Loss of mobility	£30,000

The CRU certificate lists:	
IB totalling	£5,000
IS totalling	£10,000
DLA mobility component totalling	£10,000

The compensator cannot offset against the general damages element of the award, but may offset the IB and IS paid against the loss of earnings heading. They therefore deduct a total of £15,000 from this, leaving £15,000 to be paid to the injured person.

Similarly, the compensator may offset the £10,000 of DLA paid against the loss of mobility heading, leaving £20,000 to be paid to the injured person.

The injured person has settled their claim for a total of £100,000. Following offsetting, they receive £75,000 from the compensator, plus the £25,000 they have already received from the state benefits system.

3. Exempt payments

Some compensation payments are exempt from the recovery rules:

- vaccine damage payments;
- Criminal Injuries Compensation scheme payments (see Chapter 46(3));
- payments from the Macfarlane and Eileen Trusts and the Skipton Fund;
- payments from the government-funded trust for people with Variant Creutzfeldt-Jakob disease;
- payments under the Fatal Accidents Act 1976;
- contractual sick pay and redundancy payments;
- payments made under the NHS industrial injuries scheme;
- certain trust and contractual insurance payments;
- payments under the NCB Pneumoconiosis Compensation scheme; *and*
- payments in respect of sensorineural hearing loss of less than 50dB in one or both ears.

4. Appeals

If your compensation payment has been reduced to take account of benefit recovery and you think that the certificate of recoverable benefit is wrong, you can appeal. You must attach any letters you have received from the compensator telling you that the compensation payment has been reduced. You must state under which of the 4 following grounds you are making your appeal:

- any amount, rate or period specified in the certificate is incorrect; *or*
- the certificate shows benefits that were not paid as a result of the accident, injury or disease in respect of which compensation was paid; *or*
- benefits listed which have not and are not likely to be paid to you have been brought into account; *or*
- the compensation payment made was not as a consequence of the accident, injury or disease.

You must appeal within one month of the date the compensator pays the Compensation Recovery Unit (CRU). If you apply late you must show that there are special circumstances for the delay. Appeal on form Z2, which can be downloaded from the CRU website: www.dwp.gov.uk/cru.

Warning: A tribunal dealing with an appeal against recovery is entitled to decide whether or not the benefits recovered were in fact paid in respect of the accident, injury or disease in question. Both the tribunal's decision and the evidence on which it is based can potentially raise doubt about entitlement to those benefits. Consequently, it would be wise to seek advice before lodging an appeal.
R(CR)2/02

5. For more information

For further information see the DWP guide GL27 *Compensation and social security benefits. The guide can be downloaded from the* Compensation Recovery Unit (CRU) *website: www.dwp.gov.uk/cru.*

For specific enquiries regarding the relevant law (the Social Security (Recovery of Benefits) Act 1997), you can ring the CRU Policy Liaison Section: 0191 225 2235.

For information regarding the similar scheme in Northern Ireland, contact the Compensation Recovery Unit, Social Security Agency, Magnet House, 81-93 York Street, Belfast BT15 1SS (028 9054 5855).

For a fuller explanation of the scheme, see *Deducting Benefits from Damages for Personal Injury* by Professor Richard Lewis (Oxford University Press).

P Coming to or leaving the UK

This section of the Handbook looks at:

49 Coming to the UK

1. Introduction

To qualify for most benefits you must satisfy the rules about residence and presence in Great Britain (GB). Your right to benefit may also be affected by your immigration status.

GB means England, Wales and Scotland; United Kingdom (UK) means GB plus Northern Ireland. In Northern Ireland and the Isle of Man, social security benefits come under separate legislation, but this is virtually the same as in GB, and periods of residence may count for UK benefits. In the Channel Islands the system is different but there is a reciprocal agreement that may allow periods of residence there to count for UK benefits. Periods of residence in another European Economic Area (EEA) country may count as residence in GB for those covered by European Community (EC) rules, and reciprocal agreements with some non-EEA countries include similar rules.

EEA countries – the EEA consists of the 25 member states of the European Union (EU) – Austria, Belgium, Cyprus, Czech Republic,* Denmark, Estonia,* Finland, France, Germany, Greece, Hungary,* Italy, Latvia,* Lithuania,* Luxembourg, Malta, Netherlands, Poland,* Portugal, Republic of Ireland, Slovakia,* Slovenia,* Spain, Sweden, UK (including Gibraltar, but not the Channel Islands or Isle of Man) – together with Iceland, Norway and Liechtenstein. Nationals of EEA states, as well as refugees and stateless people resident in an EEA country, who are or were employed or self-employed (and their families), are covered by more favourable EC social security rules. Generally, you count as employed or self-employed if you have paid contributions under the UK national insurance scheme or are insured under a social security scheme of another EEA country. From 1.6.02 the same rights apply to Swiss nationals and their families.

* **A8** – This term refers to the 8 EEA countries marked * above. 'A8 nationals' refers to nationals of these 8 countries. If you are an A8 national the circumstances in which you have a 'right to reside' in the UK are more restricted than for other EEA nationals. This can affect your entitlement to the benefits that include a 'right to reside' requirement (see 2 below).

Reciprocal agreements – The UK has reciprocal social security agreements with some countries (including all EEA countries except the A8 countries and Greece and Liechtenstein – the reciprocal agreement applies where you are not covered by EC rules) that may help you receive benefit abroad. Non-EEA countries covered by reciprocal agreements are Barbados, Bermuda, Canada, Isle of Man, Israel, Jamaica, Jersey & Guernsey, Mauritius, New Zealand, Philippines, Switzerland, Turkey, USA, former Yugoslavia. Each agreement differs and not all benefits are covered by each. There are also 'association' and 'co-operation' agreements with Algeria, Morocco, Tunisia and Turkey.

2. Residence and presence tests

Entitlement to many benefits depends on you satisfying the residence and presence tests for that benefit.

'Present' simply means physically present in GB throughout the whole day. (See Chapter 50 for the circumstances in which you can be treated as present in GB while you are abroad.)

You are usually 'resident' in the country where you have your home for the time being.

The term 'ordinarily resident' is not defined in regulations. You should be 'ordinarily resident' in the place where you normally live for the time being if there is a degree of continuity about your stay such that it can be described as settled.

The term 'habitually resident' is not defined in regulations. See below for how this test is applied.

The term 'right to reside' is not defined in regulations, and as this requirement was only introduced on 1.5.04 its meaning is still being clarified. Examples of those with a 'right to reside' include British citizens, those with leave to enter/remain in the UK, EEA nationals who are working (including self-employment) or (except A8 nationals) those who are genuinely seeking work. A8 nationals who are not working will have a right to reside if they have worked in the UK continuously (disregarding breaks totalling 30 days or less) for 12 months. Other people can have a right to reside depending on their circumstances. Seek advice if this requirement could affect you.

Disability benefits

For disability living allowance (DLA), attendance allowance (AA), carer's allowance (CA), severe disablement allowance (SDA) and 'no-contribution' incapacity benefit (IB), the general rules and exceptions are as follows.

The residence and presence test (general rule) – You must be present and ordinarily resident in GB, and have been present for not less than 26 of the last 52 weeks. This is a continuing test. It applies to any day for which you are claiming benefit.

If you (or your spouse, or, for DLA, your (step) parent if you are under 16) receive earnings exempt from UK income tax, you must have been present in the UK for not less than 3 of the 4 years before your claim.

DLA and AA – If you claim DLA care component for a baby under 6 months old, there is a 13-week presence test that applies until the baby's 1st birthday. If a child becomes entitled to DLA after reaching 6 months, the 26-week test applies.

The 26- or 13-week presence tests do not apply if you are accepted as terminally ill.

If these special provisions apply, the other tests, including being ordinarily resident, must still be satisfied.

SDA and 'no-contribution' IB – Once you have passed the residence and presence tests you do not need to satisfy them again while you are still in the same period of incapacity for work.

CA – The extra presence test outlined above for those with UK tax-exempt earnings does not apply.

Tax credits and child benefit

For working tax credit (WTC) and child tax credit (CTC) you (and your partner if you are making a joint claim) must be present and ordinarily resident in the UK and, for new CTC claims (other than renewal claims) made on or after 1.5.04, have a right to reside in the UK.

To be entitled to child benefit you *and* the child must be present in GB (or Northern Ireland if you are claiming there) and ordinarily resident in the UK and, for new claims made on or after 1.5.04, you must have a right to reside in the UK.

Income support, pension credit and income-based jobseeker's allowance

You must be present in GB and 'habitually resident' in the Common Travel Area (see below).

If you used to live in GB or abroad with your partner who is now abroad, they will, for income support (IS), pension credit (PC) or income-based jobseeker's allowance (JSA), be treated as your partner (and their income and capital will affect your entitlement to benefit) unless you do not intend to resume living together or the absence is likely to exceed 52 weeks. For PC, there are additional rules when your partner will cease to be treated as your partner if they are abroad (see Chapter 50(5)).

Habitual residence

Anyone making a new claim after 1.8.94 for housing benefit (HB), council tax benefit (CTB), IS, PC or income-based JSA (unless you are entitled to urgent cases payments of IS or JSA – see 3 below, or you left Montserrat after 1.11.95 because of the volcanic eruption) is only eligible if accepted as being habitually resident in the Common Travel Area (UK, Channel Islands, the Isle of Man or the Republic of Ireland). You are treated as habitually resident, and are therefore exempt from the test, if you:

- have refugee status; *or*
- have exceptional leave to enter/remain; *or*
- are not a 'person subject to immigration control' (see 3 below) and you have been deported, expelled, or otherwise legally removed from another country; *or*
- are an EEA national (see 1 above) classified as a 'worker' for the purposes of EC Regulations 1612/68 or 1251/70, or as having the 'right to reside in the UK' under EC Directives 68/360 or 73/148. The term 'worker' is not defined in EC legislation, but case law has established a number of principles. You should have worker status if you are employed doing 'genuine and effective' work (full or part time) in the UK. You have 'residence rights' if you are a worker or self-employed, or you are providing or receiving commercial services (including private healthcare), or a member of your family is in one of these groups. You may retain worker status or residence rights (in certain circumstances), even if you stop work; *or*
- are an A8 national required to register your employment with the Home Office and you either have registered or are within the first month of employment.

Only the claimant is subject to the habitual residence test. If you are one of a couple, the person most likely to satisfy (or be exempt from) the test should be the claimant.

For new claims made on or after 1.5.04 you can only satisfy the habitual residence test if you have a right to reside in the Common Travel Area. However, this requirement does not apply if your new claim is continuous with a period of entitlement to either IS, income-based JSA, PC, HB or CTB that included 30.4.04.

Case law suggests there is no definitive list of factors that determine habitual residence, but you need to show a 'settled intention' to stay here. Depending on your circumstances, you may be accepted as habitually resident from your first day of residence if you are:

- returning to the Common Travel Area and you were previously habitually resident here; *or*
- a national of, and have worked in, an EEA state (see 1 above).

In other cases a period of actual residence is likely to be required, although it may be very short.

Seek specialist advice if you are likely to be subject to the test. You can appeal against a decision that you are not habitually resident. To ensure entitlement to benefit as soon as possible, you should submit further claims while you are waiting for your appeal to be heard, and appeal each negative decision.

Note that if you are not accepted as habitually resident for the purposes of IS, income-based JSA or PC, the HB/CTB office must carry out its own test, not just follow the DWP decision.

3. Immigration status

If you are defined as a 'person subject to immigration control', unless you come under one of the exemptions below, you will be excluded from possible entitlement to the following benefits:

- attendance allowance (AA) and disability living allowance (DLA);
- carer's allowance (CA);
- child benefit;
- child tax credit (CTC) and working tax credit (WTC);
- housing benefit (HB) and council tax benefit (CTB);
- income-based jobseeker's allowance (JSA);
- income support (IS);
- no-contribution incapacity benefit (IB);
- pension credit (PC);
- severe disablement allowance (SDA);
- social fund.

Your immigration status does not prevent you claiming other benefits.

You are defined as a 'person subject to immigration control' if you are not an EEA national (see 1 above) and you:

- require leave to enter/remain in the UK but do not have it; *or*
- have leave to enter/remain in the UK subject to a condition that you do not have recourse to public funds; *or*
- are a sponsored immigrant – ie you have leave to enter/remain given as a result of a maintenance undertaking (a written undertaking, given by someone else in pursuance of the immigration rules, to be responsible for your maintenance and accommodation).

Exemptions: who can still get benefits?

You are not excluded from benefit entitlement if you are not defined as a person subject to immigration control. Examples include people with refugee status, indefinite leave to enter/remain (unless given as the result of a maintenance undertaking) or exceptional leave to enter/remain (unless it is subject to the condition that you do not have recourse to public funds – if this applies seek expert immigration advice) – including humanitarian protection or discretionary leave, or Swiss nationals.

Some groups of people (listed below) can be entitled to benefit despite being defined as a person subject to immigration control.

Warning: All the benefits listed above are classed as 'public funds' except no-contribution IB. If your immigration status is subject to a 'no recourse to public funds' condition, receiving one of these benefits (even where your partner is paid benefit on your behalf) may jeopardise your right to stay in the UK or undermine applications to the Home Office. However, the Home Office does not regard you as having 'recourse to public funds' if you fall into one of the exempt groups below.

You should get expert immigration advice (see Box P.1) before making a claim if you have concerns over 'public funds' or do not have leave to enter/remain, have overstayed the leave you had or are unsure about your immigration status, since information is exchanged between all the benefit authorities and the Home Office.

Who can get IS, PC, income-based JSA, HB, CTB?
Even if you are defined as a person subject to immigration control you are not excluded from entitlement to IS, PC, income-based JSA, HB, or CTB if you fall into one of the groups below.

❑ **You are not excluded from HB, CTB or normal payments of IS/income-based JSA if you are:**

- a national of Croatia or Turkey and you are lawfully present in the UK. Case law has held that asylum seekers with temporary admission are not lawfully present, but those who claimed asylum while having 'leave' (eg as a visitor or student) should be entitled under this provision; *or*
- a sponsored immigrant and you have been resident in the UK for 5 years (beginning on the later date of either your entry to the UK or the signing of the maintenance undertaking).

❑ **You are not excluded from PC, HB, CTB or 'urgent cases payments' of IS/income-based JSA if you:**

- claimed asylum 'on arrival' (other than on re-entry) in the UK on or before 2.4.00. The words 'on arrival' are not defined in the regulations, but case law suggests you must have entered the country through a recognised port of entry and claimed (or attempted to claim) asylum before clearing immigration control or before leaving the port of entry; *or*
- are a national of former Zaire (Democratic Republic of Congo) or Sierra Leone and you submitted a claim for asylum within the 3 months following the Home Secretary's declarations that these countries were undergoing 'significant upheaval' made on 16.5.97 and 1.7.97 respectively; *or*
- (except for income-based JSA) were entitled to IS, HB or CTB as an asylum seeker on 4.2.96, or a member of your family, covered by this group, was claiming the benefit for you on this date and you now need to claim separately from them (eg you are their ex-partner or child who ceased to be dependent). You will still be entitled if you claim again after a break; *or*
- are a sponsored immigrant and less than 5 years have passed since you entered the UK (or since the maintenance undertaking was signed) and your sponsor has (or, if more than one, they have all) died; *or*
- are on limited leave with the condition you do not have recourse to 'public funds', and you have not yet had such recourse other than under this provision, and you are dependent on funds from abroad that are temporarily disrupted, but which are reasonably expected to resume (maximum of 42 days payment per period of leave).

Urgent cases payments – These have different calculation rules not covered in this Handbook. If you are entitled to urgent cases payments of IS you do not need to fall into another eligible category (see Box B.1, Chapter 3). This means you can claim IS instead of income-based JSA.

When entitlement ends – If you are entitled to benefit as an asylum seeker, entitlement will end on the date the decision on (or abandonment of) your asylum claim (or appeal if it was against a pre-5.2.96 decision) is recorded by the Home Office and notified to you.

If your partner is subject to immigration control – If you are entitled to PC or normal payments of IS or income-based JSA, then you cannot be paid for a partner defined as a person subject to immigration control (unless, except for PC, they are within one of the exempt groups above). If you are entitled to HB or CTB or urgent cases payments of IS or income-based JSA, you should be paid for your partner whether or not they are defined as a person subject to immigration control.

EC law – A family member of an EEA or Swiss national exercising their freedom of movement rights under EC law or Swiss agreement with the EC, has a right to join them in the UK and can then claim IS, income-based JSA, PC, HB or CTB.

If you, or a member of your family who you are living with, are a national of Turkey with 'authorised and lawful' residence in GB, and are lawfully working (or have lawfully worked) in GB you may have an entitlement to income-based JSA. This may also apply, for both income-based JSA and IS, if you are a national of Algeria, Morocco or Tunisia (CJSA/4705/1999 & CIS/5707/1999) – seek expert advice.

Who can get tax credits?
Even if you are defined as a person subject to immigration control you are not excluded from tax credits if:

- you are a sponsored immigrant and either more than 5 years have passed since you entered the UK (or since the maintenance undertaking was signed) or your sponsor has (or, if more than one, they have all) died; *or*
- you are on limited leave with the condition you do not have recourse to public funds, and you have not yet had such recourse other than under this provision, and you are temporarily without funds due to funds from abroad being disrupted, but which are reasonably expected to resume (maximum of 42 days payment); *or*
- (CTC only) you are a national of Algeria, Morocco, Tunisia or Turkey and are lawfully working (or have lawfully worked) in UK; *or*
- (WTC only) you are a national of Croatia or Turkey and you are lawfully present in the UK; *or*
- (CTC only) your CTC award begins on or after 6.4.04 and immediately before it you were entitled to IS or income-based JSA for a child because you fell into either the above group, or one of the first 3 groups listed as not excluded from urgent cases payments of IS/income-based JSA (above).

If your partner is subject to immigration control – They are treated as if they were not if either you are also subject to immigration control but fall within one of the 5 exempt groups above, or you are not subject to immigration control.

Refugees
If you are granted refugee status you may be able to claim backdated IS, HB/CTB, child benefit and tax credits. (If you are aged 60 or over seek specialist advice about claiming backdated PC.) You must claim within 28 days (or 3 months for child benefit and tax credits) of receiving the letter notifying you of your refugee status. Benefit will be backdated to the later of:

- the date of your asylum application; *or*
- (except for tax credits) the date any previous award ended due to your asylum claim being refused; *or*
- 5.2.96 (or for tax credits 6.4.03).

Note that the Government intends to abolish these entitlements to backdated benefits and introduce an 'integration loan' for refugees in 2005.

Once you are granted refugee status (or exceptional leave to enter/remain, including humanitarian protection or discretionary leave), you are no longer subject to immigration control and can claim benefits under the normal rules.

Who can get disability benefits and child benefit?
Even if you are defined as a person subject to immigration control you are not excluded from AA, DLA, no-contribution IB, child benefit, SDA, and CA if:

- a member of your family is an EEA national (see 1 above); *or*
- either you, or a member of your family who you are living with, are a national of Algeria, Morocco, Tunisia or Turkey and are lawfully working (or have lawfully worked) in GB; *or*
- you are a sponsored immigrant; *or*

- (for DLA, AA, and child benefit only) you are covered by a reciprocal agreement (see 1 above); *or*
- you were in receipt of the benefit immediately before 5.2.96 (or 7.10.96 for child benefit). Your entitlement will end if:
  - your benefit is revised or superseded. Claiming child benefit for an additional child does not give rise to a revision or supersession of your existing benefit entitlement; *or*
  - you break your claim, or your award was for a fixed period and that award comes to an end; *or*
  - your claim for asylum (if any) is recorded by the Secretary of State as having been decided or abandoned.

Social fund
Even if you are defined as a person subject to immigration control you are not excluded from entitlement to the social fund if you fall into any of the exempt categories listed above. However, you must meet the other conditions of entitlement, including (with the exception of crisis loans and winter fuel payments) being in receipt of a qualifying benefit.

4. Other forms of support

Asylum support – If you have applied for asylum (or have made a claim under Article 3 of the Human Rights Convention) and your claim or appeal has not been determined, or you are a dependant of such a person, you may be able to get asylum support (accommodation and/or subsistence) if you are aged 18 or over and are accepted as destitute or likely to become destitute within 14 days. Asylum support is provided by the National Asylum Support Service (NASS). Temporary support while your application is processed and assistance in making the application to NASS is available from voluntary sector 'reception assistants', unless you are applying to NASS because you are no longer entitled to income support due to a negative asylum decision made on or after 25.9.00 and you have children, in which case your local authority should provide this.

If NASS refuses or stops your support you can, in most cases, appeal within 3 days of receiving the decision; seek immediate advice.

If you are no longer entitled to asylum support because your asylum claim and appeal (if any) have been refused you may be eligible for 'hard cases' support (full-board accommodation) from NASS; seek advice.

Help from social services – Even if you are defined as a person subject to immigration control you may be entitled to accommodation and/or other assistance from your social services department under one or more legal provisions. You may be eligible for Community Care services under section 2 of the Chronically Sick and Disabled Persons Act 1970 (see Chapter 25(5)). If you have needs which are not solely a consequence of 'destitution' or its physical effects (eg you have needs due to your age or disability) you may be entitled to accommodation and other assistance under the National Assistance Act 1948. If you are an unaccompanied child aged under 18 or you have dependent children and either you are not entitled to asylum support or the needs of your children are not being met by asylum support, you may be able to get assistance under the Children Act 1989. Remember that information is exchanged between social services and the Home Office. If you are refused assistance from your local authority, seek independent advice.

50 Leaving the UK

1. Introduction

If you travel or live abroad, you may be able to receive benefit while you are away. Some benefits (eg state pension) can be paid no matter how long you are away, while for others the conditions are more complex. The rules vary depending on the country you go to. If you go to a European Economic Area (EEA) country you may benefit from more favourable European Community (EC) social security rules. However, if you are not covered by the EC rules or a reciprocal agreement (see Chapter 49(1)) then the general rules on payment of benefits abroad apply.

This chapter looks at the general rules and indicates the benefits payable in EEA countries. But EC rules and reciprocal agreements are too varied and complex to cover here, so if you plan to go abroad get specialist advice about the effect on your benefits (see Chapter 59). Contact The International Pension Centre (see inside back cover) for information about taking your state pension abroad. For other benefits you should contact the office that pays each benefit. In each case they will need to know the purpose, destination and intended length of your visit.

Temporary absence – For many benefits, one of the conditions for payment while abroad is that your absence is temporary. For child benefit and tax credits this means the absence, at the beginning, is unlikely to exceed 52 weeks. For other benefits, the term is not defined in the regulations and in deciding whether your absence is temporary, the DWP should consider all the circumstances, including your intentions and the purpose and length of your absence. If the decision maker decides your absence is not temporary, you have a right of appeal.

2. Incapacity and maternity benefits

General rules – If you are temporarily absent from GB, you can continue to be paid incapacity benefit (IB), severe disablement allowance (SDA) or maternity allowance (MA) for the first 26 weeks of the absence, provided the Secretary of State agrees it is consistent with the proper administration of the benefits system. There is no right of appeal if the Secretary of State refuses; your only recourse is judicial review. You are not subject to the 26-week limit and do not require the Secretary of State's agreement if you are receiving disability living allowance or attendance allowance (see 6 below for when these can be paid beyond 26 weeks) or if you are a family member of a serving member of the armed forces and temporarily absent because you are living with that person. However, in all cases you must satisfy one of the following conditions:

- at the time you go abroad you have been continuously incapable of work for at least 6 months and remain continuously incapable while abroad; *or*
- you have gone abroad *'for the specific purpose of being treated'* for an illness or disability that began before you left. The treatment does not need to be the only reason you have for going abroad. However, going abroad to convalesce or for a change of air – even on your doctor's advice – is not enough. *'Being treated'* must involve some activity by another person. It does not matter whether the treatment is available in the UK or not. In some cases the claimants did not receive any treatment – but they did go abroad specifically to try and get it.

SDA and no-contribution IB – You are exempt from these conditions for SDA or no-contribution IB if you are abroad because you are living with a family member who is a serving member of the forces.

If entitlement to no-contribution IB ended solely because

you were abroad you may be able to re-claim after you return (see Chapter 14(10)).

EC – Generally, if you go to live in another EEA country or you return to the EEA country where you ordinarily live or you are authorised by the DWP to go to an EEA country specifically for medical treatment, you may be able to get short-term IB or MA there. You must get agreement from the DWP that your benefit can be paid there before you go. Long-term IB and SDA can be paid in another EEA country.

3. Statutory sick/maternity/paternity and adoption pay

You can receive these while abroad, unless your employer is not required to pay Class 1 national insurance contributions for you – eg because they are not present or resident, and do not have a place of business, in GB (or Northern Ireland); or they are exempt from the requirement due to an international treaty or convention.

4. Income support

If you are entitled immediately before you leave, you can continue receiving income support (IS) during a temporary absence abroad if:

- (except in Scotland) you are receiving treatment provided by the NHS outside GB; *or*
- the absence is unlikely to exceed 52 weeks and you continue to meet the entitlement conditions while you are away (apart from the fact that you are out of GB) and satisfy the 4 or 8 week rule below.

4-week rule – You can be paid IS for the first 4 weeks unless you are entitled to IS on the grounds that you are incapable of work (including statutory sick pay entitlement), or appealing against an incapacity for work decision, or a 'person subject to immigration control' entitled to urgent cases payments (see Chapter 49(3)), or in school or full-time non-advanced education, or involved in a trade dispute (see Box B.1, Chapter 3). If one of these applies, you can still be paid IS for the first 4 weeks if:

- you are in Northern Ireland; *or*
- you and your partner are both abroad and a disability premium, severe disability premium or any pensioner premium is applicable for the partner who is not the claimant; *or*
- you have been continuously incapable of work during the 364 days before the day you leave GB, or 196 days if you are terminally ill or entitled to disability living allowance highest rate care component (two or more periods of incapacity are treated as continuous if the break between is not more than 56 days each time); *or*
- you are incapable of work and your absence is *'for the sole purpose of receiving treatment from an appropriately qualified person for the incapacity by reason of which'* you are eligible for IS.

8-week rule – You can get IS for the first 8 weeks abroad if you are taking your dependent child abroad for medical treatment, physiotherapy or similar treatment by an appropriately qualified person.

Partner abroad – If you are the IS claimant and you stay in GB, your IS will include benefit for your partner for the first 4 weeks (or 8 weeks if they meet the conditions of the 8-week rule above). After this, benefit will be reduced. However, your partner's income and capital will affect your IS entitlement unless either you do not intend to resume living together or the absence is likely to exceed 52 weeks.

P.1 For more information

For information on benefits for people entering and leaving the UK, see *Migration and Social Security Handbook* (3rd edn) (Child Poverty Action Group). For information on support available to asylum seekers, see *Support for Asylum Seekers* (2nd edn) (Legal Action Group). For a guide to immigration law, see *Immigration, Nationality & Refugee Law Handbook* (2002 edn) (JCWI).

For immigration advice contact the Joint Council for the Welfare of Immigrants (JCWI), the Refugee Legal Centre, or a law centre (see Address List).

The DWP and Inland Revenue produce leaflets for each country covered by a reciprocal agreement with the UK as well as *Social security abroad* (NI 38) covering the rules for leaving the UK and *How to prove your identity for social security* (GL 25). Some leaflets are available in languages other than English. Leaflets are available from www.dwp.gov.uk, your local Jobcentre Plus office or The International Pension Service (see inside back cover).

5. Pension credit

You continue to be entitled to pension credit (PC) during a temporary absence from GB if you are receiving treatment provided by the NHS outside GB. Otherwise there is a limit of 4 weeks (as long as the absence is unlikely to exceed 52 weeks and you continue to satisfy the other conditions of entitlement), or 8 weeks if you are accompanying a child who lives with you or your partner in connection with treatment for a disability by an appropriately qualified person.

EC – Seek specialist advice to argue that PC can be paid in another EEA country.

Partner abroad – If one of these circumstances applies to your partner, your PC will include benefit for your partner for the relevant period of their temporary absence. After this they cease to be treated as your partner and so your benefit will be reduced.

6. Jobseeker's allowance

General rules – If you are entitled immediately before you leave you can continue receiving income-based or contribution-based jobseeker's allowance (JSA) during a temporary absence abroad if:

- (except in Scotland) you are receiving treatment provided by the NHS outside GB; *or*
- the absence is unlikely to exceed 52 weeks and you satisfy one of the rules below.

❑ You can be paid for the first 4 weeks if either you are in Northern Ireland and you continue to satisfy the conditions of entitlement while you are there, or you are abroad with your partner and a disability premium, severe disability premium or any pensioner premium is payable in respect of your partner and you are the claimant. You can also be paid for up to 4 weeks if you are aged under 25 and receive a government training allowance, but are not receiving training (although certain training courses are excluded).

❑ You can be paid for the first 8 weeks if you are taking your dependent child abroad for medical treatment, physiotherapy or similar treatment by an appropriately qualified person.

❑ If you go abroad for a job interview and are away for no more than 7 consecutive days, you can be paid for your days abroad provided you give notice in advance to the Jobcentre Plus office (in writing if required to do so) and on your return you satisfy the employment officer that you did attend the interview.

Partner abroad – The rules for income-based JSA are similar to income support (see 4). However, if you are claiming as a joint-claim couple and at the date you make your claim your partner is abroad, you will only be paid for them for the first 4 weeks if they are in Northern Ireland (and the absence is unlikely to exceed 52 weeks) or they are in receipt of a training allowance (as above) or for up to 7 days if they are attending a job interview. Otherwise you will be paid as a single person.

EC – For contribution-based JSA, if you are going to an EEA country to look for work, then, provided you have been registered with the Jobcentre Plus office for, normally, 4 weeks and satisfy the conditions of entitlement up to the date you leave the UK, you can usually get benefit in the EEA country for up to 3 months. You must comply with the procedures in the country where you are seeking work. For income-based JSA seek specialist assistance to argue the same rules should apply.

7. Attendance allowance and disability living allowance

General rules – Attendance allowance (AA) and disability living allowance (DLA) will continue to be paid for the first 26 weeks of a temporary absence abroad. You can only be paid for longer if the absence is temporary and for the specific purpose of being treated for an illness or disability that began before you left GB, and the Secretary of State agrees it is consistent with the proper administration of the benefits system to pay you for a longer period.

You can be paid for any day you are abroad if you (or a member of your family who you live with) are a serving member of the forces, or fall within certain categories of airmen, mariners and continental-shelf workers.

EC – If your AA or DLA entitlement began after 1.6.92, you cannot continue to be paid if you go to live in another EEA country (other than under the rules above for a temporary absence).

If your entitlement to AA or DLA began before 1.6.92, you may be paid your benefit without time limit in another EEA country if you, or a member of your family, have been employed or self-employed in the UK, and you continue to satisfy all the other conditions of entitlement other than the residence and presence conditions. You can then make a renewal claim while you are abroad, but you should avoid any break in entitlement between the end of an award and entitlement under the renewal claim.

8. Carer's allowance (CA)

General rules – This will be paid for the first 4 weeks of a temporary absence abroad if you go without the person you are caring for. If you go abroad temporarily specifically to care for that person, you will receive CA for as long as they receive attendance allowance (AA) or disability living allowance (DLA). You can be paid for any day you are abroad if you (or a member of your family who you live with) are a serving member of the forces, or fall within certain categories of airmen, mariners and continental-shelf workers.

EC – The rules are the same as for AA/DLA (see above).

9. Child benefit

If you are ordinarily resident in the UK and temporarily absent from GB (or Northern Ireland if you are claiming there) you continue to be entitled to child benefit for the first 8 weeks, or for the first 12 weeks if the absence is in connection with:

- your treatment for a disability or illness; *or*
- the treatment (for a disability or illness), or death, of your partner, or the sibling, parent, (great) grandparent, child (including a child you are responsible for), (great) grandchild of you or your partner.

Under these rules, if a woman gives birth while absent from GB the baby will be treated as being in GB (or Northern Ireland) for up to 12 weeks from the start of the mother's absence.

Child benefit can be paid for the first 12 weeks of your child's temporary absence abroad. It may be paid for longer if your child goes abroad:

- for the specific purpose of being treated for an illness or disability that began before they left the UK; *or*
- solely in order to receive full-time education in another EEA country or on an educational exchange or visit; *or*
- to Northern Ireland (or to GB if you are claiming in Northern Ireland).

Special rules enable child benefit to be paid for children of civil servants posted overseas, serving members of the forces, and people temporarily absent from GB because they are employed abroad if half their income is liable to UK income tax (eg a VSO volunteer). Guardian's allowance can be paid abroad for the same period as child benefit.

EC – You may be paid benefit for a child resident in another EEA country.

10. Industrial injuries disablement benefit

A basic disablement pension and retirement allowance are both payable while you are abroad. However, there are time limits for other industrial injuries benefits.

Reduced earnings allowance (REA) – is payable for the first 3 months of a temporary absence abroad if you were entitled before you left and your absence is not connected with work, or for longer if the Secretary of State agrees. If you lose REA for one day, you may lose it for good.

Constant attendance allowance and exceptionally severe disablement allowance – are payable for the first 6 months of a temporary absence abroad, or longer if the Secretary of State agrees.

EC – If you are already getting any industrial injuries benefit (including those above) before you leave, it is payable without time limit in an EEA country.

11. Retirement, widows' and bereavement benefits

These are payable no matter how long you are away. If you intend to go for longer than 6 months, let your local Jobcentre Plus office know so that arrangements can be made for paying your benefit abroad. If you are living permanently in a country outside the EEA, you can only receive the annual up-rating increases if that country has a reciprocal agreement with the UK that covers the payment of annual increases or you are covered by the co-operation and association agreements with Algeria, Morocco, Tunisia and Turkey.

You will be disqualified from a bereavement payment if you are abroad at the time of your spouse's death unless either your spouse was in GB when they died, or you returned within 4 weeks of their death, or their national insurance contribution record is sufficient for you to satisfy the contribution condition of a widowed parent's allowance or bereavement allowance.

EC – If you are living in an EEA country, you will get annual benefit increases as if you were in the UK.

12. Tax credits

If you are ordinarily resident in, but temporarily absent from, the UK you are treated as present and can therefore either claim or continue to be entitled to tax credits for the first 8 weeks, or for the first 12 weeks if the absence is in connection with:

- your treatment for a disability; *or*
- the treatment (for a disability), or death, of your partner, or the sibling, parent, (great) grandparent, child (including a child you are responsible for), (great) grandchild of you or your partner.

There are special rules for crown servants posted overseas.

EC – If you are in the UK, child tax credit can be paid for family members living in another EEA country.

A B C D E F G H I J K L M N O P Q R S

Other matters

This section of the Handbook looks at:

51 After a death

1. What to do after a death

The period after a death is really the worst time to have to look through official leaflets to find out about any financial or practical help that could be available. You don't want to have to worry about dealing with bureaucracy as well as coping with bereavement. The DWP leaflets D49 *What to do after a Death in England and Wales* or D49S *What to do after a Death in Scotland* give straightforward advice and information about all aspects of bereavement.

You can get practical help and advice from a funeral director, GP, solicitor, religious organisation, social services department or Citizens Advice Bureau. A health visitor or district nurse may help if the death was at home. If it was in hospital the ward sister or hospital chaplain could help. One of the first things you may need to do is to transfer insurance policies (eg car and home insurance) into your name.

If you need support and comfort, organisations such as Cruse, the organisation for bereavement care (Helpline 0870 1671 677), Winston's Wish, which offers a service to bereaved children and families (Helpline 0845 2030 405) and local branches of national charities such as the Multiple Sclerosis Society may help (see Address List).

2. Social fund funeral expenses

If you receive income support, income-based jobseeker's allowance, housing benefit, council tax benefit, pension credit, working tax credit (if it includes either disability element – see Chapter 18) or child tax credit (at any rate greater than the family element), you may be able to get a payment from the social fund for funeral expenses (see Chapter 9).

3. IS, JSA, PC, HB and CTB

If you are under 60 and on a low income you may be able to get income support (IS) or income-based jobseeker's allowance (JSA) (see Chapters 3 and 17 respectively). In either case, your capital must not be over £8,000 and you must not be working 16 hours or more a week. You may be eligible to claim IS if you are incapable of work, a carer or a lone parent (see Chapter 3, Box B.1). You are also eligible to claim if, on or after 9.4.01 you were aged 55-59, you have been bereaved since that date and you are claiming as a single person. If you claim JSA you will be required to be available for and actively seeking full-time work. You may get a bereavement premium in these benefits (see Chapter 4(10)).

If you are aged 60 or over and on a low income you may be able to get pension credit (PC) (see Chapter 41). This has no limits on work or capital.

For each of these benefits £10 a week of widowed parent's or widowed mother's allowance is ignored in the assessment of your income.

Late claims – If your claim for IS or JSA is late and it wasn't reasonable to expect you to claim on time because of the death of a partner, parent, son, daughter, brother or sister, your claim can be backdated for up to one month (see Chapter 57(3)). Claims for PC can be backdated for up to 12 months.

Carers – If you are getting IS (or carer's allowance – see Chapter 23) because you were caring for the person who has died, your benefit might change after 8 weeks. Chapter 24(8) explains what happens to your benefit in these circumstances.

Housing costs – If you have a mortgage and are claiming IS, income-based JSA or PC, you may be entitled to help with mortgage interest payments. If you are eligible for PC you can get this help straightaway. For IS and JSA, if your partner has died and you have a child, half the eligible mortgage interest can be included in your benefit after 8 weeks, and all of it after 26 weeks. If you don't have a child you will have to wait 39 weeks for such help. See Chapter 4(14).

Rent and council tax – Housing benefit (HB) and council tax benefit (CTB) may help to pay the rent or council tax if you are on a low income and have capital of less than £16,000. The capital limit does not apply if you get PC guarantee credit. In the assessment of your income, £15 a week of widowed parent's or widowed mother's allowance is ignored. HB and CTB may also include a bereavement premium (the rules are similar to those for IS see – Chapter 4(10)). See Chapter 7 for more details about HB and CTB.

4. Bereavement benefits

Bereavement benefits are available to both men and women whose spouses have died on or after 9.4.01. They replaced the old system of widow's benefits that only women could claim. Women whose husbands died before 9.4.01 continue to claim widow's benefits. '

There are three different bereavement benefits:

- bereavement payment – a single tax-free payment of £2,000;
- widowed parent's allowance (WPA) – if you have dependent children;
- bereavement allowance – payable for 52 weeks for those aged 45 and over when their spouse dies.

You must have been legally married; if you were in the process of divorcing, you would still qualify for bereavement benefits if your spouse died before the decree absolute was issued. In Scotland, you may also qualify for bereavement benefits and/or a state pension based on your partner's contributions, if you were married *'by cohabitation with habit and repute'*. You will, however, need to provide substantial evidence of this. Bereavement allowance and WPA are suspended for any period when you are cohabiting. If you remarry, the benefit stops altogether.

Claim bereavement benefits from your local Jobcentre Plus office. You may be required to attend a work-focused interview (see Box R.1, Chapter 57). Late claims for bereavement allowance or WPA can be backdated for up to 3 months (or 12 months when death has been difficult to establish).

A bereavement payment must be claimed within 12 months For help available to war widows and widowers see Chapter 45(8).

Bereavement payment

This is a tax-free, lump-sum payment of £2,000 for those bereaved on or after 9.4.01. You must have been under state pension age when your spouse died, unless they were not entitled to a Category A state pension.

To qualify, your spouse must have paid class 1, 2 or 3 national insurance (NI) contributions on earnings in any one tax year equal to 25 times the lower earnings limit for that year. For tax years before 6.4.75, 25 flat-rate contributions will be sufficient. If your spouse died as a result of an industrial accident or prescribed industrial disease, the contribution conditions are treated as satisfied. See Chapter 12(1) for more information about NI contributions.

Widowed parent's allowance (WPA)
WPA is a regular payment for men and women bereaved on or after 9.04.01 who have dependent children. Men widowed before 9.4.01 can also claim WPA if they have dependent children. Women who are pregnant by their late husband can also qualify. Women whose husbands died before 9.4.01 can continue to claim widowed mother's allowance (see below). WPA cannot be paid beyond state pension age (see below).

If your spouse met the NI contribution conditions, the full rate of £82.05 a week is payable. If your spouse's NI contribution record was incomplete, you will receive a proportionally reduced amount of WPA – unless they died as a result of an industrial accident or prescribed industrial disease.

If you have dependent children you should claim child tax credit at the same time that you claim WPA (see Chapter 18).

You may get an additional state pension from SERPS based on your spouse's earnings. Widowers who receive a state pension based on their late wife's contracted-out private pension may have this SERPS reduced. If you were widowed on or after 6.10.02 and your spouse was under state pension age on that date, the amount of SERPS is also reduced.

WPA for yourself is taxable. Increases for children payable on claims made before 6.4.03 are tax free.

Bereavement allowance
Bereavement allowance is payable if you were aged 45 or over when your spouse died. It is payable for 52 weeks starting from the Tuesday on or following the death of your spouse. You cannot get bereavement allowance at the same time as WPA, but you can claim bereavement allowance for the remainder of the 52 weeks if your WPA ends during that time. Bereavement allowance cannot be paid beyond state pension age (see below).

The amount you are paid is related to your age when your spouse died. Payments range from £24.62 a week if you were aged 45, up to £76.31 if you were aged 54. If you were aged 55 or over (but below state pension) age on the day your spouse died, the full-rate allowance of £82.05 may be payable. If your spouse's NI contribution record was incomplete, the amount payable is reduced, unless they died as a result of an industrial accident or prescribed industrial disease.

A bereavement allowance is taxable.

Widowed before 9.4.01
Women widowed before 9.4.01 come under the old rules for widows' benefits outlined below. Men widowed before 9.4.01 are generally not eligible for widows' benefits (but can claim widowed parent's allowance if they have dependent children). However, men who were bereaved prior to 9.4.01 and who claimed a widow's benefit but were refused, could rely on the decision of the European Court of Human Rights (*Willis v United Kingdom*), which found that the rule breached human rights law.

Widows' benefits consist of the following:

- ❑ **Widowed mother's allowance** – This is usually payable if you have dependent children. The amounts and qualifying conditions are the same as those for WPA.
- ❑ **Widow's pension** – You may get a reduced, age-related widow's pension if you were aged 45 to 54 on the day your husband died or when your widowed mother's allowance ended. If you were aged 55 to 64 on that day, you may get a full-rate pension. The amount of benefit is the same as for bereavement allowance except that a SERPS additional pension may be payable with your widow's pension. If your husband died before 11.4.88, an age-related pension is payable if you were aged 40 to 49, and a full-rate pension if you were aged 50 to 64.

What happens to other benefits?
Bereavement and widows' benefits overlap with incapacity benefit (IB), carer's allowance, severe disablement allowance, contribution-based jobseeker's allowance, maternity allowance, unemployability supplement and state pension. You receive an amount equal to the higher of the overlapped benefits.

If your husband died before 11.4.88 and you get industrial death benefit, it is paid in full on top of any transitional IB (see Box E.10, Chapter 14) or state pension you are entitled to based on your own NI contributions.

When you reach pension age
Widowed parent's allowance and bereavement allowance cannot be paid beyond state pension age (60 for women, 65 for men). Widow's pension and, as long as you still have dependent children, widowed mother's allowance can be paid until your 65th birthday. If you also claim a state pension you cannot receive both; you'll receive whichever is the higher.

When you reach state pension age, you will be entitled to a Category B state pension if you have not remarried before state pension age, or to a Category A state pension based on your own NI contributions record and including your spouse's record if that would give you a higher state pension. See DWP leaflet PM2 *State Pensions – Your guide* for details.

5. Special rules for incapacity benefit

If you are incapable of work but don't have enough national insurance (NI) contributions to qualify for incapacity benefit (IB), special rules for widows and widowers may help you. However, these rules only apply if your spouse died before 9.4.01. For women, you are entitled to long-term IB if:

- you were not entitled to widowed mother's allowance (WMA) on your husband's death, or entitlement has ended; *and*
- you are entitled to a reduced-rate widow's pension, or you don't get a pension because you were under 45 when your husband died or WMA ended; *and*
- you were incapable of work on your husband's death or when your WMA ends (and this was after 5.4.79); *and*
- you are in the same 'period of incapacity for work' (see Box E.8, Chapter 14) that began before your husband died or WMA ended, and have been incapable of work for 52 weeks. If you are terminally ill, IB is payable after 28 weeks of incapacity.

If you get a reduced-rate widow's pension, IB tops it up to the standard long-term IB rate (see Chapter 14(4)). So if you were getting severe disablement allowance when your husband died, you will switch to IB when your WMA ends if you are not then entitled to widow's pension, or if it is lower than your IB entitlement.

Once you reach state pension age, your IB will stop. You will be entitled to a full state pension even if you do not have sufficient NI contributions (see Chapter 42).

For men, you can qualify for IB on the same basis if you were incapable of work on your wife's death, or within 13 weeks afterwards.

6. Death of a child

Benefits will be affected by the death of your child, but dealing with different agencies after such a loss may be impossible. Since the agencies concerned do need to be informed quickly, it may be appropriate to ask someone to make the calls on your behalf, be they an advice worker or a good friend. Make sure they are aware that the office dealing with each different benefit will need to be informed.

Some benefits will continue for 8 weeks after the death of a child. These include carer's allowance, child benefit, child tax credit, and the carer premium as well as child allowances paid in means-tested benefits (eg housing and council tax benefit).

There are organisations that provide support and comfort to bereaved parents and families. There is the national Child Death Helpline (0800 282 986) and the Compassionate Friends Helpline (08451 232 304).

52 Health benefits

1. Who qualifies for help?

Some people qualify automatically for help with NHS charges, vouchers for glasses, and hospital travel fares (including travel abroad for NHS treatment) because of their age or circumstances. Others can qualify for full or partial help with NHS charges, hospital travel costs and vouchers for glasses on the basis of low income. If you qualify on low-income grounds, your partner and dependent children also qualify. NHS leaflets HC11 and HC12 explain the help available with health costs (available from the Department of Health publications orderline: 08701 555 455). The Prescription Pricing Authority manages the health benefits scheme.

2. Prescription charges

Prescriptions cost £6.50 (in 2005/06) for each item (but less in Wales; probably £4, and £3 from October 2005), so it is important to take advantage of exemptions from charges, or prepayment certificates (which save money on frequent prescriptions). If you are a hospital outpatient, exemptions from charges made by hospitals for prescribed drugs are the same as those listed below.

Who is automatically exempt?

You can get free prescriptions if you are:

- under 16 (under 25 in Wales), or under 19 and in full-time education;
- aged 60 or over;
- receiving income support or income-based jobseeker's allowance, or you would be but for the fact that your entitlement is less than 10 pence;
- the partner or dependent child of someone who gets one of the benefits listed above.

Who can get an exemption certificate?

You can get an exemption certificate for free NHS prescriptions if you:

- are pregnant or have given birth in the previous 12 months. You can get form FW8 from your doctor, midwife or health visitor;
- receiving pension credit (PC) guarantee credit;
- receive working tax credit (WTC) with a disability or severe disability element *or* child tax credit with or without any rate of WTC, *and* your relevant income for tax credit purposes is £15,050 or less;
- have a specified condition (see below);
- are a war/service pensioner (the prescription must be for your accepted war disablement);
- qualify under the low income scheme for an HC2 (full help) certificate (see 5);
- are a 16/17-year-old leaving the care of an English or Welsh local authority and are wholly or partly maintained by a local authority;
- are an asylum seeker, or their partner or dependent child, supported by the National Asylum Support Services.

If you qualify for a tax credit exemption certificate, the Prescription Pricing Authority will send it to you when your award has been confirmed by the Inland Revenue. This may take several weeks, so if you need prescriptions while waiting, you must pay and obtain a receipt (ask the pharmacist for form FP57). You can claim a refund later (see below). Your exemption certificate is valid until the end of the tax year, regardless of any changes to your tax credit entitlement. If you receive PC, your exemption certificate will be included with your award notice.

What are the specified conditions ?

If you have one of the conditions listed below, you are entitled to an exemption certificate:

- a continuing physical disability that prevents you from leaving home without the help of another person (a temporary disability is excluded, even if it is likely to last a few months);
- a permanent fistula (eg caecostomy, colostomy, laryngostomy or ileostomy) requiring continuous surgical dressing or an appliance;
- diabetes mellitus (except where treatment is by diet alone), myxoedema, hypoparathyroidism, diabetes insipidus or other forms of hypopituitarism, forms of hypoadrenalism (including Addison's disease) for which specific substitution therapy is essential, and myasthenia gravis;
- epilepsy, requiring continuous anti-convulsive therapy.

Claim on form FP92A (EC92A in Scotland, FP92W in Wales), available from your doctor.

How to claim

Complete and sign the declaration on the back of the prescription form. The pharmacist will ask you to provide evidence that you are eligible for free prescriptions. When you collect your prescription take your exemption certificate, prepayment certificate or DWP award letter. You should not be refused the prescription if you do not have the evidence but your entitlement may be checked later and if you were not exempt you will be asked to pay the prescription charge. You may also be charged a penalty of up to 5 times the cost of the prescription, subject to a £100 maximum.

Refunds – You can claim a refund within 3 months (later if you have good cause) of the date you paid for treatment if you should have been entitled to help. When you pay ask your pharmacist for receipt form FP57 (WP57 in Wales, EC57 in Scotland) and send this with your claim on form HC5. See booklet HC11 for details of where to send your claim.

What is a prescription prepayment certificate?

If you are not exempt from prescription charges, or your income is too high to get the HC2 (full help) certificate (see 5), a prepayment certificate is the only way to reduce prescription costs. A 4-month certificate costs £33.90 (£20.93 in Wales from October 2004) and a year's certificate costs £93.20 (£57.46 in Wales; expected to be reduced October 2005) in 2005/06; it saves money if you need more than 5 items in 4 months or 14 items in a year.

You apply on form FP95 (or EC95 in Scotland), available from pharmacists, the Department of Health publications orderline (08701 555 455) or their website: www.dh.gov.uk/helpwithhealthcosts. You can also apply by ringing the Prescription Pricing Authority on 0845 850 0030 and paying with a debit or credit card.

3. Sight tests and glasses

You and any partner or dependent children, qualify for free NHS eyesight tests and vouchers for glasses or contact lenses if you:

- are under 16, or under 19 and in full-time education;
- are a 16/17-year-old leaving the care of an English or Welsh local authority and are wholly or partly maintained by a local authority and named on an HC2 certificate;
- receive pension credit guarantee credit;
- are a war/service pensioner (the need must be due to your accepted war disablement);
- are receiving income support or income-based jobseeker's allowance, or you would be but for the fact that your entitlement is less than 10 pence;
- receive working tax credit (WTC) with a disability or severe disability element *or* child tax credit with or without any rate of WTC, *and* your relevant income for tax credit purposes is £15,050 or less, and you are named on a valid NHS tax credit exemption certificate;
- need complex or powerful lenses – you qualify automatically for lower-rate vouchers (and free eye tests);
- are an asylum seeker supported by the National Asylum Support Services and named on an HC2 certificate.

In addition, NHS eyesight tests are free if you are:

- aged 60 or over;
- registered blind or partially sighted;
- diagnosed as having diabetes or glaucoma, or you are considered to be at risk of glaucoma, or you are aged 40 or over and are the parent, brother, sister or child of a person with glaucoma.

You may also qualify for vouchers for glasses or contact lenses, and help towards the cost of sight tests, if your income is low (see below). You must ask for a voucher when you have your eyes tested. The value of the voucher depends on the strength of the lenses you need, with additions for clinically necessary prisms or tints. You will usually be asked to supply evidence that you qualify. When you buy your glasses, give the supplier your voucher. If the glasses cost more, you will have to pay the extra.

Low income scheme – See 5 below for details. If you don't already have a current HC2 (full help) or HC3 (partial help) certificate and believe you qualify, you should apply to the Prescription Pricing Authority on form HC1, available from the Department of Health publications orderline: 08701 555 455. If you have an HC2 certificate your eye tests are free.

Refunds – You can claim a refund within 3 months (later if you have good cause) of the date you paid for treatment if you should have been entitled to help. When you pay ask your optician for a receipt and send this with your claim on form HC5. See booklet HC11 for details of where to send your claim.

4. Free NHS dental treatment

You qualify for free NHS dentures and dental treatment if you:

- are aged under 18;
- are under 19 and in full-time education;
- are pregnant – if you were pregnant when the dentist accepted you for treatment;
- have given birth in the past year – if you start a course of dental treatment before your child's first birthday;
- are receiving income support or income-based jobseeker's allowance, or you would be but for the fact that your entitlement is less than 10 pence;
- receive working tax credit (WTC) with a disability or severe disability element *or* child tax credit with or without any rate of WTC, *and* your relevant income for tax credit purposes is £15,050 or less, and you are named on a valid NHS tax credit exemption certificate;
- receive pension credit guarantee credit;
- are an asylum seeker supported by the National Asylum Support Services and are named on an HC2 certificate;
- are the partner or dependent child of a person who gets one of the benefits listed above.

In England, war/service pensioners may be entitled to free dental treatment if the treatment is for their pensionable disability. In Wales, those aged under 25 or 60 and over are entitled to a free NHS dental examination.

You may also be entitled if you are a 16/17-year-old leaving the care of an English or Welsh local authority and are wholly or partly maintained by a local authority.

Tell your dentist you qualify (you will usually be asked to provide evidence) and fill in the declaration on the form they give you.

Low income scheme – See 5 below for details. If you don't already have a current HC2 (full help) or HC3 (partial help) certificate and believe you qualify, you should apply to the Prescription Pricing Authority on form HC1, available from the Department of Health publications orderline: 08701 555 455.

Refunds – You can claim a refund within 3 months (later if you have good cause) of the date you paid for treatment if you should have been entitled to help. When you pay ask your dentist for a receipt form FP64 (GP17D in Scotland) and send this with your claim on form HC5. See booklet HC11 for details of where to send your claim.

5. Low income scheme

The low income scheme for help with NHS charges and optical vouchers is operated by the Patient Services section of the Prescription Pricing Authority (PPA). If your capital is £8,000 or less, or £12,250 or less if you or your partner are aged 60 or over, you may be eligible for help. The capital limit is £20,500 if you live permanently in a care home.

If your income is less than or equal to your requirements (plus 50% of any prescription charge), you are entitled to full help with any NHS charges and to vouchers towards the cost of glasses. The PPA will send you an HC2 certificate.

If your income is higher than your requirements by more than 50% of the prescription charge, you cannot get help with the cost of NHS prescriptions. However, you may get some help with other NHS charges and travel expenses to and from a Disablement Services centre or a hospital for NHS treatment. The PPA will send you an HC3 certificate (partial help) to show you how much you have to contribute towards NHS charges and travel expenses.

For travelling expenses, you'll get the difference between your excess income and your total fares in any week (Sunday through to Saturday). For sight tests, you'll get the difference between the sight test fee and your excess income. For glasses, the maximum voucher value is reduced by twice your excess income. For dental charges, your maximum contribution is 3 times your excess income.

The low income assessment

The assessment of income and capital is broadly the same as for income support (see Chapter 5), but there are some differences.

- ❑ If you live in a care home, the capital limit is £20,500.
- ❑ If you are on strike, your pre-strike income is taken into account.
- ❑ The £10 disregard for student loans is only available if your assessment includes a premium, or you get disabled students' allowance because of deafness, or where you are not a student but your partner is.

Your requirements are worked out in almost the same way as the housing benefit (HB) applicable amount, including premiums (see Chapter 7(25)). There are some significant differences.

- A disability premium can be included after 28 weeks of incapacity, rather than 52 weeks.
- All lone parents get the lone parent rate of the family premium.
- If you are a lone parent aged 60 or over your requirements are calculated in the same way as for pension credit (see Chapter 41).
- For children, the personal allowance at age 16 is not aligned with the school year as it is with HB, but increases on the child's 16th birthday.
- Generally, your net weekly housing costs are also taken into account, including: mortgage capital repayments; payments on an endowment policy in connection with buying your home; repayments of interest and capital on a loan to adapt your home for the special needs of a disabled person; rent payments (less any HB); and council tax (less council tax benefit). Amounts for non-dependants are deducted (see Chapter 7(22)).

How do you claim?
Claim on form HC1, available from Jobcentre Plus offices, the PPA (0845 850 1166) or the Department of Health publications orderline: 08701 555 455. NHS hospitals, doctors, dentists, opticians and advice agencies may also have the form. If you are unable to act for yourself, someone else can claim for you. Claim on form HC1(SC) if you live in a care home and the local authority helps with the fees, or you are a 16/17-year-old care leaver and a local authority supports you.

If you haven't claimed before or don't have a current HC2 or HC3 certificate, and have just paid for dental treatment, etc you will also need to claim on form HC5 for a refund within 3 months of paying.

After you have claimed, the PPA will send you a decision. If you are entitled to full help, they will send an HC2 certificate. If you are entitled to partial help, they will send an HC3 certificate.

How long does the certificate last? – Each HC2 or HC3 certificate lasts for 6 or 12 months. It will last for 12 months if you are aged 60 or over, or entitled to a disability premium (as long as you don't have a partner working 16 hours or more a week), or if you live in a care home placed by the local authority. You should make a repeat claim on form HC1 4 weeks before the end of your current certificate. If your circumstances change during the currency of a certificate, you can make a new claim to the PPA and they will issue a new certificate showing your revised entitlement.

If you are not happy with the decision – There is no right of appeal but you can write to the PPA and ask them to reconsider their decision (Independent Review Section, PPA, PO Box 993, Newcastle-upon-Tyne, NE99 2TZ).

6. Free milk and vitamins

You qualify automatically if you or a dependant:

- are pregnant and receive income support (IS), income-based jobseeker's allowance (JSA), pension credit (PC) guarantee credit, or child tax credit (CTC) (but not working tax credit – WTC) and your relevant income is less than £13,910 (or you are a family member of a person thus entitled);
- you have a child under 5 and receive IS or income-based JSA, or CTC (but not WTC) and your relevant income is less than £13,910 (see Chapter 18).

If your relevant income is between £13,910 and £15,050, you will receive infant formula instead of milk.

Free milk is also available for any child under 5 who is looked after for at least 2 hours a day by a registered childminder or daycare provider, local authority, school, or workplace nursery which is exempt from registration.

A child with a learning and/or physical disability aged 5-16 years old who is not a registered pupil at a school may receive free milk (see Chapter 35(1)).

For more information, get leaflet WMV:G1 or the NHS welfare foods leaflet *Free Milk For Pregnant Women* from your local Jobcentre Plus office or your midwife, or ring the Token Distribution Unit (0845 850 1032). If you receive CTC you do not need to make a claim, as the Inland Revenue will notify the Department of Health that you qualify.

The Welfare Food Scheme is currently being reviewed and will be replaced by Healthy Start. This introduces weekly vouchers that can be used to buy fresh fruit and vegetables, as well as milk. It is anticipated that the new arrangements will be piloted in Devon during 2005 and be rolled out nationally early in 2006.

53 Christmas bonus

1. What is the Christmas bonus?

This is a tax-free payment of £10 paid in December with certain social security benefits. It is not taken into account as income for means-tested benefits.

2. How is it paid?

Your Christmas bonus will be paid with your usual benefit payment from the week beginning Monday 5.12.05. If you have not received the bonus by the end of December, contact your local Jobcentre Plus or Pension Service office.

3. Who qualifies for it?

You will be entitled to a Christmas bonus if, in the week beginning 5.12.05 (the relevant week):

- you are present or ordinarily resident in the UK, the Channel Islands, the Isle of Man, Gibraltar or any European Economic Area country or Switzerland (see Chapters 49 and 50); *and*
- you are entitled to a payment of one of a list of qualifying benefits for a period which includes a day in the week beginning 5.12.05. This list includes: attendance allowance, carer's allowance, disability living allowance, some recipients of industrial injuries disablement benefit (including industrial death benefit), long-term incapacity benefit, pension credit (PC), severe disablement allowance, state pension, war disablement or widow's pension, widow's pension or widowed mother's (or parent's) allowance.

If each of a couple meets these qualifying conditions, each will be paid the £10 bonus. If you receive more than one qualifying benefit you will only receive one bonus. However, if you and your partner are both over state pension age but your partner does not receive a bonus in their own right, you will get an extra £10 bonus for your partner if you are entitled, or treated as entitled, to a dependant's addition for them, or if the only benefit you get is PC.

54 Income tax

1. Introduction

This is a brief outline of some basic income tax facts. Your local Inland Revenue Enquiry Centre can help with tax enquiries. For independent advice, contact a Citizens Advice Bureau, or TaxAid, an independent registered charity based at Room 304, Linton House, 164-180 Union Street, London SE1 0LH (020 7803 4959).

To check if you are paying the right amount of tax you

need to know what income is taxable, the allowances you are entitled to, and the appropriate rate of income tax. The amounts change from year to year (from 6 April) so find out the amounts for the year you want to check. The figures and allowances in this chapter are for 6.4.05 to 5.4.06.

2. Income

Some income is exempt from tax (eg interest on an ISA account) and so is ignored completely when working out your tax. Other income (eg earnings) is taxable. You are allowed tax relief on certain outgoings (eg pension contributions), but this is often deducted at source.

Which benefits are taxable?

The following benefits are the only ones that are taxable:

- bereavement allowance;
- carer's allowance;
- higher rate short-term incapacity benefit (IB);
- long-term IB (but not if you transferred from invalidity benefit – see Box E.9, Chapter 14);
- income support if you are directly involved in a trade dispute;
- invalidity allowance paid with a state pension;
- industrial death benefit;
- jobseeker's allowance;
- state pension;
- statutory adoption, maternity, paternity, sick pay;
- adult dependants' additions paid with these benefits;
- widowed mother's/parent's allowance and widow's pension.

3. Tax allowances

You are entitled to a personal allowance. You may also be entitled to a blind person's allowance. The children's tax credit, a form of tax allowance, was merged into child tax credit in April 2003 (see Chapter 18). All other tax allowances were abolished from April 2000, although married couples can continue to receive their married couple's allowance where either partner was born before 6.4.35.

The tax allowances that have now been abolished were restricted to give a reduced amount of tax relief (15% from April 1995; 10% from April 1999). These were the married couple's allowance, additional personal allowance and widow's bereavement allowance.

If you have not had the tax allowances due to you, write to your local Inland Revenue Enquiry Centre with the details. You can claim for the last 6 complete tax years, and if you have overpaid tax you will get a refund. In the tax year 2005/06 you can claim a refund back to 1999/2000.

Personal allowance

Everyone, male or female, married or not, has a personal allowance that can be set against all income.

Age	personal allowance
Under 65	£4,895
65-74	£7,090
75 or over	£7,220

You can claim the appropriate higher allowance for the complete year if your 65th or 75th birthday falls at any time during the tax year. The higher allowances for those aged 65 or over are reduced if your total income is over £19,500 for the 2005/06 tax year. For each £2 extra income over £19,500, £1 is deducted. But it won't be reduced below the basic personal allowance. A husband and wife each have a separate total income limit.

If you don't use up your full personal allowance, you cannot transfer it to a partner or carry it forward to future tax years.

Blind person's allowance

You will get an allowance of £1,610 if you are registered blind (but not if you are registered partially-sighted). A married couple can transfer any surplus allowance from one to the other. If both husband and wife are registered blind, it is therefore possible for one of them to get both their own blind person's allowance and the other's surplus allowance. You can receive the allowance for the tax year before the one in which you are registered as blind, provided you had obtained the evidence for registration (eg ophthalmologist's certificate) before the end of that tax year.

Married couple's allowance

This is an extra allowance for a married couple who live together where at least one of the partners was born before 6.4.35. The rate depends on the age of the older partner.

Age of older partner	married couple's allowance
65 before 6.4.00	£5,905
75 or over	£5,975

Tax relief on married couple's allowance is restricted to 10%. It may be reduced if the husband's income is above the £19,500 income limit (by £1 for every £2 over the limit). It only starts to be affected if his personal allowance has been reduced to the basic personal allowance and it cannot be reduced below a minimum of £2,280.

4. Income tax rates

Taxable income	rate for tax year 2005/06
The first £2,090	10% (lower rate)
Between £2,091 and £32,400	22% (basic rate)
Above £32,400	40% (higher rate)

5. Working out your tax

Step 1: Work out your total income
Add up income from all sources for the tax year (which runs from 6 April to 5 April). Include taxable benefit, but not exempt income.

Step 2: Work out your taxable income
Deduct your personal allowance (plus the blind person's allowance if you qualify) from your total income in Step 1.

Step 3: Work out your tax
Add 10% of the first £2,090 of your taxable income to 22% of your taxable income between £2,091 and £32,400. Add to that 40% of all your income above £32,400.

Step 4: Work out the tax you are due to pay
If you get married couple's allowance (which gives only restricted tax relief), work out 10% of this and deduct the result from the tax payable in Step 3. This is the tax you will have to pay.

Example: James is aged 72 and is married to Annie who is aged 70. He is registered blind. He gets an occupational pension of £7,296 for this tax year and state pension of £6,830.

Step 1: James' total income	
Occupational pension	£7,296
State pension	£6,830
Total income	*£14,126*

Step 2: James' taxable income	
Personal allowance, aged 65-74	£7,090
Blind person's allowance	£1,610
Total personal allowances	*£8,700*
Subtract allowances from income	
Taxable income	*£5,426*

A B C D E F G H I J K L M N O P Q R S

Step 3: James' tax

10% of first £2,090	£209.00
22% of next £3,336	£733.92
Total tax due	*£942.92*

Step 4: James is due to pay

Tax due	£942.92
Less 10% of married couple's allowance of £5,905	£590.05
Tax payable	*£352.87*

6. Notice of coding

If you have earnings or an occupational pension you will generally have tax deducted under PAYE (Pay As You Earn). You should receive a notice of coding setting out details of personal allowances, with any necessary adjustments, that are to be set against income.

For example, if you are a single person under 65 and registered blind, you would get total allowances of £6,505 (personal allowance of £4,895 + blind person's allowance of £1,610). Your code would be 650L – the final digit of your allowance is replaced by the letter L. The letters at the end of tax codes give information about the allowances you get.

Tax code letters

- L basic personal allowance
- P personal allowance (aged 65-74)
- Y personal allowance (aged 75 or over)
- V personal allowance plus married couple's allowance (aged 65-74)
- T most other cases.

There are 5 special cases that either do not have numbers or have numbers that do not show the amount of allowances.

- BR no allowances; tax is deducted at basic rate (22%) on every pound of income
- D tax is deducted at a higher rate (40%)
- K amounts to be taken away from your allowances are more than the total allowances. Negative allowances show the amount to be added to your pay or pension on which tax is to be paid
- NT no tax is to be deducted
- OT no allowances; tax is deducted at the appropriate rate on every pound of income.

7. Tax refunds

If you have paid too much tax you can claim a refund for 6 years back as well as the current tax year. Write to your local Inland Revenue Enquiry Centre with the details, including your national insurance number and any tax reference you have. You can telephone the Enquiry Centre for guidance on how to make a written claim.

If you have to give up work and your income drops, any refund due to you can be paid after 4 weeks of leaving work. Send your P45 to the Inland Revenue Enquiry Centre. You will need to estimate your income for the remainder of the tax year. If you have left work and are signing on for jobseeker's allowance, you can't get a tax refund until the end of the tax year.

Savings

Most income from savings is received after deduction of tax by the bank, building society, etc. If you have income, including interest (gross) amounting to less than your total personal allowances, you are entitled to receive interest from banks, building societies, etc without deduction of tax. Ask your bank or building society for an R85 form.

The rate of income tax deducted from interest credited to depositors (eg by banks and building societies) is 20%. There is no further tax to pay by most depositors even if you are normally liable at the basic rate of 22%. (Further tax is payable only if you are liable to pay tax at the higher rate of 40%.) If your taxable income including interest is less than £2,090 above your personal allowances, you are only liable to pay tax at the rate of 10% on interest from savings. You can claim a refund from the Inland Revenue. Ask your local Inland Revenue Enquiry Centre for form R40.

The rate of income tax deducted from dividends (known as a tax credit) is 10%. As in the case of interest, there is no further tax to pay unless you are liable to pay tax at the higher rate of 40%. However, unlike in the case of interest, even if your taxable income including savings is less than your personal allowances, you cannot claim a refund for the tax credit from the Inland Revenue.

8. Arrears of tax

If you have not paid enough tax, the Inland Revenue (IR) can claim it from you. Generally, they must do so within 6 years. If there are special circumstances (eg tax evasion) there is no time limit, and there may be penalties.

In certain circumstances, arrears of tax are wholly or partly waived if they have arisen through the failure of the IR to take account of information you have given them so that you could reasonably believe your affairs were in order. This concession is normally given where you are notified of the arrears after the end of the tax year following that in which the IR received information indicating that you had underpaid tax. For example, if in 2003/04 the IR received information that you had underpaid tax, you may claim a waiver of liability if the arrears are not notified to you by 5.4.05.

If you believe this applies to you, write to your local Inland Revenue Enquiry Centre claiming a waiver under extra statutory concession A19.

9. Tax returns and keeping records

You may be asked to complete a tax return, particularly if your circumstances have changed. However, usually only self-employed people and tax payers with complex tax affairs are asked to do this every year. If in any tax year you receive income or capital gains that should be taxed and which the Inland Revenue (IR) do not know about, you should notify them within 6 months of the end of the year. If you become self-employed, you must register with the IR within 3 months (call 0845 915 4515) or a penalty up to £100 will be imposed.

You should keep records of your income and capital gains to enable you to complete a tax return, in case it is required. Usually records should be kept for 22 months after the end of the tax year to which they relate. If you are self-employed or have rental income this period is extended by 4 years.

If you regularly complete a tax return, it will be sent to you shortly after the end of the tax year; eg for the tax year ended 5.4.05, you should receive your blank tax return by the end of April 2005. If you want the IR to calculate your tax or to collect any arrears through your PAYE code, you should complete and send back the tax return by 30.9.05. Alternatively, under self-assessment, you may calculate your own tax, in which case you have until 31.1.06 to complete your tax return, including your calculation of the tax you should pay or be refunded. If tax is payable, it should be paid by 31.1.06. There is a penalty of up to £100 if the return is not sent back by 31.1.06. This penalty cannot exceed the tax payable. So if you file your return after the deadline and this shows that a refund was due, the penalty should be cancelled.

55 Disability Discrimination Act

1. What is the DDA and who does it cover?

The Disability Discrimination Act 1995 (DDA) makes it unlawful to discriminate against disabled people in connection with employment, education, the provision of goods, facilities and services or the disposal or management of premises, and allows the Government to set standards and targets for accessible public transport.

The DDA defines disability as *'a physical or mental impairment which has a substantial and long-term adverse effect on [your] ability to carry out normal day-to-day activities'*. If you can show that you come within this definition, you will have the protection of the Act.

'Impairment' includes sensory impairments (for example, blindness or deafness), learning disabilities, and mental illness which is a clinically well recognised condition. *'Substantial'* means *'more than minor or trivial'*. *'Long-term'* means effects that have lasted at least 12 months, or are likely to last at least 12 months, or are likely to last for the rest of your life (if that is less than 12 months). Conditions that are likely to recur such as epilepsy or asthma will be considered as long term. The definition also includes you if you have had a disability in the past that meets the definition in the DDA, even if you no longer have that disability. You are covered by the Act if you have a severe disfigurement, even though it may not affect your ability to carry out normal activities.

'Day-to-day activities' are defined as activities involving: moving from place to place; manual dexterity; physical co-ordination; continence; the ability to lift, carry or move ordinary objects; speech, hearing or eyesight; memory or the ability to concentrate, learn or understand; and being able to recognise physical danger.

If you have a progressive condition (eg cancer or multiple sclerosis) you will not be covered simply because your condition has been diagnosed. You will only come under the definition used in the DDA from the time that your condition has an effect on your ability to carry out day-to-day activities. The effect does not need to be substantial as long as it would be expected eventually to become substantial. You will not be covered by the Act just because you have a genetic predisposition to a particular condition, such as thalassaemia.

Any steps taken to treat or correct your disability (eg hearing aid, artificial limb or medication) are ignored when considering whether your impairment has a substantial adverse effect. An exception is made if you wear glasses or contact lenses, in that it is the effect on your vision with the lenses that is considered.

If you are blind or partially sighted you automatically meet the DDA definition if you are registered with your local authority as blind or partially sighted, or if a consultant ophthalmologist has certified that you are blind or partially sighted.

The Government has published guidance to help you work out if you come under the definition of disability. You can get a copy from The Stationery Office or from the Disability Rights Commission website (see Box Q.1).

The DDA protects disabled people who take on a case or make a complaint under the DDA and also people victimised by service providers for helping a disabled person to make a complaint, give evidence or take a case under the DDA. This is called 'victimisation'. For example, a non-disabled woman gives evidence when a deaf man brings a case against a pub under the DDA. The next time the non-disabled woman goes to the pub, the bar manager refuses to serve her. This is an example of victimisation, and the woman could bring her own case to court under the DDA against the pub.

The DDA says discrimination occurs when service providers treat disabled people less favourably because of their disability and the treatment cannot be justified.

2. Your employment rights – DDA Part 2

It is unlawful for an employer to treat you less favourably than someone else for a reason related to your disability, unless they can show such treatment is justified. The DDA covers almost all employment – except the Armed Forces, anyone who works entirely or mainly outside the UK, and some volunteers. The DDA covers temporary staff, contract workers and permanent employees, and all employment matters, including recruitment and selection, training, promotion, dismissal and redundancy. It also covers harassment.

Since 1.10.04, the DDA also covers employment agencies, work experience (including making reasonable adjustments) and qualifying bodies.

Employers are liable (ie legally responsible) for the actions of their employees and agents (eg a recruitment agency which deliberately discriminates on the authority of the employer). The Act also covers discrimination in occupational pension schemes and insurance obtained through employers – eg health insurance. There is no qualifying period of employment to bring a discrimination claim, and there is no cap on compensation.

Trade organisations (eg trade unions) have a duty under the DDA not to discriminate against members or potential members and are required to make *'reasonable adjustments'* for their existing and potential members (see below).

Since 1.10.04, there are 4 different types of employment discrimination.

- ❑ Direct discrimination: discrimination on the ground of someone's disability – this includes harassment.
- ❑ Disability-related discrimination: the reason is linked to the disability but is not the disability itself.
- ❑ Failure to make reasonable adjustments.
- ❑ Victimisation.

Only the second can be justified; employers can justify disability-related discrimination if in the circumstances it is for a material and substantial reason. *'Material'* means that there must be a reasonably strong link between the employer's reason and the circumstances of the individual case. Refusing to employ someone simply because they are disabled would not be material. *'Substantial'* means that the reason for the discrimination must be more than minor or trivial. A reason will be substantial if it has real weight. An unsupported refusal to employ someone or make adjustments would not be substantial. The employer has to prove this.

Reasonable adjustments

The DDA requires employers to make *'reasonable adjustments'* (changes) to the workplace and to employment arrangements, including recruitment, so that a disabled employee or job applicant is not at any substantial disadvantage. Reasonable adjustments include changes to the physical environment, eg widening a doorway to allow for wheelchair access or allocating a specific parking space for a disabled person. The term includes changes to arrangements in the workplace such as flexible working hours, purchasing specialised equipment, providing additional training or allowing time off for treatment. Reasonable adjustments also include providing an assistant or communications support – eg BSL interpreters.

If your employer does not own premises but rents them, then the landlord cannot unreasonably refuse permission for the premises to be altered to accommodate you. However, they may attach reasonable conditions to their permission (eg returning the premises to the original condition when vacating them). If your employer does not make a reasonable adjustment because the landlord unreasonably refuses permission for the premises to be altered, then you could take your employer to the Employment Tribunal, and either you or your employer could ask the Tribunal to make the landlord a party to the case. This means that the landlord would have to go the Tribunal as well.

The Disability Rights Commission (DRC) codes of practice on employment and occupation and on trade organisations give more information and examples on these issues. You can get these from the DRC website.

3. Access to goods and services – DDA Part 3

It is unlawful for organisations (service providers) who provide goods, facilities or services in the UK directly to the general public to discriminate against disabled people. It does not matter whether the services are free or paid for. Service providers include: shops, hotels, banks, cinemas, restaurants; courts and solicitors; private education providers, non-educational activities in schools, colleges and universities (eg parents' evenings), students' unions; telecommunications companies, railway stations, libraries, swimming pools; healthcare, social and housing services; government offices; and voluntary services such as advice centres. Insurance companies are covered but special rules apply.

However, not all service providers are covered by the DDA. Private clubs and associations are exempt from the Act in relation to serving their members. Part 3 does not cover the manufacture and design of products, and does not apply to the use of any means of transport – eg buses, ships, planes or trains. However, stations and booking facilities are covered by Part 3.

You may have been discriminated against if you were treated less favourably than someone else for a reason relating to your disability – eg a service provider refused to serve you or offered you a lower standard of service or service on less favourable terms. However, the DDA allows service providers to treat a disabled person less favourably in some situations – called *'justification'*. There are 5 conditions for such justification:

- **Health and safety** – A service provider can, for example, refuse to provide a service or provide a lower standard of service if in doing so a genuine health and safety risk occurs for you or anyone else.
- **Incapacity to enter into a contract** – A service provider does not have to enter into a contract with someone – eg a customer with senile dementia – who is not capable of entering into a legally enforceable agreement or of giving informed consent. However, a service provider would need to consider if it would help to provide a document in more simple language. This does not apply if someone else deals with your affairs.
- **The service provider is otherwise unable to provide the service** – It may take longer to provide you with a service because of your communication needs, eg you need a BSL interpreter for a training course. Although the interpreter is running late, the service provider starts the training because if they wait, they will not be able to get through all of the information. This would be less favourable treatment, but necessary to provide the service to other people. The treatment is only justified if otherwise it would not be possible to provide the service to the other members of the public.
- **Discrimination is necessary to provide the service to the disabled person or other members of the public** – The service provider can justify treatment to a lower standard or in a worse manner if the discrimination is necessary to provide a service to you, or to provide a service to other members of the public. For example, it may take a service provider a little longer to provide you with a service if you have communication needs. This is a lower standard of service, but necessary in order to provide you with that service.
- **Greater expense** – If the service is individually tailored to your needs it may cost the provider more to do so. For example, a customer needs a bed specially made to accommodate her disability and the store charges more than for a standard one, because the special bed costs more to make.

Service providers can only use these five reasons and they have to prove that at least one applies. Service providers are legally responsible for any discrimination by their employees or anyone else who works as part of their business – eg contractors.

Reasonable adjustments

Service providers must make adjustments to their service(s) where without the adjustments it is impossible or unreasonably difficult for a disabled person to access the service.

There are 4 types of reasonable adjustment.

- Changing the way a service is provided – 'practices, policies or procedures' – eg producing statements in large print.
- Providing an additional aid or service if this will help or enable you to access the service – eg communication support.
- Providing the service in an alternative way – eg if the business' premises are inaccessible, home visits to some clients could be offered.
- Removing or altering physical features, such as doors, lighting or glass screens, if these create barriers to accessing the service, or providing a reasonable means of avoiding them.

The first three duties came into force on 1.10.99, the 4th on 1.10.04.

Service providers only have to do what is reasonable. This can depend on a number of things, including how practicable it is to make the adjustment and the cost. Service providers have to plan ahead to meet these duties, and will have to comply even if they do not know that someone is disabled. Providers must not charge disabled people for making reasonable adjustments.

4. Housing

It is unlawful for anyone letting or selling land or property to discriminate against disabled people. Most types of premises are covered (ie houses, flats, bedsits and business premises) as is housing maintained by local authorities or housing associations. Hotels and guest houses are covered by the Goods and Services section of the Act, as is the provision of general housing information and advice (see 3).

The DDA applies to most agencies involved in letting, selling or managing rented property, including local authorities, housing associations, private landlords, estate agencies, accommodation agencies, banks and building societies, property developers, and owner occupiers.

You will have been discriminated against if you are treated less favourably than someone else for a reason relating to your disability and this treatment cannot be justified. For example, if you were charged a higher rent or a higher deposit than other tenants for a reason related to your disability and this could not be justified, your landlord would be guilty of discrimination.

The Act also makes the harassment of disabled people unlawful. If the landlord or person managing the premises restricts or prevents a disabled person from using any benefits or facilities, this can be unlawful discrimination. For example, it may be unlawful if a property management company refuses to allow a tenant's child to use the communal garden because the child has attention deficit disorder and other tenants object to them using the garden. There are specific justification conditions that landlords can rely on.

The Act exempts landlords who let rooms to 6 or fewer people in their own homes and there is no legal obligation on anyone selling or letting property to alter the premises in order to make them accessible for you. The DDA does not cover a sale arranged without an estate agent.

The DDA does not require landlords to make reasonable adjustments to premises, but estate agents could be covered by Part 3 – eg they must produce accessible information and not refuse to deal with disabled enquirers.

The Disability Rights Commission *Code of Practice on Goods, Services, Facilities and Premises* gives more information and guidance on these issues (see Box Q.1). For information in Northern Ireland, visit the Equality Commission for Northern Ireland website: www.equalityni.org.

5. Education

Since 1.9.02, it has been unlawful for education providers to discriminate against pupils and students on the grounds of disability. This duty applies to admissions, education and related services and exclusions.

Schools in England, Scotland and Wales have to ensure that disabled pupils are not treated less favourably, and have to make reasonable adjustments to avoid putting disabled pupils at a substantial disadvantage. However, auxiliary aids and services are provided through the existing special educational needs framework and physical accessibility will be achieved through longer-term strategic planning.

These duties apply to all schools, including publicly funded and independent schools, mainstream and special schools, pupil referral units and school sixth forms. They also apply to local education authority and education authority maintained nursery schools and classes, and to nursery provision at independent and grant-aided schools. Private, voluntary and statutory providers of nursery education that are not constituted as schools are covered by the Goods and Services provisions of the DDA (see 3).

Post-16 education providers include further, higher, adult and community education and the statutory youth service. It is unlawful for them to treat disabled students less favourably and they have a duty to make certain reasonable adjustments. Since 1.9.03 providers have had to provide auxiliary aids and services, and from 1.9.05 will need to make physical alterations to their premises. In some cases, the Goods and Services provisions of the DDA may apply instead. These include services provided by student unions, institutions of further and higher education to members of the public other than students, or private and voluntary sector education providers. The DDA does not yet apply to education in Northern Ireland (as of February 2005).

The Disability Rights Commission codes of practice on education give more information and examples on these issues (see Box Q.1).

6. Transport

The Public Transport Vehicles section of the Act covers taxis, buses, coaches, trains and trams. Airports, bus and rail stations, etc are covered under the Goods and Services section of the Act (see 3 above). The Act gives the Government the power to require all new public transport vehicles and newly licensed taxis to be accessible to disabled people. However, the Act also gives the Government fairly wide powers to grant exemptions. Since April 2001 licensed taxis are not allowed to refuse to carry or charge more for a disabled person accompanied by a guide or assistance dog. Drivers can ask to be exempt from this duty on medical grounds. A similar duty for private hire vehicles became law in April 2004.

The transport part of the Act has not yet been fully implemented. The train and tram regulations came into force on 1.1.99. Public service vehicle regulations covering all new buses and coaches came into force on 31.12.00. The Department for Transport can provide information on the transport provisions of the Act (see Box Q.1). There is a voluntary code of practice which covers air travel. The DDA does not cover aircraft.

7. Enforcing your rights

If you think you have been discriminated against under the employment provisions of the DDA you can make a complaint to an Employment Tribunal. The complaint must be registered with the Tribunal within 3 months of the discriminatory act – eg the date you were dismissed. In some circumstances there is a legal requirement to use a grievance or disciplinary procedure first. If this applies, you have an extra 3 months to bring a claim. If you don't use the procedure when you have to, the Tribunal will reject your claim.

The DDA has a questionnaire procedure to enable you to

Q.1 For more information

There is a range of government booklets covering different aspects of the DDA available free from the Disability Rights Commission (DRC) Helpline (0845 762 2633; Textphone 0845 762 2644). Booklets and advice can be obtained from: DRC Information, FREEPOST, MID 02164, Stratford-upon-Avon CV37 9BR, website: www.drc-gb.org. Information is available in Welsh, Braille, audio cassette and as a special pack for people with learning disabilities.

You can buy copies of codes of practice and guidance from The Stationery Office bookshops. Ring 0870 600 5522 or visit: www.tso.co.uk.

- *Guidance on Matters to be Taken into Account in Determining Questions Relating to the Definition of Disability* (£7.50)
- *Code of Practice – Rights of Access. Goods, Facilities, Services and Premises* (£13.95)
- *Code of Practice Employment and Occupation* (£12.95)
- *Code of Practice –Trade Organisations and Qualifications Bodies* (£9.95)
- *Code of Practice for Schools – DDA 1995: Part 4A*
- *Code of Practice for providers of Post 16 education and related services – DDA 1995: Part 4*

Information about the transport provisions of the Act, and the *Access to Air Travel: Code of Practice* can be obtained from the Mobility and Inclusion Unit, Department for Transport, 1/18 Great Minster House, 76 Marsham Street, London SW1P 4DR (020 7944 6100; Textphone 020 7944 3277, www.dft.gov.uk).

Guidance on providing British Sign Language/English interpreters under the Disability Discrimination Act 1995 – published by RNID/BDA/DRC. Available from RNID Information Line 0808 808 0123 or www.rnid.org.uk

Further information on the DDA and copies of the codes are available at: www.disability.gov.uk and at: www.drc-gb.org.

Advice

You may find it helpful to contact: DRC, RNIB, RADAR, RNID, the Disability Law Service, a local law centre (see Address list) or Citizens Advice Bureau. Contact Disability Alliance for advice on social security matters only. Our advisers are not experts on the DDA.

Useful books include *Disability Discrimination – Law and Practice* (4th edn) by Brian J Doyle (Jordans), *Disability Discrimination Act* by Caroline Gooding (Blackstone Press), and *Disability Discrimination Claims* by Catherine Casserley and Bela Gor (Jordans).

ask the employer questions. This can help you decide whether you have a strong case. If you are a trade union member, seek assistance from your union.

Rights under the goods and services and post-16 education provisions of the Act are enforceable through the County Court (the Sheriff Court in Scotland). You have to take the case to court within 6 months of the discriminatory act, eg the date when you were refused service. You can make a complaint to the Pensions Ombudsman if you think the managers of a pension scheme have discriminated against you (see Box N.2, Chapter 42).

Rights under the education provisions that apply to schools in England and Wales are enforceable through the Special Educational Needs and Disability Tribunal. Claims of unlawful discrimination in respect of a refusal to admit to, and permanent exclusions from, maintained schools and City Academies are heard by admissions appeal panels or independent appeals panels. All DDA claims against schools in Scotland are enforceable through the Sheriff Court. You have to take a case to court or the tribunal within 6 months of the date of the discriminatory act.

If you are successful in a tribunal or court you can obtain damages for financial loss or hurt feelings. The Special Educational Needs and Disability Tribunal and Sheriff Court cannot award financial compensation in claims against schools. Courts can also order service providers to make adjustments, in some circumstances. Tribunals can recommend that an employer makes an adjustment. Courts and tribunals can also make a declaration stating publicly that you were discriminated against because of your disability.

56 TV licence concessions

1. Do you need a TV licence?

You need a TV licence to install or use any equipment to receive television programme services. This includes a television set, video recorder, set-top box, computer with a broadcast card or any other TV-receiving equipment. A TV licence covers you and anyone else living at the premises occupied by you at the address listed on the licence.

A full-fee colour TV licence costs £126.50 a year; for a black and white TV it is £42. Concessions are available for people aged 75 or over, registered blind or in certain cases living in care homes or sheltered housing.

For further information go to www.tvlicensing.co.uk.

2. Aged 75 or over

For anyone aged 75 or over the TV licence is free for your main home but not for a second home. Although free, you do still need to have a licence. If your 75th birthday will fall in the year covered by the next licence, you can buy a short-term licence to cover you until your birthday, or you can claim a refund on an existing licence for the months since you reached age 75. To get your over-75 licence you need to provide TV Licensing with your date of birth and national insurance number. If TV Licensing can verify these details, the over-75 licence is renewed automatically and you don't have to apply for a new one each year. If the over-75 licence-holder dies, the TV licence continues to cover your household until it runs out.

3. Registered blind

There is a 50% discount on the licence fee if you are registered blind (not partially sighted) – ie £63.25 for a colour TV, £21 for a black and white TV. Anyone in the household who is registered blind (including children) can apply for the 50% discount, but the licence must be transferred into that person's name. You can apply for a discount for a second home as well as your main home.

When your licence is due for renewal, take your renewal form and local authority registration document to the post office or send them to the Concessionary Licensing Centre (see 4 below for address). If you don't have your registration document, you can get a copy from the social services (social work in Scotland) department. You should only need to do this initially. When you first register as blind with social services, you can get a 50% discount on your existing licence. For further enquiries call 0870 241 6468.

You do not need a licence for a TV sound-only receiver. These are available from Portset (01489 896837).

4. Care homes

The concessionary £5 licence is called the Accommodation for Residential Care (ARC) licence. To qualify for the ARC licence you must:

- live in a care home; *or*
- live in local authority or housing association sheltered housing with a warden who lives or works there for at least 30 hours a week, and which:
  - has at least 4 flats (with no more than a quarter of properties bought under the 'right to buy'); *and*
  - is occupied only by disabled people or retired people over age 60.

If you are over 75, the licence is free. The warden will apply for your free licence at the same time as applying for the concessionary licence for other residents.

When you move into a care home, you may get a refund for the remainder of your existing licence at your previous home. The warden should apply for you. Write to: The Concessionary Licensing Centre, TV Licensing, Bristol BS98 1TL (0870 240 1291).

This section of the Handbook looks at:

Claims and appeals R

A B C D E F G H I J K L M N O P Q R S

57 Claims and payments

1. Making a claim

For details about how to claim each benefit, see the relevant chapter about that benefit. Here we look at some of the common rules and problems about claiming.

In order to get any benefit, you.have to claim it. You should claim (or ask the DWP for advice) as soon as you think you might qualify. If you are in any doubt, claim anyway. If you cannot make enquiries or claim yourself, get someone else to do so; the DWP can accept a claim made by someone else on your behalf. For anyone who can't claim for themselves because of mental incapacity, the DWP can appoint someone to act on their behalf (see 4) but don't delay claiming in the meantime.

If you haven't got the proper claim-form and are worried about missing some benefit, note that the decision maker has discretion to accept anything written *'as sufficient in the circumstances of any particular case'* to count as a claim (except for income support and jobseeker's allowance – see 2). If the decision maker accepts it as a claim, the date that earlier letter or other document was received in a DWP office counts as your date of claim. Arrears of benefit will be payable from that date (or from the pay day following it).

Examples of cases where you could ask the DWP to exercise this discretion include when:

- you wrote to the DWP to say you wanted to claim a particular benefit and asked them for the claim-form;
- you wrote a general letter to the DWP explaining your situation and asked what help you could get;
- you wrote about a deterioration in your condition in an appeal letter.

You can ask the decision maker to reconsider but there is no right of appeal to a tribunal if the decision maker refuses to exercise this discretion.

National insurance numbers – To be entitled to most benefits, you must give your national insurance (NI) number when you claim, and your partner's if you are claiming for them, and enough information to confirm that the number belongs to you.

If you don't know your number or you're not sure of it, it is enough to give sufficient information to allow the DWP to trace it. Normally, the personal details you give on the claim-form are enough. If the DWP wants more evidence, they will let you know.

If you don't have an NI number, you are still entitled to benefit as long as you apply for a number and provide enough information and evidence for one to be allocated to you. Apply at your local Jobcentre Plus office.

2. Date of claim

The date your claim is 'made' is the day it is received, properly completed, in a DWP office (or Inland Revenue office for tax credits). Sometimes your claim can be treated as though it were made on an earlier date.

- For disability living allowance and attendance allowance, your date of claim is the date you requested a claim-form from the DWP or their Benefit Enquiry Line, as long as you return the completed claim-form within 6 weeks (see Chapter 20(23) for details).
- For pension credit (PC), your date of claim is the date you informed the DWP or local authority office of your intention to claim PC, as long as you provide all the information and evidence that they require within one month (unless an extension is agreed).
- If you make a 'defective' claim (ie one not properly completed in accordance with the instructions on the form) or you don't use the correct form, you may have the claim referred back to you or be given the correct form. If it is referred back to you, then if you return the properly completed claim-form within one month of it being sent to you, your claim must be treated as though the original defective claim had been properly made. You can appeal against a decision to disallow benefit on the basis that the claim was defective.

For income support (IS) and jobseeker's allowance (JSA) there are stricter rules.

Claims for income support

Your date of claim for IS is the date you first told the DWP you wanted to claim, as long as you return the claim-form fully completed with all the information and supporting documents required on the form within one month. Until you do this, you have not made your claim unless you can show that one of the following reasons applies in your case.

- You have a *'physical, learning, mental or communication difficulty'* and it is not reasonably practicable for you to get help with your claim or get the required information or evidence.
- The information or evidence required:
  - does not exist; *or*
  - can only be obtained at serious risk of physical or mental harm to you; *or*
  - can only be obtained from a third party and it's not reasonably practicable for you to get it from them.

Reg 4(1B), SS (Claims and Payments) Regs 1987

Send in your claim-form explaining your difficulties, or call the DWP (or get someone else to contact them for you). As long as you do this within one month and the DWP accepts your reasons, your date of claim will be the date you first told the DWP you wanted to claim.

If there is other evidence needed to decide your claim but it is not specified in the claim-form, it does not affect your date of claim if you can't provide it with your claim.

Claims for JSA
Your date of claim is the date you asked for a claim-form, as long as you provide a fully completed claim-form and all the required evidence by the time you attend your 'new jobseeker interview' (or during the interview). If either member of a joint-claim couple does not attend the interview with their claim-form and evidence, the date of claim is the date that one of them does so.

If you can't complete the form or get all the evidence for one of the reasons outlined above for IS, your claim can still be accepted. If you haven't got all the evidence or need more time to complete the form, the time limit can be extended by up to one month from the date you first asked for the claim-form.

3. Backdating delayed claims

The time limits for claiming benefits are given in Box R.3.

Income support (IS) and jobseeker's allowance (JSA) can

R.1 The new claims process and 'work-focused' interviews

Jobcentre Plus offices administer benefits for people of working age. Although several of the benefits that they administer are paid to people who are not able to work, there is always a 'work focus' in the way that they operate. This will usually involve you attending a 'work-focused' interview.

Most claimants are expected to make initial contact by phone to a Jobcentre Plus Contact Centre, which will provide advice on both employment prospects and benefits. Your personal details will be taken over the phone. At this point you may be submitted for a job, if you are thought to be 'job ready'. If you are not found work immediately or this is not appropriate in your case you should be sent the relevant claim forms. An appointment can then be made for you to attend a work-focused interview.

We describe the claims process for jobseeker's allowance (JSA) separately in Chapter 17(3).

Work-focused interviews

You are required to attend a work-focused interview if you make a claim for the following benefits:

- income support (IS);
- carer's allowance (CA);
- incapacity benefit (IB); *or*
- any bereavement benefit.

In this interview a personal adviser will discuss your work prospects. If you don't attend the interview without good cause, your claim will lapse or your benefit will be reduced. So if you are claiming a benefit such as CA or IB because you have recently been forced by your circumstances to give up work, you should still attend the interview, even if you feel it is inappropriate for you.

You are also required to take part in such an interview if your partner is claiming extra for you on IS, income-based JSA, IB, severe disablement allowance (SDA) or CA.

An interview for one benefit counts for all others, so you won't have to go through separate interviews for each benefit you claim.

Who is not required to attend?

You are not required to attend a work-focused interview in the following circumstances.

- ❑ You are aged 60 or over.
- ❑ You are working 16 hours or more a week.
- ❑ You are also claiming JSA, unless you are a member of a joint-claim couple who is excused from meeting JSA conditions.

The requirement to attend, however, can be waived altogether or deferred to a later date, at the discretion of the personal adviser.

Attendance is waived – The personal adviser can waive attendance if they consider that an interview would *'not be of assistance'* to you or *'appropriate in the circumstances'*. Once attendance has been waived you are treated as if you had taken part in the interview.

Attendance is deferred – Similarly attendance can be deferred if the personal adviser considers that an interview would not be of assistance to you or appropriate in the circumstances at that particular time. Guidance suggests circumstances where it may be reasonable to defer the interview. These are when you are:

- at a time of major change, for example you have just been made homeless or are a single parent who has recently had a baby; *or*
- emotionally distressed because, for example, a close relation has died or a relationship has broken down; *or*
- too ill to attend the interview because, for example, you are recovering from a serious illness or operation; *or*
- likely to claim benefit only for a short period because, for example, you are a homeless person staying in short-stay accommodation or you are expected to start full-time work shortly.

This is not an exhaustive list. There may be other circumstances in which it would not be reasonable to expect you to attend an interview.

(DMG Vol 1 para 05338)

Where the interview is deferred, the personal adviser will seek agreement with you on another date when it will be appropriate to hold the interview. For benefit purposes, you will be treated for the time being as having taken part in an interview.

It is best to contact the personal adviser in advance and explain any circumstances that might make an interview inappropriate or of no help to you. However, most people are expected to attend, even if, for example, they are claiming benefit because they can't work now and any chance of working in the future seems remote.

At the interview

At the interview you will first be seen by a benefits expert, who will help you with claim-forms and give you information about your benefits position. A personal adviser will then see you for the work-focused interview. To pass the interview requirement, you must not only turn up for the interview at the right time, but also take part in it. You are expected to answer questions about your educational qualifications, any vocational training you have undertaken, your employment history, your work-related skills, any paid or unpaid work you are doing and any caring or childcare responsibilities you have. You may also be asked about any medical condition which in your opinion puts you at a disadvantage in getting a job. This may involve discussing a capability report provided by the DWP doctor who examined you for your IB (see Box E.3, Chapter 11). Because the law says you must give *'appropriate'* information, you should only be required to discuss personal issues about your disability or health in so far as you consider it to be relevant to your employment prospects. Participation in these work-focused interviews should not adversely affect your claim for IB.

You are not required to do any more than take part in the interview. Actually attending training, following up on a job vacancy or doing anything else the personal adviser suggests is entirely up to you.

be backdated for up to either one month or 3 months in the limited circumstances described below. Housing benefit (HB) and council tax benefit (CTB) can be backdated for up to a year if you have good cause for the delay in claiming (see Chapter 7(17)). For other benefits, there is no extension to the time limits for claiming, no matter how good your reasons are for not applying earlier – unless, in some cases, it is because of a delay in the award of a qualifying benefit.

If you want to claim benefit for an earlier period, make sure you say this on your claim-form.

Delays in qualifying benefits
Entitlement to some benefits may depend on you, a member of your family or someone else getting another qualifying benefit. For example, carer's allowance depends on the person you look after receiving attendance allowance or disability living allowance (DLA) middle or highest rate care component.

If you are aged under 18, you will be referred to the Careers Service or Connexions for help on education and training. You must attend an interview arranged with them.

What if you don't attend the interview?

Unless you can show that you have good cause for not attending a work-focused interview, your claim will lapse. If the interview had been deferred, with the result that benefit was already in payment, then entitlement will stop. You have just 5 working days to tell them why you missed the interview; if you leave it any later, you must show that you couldn't reasonably have told the personal adviser within the 5 days.

So, if you make a claim for IS, housing benefit (HB) and council tax benefit (CTB) and don't attend the work-focused interview, your IS, HB and CTB claims all lapse. You should claim again, and appeal against the decision if you think it's wrong (see below). You may be able to claim a crisis loan in the meantime, although these are very limited (see Chapter 10(6)).

In deciding whether you have good cause for not attending the interview, the personal adviser must consider the following:

- because of your disability it was impossible for you to attend at the given time;
- you misunderstood the requirement to take part in the interview because of learning disabilities, language or literacy difficulties, or because you were given misleading official information;
- you had a medical or dental appointment and it would have been unreasonable to rearrange it;
- you had transport difficulties and had no reasonable alternative;
- you couldn't attend on that day or time because of your religion;
- you had a job interview or were pursuing self-employed work;
- you or a dependant or someone you care for became ill or had an accident;
- you were at a funeral of a close friend or relative that day.

This list is not exhaustive and the personal adviser can consider other reasons.

Interviews at later trigger points

Once you've had your first work-focused interview, you will normally only be asked back when certain events happen to trigger another interview (see below for exceptions). Existing SDA claimants will also be expected to attend these interviews. The trigger points are:

- you are a lone parent over 18 who does not claim IB or SDA and it has been more than 6 months since your first interview or more than 12 months since your second or later interview;
- following a personal capability assessment – but not if your benefit is stopped following the assessment;
- CA entitlement stops but you continue to be entitled to another of the specified benefits listed above;
- you start or stop part-time work of less than 16 hours a week;
- you finish an education or training course arranged by your personal adviser;
- you reach the age of 18;
- you have not had such an interview in the last 3 years.

As for the first work-focused interview, in some circumstances you won't be required to attend or the interview may be deferred to a later date (see above).

What if you don't attend the interview? – Unless you have good cause for not attending (see above), a deduction of £11.24 a week is made from your benefit. The deduction continues until you do actually attend a work-focused interview or reach the age of 60.

More frequent interviews

Pathways to Work – A more intensive regime of work-focused interviews for people claiming incapacity benefits has been introduced in those parts of the country operating under Pathways to Work. These are covered in more detail in Box F.2, Chapter 16.

'Working Neighbourhoods' – Another more intensive regime of work-focused interviews operates in those areas where Working Neighbourhood pilots have been introduced (Tower Hamlets, Knowsley, Wirral, Sheffield, Newcastle-upon Tyne, Birmingham, Middlesbrough, Swansea, Great Yarmouth, Hastings and Glasgow). If you live in one of these areas, you are affected if you are over 18 and either you or your partner are claiming IS or IB. You will need to attend a series of up to 8 work-focused interviews separated by intervals of 13 weeks.

Quarterly interviews for lone parents – In another set of pilot areas, lone parents are expected to attend work-focused interviews every 13 weeks. The areas covered are the education authority areas of Aberdeenshire, Bradford, Fife, Greenwich, Haringay, Leicestershire, Lewisham, Sandwell and Torfaen. Quarterly interviews will apply if you are a lone parent claiming IS (other than on the basis of incapacity) and your youngest child is at least 12.

Challenging a decision

Personal advisers make decisions on whether you have complied with the requirement to take part in an interview and whether you have good cause for failing to attend. You can appeal against their decision within one month of the decision being posted to you (see Chapter 58). Alternatively, you can ask them to reconsider and revise the decision; within one month for any reason, or outside of one month if it arose from an official error (see Box R.5). In each case, any arrears due are paid back in full if you are successful. There is no right of appeal about waivers and deferrals, although you can ask the personal adviser to reconsider.

Welfare Reform and Pensions Act 1999
The Social Security (Work-focused Interviews) Regulations 2000
The Social Security (Jobcentre Plus Interviews) Regulations 2002
The Social Security (Incapacity Benefit Work focused Interviews) Regulations 2003

The general rule – Claim straight away, don't wait for a decision on the qualifying benefit. If your first claim is refused because the qualifying benefit has not yet been awarded, claim again once you do get a decision awarding the qualifying benefit. As long as you do this within 3 months of the decision awarding the qualifying benefit (which might be after a revision or an appeal if the qualifying benefit is refused initially), that second claim can be backdated to the date of the first claim, or to the date from which the qualifying benefit is awarded if that is later. Bear in mind that on the date you first claim, if you have not already claimed the qualifying benefit you have another 10 days to do so. If you wait longer than 10 days, a second claim made once the qualifying benefit is awarded cannot be backdated in this way.

Where entitlement to one benefit depends on another, if one stops the other stops too. In this case, if you challenge the decision on the qualifying benefit and it is reinstated, make a fresh claim for the other benefit within 3 months of the date of the decision to reinstate the qualifying benefit and the other benefit will then be fully backdated. For example, if your incapacity benefit (IB) is stopped you may, as a consequence, also lose entitlement to IS. If you get back your IB after a successful appeal, make a fresh claim for IS and it will be paid again from when it was stopped. For more about IS, see Chapter 6(2).

Exceptions – The rule above applies to almost all benefits with the following exceptions.

- Where entitlement to either working or child tax credit is dependent on the disability, severe disability, disabled child or severely disabled child element being included (see Chapter 18(4,7 and 8)), the rule is slightly different. On the date you claim the tax credit you must already have claimed the qualifying benefit – you do not have a further 10 days to claim it. Once the qualifying benefit is awarded, claim the tax credit again within 3 months of the decision and the claim will be backdated to the first tax credit claim. The normal 3-month backdating of this first tax credit claim will not apply, however, when the qualifying benefit became payable less than 3 months before the tax credit claim was made. In this case, the tax credit can only be paid from the date that the qualifying benefit became payable.
- If your IB is stopped (because you are no longer deemed incapable of work) while you are waiting to hear about a claim for DLA (or constant attendance allowance), you should reclaim IB within 3 months of the decision awarding you DLA highest rate care component. Your new IB claim will be backdated to the end of your earlier IB entitlement, or to the date from which DLA is payable, if that is later.

R.2 Interchange of claims

If you make a claim for one benefit, then find you should have claimed a different benefit instead, or you were also entitled to a different benefit, the rules on interchanging benefit claims may help you get arrears of benefit beyond the usual limits. Your original claim may be treated as a claim for another benefit, either as an alternative to the original claim or in addition. But not all benefits can count as a claim for any other. Within each group below, the benefits listed are interchangeable with each other:

- incapacity benefit, maternity allowance;
- state pension of any category, widow's benefit/ bereavement benefit;
- disability living allowance, attendance allowance, industrial injuries constant attendance allowance;
- child benefit, guardian's allowance, an addition for a child dependant (with non-means-tested benefits prior to April 2003), maternity allowance claimed after confinement;
- a claim for income support can be treated as a claim for carer's allowance, but not the other way round.

Reg 9 and Schedule 1 Social Security (Claims & Payments) Regs 1987

If the decision maker treats one claim as another, then the date of the original claim counts as the date of claim for the alternative benefit and arrears may be payable from then. However, the overlapping benefit rules could prevent some or all of the arrears being payable.

You cannot appeal against a decision on whether to treat a claim for one benefit as a claim for another but you can ask the decision maker to look at the decision again (see 'Ground 9' in Box R.5).

Backdating IS and JSA

Administrative reasons: one-month backdating

IS or JSA can be backdated for up to one month if any one or more of the administrative reasons below apply, as a result of which you could not reasonably have been expected to make the claim earlier.

- You couldn't attend the Jobcentre Plus office to make your claim either because it was closed or because of transport difficulties, and there were no alternative arrangements available.
- There were adverse postal conditions.
- You were not sent notice of the end of entitlement to a previous benefit until after it actually ended.
- You stopped being part of a couple within one month before claiming.
- You claimed JSA after your partner had failed to attend a work-focused interview.
- Your partner, parent, son, daughter, brother or sister died within one month before claiming.

Reg 19(6), (7) SS (Claims & Payments) Regs 1987

Special reasons: 3-month backdating

IS and JSA can be backdated for up to 3 months if any one or more of the special reasons below apply, as a result of which you could not reasonably have been expected to make the claim earlier.

- You have difficulty communicating either because you are deaf or blind, or because you have learning, language or literacy difficulties, and it was not reasonably practicable for you to get help to make your claim. The test is about your ability to get help and not whether someone should have offered it.
- You are ill or disabled and it was not reasonably practicable for you to get help to make your claim (this is not accepted as a special reason for JSA). There is no definition of 'ill' or 'disabled' in the regulation.
- You were caring for someone who is ill or disabled and it was not reasonably practicable for you to get help to make your claim. You don't have to live with the person or be related to them.
- You were given information by an official of the DWP which led you to believe that your claim would not succeed. This may include a situation where you were only advised to claim IB when in fact you should have claimed IS. What you understood from the information you were given may have been affected by your disability or communication difficulties and this should be taken into account.
- You were given written advice by a solicitor or other professional adviser, a medical practitioner, a local authority, or a person working in a Citizens Advice Bureau or similar advice agency, which led you to believe that your claim would not succeed.

- ❑ You or your partner were given written information about your income or capital by an employer or ex-employer, or a bank or building society, which led you to believe that your claim would not succeed.
- ❑ You were required to deal with a domestic emergency affecting you and it was not reasonably practicable for you to get help to make your claim.
- ❑ You were prevented by bad weather from attending the Jobcentre Plus office.

Reg 19(4), (5) SS (Claims & Payments) Regs 1987

You should give full details of your reasons for claiming late on your claim-form. You can appeal if you disagree with the decision on backdating.

Test cases

If you are claiming following a test case, any backdating that might apply under the normal rules is generally limited to the date the test case decision was given. See Chapter 58(6).

4. Appointees

If a person is or might be entitled to benefit and cannot act for themselves, the decision maker can appoint someone aged 18 or over, an 'appointee', to act on their behalf. An appointee is usually a relative or friend, but can also be a body of people such as a firm of solicitors or a housing association. An appointment may be appropriate, for example, if the claimant is a child or is unable to act for themselves because of a severe learning disability, mental illness or senility. Contact the office dealing with the claim and they will make the arrangements. See DWP leaflet GL21.

If you are the appointee, then it is your responsibility to deal with the claim, including, for example, notifying changes of circumstances. It is the appointee who is responsible for claiming on time and whose own circumstances will be relevant in deciding whether there are special reasons for backdating a delayed claim, or for not providing all the documentary evidence required for a claim.

If you claimed disability living allowance (DLA) for your child, you will have been appointed by the Secretary of State to act on your child's behalf, but only in relation to DLA. If your child is unable to act for themselves when they reach 16 and you continue to claim and receive DLA for them, you will have a full appointment covering almost all benefits.

If you are appointed to act for the claimant in relation to one benefit, that appointment covers all non-means-tested benefits as well as income support, tax credits, and maternity, cold weather and funeral payments from the social fund. Separate appointments have to be made for housing benefit and for council tax benefit.

5. Payments

Your benefit is normally paid directly into a bank, building society or post office account. Prior to April 2005 many people had their benefit paid through order books which could be cashed at post offices. Post office card accounts have been developed to ensure that people still have the option of collecting their money at post offices. These card accounts only accept the payment in of benefits or tax credits and only allow cash withdrawal at post offices. You can nominate someone else to withdraw your money for you; they will then be issued with the card.

If, for some reason, you are unable to open or use any of the above accounts then you will be paid by cheque instead.

Certain benefits are paid through your wages – ie statutory sick, maternity, paternity and adoption pay. Working tax credit is currently also paid through your wages, except for any childcare element, which is paid to the main carer along with child tax credit, usually by direct payment.

Compensation for delays – You may be due compensation if payments are delayed – eg because of a delay in processing your claim, or you claimed late because of wrong official advice. See Chapter 60(2).

Lost payments – If you are paid in the normal fashion by direct payments and lose your PIN number you may need to

R.3 Time limits for claiming benefit

Benefit	Time limit
Disability living allowance, attendance allowance	
■ initial claim	immediate
■ renewal claim	immediate
Income support, jobseeker's allowance	immediate
Social fund	
■ Sure Start maternity grant	from 11 weeks before expected week of birth, up to 3 months after date of birth or adoption or parental order
■ funeral expenses	from the date of death to 3 months after date of funeral
Carer's allowance	3 months
Incapacity benefit	3 months
State pension	3 months (prior to 7.7.05). Claims made on or after 7.7.05 can be backdated to 6.4.05 (see Chapter 42(6)).
Pension credit	12 months
Tax credits	3 months
Bereavement allowance, child benefit, guardian's allowance, maternity allowance, widowed parents' allowance, dependants' additions (not income support)	3 months
Bereavement payment	12 months
Industrial injuries disablement benefit	3 months (from 15 weeks after date of accident, etc)

Reg 19 and Schedule 4, SS (Claims & Payments) Regs

The time limits are not generally cut-off points for claiming benefit, but just limit the extent to which your benefit can be backdated: eg if you claim carer's allowance it can be automatically backdated for 3 months.

However, in the case of industrial injuries disablement benefit, you must claim within 5 years of working in the prescribed occupation for occupational deafness, or 10 years for occupational asthma, otherwise you lose entitlement completely (see Chapter 44). For some benefits the time limits can be extended in certain circumstances (see 3).

A B C D E F G H I J K L M N O P Q R S

claim a social fund crisis loan if the matter takes a while to sort out.

If you are still paid by cheque and this goes missing or is stolen after you have received it, tell the office dealing with your claim immediately and ask them for a replacement. Confirm this in writing. Even if a payment has been cashed by someone else, the DWP should replace it provided they accept you did not get the payment and there is no fraud on your part. If there is a delay, seek advice from a CAB or other local advice centre. You might be eligible for a social fund crisis loan in the meantime. If the DWP refuses to replace it, seek legal advice (see Chapter 59). You cannot appeal in the usual way but you may be able to take action in the county court against the Secretary of State.

6. Overpayments

An overpayment of benefit is recoverable if it was overpaid because you failed to disclose a 'material fact', or you misrepresented a material fact. This is so even if you acted in all innocence. A recent tribunal of Commissioners (CIS/4348/2003) has decided that once a fact is 'known' to you and the duty to report it has been made clear to you, you cannot argue that due to the particular circumstances of your case (eg mental disability) disclosure of the fact could not reasonably have been expected. (Leave to appeal has been granted to the claimant in this case, so appeals dealing with 'failure to disclose' arguments should be stayed until this case has been decided by the Court of Appeal.)

In deciding whether there has been an overpayment, the decision maker must first revise or supersede your entitlement to benefit and decide how much you should have been paid. The decision maker will then decide whether:

- you failed to notify the relevant office (ie the office that normally deals with the benefit concerned) about a material fact on the relevant date or as soon as possible afterwards; *or*
- you misrepresented a material fact – ie made an incorrect statement.

In either case, the overpayment would be recoverable.

A 'material' fact is one that would have affected the amount of your benefit. A 'fact' is not the same as a conclusion drawn from fact. For example, the conclusion that you are 'incapable of work' is drawn from the facts of your case. The onus of proof is on the decision maker to identify the material fact which you failed to disclose or misrepresented.

The DWP has recently won its case at the House of Lords against the Court of Appeal *Hinchy* decision, which held that a claimant could not fail to disclose to one DWP office a benefit decision taken by another DWP office. Consequently, when a decision is made on one benefit that could affect entitlement to another, you are under a duty to inform the office dealing with the potentially affected benefit.

The overpayment test is common to income support (IS), income-based jobseeker's allowance (JSA), pension credit (PC), social fund grants and loans, and to almost all of the non-means-tested benefits. There is a different test for housing benefit (HB) and council tax benefit (CTB) (see Chapter 7(19)). Generally, the Inland Revenue has greater flexibility in dealing with changes of circumstances in respect of tax credits, with a continual process of adjusting what they overpaid or underpaid you one year with what they will pay you in the next year (see Box G.4, Chapter 19). Notwithstanding this flexibility, overpayments due to fraud or negligence can be dealt with by a penalty system (see Chapter 18(12)).

If the overpayment is not recoverable

If it is not recoverable under the legislation, you do not need to pay back the overpayment. Nevertheless, the DWP may write and ask you to pay it back. You should not feel under pressure to do so. If you're not sure whether you are obliged to pay back an overpayment, seek advice from a local advice centre. Note that the DWP may mention the possibility of taking proceedings through the courts to recover the overpayment under common law. In practice, this is not something they are likely to do. But if they take this any further, seek legal advice immediately.

Incapacity and disability benefits

Where there has been an improvement in your condition and you didn't know that you should have reported this, you should not be left with an overpayment. Similarly, where the effect of your incapacity or disability proves not to be as severe as it was originally believed, and you didn't know you should have reported the mistake in the original information, you should not be left with an overpayment. The reduction in your benefit in either case should thus not be backdated. You should appeal against the decision that you were paid the wrong amount of benefit for the earlier period. See Box R.5 under 'Ground 1' and 'Ground 6' for details.

Appointees and others

Overpayments can be recovered from third parties if it is they who have failed to disclose or misrepresented the material fact. If it is an appointee acting on behalf of the claimant, the decision maker may decide that the overpayment is recoverable from both the claimant and the appointee. Alternatively, the decision maker may decide the overpayment is recoverable from either one or the other. As a general rule, where the appointee has retained the benefit instead of paying it to, or applying it for the benefit of, the claimant, only the appointee is liable. Where the appointee has acted with due care and diligence, only the claimant is liable.
R(IS)5/03

Appeals

You can appeal against a decision that you were paid the wrong amount of benefit. You can also appeal against a decision that the overpayment is recoverable and against decisions relating to the period of the overpayment, from whom it is recoverable and the amount owed.

Amount of the overpayment

If you have been overpaid any benefit, and the overpayment resulted from your misrepresentation of, or failure to disclose, a material fact, the amount of the overpayment is reduced by:

- any amount of the overpayment of benefit which has been offset against arrears of entitlement in a later award (generally because of a change in the rate of award of a benefit you had already claimed);
- any extra IS, income-based JSA or PC you should have been paid, not necessarily for the same period as the overpayment. If the overpayment is of some other benefit, then again the decision maker must consider an offset of IS even if there is no connection between the periods in which the different benefits were payable (R(IS)5/92, CSIS/8/95).

If you had not claimed any benefit (such as IS), but would have been entitled to it had you not been overpaid another benefit, put in a claim and ask for it to be backdated if you have 'special reasons' (see 3). If successful, you can ask for an abatement of the overpayment against what you should have received under the other benefit.

The law on overpayments is found in sections 71 and 74 of the Social Security Administration Act 1992, and in the Social Security (Payments on Account, Overpayments and Recovery) Regulations 1988, as well as in case law. For more details about the nature of the overpayment test, read the notes to section 71 in *Social Security: Legislation 2004 Volume III* (see Box R.9).

Diminishing capital

If you have been overpaid IS, income-based JSA or PC because you didn't tell the DWP about all your capital resources, or you misrepresented the nature of your capital, allowance is made for capital you would have spent had you not been paid benefit. At the end of each 13-week period, starting with the first day of the overpayment, your capital is treated as having been reduced by the amount of IS, income-based JSA or PC you had been overpaid during that quarter. At the same time, any tariff income would be recalculated.

Your capital cannot be treated as diminished in this way over any period shorter than 13 weeks. But, if you actually spent any of that undeclared capital during the overpayment period, the overpayment would end on the day your capital reached the appropriate limit – assuming that the notional capital rules don't apply (see Chapter 5(15)). The treatment of diminishing capital under this rule would also apply to the reduced amount.

The diminishing capital principle applies also to CTB (under reg 89, CTB Regs), and to HB (under reg 103, HB Regs). Note that the diminishing capital principle is different from the diminishing notional capital principle explained in Chapter 5(15).

Fraud and penalties

It is fraud if you dishonestly or knowingly make a false statement or provide a false document or information, in order to get benefit or more benefit. It is also fraud if:

- there has been a change of circumstances affecting entitlement to your or another person's benefit; *and*
- the change is not excluded by regulations from changes that are required to be notified; *and*
- you know that the change affects your own, or the other person's entitlement; *and*
- you dishonestly fail to give a prompt notification of the change in *'the prescribed manner to the prescribed person'* (eg giving notice in writing to the relevant authority).

These rules apply to appointees or to anyone else with a right to receive benefit on behalf of another person. They also apply to third parties such as landlords, where they know, or would be expected to know, of changes with respect to a tenant's occupation of a dwelling or a tenant's liability to make payments in respect of that dwelling.

When fraud is suspected, the DWP (or local authority for HB and CTB) may ask you to attend an interview with a fraud officer. Seek advice beforehand and if possible take a friend who is not involved in the matter with you. They may decide not to prosecute, even if they believe you to have committed fraud. But if you are found guilty of fraud, the court can fine you or imprison you or both.

If the DWP or local authority believe they have enough evidence to successfully prosecute, they may give you the option of paying a penalty as an alternative to prosecution. The penalty is fixed at 30% of the overpayment. You also have to repay the overpayment. You have 28 days to change your mind if you have agreed to pay a penalty.

A formal caution may be offered as an alternative to prosecution in England and Wales (not in Scotland). This is an administrative practice in the DWP; it is not a criminal conviction. But if you are later found guilty of another offence, the formal caution may be used in court for sentencing purposes.

Different rules apply to tax credits, which have a penalty system in place (see Chapter 18(12)). Where the Inland Revenue believes fraud is involved, they may prosecute in the courts.

If you are accused of fraud, get legal advice as soon as you can. Contact details for local law centres are in the address list. Alternatively, a Citizens Advice Bureau may be able to help.

Benefit sanctions

Sanctions, where benefits are removed or reduced, can be imposed if you are convicted of one or more benefit offences in two separate sets of proceedings within a 3-year period, where those offences have not previously been taken into account. These offences, which must have been committed since 1.4.02, can be with respect to any benefit (including war pensions) other than statutory sick pay, statutory maternity pay, maternity allowance and working families' and disabled person's tax credits. A similar list of benefits can consequently be sanctioned, excepting also state pension, graduated retirement pension, disability living allowance, attendance allowance, child benefit, guardian's allowance, social fund payments and the Christmas bonus. The sanction period will be for 13 weeks, during which time no sanctioned benefit will usually be payable. The only exceptions to this are IS, JSA (see Chapter 17(9)), HB, CTB and PC, where reductions of benefit, rather than their complete removal, are made instead.

Social Security Fraud Act 2001

58 Decisions, revisions and appeals

In this chapter we look at:

1. Who makes decisions?

The Secretary of State for Work and Pensions is responsible for decision making on almost all social security benefits but in practice decisions are made on her/his behalf by a decision maker.

Decisions on appeal are made by an appeal tribunal. Appeal tribunals are run by a DWP agency called The Appeals Service. The President of The Appeals Service and the members of the panel who act as tribunal members are independent of the DWP.

Appeals against decisions of appeal tribunals are made to the Social Security Commissioners.

Legislation is currently progressing to reform appeal provision. This will include the incorporation of benefit appeals tribunals into a unified system of tribunals and the replacement of the Social Security Commissioners with a new second-tier tribunal. The first of the reforms to take effect, the transfer of The Appeals Service to the new unified Tribunals Service, is expected to take place in April 2007.

Some decisions are made by the Inland Revenue (IR) but use the same appeal system.

- **Working tax credit, child tax credit, child benefit and guardian's allowance** – Decisions are made by an officer of the IR based in the Tax Credit Office in Preston or the Child Benefit Office in Newcastle-upon-Tyne. The tax credits' decision-making process is different to that of social security benefits (see Chapter 18(13)). However, decisions on appeal are currently made by an appeal tribunal, though it is intended that tax credit appeals will eventually go to a tax tribunal.
- **National insurance (NI) credits and home responsibilities protection** – The Secretary of State is responsible for decision making, but in practice decisions are made on her/his behalf by officers of the IR based in the NI Contributions Office. Decisions on appeal are made by an appeal tribunal.

Decisions on NI contributions and employed earner status are made by the IR. Appeals are usually made to the Income Tax General Commissioners.

Housing benefit (HB) and council tax benefit (CTB) have a decisions and appeals system similar to other benefits. Decisions are made by an officer of the local authority. The ways of changing decisions described in this chapter apply equally to decisions on HB and CTB, unless otherwise stated. Decisions on appeal are made by an appeal tribunal.

There are separate systems for social fund community care grants and loans (Chapter 10), statutory sick pay (Chapter 13(10)), statutory maternity, paternity and adoption pay (Chapter 34) and war disablement pensions (Chapter 45(9 and 10)). There are modified rules for vaccine damage payments (Chapter 47(5)).

2. Ways of changing decisions

Once a decision is made it stands and is binding until one of the specific methods given in the law for changing decisions is set in motion. Even a decision given without legal authority counts as an effective decision until such time as it is challenged.

Changing a decision made by a decision maker

There are 4 ways of changing a decision made by a decision maker on behalf of the Secretary of State:

- correct an accidental error;
- revise the decision;
- supersede the decision;
- appeal against the decision.

Correcting an accidental error – An 'accidental' error in a decision can be corrected by the decision maker. Arithmetical or clerical errors can be corrected in this way. There is no time limit. However, correction is discretionary and there is no appeal against a refusal to correct.

If the decision is corrected, the dispute period (see 3) and time limit for lodging an appeal will start from when notice of the corrected decision is given. If a decision is not corrected, however, the original dispute period and appeal time limits remain in place. Consequently, if you have asked for a decision to be corrected and are awaiting a response, ensure that in the meantime you ask for a revision or lodge an appeal within the appropriate time limits, just in case the decision is not corrected.

Revisions, supersessions and appeals are covered in 3 to 16 below.

Changing a decision made by an appeal tribunal

There are 4 ways of changing a decision made by an appeal tribunal:

- correct an accidental error;
- set aside the decision;
- supersede the decision;
- appeal against the decision.

These are covered in more detail in 17 and 18 below.

Old review and appeal rules

The current decision and appeal system dates from 1999. Where an appeal concerns a decision that was made under the old review rules and these are at issue in the appeal, the tribunal must consider the rules that applied at the time. So, for example, it is the old grounds for review that need be satisfied and old backdating rules that apply to any subsequent award. See *Disability Rights Handbook* 24th edition, Chapter 57.

3. 'Any grounds' revisions

There is a 'dispute period' of one month from the date the decision is sent to you in which you can ask a decision maker to revise the decision on 'any grounds'. This means the decision can be revised for any reason other than a later change of circumstances. (If your circumstances have changed, you must make a fresh claim or ask for the award to be superseded – see Box R.5.) The time limit can be extended in special circumstances (see below). Outside of the dispute period, while it is possible for decisions to be revised, it is only where certain grounds are satisfied (see 4 and Box R.5).

A decision of an appeal tribunal cannot be changed by an 'any grounds' revision; see 17 for what to do if you disagree with a tribunal decision.

'Any grounds' revision or appeal?

The letter giving you the decision should explain your right either to ask for an 'any grounds' revision or to appeal. Normally you have a choice, but there are some decisions that carry no right of appeal (see 7).

Asking for a decision to be revised is a quicker way of getting a decision changed than an appeal. Additionally, if you appeal straight away you lose one opportunity of having the case looked at again. With an 'any grounds' revision, the DWP simply takes another look at the decision, including any further evidence you supply, to see if they think it is correct. Normally, a different decision maker will look at the case. You will have a further month to appeal if you are still not satisfied with the new decision. Appeals are covered in more detail in 7-17 below.

How do you ask for a revision?

It is most important to act within the one-month time limit. If you don't, you could miss out on arrears of benefit or even find that you can't challenge the decision at all. A telephone call to the DWP can set up the revision. However, if you do this, confirm your request in writing and keep a copy if you can. If you are anywhere near the deadline, you should phone the appropriate office to register the revision and tell them you will write with more details, otherwise any delay in the post could result in your revision request being out of time. For housing benefit (HB) and council tax benefit (CTB), your request must be in writing to the local authority. Once you have posted a revision request, ring the office you sent it to a few days later, to ensure that they have actually received it.

An 'any grounds' revision can be made for any reason, but you should explain exactly how and why you think the decision is wrong. If you can, provide evidence to back up your argument. If you cannot send this off straight away, inform the office dealing with the claim. They should allow you one month from the date your revision is registered to send them such evidence, but they have the discretion to extend this period.

Written reasons for the decision
If the decision did not include reasons, you can ask for a written statement. You must do this within one month of the day the decision is sent to you. If you ask for the written statement within one month and it is provided within that period, the one-month time limit is extended by 14 days; if it is provided outside one month, you will be given an extra 14 days from the date it is provided. With HB and CTB, however, in calculating the time limit any days between the date that the local authority receives your request for a statement and the date they actually provide it are ignored. Unfortunately, you can't always tell from the decision letter whether or not reasons are actually included and the written statement you are then sent later often does not cast a great deal more light on the matter. Consequently, it is advisable to submit your application for a revision within the one-month time limit, even if you are still waiting for a written statement.

The time limit
You must ask for an 'any grounds' revision (or an appeal) within one month of the day the decision is sent to you, unless you have requested a written statement as above. This means your request must be received at the right office no later than one calendar month starting from the day after the date the decision was posted to you. The address of the office to contact is on the decision letter. The date the decision is posted is usually taken to be the date on the decision letter.

For example, if the date given on the decision letter is 10 October 2005, your request must be received on or before 10 November 2005. If the date of the decision letter is 31 January 2006, your request must be received on or before 28 February 2006 (the last day of the calendar month).

Keep a record of the date you make your request. If you take a letter into the office, ask for a dated receipt.

DWP guidance advises decision makers to accept requests received one day late unless they are completely certain the decision letter was actually posted on the same day as the date on the letter (para 03063, Vol 1, *Decision Makers Guide*).

Extending the time limit
If you have missed the deadline, there are two options.

❑ Ask for a late 'any grounds' revision. It is not impossible to have the dispute period extended but there are strict conditions to meet (see below). The advantage is that if a late application is accepted, the decision can still be revised for any reason – you are not limited to certain grounds. Also, if you are successful, benefit can be fully backdated.
❑ See if there are grounds for the decision to be revised or superseded outside the dispute period. However, for a supersession, arrears of benefit are normally limited to the date you apply. See 4 and 5 below and Box R.5.

If you are asking for a late 'any grounds' revision (or a late appeal), it is worth asking the decision maker to treat your letter as a request for a supersession if the late revision or appeal is not allowed. That way you will avoid a delay in the supersession and avoid missing out on backdated benefit.

Late revisions – An application for a late 'any grounds' revision may be accepted if:

- it is reasonable to grant the application;
- the application for revision has 'merit' – this is not defined but if there is no prospect of success, the application for a late revision will probably be refused; *and*
- the delay was caused by special circumstances – you must show that it was not practicable for you to apply in time. The longer the delay, the better the reason must be. It won't count that you simply didn't know or understand the law or the time limits involved.

A reinterpretation of the law by a Commissioner or court does not enable a late 'any grounds' revision to be made (but it may allow a supersession for error of law – see Box R.5).

Apply for a late 'any grounds' revision in writing; include the name of the benefit concerned, the date of the decision, why you think it should be revised and details of your reasons for the delay. You cannot get a late 'any grounds' revision more than 13 months (plus any short extensions allowed due to delays in sending you the written statement – see above) after the date the decision was sent to you. If you are refused a late revision once, you cannot apply again.

Late appeals – The rules are slightly different (see 7 below).

The revised decision
You will get a written decision about your application for a revision. This should also explain your right to appeal. The revised decision takes effect from the date on which the earlier decision took effect, so benefit can be backdated to the original date of claim.

Appeal rights – You have a fresh right of appeal within one month of being sent the revised decision. Similarly, if the decision maker decides not to revise the decision, they will write to tell you. You have a further month to appeal against the original decision from the date the notification is sent to you.

R.4 Backdating

A *revised* decision takes effect from the date the earlier decision took effect, so benefit is fully backdated. A *superseded* decision generally only takes effect from the date you apply for the decision to be superseded, so benefit can only be backdated to this date. Exceptions to the rule are listed below.

Event	Backdating
Award of a qualifying benefit	Full backdating to start of existing award or date qualifying award starts (if later)
Following a reinterpretation of the law in a test case	Backdating to date of test case decision
Change of circumstances	
■ notified within one month	Backdating to date of change
■ for DLA/AA – notified within one month of completing 3- or 6-month qualifying period for new rate or component	Backdating to end of qualifying period
■ notified after one month	No backdating
■ notified after one month (but within 13 months) – special circumstances for the delay	Backdating to date of change
Official error	
■ all benefits	Full backdating
For incapacity benefit	
■ exempted from personal capability assessment	Backdating to date of exemption
■ DLA highest rate care component awarded	Long-term rate fully backdated

4. 'Any time' revisions and supersessions

It is always best to challenge a decision within the dispute period if you can. However, this is not always possible; your circumstances might change later or you might only realise later that the decision was wrong. You can go back to the DWP or local authority at any time to ask them to reconsider a decision, however long ago the decision was made, but you must first show that certain grounds are satisfied (see Box R.5). If the grounds are satisfied, the decision maker will normally '*supersede*' the decision although, in some cases, they will carry out an 'any time' revision.

What's the difference between revising and superseding a decision? – Broadly speaking, a decision is revised if it was wrong at the time it first had effect. A revised decision takes effect from the same date as the original decision, so benefit is fully backdated. On the other hand, a decision is generally superseded where there is a later change and usually there is no backdating. See Box R.4 for a quick guide to the

R.5 Grounds for revising or superseding a decision

Outside the dispute period, a decision can only be looked at again for certain reasons. If at least one of the grounds outlined in this box is met, a decision can be either revised or superseded. We have called them 'Ground 1', 'Ground 2' and so on, for convenience, but, these numbers are not used officially, so you must clearly state your grounds in your application. We include all the principle grounds here; the full list is contained within regs 3 and 6 of the SSCS (D&A) Regs 99 and regs 4 and 7 of the Housing Benefit and Council Tax Benefit (Decisions and Appeals) Regulations 2001.

If you ask for the decision to be looked at again, the onus is on you to show that one or more of the grounds are satisfied. The decision maker can decide for themselves to revise or supersede the decision and if they do, they must show that the grounds are satisfied. If none of these grounds are met, the decision cannot be changed, no matter how wrong that decision may be.

CDLA/3875/2001

Note that a decision made by an appeal tribunal or Commissioner can be superseded (not revised), but not on the basis of 'error of law', so Grounds 2 and 4 are not available to you.

Ground 1: Change of circumstances

Any decision can be *superseded* if there has been a *'relevant change of circumstances since [it] had effect'*, or such a change is anticipated.

What changes are 'relevant'? – A change of circumstances is 'relevant' if it calls for serious consideration by the decision maker and could (but not necessarily would) potentially change some aspect of the award such as the amount or length of the award.

For example, if you have the lowest rate of the disability living allowance (DLA) care component for part-time day care needs, and your condition deteriorates so that you need more help with personal care throughout the day, that is a relevant change of circumstances because it could lead to entitlement to the middle rate.

Note the following points.

- If the original decision was to refuse benefit completely, that decision cannot be superseded only because there has been a later change of circumstances. The original decision remains correct and you must make a fresh claim, or alternatively your application for a supersession will be treated as a fresh claim.
- For incapacity-related benefits, a new report from a DWP doctor enables a decision to be superseded (see Ground 3 below). But for other benefits, such as DLA, a different medical opinion does not in itself amount to a relevant change of circumstances. However, the findings of an up-to-date medical examination and report may be evidence of an actual change of circumstances (eg that you have developed a new medical condition or that your condition has deteriorated).
- A change in the legislation counts as a relevant change of circumstances and a supersession can take effect from the date on which the change in the legislation had effect. However, a decision of the court or a Commissioner's decision does not count as a relevant change of circumstances.
- If there has been a change of circumstances which occurred after a decision under appeal was made, but only came to light during the appeal process, the decision maker can supersede the tribunal's decision to take account of the change.
- When a DLA renewal decision has already been made, if your condition improves (more than anticipated) or does not deteriorate (as anticipated) between the date of the renewal decision and the effective date of renewal, the decision maker can *revise* rather than supersede the decision.

Reg 13C(3) Social Security (Claims and Payments) Regulations 1987 (see also CIB/4751/02 et al)

The backdating rules following a change of circumstances are described in Chapter 58(5).

Ground 2: Error of law

A decision can be *superseded* if it was based on a mistake about the law (eg the decision maker misinterpreted the relevant law or applied the wrong regulation). Such a decision can be *revised* instead (hence you can get full backdating of benefit) if the error of law is also an official error (see 'Ground 4').

Note that a decision of an appeal tribunal or a Commissioner cannot be superseded on the basis of an error of law. You may, however, be able to appeal further (see Chapter 58(17)).

Ground 3: New medical report

A decision maker can *supersede* any decision that you are incapable of work under the personal capability assessment (including a decision made by a tribunal or Commissioner) when they get a new medical report on your incapacity from a DWP doctor. However, once the decision maker has decided that this ground applies, they still need to consider whether or not you are incapable of work. In doing so, they should look at all the relevant evidence with respect to your incapacity, which may include medical evidence from earlier periods (CSIB/1266/2000).

Ground 4: Official error

A decision can be *revised* if it arose from an official error by the DWP or local authority, as long as no one outside the department or authority caused or materially contributed to the error.

The revised decision generally takes effect from the same date as the original decision, so benefit can be fully backdated no matter how long ago the original decision was made. However, if a later decision of a Commissioner or court in another case (a test case) shows that there is an error of law in a decision on your award, it cannot be revised for official error. Instead, it is *superseded* for error of law and arrears can only be backdated to the date of the test case.

backdating rules. Whether a decision should be revised or superseded depends on which of the grounds (listed in Box R.5) are satisfied.

Don't worry if you're not sure which it should be. The decision maker can treat an application for a supersession as one for an 'any time' revision, and vice versa.

Applying for a decision to be revised or superseded
It is best to put a request for a decision to be revised or superseded in writing. In the case of housing benefit (HB) and council tax benefit (CTB), this is the only option but with other benefits you can phone or go in person to the appropriate office if you prefer. However, if you do this, you should confirm your request in writing. Check which one or more of the grounds (listed in Box R.5) apply, and state these in your letter. Give reasons why you think those grounds are satisfied. The decision maker need not take into account anything that is not raised by your application. So make sure

Ground 5: Award of a qualifying benefit
If you or your partner or dependent child become entitled to another qualifying benefit or to an increase in a qualifying benefit, your existing award can be *revised* or *superseded*. Benefit can then be fully backdated to the start of the existing award (by revision) or to the start of the award of the qualifying benefit, if that is later (by supersession). For example, if you are claiming income support (IS) and then make a claim for DLA, which is awarded after a delay, your IS award can be superseded and the disability premium fully backdated to the start of the DLA award.

This rule can apply to increase entitlement to a benefit you already have. If you don't have an existing award, see Chapter 57(3) for rules on backdating claims. See also Chapter 6(2).

A decision maker can *revise* a decision on reduced earnings allowance (REA) when a claim to REA has been disallowed because of a decision that there was no assessment of disablement (ie you are found not to have a prescribed disease or a loss of faculty (see Chapter 44(14)), and the latter decision is either revised by a decision maker or changed at appeal.

A decision maker can *revise* a decision on IS or pension credit (PC) when a non-dependant living with you is awarded backdated benefit (eg attendance allowance) such that you can become entitled to the severe disability premium (or the PC equivalent) from the beginning of your IS or PC claim. If, however, the non-dependant's benefit is awarded from a date after the start of your IS or PC award, the decision maker can *supersede* the decision.

Ground 6: Incorrect facts
Any decision can be *superseded* if it was made in ignorance of a material fact or was based on a mistake about a material fact. For example, when you filled in your DLA claim-form maybe you underestimated the help you need with personal care. If you give the DWP this information now, they can supersede the decision.

The new decision only takes effect from the day you apply for the original decision to be superseded. This applies equally where it is a decision of an appeal tribunal or Commissioner that is being superseded. There is generally no backdating (see Box R.4).

If you think the DWP or local authority made a mistake and neither you nor anyone else outside the department or authority contributed to the mistake, this may be an official error (see 'Ground 4' above). You can get full backdating of arrears if there has been an official error.

Mistakes in your favour – The general rule is that if you were paid more benefit than you were entitled to because a decision was made in ignorance of a relevant fact of your case or based on a mistake about such a fact, a decision maker can *revise* the decision at any time (or *supersede* the decision if it was made by an appeal tribunal or Commissioner). The new decision takes effect from the same date as the original decision took effect (or where the decision was made by an appeal tribunal or Commissioner, from the date that decision took effect). If there is any overpayment, the decision maker must then go on to consider whether it is recoverable under the normal overpayment rules (see Chapter 57(6)).

The same rule applies whenever the original decision was more advantageous to you than it should have been (see Chapter 58(9)), unless the special protection for disability and incapacity-related benefits applies.

Disability and incapacity-related benefits – A cut in benefit won't be backdated if the decision maker is satisfied that at the time of the original decision you didn't know and couldn't *'reasonably have been expected to know'* of the fact in question and that it was relevant. For more about this rule, see Chapter 58(5) under 'What if your benefit goes down?'

Ground 7: Revision during the appeal process
As long as an appeal has been lodged within the time limits (see Chapter 58(7)), a decision maker can *revise* a decision at any time prior to the appeal being determined. This means, for example, that if further evidence follows on from an adjourned hearing, the decision maker can revise the original decision, thus making it likely that a further hearing will be unnecessary.

Ground 8: Following the appeal outcome of an earlier decision
A decision can be *revised* at any time following an appeal determination of an earlier, related decision. For example; you appeal against a decision that you are capable of work following a personal capability assessment. You also claim incapacity benefit again, which is in turn disallowed. The appeal against the earlier decision turns out to be successful, so benefit is paid up to the date of the new claim. The decision maker can now *revise* the second decision and thus award benefit from the date of the new claim as well.

Ground 9: No appeal rights
A decision that carries no right of appeal can be either *revised* or *superseded*. These decisions include most administrative decisions about claims and payment of benefit (see Chapter 58(7)). This means that although you can't appeal, you can ask the decision maker to reconsider the decision at any time without needing to show any special grounds.

Ground 10: Sanctions
If a decision maker wishes to impose a sanction, any decision that jobseeker's allowance (JSA) is payable can be *superseded*, including one made by an appeal tribunal or Commissioner. A decision to apply a sanction to your JSA can in turn be *revised*. So if you are outside the dispute period, you can still challenge a sanction. The new decision takes effect from the same date as the original decision. If the sanction is lifted, arrears of benefit can be fully backdated.

you give all the reasons why you think the decision should be changed. If you can, provide evidence to back up your argument. If you cannot send this off straight away, inform the appropriate office. Keep a copy of your letter and any evidence you may include with it.

Warning: A disability living allowance (DLA) award consists of one or both DLA components. If you ask for one DLA component to be increased or request a component you don't already have, the decision maker could well decide to question your existing entitlement to the other component. So it is advisable to obtain medical evidence to support your request prior to contacting the DWP. If you are happy with the level of one component you are already getting, you should clearly say so in your application, as the DWP *'need not consider any issue that is not raised by the application'*. This will not, however, afford cast-iron protection for your existing award.

Appeal rights

If one of the grounds in Box R.5 is satisfied, the original decision can be either revised or superseded. The result of this may be to confirm the original decision or to change it. As long as the decision maker makes a decision either to revise, supersede or not to supersede (if the decision maker decides not to supersede they will confirm the original decision as correct), then you have a right of appeal. In rare circumstances, where the application for supersession is obviously hopeless, the decision maker can refuse to make a decision and will simply notify you that the decision is not superseded. Since there is no decision, there is no right of appeal. Such a refusal should only occur where the supersession request is obviously irrelevant or where it could not possibly result in a different award.

Wood v Sec of State for Work and Pensions 2003 EWCA (Reported as R(DLA)1/03)

If you can't appeal, you can always apply again for the decision to be superseded, particularly if your condition gets worse.

For appeal rights within the dispute period, see 3.

5. Backdating after a change of circumstances

If your circumstances change and a decision is superseded, the extent to which benefit can be backdated will depend on the circumstances of the case. You should tell the DWP or local authority about the change of circumstances as soon as you can. If you notify the change within one month, benefit is fully backdated to the date of the change.

For disability living allowance (DLA) and attendance allowance (AA), if you are applying to move up a rate or applying for another component, benefit can be paid from the first pay day after you first satisfy the 3-month or 6-month backwards qualifying period (see Chapters 20(4) and 21(2)) as long as you notify the change of circumstances within a month of completing the qualifying period. For example, if your need for extra care would have satisfied the disability test for a higher rate more than 4 months before you apply, an increase in DLA won't be backdated unless, as explained below, you have special reasons for the delay in telling the DWP. If you only know the month and not the day you would have passed the disability test for the higher rate or other component, the DWP is advised to assume it to be the end of that month (para 04410, Vol 1, *Decision Makers Guide*).

If you tell the DWP or local authority about a change of circumstances that happened more than a month ago, you can still get full backdating to the date of the change if you can show there are special reasons for the delay and you apply within 13 months of the date of the change. Write to the appropriate office giving details of the change of circumstances and reasons for not telling them earlier.

The decision maker must be satisfied that:

- it is reasonable to grant the application; *and*
- the change is relevant to the decision that is to be superseded (see 'Ground 1' in Box R.5); *and*
- there are special circumstances that are relevant to the application; *and*
- because of the special circumstances it was not practicable for you to notify the change of circumstances within a month (eg because of serious illness).

The longer the delay, the better the reason must be. The decision maker won't take account of the fact that you simply didn't know of the time limits or the law, or that a Commissioner or court has reinterpreted the law.

What if your benefit goes down? – If your circumstances change, and as a result your benefit goes down or stops, the general rule is that the reduction is put into effect back to the date of the change of circumstances, no matter when you reported it. The same applies whenever the decision is not advantageous to you (see 9). If the DWP or local authority decide you have been paid too much benefit, they may try to recover the overpayment (see Chapter 57(6)).

There are exceptions, however, for the following:

- the disability tests for DLA or AA;
- disablement for severe disablement allowance or industrial injuries benefits;
- incapacity for work for income support (IS), incapacity benefit (IB) or severe disablement allowance.

For these benefits, the reduction is only backdated if you knew or could reasonably have been expected to know that the change should have been notified. In this case the reduction is backdated to the date you ought to have told them.

The same applies to any consequent change to a linked benefit. For example: if DLA care component is stopped following a periodic enquiry and you could not reasonably have been expected to know that you should have told the DWP about a reduction in your care needs, DLA entitlement and any disability premium included in IS will only stop from the date of the new decision.

In deciding whether you *'reasonably could have been expected to know'* that you should have notified the change, decision makers are advised to take into account:

- how much you knew about the reasons for awarding you benefit;
- what information was given to you about notifying changes of circumstances;
- your ability to recognise when a gradual improvement results in a relevant change of circumstances. A slight change in your care or mobility needs, or your ability to carry out activities in the personal capability assessment of incapacity, would not normally be a change which you could reasonably be expected to notify. However, where the change is gradual there may be a point at which you could reasonably be expected to know that a change should be reported.

Para 04239/40, Vol 1, Decision Makers Guide.

6. When a test case is pending

If you make a claim or ask for a decision to be revised or superseded, and your entitlement might be affected by a matter of law which is under appeal in the courts in another case, ie the 'test case', the decision maker may choose to postpone making a decision in your case until the test case has been decided. Alternatively, they may choose to make the decision in your case as though the test case had already been decided in a way that was unfavourable to you. If the test case turns out differently, the decision maker must then go back and revise the decision accordingly.

Generally, when the decision maker makes a decision in your case after a decision in a test case, arrears of benefit are restricted to the date of the test case decision.

If you have appealed – The outcome of your appeal may

depend in some way on the result of another case pending at the courts. If this happens, the decision maker may ask the tribunal or Commissioner to do one of the following:

- not to decide the appeal, but to refer it back to them. The appeal will be held until the test case is decided. Then the decision maker will revise or supersede the decision as appropriate;
- to deal with the appeal. The tribunal or Commissioner will either hold the appeal until the test case has been decided, or determine it as if the test case has been decided in a way that is unfavourable to you. If the result of the test case is then favourable, the decision should be superseded.

7. Appeals

You have a right to appeal to an appeal tribunal against any decision on a claim for benefit or against any decision which revises or supersedes another decision, unless it is specifically listed in law as one with no right of appeal. There is no right of appeal against:

- most administrative decisions about claims and payment of benefit (but not decisions on whether or not claims are 'defective' – see Chapter 57(2)). An extensive list is now clearly defined in law (see legal references below);
- entitlement to industrial injuries constant attendance allowance or exceptionally severe disablement allowance, or Christmas bonus; *or*
- that part of a decision which adopts a rent officer's decision; *or*
- decisions to postpone or make temporary unfavourable determinations when a test case is pending (see 6).

The full list is in Schedule 2 SSA 98; reg 27 and Schedule 2 SSCS(D&A)Regs 99; reg 16 and Schedule HB & CTB(D&A)Regs 01.

If you do not have a right to appeal, you can ask for the decision to be revised or superseded (see 'Ground 9' in Box R.5). Judicial review may also be a possibility, but you will need expert advice from a law centre or solicitor.

You must be given a written decision and informed of your right to appeal. You can ask for written reasons for the decision if they were not included with the decision (see below).

Time limits for appeal

Your appeal request must be received at the DWP or local authority office (in each case at the office which sent you the decision) within one calendar month of the date the decision was sent to you. For example, if the decision was sent to you on 7 July, your appeal must be received at the relevant office by 7 August at the latest. For tax credits, your appeal must be received at the office that sent you the decision within 30 days of the date the decision was sent to you. The date the decision is sent to you is usually taken to be the date on the letter. If there is a dispute about whether or not your appeal was made within the time limit, the dispute should be referred to a legally qualified tribunal member for a decision.

You can ask for written reasons for the decision if they were not included with the decision. You must do this within one month of the day the decision is sent to you. If you ask for the written reasons within one month and they are provided within that period, the one-month time limit is extended by 14 days; if they are provided outside one month you will be given an extra 14 days from the date they are provided. With housing benefit and council tax benefit, however, in calculating the time limit any days between the date that the local authority receives your request for a statement and the date they actually provide it are ignored. It is not always clear, however, whether the original decision did or did not include reasons, so do not rely on having extra time to appeal if there is any doubt.

It is most important that you appeal within the time limit. Although it is not impossible to get an appeal admitted late, there are strict conditions to satisfy before a late appeal will be accepted.

Late appeal

If you miss the deadline, a late appeal can be accepted in certain limited circumstances. An application for a late appeal must be made in writing and will first be considered by a decision maker. They will decide whether it is in the interests of justice to allow a late appeal and in doing so will consider whether or not there were 'special circumstances' which are relevant to the delay. These are that:

- you, your partner or a dependant has died or suffered serious illness; *or*
- you live outside the UK; *or*
- normal postal services were disrupted; *or*
- some other *'wholly exceptional'* circumstances occurred.

The longer the delay, the better the reasons must be. No account is taken of the fact that you or your adviser did not know or understand the law or the time limits involved, nor that a Commissioner or the court has reinterpreted the law.

If the decision maker cannot accept the late appeal they must then refer it to The Appeals Service, where a legally qualified tribunal member decides whether to accept it. Not only can the tribunal member accept a late appeal if they feel it is in the interests of justice to do so, but they can also accept a late appeal if they are satisfied there are *'reasonable prospects that the appeal will be successful'*. If you are turned down, you can't appeal or ask again. So make sure you give full details of all the relevant special circumstances that apply in your case. The time limit cannot be extended for more than one year after the end of the normal period for appealing.

8. Making an appeal

You must apply in writing, preferably using the appropriate appeal form. For most benefits this will be the GL24, which you get from the DWP. The Inland Revenue provides the TC/AP appeal form for tax credits and the CH24A appeal form for child benefit and guardian's allowance. For housing benefit and council tax benefit, your local authority will provide their own, approved appeal form.

On the appeal form you must give details of the decision you wish to appeal against (eg which benefit is involved and the date of the decision) and details of why and how you think the decision is wrong. For tax credits, tribunals will only consider grounds of appeal not made on the appeal form if they consider that the omission was not *'wilful or unreasonable'*. Sign the appeal form and make sure it is received at the appropriate office within the one-month (or for tax credits, 30-day) time limit.

9. What happens when you appeal?

When they receive your appeal, the decision maker will first check to see if they can revise the decision you are appealing against.

R.6 Human Rights Act

The Human Rights Act 1998 incorporated into UK law the rights guaranteed under the European Convention on Human Rights. Arguments based on Convention rights may be made in social security appeals against decisions made since 2.10.00. Decision makers, tribunals and Commissioners are obliged to interpret the law in a way that is consistent with the Act as far as they are able. You should seek legal advice if you think it may apply in your case.

You can find the Human Rights Act and detailed commentary on its provisions in *Social Security: Legislation 2004 Volume III* (Sweet & Maxwell).

If it is revised, your appeal lapses if the new decision is more advantageous to you – even if it does not give you everything you wanted. To continue with your appeal, you must now make a new appeal against the revised decision within one month (or for tax credits, 30 days) of this decision.

If it is revised but the new decision is not more advantageous to you, your appeal will go ahead against the revised decision. You have another month in which to provide further arguments and evidence for your appeal against the new decision. The decision maker could decide to revise the decision yet again in the light of the further information and evidence you provide. Otherwise the appeal will go forward for hearing.

When is a decision more 'advantageous'?

A decision is more 'advantageous' to you if:

- more benefit is paid (or would have been but for some restriction, suspension or disqualification);
- the award is for a longer period;
- a denial or disqualification of benefit is lifted wholly or partly;
- an amount of recoverable overpaid benefit is reduced or decided not to be recoverable;
- it reverses a decision to pay benefit to a third party;
- it reverses a decision that an accident was not an industrial accident;
- you will get some financial gain.

This list is not exhaustive.

Note that a decision maker can revise a decision at any time prior to the appeal being determined (see 'Ground 7' in Box R.5).

10. Striking out an appeal

The clerk to the appeal tribunal may decide to strike out your appeal if:

- the tribunal does not have jurisdiction to deal with the appeal (eg it is about a decision that does not carry a right of appeal);
- you fail to 'proceed' with the appeal (eg you appeal outside the absolute time limit of 13 months);
- you fail to comply with a direction given to you (eg you don't return forms within the deadlines; usually you have just 14 days to return forms so it is best to phone the clerk if you think you'll miss a deadline).

The Appeals Service will write to you if your appeal has been struck out.

Reinstatement – You can ask for your appeal to be reinstated but you must do so in writing within one month of the date of issue of the order to strike out, stating why you believe the appeal should not have been struck out. In limited circumstances the clerk to the appeal tribunal can reinstate the appeal where there are *'reasonable grounds'* to do so. If they are not satisfied that there are reasonable grounds, they should then refer the request to a legally qualified tribunal member. The tribunal member can reinstate the appeal if they are satisfied that there are reasonable grounds to do so, or that it was not an appeal that could be struck out under the rules, or it is not in the interests of justice for the appeal to be struck out.

11. Withdrawing an appeal

You have the right to withdraw your appeal at any time before it is decided. You do not need the agreement of the DWP, local authority or tribunal chairperson. If you haven't received the appeal submission yet, just write to the decision maker at the office dealing with your claim. Otherwise write to the clerk to the appeal tribunal stating that you wish to withdraw the appeal. You can withdraw the appeal at the hearing itself if you wish.

Tax credit appeals can only be withdrawn with the agreement of the Inland Revenue, and may be withdrawn at any time before the appeal is heard (but not at the hearing

R.7 Commissioners' decisions

A number of Social Security Commissioners' decisions are quoted in this Handbook. These decisions are part of case law, setting precedents which must be followed in similar cases.

In general, decisions of the courts are binding on Commissioners, tribunals and decision makers. Though Commissioners speak with equal authority (see R(I)12/75, p19–22), a decision of a Tribunal of Commissioners should be followed in preference to a decision of a single Commissioner. A reported decision of a single Commissioner may be given more weight than an unreported one. Nonetheless, decision makers and tribunals are free to follow whichever decision they consider to be correct. There is no obligation on tribunals to prefer an earlier decision to a later one, or vice versa.

The most important decisions are published or reported. See Box R.9 for where to get copies.

Reported decisions – These are referred to as, for example, R(IB)2/99; R = reported; (IB) = the series initial, in this case standing for incapacity benefit; 2/99 = the second decision in that series reported in 1999 (Since 2000 the date will refer to the point the decision was published by the DWP.)

Unreported decisions – These are referred to as, for example, CA/140/85. Where: C = Commissioner; A = the series initial; 140 = the number of the file; 85 = the year in which the file was opened by the Commissioner. Decisions made in Scotland are identified with an S, as in CSDLA/121/97.

Between 1982 and the beginning of 2002 unreported decisions of more general significance were starred; some went on to be reported at a later stage.

Series initials

(A)	attendance allowance
(CR)	compensation recovery
(DLA)	disability living allowance
(DWA)	disability working allowance
(F)	child benefit, formerly family allowance
(FC)	family credit
(G)	general: includes benefits not covered in other categories, such as carer's allowance, maternity allowance and widows' benefits
(H)	housing benefit and council tax benefit
(HR)	home responsibilities protection
(I)	industrial injuries benefits
(IB)	incapacity benefit
(IS)	income support
(JSA)	jobseeker's allowance
(M)	mobility allowance
(P)	retirement or state pensions
(PC)	pension credit
(S)	sickness and invalidity benefit and severe disablement allowance
(SB)	supplementary benefit
(SSP)	statutory sick pay
(TC)	tax credits
(U)	unemployment benefit

itself). Note that a tax credit appeal can be settled by agreement between the claimant and the Inland Revenue. If there is agreement then the appeal lapses; it does not have to be withdrawn, even where there is no change in the decision.

12. Opting for an oral hearing

When your appeal is lodged, you will get an initial acknowledgement. When the DWP, Inland Revenue or local authority send your appeal to The Appeals Service, they will also send you a copy of their submission on your case together with a pre-hearing enquiry form. This asks you to choose whether you want an oral hearing or a paper hearing – in other words, do you want to attend the hearing in person. Make sure you return the enquiry form within 14 days, otherwise your appeal could be struck out (see 10).

In most cases, it is better to ask for an oral hearing. In some cases, it will be crucial for the success of your appeal. This is particularly true of cases involving any medical or disability questions (eg decisions about incapacity for work or entitlement to disability living allowance). For example, it may not become obvious until the tribunal asks you questions at the appeal hearing as to your ability to perform the activities in the personal capability assessment of incapacity. In 2002, only 14% of paper hearings with respect to these were successful, as compared with 51% where there was an oral hearing.

13. Preparing your case

Read the submission sent to you so you can see where you might need to dispute it. If you haven't already done so, see if there is a local advice centre that can advise you and maybe support you at the hearing itself (see Chapter 59).

The tribunal need not consider any issue that is not raised by the appeal. Hence it is important to give as much detail as you can about why and how you think the decision is wrong. On the other hand, if there is part of your award that you are happy with, you should say so. It is important to remember that the tribunal can only consider circumstances that existed at the time of the decision that you are appealing against. So if your circumstances change while you are waiting for the appeal to be heard, you should consider making another claim (see 14 below).

Check the law

Tribunals must make decisions in accordance with the legislation and case law by applying these to the particular facts of your situation.

Legislation is made up of Acts and Regulations. The appeal papers should refer to the parts of the legislation relevant to your appeal. You can look these up in *The Law Relating to Social Security* (see Box R.9).

Case law is found in decisions of the Social Security Commissioners and the courts. Decisions made by the Social Security Commissioners set precedents (see Box R.7). If the principles and facts of a Commissioner's decision are similar to those in your own case, the tribunal should follow that decision. The appeal papers should refer you to any relevant decisions; it is always worth checking these. But there may be other Commissioners' decisions that are more helpful for your appeal. For reported decisions read *Neligan* (see Box R.9); find the decisions quoted in the appeal papers and look at the other decisions in the pages around them. In really complex cases, you should read every reported decision on that topic.

Sort out the facts and evidence

Once you have looked at the legislation and case law, you may have a clearer idea of which facts are important for your appeal and what extra evidence you might need. Almost all appeals concern a dispute about the facts, or a different interpretation of the same facts. So if you feel confused about the law – then just concentrate on the facts.

You do not have to prove any fact 'beyond all reasonable doubt'. You just have to prove your case on a balance of probabilities. Your word is just as much 'evidence' as a bit of paper is. But if you get other evidence to back up what you are saying, this helps tip the balance your way.

If you read through the chapter on the benefit you are appealing about, you should get a good idea of what facts could be important. A local advice agency may also be able to help sort out which facts are important and what other evidence you might need. They might also be able to represent you. In some cases you might need to call witnesses – so you'll need to get their agreement beforehand. Try to make sure that their account will back up your case.

It is best to send in any further evidence and details of your case in advance of the tribunal hearing. Make a copy and take it with you to the hearing.

Getting medical evidence

If your appeal concerns a medical question (eg whether or not you are 'virtually unable to walk'), try to obtain supportive medical evidence, which you should send in before the hearing.

Bear in mind that the tribunal can only consider your circumstances up to the date of the decision you are appealing against. You can still get medical evidence later but it should relate to the circumstances as they were up to the time of the decision under appeal.

The evidence can come from medical professionals such as your GP, specialist nurse, physiotherapist or hospital consultant. When you ask them to give you a letter or statement it is best to put to them specific questions, so you get answers that are directly relevant to the case and not a vague comment about your general condition. Make sure that they are aware of your condition and how it relates to the questions of the case; if you have kept a diary in respect of disability living allowance (see Chapter 20(15)), provide them with a copy.

If the appeal papers contain a report from a DWP doctor, read it carefully to see where you might need to get your own medical evidence to counter what is said in the report. Make sure you ask your doctor or nurse, etc to comment specifically on the points in dispute. For example, if you disagree with a DWP doctor's report that says you can walk 100 metres without severe discomfort, ask for an opinion of how far you can walk without severe discomfort.

You can argue that your own doctor's evidence should carry more weight than that of a DWP doctor. Your doctor has probably spent more time examining you and knows you better, or perhaps is a specialist in your condition.
CDLA/1850/2001

Difficulties obtaining evidence? – If you have problems obtaining evidence from one of the professionals treating you, the Legal Aid scheme may cover the cost of a medical report from an independent consultant or specialist through a solicitor or advice agency contracted with the Legal Services Commission (see Chapter 59).

If you think you will be unable to get supportive medical evidence by the time of the hearing, you can ask for a postponement to allow you more time to obtain it (see 16). If, however, you consider that such evidence is unlikely to be forthcoming, the lawyer chairperson at the tribunal can still refer you for an examination if they think it is necessary to obtain a medical report to help them decide the appeal. You can ask the tribunal to make such a referral and if you have a list of specific questions that you consider need to be answered at the appeal, ask the tribunal to agree that those questions be put to the doctor.
S. 20 SSA 98 and reg 41, SSCS(D&A) Regs 99

There is no rule that you must have corroborating medical

or other evidence. You can go ahead with your appeal even if you can't get supporting evidence.

14. If your circumstances change before the appeal

It can take some months for your appeal to be heard and your circumstances may change in the meantime. The tribunal can only look at your situation as it was up to the time of the decision you are appealing against. They decide whether the decision was correct at the time it was made on the basis of what was known at that time. If your situation has changed between the decision and the tribunal hearing, they can't take that into account. The only exceptions are if the change was one that was almost certain to occur, such as you reaching a certain age, or in the case of disability living allowance renewals, when the change took place after the renewal decision was made but before it took effect.

If your circumstances do change while your appeal is pending and you think you might begin to qualify for the benefit concerned, you should make a fresh claim. If you are already getting the benefit, notify the DWP or local authority about your change of circumstances so that they can consider superseding the award. If you don't, and your appeal is unsuccessful, you could lose out because of the strict rules on backdating.

If the new claim is unsuccessful or the decision maker refuses to supersede your award, it is important to put in a second appeal. This is because the tribunal hearing the first appeal cannot consider the period covered by the second claim. You could find that benefit is put into payment by a first successful appeal then stopped from the date of the unsuccessful claim. While it is true that the decision maker can revise the decision on the second claim following the successful first appeal (see 'Ground 8' in Box R.5), there is no guarantee that this will happen every time. So to be on the safe side, lodge the second appeal. You can ask that a single tribunal hears all the appeals together. For appeals on incapacity for work, see also Chapter 11(11) and (12).

15. Special needs and access to the hearing

If you have any special needs, check with the tribunal clerk beforehand about accessibility, what facilities are available, and how your needs can be met to enable you to be present at your hearing and get home within a reasonable time after the hearing. You can and should ask for whatever you need. Whether The Appeals Service can arrange or provide it is a separate matter – if they cannot, seek advice.

For example, if it is too far for you to walk easily to the tribunal room from the nearest point at which a car can set you down, ask for a wheelchair to be waiting for you. If you need any breaks during a hearing (eg to go to the toilet, to take food, liquids or medication, to stretch your legs, or to change position), ask for them – it helps if the tribunal are aware beforehand of what you might need.

If the premises aren't accessible to you, the tribunal should adjourn to a time and place where you can be present.
CI/112/84

Domiciliary tribunals – If you exercise your right to opt for an oral hearing of your appeal, The Appeals Service can, if necessary, arrange for the tribunal to hear your appeal at your home (a 'domiciliary hearing'). You should provide medical evidence of your need for a domiciliary hearing.

The tribunal will normally sit to hear the case to decide whether to adjourn for a domiciliary hearing. The tribunal should fully consider your request for such a hearing; if they go ahead in your absence they must be satisfied there is already sufficient evidence before them for a full appeal or that there are other ways to get the evidence they need (eg by referring you for a medical report).
CIB/2751/02

If you are reluctant to have them visit your home, perhaps because you don't have enough room, a local disability group may know of a suitable and fully accessible venue which could be used instead.

16. At the hearing

You must be given at least 14 days' notice of the time and place of the hearing, starting from the day the hearing notice is sent to you. As The Appeals Service aims to provide you with a hearing date as soon as they receive your completed pre-hearing enquiry form (see 12), you may well have considerably more notice than this.

Asking for a postponement

If the date is inconvenient or it doesn't give you enough time to prepare your case, write to the clerk to the tribunal and ask if the hearing can be postponed. If time is short, you can telephone the clerk (the number will be at the top of the hearing notice) but you should also write to confirm your request. The same applies if you find that you are ill before or on the day. If you have a sudden domestic difficulty or the case was listed in error, the clerk will generally make the decision on whether to grant a postponement. But in other cases, a legally qualified tribunal member will deal with the request. If you have asked for a postponement because of insufficient notice and you have not had the postponement confirmed, it is best to go along to the hearing anyway, just in case your request is refused.

Who is at the hearing?

You and your representative – It is always best to attend the hearing yourself – see 15 above if there is a problem with access. You are entitled to have someone with you to represent you (see Chapter 59) and you can also bring a companion for support. Both you and your representative have the right to speak, and you can also call witnesses if you want to.

The tribunal members – The appeal tribunal itself is made up of a lawyer chairperson and possibly one or two other people, depending on the issue under appeal:

- disability living allowance, attendance allowance, disability and incapacity questions relating to working tax credit and child tax credit – a lawyer, a doctor and a person experienced in the needs of disabled people (the disability member);
- personal capability assessment – a lawyer and a doctor;
- severe disablement allowance, industrial injuries benefit – a lawyer and one or two doctors;
- difficult financial matters about trust funds or business accounts – a lawyer and an accountant;
- declaration of industrial accident, any other matter – a lawyer.

The tribunal cannot go ahead unless all the tribunal members are present. Members are drawn from a panel of suitably qualified people appointed by the Lord Chancellor.

The 'disability member' is a person who is *'experienced in dealing with the needs of disabled persons... in a professional or voluntary capacity... or because they are themselves disabled'*. They cannot be a medical practitioner, but could be a paramedic such as a physiotherapist or a nurse.

To avoid a conflict of interest, the tribunal must not include a doctor who has ever provided advice or prepared a report about you, or has ever been your regular doctor.

Although the President of the appeals tribunals may decide to include an additional member on a tribunal there can never be more than 3 tribunal members. The appeal tribunal itself may decide it needs to call on an expert to attend the hearing or to give a written report, but this person won't take part in the appeal tribunal's deliberations.

Others – Apart from the tribunal members, there may be a presenting officer (who is a decision maker, but not necessarily the one who made the decision) to put the DWP, Inland Revenue or local authority case. The presenting officer should also identify any points in your favour. This is because the procedure is inquisitorial, and not adversarial (with you against the presenting officer). There will also be a clerk who will deal with administrative matters that arise during the hearing, such as photocopying documents, and there could be someone to assist the clerk or the tribunal.

If the tribunal chairperson agrees, any other person can be present during the hearing (including another friend) but they cannot take part in the proceedings. The hearing will be open to the public unless the tribunal chairperson decides otherwise. They might be persuaded if it was put to them that a private hearing was required for the protection of the private or family life of one or more parties to the proceedings. Otherwise, in practice, the only members of the public who are likely to be present are other claimants (so that they can see what happens before their own appeal is heard) or advisers (to help them in their work).

What happens at the hearing?
The hearing itself should be fairly informal. The tribunal chairperson will begin by introducing the members of the tribunal and explaining its role. They will then usually clarify what they understand to be the issues before them. They will want to determine those aspects of your case that are being disputed and any that are not. If there is a presenting officer, the chairperson will usually ask them to present the decision maker's case first.

You will then be asked to explain your case. It is useful to put your main points in writing so you don't forget anything. If you are interrupted, ask tactfully if you can make all your points before answering questions. Wherever possible, back up your argument with documentary evidence (eg bills, doctor's letter, etc). At the end of your statement, repeat the decision you want the tribunal to make. You can question the presenting officer, if there is one, and any witnesses. Listen carefully to what they have to say, and be prepared to ask questions if you think the facts are being misrepresented. Once the tribunal is satisfied that each party has had the opportunity to present its case, the chairperson will ask you to leave the tribunal room while they make their deliberations.

Medical examinations – For a severe disablement allowance or industrial injuries appeal involving an assessment of the extent of your disability, the doctor on the tribunal will examine you in private, usually at the end of the hearing.

The tribunal cannot carry out a physical examination for any other benefit. They cannot ask you to undergo a walking test for the mobility component of disability living allowance. They will, however, see how you walk into and out of the room, as well as observing how you cope with what might be a lengthy hearing.

Claiming expenses
You can claim travelling expenses for yourself, and compensation for loss of earnings can be claimed up to a set maximum. You can also claim childminding expenses and subsistence allowance if you are away from home or work for more than 2½ hours. If you are not sure what you, or someone with you, can claim, ask the tribunal clerk: phone the number on the hearing notice.

17. The appeal decision

You will get a decision notice on the day of the hearing or soon after. A copy is sent to the department that made the original decision so that they can put the tribunal decision into effect and pay you any benefit owed.

If the appeal is unsuccessful, you should ask for a more detailed explanation, the 'statement of reasons' for the decision. If you want to appeal to a Social Security Commissioner, you need this statement, so make sure you write and ask for it within the one-month time limit.

Once you have had the opportunity to read the statement of reasons, it should be clear to you how and why you have been unsuccessful. If it is not, this may be an error of law (see Box R.8) and it may be possible to appeal further to a Commissioner.

If you disagree with the decision
A decision of an appeal tribunal can be changed in the following ways:

- appeal to a Commissioner if there is an error of law – see 18 below (if you are out of time to appeal, see below for some ideas of what to do);
- apply for the decision to be set aside (see below);
- apply to the tribunal clerk to correct an accidental error (see below);
- apply to the DWP or local authority to supersede the decision if there has been a relevant change of circumstances or such a change is anticipated (see 'Ground 1' in Box R.5). This can include a change of circumstances that occurred after the decision under appeal was made but which only came to light during the appeal process (the tribunal would have been prevented from taking the change into account itself);
- apply to the DWP or local authority to supersede the

R.8 Errors of law

Can you understand the decision?
From reading the full written decision of any tribunal, it must be clear what they decided, and why they made the decision. If you put forward specific arguments, it must be clear how and why they dealt with your arguments. From the decision it must also be clear that the tribunal understood and correctly applied the legislation and case law relevant to the decision.

Errors of law are also relevant if you (or the decision maker) are seeking to supersede a previous decision on this ground (see 'Ground 2' in Box R.5).

Identifying errors of law
R(A)1/72 lists the tests to be applied in deciding whether a decision is erroneous in law. Generally, a decision will be wrong in law if any of the following apply.

- ❑ There has been any breach of the rules of natural justice (that is, loosely, incorrect or unfair procedures).
- ❑ The tribunal has failed to make sufficient findings of fact on the key questions at issue so as to enable it properly to come to a decision.
- ❑ The tribunal has failed to give adequate reasons for the decision. (Listing a string of Commissioners' decisions and/or legal references, or repeating the question at issue in the appeal, is not good enough.)
- ❑ The decision contains a misdirection or misunderstanding of the relevant law. (For example, if a tribunal's decision shows they thought 'required' meant only medically required, rather than reasonably required, they would have erred in law. They would have made the decision on the basis of a wrong construction, or understanding, of the law, and the meaning of the words used in the law.)
- ❑ There is no evidence supporting their decision.
- ❑ The facts found were such that no person acting judicially and properly instructed about the relevant law could have come to the decision. (There must be a clear inconsistency here between the facts of the case and the decision.)

decision if it was made in ignorance of any material fact, or was based on a mistake about any material fact (see 'Ground 6' in Box R.5).

Setting aside for procedural reasons – A decision may be set aside by a legally qualified tribunal member, if it 'appears just' to do so because:

- a document relevant to the appeal wasn't sent to or received (or received in sufficient time) by any party to the proceedings, their representative or the tribunal; *or*
- a party to the proceedings or a representative wasn't present at the hearing; but if you did not opt for an oral hearing (see 12 above), the decision can only be set aside on this ground if *'the interests of justice manifestly so require'*.

You must apply in writing to have the decision set aside within one month of either the date the decision was sent to you or the date the statement of reasons was sent to you.

The time limit can be extended by up to one year where there are special circumstances. The rules for these are similar to those for late appeals – see 7 above. However, in this case the legally qualified tribunal member must be satisfied that it is in the interests of justice to extend the time limit and, if it is extended, that there are reasonable prospects that the application to set aside will be successful.

Setting aside means the tribunal decision is wiped out and there can be a fresh hearing before a new appeal tribunal. You cannot appeal against a refusal to set aside, but it does start afresh the time limits for applying for a statement of reasons for the original decision or for leave to appeal to a Commissioner. This does not apply, however, where the legally qualified tribunal member has refused to accept a late application for setting aside.

Correcting an accidental error – An 'accidental' error in a decision of an appeal tribunal can be corrected by the tribunal clerk or a legally qualified tribunal member. Arithmetical or clerical errors can be corrected in this way (eg from the record of the decision it is clear that they accidentally gave the wrong starting date for an award of benefit). There is no time limit. Write to the clerk to the tribunal. However, correction is discretionary and there is no right to appeal against a refusal to correct.

If the decision is corrected, time limits start afresh for applying for a statement of reasons for the original decision or for leave to appeal to a Commissioner. A refusal to correct does not extend the time limits, however.

If you can't appeal to a Commissioner – If you think there is an error of law in the decision but you are out of time for appealing, try one of the following.

- ❑ Make a fresh claim for benefit. The normal rules for backdating claims apply.
- ❑ If you still have an award of benefit, check to see if the decision can be superseded if it was made in ignorance of a material fact or was based on a mistake about a material fact (see 'Ground 6' in Box R.5). Very often what counts as a material fact depends on how the law is interpreted and on the understanding of the nature of the tests required by the law. If an error of law has been made, it is likely that the tribunal or Commissioner won't have explored all the relevant facts. If a supersession on the basis of mistake or ignorance about the facts is possible, then the whole decision is considered afresh and the current interpretation of the law applied.
- ❑ If you still have an award of benefit and there has been a change of circumstances since the tribunal or Commissioner decision, the decision maker can correct the error of law when they supersede the decision. This is because once you tell the DWP or local authority about

R.9 For more information

The Acts and Regulations

- Social Security Act 1998 (abbreviated in this chapter to SSA 98)
- The Social Security and Child Support (Decisions and Appeals) Regulations 1999 (abbreviated in this chapter to SSCS (D&A) Regs 99)
- The Social Security Commissioners (Procedure) Regulations 1999
- Child Support, Pensions and Social Security Act 2000
- The Housing Benefit and Council Tax Benefit (Decisions and Appeals) Regulations 2001
- Tax Credits Act 2002
- The State Pension Credit Act 2002
- The Tax Credits (Appeals) (No. 2) Regulations 2002

These cover most of the rules on decision making and appeals procedures. You can buy individual Acts and Regulations from The Stationery Office, PO Box 29, Norwich NR3 1GN (0870 600 5522, Textphone 0870 240 3701) or look them up on the HMSO website: www.legislation.hmso.gov.uk. Most have been amended, but you can find consolidated and updated legislation in: *The Law Relating to Social Security* (The Blue Volumes) distributed by Corporate Document Services (see Chapter 61) or available on our website: www.disabilityalliance.org/links2.htm.

Reference books

Tribunal members are issued with: *Social Security: Legislation 2004 Volumes I, II, III* and *IV* (Sweet & Maxwell). These books have detailed footnotes explaining the legislation and highlighting relevant case law. Make sure you look at the latest editions.

Case law

- *Neligan – Social Security Case Law – Digest of Commissioners' Decisions* – available from Corporate Document Services and also on our website: www.disabilityalliance.org/links2.htm. This outlines the main reported decisions. In tricky cases it is unlikely to give you enough information and you will need to look up the full reported decisions.

All Commissioners' decisions are available from their office individually on request at a small charge (see inside back cover for their address). Decisions are also available on the Commissioners' website (www.osscsc.gov.uk) where reported decisions from 1991 and selected unreported decisions deemed to be of interest from 2002 are published.

Interpreting law

- *Decision Makers Guide* (Corporate Document Services)
- *Medical Assessment Framework* (Corporate Document Services) – To help decide industrial injuries disablement benefit
- *Social Fund Guide* (Corporate Document Services)
- *Incapacity Benefit Handbook for Approved Doctors* (Corporate Document Services)
- *Disability Handbook* (The Stationery Office)

All are available on our website: www.disabilityalliance.org/links2.htm.

Your local library may have copies of all, or some, of these publications. You can also consult DWP publications at your local social security or Jobcentre Plus office – it is best to phone or write beforehand to make an appointment. Much recent law, case law and official guidance is available on our website: www.disabilityalliance.org/links2.htm.

the change of circumstances, as long as they agree the change is relevant, then all aspects of the decision can be reconsidered.

18. Appeals to the Commissioners

You can only appeal to a Commissioner if there is an error of law in the decision of the appeal tribunal (see Box R.8). You cannot appeal about the facts. But it is sometimes hard to separate the law from the facts, so it is worth asking an experienced adviser to check the decision. Don't delay, as there are strict deadlines to be met. To appeal to a Commissioner, you must take the following steps.

Step 1: Ask for a 'statement of reasons' for the decision within one month of the date the decision notice was given or sent to you. The time limit can be extended to 3 months if you can show there are special circumstances for your application being late. The rules are the same as those for late appeals to a tribunal (see 7), except in this case there is not the option of having a late application accepted simply because there are reasonable prospects that the further appeal will succeed.

Step 2: Apply for leave to appeal to the tribunal chairperson within one month of being sent the statement of reasons. Ask the tribunal clerk for form OSSC1 or write a letter setting out the reasons why you think the decision was legally wrong. Head it *'Application for leave to appeal to the Commissioner'*. Send your OSSC1 form or letter to the clerk to the tribunal and include a copy of the statement of reasons for the decision. The chairperson cannot give leave to appeal if you do not have this statement of reasons.

Step 3: If the chairperson refuses leave to appeal, apply for leave to appeal directly to the Commissioner within one month of being sent the notice refusing leave. With your OSSC1 form or letter, enclose a copy of each of the following: the tribunal decision notice, the tribunal's statement of reasons and the notice refusing leave to appeal. Send these to the Commissioners Office (see inside back cover). If you are posting this to them and you are close to the time limit, it would be advisable to record the delivery. Although *'a properly addressed notice'* is effective from the day it is sent, you may be required to prove this if it arrives late. If leave to appeal was refused because you did not have the statement of reasons, the Commissioner has discretion to admit the appeal, but this is not guaranteed; the Commissioner will wish to know why you do not have a statement of reasons.

Step 4: If leave to appeal is given, you must then appeal to the Commissioner within one month of being sent the notice granting leave. You will be sent a form on which to do this.

If you miss the deadline, you may be able to have a late appeal accepted for 'special reasons'. The final cut-off for a late appeal is 13 months from the date the statement of reasons was sent to you. See below.

The decision maker has the same rights of appeal as yourself.

Setting aside for error of law

There is a quick procedure to set aside the tribunal decision without the appeal going to the Commissioner. When you apply for leave to appeal, the tribunal chairperson may set aside the decision of the tribunal if they consider there is an error of law. They must do this when the decision maker agrees with you that there has been such an error. When a decision has been set aside, the appeal will be heard again either by the same tribunal or by a new one.

Payment pending appeal

Until your appeal is settled, the DWP, Inland Revenue or local authority will put the decision of the tribunal into effect. However, if the decision maker proposes to appeal, then payment of the disputed benefit may be suspended and you won't be paid until the appeal is finally decided. If this causes hardship, ask the relevant office to consider lifting the suspension.

Late applications for leave to appeal to a Commissioner

If you miss the one-month time limit for applying for leave to appeal, you can make a late application up to 13 months from the date you were sent the statement of reasons. A legally qualified tribunal member can accept a late application if there are special reasons. This is at their discretion. The strict rules that apply to late appeals to a tribunal do not apply here.

If a late application is refused, you can apply directly to the Commissioner for leave to appeal. The Commissioner can consider your late application if there are special reasons and you are within the 13-month deadline.

If you can't get a late appeal, but you think there is an error of law, see 17 above.

The Commissioner's decision

If a Commissioner finds that an appeal tribunal decision is wrong in law (see Box R.8):

- they can give the decision they consider the tribunal should have given, if they can do so without making fresh or further findings of fact; *or*
- if they consider it expedient, the Commissioner can make fresh or further findings of fact, and then give a decision in the light of them; *or*
- if there aren't enough findings of fact, and the Commissioner doesn't think it expedient to look at the evidence afresh, the case must be referred back to a tribunal. The Commissioner will give the tribunal directions so that they can make a fresh decision along the right lines.

A quicker procedure can be used where both parties agree there is an error of law. If the decision maker supports your case and you agree with their submission to the Commissioner, the Commissioner may then set aside the tribunal's decision straight away and refer it back to a tribunal with short directions to guide them.

S Help and Information

This section of the Handbook looks at:

59 Getting advice

1. Who can help you?

Your local Citizens Advice Bureau (CAB) can help with benefits advice and many other matters. You can also get application forms and leaflets from them. The CAB may be able to represent you if you have a problem or an appeal. If not, they may be able to tell you if there is another local organisation which could help. There might also be other independent advice centres locally which provide services similar to the CAB. Your local council might have a welfare rights service that could help or, if not, they are likely to be able to give you a list of local advice centres. Contact your town hall for information. A local DIAL (Disability Information and Advice Line) group or other disablement advice centre may be able to offer advice and, in some cases, may be willing to represent you. See the Address List for a list of DIAL groups.

2. Free legal help

Most solicitors will not be familiar with the intricacies of the social security system. So your first step should normally be to see what advice or help your local CAB, DIAL or other advice agency can give you. Also, some firms of solicitors, particularly those who have contracts with the Legal Services Commission, employ welfare rights specialists who can help with benefit matters.

If you live or work in the catchment area of a law centre, contact them to see if they can help. Law centres can usually give benefits advice as well as help in other areas of the law such as housing, employment and immigration. See the Address List for details of local law centres. Your CAB may have volunteer lawyers and can possibly refer you to one at a special advice session. Many trade unions offer free legal advice to their members.

Free legal advice can also be obtained from the Community Legal Service Direct national helpline (0845 345 4345).

Legal Aid – In England and Wales, the Community Legal Service (CLS) organises free legal advice or Legal Aid through participating solicitors and advice agencies. Anyone who receives income support, income-based jobseeker's allowance or pension credit (guarantee credit) automatically qualifies for Legal Aid if their capital is below the set limit. Other people, in or out of work, may qualify if their savings and income are low enough; you can use the calculator on the CLS website (www.clsdirect.org.uk) to work out if you may be entitled to Legal Aid. Not all solicitors are part of the scheme – only those who are contracted with the Legal Services Commission. Look on the CLS website or ring 0845 608 1122 (Textphone 0845 609 6677) for details of participating solicitors and advice agencies.

The Scottish Legal Aid Board manages Legal Aid in Scotland. Look on their website (www.slab.org.uk) or ring 0131 226 7411 for details of participating solicitors.

Legal Aid can cover the cost of preparing for a tribunal – eg writing letters, getting a medical report, advising you on the law, or preparing a written submission for you to hand to the tribunal. However, it does not cover actual representation at a tribunal hearing.

Injured in an accident – If you have been injured in an accident, you can arrange for a free legal consultation with a local solicitor specialising in injury claims, by phoning The Accident Line on Freephone 0500 192939. Alternatively, your union may be able to arrange a solicitor for you.

Making a will – The free CLS Legal Aid scheme covers making a will for specific groups of people only, including most people with disabilities, people aged 70 or over, a parent of a disabled person who wants to provide for that person in their will, and a lone parent wishing to appoint a guardian for their child in a will.

60 Making a complaint

1. Complaints about the DWP

When a DWP agency has made a mistake you can expect them to explain what went wrong and why, and to apologise. They should not treat you any differently just because you have complained. Each DWP agency has its own complaints procedures. You can ask the office you have been dealing with for their complaints leaflet and customer charter.

To make a complaint, start by contacting the person you dealt with, or that person's manager. It may be possible to sort things out easily. It is always best to complain as soon as something goes wrong. Don't wait until you get a decision on your claim – a complaint will not prejudice your chances of a successful decision on your claim.

If the problem is not resolved, you can take the following steps.

- ❑ Contact the Office Manager at the office dealing with your claim.
- ❑ If your complaint is with a Jobcentre Plus office and you are not satisfied with the response from the Office Manager, you should then contact the District Manager.
- ❑ If you are not satisfied with the response from the Office Manager (or District Manager) you should write to the Chief Executive of that agency (see inside back cover).
- ❑ If a problem continues for some time, it can be helpful to involve your MP. You can do this at any point.
- ❑ Where your case involves maladministration, you can complain to the Ombudsman (see 5 below).

Ask the DWP for their leaflet on comments and complaints. If your complaint is about a DWP medical examination, see 3 below.

2. Compensation

There are a number of ways in which you can claim compensation or financial redress when you have lost money because of delays or mistakes made by the DWP or because you have received wrong or misleading advice from them.

Extra-statutory compensation

You may get extra-statutory compensation if you lose entitlement to a benefit because of wrong or misleading official advice and the normal statutory channels are not available to you – eg you fail to claim a benefit because you were told you were not eligible for it and you are only granted arrears of benefit for a limited period. Write, asking for compensation, to the office handling your benefit.

Ex-gratia payments

Financial losses – If you lose money because of delays or mistakes by the DWP in paying your benefit, you can ask them for a discretionary 'ex-gratia' special payment to cover your actual financial losses (eg the cost of phone calls, stamps and stationery, bank charges, etc). The delay or mistake need not have lasted for any set period of time. It is enough if you have had a financial loss as a result.

Consolatory payments – In very exceptional circumstances where maladministration has had a directly adverse affect on your life you can ask for a consolatory payment. This may be appropriate where an official error has resulted in gross inconvenience, embarrassment, humiliation or unnecessary personal intrusion, or has caused you severe distress, which has significantly impacted on your physical or mental health. You need not have had any financial loss.

Unreasonable or exceptional delays – If the DWP delays paying benefit, you can also get ex-gratia payments to cover the interest (at fixed rates) on the arrears of benefit. Such payments may be made if:

- the arrears of benefit are £100 or more; *and*
- a significant part of the delay is due to DWP maladministration; *and*
- the compensation would be at least £10; *and*
- the delay was unreasonable or exceptional. 'Delay indicators' provide a guide to measure this (see below).

Claims and underpayments – If you are paid benefit on a claim, or arrears from an underpayment of benefit following a revision or supersession, compensation is payable, where the above criteria are met, if correct payment on that claim has been delayed beyond a set period, called the 'delay indicator'.

Delay indicators	**months**
DLA and AA	
– new claims	7
– DLA renewal claims	9
– AA renewal claims	7
– 'Special rules' claims	2
Carer's allowance	9
Incapacity benefit	4
Income support	2
Industrial injuries disablement benefit	12
Jobseeker's allowance	3

Current claims – Compensation becomes payable if your benefit payments are interrupted for 3 months.

If you qualify for compensation – Interest is payable on all the benefit owed to you for each complete tax year. It starts to accrue from the end of the set period, but is worked out on all the arrears. Compound interest is only calculated if the delay in payment is over 10 years.

Write to the office handling your claim to ask for compensation. They may, however, offset any overpayments previously judged to be non-recoverable. They can only do this if a decision maker has decided there was an overpayment and you were notified of it. You could consider challenging that overpayment decision in order to remove the offset.

Guidance on the various kinds of compensation payable is contained in the DWP guidance *Financial Redress for Maladministration*, which includes details of delay indicators and the method of calculating interest. You can ask to see a copy of this guidance at your local Jobcentre Plus office; it is also on our website: www.disabilityalliance.org/links2.htm.

3. Complaints about DWP medical examinations

To make a complaint about a doctor who has carried out a medical examination on behalf of the DWP, or about facilities at, or conduct of, a medical examination, you can take the following steps.

- ❑ Write to the Medical Services Centre at the address on your medical appointment letter. You could use the tear-off slip on the Medical Services leaflet *Comments, complaints and suggestions*, available at the Medical Examination Centre. The Medical Services Customer Relations Team will handle your complaint. They are based at Government Buildings, Lawnswood, Leeds LS16 5PU (tel 0113 230 9175). They will acknowledge your complaint and aim to fully respond to the issues you have raised, in writing, within 20 working days.
- ❑ If you are not satisfied with the response, write back to the Customer Relations Team. Your complaint will be passed to one of their senior managers, who will review the case.
- ❑ The next step, if you are not satisfied, is to write to the Customer Relations Team and ask for your complaint to be referred to a local independent complaints panel, called an Independent Tier.
- ❑ If the problem is not sorted out and involves maladministration, you can complain to the Parliamentary Ombudsman. Ombudsmen cannot concern themselves with a DWP doctor's clinical findings. They can, however, examine complaints about the way a medical examination was conducted – eg the doctor was rude or insensitive (see 5).
- ❑ You can write to the Director of Medical Services (see inside back cover).

4. Health and social services

There is a standard complaints procedure you can use if you are not happy with care services provided by the social services or social work department. You might also want to take up the matter with a local councillor or MP. Chapter 25(7) outlines the steps you can take.

For complaints about hospitals, GPs and NHS services, the best starting point is your local patient advocacy and liaison service (PALS) in England and Wales, local health council in Scotland, or health and social services council in Northern Ireland. They can advise you on the right procedure to use, and might also be able to help you to make your complaint. Patients who are detained in hospitals or care homes under the Mental Health Act can contact The Mental Health Act Commission who will look into the complaint. In Scotland, contact the Mental Welfare Commission for Scotland. See the Address List.

5. Complaining to the Ombudsman

Complaining to an Ombudsman is not an alternative to the normal appeals process, nor is it an extension of that process. You would normally complain to an Ombudsman about the way a decision was taken or the way you were treated, rather than about the actual decision itself. Before you can complain to an Ombudsman, you should first use the normal complaints procedure. It is best to keep a copy of your letter of complaint and of anything connected with it. If you are still not satisfied, you should normally approach an MP (see below) and ask that your complaint be referred to the Ombudsman. You do not have to pay a fee to make a complaint.

Contact details for Ombudsmen are at the end of the Address List. Information can also be obtained from the website: www.bioa.org.uk.

An Ombudsman investigates whether maladministration has caused injustice. Ombudsmen do not investigate personnel matters, except in some cases the Northern Ireland Ombudsman.

Maladministration – This includes such things as bias, prejudice, incorrect action, unreasonable delay, failure to follow (or have) proper procedures and rules.

Injustice – This does not only cover financial and other material or tangible loss but also includes inconvenience, anxiety or stress, and even a sense of outrage about the way in which something has been done.

Ombudsmen have powers similar to those of High Court (Court of Session in Scotland) for obtaining evidence.

If an Ombudsman upholds your complaint, they will expect the body against which you have complained to provide you with some remedy. This may be an apology, a change in procedures, financial compensation, or any combination of these or similar measures.

You need to complain to the correct Ombudsman. In Britain you complain to:

- Parliamentary Ombudsman about central government (eg the DWP);
- Local Government Ombudsman about local government (eg local authority housing benefit offices or social services departments);
- Health Service Ombudsman about health authorities and trusts, doctors, dentists, opticians, etc. They can also investigate cases where maladministration has caused hardship, complaints about clinical judgements, and complaints about the refusal of access to official information.

There is only one government Ombudsman in Northern Ireland.

For devolved matters, there is a separate Scottish Public Services Ombudsman and a Welsh Administration Ombudsman. The Scottish Public Services Ombudsman deals with complaints about the Scottish Executive and its agencies and other public bodies including health, housing and social services.

You can ask your Citizens Advice Bureau (CAB) to check with the Ombudsman first if you want to make sure that an Ombudsman can investigate a complaint against a particular government body, such as a quango.

You can complain directly to any of the Ombudsmen except the Parliamentary Ombudsman and, in cases concerning central government, the Northern Ireland Ombudsman.

Only an MP can refer a complaint to the Parliamentary Ombudsman. You should normally approach your own MP and only approach another MP if yours has refused to refer your complaint. If you do approach an MP for another constituency, they will usually contact your own MP before they decide whether to refer your complaint.

Other Ombudsmen

As well as the government Ombudsmen, there are several other Ombudsmen, including the Financial Ombudsman, Independent Housing Ombudsman and the Legal Services Ombudsman. Your CAB can give you their addresses and advise you whether one of them can help you. For information about the Pensions Ombudsman, see Box N.2 in Chapter 42.

61 Useful publications

1. Benefits guides

In many chapters in this Handbook we suggest other sources of information (law, guidance and reference books) specific to the benefit or other rights described in the chapter. Look in boxes called 'For more information'. Listed below are a selection of other guides.

- *Guide to Housing Benefit and Council Tax Benefit 2005/2006.* Published jointly by the Chartered Institute of Housing and Shelter. £21.50
- *Welfare Benefits and Tax Credits Handbook 2005/2006.* Published by Child Poverty Action Group. £33 (£8 for claimants)
- *Your Rights 2005-2006 – a guide to money benefits for older people.* Published by Age Concern England. £5.99
- *Child Support Handbook 2005/2006.* Published by Child Poverty Action Group. £21.50 (£6 for claimants)
- *Council Tax Handbook 2005, 6th edition.* Published by Child Poverty Action Group (due Autumn 2005). £15
- *Paying for Care Handbook 2005/2006, 5th edition – a guide to community and residential care* (due Autumn 2005). Published by Child Poverty Action Group. £18.50
- *A Practical Guide for Disabled People: Where to find information, services and equipment* – information on a wide range of government and voluntary services. Also available in Braille and on audio cassette. Quote reference 29614 when ordering. Free from: Department of Health, PO Box 777, London SE1 6XH (0800 555777, website: www.dh.gov.uk)

2. DWP leaflets and guidance

The DWP leaflets mentioned in this Handbook should be available from your local Jobcentre Plus office. You can buy official DWP guidance from: Corporate Document Services, 7 Eastgate, Leeds LS2 7LY, or ring their orderline: 0113 399 4040. You can see copies of official guidance at your local Jobcentre Plus office or on the DWP website: www.dwp.gov.uk.

3. Disability Alliance publications

In addition to this Handbook we publish several guides and bulletins on matters relating to disability and welfare rights. The following is a list of current publications. Future publications will be advertised in our bulletins.

- *Disability Rights Bulletin* (published Summer, Winter and Spring 2005/2006) – updates this Handbook and includes articles on disability issues. £3.75 each or £11.25 for the full set
- *Benefits! Where do I stand?* (2004) – a guide for people with mental health problems who are considering moving into work. Produced in partnership with Salford Training & Employment Partnership and Salford Welfare Rights Service. £5 (£3 for claimants)
- *Charges for Community Care Services – A guide for disabled people and carers in England and Wales* (2002) – will assist disabled people, their carers and advisers to make informed choices about the options available to them. £4 (£2.50 for claimants)
- *Claiming Disability Living Allowance - A self-help guide for disabled people aged 16-64* (2004) – explains the DLA qualifying conditions, takes you through the claim-form step by step, and advises what to do if you are unhappy with a decision. £5 (£3 for claimants)
- *Claiming Attendance Allowance – A self-help guide for people aged 65 and over with a long-term health problem or disability* (2003) – explains the qualifying conditions, takes you through the claim-form step by step and advises what to do if you are unhappy with a decision. £5 (£3 for claimants)
- *Tell it like it is – A self-help guide to claiming disability living allowance for a child with disabilities or special needs* (2004) – explains the qualifying conditions, takes you through the claim-form step by step, and identifies other benefits to which you or your child may be entitled. £6 (£4 for claimants)
- *Claim it right! – A self-help guide to claiming disability living allowance for adults and children with sickle cell*

disorders (2004) – explains the DLA qualifying conditions, takes you through the claim-form step by step, and includes a chapter on keeping a diary to provide evidence for the claim. £6 (£4 for claimants)

- *The way to work – A guide to benefits and tax credits for mental health professionals* (2004) – will enable mental health professionals to help their clients make informed decisions when moving into work. £8.50 (£4 for claimants)
- *Moving into work – A disabled person's guide to the benefits, tax credits and other help available when considering any kind of work* (2003, updated 2005) – covers the support available from the benefits and tax credits systems and government schemes. £5 (£3 for claimants)
- *Out of sight* (2003) – a policy report examining how ethnic minority claimants who are either disabled or caring for a disabled person experience the benefits system. It focuses on non-English speakers, particularly Asian women, and identifies many deficiencies in the system. £8.50
- *Self-employment – why not? – A disabled person's guide to the benefits, tax credits and other help available when considering self-employment* (2003, updated 2005) – covers the support available from the benefits and tax credits systems and government schemes. £5 (£3 for claimants)

Organisations can become members of Disability Alliance and receive a free copy of all our current publications. See back cover for contact details.

Address list

Organisations

Using the address list

General and specialist organisations dealing in some way with disability issues are listed. The main A-Z section lists organisations that cover England or all of the UK. Organisations based in Northern Ireland, Scotland and Wales are listed separately. We do not have space to list local organisations and instead provide a list of DIAL UK local groups as a first point of contact.

Lists are organised alphabetically. Entries beginning with the words National, British, etc are listed by the disability or community they serve, eg 'Schizophrenia, National Fellowship' or 'Deaf Association, The British'.

Acronyms such as BILD (British Institute of Learning Disabilities) are generally listed by disability (Learning Disabilities, British Institute of,).

Email and website addresses are not included. The best starting point for a list of organisations and their website addresses is www.disabilitynet.co.uk.

England and UK-wide

A

Ability Net, PO Box 94, Warwick CV34 5WS (01926 312847; Advice Helpline 0800 269545) *Makes mainstream computer technology accessible to people with disabilities.*

Acupuncture Council, British, 63 Jeddo Road, London W12 9HQ (020 8735 0400) *Free local list of practitioners and a leaflet on acupuncture provided on request. Large print also available.*

Advocacy Resource Exchange (ARX) (formerly CAIT), 162 Lee Valley Technopark, Ashley Road, Tottenham Hale, London N17 9LN (020 8880 4545) *The national resource and referral agency for independent advocacy.*

Afasic, 2nd Floor, 50-52 Great Sutton Street, London EC1V 0DJ (020 7490 9410; Helpline 0845 355 5577 – open 10.30am-2.30pm) *For children and young people with speech, language and communication impairments.*

African-Caribbeans, Organisation of Blind, 1st Floor, Gloucester House, 8 Camberwell New Road, London SE5 0RZ (020 7735 3400)

Age Concern England, Astral House, 1268 London Road, London SW16 4ER (020 8765 7200)

AIDS Trust, National (NAT), New City Cloisters, 196 Old Street, London EC1V 9FR (020 7814 6767) *The National AIDS Trust is the UK's leading independent policy development and campaigning organisation on HIV and AIDS.*

Alcohol Concern, Waterbridge House, 32-36 Loman Street, London SE1 0EE (020 7928 7377) *National agency on alcohol misuse. Aims to reduce impact of misuse and increase range and quality of services.*

Alcoholics Anonymous, PO Box 1, Stonebow House, Stonebow, York YO1 7NJ (01904 644026; London Helpline 020 7833 0022; National Helpline 0845 7697555)

Alzheimer's Society, Gordon House, 10 Greencoat Place, London SW1P 1PH (020 7306 0606; Helpline 0845 300 0336 – open 8am-6pm) *Advice and support for those coping with dementia.*

Amnesia – see *Headway*

Ankylosing Spondylitis Society, National, PO Box 179, Mayfield, East Sussex TN20 6ZL (01435 873527)

Arise – The Scoliosis Research Trust, The Graham Hill Unit, Royal National Orthopaedic Hospital Trust, Brockley Hill, Stanmore, Middlesex HA7 4LP (020 8954 8939) *Information on scoliosis for patients and professionals.*

Arthritis Care, 18 Stephenson Way, London NW1 2HD (020 7380 6500; Helpline 0808 800 4050) *Empowering people with arthritis.*

Arthritis, Horder Centre for, St John's Road, Crowborough, East Sussex TN6 1XP (01892 665577) *Specialists in bone replacement surgery.*

Arthritis and Musculoskeletal Alliance (ARMA), 41 Eagle Street, London WC1R 4TL (020 7841 5191)

ASBAH (Association for Spina Bifida and Hydrocephalus), ASBAH House, 42 Park Road, Peterborough PE1 2UQ (01733 555988)

Asian Disability Network (ADN), Noor House, 11 Bradford Lane, Laisterdyke, Bradford BD3 8LP (01274 224444; Minicom 01274 201860; Fax 01274 229444) *Nothing about us without us: breaking down barriers to real inclusion.*

Asian People's Disability Alliance (APDA), The Disability Alliance Centre, The Old Refectory, Central Middlesex Hospital, Acton Lane, London NW10 7NS (020 8961 6773) *Respite care, advice and advocacy, day care for elderly Asians and disabled people, IT training, sports and leisure and home help service.*

Asthma UK, Providence House, Providence Place, London N1 0NT (020 7226 2260; Adviceline 0845 701 0203)

Ataxia UK, 10 Winchester House, Kennington Park, Cranmer Road, London SW9 6EJ (020 7582 1444; Helpline 020 7820 3900) *Friedreich's and other cerebellar ataxias. Information, advice, support and publications. Working with and for people affected by ataxia.*

Autistic Society, National, 393 City Road, London EC1V 1NG (020 7833 2299; Autism Helpline 0845 070 4004 – open Mon-Fri 10am-4pm) *Offers information and advice to people with autistic spectrum disorders.*

B

BackCare, 16 Elmtree Road, Teddington, Middlesex TW11 8ST (020 8977 5474; Helpline 0870 950 0275 – Mon and Fri 9am-12pm; Wed 6pm-9pm) *Support for people with back pain, helpline and local branches.*

Barnardo's, Tanners Lane, Barkingside, Essex IG6 1QG (020 8550 8822) *Social care and educational services for disabled children, young people and their families.*

BDF Newlife (previously known as Birth Defects Foundation), BDF Centre, Hemlock Way, Cannock, Staffordshire WS11 7GF (Helpline 08700 707020) *Support and information for anyone affected by birth defects, particularly Noonan Syndrome.*

Blind, General Welfare of the, 276 York Way, London N7 9PH (020 7619 1650) *Sheltered workshops for blind and disabled people.*

Blind, Guide Dogs for the, Hillfields, Burghfield Common, Reading, Berkshire RG7 3YG (0118 983 5555)

Blind, National Federation of the, Sir John Wilson House, 215 Kirkgate, Wakefield WF1 1JG (01924 291313) *Campaigning and self-help organisation.*

Blind, National Library for the, Far Cromwell Road, Bredbury, Stockport, Cheshire SK6 2SG (0161 355 2000) *Free and post-free lending service in Braille and Moon books, Braille music and website access to electronic books and information services. Leading national agency in the provision of library services for visually impaired people. Open Mon-Fri 8.30am-4pm.*

Blind, Royal National Institute of the (RNIB), 105 Judd Street, London WC1H 9NE (Helpline 0845 766 9999) *Provides expert advice, assistance and* *information on benefits, equipment, employment and support to anyone with a sight problem. Campaigns for the rights of people with sight problems, and encourages research into the prevention of eye disease.*

Blind and Disabled, National League of the, Central Office, Swinton House, 324 Gray's Inn Road, London WC1X 8DD (020 7239 1262) *Trade union campaigning for employment and civil rights.*

Blind Children's Society, National, Bradbury House, Market Street, Highbridge, Somerset TA9 3BW (01278 764764) *Provides educational equipment, customised large-print books, advocacy; will pay for recreational activities.*

Blind People, Action for, 14-16 Verney Road, London SE16 3DZ (020 7635 4800; National Helpline 0800 915 4666) *Employment, housing, leisure and a national specialist information and support service, also specialist advice on social security benefits.*

Bliss – The Premature Baby Charity, 68 South Lambeth Road, London SW8 1RL (020 7820 9471; Freephone Helpline 0500 618140) *Supports families of premature and sick babies.*

Brain and Spine Foundation, 7 Winchester House, Kennington Park, Cranmer Road, London SW9 6EJ (020 7793 5900; Helpline 0808 808 1000 – Mon, Tues, Thurs, Fri 9am-1pm, Wed 10am-6pm) *Information and support by people trained in understanding neurological disorders.*

BREAK, Davison House, 1 Montague Road, Sheringham, Norfolk NR26 8WN (01263 822161) *Holidays, short breaks and respite care for children and adults with learning disabilities.*

Breast Cancer Care, Kiln House, 210 New Kings Road, London SW6 4NZ (020 7384 2984; Helpline 0808 800 6000; Helpline Textphone 0808 800 6001) *Information and support.*

British Legion, The Royal, 48 Pall Mall, London SW1Y 5JY (020 7973 7200; Helpline 0845 725725)

Brittle Bone Society, 30 Guthrie Street, Dundee DD1 5BS (01382 204446; Freephone Helpline 08000 282459)

C

Calibre Cassette Library, Aylesbury, Buckinghamshire HP22 5XQ (01296 432339) *Free postal cassette library for blind, partially sighted or print-disabled adults and children.*

Cancer, Association for New Approaches to, PO Box 194, Chertsey, Surrey KT16 0WJ (Freephone 0800 389 2662) *Works alongside conventional treatment, and guides patients and families to their nearest source of complementary therapy.*

Cancer BACUP, 3 Bath Place, Rivington Street, London EC2A 3JR (Freephone 0808 800 1234 – Mon-Fri 9am-8pm) *Information and support for anyone affected by any type of cancer. Ring for details of walk-in centres.*

Cancer Care, Marie Curie, 89 Albert Embankment, London SE1 7TP (020 7599 7777) *Provides high-quality nursing free of charge to give terminally ill people the choice of dying at home supported by their families.*

Cancer Relief – see *Macmillan Cancer Relief*

Cancer Research UK, PO Box 123, 61 Lincolns Inn Field, London WC2A 3PX (020 7009 8820)

Cardiomyopathy Association, 40 The Metro Centre, Tolpits Lane, Watford, Hertfordshire WD18 9SB (01923 249977) *Provides information for people with cardiomyopathy and for medical professionals.*

Care and Repair England, The Renewal Trust Business Centre, 3 Hawksworth Street, Nottingham NG3 2EG (0115 982 1527)

Carers UK, Ruth Pitter House, 20-25 Glasshouse Yard, London EC1A 4JT (020 7490 8818; Textphone 020 7251 8969; Freephone CarersLine 0808 808 7777 – open Wed and Thurs 10-12am, 2-4pm) *Provides information and advice on all aspects of caring to carers and professionals.*

Cerebral Palsy – see *Scope*

Child Death Helpline, c/o Great Ormond Street NHS Trust, Great Ormond Street, London WC1N 3JH (020 7813 8551; Freephone Helpline 0800 282 986) Also: Alder Hey Children's Hospital, Eaton Road, Liverpool L12 2AJ (0151 252 5391) *A helpline for anyone affected by the death of a child, teenager or young adult. Information packs and flyers are also available.*

Child Growth Foundation, 2 Mayfield Avenue, London W4 1PW (020 8994 7625; publications 0131 553 6553) *Supports families and patients who have conditions that affect growth.*

Child Poverty Action Group (CPAG), 94 White Lion Street, London N1 9PF (020 7837 7979; Advice line for advisers 020 7833 4627 – Mon-Fri 2-4pm) *Benefits handbooks for claimants and advisers; consultancy and training for advisers.*

Children, Action for Sick, c/o National Children's Bureau, 8 Wakley Street, London EC1V 7QE (Helpline 0800 074 4519) *Offers support and advice for the parents/carers of sick children. Campaigns to improve the quality of healthcare for children. Services include publications for parents/carers and professionals and a branch support network.*

Children with Heart Disorders, The Association for, Mrs Gill Hitchen, 26 Elizabeth Drive, Helmshore, Rossendale, Lancashire BB4 4JB (01706 213632)

Children's Bureau, National (including Council for Disabled Children), 8 Wakley Street, London EC1V 7QE (020 7843 6000)

Children's Legal Centre, University of Essex, Wivenhoe Park, Colchester, Essex CO4 3SQ (01206 872466)

Children's Liver Disease Foundation, 36 Great Charles Street, Birmingham B3 3JY (0121 212 3839) *Funds research, provides education and gives emotional support.*

Chinese Mental Health Association (CMHA), 2/F Zenith House, 155 Curtain Road, London EC2A 3QY (020 7613 1008)

Chinese National Healthy Living Centre, 29-30 Soho Square, London W1D 3QS (020 7534 6547)

Citizens Advice, Myddelton House, 115-123 Pentonville Road, London N1 9LZ (020 7833 2181) *Provides details of your local Citizens Advice Bureau.*

Coalition on Charging, c/o National Centre for Independent Living, 250 Kennington Lane, London SE11 5RD (020 7587 1663)

Colitis and Crohn's Disease, National Association for, 4 Beaumont House, Sutton Road, St Albans, Hertfordshire AL1 5HH (Helpline 0845 130 2233; NACC-in-Contact Support Line 0845 130 3344; Administration 01727 830038)

Colostomy Association, British, 15 Station Road, Reading, Berkshire RG1 1LG (Freephone Helpline 0800 328 4257 – 7-day service, 24 hours) *Advice on living with a colostomy and returning to a full life after surgery.*

Combat Stress – see *Ex-Services Mental Welfare Society*

Community Service Volunteers, 237 Pentonville Road, London N1 9NJ (020 7278 6601)

Compassionate Friends, Nationwide, 53 North Street, Bristol BS3 1EN (0845 120 3785; Helpline 0845 123 2304 – open daily 10am-4pm and 6.30-10.30pm) *Nationwide support from bereaved parent to bereaved parent and their immediate families.*

CONSENT (Consultancy, Sexuality, Education and Training), The Eric Shepherd Unit, Woodside Road, Abbots Langley, Hertfordshire WD5 0HT (01923 670796) *Direct work and training for staff, carers and people with learning disabilities on issues of sexuality.*

Contact a Family, 209-211 City Road, London EC1V 1JN (020 7608 8700; Helpline 0808 808 3555; Minicom 0808 808 3556) *Advice and support for families caring for disabled children, including those with rare disorders.*

Contact the Elderly, 15 Henrietta Street, London WC2E 8QG (Head Office 020 7240 0630; Freephone 0800 716543) *Friendship and regular monthly outings for elderly people who live alone without family support.*

Continence Foundation, 307 Hatton Square, 16 Baldwins Gardens, London EC1N 7RJ (Helpline 0845 345 0165 – open Mon-Fri 9.30am-1pm)

Counsel and Care, Twyman House, 16 Bonny Street, London NW1 9PG (020 7241 8555; Advice Line 0845 300 7585 – open Mon-Fri 10am-1pm) *Advice service on community care, benefits, care at home, residential care and financial* *help for older people.*

Counselling and Psychotherapy, British Association for, BACP House, 35-37 Albert Street, Rugby, Warwickshire CV21 2SG (0870 443 5252; Textphone 0870 443 5162) *Lists of counsellors, counselling agencies and local agencies available by post or from the website.*

Crossroads – Caring for Carers, Information and Communications Department, 3rd Floor, 49 Charles Street, Cardiff CF10 2GD (0845 450 0350) *Committed to providing practical support where it is most needed. Trained carer support workers take over caring tasks in the home to provide carers with a break.*

Cruse Bereavement Care, 126 Sheen Road, Richmond TW9 1UR (020 8939 9530; Helpline 0870 167 1677) *Counselling, support groups, information, advice and publications.*

Cued Speech Association UK, 9 Duke Street, Dartmouth, Devon TQ6 9PY (Voice and Textphone 01803 832784) *Training and information about Cued Speech, spoken language accessed through vision, for deaf people.*

Cystic Fibrosis Trust, 11 London Road, Bromley, Kent BR1 1BY (020 8464 7211; Helpline 0845 851 1000) *Provides support services for families and individuals with cystic fibrosis.*

D

Daycare Trust – The National Childcare Campaign, 21 St Georges Road, London SE1 6ES (Hotline 020 7840 3350 – open Mon-Fri 10am-5pm) *Provides information and advice on childcare issues.*

Deaf Association, The British, 1-3 Worship Street, London EC2A 2AB (020 7588 3520; Freephone Textphone 0800 652 2965; Helpline 08770 3300; Videophone 020 7496 9539; Fax 020 7588 3527)

Deaf Children's Society, National, 15 Dufferin Street, London EC1Y 8UR (Voice and Textphone 020 7490 8656; Freephone Helpline (Voice and Textphone) 0808 800 8880 – Mon-Fri 10am-5pm) *Information and support for families of deaf children and young people, including information on education, benefits, audiology and technology.*

Deaf People, Royal Association for, Head Office, Walsingham Road, Colchester, Essex CO2 7BP (01206 509509; Textphone 01206 711260; Fax 01206 769755) *Sign language interpreting service and communication and general support for deaf people.*

Deaf People, Royal National Institute for, (RNID), 19-23 Featherstone Street, London EC1Y 8SL (Voice 020 7296 8000; Textphone 020 7296 8001; Freephone Information Line 0808 808 0123; Freephone Text Information Line 0808 808 9000; Freephone Tinnitus Information Line 0808 808 6666; Freephone Text Tinnitus Helpline 0808 808 0007; Fax 020 7296 8199) *Campaigns for a better quality of life for people with hearing impairment, provides services and undertakes research.*

Deafplus, Prospect Hall, 12 College Walk, Selly Oak, Birmingham B29 6LE (Voice and Text 0121 415 2080; 0121 415 2081) *Aims to improve the quality of life for deaf people through contact, information and training.*

Deafblind UK, National Centre for Deafblindness, John and Luuie Van Geest Place, Cygnet road, Hampton, Peterborough PE7 8FD (01733 358100; 24-hour Helpline 0800 132320) *Provides comprehensive services for deafblind members, their support assistants and professionals who work with them. Also campaigns to challenge the prejudice faced by deafblind people.*

Deafblind and Rubella Association, The National – see *Sense*

Deafened People, The LINK Centre for, 19 Hartfield Road, Eastbourne, East Sussex BN21 2AR (01323 638230; Textphone 01323 739998) *Rehabilitation courses for deafened adults, outreach volunteers, social support groups, self-management programmes and training for professionals.*

DEBRA, DEBRA House, 13 Wellington Business Park, Dukes Ride, Crowthorne, Berkshire RG45 6LS (01344 771961) *Provides assistance to people with all types of epidermolysis bullosa.*

Depression Alliance, Suite 212, Spitfire Studios, 63-71 Collier Street, London N1 9BE (0845 123 2320) *Provides information and support to those affected by depression.*

Diabetes UK, 10 Parkway, London NW1 7AA (020 7424 1000; Careline 0845 120 2960) *Support and information on diabetes.*

DIAL, Local groups and members, see pages 274-276

DIAL UK, St Catherine's, Tickhill Road, Doncaster DN4 8QN (Voice and Textphone [use voice announcer] 01302 310123) *National organisation for the DIAL network – 160 disability advice centres run by and for disabled people.*

Disabilities Trust, The, 32 Market Place, Burgess Hill, West Sussex RH15 9NP (01444 239123) *Care, accommodation and rehabilitation for adults with acquired brain injury, autism, physical impairments and learning difficulties. The trust runs a school for children with autism in Berkshire.*

Disability and Oral Health, The British Society for, Mrs Alison Dougall, The Dental Department, Royal Leamington Spa, Rehabilitation Hospital, Heathcote Lane, Leamington Spa, Warwickshire CV34 6SR (Contact for healthcare professionals – 01926 317726)

Disability Consultancy, RNIB &, 1st Floor, 105 Judd Street, London WC1H 9NE (Voicemail: 020 7391 2331) *Disability Discrimination Act workplace compliance assessments and training.*

Disability Equipment Register, 4 Chatterton Road, Yate, Bristol BS37 4BJ (01454 318818) *Nationwide service to buy and sell used disability equipment directly from or to other users.*

Disability Foundation, The, based at Royal National Orthopaedic Hospital, Brockley Hill, Stanmore, Middlesex HA7 4LP (020 8954 7373)

Disability Law Service, Ground Floor, 39-45 Cavell Street, London E1 2BP (020 7791 9800; Textphone 020 7791 9801) *Free legal advice and information for disabled people, their families, enablers and carers.*

Disability, Pregnancy and Parenthood International, National Centre for Disabled Parents, Unit F9, 89-93 Fonthill Road, London N4 3JH (020 7263 3088; Textphone 0800 018 9949; Resource Centre 0800 018 4730 – Mon-Fri 10am-4pm) *Information on pregnancy and parenthood for disabled people and professionals. Book appointment to try out small baby equipment and see publications.*

Disability Resource Team, 2nd Floor, 6 Park Road, Teddington, Middlesex TW11 0AA (020 8943 0022) *Disability training, consultancy and transcription services.*

Disability Rights Commission, Helpline, FREEPOST MID02164, Stratford-upon-Avon CV37 9BR (Helpline 0845 762 2633; Textphone 0845 762 2644)

Disability Sport England, Unit 4G, 784-788 High Road, Tottenham, London N17 0DA (020 8801 4466)

Disabled Drivers' Association, The, National Headquarters, Ashwellthorpe, Norwich NR16 1EX (0870 770 3333) *Self-help association aiming for independence through mobility.*

Disabled Drivers' Motor Club, Cottingham Way, Thrapston, Northamptonshire NN14 4PL (01832 734724) *Advice for disabled motorists. Various discounts and concessions available.*

Disabled Living Centres Council, Redbank House, 4 St Chad's Street, Manchester M8 8QA (0161 834 1044) *Co-ordinates work of Disabled Living Centres UK-wide. List of centres available.*

Disabled Living Foundation, 380-384 Harrow Road, London W9 2HU (020 7289 6111; Helpline 0845 130 9177; Textphone 020 7432 8009) *Information and advice about daily living equipment for disabled people.*

Disabled Motorists Federation, c/o Chester-Le-Street District CVS Volunteer Centre, Clarence Terrace, Chester-Le-Street, County Durham DH3 3DQ (0191 416 3172) *Free information given to all disabled people and their carers on travel in general and motoring in particular.*

Disabled Parents Network, 89-93 Fonthill Road, London N4 3JH (Helpline 0870 241 0450) *Operates a peer support register that is open to all disabled parents, circulates newsletter to members. Helpline operated by disabled parent volunteers.*

Disabled People, British Council

of (BCODP), Litchurch Plaza, Litchurch Lane, Derby DE24 8AA (01332 295551; Textphone 01332 295581; Fax 01332 295580) *Support for organisations of disabled people.*

Disabled People, Queen Elizabeth's Foundation for, Leatherhead Court, Leatherhead, Surrey KT22 0BN (01372 841100) *Four centres including training college, mobility centre, brain injury rehabilitation.*

Disabled Professionals, Association of, (ADP), Jane Hunt, BCM ADP, London WC1N 3XX (01204 431638)

Disfigurement Guidance Centre – Skinlaser Today, PO Box 7, Cupar, Fife KY15 4PF (01337 870281) *Information, help, publications including Skinlaser directory and cosmetic handbook; sae essential for reply.*

Down's Heart Group, PO Box 4260, Dunstable LU6 2ZT (0845 166 8061) *Support and information relating to heart problems associated with Down's Syndrome.*

Down's Syndrome Association, Langdon Down Centre, 2a Langdon Park, Teddington TW11 9PS (0845 230 0372)

Dyslexia Association, British, 98 London Road, Reading RG1 5AU (0118 966 2677; Helpline 0118 966 8271) *National charity representing the dyslexia population.*

Dyslexia Institute, Park House, Wick Road, Egham, Surrey TW20 0HH (01784 222300) *Nationwide service offering educational assessment, teaching, training and advice.*

Dystonia Society, 46/47 Britton Street, London EC1M 5UJ (020 7490 5671) *Support for those affected by dystonia, a neurological movement disorder.*

E

Eating Disorders Association, 1st Floor, Wensum House, 103 Prince of Wales Road, Norwich NR1 1DW (0870 770 3256; Adult Helpline 0845 634 1414 – Mon-Fri 8.30am-8.30pm, Sat 1.30pm-4.30pm; Youth Helpline 0845 634 7650 – Mon-Fri 4-6pm, Sat 1-4.30pm; Textphone 01603 753322)

Eczema Society, National, Hill House, Highgate Hill, London N19 5NA (020 7281 3553; Helpline 0870 241 3604)

Education, The Alliance for Inclusive, Unit 2, 70 South Lambeth Road, London SW8 1RL (020 7735 5277) *Campaigns to achieve an inclusive education system.*

Employment Opportunities for People with Disabilities, 53 New Broad Street, London EC2M 1SL (Voice 020 7448 5420; Textphone 020 7374 6684; Fax 020 7374 4913) *Working with people with disabilities, business partners and government agencies to help people with disabilities find and retain employment).*

Environments, Centre for Accessible, Nutmeg House, 60 Gainsford Street, London SE1 2NY (Voice and Textphone 020 7357 8182) *Information, training and consultancy on the design of accessible buildings.*

Epilepsy Action (The British Epilepsy Association), New Anstey House, Gate Way Drive, Yeadon, Leeds LS19 7XY (0113 210 8800; Helpline 0808 800 5050; Fax Helpline 0808 800 5555)

Epilepsy, National Society for, Chesham Lane, Chalfont St Peter, Buckinghamshire SL9 0RJ (01494 601300; Helpline 01494 601400) *Medical services including in-patient assessment and out-patients; long-term care, supported living, information and education service available to anyone wanting to know more about epilepsy training.*

Equal Opportunities Commission, Arndale House, Arndale Centre, Manchester M4 3EQ (Helpline 0845 601 5901; Typetalk 1800 10845 601 5901)

Ex-Services Mental Welfare Society (Combat Stress), Head Office, Tyrwhitt House, Oaklawn Road, Leatherhead, Surrey KT22 0BX (01372 841600)

F

Family Fund, PO Box 50, York YO1 9ZX (0845 1304542; Textphone 01904 658085) *Financial help and information for families with severely disabled seriously ill children aged 16 and under.*

Family Service Units (FSU), 207 Old Marylebone Road, London NW1 5QP (020 7402 5175; Fax 020 7724 1829) *A national charity providing support services to children and families who are at risk of social exclusion.*

Family Welfare Association, 501-505 Kingsland Road, London E8 4AU (020 7254 6251) *Family support, mental health services, grants for people in need and educational grants advice.*

Far East (Prisoners of War and Internees) Fund, The Laurels, High Street, Child Okeford, Blanford Forum, Dorset DT11 8EH (01258 863691)

Fostering Network, 87 Blackfriars Road, London SE1 8HA (020 7620 6400; Helpline 020 7620 2100 – open Mon-Fri 12.30-4pm; Information Line 020 7261 1884 – open Wed-Fri 12-3pm)

Foundations, Bleaklow House, Howard Town Mill, Glossop SK13 8HT (01457 891909) *Advice for home owners or private sector tenants who are older, disabled or on low income on repairing, improving, maintaining or adapting their home.*

Friends of Fashion Services, The Greenfield Centre, Green Lane, Baildon BD17 5JS (01274 597487) *Made-to-measure service. Moving to a new address in early 2005, but will be able to collect post from the above address.*

G

Gauchers Association, 25 West Cottages, London NW6 1RJ (020 7433 1121) *Provides information on Gauchers disease to families and doctors.*

Gemma, BM Box 5700, London WC1N 3XX *National friendship network of disabled and non-disabled lesbian and bisexual women.*

Gingerbread, 7 Sovereign Close, London E1W 3HW (020 7488 9300; Advice Line 0800 018 4318) *Support network for lone parent families.*

GLAD (Greater London Action on Disability) – see page 272.

Guillain-Barre Syndrome Support Group, c/o Lincolnshire County Council, Council Offices, Eastgate, Sleaford, Lincolnshire NG34 7EB (01529 304615)

H

3H Fund (Help the Handicapped Holiday), 147a Camden Road, Tunbridge Wells, Kent TN1 2RA (01892 547474) *Organises six holidays a year for physically disabled people and runs a UK holiday grant programme for people with any disability, given sufficient funds.*

Haemophilia Society, First Floor, Petersham House, 57a Hatton Garden, London EC1N 8JG (020 7831 1020; Helpline 0800 018 6068)

Headlines – The Cranio Facial Support Group, 128 Beesmoor Road, Frampton Cotterell, Bristol BS36 2JP (01454 850557) *Information, advice, support, and contact for people and their families having or dealing with Craniosynostosis and associated conditions, including Apert, Crouzon, Pfeiffer, Cloverleaf Skull, Saethre-Chotzen and Muenke syndromes, and Single or Multi-Suture Craniosyntosis.*

Headway – The Brain Injury Association, 4 King Edward Court, King Edward Street, Nottingham NG1 1EW (0115 924 0800; Helpline 0808 800 2244) *Help, information and support for people with head injuries, their families and carers.*

Hearing Concern, 4th Floor, 275-281 King Street, Hammersmith, London W6 9LZ (020 8233 2929; Textphone 020 8233 2934; Helpdesk Voice and Textphone 0845 074 4600) *Self-help clubs, advisory and information service for deaf and hard-of-hearing people.*

Heart Foundation, British, 14 Fitzhardinge Street, London W1H 6DH (020 7935 0185)

Help the Aged, 207-221 Pentonville Road, London N1 9UZ (020 7278 1114; SeniorLine 0808 800 6565) *Free advice and information for older people and their carers about benefits, community and residential care.*

HoDis (National Disabled Persons Housing Service), 17 Priory Street, York YO1 6ET (01904 653888) *Promoting housing resources for disabled people in the UK, including provision of local disability housing services. Referrals* *preferred by email or letter.*

Holiday Homes Trust, Scouts, Gilwell Park, Chingford, London E4 7QW (020 8433 7290) *Low-cost, self-catering holidays for disabled and disadvantaged people on fully commercial holiday parks (no scouting connection necessary).*

Home Care Association, UK, 42b Banstead Road, Carshalton Beeches, Surrey SM5 3NW (020 8288 1551) *Professional association for domiciliary care agencies. Provides lists of local agencies.*

Home Farm Trust Ltd, Merchants House, Wapping Road, Bristol BS1 4RW (0117 930 2600) *Provides a range of services for people with learning difficulties including residential care, supported living, supported employment, advocacy and family carer support service.*

Homeless Link, 1st Floor, 10-13 Rushworth Street, London SE1 0RB (020 7960 3010) *Represents more than 700 agencies working with homeless people across England and Wales.*

Huntington's Disease Association, 108 Battersea High Street, London SW11 3HP (020 7223 7000) *Support to families and professionals affected by Huntington's disease.*

Hydrocephalus – see *ASBAH*

Hyperactive Children's Support Group, 71 Whyke Lane, Chichester, West Sussex PO19 7PD (01243 551313)

I

I CAN Charity, 4 Dyer's Buildings, Holborn, London EC1N 2QP (0845 225 4071) *Helps children across the UK with communication difficulties.*

IA (The Ileostomy and Internal Pouch Support Group), Peverill House, 1-5 Mill Road, Ballyclare, Co. Antrim BT39 9DR (028 9334 4043; Freephone 0800 0184 724) *Helps people return to active lives following surgery for removal of the colon. Local groups UK-wide.*

IBS Network, Moving to new address – ring for details (0114 261 1531; Helpline 01543 492 192 – open Mon-Fri 6-8pm and Sat 10am-12pm) *Provides a comprehensive support service for the self-management and long-term management solution of IBS (irritable bowel syndrome). Helpline answered by IBS specialist nurses.*

Immigrants, Joint Council for the Welfare of, 115 Old Street, London EC1V 9RT (020 7251 8708; Advice Line for individuals 020 7251 8706 – Tue and Thu 2-5pm) *Campaigns for justice in immigration, nationality and refugee law and policy.*

Incapacity Action, 104 Cornwallis Circle, Whitstable, Kent CT5 1DT *Campaigning for benefits for disabled people. Send sae for information.*

Independent Living, National Centre for, 250 Kennington Lane, London SE11 5RD (020 7587 1663; Textphone 020 7587 1177) *Provides information, consultancy and training on personal assistance and direct payments.*

Independent Living Alternatives, Trafalgar House, Grenville Place, London NW7 3SA (020 8906 9265) *Support and advice on employing personal assistants.*

Independent Living Fund, PO Box 7525, Nottingham NG2 4ZT (0845 601 8815; Textphone 0845 601 8816) *A government-funded trust to help severely disabled people aged 16-65 pay for personal or domestic care, on top of social services provision.*

J

JAMI (Jewish Association for the Mentally Ill), 16A North End Road, London NW11 7PH (020 8458 2223)

JCWI – see *Immigrants, Joint Council for the Welfare of*

Jewish Blind and Disabled, 35 Langstone Way, Mill Hill East, Bittacy Hill, London NW7 1GT (020 8371 6611) *Sheltered housing for visually impaired, blind and disabled people.*

John Grooms, 50 Scrutton Street, London EC2A 4XQ (020 7452 2000) *Residential and nursing care, housing and holidays for people with physical disabilities.*

K

Kidney Patient Association, British, Bordon, Hampshire GU35 9JZ (01420 472021/2) *Financial help and advice.*

Kids, 49 Mecklenburgh Square, London WC1N 2NY (020 7520 0405) *Provides services for children with special needs and disabilities, including adventure playgrounds, home-based learning, respite care, family support and information.*

L

Laryngectomy Clubs, National Association of (NALC), Ground Floor, 6 Rickett Street, London SW6 1RU (020 7381 9993)

Law centres, see pages 276-277

Law Centres Federation, Duchess House, 18-19 Warren Street, London W1T 5LR (020 7387 8570) *Information on your nearest law centre.*

Learning Difficulties – Values into Action, Oxford House, Derbyshire Street, London E2 6HG (020 7729 5436) *Campaigns for the right of people with learning difficulties to live ordinary lives in the community.*

Learning Disabilities, British Institute of (BILD), Campion House, Green Street, Kidderminster, Worcestershire DY10 1JL (01562 723010) *Provides education, training, information, publications, journals, membership services, research and consultancy for people with learning disabilities.*

Learning Disabilities, The Foundation for People with, 83 Victoria Street, London SW1H 0HW (020 7802 0300)

Leonard Cheshire, 30 Millbank, London SW1P 4QD (020 7802 8200) *Provides a wide range of support services to disabled people throughout the UK.*

Leukaemia Research Fund, Correspondence: 43 Great Ormond Street, London WC1N 3JJ, Walk-in: 39-40 Eagle Street, London WC1R 4TH (020 7405 0101) *Booklets on leukaemia and related blood cancers.*

Liberty (The National Council for Civil Liberties), 21 Tabard Street, London SE1 4LA (020 7403 3888; Human Rights Legal Advice Line 0845 123 2307 – open Mon and Thur 6.30-8.30pm, Wed 12.30-2.30pm)

Limbless Association, Rehabilitation Centre, Roehampton Lane, London SW15 5PR (020 8788 1777)

Limbless Ex-Service Men's Association, British (BLESMA), Frankland Moore House, 185-187 High Road, Chadwell Heath, Romford, Essex RM6 6NA (020 8590 1124)

Listening Books, 12 Lant Street, London SE1 1QH (020 7407 9417) *A postal library of audio books for adults and children who can't read due to disability or illness.*

Long-Term Medical Conditions Alliance (LMCA), Unit 202, 16 Baldwins Gardens, London EC1N 7RJ (020 7813 3637) *Aims to bring together national voluntary organisations which want to meet the needs of people with long-term medical conditions.*

Lupus UK, St James House, Eastern Road, Romford, Essex RM1 3NH (01708 731251) *Self-help and fundraising.*

M

Macfarlane Trust, Alliance House, 12 Caxton Street, London SW1H 0QS (020 7808 1170; Fax 020 7808 1169) *Provision of grants and non-financial services to people infected with HIV through treatment with contaminated blood products.*

Macmillan Cancer Relief, 89 Albert Embankment, London SE1 7UQ (020 7840 7840; Macmillan CancerLine 0808 808 2020) *Information on cancer support services, including Macmillan nurses, local self-help groups; Macmillan grants for patients in financial need; advice on other sources of financial help for people affected by cancer.*

Manic Depression Fellowship, Castle Works, 21 St George's Road, London SE1 6ES (020 7793 2600) *User-led mental health charity working to enable people affected by manic depression (bi-polar affective disorder) to take control of their lives.*

Maternity Alliance, Unit 3.3, 2-6 Northburgh Street, London EC1V 0AY (020 7490 7639; Information line 020 7490 7638) *Pressure group, advice and information on maternity rights at work and benefits.*

ME (Myalgic Encephalomyelitis), Action for, PO Box 1302, Wells, Somerset BA5 1YE (0845 123 2380)
ME Association, The, 4 Top Angel, Buckingham Industrial Park, Buckingham MK18 1TH (ME Connect 0870 444 1835 – open every day 10-12am, 2-4pm & 7-9pm)
Medic Alert Foundation, 1 Bridge Wharf, 156 Caledonian Road, London N1 9UU (Freephone 0800 581 420) *Provides emergency medical identification bracelets or necklets for people with hidden medical conditions or allergies, supported by 24-hr emergency line.*
Mencap Society, Royal, 123 Golden Lane, London EC1Y 0RT (020 7454 0454)
Meningitis Trust, The, Fern House, Bath Road, Stroud, Gloucestershire GL5 3TJ (01453 768000; 24-hour Helpline 0845 600 0800)
Mental After Care Association (MACA), 1st Floor, Lincoln House, 296-302 High Holborn, London WC1V 7JH (020 7061 3400) *Community and hospital-based services for people with mental health needs.*
Mental Health Act Commission, Maid Marian House, 56 Houndsgate, Nottingham NG1 6BG (0115 943 7100) *Special health authority safeguarding the rights of people detained under the Mental Health Act.*
Mental Health Foundation, Sea Containers House, 9th Floor, 20 Upper Ground, London SE1 9QB (020 7803 1100; Fax 020 803 1111)
Migraine Action Association, Unit 6, Oakley Hay Lodge Business Park, Great Folds Road, Great Oakley, Northants NN18 9AS (01536 461333) *Research, newsletter, leaflets, free information service.*
Migraine Trust, 2nd Floor, 55-56 Russell Square, London WC1B 4HP (020 7436 1336) *Information, helpline, factsheets, newsletter and educational service.*
Mind (The National Association of Mental Health), Granta House, 15-19 Broadway, London E15 4BQ (020 8519 2122; Mind Info Line 0845 766 0163 – open Mon-Fri 9.15am-5.15pm) *Mental health information service.*
Mobility Centre, Queen Elizabeth's Foundation, Damson Way, Fountain Drive, Carshalton, Surrey SM5 4NR (020 8770 1151) *Free information service, assessments for car drivers, passengers and wheelchair users. Driving tuition and residential accommodation.*
Motability, Goodman House, Station Approach, Harlow, Essex CM20 2ET (0845 456 4566) *The Motability scheme allows you to lease or buy a car, or a powered wheelchair or scooter, by using the higher rate mobility component of your disability living allowance or your war pensions' mobility supplement.*
Motor Neurone Disease Association, PO Box 246, Northampton NN1 2PR (01604 250505; Helpline 08457 626262)
Mucopolysaccharide Diseases, The Society for, 46 Woodside Road, Amersham, Buckinghamshire HP6 6AJ (01494 434156) *Support, advocacy and help for families.*
Multiple Sclerosis Resource Centre, 7 Peartree Business Centre, Peartree Road, Stanway, Colchester, Essex CO3 0JN (01206 505444; MS 24-hour counselling service 0800 783 0518 then press '1' to access) *Information, bi-monthly 'New Pathways' magazine, benefits advice, counselling by phone.*
Multiple Sclerosis Society of Great Britain and Northern Ireland, MS National Centre, 372 Edgware Road, London NW2 6ND (020 8438 0700; Helpline 0808 800 8000 – open 9am-9pm)
Muscular Dystrophy Campaign, 7-11 Prescott Place, London SW4 6BS (020 7720 8055)
Myasthenia Gravis Association, Central Office, Keynes House, Chester Park, Alfreton Road, Derby DE21 4AS (01332 290219)

N

Narcolepsy Association (UK), Craven House, 1st Floor, 121 Kingsway, London WC2B 6PA (0845 450 0394) *Support, information and guidance to those affected and their families.*
National Association of Citizens' Advice Bureaux (NACAB) – see *Citizens' Advice*
NCH, 85 Highbury Park, London N5 1UD (020 7704 7000; Helpline 0845 7626 579) *Community and residential projects for children with disabilities.*
NCVO – see *Voluntary Organisations, National Council of*
Neurodisability Service, Great Ormond Street Hospital NHS Trust, Wolfson Centre, Mecklenburgh Square, London WC1N 2AP (020 7837 7618) *Assessment and advice on children with complex neuro-developmental problems.*
Neurofibromatosis Association, The, Quayside House, 38 High Street, Kingston upon Thames KT1 1HL (020 8439 1234; Fax 020 8439 1200)
Norwood, Broadway House, 80-82 The Broadway, Stanmore, Middlesex HA7 4HB (020 8954 4555 – Mon-Thur all day, Fri am) *Services for children, families and adults coping with learning and physical disabilities and social disadvantage.*
Not Forgotten Association, 2 Grosvenor Gardens, London SW1W 0DH (020 7730 2400) *Services for disabled ex-service people, TVs, holidays, entertainment and outings.*
NSPCC (National Society for the Prevention of Cruelty to Children), Weston House, 42 Curtain Road, London EC2A 3NH (020 7825 2500) Helpline: 0808 800 5000 Helpline Textphone: 0800 056 0566; Welsh Helpline: 0808 100 12524; Bengali: 0800 096 7714; Gujarati: 0800 096 7715; Hindi: 0800 096 7716;Punjabi: 0800 096 7717; Urdu: 0800 096 7718 *Runs a network of child protection services and programmes.*

O

Occupational and Environmental Diseases Association (OEDA), Mitre House, 66 Abbey Road, Bush Hill Park, Enfield EN1 2QN (020 8360 8490) *Asbestos research and information.*
One Parent Families, 255 Kentish Town Road, London NW5 2LX (020 7428 5400; Helpline 0800 018 5026)
Organic Acidaemias UK, Mrs E Priddy, 5 Saxon Road, Ashford, Middlesex TW15 1QL (01784 245989) *Arranges contacts between families of children with organic acidaemias.*
Osteoporosis Society, National, Camerton, Bath BA2 0PJ (01761 471771; Helpline 0845 450 0230 – Mon-Fri 10am-3pm)

P

Paget's Disease, National Association for the Relief of, 323 Manchester Road, Walkden, Worsley, Manchester M28 3HH (0161 799 4646)
Pain Society, The British, 21 Portland Place, London W1B 1PY (020 7631 8870)
Parkinson's Disease Society of the UK, 215 Vauxhall Bridge Road, London SW1V 1EJ (020 7931 8080)
Parents for Inclusion, Unit 2, 70 South Lambeth Road, London SW8 1RL (Freephone Inclusion Helpline 0800 652 3145) *For parents who want their disabled children included in mainstream education. Support groups for parents with early years and school-age children, and Planning Positive training.*
Partially Sighted Society, Queens Road, Doncaster, South Yorks DN1 2NX, or PO Box 322, Doncaster DN1 2XA (01302 323132)
Patients' Association, The, PO Box 935, Harrow, Middlesex HA1 3YJ (020 8423 9111; Helpline 0845 608 4455) *Help and advice for patients. Leaflets and self-help directory available.*
Pensions Advisory Service (OPAS), 11 Belgrave Road, London SW1V 1RB (0845 601 2923) *Free help to people with personal, occupational or state pension queries.*
People First, 3rd Floor, 299 Kentish Town Road, London NW5 2TJ (020 7485 6660) *Independent self-advocacy organisation run by and for people with learning difficulties. Send sae for details.*
PHAB England, Summit House, 50 Wandle Road, Croydon CR0 1DF (020 8667 9443) *Clubs and holidays to bring disabled and able-bodied people together on equal terms.*
Polio Fellowship, British, Eagle Office Centre, The Runway, South Ruislip, Middlesex HA4 6SE (Freephone 0800 018 0586)
Prader-Willi Syndrome Association (UK), 125a London Road, Derby DE1 2QQ (01332 365676; Helpline 01332 360400)
Premenstrual Syndrome, National Association for (NAPS), 41 Old

Road, East Peckham, Kent TN12 5AP (0870 777 2178; Helpline 0870 777 2177)

Primary Immunodeficiency Association, Alliance House, 12 Caxton Street, London SW1H 0QS (020 7976 7640) *Information on treatment and care of primary immunodeficiencies and advice on benefits.*

Psoriasis Association, Milton House, 7 Milton Street, Northampton NN2 7JG (01604 711129; Local rate number 0845 676 0076)

Psychiatric Rehabilitation Association, Bayford Mews, Bayford Street, London E8 3SF (020 8985 3570; 24-hour answerphone 020 8985 3570) *Provides a range of services to people recovering from long-term mental health problems.*

Q

QUIT, Ground Floor, 211 Old Street, London EC1V 9NR (020 7251 1551; Quitline 0800 002200 – Mon-Sun 9am-9pm) *Help for those wanting to, or those helping someone else to, quit smoking.*

R

Racial Equality, Commission for (CRE), St Dunstan's House, 201-211 Borough High Street SE1 1GZ (020 7939 0000)

RADAR (Royal Association for Disability and Rehabilitation), 12 City Forum, 250 City Road, London EC1V 8AF (020 7250 3222; Textphone 020 7250 4119) *National disability campaigning and information service.*

Rathbone's Special Education Advice Line, 4th Floor, Churchgate House, 56 Oxford Street, Manchester M1 6EU (National 08707 461045; Advice Line 0800 917 6790; Parents who speak Urdu, Punjabi, Gujarati, Bengali and Hindi can ring the Advice Line) *Provides advice on special needs education to parents of children with learning difficulties.*

Raynaud's and Scleroderma Association, 112 Crewe Road, Alsager, Cheshire ST7 2JA (01270 872776) *Support, advice, newsletters, publications.*

Reach, National Co-ordinator, PO Box 54, Helston TR13 8WD (0845 130 6225) *Advice and information for children with hand or arm deficiency.*

Real Life Options, Churchill House, 29 Mill Hill Road, Pontefract, West Yorkshire WF8 4HY (01977 781800) *Care homes, supported living, outreach and short breaks for people with severe learning disabilities, within Northern England, Nottinghamshire, North London, Fife, Angus and Glasgow.*

Refugee Action, The Old Fire Station, 150 Waterloo Road, London SE1 8SB (020 7654 7700)

Refugee Legal Centre, 153-157 Commercial Road, London E1 2DA (020 7780 3200; Advice 020 7780 3220; Detention Line 0800 592398)

REMAP, Mary-Ann Mitchell, National Organiser, D9 Chaucer Business Park, Kemsing, Sevenoaks, Kent TN15 6YU (0845 130 0456) *Makes or adapts aids for disabled people when not commercially available, at no charge to the disabled person.*

Remploy Ltd, Stonecourt, Siskin Drive, Coventry CV3 4FJ (0845 601 5878; Textphone 0845 600 9228) *The UK's leading provider of employment opportunities for disabled people.*

Restricted Growth Association, RGA Office, PO Box 4744, Dorchester DT2 9FA (01308 898445) *Information and support for those affected by restricted growth.*

Rethink (National Schizophrenia Fellowship), 30 Tabernacle Street, London EC2A 4DD (0845 456 0455; Advice Line 020 8974 6814 – open Tues and Thur 10am-1pm) *Free pack available.*

Retinitis Pigmentosa Society, British, PO Box 350, Buckingham MK18 1GZ (01280 821334; 0845 123 2354)

Retirement Pensions Associations, National Federation of (Pensioners Voice), Thwaites House, Railway Road, Blackburn, Lancashire BB1 5AX (01254 52606)

Rett Syndrome Association UK, 113 Friern Barnet Road, London N11 3EU (0870 770 3266; 020 8361 5161) *Provides information, advice and support to parents, carers, siblings and professionals involved with a child or adult who has Rett Syndrome.*

Ricability, 30 Angel Gate, City Road, London EC1V 2PT (020 7427 2460; Textphone 020 7247 2469) *An independent research charity that publishes free, unbiased consumer guides for disabled people.*

Riding for the Disabled Association, Lavinia Norfolk House, Avenue 'R', Stoneleigh Park, Warwickshire CV8 2LY (0845 658 1082)

Roadpeace, PO Box 2579, London NW10 3PW (020 8838 5102; Helpline 0845 450 0355) *The national charity for road traffic victims. Provides vital support, information and advocacy for bereaved and injured.*

Royal Air Forces Association, 117½ Loughborough Road, Leicester, LE4 5ND (0116 266 5224) *Providing welfare support to serving and former RAF personnel and dependants.*

Royal National Institute for Deaf People (RNID) – see *Deaf People, Royal National Institute for*

Royal National Institute of the Blind (RNIB) – see *Blind, Royal National Institute of the*

S

St Dunstan's for Blind ex-Service Men and Women, 12-14 Harcourt Street, London W1H 4HD (020 7723 5021) *An independent future for blind ex-Service men and women.*

St Loye's Foundation for Training Disabled People for Employment, Fairfield House, Topsham Road, Exeter, Devon EX2 6EP (01392 255428) *Residential assessment, vocational training and employment placement.*

SANE, 1st Floor, Cityside House, 40 Adler Street, London E1 1EE (020 7375 1002; SANELINE 0845 767 8000 – open noon-2am) *Helpline providing information and support for anyone affected by mental health problems.*

Schizophrenia Association of Great Britain, Bryn Hyfryd, The Crescent, Bangor, Gwynedd LL57 2AG (01248 354048) *Helpline and free information packs including nutritional advice.*

Schizophrenia, National Fellowship – see *Rethink*

Scoliosis Research Trust – see *Arise*

Scope PO Box 833, Milton Keynes, Buckinghamshire MK12 5NY (Cerebral Palsy Helpline 0808 800 3333)

Sense, The National Deafblind & Rubella Association, 11-13 Clifton Terrace, Finsbury Park, London N4 3SR (020 7272 7774; Textphone 020 7272 9648; Fax 020 7272 6012)

Sequal Trust, The, 3 Ploughmans Corner, Wharf Road, Ellesmere, Shropshire SY12 0EJ (01691 624222) *Assessment and provision of communication aids.*

Shaftesbury Society, 16 Kingston Road, London SW19 1JZ (020 8239 5555; 0845 330 6033) *Residential centres, day care centres, supported living, schools and colleges.*

Shaw Trust, Shaw House, Epsom Square, White Horse Business Park, Trowbridge, Wiltshire BA14 0XJ (01225 716350; Minicom 0845 769 7288) *Job preparation, job finding, job support, job retention and job creation.*

Shelter (National Campaign for Homeless People), 88 Old Street, London EC1V 9HU (020 7505 2000; Freephone Helpline 0808 800 4444) *Provides information, advice and advocacy to homeless and badly housed people.*

Sickle Cell Society, 54 Station Road, London NW10 4UA (020 8961 7795; 020 8961 4006) *Information, counselling and caring for those with sickle cell disorders and their families.*

Skill – National Bureau for Students with Disabilities, Chapter House, 18-20 Crucifix Lane, London SE1 3JW (Voice and Textphone 020 7450 0620; Helpline, Voice 0800 328 5050 – open Tues 11.30am-1.30pm, Thur 1.30-3.30pm; Textphone 0800 068 2422) *Aims to develop opportunities for people with disabilities and learning difficulties in post-16 employment education and training.*

Skin Foundation, British, 4 Fitzroy Square, London W1T 5HQ (020 7383 0266)

Snowdon Award Scheme, The, 22 City Business Centre, 6 Brighton Road, Horsham, West Sussex RH13 5BB (01403 211 252) *Grants to help physically* *disabled students with the extra costs of higher or further education and training.*

Social Workers, British Association of (BASW),16 Kent Street, Birmingham B5 6RD (0121 622 3911) *BASW is the largest professional association representing social work and social workers in the UK.*

Solicitors with Disabilities, Group for (GSD), The Law Society, 114 Chancery Lane, London WC2A 1PL (020 7320 5793) *Aims to achieve equality for disabled people, solicitors and their clients. Calls taken from professionals only.*

Spastics Society – see *Scope*

Speakability, 1 Royal Street, London SE1 7LL (020 7261 9572; Helpline 0808 808 9572) *Information, advice and support for people who have aphasia or dyphasia (difficulty communicating after stroke or brain injury).*

Special Education Advice, Independent Panel for, 6 Carlow Mews, Woodbridge, Suffolk IP12 1EA (01394 380518; Advice 0800 018 4016 – Mon-Thur 10am-4pm, Fri 10am-1pm) *Free and independent advice and support to parents of children with special educational needs.*

Speech Impaired Children, Association For All – see *Afasic*

Spina Bifida – see *ASBAH*

Spinal Injuries Association, Suite J, 3rd Floor, Acorn House, 387-391 Midsummer Boulevard, Central Milton Keynes MK9 3HP (0845 678 6633; Freephone 0800 980 0501)

Spinal Muscular Atrophy, Jennifer Trust for, Elta House, Birmingham Road, Stratford-upon-Avon, Warwickshire CV37 0AQ (0870 774 3651)

SSAFA Forces Help, Special Needs and Disability Advisor, 19 Queen Elizabeth Street, London SE1 2LP (020 7403 8783; Special Needs and Disability Advisor 020 7463 9234)

Stammering Association, The British, 15 Old Ford Road, London E2 9PJ (020 8983 1003; Helpline 0845 603 2001 – open Mon-Thur 10am-1pm, 2-4pm and 7-9pm)

Stroke Association, The, Stroke House, 240 City Road, London EC1Y 2PR (020 7566 0300; National Stroke Helpline 0845 303 3100) *Information, support, publications, regional centre details for local stroke clubs, welfare grants.*

Strokes, Different, 9 Canon Harnett Court, Wolverton Mill, Milton Keynes MK12 5NF (0845 130 7172) *Support for younger stroke survivors.*

Students, National Union of, Nelson Mandela House, 461 Holloway Road, London N7 6LZ (020 7272 8900)

T

Terrence Higgins Trust, 52-54 Gray's Inn Road, London WC1X 8JU (020 7831 0330; Helpline 0845 1221 200 – Mon-Fri 10am-10pm, Sat & Sun 12-6pm) *Legal, welfare and housing advice and support for people with HIV and AIDS.*

Thalassaemia Society, UK, 19 The Broadway, Southgate, London N14 6PH (020 8882 0011; Freephone 0800 731 1109) *Education, information, counselling. Publicity available in Greek, Italian, Chinese, Turkish, Arabic, Hebrew, Portuguese and Asian languages.*

Thalidomide Society, The, 19 Central Avenue, Pinner, Middlesex HA5 5BT (020 8868 5309) *Support and information for people with thalidomide and similar impairments.*

Thrive (formerly Society for Horticultural Therapy), Geoffrey Udall Centre, Beech Hill, Reading RG7 2AT (0118 988 5688) *National charity that uses gardening to improve the lives of disabled, disadvantaged and older people.*

Tinnitus Association, British, Ground Floor, Unit 5, Acorn Business Park, Woodseats Close, Sheffield S8 0TB (0114 250 9922; Freephone 0800 018 0527) *Provides information, promotes self-help, raises awareness and funds research.*

Tracheo-Oesophageal Fistula Support, St George's Centre, 91 Victoria Road, Netherfield, Nottingham NG4 2NN (0115 961 3092) *Helping children born unable to swallow.*

Tripscope, The Vassall Centre, Gill Avenue, Bristol BS16 2QQ (Voice and Text 08457 585641) *Advice and information on planning or coping with transport in the UK and abroad.*

Tuberous Sclerosis Association, PO Box 9644, Bromsgrove B61 0FP (01527 871898) *Provides support and information and promotes research.*

Turning Point, New Loom House, 101 Backchurch Lane, London E1 1LU (020 7702 2300) *Help with alcohol, drugs, mental health and learning disabilities.*

Typetalk, John Wood House, Glacier Building, Harrington Road, Brunswick Business Park, Liverpool L3 4DF (0151 709 9494; Helpline Voice 0800 7311888; Text 0800 500888. To make a call dial 18001 [text] or 18002 [hearing] plus full telephone number. Dial 18000 for emergency operator [text only]) *Telephone relay service for deaf, deafblind and speech impaired people.*

U

Urostomy Association, Central Office, 18 Foxglove Avenue, Uttoxeter, Staffordshire, ST14 8UN (0870 770 7931) *Support for people who are about to have or who have had surgery for urinary diversion of any kind.*

V

Vision Homes Association, Quadrant West, 210-222 Hagley Road West, Oldbury, West Midlands B68 0NP (0121 434 4644) *Provides 24-hour support for people with visual impairments and additional disabilities.*

Vitalise (formerly Winged Fellowship Trust), 12 City Forum, 250 City Road, London EC1V 8AF (0845 345 1972) *National charity providing breaks for disabled and visually impaired people and their carers.*

Voluntary Organisations, National Council of (NCVO), Regent's Wharf, 8 All Saints' Street, London N1 9RL (020 7713 6161; Helpline 0800 2798 798; Helpline Textphone 0800 018 8111)

W

Williams Syndrome Foundation (incorporating Infantile Hypercalcaemia), 161 High Street, Tonbridge, Kent TN9 1BX (01732 365152)

Wireless for the Blind Fund, British, Gabriel House, 34 New Road, Chatham, Kent ME4 4QR (01634 832501) *Provides radios/cassette players to registered blind and registered partially-sighted people.*

Women, Rights of, 52-54 Featherstone Street, London EC1Y 8RT (020 7251 6575/6; Advice 020 7251 6577; Sexual Violence Line (London only) 020 7251 8887) *Provides free confidential legal advice to women living in England and Wales.*

Women's Aid Federation, England, PO Box 391, Bristol BS99 7WS (0117 944 4411; 24-hour Helpline 0808 2000 247) *Campaigns to end violence against women and children. Provides advice and information or referral to a refuge.*

Women's Alcohol Centre, 66a Drayton Park, London N5 1ND (020 7226 4581) *Alcohol-focused one-to-one sessions, group work, complementary therapies, residential rehabilitation, alcohol assessment and referral to appropriate agencies. No wheelchair access.*

Women's Health, 52-54 Featherstone Street, London EC1Y 8RT (Helpline 0845 125 5254 – Mon-Fri 9.30am-1.30pm; Textphone 020 7490 5489) *Information and support on gynaecological and sexual health issues.*

WRVS, Garden House, Milton Hill, Steventon, Abingdon, Oxfordshire OX13 6AD (01235 442900) *Provides care and practical help for socially isolated elderly people, often through referral from social services.*

London-wide

Artsline, 54 Chalton Street, London NW1 1HS (Tel and Textphone 020 7388 2227) *Advice and information service for disabled people on access to London's arts and entertainment venues, and tourist attractions.*

Black Disabled People's Association, PO Box 7610, London NW6 5BN (020 8933 3826) *Independent living and research of and for black disabled people.*

Blind, Metropolitan Society for

the, Lantern House, 102 Bermondsey Street, London SE1 3UB (020 7403 6184) *Home visiting, audio equipment, small grants, advice and advocacy.*
Children with Cerebral Palsy, The Hornsey Trust for, Conductive Education Centre, 54 Muswell Hill, London N10 3ST (020 8444 7242) *Conductive education, advice and support for children with cerebral palsy up to age 7.*
DIAL, Local groups and members, see pages 274-276
Free Representation Unit (FRU), 6th Floor, Peer House, 289-293 High Holborn, London WC1V 7HZ (020 7611 9555) *Provides representation for employment and social security tribunals, criminal injuries compensation and limited immigration cases in the London area. Claimants must contact FRU via a Citizens Advice Bureau, law centre or other referral agency.*
Greater London Action on Disability (GLAD), 336 Brixton Road, London SW9 7AA (020 7346 5800; Textphone 020 7346 5811) *Information, publications, newsletter, training and campaigning.*
Law Centres, see pages 276-277
Kith and Kids, The Irish Centre, Pretoria Road, London N17 8DX (020 8801 7432) *Running holidays, weekends, friendship, family support and advocacy projects.*
Naz Project London, Palingswick House, 241 King Street, London W6 9LP (020 8741 1879) *HIV, AIDS and sexual health agency for South Asian, Middle Eastern, North African and Latin American communities.*
Parents for Children, 253-254 Upper Street, Islington, London N1 1RY (020 7288 4320; 0845 307 6653) *Specialist fostering and adoption agency, placing children with exceptional needs.*
Richard Dimbleby Cancer Information and Support Service, 2nd Floor, Lambeth Wing, St Thomas' Hospital, Lambeth Palace Road, London SE1 7EH (020 7188 5918) *Drop-in information service with psychological support and complementary therapies.*
Shape London, LVSRC, 356 Holloway Road, London N7 6PA (020 7619 6160; Textphone 020 7619 6161 – Mon-Fri 10am-6pm) *Disability arts agency, workshops, training, festivals, ticket scheme, deaf arts.*
Transport for All, 336 Brixton Road, London SW9 7AA (020 7737 2339; Fax 020 7737 2231) *Accessible travel information and assistance for the disabled and elderly.*
Women's Therapy Centre, 10 Manor Gardens, London N7 6JS (Admin 020 7263 7860; Appointments and referrals 020 7263 6200; Fax 020 7281 7879) *Provides individual and group psychotherapy for women of 18 and over. A limited number of spaces are reserved for women with disabilities.*

Northern Ireland

Age Concern, Northern Ireland, 3 Lower Crescent, Belfast BT7 1NR (028 9024 5729; Advice Line 028 9032 5055 – Mon-Fri 9.30am-1pm) *A voluntary organisation committed, through campaigning, community development and service provision, to improving the quality of life of all older people and promoting their rights as active, involved and equal citizens.*
Alzheimer's Society, NI Regional Office, 86 Eglantine Avenue, Belfast BT9 6EU (028 9066 4100)
Arthritis Care Northern Ireland, 115 Enkalon Business Park, 25 Randalstown Road, Antrim BT41 4LJ (028 9448 1380; Helpline 0808 800 4050) *Works on behalf of over 230,000 people in NI who are affected by arthritis. Provides services and support for people with all types of arthritis, their families and those who work with them.*
Blind, Royal National Institute for the, Northern Ireland, 40 Linenhall Street, Belfast BT2 8BA (028 9032 9373; Fax 028 9027 8119; National Helpline 0845 766 9999)
Carers Northern Ireland, 58 Howard Street, Belfast BT1 6PJ (028 9043 9843) *Free information for carers on all aspects of caring.*
Cedar Foundation, The, Malcolm Sinclair House, 31 Ulsterville Avenue, Belfast BT9 7AS (028 9066 6188) *Training, accommodation and support for people with physical disabilities.*
Chest, Heart and Stroke Association Northern Ireland, 22 Great Victoria Street, Belfast BT2 7LX (028 9032 0184; Helpline 0845 769 7299; Cardiac Liaison Sister Helpline 0845 6011 658)
Disability Action, Portside Business Park, 189 Airport Road West, Belfast BT3 9ED (028 9029 7880) *Aims to ensure disabled people attain their rights. Information and library service.*
Down's Syndrome Association Northern Ireland, Graham House, Knockbracken Healthcare Park, Saintfield Road, Belfast BT8 8BH (028 9070 4606)
Educational Guidance Services Adult (EGSA), 4th Floor, 40 Linenhall Street, Belfast BT2 8BA (028 9024 4274) *Connecting adults with learning.*
Extra Care for Elderly People, 11 Wellington Park, Belfast BT9 6DJ (028 9068 3273) *Domiciliary care for carers in most of Northern Ireland.*
Families in Contact, c/o Mrs Janice McKee, 6 Greycastle Manor, Belfast BT6 9QT (028 9079 4048) *Families with disabled children/young people supporting each other.*
Fibromyalgia Support (NI), 4 Springwell Drive, Groomsport, BT19 6JX (Helpline 0870 990 9220 – open Mon-Fri 10.30am-5pm) *Support and information on fibromyalgia.*
Help the Aged, Ascot House, Shaftesbury Square, Belfast, BT2 7DB (028 9023 0666; Senior Line 0808 808 7575 – Mon-Fri 9am-4pm) *Free advice and information for older people and their carers about benefits, community and residential care.*
Law Centres, see pages 276-277
Mencap in Northern Ireland, Segal House, 4 Annadale Avenue, Belfast BT7 3JH (028 9069 1351; Information Service 0845 7636 227 – 9.15am-5.15pm) *Mencap offers information, support and a range of services for children and adults with a learning disability, and campaigns for choice, opportunity and respect for people with a learning disability and their families.*
Meningitis Trust, PO Box 207, Newtownards BT23 8ZT (0845 6000 800 – open 24 hours)
Mental Health, Northern Ireland Association for, 80 University Street, Belfast BT7 1HE (028 9032 8474)
Multiple Sclerosis Society NI, The Resource Centre, 34 Annadale Avenue, Belfast BT7 3JJ (028 9080 2802)
Nation Union of Students (NUS-USI), 29 Bedford Street, Belfast BT2 7EJ (028 9024 4641)
PHAB (NI) Independent Living Limited, Jennymount Business Park, North Derby Street, Belfast BT15 3HN (028 9050 4800) *Quality housing and support for young people, and day care facilities.*
Polio Fellowship, Northern Ireland, Mrs Helen Chapman, 89 South Parade, Belfast BT7 2GN (028 9064 0586)
Shelter, Northern Ireland, 58 Howard Street, Belfast BT1 6RJ (028 9024 7752). Also at 13 Dock Street, Strabane BT82 8EG (028 7188 2145; Freephone 0800 028 6686) and 12b Foundry Lane, Omagh BT78 1ED (028 8225 9000)
Spina Bifida and Hydrocephalus, The Association for (ASBAH), NI Region, Graham House, Knockbracken Healthcare Park, Saintfield Road, Belfast BT8 8BH (028 9079 8878)
Women's Aid, Northern Ireland, 129 University Street, Belfast BT7 1HP (028 9024 9041; 24-hour Helpline 028 9033 1818)

Scotland

Age Concern Scotland, Leonard Small House, 113 Rose Street, Edinburgh EH2 3DT (0131 220 3345; Free Information Line 0800 00 99 66) *Factsheets on older people's issues.*
Alcohol Focus Scotland, 2nd Floor, 166 Buchanan Street, Glasgow G1 2LW (0141 572 6700) *Provides information and training on alcohol issues, and campaigns to influence alcohol policy.*
Alzheimer Scotland – Action on Dementia, 22 Drumsheugh Gardens, Edinburgh EH3 7RN (24-hr Freephone Helpline 0808 808 3000) *Wide range of information and support for people with dementia and their carers.*
Asbestos, Clydeside Action on, 245 High Street, Glasgow G4 0QR (0141 552 8852)
Autism, The Scottish Society for,

Hilton House, Alloa Business Park, Whins Road, Alloa FK10 3SA (01259 720044) *Provides services for people of all ages coping with autism in Scotland.*

Capability Scotland, Westerlea, 11 Ellersly Road, Edinburgh EH12 6HY (0131 313 5510) *Provides a wide range of services and support for disabled children and adults.*

Chest, Heart and Stroke Scotland, 65 North Castle Street, Edinburgh EH2 3LT (0131 225 6963; Advice Line 0845 077 6000 – Mon-Fri 9.30am-12pm and 1.30-4pm)

Child Poverty Action Group (CPAG) in Scotland, Unit 9, Ladywell Centre, 94 Duke Street, Glasgow G4 0UW (0141 552 3303; Advice line 0141 552 0552 – open Tue, Wed and Thur 10am-noon)

Children's Fund, Challenger, Cunningham Unit, Astley Ainslie Hospital, 133 Grange Loan, Edinburgh EH9 2HL (0131 537 9093) *Considers grants for anything not provided by statutory sources to physically disabled children under 18 living in Scotland.*

Crossroads (Scotland) – Caring for Carers, 24 George Square, Glasgow G2 1EG (0141 226 3793; Carers Information and Support Line 0141 353 6504 – Mon-Thur 9am-5pm and Fri 9am-4pm available in Glasgow area) *Provides respite relief for carers.*

Deafness, Scottish Council on, Central Chambers Suite 62, 93 Hope Street, Glasgow G2 6LD (0141 248 2474; Textphone 0141 248 2477; Fax 0141 248 2479)

Deafblind Scotland, 21 Alexandra Avenue, Lenzie, Glasgow G66 5BG (Voice and Textphone 0141 777 6111; Helpline 0800 132320; Fax 0141 775 3311)

DIAL, Local groups and members, see pages 274-276

Disability Information Service, Dundas Resource Centre, Oxgang Road, Grangemouth FK3 9EF (Voice and Textphone 01324 504304) *Advice and information service for people with disabilities, carers and professionals in the Falkirk Council area.*

Disability Sport, Scottish, Caledonia House, South Gyle, Edinburgh EH12 9DQ (0131 317 1130; Fax 0131 317 1075)

Disablement Income Group Scotland, 5 Quayside Street, Edinburgh EH6 6EJ (0131 555 2811) *Free information and advice on benefits for disabled people and carers in Scotland.*

Down's Syndrome Scotland, 158-160 Balgreen Road, Edinburgh EH11 3AU (0131 313 4225)

Dyslexia Scotland, Stirling Business Centre, Wellgreen, Stirling FK8 2DZ (Helpline 0844 800 8484)

Earl Haig Fund Scotland, The, New Haig House, Logie Green Road, Edinburgh EH7 4HR (0131 557 2782); Suites 206 & 207, The Pentagon Centre, 36 Washington Street, Glasgow G3 8AZ (0141 221 8141) *Assists ex-service personnel and their dependants who reside in Scotland.*

Energy Action Scotland, Suite 4a, Ingram House, 227 Ingram Street, Glasgow G1 1DA (0141 226 3064) *Promotes affordable warmth and an end to fuel poverty.*

Epilepsy Scotland, 48 Govan Road, Glasgow G51 1JL (0141 427 4911; Freephone Helpline 0808 800 2200 – open Mon-Fri 10am-4pm, Thur 10am-6pm)

FABB Scotland, Norton Park, 57 Albion Road, Edinburgh EH7 5QY (0131 475 2313 – open Mon-Fri 10am-4pm) *Facilitating access and breaking barriers through leisure and education.*

Help the Aged, 11 Granton Square Edinburgh, EH5 1HX (0131 551 6331; National Senior Line 08008 800 6565) *Free advice and information for older people and their carers about benefits, community and residential care.*

Huntington's Association, Scottish, Thistle House, 61 Main Road, Elderslie PA5 9BA (01505 322245)

Law centres, see pages 276-277

Law Society of Scotland, 26 Drumsheugh Gardens, Edinburgh EH3 7YR (0131 226 7411) *Provides details of Scottish solicitors.*

Lead Scotland (Linking Education and Disability), Queen Margaret University College, Clerwood Terrace, Edinburgh EH12 8TS (0131 317 3439; Fax 0131 339 7198) *Supports disabled adults into learning.*

Meningitis Trust, PO box 19554, Renfrew PA4 0JD (0845 120 2123; 24-hr nurse-led Helpline 08455 6000 800) *24-hour support for those whose lives have been affected by meningitis.*

Mental Health, Scottish Association for, Cumbrae House, 15 Carlton Court, Glasgow G5 9JP (0141 568 7000)

Mental Health Foundation, 5th Floor, Merchants House, 30 George Square Glasgow G2 1EG (0141 572 0125) *A campaign organisation which also provides a range of information for people with mental health problems. (Not a drop-in office.)*

Mental Welfare Commission for Scotland, K Floor, Argyle House, 3 Lady Lawson Street, Edinburgh EH3 9SH (0131 222 6111) *Independent organisation to safeguard the rights of people with a mental illness or learning disability in Scotland.*

Mental Welfare Society, Ex-Services, Hollybush House, Hollybush, by Ayr KA6 7EA (01292 560214; 01292 560322)

Motor Neurone Disease Association, Scottish, 76 Firhill Road, Glasgow G20 7BA (0141 945 1077) *Provides care and support for people with motor neurone disease.*

Multiple Sclerosis Society Scotland, National Office, Ratho Park, 88 Glasgow Road, Ratho Station, Newbridge EH28 8PP (0131 335 4050; Fax 0131 335 4051; National Helpline 0808 800 8000)

National Union of Students Scotland, 29 Forth Street, Edinburgh EH1 3LE (0131 556 6598)

Options for Independence, British Red Cross, Alexandra House, 204 Bath Street, Glasgow G2 4HL (0141 332 9591) *Adults with physical disabilities – provides a range of residential and community support services to meet individual's independence objectives.*

PHACE Scotland, Top Floor, 134 Douglas Street, Glasgow G2 4HF (0141 332 38373838; Fax 0141 332 3755) and Grampian Service, 11 Waverley Place, Aberdeen AB10 1XH (0845 241 2151; Fax 0845 241 2152) *Provides practical and emotional support for people infected with or affected by HIV/AIDS.*

Red Cross Society, British (Head Office, Scotland), Alexandra House, 204 Bath Street, Glasgow G2 4HL (0141 332 9591) *Local branches provide medical equipment loans, transport, escort home from hospital, therapeutic care and domiciliary respite.*

Refugee Council, Scottish, 5 Cadogan Square (170 Blythswood Court) Glasgow G2 7PH (0141 248 9799; Helpline 0800 085 6087 – open Mon-Fri 9.30am-4.30pm)

Sense Scotland, 43 Middlesex Street, Glasgow G41 1EE (0141 429 0294)

Shelter Scotland, 4th Floor, Scotiabank House, 6 South Charlotte Street, Edinburgh EH2 4AW (0131 473 7170; 24-hour Freephone Shelterline 0808 800 4444)

Sign Language Interpreters, Scottish Association of, Donaldson's College, West Coates, Edinburgh EH12 5JJ (Voice and Text 0131 347 5601) *Holds register of interpreters for Scotland, and provides training.*

Spina Bifida Association, Scottish, 190 Queensferry Road, Edinburgh EH4 2BW (0131 332 0743; Family Support Service Helpline 0845 911 1112) *For people with spina bifida, hydrocephalus and allied disorders, their carers and families.*

Spinal Injuries Scotland, Festival Business Park, 150 Brand Street, Govan, Glasgow G51 1DH (0141 314 0056; Helpline 0141 314 0057)

Thistle Foundation, The, Niddrie Mains Road, Edinburgh EH16 4EA (0131 661 3366) *Accommodation and support for disabled people and their families.*

Turning Point Scotland, 54 Govan Road, Glasgow G51 1JL (0141 427 8200) *Support for people with drugs, alcohol and mental health problems, and learning disabilities.*

Women's Aid, Scottish, 2nd Floor, 132 Rose Street, Edinburgh EH2 3JD (0131 226 6606; 24-hr Scottish Domestic Abuse Helpline 0800 027 1234)

Wales

Agoriad Cyf, Porth Penrhyn, Bangor, Gwynedd LL57 4HN (01248 361392; Fax 01248 372050); Ground Floor Office, Swyddfeydd NFU, Dolgellau, Gwynedd LL40 2NJ (01341 421440); 1 Allt Salem, Pwllheli, Gwynedd LL53 5DU (01758 613015) *Providing training and support* *for disabled people to help them into employment in North Wales.*

Arts Disability Wales, Sbectrwm, The Old School, Bwlch Road, Fairwater, Cardiff CF5 3EF (Voice and Textphone 029 2055 1040)

ASBAH in Wales, 4 Llys y Fedwen, Parc Menai, Bangor, Gwynedd LL57 4BL (01248 671345) *Services to those with spina bifida and/or hydrocephalus.*

DIAL, Local groups and members, see pages 274-276

Disability Wales, Wernddu Court, Caerphilly Business Park, Van Road, Caerphilly CF83 3ED (029 2088 7325; Helpline 0800 731 6282 – Mon and Fri 10am-1pm) *National association of disability groups in Wales.*

Disablement Welfare Rights, Canolfan Lafan, 2 Glanrafon, Bangor, Gwynedd LL57 1LH (01248 352227) *Anglesey and Gwynedd only.*

Drugaid, 1A Bartlett Street, Caerphilly, CF83 1JS (029 2088 1000); 16 Clive Street, Caerphilly CF83 1GE (029 2086 8675); MIDAS, 2nd Floor Oldway House, Castle Street, Merthyr Tydfil CF47 8UX (01685 721991) *Counselling, information and support to drug and alcohol users.*

Help the Aged, 12 Cathedral Rd, Cardiff CF11 9LJ (029 2034 6550; Fax 029 2039 0898) *Free advice and information for older people and their carers about benefits, community and residential care. Major campaigner for older people's rights in Wales.*

Law centres, see pages 276-77

Manic Depression Fellowship Wales, 1 Palmyra Place, Newport NP20 4EJ (Helpline 08456 340 080 – Mon-Fri 9.30am-4pm) *User-led mental health charity working to enable people affected by manic depression (bi-polar affective disorder) to take control of their lives.*

Mencap Cymru, 31 Lambourne Crescent, Cardiff Business Park, Llanishen Cardiff CF14 5GF (029 2074 7588; Wales Learning Disability Helpline 0808 8000 300) *For support and information on a wide range of learning disability issues. Please contact the Wales Learning Disability Helpline.*

Meningitis Trust, PO Box 89, Carmarthen SA31 2YG (0845 120 4886; 24-hr nurse-led helpline 0845 6000 800)

National Union of Students, Wales, 13 Lambourne Crescent, Cardiff Business Park, Llanishen, Cardiff CF14 5GF (029 2037 5980)

Scope Cymru, Wales Area Office, The Wharf, Schooner Way, Cardiff CF10 4EU (029 2046 1703; CP National Helpline 0808 800 3333 – Mon-Fri 9am-9pm, Sat & Sun 2-6pm)

Shelter Cymru, 25 Walter Road, Swansea SA1 5NN (01792 469400; Shelterline 0808 800 4444) *Operating advice surgeries in all local authority areas.*

Shopmobility Newport, 193 Upper Dock Street, Newport, Gwent NP20 1DB (01633 673845) *Provides electrically powered wheelchairs, scooters and manual wheelchairs. Free loan of manually powered wheelchairs available within city centre.*

Wales Council for the Blind, 3rd Floor, Shand House, 20 Newport Road, Cardiff CF24 0DB (029 2047 3954)

Wales Council for the Deaf, Glenview House, Courthouse Street, Pontypridd CF37 1JY (01443 485687; Textphone 01443 485686)

DIAL groups and members

There are around 160 DIAL member organisations in the UK; and those listed below offer advice or case work in welfare benefits. (Listings start with the catchment area for the organisation.) For details of DIAL member organisations offering benefits information, or help with any other issue, please contact DIAL UK on 01302 310123.

England

Barnsley Metropolitan District – DIAL Barnsley, 9 Doncaster Road, Barnsley, South Yorkshire S70 1TH (01226 240273 – Mon-Thur 9am-5pm, Fri 9am-2pm)

Bath and North East Somerset – SWAN Advice Network, Leigh House, 1 Wells Hill, Radstock, Somerset BA3 3RN (01761 437176 – 10am-12pm)

Bedfordshire – Disability Resource Centre (Dunstable), Poynters House, Poynters Road, Dunstable, Bedfordshire LU5 4TP (01583 470900)

Blackpool, Wyre and Fylde – Disability Information & Support (Blackpool, Wyre & Fylde), 52 Clifton Street, Blackpool, Lancashire FY1 1JP (01253 625553 – 10am-4pm)

Blyth Valley – Blyth Valley Disabled Forum, The Eric Tollhurst Centre, 3-13 Quay Road, Blyth, Northumberland NE24 2AS (01670 364657)

Bradford Metropolitan District – Disability Advice Bradford, 103 Dockfield Road, Shipley, West Yorkshire BD17 7AR (01274 594173 – Mon-Thur 9.30am-12.15pm and 12.45pm-3.15pm, Fri 9.30am-2pm)

Brighton and Hove – Disability Advice Centre (Brighton & Hove), 6 Hove Manor, Hove Street, Hove, East Sussex BN3 2DF (01273 203016 – 10am-4pm)

Buckinghamshire – Bucks Disability Information Network, Brookside Centre, Station Way, Aylesbury, Buckinghamshire HP20 2SQ (01296 487924 – 10am-4pm)

Buckinghamshire (South) and Berkshire (North) – DIAL High Wycombe, Family Centre, Richardson Street West, High Wycombe, Buckinghamshire HP11 2SB (01494 442601 – Tues-Thur 10am-4pm)

Calderdale – Calderdale DART, Harrison House, 10 Harrison Road, Halifax, West Yorkshire HX1 2AF (01422 346040 – Mon, Tues & Thur 10am-4pm, Fri 10am-3pm)

Cambridgeshire (not Huntingdonshire) – Directions Plus, 1 Orwell Furlong, Cowley Road, Cambridge, Cambridgeshire CB4 0WY (01223 569600 – 10am-12.30pm and 1.30pm-4pm)

Carlisle and Eden – Disability Association Carlisle & Eden, Disability Information Centre, Regents Court, Kingmoor Business Park, Carlisle, Cumbria CA6 4SJ (0845 1249 300)

Cheshire & North Flintshire – DIAL House Chester, DIAL House, Hamilton Place, Chester, Cheshire CH1 2BH (01244 345655 – 10am-4pm)

Derby – Disability Direct, 227 Normanton Road, Derby, Derbyshire DE23 6UT (01332 299449 – 9.30am-4pm)

Doncaster – DIAL Doncaster, Unit 9, Shaw Wood Business Park, Shaw Wood Way, Doncaster, South Yorkshire DN2 5TB (01302 327800 – Mon-Fri 9.30am-4pm, Fri 9.30am-3pm)

Dorset (East) – Disability Wessex, Ground Floor, 5 Stratfield Faye, 22 Wellington Road, Bournemouth BH8 8JN (01202 300230 – 10am-4pm)

Essex – Essex Disabled People's Association, Moulsham Mill, Parkway, Chelmsford, Essex CM2 7PX (0870 8736 333)

Essex (South) – DIAL Basildon, 1st Floor, The Basildon Centre, St Martin's Square, Basildon, Essex SS14 1DL (0845 450 3001/3002 – 10am-4pm)

Hampshire (South East) – Frank Sorrell Centre, Prince Albert Road, Southsea, Hampshire PO4 9HR (02392 824853 – 10am-4pm)

Herefordshire – ABLE Hereford, The Warehouse, Coningsby Street, Hereford, Herefordshire HR1 2DY (01432 27770)

Hertfordshire – DISH (Disability Information Service Hertfordshire), 45 Grosvenor Road, St Albans, Hertfordshire AL1 3AW (0800 181067 – 10am-3pm)

Huntingdonshire – Disability Information Service Huntingdonshire, Pendrill Court, Papworth Everard, Cambridgeshire CB3 8UY (01480 830833 – 9.30am-2.30pm)

Ipswich – Ipswich Disabled Advice Bureau, 19 Tower Street, Ipswich, Suffolk IP1 3BE (01473 217313 – Tue-Fri 10am-2pm)

Kent (North) – DIAL Kent, 9a Gorrell Road, Whitstable, Kent CT5 1RN (01227 771155 – Mon, Tue, Wed 10am-2pm, Thur, Fri 10am-1pm)

Kent (North West) – DIAL North West Kent, Ground Floor, Cygnet House, 132 Windmill Street, Gravesend, Kent DA12 1BQ (01474 537666 – 11am-3pm)

Lancashire (West) – West Lancashire Disability Helpline, 49 Westgate, Sandy Lane, Skelmersdale, Lancashire WN8 8LP (0800 220676 – 24-hr answerphone)

Leeds metropolitan district – DIAL

Leeds, The Mary Thornton Suite, Armley Grange Drive, Leeds, West Yorkshire LS12 3QH (0113 214 3630 – 10.30am-3.30pm)
Leicestershire and Rutland – MOSAIC, 2 Richard III Road, Leicester, Leicestershire LE3 5QT (0116 262 6900 – Mon-Thur 9am-5pm, Fri 9am-4.30pm)
Lincolnshire (North) – Carers' Support Centre, 11 Redcombe Lane, Brigg, Lincolnshire DN20 8AU (01652 650585)
Lowestoft and Waveney area – DIAL Lowestoft & Waveney, Waveney Centre for Independent Living, 161 Rotterdam Road, Lowestoft, Suffolk NR32 2EZ (01502 511333 – 9am-3pm)
Midlands (West) – Disability West Midlands, Prospect Hall, College Walk, Selly Oak, Birmingham B29 6LE (0121 414 1616)
Midlands (West) – FRESHWINDS, Freshwinds House, 22 George Road, Edgbaston, Birmingham B15 1PJ (0121 456 8100)
New Forest – New Forest Disability Information Service, 6 Osborne Road, New Milton, Hampshire BH25 6AD (01425 628750)
Northern England – Disability North, Information and Advisory Service, The Dene Centre, Castles Farm Road, Newcastle-upon-Tyne, Tyne & Wear NE3 1PH (0191 284 0480)
Nuneaton and Bedworth borough – DIAL Nuneaton & Bedworth, New Ramsden Centre, School Walk, Attleborough, Nuneaton, Warwickshire CV11 4PJ (024 7634 9954 – Mon-Thur 9am-4pm)
Peterborough area – DIAL Peterbrough, The Kingfisher Centre, The Cresset, Bretton, Peterborough, Cambridgeshire PE3 8DX (01733 265551 – Mon-Thur 10am-4pm)
Plymouth area – Disability Information & Advice Centre, Ernest English House, Buckwell Street, Plymouth, Devon PL1 2DA (01752 201065 – Mon 9am-1pm, Tue-Fri 9am-1pm and 2pm-5pm)
Preston – Preston DISC, 103 Church Street, Preston, Lancashire PR1 3BS (01772 558863 – 9am-4pm)
Rotherham area – Rotherham's Disability Information Service, c/o Central Library, Walker Place, Rotherham, South Yorkshire S65 1JH (01709 373658 – 10am-4pm)
St Helens – DASH (Disability Advice & Information St Helens), Central Library, Victoria Square, St Helens, Merseyside WA10 1DY (01744 453053)
Sandwell borough – CARES Sandwell, The Carers Centre, 2 Bearwood Road, Smethwick, West Midlands B66 4HH (0121 558 7003)
Scarborough – Scarborough & District Disablement Action Group, Allat House, 5 West Parade Road, Scarborough, North Yorkshire YO12 5ED (01723 379397)
Selby district council – DIAL Selby & District, 12 Park Street, Selby, North Yorkshire YO8 4PW (01757 210495 – 10am-3pm)
Shropshire, Telford and Wrekin – DIAL Shropshire Telford & Wrekin, Ground Floor, Allison House, Oxon Business Park, Shrewsbury, Shropshire SY3 5HJ (01743 240404 – 9am-4pm)
Solihull borough – DIAL Solihull, Lowbrook Centre, Chichester Grove, Chelmsley Wood, West Midlands B37 5RZ (0121 770 0333 – 10am-3pm)
Somerset (North) – DIAL Weston-super-Mare, Room 5, Roselawn, 28 Walliscote Road, Weston-super-Mare, Somerset BS23 1UJ (01934 419426 – Tue and Thur 12pm-4pm)
Southend borough – DIAL Southend, 29-31 Alexandra Street, Southend on Sea, Essex SS1 1BW (0172 356031 – 10am-4pm)
Suffolk coastal area – Disability Advice Service (East Suffolk), Cedar House, Pytches Road, Woodbridge, Suffolk IP12 1EP (01394 387070 – Tue, Thur and Fri 10am-2pm)
Suffolk (Mid and South East) – Rethink Disability Advice Service, Red Gables, Ipswich Road, Stowmarket, Suffolk IP14 1BE (01449 672781; Typetalk 01449 775999)
Suffolk (West) – Rethink Disability Advice Service, West Suffolk Disability Resource Centre, Papworth House, 4 Bunting Road, Bury St Edmonds, Suffolk IP32 7BX (01284 748800 – Mon-Thur 10am-3pm)
Warwickshire – Council of Disabled People Warwickshire, Rehabilitation Hospital, Heathcote Lane, Leamington, Warwickshire CV34 6SR (01926 889349)
Wigan and Leigh – Paveways, Citizens Advice Bureau Disability Helpline, Hunter Lodge Clubhouse, Hunter Road, Wigan, Manchester WN5 0QD (01942 519909 – Mon-Thur 10am-3pm)
Wiltshire – Wiltshire & Bath Independent Living Centre, Independent Living Centre, St George's Road, Semington, Wiltshire BA14 6JQ (01380 871007)
Worcestershire (North) – DIAL North Worcestershire, Social Education Centre, Habberley Road, Kidderminster, Worcestershire DY11 6AB (0800 970 7202 – 10am-4pm)
Worcestershire (South) – DIAL South Worcestershire, 54 Friary Walk, Crowngate Centre, Worcester, Worcestershire WR1 3LE (01905 27790; Typetalk 01905 22191 – 9am-1pm)
York – Disability Information & Advice Centre (York), Room 2 Nursery Block, Priory Street Centre, 17 Priory Street, York, North Yorkshire YO1 6ET (01904 638467 – 10am-3pm)

London

Camden – DISC (Disability in Camden), 58 Phoenix Road, Camden, London NW1 1EU (020 7387 1466 – Mon, Tue, Thur, Fri 10am-4pm)
Greenwich borough – Greenwich Association of Disabled People, The Forum @ Greenwich, Trafalgar Road, Greenwich, London SE10 9EQ (020 8305 2221)
Hounslow borough – Disability Network Hounslow, 121c High Street, Brentford, Hounslow, London TW8 8AT (020 8758 2048)
Lambeth – Disability Advice Service Lambeth, 336 Brixton Road, Lambeth, London SW9 7AA (020 7738 5656 – 11am-1pm)
London area – GLAD (Greater London Action on Disability), 336 Brixton Road, London SW9 7AA (020 7346 5800)
Richmond borough – Richmond Advice & Information on Disability, Disability Action and Advice Centre, 4 Waldegrave Road, Teddington, Richmond, London TW11 8HT (020 8831 6070 – 11am-4pm)
Waltham Forest – DIAL Waltham Forest, Community Place, 806 High Road, Leyton, London E10 6AE (020 8539 8884 – Mon, Tue, Thur & Fri 10am-4pm)
Wandsworth borough – Wandsworth Disabled Advice Service, 5th Floor, Bedford House, 215 Balham High Road, Balham, Wandsworth, London SW17 7BQ (020 8333 6949 – 10am-4pm)

Scotland

Dunbartonshire (East) – Contact Point in East Dunbartonshire, The Park Centre, 45 Kerr Street, Kirkintilloch G66 1LF (0141 578 0183)
Glasgow areas G11 to G15 – The Three Eyes Project, 52 Knightscliffe Avenue, Knightscliffe, Glasgow G13 2TE (0141 954 8432)
Lanarkshire (South) – South Lanarkshire Disability Forum, 42 Campbell Street, Hamilton, South Lanarkshire ML3 6AS (01698 307733 Mon-Thur 9am-4.30pm, Fri 9am-4pm)

Wales

Anglesey (North) – Taran Information Service, Centre for Integrated Living, Canolfan Mona Industrial Estate, Llangefni, Anglesey LL77 7JA (01248 750249 – 10am-4pm)
Anglesey and Gwynedd – Disablement Welfare Rights, Canolfan Lafan, 2 Glanrafon, Bangor, Gwynedd LL57 1LH (01248 352227)
Carmarthenshire – CATCH UP Ltd, 4 Coleshill Terrace, Llanelli, Carmarthenshire SA15 3DB (01554 776850 – Mon-Thur 9.30am-3.30pm, Fri 9.30am-3pm)
Pembrokeshire – Connect DRA, Lynden Lea, Goodwick Hill, Goodwick, Pembrokeshire SA64 0EX (01348 873884 – Mon, Tue, Thur & Fri 9am-3pm)
Swansea, Neath, Port Talbot – DIAL Swansea, Neath, Port

Talbot, Brondeg House, St Johns Road, Manseltown, Swansea SA5 8PR (01792 588322 – 10am-3.30pm)
Torfaen – Disability Advice Project, 125 The Highway, New Inn, Pontypool, Torfaen NP4 0PH (01495 763778 – Mon-Thur 10am-4pm)

Law centres

Law centres provide free legal advice. They are usually restricted to providing services in a specific area and are unlikely to be able to help if you do not live or work in their area. Ring first to check if they can help you.

UK-wide

Disability Law Service, Ground Floor, 39-45 Cavell Street, London E1 2BP (020 7791 9800; Textphone 020 7791 9801)

England

Avon and Bristol Law Centre, 2 Moon Street, Bristol BS2 8QE (0117 924 8662)
Bradford Law Centre, 31 Manor Row, Bradford BD1 4PS (01274 306617)
Bury Law Centre, 19 Knowsley Street, Bury, Lancs BL9 0ST (0161 272 0666)
Carlisle Law Centre, 8 Spencer Street, Carlisle, Cumbria CA1 1BG (01228 515129)
Chesterfield Law Centre, 44 Park Road, Chesterfield S40 1XZ (01246 550674)
Coventry Law Centre, The Bridge, Broadgate, Coventry CV1 1NG (024 7622 3053)
Derby Law Centre, Balcony B5, Market Hall, Derby DE1 2DB (01332 344557)
Devon Law Centre, Virginia House, 40 Looe Street, Plymouth, Devon PL4 0EB (01752 519794)
Gateshead Law Centre, 1 Walker Terrace, Gateshead NE8 1EB (0191 440 8575)
Gloucester Law Centre, 3rd Floor, 75-81 Eastgate Street, Gloucester GL1 1PN (01452 423492)
Greater Manchester Immigration Aid Unit, 1 Delaunays Road, Crumpsall Green, Manchester M8 9QS (0161 740 7722)
Harehills and Chapeltown Law Centre, 263 Roundhay Road, Leeds LS8 4HS (0113 249 1100)
Humberside Law Centre, 95 Alfred Gelder Street, Hull HU1 1EP (01482 211180)
Isle of Wight Law Centre, Exchange House, Saint Cross Lane, Newport, Isle of Wight PO30 5BZ (01983 523492)
Leicester Law Centre, 1st Floor, International House, 125-133 Granby Street, Leicester LE1 6FD (0116 255 3781)
Liverpool 8 Law Centre, 34-36 Princes Road, Liverpool L8 1TH (0151 709 7222)
Luton Law Centre, 28 Clarendon Road, Luton, Bedfordshire LU2 7PQ (01582 481000)
Newcastle Law Centre, 1st Floor, 1 Charlotte Square, Newcastle Upon Tyne NE1 4XE (0191 230 4777)
North Manchester Law Centre, Unit A, Harpurhey District Centre, off Rochdale Road, Harpurhey, Manchester M9 4DH (0161 205 5040)
Nottingham Law Centre, 119 Radford Road, Nottingham NG7 5DU (0115 978 7813)
Oldham Law Centre, 1st Floor, Archway House, Bridge Street, Oldham OL1 1ED (0161 627 0925)
Rochdale Law Centre, Smith Street, Rochdale OL16 1HE (01706 657766)
Saltley and Nechells Law Centre, 2 Alum Rock Road, Saltley, Birmingham B8 1JB (0121 328 2307)
Sheffield Law Centre, 1st Floor, Waverley House, 10 Joiner Street, Sheffield S3 8GW (0114 273 1888)
South Manchester Law Centre, 584 Stockport Road, Manchester M13 0RQ (0161 225 5111)
Stockport Law Centre, 85 Wellington Road South, Stockport SK1 3SL (0161 476 6336)
Vauxhall Community Law and Information Centre, VNC Millennium Resource Centre, 1-3 St Augustine Street, Liverpool L5 8UX (0151 330 0239)
Warrington Law Centre, 64-66 Bewsey Street, Warrington, Cheshire WA2 7JE (01925 651104)
Wiltshire Law Centre, Temple House, 115-118 Commercial Road, Swindon, Wiltshire SN1 5PL (01793 486926; Textphone 01793 611326)
Wythenshawe Law Centre, 260 Brownley Road, Wythenshawe, Manchester M22 5EB (0161 498 0905/6)

London

Barnet Law Service (Law Centre), 9 Bell Lane, London NW4 2BP (020 8203 4141)
Battersea Law Centre, (a South West London Law Centre), 14 York Road, London SW11 1LJ (020 7585 0716)
Brent Community Law Centre, 389 High Road, Willesden, London NW10 2JR (020 8451 1122)
Cambridge House Law Centre, 137 Camberwell Road, London SE5 0HF (020 7703 3051)
Camden Community Law Centre, 2 Prince of Wales Road, London NW5 3LG (020 7284 6510)
Central London Law Centre, 19 Whitcomb Street, London WC2H 7HA (020 7839 2998)
Croydon and Sutton Law Centre, (a South West London Law Centre), 4th Floor, Oakley House, 1a Katherine Street, Croydon CR0 1NX (020 8667 9226)
Enfield Law Centre, 38 Market Square, Edmonton Green, London N9 0TZ (020 8807 8888)
Greenwich Community Law Centre, 187 Trafalgar Road, London SE10 9EQ (020 8853 2550)
Hackney Community Law Centre, 8 Lower Clapton Road, London E5 0PD (020 8985 8364)
Hammersmith and Fulham Law Centre, 142-144 King Street, London W6 0QU (020 8741 4021)
Hillingdon Law Centre, 12 Harold Avenue, Hayes, Middlesex UB3 4QW (020 8561 9400)
Hounslow Law Centre, 51 Lampton Road, Hounslow, Middlesex TW3 1LY (020 8570 9505)
Islington Law Centre, 161 Hornsey Road, London N7 6DU (020 7607 2461)
Kingston and Richmond Law Centre, (a South West London Law Centre), Siddeley House, 50 Canbury Park Road, Kingston KT2 6LX (020 8547 2882)
Lewisham Law Centre, 28 Deptford High Street, London SE8 4AF (020 8692 5355)
Mary Ward Legal Centre, 26-27 Boswell Street, London WC1N 3JZ (020 7831 7079)
North Kensington Law Centre, 74 Golborne Road, London W10 5PS (020 8969 7473)
North Lambeth Law Centre, 14 Bowden Street, London SE11 5DS (020 7582 4373)
Paddington Law Centre, 439 Harrow Road, London W10 4RE (020 8960 3155)
Plumstead Law Centre, 105 Plumstead High Street, London SE18 1SB (020 8855 9817)
Southwark Law Centre, Hanover Park House, 14-16 Hanover Park, London SE15 5HS (020 7732 2008)
Springfield Advice and Law Centre, Springfield University Hospital, Admissions Building, 61 Glenburnie Road, London SW17 7DJ (020 8767 6884)
Thamesmead Law Centre, (attached to Plumstead Community Law Centre) St Paul's Church, Bentham Road, London SE28 8AS (020 8311 0555)
Tottenham Law Centre, 754-758 High Road, London N17 0AL (020 8808 5354)
Tower Hamlets Law Centre, 214 Whitechapel Road, London E1 1BJ (020 7247 8998)
Wandsworth and Merton Law Centre, (a South West London Law Centre), 101a Tooting High Street, London SW17 0SU (020 8767 2777); South London Tamil Welfare Office, 36 High Street, Colliers Wood SW19 (020 8543 4069)

Northern Ireland

Law Centre (NI), 124 Donegall Street, Belfast BT1 2GY (028 9024 4401); Western Area Office, 9 Clarendon Street, Derry BT48 7EP (028 7126 2433)

Scotland

Castlemilk Law and Money Advice Centre, 32 Dougrie Drive, Castlemilk, Glasgow G45 9AD (0141 634 0313)

Disability Legal Services, 27 Hills Road, Strathaven ML10 6LQ (Tel and Fax 01347 523134)

Drumchapel Law and Money Advice Centre, Unit 28, 42 Dalsetter Avenue, Drumchapel, Glasgow G15 8TE (0141 944 0507; 0141 944 0281)

Dundee North Law Centre, Top Floor, 20 Granpian Gardens, Fintry Dundee DD4 9QZ (01382 432 458)

East End Community Law Centre, Units 21 and 22, Ladywell Business Centre, 94 Duke Street, Glasgow G4 0UW (0141 552 6666) and 3rd Floor, Princes House, Shandwick Place, Edinburgh EH2 4RG (0131 228 9993)

Ethnic Minorities Law Centre, 41 St Vincent Place, 2nd Floor, Glasgow G1 2ER (0141 204 2888)

Govan Law Centre, 47 Burleigh Street, Govan Cross, Glasgow G51 3LB (0141 440 2503)

Legal Services Agency, 3rd Floor, Fleming House, 134 Renfrew Street, Glasgow G3 6ST (0141 353 3354)

Paisley Law Centre, 65 George Street, Paisley PA1 2JY (0141 561 7266)

Scottish Child Law Centre, 54 East Crosscauseway, Edinburgh EH8 9HD (0131 667 6333; Freephone for under-18s 0800 328 8970)

The West Dumbartonshire Community Law Service, 120 Dumbarton Road, Clydebank G81 1UG (0141 952 7070; Fax 0141 952 9086)

Wales

Cardiff Law Centre, 41-42 Clifton Street, Adamsdown, Cardiff CF24 1LS (029 2049 8117)

Ombudsmen

Parliamentary Ombudsman
Deals with complaints about central government, for England and Wales. Only an MP can refer a complaint to the Parliamentary Ombudsman.
Millbank Tower, Millbank, London SW1P 4QP (0845 015 4033; 020 7217 4163)

Health Service Ombudsman
Deals with complaints about health authorities and trusts, doctors, dentists, opticians, etc.
England: Millbank Tower, Millbank, London SW1P 4QP (020 7217 4051)
Wales: 5th Floor, Capital Tower House, Greyfriars Road, Cardiff CF10 3AG (029 2039 4621)

Local Government Ombudsman
Deals with complaints about local government.
England (area 1): Tony Redmond, Local Government Ombudsman, 10th Floor, Millbank Tower, Millbank, London SW1P 4QP (020 7217 4620)
London boroughs north of the River Thames (including Richmond but not including Harrow or Tower Hamlets), Essex, Kent, Surrey, Suffolk, East and West Sussex, Berkshire, Buckinghamshire, Hertfordshire and the City of Coventry.
England (area 2): Patricia Thomas, Local Government Ombudsman, Beverley House, 17 Shipton Road, York YO30 5FZ (01904 380200)
London Borough of Tower Hamlets, City of Birmingham, Cheshire, Derbyshire, Nottinghamshire, Lincolnshire and the north of England (except the cities of York and Lancaster).
England (area 3): Jerry White, Local Government Ombudsman, The Oaks No. 2, Westwood Way, Westwood Business Park, Coventry CV4 8JB (024 7682 0000)
London boroughs south of the River Thames (except Richmond) and Harrow; the cities of York and Lancaster; and the rest of England not included in areas 1 and 2.
Wales: Adam Peat, Public Services Ombudsman, 1 Oldfield Road, Pencoed CF35 5LJ (01656 641150; Fax 01656 641199)

Northern Ireland Ombudsman
Deals with complaints about Northern Ireland government departments and their agencies and public bodies including health and personal social services.
Tom Frawley, Progressive House, 33 Wellington Place, Belfast BT1 6HN; Freepost: The Ombudsman, Freepost BEL 1478, Belfast BT1 6BR (028 9023 3821; Freephone: 0800 343424)

Scottish Public Services Ombudsman
Deals with complaints about the Scottish Executive and its agencies and other public bodies including health, housing and social services.
Professor Alice Brown, Ombudsman, 4 Melville Street, Edinburgh EH3 7NS (0870 011 5378)

Index

A

B

D

I

R

S

T

U

V